One of the Holy Trinity
✢ Suffered for Us ✢

The Reverend William C. Weinrich

ONE OF THE HOLY TRINITY
✛ SUFFERED FOR US ✛

Essays in Honor of **William Weinrich**

Edited by
James Bushur

ISBN 978-1-935035-43-5

Printed in the United States of America

CONTENTS

PART ONE: EVANGELION

CONTRIBUTORS

PART ONE: EVANGELION

DEAN O. WENTHE is Professor of Exegetical Theology and President Emeritus of Concordia Theological Seminary, Fort Wayne, Indiana, and President of the Concordia University System for the Luther Church—Missouri Synod.

JAMES W. VOELZ is Graduate Professor of Exegetical Theology and holds the Dr. Jack Dean Kingsbury Chair of New Testament Theology at Concordia Seminary, Saint Louis, Missouri.

ARTHUR A. JUST JR is Professor of Exegetical Theology at Concordia Theological Seminary, and Associate Executive Director of International Mission in Theological Education.

BRUCE SCHUCHARD is Professor of Exegetical Theology at Concordia Seminary, St. Louis, Missouri.

CHARLES A. GIESCHEN is Academic Dean and Professor of Exegetical Theology at Concordia Theological Seminary, Fort Wayne, Indiana.

PETER J. SCAER is Associate Professor of Exegetical Theology and Director of the Master of Arts Program at Concordia Theological Seminary, Fort Wayne, Indiana.

CHAD D. KENDALL is associate pastor at St. John Lutheran Church in Wheaton, Illinois, and Adjunct Professor at Concordia University, Chicago and Concordia Theological Seminary, Fort Wayne, Indiana.

PART TWO: THEOLOGIA

DAVID P. SCAER is Chairman of the Department of Systematic Theology and Professor of Biblical and Systematic Theology at Concordia Theological Seminary, Fort Wayne, Indiana.

D. RICHARD STUCKWISCH is pastor of Emmaus Evangelical Lutheran Church in South Bend, Indiana.

PAUL GREGORY ALMS is the pastor of St. Paul Lutheran Church, Catonsville, Maryland.

ALEXEY STRELTSOV is the rector of Theological Seminary of Siberian Evangelical Lutheran Church, Novosibirsk, Russia.

JAMES G. BUSHUR is Associate Professor of Historical Theology, Director of Deaconess Formation, and holds The Carl and Erna Weinrich Chair in New Testament and Early Church Studies at Concordia Theological Seminary, Fort Wayne, Indiana.

PART THREE: ECCLESIA

CAMERON A. MacKENZIE is Ellis Professor and Chairman of the Department of Historical Theology at Concordia Theological Seminary, Fort Wayne, Indiana.

TIMOTHY C. J. QUILL is Professor Emeritus of Pastoral Theology and Missions at Concordia Theological Seminary, Fort Wayne, Indiana, and General Secretary of the International Lutheran Council.

K. DETLEV SCHULZ is Professor of Pastoral Ministry and Missions, Director of the PhD program in Missiology, and Dean of Graduate Studies at Concordia Theological Seminary, Fort Wayne, Indiana.

SCOTT STIEGEMEYER is Assistant Professor of Bioethics and Theology at Concordia University in Irvine, California.

WALLACE SCHULZ is Editor, Good News, magazine.

GINO R. MARCHETTI II is pastor of St. Peter's Lutheran Church of Warsaw, Indiana.

FOREWORD

✝

Justin Martyr, the great apologist of the second century, favored the following aphorism: Δεδιδάγμεθα καὶ διδάσκομεν. It means "as we have been taught so we teach." This axiom expresses the early Christian conviction that theology properly consists in the divine conversation that ever moves in reciprocal fashion between the Father, Son, and Holy Spirit. This divine conversation is opened up to humanity through the eternal Word of God, who becomes flesh and dwells among us. Thus, for Justin Martyr, this axiom—"as we have been taught so we teach"—defines the whole life of the church. This aphorism certainly also characterizes the life and work of Rev. Dr. William C. Weinrich, whom this festschrift celebrates as a true gift from God to us—his students, colleagues, and friends.

In the fall of 1989, I, the editor of this festschrift, was introduced to this divine conversation in one of my first classes simply called Early Church. No one called it Early Church History. We simply omitted the word *History* and called it Early Church. (Of course, this may have been a simple abbreviation.) However, I like to think that it had something to do with the way the course was taught. Weinrich did not simply lecture *about* early Christian conflicts and theologians as if they were dead relics of a distant past. Rather, to hear Weinrich speak was to hear the theological vision of the early church come to new life. He did not merely speak *about* Athanasius; rather, it was as if Athanasius himself was in the very room forcing us to take his theological vision seriously. Now, it was surprising for some of us that Athanasius spoke with an Oklahoman accent. Yet Weinrich made us believe it anyway. His teaching style bears a passionate devotion to Christ, a personal experience in ministry, and a genuine love for students that have made Weinrich consistently one of the most effective teachers at Concordia Theological Seminary, Fort Wayne, Indiana. Irenaeus, a second century bishop, describes Clement of Rome as one who had the apostolic preaching "echoing in his ears." I resonate with this experience. There are times when I am teaching that I can sense Weinrich's thoughts and words forming in my mind. Thus, it is my privilege and joy to be the editor of this festschrift in honor of Dr. William C. Weinrich under the following title: *One of the Holy Trinity Suffered for Us.*

"One of the Holy Trinity suffered for us." This formula was the test for orthodox Christology proposed by the Scythian monks in the first half of the sixth century. The Scythian monks made this proposal due to a perceived revival of the Nestorian heresy following the council of Chalcedon (451 AD). Initially, this formula was met with resistance. However, the formula was finally championed by the Emperor Justinian and became the heart of the orthodox confession made at the second council of Constantinople (553 AD). In many ways, this formula recapitulates the profound theological struggle of the first five hundred years of the church. Since the council of Nicaea, the church struggled to find language that could adequately articulate what she was experiencing at the baptismal font, in the Scriptures, and around the Eucharistic altar. For the orthodox fathers, salvation depended upon God's direct and immediate communion with humanity. Such an intimate communion is precisely what this formula expresses (or "bespeaks," as Weinrich would say). In the person of the Son, God himself suffers. In other words—and this is a hallmark of Weinrich's teaching—the cross of Christ means that there is no barrier between his divinity and our humanity; no boundary separating his righteousness from our sin; no gap dividing his glory from our humiliation or his life from our death. Thus, this formula testifies to the ultimate triumph of the Nicene Creed and the Trinitarian faith confessed therein.

There is no better formula to use in honor of Dr. William Weinrich. For over forty years, he has taught, confessed, and embodied the faith of Nicaea. He stands among us as a recapitulation of the ancient faith that is always regenerating at the font, forgiving in the absolution, catechizing from the pulpit, nourishing and perfecting at the altar. Weinrich abides among us as a true father of the "faith once handed over to the saints" (Jude 3). While ancient, this faith becomes ever new in those who confess it. The contributing authors in this festschrift count it a great blessing to call Dr. Weinrich our teacher, colleague, and friend. Accordingly, we now ask you to join us in honoring him as a true teacher of the church (Doctor Ecclesiae). Δεδιδάγμεθα καὶ διδάσκομεν: As we have been taught so may we ever continue to teach!

Part One
EVANGELION

Since joining the faculty of Concordia Theological Seminary, Fort Wayne, Indiana in 1975, a hallmark of Dr. William Weinrich's work has been his interest in the Gospels, especially the tradition of St. John. Weinrich compiled the *Ancient Christian Commentary on Revelation* and has translated several Latin and Greek patristic commentaries on *Revelation.* Weinrich is also in the process of writing the *Concordia Commentary* on John's Gospel. In his exegetical work, Weinrich has emphasized that the Scriptures belong to the church; it is in the sanctuary—the gathering of the baptized around font, pulpit, and altar—that the Scriptures are heard in the Spirit as the direct discourse of the Father through His Son. The essays in this section give thanks to God for Dr. Weinrich's exegetical work and testify to the rich theological conversation in which Weinrich has been and continues to be a significant contributor.

Order of Contributors: Dean Wenthe, James Voelz, Arthur Just, Bruce Schuchard, Charles Gieschen, Peter Scaer, Chad Kendall

Part Two
THEOLOGIA

As professor of church history, Dr. Weinrich has spent his professional life engaged in the task of forming students for ministry in the church. As academic dean of Concordia Theological Seminary, Weinrich took up the monumental task of reforming the curriculum—a reform that continues to shape the culture of the seminary to this day. Weinrich's leadership in reforming the curriculum recognized that the seminary's primary mission is not to prepare students for the secular academy but for the sacred fellowship of the church. Rather than exegetes, systematicians, historians, or professionals, pastors are called to be "theologians" in the truest sense of the term; that is, to take their place within God's direct discourse with his people. For Weinrich, the vocation of theologian is an ancient one including countless saints, martyrs, catechists, and bishops such as Ignatius of Antioch, Polycarp, Irenaeus, and Athanasius. To enter the vocation of theologian is to enter a divine conversation that has its root within the fellowship of the Trinity and continues in the one, holy, catholic, and apostolic church throughout the ages. Essays in this section give thanks to God for Dr. Weinrich's work in patristic theology and for his clear confession of the Trinitarian and Christological foundations of the Nicene Creed.

Order of Contributors: David Scaer, Richard Stuckwisch, Gregory Alms, Alexei Streltsov, James Bushur

Part Three

ECCLESIA

Dr. Weinrich has served the Lutheran Church—Missouri Synod as synodical vice president (1998–2004), a member of the CTCR (1992–2001), and chaplain in the Air National Guard for thirty years achieving the rank of Lieutenant Colonel. Weinrich has also served the church internationally, contributing to the work in Russia and serving as Rector of the seminary in Latvia. From such service, it is clear that Weinrich's life demonstrates his love for the church. All true theology must have its *telos* in the gathering of God's people around Christ. The one, holy, catholic, and apostolic church—present from the beginning in the Spirit, constituted in the body of Jesus, and perfected in the eschaton as the bride of Christ—is the reality that has fueled Weinrich's theological vision and his practical service of God's people. The essays in this section give thanks to God for Dr. Weinrich's selfless service to the church and for his exemplary leadership of the seminary in the challenging circumstances of our contemporary cultural context.

Order of Contributors: Cameron Mackenzie, Timothy Quill, Detlev Schulz, Scott Stiegemeyer, Wallace Schulz, Gino Marchetti II

JAMES BUSHUR, EDITOR

a special thanks to
JOSHUA WOELMER
for his assistance

IN HONOR OF FATHERS

AN ENCOMIUM FOR
DR. WILLIAM WEINRICH

☨

"We believe in one God, the Father . . . ." The Nicene Creed expresses what is most fundamental to the faith of orthodox Christianity. Before all else, even before confessing God as Creator, the church calls him "Father." While God's patriarchy may grate on the sensibilities of some in our contemporary culture, it nevertheless expresses the very core of the ancient church and the gospel she handed over to her children. At the heart of Jesus' conflict with his Jewish opponents is his incessant practice of "calling God his own Father and, thus, making himself equal with God" (John 5:18). Yet, as the raising of Lazarus demonstrates, Jesus is crucified because the Father listens when Jesus calls upon him and does what he asks (John 11). Finally, John's Gospel ends with Jesus giving his disciples a share in his own sonship. At the tomb, Mary Magdalene is entrusted with the sacred message, "Go to my brethren and say to them, 'I am ascending to my Father and your Father'" (John 20:17). It is precisely this transition from the first person singular "my" to the second person plural "your" that defines the faith of early Christians. In Holy Baptism, a new humanity is generated, "not from blood, nor from the desire of the flesh, nor from the desire of man, but from God" (John 1:13). Begotten from above by water and the Spirit, Christians receive a place in Jesus' own eternal Sonship and therefore confess as of first importance, "We believe in one God, the Father."

Yet what does this confession actually mean? In our contemporary landscape, fatherhood has lost much of its theological significance. The sexual union has been separated from procreation and has therefore lost its sanctified character. As a consequence, fatherhood is no longer considered a sacred vocation to which men aspire as the fulfillment of their masculinity. Rather, fatherhood is often the consequence of failed contraception and identified with an accidental vocation to be avoided more often than not. Through the proliferation of serial marriage and divorce, fatherhood has been reduced to a distant relationship mainly constituted in the duty of financial support. Through the recognition of genderless marriage, fatherhood is being repudiated as essential to the family and chiseled out of the foundation upon which human society rests.

For the ancient church, fatherhood is the *arche* or sacred source from which children draw their lives, their identities, and their destinies. The accomplishment of the ancient directive to "know oneself" demands reflection upon the fundamental source of one's own being and life. Fathers are thus to be honored in accord with the fourth commandment, not as the materialistic first cause of one's biological existence. Rather, fathers form the very ontological fountain from which the whole family draws its subsistence and by which its relations are ordered and structured. The theological significance of fatherhood is sown into the very fabric of the Scriptures. The whole family of humanity is already present in Adam. The rescue of Noah must include the salvation of his family and the whole of creation. The reconciliation between Jacob and Esau begins when God calls Jacob to return to "the land of his father" (Gen 31:3). Their shared generation from a common father makes Jacob and Esau brothers and encourages the embrace of a happy reunion. Esau may have been "hated" by God but perhaps finds a place in the family of God through restored fellowship with his brother, Jacob, the one whom God loves.

However, early Christians claimed that through baptism their own being and life did not merely originate in human fathers. They claimed the right to call God "Father" and believed their own identity to be grounded in the eternal fellowship of the Holy Trinity. According to the Nicene Creed, the reality of baptism does not begin when water is applied or even when the rite is instituted by Christ. It has its beginning in the Father's eternal generation of the Son in the Holy Spirit. Thus, God does not become a father, play the part of a father, or appear to be like a father. Rather, God *is* Father precisely because he subsists eternally as the generative source of the Son. From this perspective, if the church is to understand her own identity truly, then she must ever reflect upon the theological source of her subsistence in the eternal fellowship of the Holy Trinity. There is nothing more fundamental to the church's confession than the first words of her creed: "We believe in one God, the Father . . . ."

The essays collected in this volume constitute an encomium giving thanks to our Father in heaven for blessing the church with Dr. William Weinrich. The purpose of a non-Christian encomium is to praise an individual; the purpose of a Christian encomium is to recognize the way God accomplishes his purpose in and through the individual being honored. Dr. Weinrich joined the faculty of Concordia Theological

Seminary, Springfield, Illinois, in 1975. The seminary then moved to its present location in Fort Wayne, Indiana the next year. For the Lutheran Church—Missouri Synod (LCMS), it was a time of confessional crisis. During his tenure as *Doctor Ecclesiae*, Weinrich has proved to be much more than merely a scholar, historian, or theologian. He has lived among us, first of all, as a true witness to Christ and the confessional tradition of "the one, holy, catholic, and apostolic church."

The title of witness or martyr is truly appropriate, given its prominence in the Johannine tradition and the fact that Weinrich began his academic work with a thesis on early Christian martyrdom.[1] A witness is not one who simply recalls past events and, therefore, speaks as a spectator viewing them from a safe and distant location. Instead of the past tense, the true witness speaks in the present tense: "That which was from the beginning . . . which we have seen and touched with our hands . . . we are bearing witness and proclaiming to you" (1 John 1:1–2). The martyr does not possess a truth of the past as much as he is possessed by the truth in the present. For St. John the Evangelist, it is as if the truth actively enters the witness through the eyes and remains a living reality in him. The truth dwells in the martyr, inspiring his mind, filling his soul, moving his lips, and forming his life. Like Nathaniel and Thomas in the fourth Gospel, Weinrich is a true witness to "the greater things," "the opening of heaven," which takes place when the side of Christ is torn asunder so that we might be grafted into his body as branches in the vine.

When Weinrich teaches the Gospel of John and the theology of the early church fathers, he does not merely lecture or instruct; he bears witness. He does not speak about the ancients as men speak of the dead, nor does he explain their theological vision as a relic of a distant, inaccessible past. Rather, in his lectures, the theological confession of the ancients becomes a living reality for his students. He presents the Nicene Creed not as mere words and doctrines that belong to the church's historical record but as the symbol of a living conflict that may have had its origins in the fourth century yet remains an ever-present struggle. In his classroom, it is as if St. John, Ignatius of Antioch, or perhaps Athanasius himself stands among us expounding his own convictions with passionate force. In Weinrich, ancient theologians become fathers of the faith, whose theological convictions do not merely invite our understanding but call forth our faith, give shape to our identity, and even demand our allegiance.

In the 1970s, the church needed a new Athanasius; she has been blessed with Dr. William Weinrich. Weinrich has shared the story of the

---

1. William Weinrich, *Spirit and Martyrdom: A Study of the Work of the Holy Spirit in Contexts of Persecution and Martyrdom in the New Testament and Early Christian Literature*, (Washington DC: University Press of America, 1981).

way he began his tenure at Concordia Theological Seminary. In one of his first encounters with Dr. David Scaer, Weinrich expressed his loyalty to Athanasius and the faith of the Nicene Creed. Every theologian is a product of his sources, and such sources can be compared to a geographical landscape where one chooses to sink his roots and to build his home. In response to the theological crisis in the LCMS in the 1970s, conservative theologians naturally sought stability and security in the Lutheran dogmaticians and the age of Lutheran orthodoxy. In these sources, they could find a rather clear and concise summary of orthodox Lutheran tradition. The Lutheran dogmaticians were more than helpful; they were convenient, offering a shorthand compendium of the theological principles that expressed the authentic core of orthodox Lutheranism. The Lutheran dogmaticians were also scholastic in method of analysis and mode of presentation, which seemed to supply conservative theologians with an effective arsenal for their conflict with the secular academy. Yet, the danger in this reaction was the pragmatic reduction of the sources used for theological reflection and, consequently, the narrowing of the theological vision of the LCMS.

The idea that the theological crisis of the 1970s was a battle for the Bible is somewhat misleading. The debate was not exegetical in nature nor was the biblical text the sole battlefield for the conflict. Rather, the two sides differed concerning the appropriate settings for theological reflection and exegetical engagement with Scripture. One side, following the momentum of the Enlightenment and mainstream Christianity, recognized that theological reflection primarily takes place within the walls of academia. In the secular academy, the Bible was analyzed in light of the advances of the social sciences and according to the same scientific methods of interpretation used to examine any other ancient artifact. Following Friedrich Schleiermacher, the academic scholars directed the flow of the Modernist stream toward the universalizing of theological reflection by grounding it in the natural religious impulses of humankind. Conservatives sought to resist this tidal wave of secularism. Against this academic universalism, conservatives tended to withdraw into more parochial settings and to root themselves in firmer ground. For conservative Lutherans, the most appealing landscape for theological reflection was the Reformation as interpreted through the tradition of post-Reformation Lutheran orthodoxy.

Thus, the 1970s battle for the Bible in the LCMS was not primarily exegetical or even theological but cultural—the secular culture of the modern academy versus the theological culture of Lutheran orthodoxy. This conflict was cultural because each side argued from radically different sources. "Liberals" believed that unless they engaged in the theological conversation of the modern academy, the Lutheran church would fall into sectarianism and irrelevant obscurantism. "Conservatives" believed that, in this engagement with academia, Lutherans must maintain the core of their Lutheran identity, which they found in orthodox Lutheran dogmaticians of the post-Reformation era. Without a common setting or foundation for their debate, the two sides could never truly engage each other and the conflict could never reach a satisfactory resolution. The conflict has been, even to this day, a little like modern warfare, in which each side remains confined within the boundaries of its own territory and launches missiles from afar. Unless the warring parties engage the same battlefield, there will be no real or lasting resolution.

What has been desperately needed in this debate is a common theological geography. Indeed, geographically speaking, "liberal" theologians had the strategic advantage. Like Lot, they chose to settle in the wide landscape of the modern, ecumenical academy. This theological Promised Land seemed to open up to an endless horizon that would stretch into the future, full of theological possibilities. However, today this promising land looks more and more like Sodom and Gomorrah, a land destined to be a lifeless desert. "Conservative" theologians, on the other hand, seemed content to retreat into the ever-narrowing plantation of Lutheran orthodoxy, a theological oasis in the midst of an ever-expanding desert.

On the basis of his theological work, I would argue that William Weinrich has stood in our midst as a witness to another land. However, he is not like Moses, who merely received a tantalizing glimpse of a land he would never reach; rather, he is more like Joshua and Caleb, who found a rich and fertile land and only reluctantly returned to the Israelite camp to testify to what they had seen and experienced. For Weinrich, the sources for theological reflection could not be reduced to the parochial pastures of the Reformers and their successors. Rather, theological reflection must spread out into the broad, catholic landscape of the ancient church. While most were arguing about the walls and roof of the contemporary church, Weinrich pointed to the foundational pillars, upon which the church was first constructed and without which all would certainly crumble.

For Weinrich, the living presence of Christ, the fourfold narrative of the gospel, and the confession of the early church as embodied in the Nicene Creed constitute the catholic foundation within which the Lutheran church must subsist if she is to be church in any real sense. In this way, Weinrich shares the spirit of the first Lutheran confessors who gave priority to the Nicene Creed in the *Book of Concord* and began their testimony at Augsburg with an article on God, expressing loyalty to "the decree of the Council of Nicaea."[2] However, in the teaching of our friend and colleague, the firm pillars of the ancient church—Irenaeus, Athanasius, Cyril of Alexandria, etc.—are not merely dead objects of research from a distant past. They are true fathers who stood at baptismal fonts, filled pulpits, and presided at altars. In this way, they are living stones joined to the chief cornerstone in the very foundations of the church. In and through their lives, the theological landscape of the church was cultivated. From this rich field, we have been generated and continue to be nourished. To ignore these ancient fathers is not merely to lose a valuable commodity, a part of our history, or a dimension of our theological heritage. It is to become theological orphans who have forgotten from whence they have come.

Thus, these essays are offered as an encomium honoring the life and work of Dr. William Weinrich; yet, they also constitute a call to the church to reflect once again on the very catholic and apostolic origins of the faith as delivered by our fathers. In this festschrift, we recognize our teacher, friend, and colleague as a faithful witness to the truth. His very life is a living testimony calling the whole church to remember her birthplace and, like the prodigal son, to "come to her senses" and return to her fatherland. However, personally, I will go a step further and acknowledge Dr. Weinrich as my theological father. By this designation, I mean that the very truth that has lived in him and borne witness through his voice has entered my ears and found a dwelling in my life. For me, the church fathers—Ignatius, Irenaeus, Athanasius, Gregory Nazianzen, Cyril of Alexandria, and the like—will always be heard with an ever so slight Oklahoman accent.

In the copy of his thesis on martyrdom supplied to the Walther Library on September 11, 1981, Weinrich inscribed these words: "in the hope that this book may help our students comprehend the centrality of the cross of Christ in the Christian's existence." This sentiment expresses something truly fundamental and authentic concerning the subject of this encomium. The purpose of his work has not been academic honors, peer recognition, or personal popularity. Rather, like a true martyr, Weinrich has laid down his life for Christ and for the benefit of his students. In relation to Christ, he is a true witness. In relation to his students, he is more than a teacher or guide; he is a theological father, that is, an image of God's own fatherhood. For, as one of his students, I can bear witness that what he taught has profoundly shaped my own relationship to God. "He who has seen me," says Christ, our Lord, "has seen the Father" (John 14:9). Jesus' words demonstrate that the revelation

---

2. Concordia *Triglotta*, AC I.

of God is never a transcendent monologue but an intimate, communal conversation. Through Weinrich's teaching, countless students have been invited and even initiated into this divine conversation.

Weinrich's lectures are direct, forceful, and challenging, and so demand the very best from his students. Like a true father, he teaches his students with the urgent hope and the firm conviction that God can make them more than what they are in the present. With this conviction, he not only entered the classroom as a professor but also revised the curriculum as academic dean. With his revision of the curriculum, Weinrich sought to do more than merely update the form of seminary education. He challenged us to consider the true theological mission of seminary training. The purpose of the seminary is not to produce academic scholars but faithful martyrs ready to lay down their lives for their beloved. Thus, theological education must do more than influence the intellect; it seeks to conform the whole person—body, heart, and soul—to the image of Christ and him crucified. In and through his faithful witness, Weinrich has become a true father, testifying to Christ, who is the truth eternally generated out of the bosom of the Father, eternally fruitful through his holy passion, and eternally subsisting within the ecclesial fellowship of the Spirit. On behalf of the authors in this festschrift, it is my privilege as editor to express the great joy that is ours to share in this fellowship of the Spirit with our teacher, colleague, and friend. It is an honor to confess with him our faith "in one God, the Father . . ." and to become fellow martyrs with him of the same Christ Jesus our Lord. For Dr. William Weinrich's faithful witness, let us all give thanks and praise to the Father, Son, and Holy Spirit, one God, now and forever. Amen.

To Christ be all the glory forever and ever. Amen.

WORKS OF WILLIAM C. WEINRICH

COMPILED SEPTEMBER 2018
BY ROBERT E. SMITH

✝

ARTICLES

"Antichrist in the Early Church." *Concordia Theological Quarterly* 49, no. 2–3 (1985): 135–47.
http://www.ctsfw.net/media/pdfs/weinrichantichristearlychurch.pdf.

"At the Edge of Subscription: The *Abusus* Doctrine in the Formula of Concord—*Doctrina* or *Ratio*?" *Concordia Theological Quarterly* 73, no. 3 (2009): 257–69.
http://www.ctsfw.net/media/pdfs/WeinrichAttheEdgeofSubscription.pdf.

"Called and Ordained: Reflections on the New Testament View of the Office of the Ministry." *Logia* 2, no. 1 (1993): 20–27.
http://www.ctsfw.net/media/pdfs/WeinrichCalledandOrdained.pdf.

"*Creation Ex Nihilo*: The Way of God." *Logia* 4, no. 2 (1995): 37–42.

"Cyprian, Donatism, Augustine, and Augustana VIII: Remarks on the Church and the Validity of Sacraments." *Concordia Theological Quarterly* 55, no. 4 (1991): 267–96.
http://www.ctsfw.net/media/pdfs/weinrichcypriandonatism.pdf.

"Death and Martyrdom: An Important Aspect of Early Christian Eschatology." *Concordia Theological Quarterly* 66, no. 4 (2002): 327–38.
http://www.ctsfw.net/media/pdfs/weinrichdeathandmartyrdom.pdf.

"The Doctrine of Christ in Theological Education." *Concordia Theological Quarterly* 73, no. 2 (2009): 179–82.
http://www.ctsfw.net/media/pdfs/CTQTheologicalObserver73-2.pdf.

"Evangelism in the Early Church." *Concordia Theological Quarterly* 45, no. 1–2 (1981): 61–75.
http://www.ctsfw.net/media/pdfs/weinrichevangelismintheearlychurch.pdf.

"Father, Son, and Spirit Is God: What Is the Point?" *Concordia Theological Quarterly* 75, no. 1–2 (2011): 27–42.
http://www.ctsfw.net/media/pdfs/WeinrichFatherSonSpirit.pdf.

"Fellowship in Christ Is the Church and Salvation." *For the Life of the World* 5, no. 1 (2001): 8–10.
http://www.ctsfw.net/media/pdfs/FellowshipinChristIstheChurchandSalvationWeinrich.pdf.

"Feminism in the Church: The Issue of Our Day." *Concordia Theological Quarterly* 50, no. 2 (1986): 139–44.
http://www.ctsfw.net/media/pdfs/TheoObserver50-2.pdf.

"God Did Not Create Death: Athanasius on the Atonement." *Concordia Theological Quarterly* 72, no. 4 (2008): 291–304.
http://www.ctsfw.net/media/pdfs/weinrichgoddidnotcreatdeath.pdf.

"The Holy Supper: A Taste of Heaven." *For the Life of the World* 4, no. 1 (2000): 6–7.
http://www.ctsfw.net/media/pdfs/HolySupperATasteofHeavenWeinrich.pdf.

"The Image of the Wheat Stalk and the Vine Twig in the Adversus Haereses of Irenaeus of Lyons." *Concordia Theological Quarterly* 62, no. 3 (1998): 219–27. http://www.ctsfw.net/media/pdfs/weinrichwcimageofwheatstalk.pdf.

"Introduction to 'Man as Male and Female: Created in the Image of God.'" *Concordia Theological Quarterly* 68, no. 1 (2004): 3–96.
http://www.ctsfw.net/media/pdfs/WeinrichIntroductiontoManasMaleandFemale.pdf.

"Introduction to 'What Does This Mean? A Symposium.'" *Concordia Theological Quarterly* 62, no. 3 (1998): 165–67.
http://www.ctsfw.net/media/pdfs/WhatDoesThisMeanSymposium.pdf.

"Man and Woman in Christ." *Lutheran Forum* 29, no. 2 (1995): 43–45.

"Man as Cyborg: A New Challenge." *For the Life of the World* 16, no. 1 (2012): 10–12. http://www.ctsfw.net/media/pdfs/WeinrichManasCyborg.pdf.

"Martin H. Scharlemann." *Concordia Theological Quarterly* 47, no. 1 (1983): 31–32. http://www.ctsfw.net/media/pdfs/TheoObserver47-1.pdf.

"The New WELS Creed." *Concordia Theological Quarterly* 56, no. 4 (1992): 201–6. http://www.ctsfw.net/media/pdfs/TheoObserver56-2,3.pdf.

"The New WELS Creed: Again." *Concordia Theological Quarterly* 57, no. 1 (1993): 116–25. http://www.ctsfw.net/media/pdfs/TheoObserver57-1,2.pdf.

"Patristic Exegesis as Ecclesial and Sacramental." *Concordia Theological Quarterly* 64, no. 1 (2000): 21–38.
http://www.ctsfw.net/media/pdfs/weinrichpatristicexegesis.pdf.

"Paul Davies & Critics: An Exchange." *First Things* 58 (1995): 3.

"Renewal of the Mind." *For the Life of the World* 9, no. 4 (2005): 7–8.
http://www.ctsfw.net/media/pdfs/RenewaloftheMindWeinrich.pdf.

"The Same Yesterday, Today, and Forever: Jesus as Timekeeper." *Concordia Theological Quarterly* 78, no. 3–4 (2014): 3–15.
http://www.ctsfw.net/media/pdfs/WeinrichSameYesterdayTodayandForever.pdf.

"Should a Layman Discharge the Duties of the Holy Ministry?" *Concordia Theological Quarterly* 68, no. 3–4 (2004): 207–29.
http://www.ctsfw.net/media/pdfs/weinrichlaymandutiesministry.pdf.

"The Spirit of Holiness: The Holiness of Man." *Concordia Theological Quarterly* 70, no. 3–4 (2006): 253–68.
http://www.ctsfw.net/media/pdfs/weinrichspiritofholiness.pdf.

"Trinitarian Reality as Christian Truth: Reflections on Greek Patristic Discussion." *Concordia Theological Quarterly* 67, no. 3–4 (2003): 335–46.
http://www.ctsfw.net/media/pdfs/WeinrichTrinitarianReality.pdf.

"Work and Reality in Latvia." *Concordia Theological Quarterly* 73, no. 2 (2009): 177–79.
http://www.ctsfw.net/media/pdfs/WorkandRealityinLatviaWeinrich.pdf.

COLLABORATIVE ARTICLES

Weinrich, William C., and G. Waldemar Degner. "The Council on Biblical Manhood and Womanhood: The Danvers Statement." *Concordia Theological Quarterly* 53, no. 1–2 (1989): 92–96.
http://www.ctsfw.net/media/pdfs/TheoObserver53-1,2.pdf.

Weinrich, William C., David P. Scaer, Richard E. Muller, Kurt E. Marquart, and Lawrence R. Rast Jr. "Joint Lutheran/Roman Catholic Declaration on Justification: A Response." *Concordia Theological Quarterly* 62, no. 2 (1998): 63–106.
http://www.ctsfw.net/media/pdfs/JointLutheran-RomanCatholicDeclarationResponse.pdf.

Weinrich, William C., Dean O. Wenthe. "Neo-Donatism or Neo-Docetism." *Concordia Theological Quarterly* 54, no. 2–3 (1990): 208–12.
http://www.ctsfw.net/media/pdfs/TheoObserver54-2,3.pdf.

BOOKS

Apocalipsis. Edited by Thomas C. Oden. Translated by Marcelo Merino. Vol. 12. La Biblia comentada por los Padres de la Iglesia y otros autores de la época patrística. Nuevo Testamento. Madrid: Ciudad Nueva, 2010.

Apocalisse. Edited by Chiara Spuntarelli. La Bibbia commentata dai padri. Nuovo Testamento 12; Roma: Città Nuova, 2008.

Early Christian Popular Literature. Fort Wayne, IN: Concordia Theological Seminary Press, 1984.

"It Is Not Given to Women to Teach": A Lex in Search of a Ratio. Fort Wayne, IN: Concordia Theological Seminary, 1993. http://www.ctsfw.net/media/pdfs/WeinrichItIsNotGiven.pdf.

John 1:1–7:1. Concordia Commentary. St. Louis, MO: Concordia Publishing House, 2015.

Patristic readings. Fort Wayne, IN: Concordia Theological Seminary Press, 1984.

Readings in Early Church History. Fort Wayne, IN: Concordia Theological Seminary Press, 1988.

Revelation. Vol. 12. Ancient Christian Commentary on Scripture. Downers Grove, IL: InterVarsity Press, 2005.

Spirit and Martyrdom : A Study of the Work of the Holy Spirit in Contexts of Persecution and Martyrdom in the New Testament and Early Christian Literature. Washington, DC: University Press of America, 1981.

요한 묵시록. Vol. 14. Ancient Christian commentary on Scripture. New Testament. 칠곡군: 분도출판사, 2010.

啟示錄 = *Qi shi lu.* Vol. 13. 古代基督信=Gu dai ji du xin yang sheng jing zhu shi cong shu. xin yue pian. 新北市 : 校園書房 = Xin bei shi : Xiao yuan shu fang, 2011.

The Service of Women in Congregational and Synodical Offices. [St. Louis, MO]: Commission on Theology and Church Relations. Lutheran Church—Missouri Synod], 1994.

COLLABORATIVE BOOKS

Scaer, David P., Richard E. Muller, Kurt E. Marquart, William C. Weinrich, Lawrence R. Rast Jr, Charles P. Arand, and Jerald Eickmann. *The Joint Declaration on the Doctrine of Justification in Confessional Lutheran Perspective.* St Louis, MO: Commission on Theology and Church Relations, 1999.

Weinrich, William C., Robert A. Dargatz, Cameron A. MacKenzie, Norman E. Nagel, and James W. Voelz. *Dissenting Opinion on Women in Congregational Offices.* St Louis, MO: Commission on Theology and Church Relations. Lutheran Church—Missouri Synod, 1994.

Weinrich, William C., David P. Scaer, Kurt E. Marquart, Richard E. Muller, and Lawrence R. Rast Jr. *The Formula of Agreement in Confessional Lutheran Perspective.* St Louis, MO: Office of the President. Lutheran Church—Missouri Synod, 1999.

TRANSLATED BOOKS

Hippolytus of Rome. *An Address on the Holy Theophanies.* Translated by William C. Weinrich. Fort Wayne, IN: Concordia Theological Seminary, 2012. http://www.ctsfw.net/media/pdfs/HippolytusIAddressontheHolyTheophanies.pdf.

Oikoumenios and Andrew, Archbishop of Caesarea. *Greek Commentaries on Revelation.* Edited by Thomas C. Oden. Translated by William C. Weinrich. Ancient Christian Texts. Downers Grove, IL: IVP Academic, 2011.

Victorinus, Bishop of Poetovio, Apringius, Bishop of Beja, Caesarius of Arles, and Bede, the Venerable. *Latin Commentaries on Revelation.* Translated by William C. Weinrich. Ancient Christian Texts. Downers Grove, IL: IVP Academic, 2011.

CHAPTERS

"Church Fellowship in the Early Church." In *Church Fellowship*, edited by Chris Christophersen Boshoven, 2:8–20. The Pieper Lectures. Crestwood, MO: The Luther Academy, 1998.

"Doubting 'Doubting Thomas.'" In *The Press of the Text: Biblical Studies in Honor of James W. Voelz*, edited by Andrew H. Bartelt, Jeffrey J. Kloha, and Paul R. Raabe, 254–69. Eugene, OR: Pickwick Publications, 2017.

"Early Christian Catechetics: An Historical and Theological Construction." In *Luther's Catechisms – 450 Years: Essays Commemorating the Small and Large Catechisms of Dr Martin Luther*, 65–73, 1979.

"Ecclesial Polity and Governance in the Early Church." In *Church Polity and Politics: Papers Presented at the Congress on the Lutheran Confessions, Itasca, Illinois, April 3–5, 1997*, edited by John R. Fehrmann and Daniel Preus, 94–106. Luther Academy Lecture Series 4. Crestwood, MO : Luther Academy, 1997.

Editor's Preface. In *The New Testament Age: Essays in Honor of Bo Reicke*, edited by William C. Weinrich, 1: ix–x. Macon, GA: Mercer, 1984.

"Feminist Hermeneutics and Biblical Interpretation." In *Confessional Lutheran Ethics: Papers Presented at the Congress on the Lutheran Confessions, Itasca, Illinois, April 16-18, 1998*, edited by Jennifer H. Maxfield and Bethany Preus. Luther Academy Lecture Series 5. St. Louis, MO: Luther Academy, 2009.

"Gnosticism: Alive and Well in the Twentieth Century Church." In *Theological Papers: Presented at the Campus Pastor's Conference, November 2-3, 1992, University Lutheran Chapel, Minneapolis, Minnesota*, edited by James H. Cavener. [Minneapolis, MN]: University Lutheran Chapel], 1993.

"*Homo Theologicus*: Aspects of a Lutheran Doctrine of Man." In *Personal Identity in Theological Perspective*, 29–44, 2006.

"'It Is Not Given to Women to Teach': A Lex in Search of a Ratio." In *Church and Ministry Today : Three Confessional Lutheran Essays : Preus - Marquart - Weinrich*, edited by John A. Maxfield, 173–215. St. Louis, MO: Luther Academy, 2001.

"'It Is Not Given to Women to Teach': A Lex in Search of a Ratio." In *Women Pastors?* edited by Matthew C. Harrison and John T. Pless, 3rd ed., 461–95. St. Louis, MO: Concordia Pub. House, 2012.

"Leviticus as a Christian Book : Patristic Instances." In *You, My People, Shall Be Holy: A Festschrift in Honour of John W. Kleinig / Stephenson, John R. ; (John Raymond),; Editor.; (Editor)*, 297–312. St. Catharines, Ontario, Canada: Concordia Lutheran Theological Seminary, 2013.

"On the Holy Pascha." In *The Restoration of Creation in Christ: Essays in Honor of Dean O. Wenthe*, edited by Dean O. Wenthe and Arthur A. Just Jr, 19–35. St. Louis: Concordia Publishing House, 2014.

"Response." In *Applying the Scriptures: Papers from ICBI Summit III*, 36–43, 1987.

"Should a Layman Discharge the Duties of the Ministry?" In *Mysteria Dei: Essays in Honor of Kurt Marquart*, edited by Paul Timothy McCain and John R. Stephenson, 341–357. Fort Wayne, IN: Concordia Theological Seminary Press, 1999.

"Speech of the Heart; Speech of God: Augustine's Use of Psalm 4 in Confessions 9.4." In *Day by Day We Magnify Thee : Psalms in the Life of the Church*, edited by Daniel Zager, 49–62. Journal of the Good Shepherd Institute 3. Fort Wayne, IN: Concordia Theological Seminary Press, 2003.

"St. Paul and the Early Church." In *God's Mission in Action: A Booklet of Essays Delivered at the First Annual Missions Congress, Concordia Theological Seminary, Fort Wayne, Indiana, April 24-27, 1986*, edited by Eugene W. Bunkowske and Michael A. Nichol, 28–52. The Great Commission Resource Library Book Series 1. Fort Wayne, IN: Great Commission Resource Library, 1986.

"The Concept of the Church in Ignatius of Antioch." In *Good News in History: Essays in Honor of Bo Reicke*, edited by Ed L. Miller, 137–150. Scholars Press Homage Series. Atlanta, GA: Scholars Press, 1993.

"The Face of Christ as the Hope of the World: Missiology as Making Christ Present." In *All Theology Is Christology: Essays in Honor of David P. Scaer*, edited by Dean O. Wenthe and David P. Scaer, 215–227. Fort Wayne, IN: Concordia Theological Seminary Press, 2000.

"The Holy Supper: A Taste of Heaven." In *We Believe : Essays on the Catechism as Drawn from For the Life of the World*, edited by Scott C. Klemsz, 129–133. Fort Wayne, IN: Concordia Theological Seminary Press, 2000.

"The Lutheran Reformation and the Early Church." In *Lutheran Catholicity*, edited by John A. Maxfield, 5:1–15. The Pieper Lectures. St. Louis, MO: Concordia Historical Institute, 2001.

"The Virtuous Anger of God: Lactantius' De Ira Dei in Conversation with the Philosophy of Antiquity." In *Ad Fontes Witebergenses: Select Proceedings of "Lutheranism and the Classics II: Reading the Church Fathers," Concordia Theological Seminary, September 28-29, 2012 / Springer, Carl P. E., ; Editor.*, edited by James A. Kellerman, 53–69. Fort Wayne, IN: Lutheran Legacy, 2014.

"Women in the History of the Church : Learned and Holy, but Not Pastors." In *Recovering Biblical Manhood and Womanhood: A Response to Evangelical Feminism*, edited by John Piper and Wayne A. Grudem, 263–279, 512–516. Wheaton, IL: Crossway Books, 1991.

"Women in the History of the Church: The Ordination of Women in Biblical Lutheran Perspective: A Collection of Essays." In *Women Pastors?*, edited by Matthew C. Harrison and John T. Pless, 3rd ed., 171–96. St. Louis, MO: Concordia Pub. House, 2012.

✦ WILLIAM C. WEINRICH

CLASS NOTES

Early Church History: A Compendium of the Course as It Is Taught by Dr. William Weinrich. Edited by Richard D. Stuckwisch. Fort Wayne, IN: Concordia Theological Seminary Press, 1990.
http://www.ctsfw.net/media/pdfs/StuckwischEarlyChurchHistory.pdf.

DISSERTATION

"Spirit and Martyrdom: A Study of the Work of the Holy Spirit in Contexts of Persecution and Martyrdom in the New Testament and Early Christian Literature." Ph. D., University of Basel, 1977.

RECORDED PRESENTATIONS

Baptism & the Baptismal Life. Audiocassette. Divine Service Institute at St. Paul's Lecture. Fort Wayne, IN: St. Paul's Lutheran Church, 1994.

Called and Ordained: A Theological Forum on the Holy Ministry. Audiocassette. Vincennes, IN: Logia Tape Productions, 1990.

Chalcedon, A.D. 451: What Was It All About and Does It Matter? Mp3. 24th Symposium on the Lutheran Confessions. Fort Wayne, IN: Concordia Theological Seminary, 2001.
https://video.ctsfw.edu/media/Confessions+-+Chalcedon%2C+A.D.+451A+What+Was+It+All+About+and+Does+It+MatterF/1_8gied138/86967591.

Christian Sacramental Living: Christology and Sacramentality in the Gospel According to St. John. Lutheran Catechetical Society, 2011.

Creatio Ex Nihilo. Audiocassette. Vol. 4. 7 vols. 16th Annual Symposium on the Lutheran Confessions. Fort Wayne, IN: Concordia Theological Seminary, 1993.

Creatio Ex Nihilo. VHS. Vol. 4. 7 vols. 16th Annual Symposium on the Lutheran Confessions. Fort Wayne, IN: Concordia Theological Seminary, 1993.

Death and Martyrdom: Eschatology in the Early Church. Mp3. 23rd Symposium on the Lutheran Confessions. Fort Wayne, IN: Concordia Theological Seminary, 2000. https://video.ctsfw.edu/media/Confessions+-+Death+and+MartyrdomA+Eschatology+in+the+Early+Church/1_6vvzaook/86967571.

Donatism, Augustine, and Augustana VIII. Audiocassette. Vol. 1. 7 vols. 14th Annual Symposium on the Lutheran Confessions. Fort Wayne, IN: Concordia Theological Seminary, 1991.

Donatism, Augustine, and Augustana VIII. VHS. Vol. 1. 8 vols. 14th Annual Symposium on the Lutheran Confessions. Fort Wayne, IN: Concordia Theological Seminary, 1991.

The Early Church Fathers on Worship. Audiocassette. Divine Service Institute at St. Paul's Lecture. Fort Wayne, IN: St. Paul's Lutheran Church, 1995.

Early Church's Views on Biblical Passages Traditionally Taken as References to the Antichrist. Audiocassette. Vol. 3. 10 vols. 8th Annual Symposium on the Lutheran Confessions, 1985.

Fellowship Lecture: "Fellowship in the Early Church." Audiocassette. Fort Wayne, IN: Concordia Theological Seminary, 1980.

Gender Inclusive Bibles. Audiocassette. Issues, Etc. [St. Louis]: [KFUO], 1999.

Gnosticism. CD. Issues, Etc. [St. Louis]: [KFUO], 2000.

Gnosticism: Then and Now. Audiocassette. 2 vols. Vincennes, IN: Logia Tape Productions, 1990.

God Did Not Make Death (Wisdom 1:13): The Sacrifice of Christ as the Life of Man: Athanasius on the Atonement. Mp4. 31st Symposium on the Lutheran Confessions. Fort Wayne, IN: Concordia Theological Seminary, 2008. https://video.ctsfw.edu/media/Confessions+-+God+Did+Not+Make+Death+%28Wisdom+1A13%29A+The+Sacrifice+of+Christ+as+the+Life+of+ManA+Athanasius+on+the+Atonement/1_iz868nf7/86967691.

God the Son and the Church as the Body of Christ. Audiocassette. Vol. 3. 8 vols. 17th Annual Symposium on the Lutheran Confessions. Fort Wayne, IN: Concordia Theological Seminary, 1994.

God the Son and the Church as the Body of Christ. Audiocassette. Vol. 3. 8 vols. 17th Annual Symposium on the Lutheran Confessions. Fort Wayne, IN: Concordia Theological Seminary, 1994.

The Holy Spirit and the Redemption of Man. Mp3. 29th Symposium on the Lutheran Confessions. Fort Wayne, IN: Concordia Theological Seminary, 2006. https://video.ctsfw.edu/media/Confessions+-+The+Holy+Spirit+and+the+Redemption+of+Man/1_u8aydysc/86967671.

The Holy Trinity: What's the Point? Mp3. 33rd Symposium on the Lutheran Confessions. Fort Wayne, IN: Concordia Theological Seminary, 2010. https://video.ctsfw.edu/media/Confessions+-+The+Holy+TrinityA+What%27s+the+PointF+-+Audio/1_v2daua5a/86967741.

The Holy Trinity: What's the Point? Mp4. 33rd Symposium on the Lutheran Confessions. Fort Wayne, IN: Concordia Theological Seminary, 2010. http://media.ctsfw.edu.s3.amazonaws.com/symposia/2010/19-Weinrich-100119.m4v.

Jesus on Unity. CD. Issues, Etc. [St. Louis]: [KFUO], 2000.

Missions, St. Paul and the Early Church. VHS. Vol. 1. 5 vols. God's Mission in Action. Fort Wayne, IN: Concordia Theological Seminary, 1986.

The Patristic Doctrine of the Trinity. Mp3. 27th Symposium on the Lutheran Confessions. Fort Wayne, IN: Concordia Theological Seminary, 2004. https://video.ctsfw.edu/media/Confessions+-+The+Patristic+Doctrine+of+the+Trinity/1_argwgnt0/86967651.

Patristic Exegesis as Sacramental and Ecclesial. Mp3. 22nd Symposium on the Lutheran Confessions. Fort Wayne, IN: Concordia Theological Seminary, 1999. https://video.ctsfw.edu/media/Confession+-+Patristic+Exegesis+as+Sacramental+and+Ecclesial/1_436kpx9m/86967561.

The Role of Women in the Liturgical Context. Audiocassette. Divine Service Institute at St. Paul's Lecture. Fort Wayne, IN: St. Paul's Lutheran Church, 1995.

Three Identifying Authorities: Looking at Situations of Pastoral Practice. Reaching Back to the Early Church. CD. Vol. 3. 6 vols. Identifying Authorities: The Limits of Theological Diversity and Confessional Unity. St. Louis: Concordia Seminary Media Services, 2003.

The Virtuous Anger of God: Lactantius' De Ira Dei in Conversation with the Philosophy of the Third Century. Mp3. Lutheranism and the Classics 2012. Fort Wayne, IN: Concordia Theological Seminary, 2012. http://media.ctsfw.edu.s3.amazonaws.com/events/conferences/Dr_William_C_Weinrich_The_Virtuous_Anger_of_God_Lactantius_De_ira_dei_in_conversation_with_the_Philosophy_of_the_Third_Century_Lutheranism_in_the_Classics_2012.mp3.

What Makes a Hermeneutic Lutheran? VHS. Vol. 2. 4 vols. Hermeneutics Lectures. Fort Wayne, IN: Concordia Theological Seminary, 1999.

REVIEWS

"*At the Lighting of the Lamps: Hymns of the Ancient Church* by John A. McGuckin." *Concordia Theological Quarterly* 62, no. 2 (1998): 156–57. http://www.ctsfw.net/media/pdfs/CTQBookReview62-2.pdf.

"*Athenagorae Qui Fertur De Resurrectione Mortuorum* by Miroslav Marcovich." *Journal of Early Christian Studies* 10, no. 3 (2002): 392–93.

"*Augustine* by Henry Chadwick." *Concordia Theological Quarterly* 51, no. 2–3 (1987): 216–216. http://www.ctsfw.net/media/pdfs/BookReviews51-2,3.pdf.

"*Augustine: His Life and Thought* by Warren Thomas Smith." *Concordia Theological Quarterly* 45, no. 4 (October 1981): 329–329. http://search.ebscohost.com/login.aspx?direct=true&db=lsdar&AN=ATLA0000522034&site=ehost-live&scope=site.

"*Beginning to Read the Fathers* by Boniface Ramsay." *Concordia Theological Quarterly* 50, no. 2 (1986): 153–54. http://www.ctsfw.net/media/pdfs/BookReviews50-2.pdf.

"*Celsus on the True Doctrine: A Doctrine against the Christians* by R. Joseph Hoffmann." *Concordia Theological Quarterly* 51, no. 4 (1987): 296–97. http://www.ctsfw.net/media/pdfs/BookReviews51-4.pdf.

"*Christ in Christian Tradition, v 2, Pt 4: The Church of Alexandria with Nubia and Ethiopia after 451* by Alois Grillmeier." *Church History* 68, no. 2 (1999): 430–32.

"*Christian Contradictions: The Structures of Lutheran and Catholic Thought* by Daphne Hampson." *Concordia Theological Quarterly* 68, no. 2 (2004): 157–60. http://www.ctsfw.net/media/pdfs/CTQBookReview68-2.pdf.

"*Christians and the Military: The Early Experience* by John Helgeland, Robert J. Daly, and J. Patout Bums." *Concordia Theological Quarterly* 49, no. 4 (1985): 315–16. http://www.ctsfw.net/media/pdfs/BookReviews49-4.pdf.

"*The Christological Controversy* by Richard A. Norris Jr." *Concordia Theological Quarterly* 45, no. 4 (1981): 327–28. http://www.ctsfw.net/media/pdfs/BookReviews45-4.pdf.

"*The Church under Siege* by M. A. Smith." *Concordia Theological Quarterly* 42, no. 4 (1978): 450–52. http://www.ctsfw.net/media/pdfs/BookReviews42-4.pdf.

"*Clement of Alexandria: A Study in Christian Platonism and Gnosticism* by Salvatore Romano Clemente Lilla." *Theologische Zeitschrift* 30, no. 1 (1974): 41–42.

"*Creeds, Councils and Christ* by Gerald Bray." *Concordia Theological Quarterly* 49, no. 2–3 (1985): 234–36.
http://www.ctsfw.net/media/pdfs/CTQBookReview49-2,3.pdf.

"*The Dark Side of the Millennium* by Arthur H. Lewis." *Concordia Theological Quarterly* 45, no. 1–2 (1981): 123–24.

"*Dietrich Bonhoeffer* by Dallas M. Roark." *Concordia Theological Quarterly* 41, no. 4 (1977): 101–2. http://www.ctsfw.net/media/pdfs/BookReviews41-4.pdf.

"*Faith and Practice in the Early Church: Foundations for Contemporary Theology* by Carl A. Volz." *Concordia Theological Quarterly* 49, no. 2–3 (1985): 223–24. http://www.ctsfw.net/media/pdfs/CTQBookReview49-2,3.pdf.

"*The First Seven Ecumenical Councils, 325-787: Their History and Theology* by Leo Donald Davis." *Concordia Theological Quarterly* 53, no. 4 (1989): 309–10. http://www.ctsfw.net/media/pdfs/BookReviews53-4.pdf.

"*From Nicaea to Chalcedon: A Guide to the Literature and Its Background* by Frances Young." *Concordia Theological Quarterly* 49, no. 4 (1985): 314–15. http://www.ctsfw.net/media/pdfs/BookReviews49-4.pdf.

"*From the Council of the Chalcedon (451) to Gregory the Great (590-604): The Church of Alexandria with Nubia and Ethiopia After 451* by Aloys Grillmeier." *Church History* 68, no. 2 (1999): 430.

"*God and Man in Time: A Christian Approach to Historiography* by Earle E. Cairns." *Concordia Theological Quarterly* 45, no. 4 (1981): 325–26. http://www.ctsfw.net/media/pdfs/BookReviews45-4.pdf.

"*History in the Making: An Introduction to the Study of the Past* by Roy Swanstrom." *Concordia Theological Quarterly* 43, no. 4 (1979): 388–89. http://www.ctsfw.net/media/pdfs/BookReviews43-4.pdf.

"*History of Christian Ethics*, Vol I From the New Testament to Augustine by George Wolfgang Forell." *Concordia Theological Quarterly* 46, no. 4 (1982): 345–46. http://www.ctsfw.net/media/pdfs/CTQBookReviews46-4.pdf.

"*Holiness and the Will of God* by Gerald Lewis Bray." *Concordia Theological Quarterly* 46, no. 4 (1982): 343–44. http://www.ctsfw.net/media/pdfs/CTQBookReviews46-4.pdf.

"*Human Face of God* by John A T. Robinson." *Theologische Zeitschrift* 32, no. 2 (1976): 118–19.

"*Incarnation: Myth or Fact* by Oskar Skarsaune." *Concordia Theological Quarterly* 56, no. 1 (1992): 60–63. http://www.ctsfw.net/media/pdfs/BookReviews56-1.pdf.

"*Leiden Als Gnade* by Helmut Millauer." *Concordia Theological Quarterly* 43, no. 4 (1979): 383–85. http://www.ctsfw.net/media/pdfs/BookReviews43-4.pdf.

"*The Letters of St Cyprian of Carthage* vol. 3 by G. W. Clarke." *Concordia Theological Quarterly* 51, no. 4 (1987): 290–290. http://www.ctsfw.net/media/pdfs/BookReviews51-4.pdf.

"*Lord Jesus Christ: Devotion to Jesus in Earliest Christianity* by Larry W. Hurtado." *Church History* 74, no. 2 (2005): 345–47.

"*The Making of the Creeds* by Frances Young." *Concordia Theological Quarterly* 58, no. 2–3 (1994): 176–78. http://www.ctsfw.net/media/pdfs/CTQBookReview58-2.pdf.

"*Major Black Religious Leaders: 1755-1940* by Henry J. Young." *Concordia Theological Quarterly* 43, no. 3 (1979): 263–65. http://www.ctsfw.net/media/pdfs/BookReviews43-3.pdf.

"*Das Martyrium Des Polykarp* by Gerd Buschmann." *Journal of Early Christian Studies* 8, no. 2 (2000): 300–302.

"*The New Testament Concept of Witness* by Allison A. Trites." *Theologische Zeitschrift* 35, no. 6 (1979): 371–72.

"*One God in Trinity: An Analysis of the Primary Dogma of Christianity* by Peter Toon and James D. Spiceland." *Concordia Theological Quarterly* 48, no. 1 (1984): 81–82. http://www.ctsfw.net/media/pdfs/BookReviews48-1.pdf.

"*One Right Reading: A Guide to Irenaeus* by Mary Ann Donovan." *Concordia Theological Quarterly* 63, no. 1 (1999): 65–67. http://www.ctsfw.net/media/pdfs/CTQBookReview63-1.pdf.

"*Prophecy in Carthage: Perpetua, Tertullian, and Cyprian* by Cecil M. Robeck Jr." *Catholic Historical Review* 82, no. 3 (1996): 494.

"*Reading Scripture with the Church Fathers* by Christopher A. Hall." *Concordia Theological Quarterly* 63, no. 1 (1999): 57–60. http://www.ctsfw.net/media/pdfs/CTQBookReview63-1.pdf.

"*Reading the Apostolic Fathers: A Student's Introduction* by Clayton N. Jefford." *Concordia Theological Quarterly* 77, no. 3–4 (July 2013): 369–70. http://www.ctsfw.net/media/pdfs/CTQBookReview77-3.pdf.

"*A Reformation Debate: Karlstadt, Emser, and Eck on Sacred Images: Three Treatises in Translation* by Bryan D. Mangrum and Giuseppe Scavizzi." *Concordia Theological Quarterly* 58, no. 2–3 (1994): 175–76. http://www.ctsfw.net/media/pdfs/CTQBookReview58-2.pdf.

✝ WILLIAM C. WEINRICH

"The Repression of the Evangelical Lutheran Church in Lithuania during the Stalinist Era by Darius Petkiinas." *Concordia Theological Quarterly* 76, no. 1–2 (2012): 188–92. http://www.ctsfw.net/media/pdfs/CTQBookReview76-1.pdf.

"The Restless Heart: The Life and Influence of St Augustine by Michael Marshall." *Concordia Theological Quarterly* 51, no. 4 (1987): 305–6. http://www.ctsfw.net/media/pdfs/BookReviews51-4.pdf.

"The Resurrection Letters of St. Athanasius, Bishop of Alexandria. 328-373 by Jack N. Sparks." *Concordia Theological Quarterly* 45, no. 4 (1981): 328–29. http://www.ctsfw.net/media/pdfs/BookReviews45-4.pdf.

"Revelation by J. P. M. Sweet." *Concordia Theological Quarterly* 45, no. 1–2 (1981): 121–22. http://www.ctsfw.net/media/pdfs/BookReviews45-1,2.pdf.

"Tertullien et Le Judaisme by Claude Aziza." *The Jewish Quarterly Review* 71, no. 2 (1980): 118–20.

"Theophilus of Antioch: The Life and Thought of a Second-Century Bishop by Rick Rogers." *Journal of Early Christian Studies* 9, no. 4 (2001): 601–3.

"Trinitarian Controversy by William G. Rusch." *Concordia Theological Quarterly* 45, no. 4 (1981): 327–28. http://www.ctsfw.net/media/pdfs/BookReviews45-4.pdf.

"The Triumph of the Meek: Why Early Christianity Succeeded by Michael Walsh." *Concordia Theological Quarterly* 51, no. 4 (1987): 314–15. http://www.ctsfw.net/media/pdfs/BookReviews51-4.pdf.

"What Are They Saying about John by Gerard S. Sloyan." *Concordia Theological Quarterly* 58, no. 2–3 (1994): 227–29. http://www.ctsfw.net/media/pdfs/CTQBookReview58-2.pdf.

"Women and the Priesthood by Thomas Hopko." *Concordia Theological Quarterly* 49, no. 2–3 (1985): 221–22. http://www.ctsfw.net/media/pdfs/CTQBookReview49-2,3.pdf.

"Women in the Church: A Biblical Study on the Role of Women in the Church by Samuele Bacchiocchi." *Concordia Theological Quarterly* 51, no. 4 (1987): 288–90. http://www.ctsfw.net/media/pdfs/BookReviews51-4.pdf.

PART ONE

EVANGELION

MORE THAN WORDS

JEREMIAH'S SACRAMENTAL RICHNESS

✛

The churchly and scholarly life of Dr. William Weinrich invites su-perlatives. As a scholar, his PhD from the University of Basel, with Dr. Bo Reicke as his Doktorvater, positioned him for a distinguished career as an author and translator. As a professor, Bill has invited students into the dense texts of patristic, Trinitarian theology. His rigorous intellectual engagement serves Christ, enhancing the church's mission more so than the fashionable but shallow appropriations of theology by a contemporary emotive culture. As Academic Dean of Concordia Theological Seminary, he led the faculty through a revision of the curriculum that was groundbreaking in its organization of theological formation. Through this curriculum, students engage in theological critique and evaluation while grounded in the central pastoral acts of Holy Baptism, Preaching, and the Eucharist.

But most striking for colleagues and friends are the integrity, fidelity, and passion that Bill brings to the theological task. The church—Christ's people—have been blessed for decades by this servant. To be among his colleagues and friends makes that blessing all the more personable and enjoyable.

One of the consistent contributions of Dr. Weinrich has been his rec-ommendation and exposition of the exegesis of the church fathers, there-by opening up fresh worlds of theological reflection on the Scriptures and freeing students from captivity only to contemporary or recent commen-taries. The following essay seeks to complement his splendid leadership in this crucial task of preserving the church's memory.

One of the refreshingly positive deployments in the world of biblical interpretation is a new window into the exegesis of earlier generations. A title that captures this dimension of biblical hermeneutics is John L. Thompson's *Reading the Bible with the Dead*.[1] Particularly salutary is the challenge this development mounts to the prideful view that only recent

---

1. John L. Thompson, *Reading the Bible with the Dead* (Grand Rapids, WI: Wm. B. Eerdmans, 2007).

3

Scriptural interpretation is worthy of consideration—a perspective that C. S. Lewis characterized as the fallacy of contemporaneity.

Evidence of the new interest in and respect for the interpretation of prior generations is obvious in the publication of two series that review patristic interpretation through the first thousand years of Christianity, book by biblical book. They are Thomas Oden's *Ancient Christian Commentary*[2] and Robert Louis Wilken's *The Church's Bible*.[3] Dr. Weinrich contributed the volume on *Revelation* in the *Ancient Christian Commentary*.[4] Through these series, a number of individual volumes have appeared that exhibit respect and openness to the exegetical and interpretive inference of early Christian Exegesis. Two are representative: Christopher Hall's *Reading Scripture with the Church Fathers*[5] and Adalbert Hamman's *How to Read the Church Fathers*.[6]

Especially inviting is the fact that the church fathers were more than mere academics or intellectual virtuosos. They were pastors who shaped their pastoral teaching and guidance of the church on the basis of the Scriptures that were, for them, inspired and authoritative. Knowledge of this early Christian exegesis deepens our capacity to hear the Scriptural witness as the *viva vox Jesu*—the living voice of Jesus through his prophets and apostles.

OLD TESTAMENT SACRAMENTS IN LUTHERAN EXEGESIS

What is true of the patristic period is also true of the Reformation period, especially in the earliest layers of Lutheran exegesis of the Old Testament, demonstrated here in several texts from Martin Luther (1483–1546), Martin Chemnitz (1522–1586), David Chytraeus (1531–1600), and Johann Gerhard (1582–1637), all of whom related Old Testament texts to Christology and the themes of grace alone and faith alone. They display a remarkable grasp of earlier patristic exegesis while framing their responses to Roman Catholic interpretation. The richness and churchly character of their exegesis is particularly displayed in that period before the rise of rationalism with its reductionist and fragmenting impulses.

One feature of this early Lutheran exegesis is especially interesting, namely, its view that there was an Old Testament sacramental system in which God joined his gracious, saving presence to specific components

2. Thomas Oden, ed., *Ancient Christian Commentary Series*, 29 vols. (Westmont, IL: InterVarsity Press).

3. Robert Louis Wilken, ed., *The Church's Bible*, 5 vols. (Grand Rapids, MI: Eerdmans, 2005–2018).

4. William C. Weinrich, ed., *Revelation*, vol. 12, Ancient Christian Commentary on Scripture (Westmont, IL: InterVarsity, 2005).

5. Christopher Hall, *Reading Scripture with the Church Fathers* (Westmont, IL: InterVarsity, 1998).

6. Adalbert Hamman, *How to Read the Church Fathers* (New York: Crossroad, 1993).

of creation—a view that benefits and builds on a thorough knowledge of the patristic authors. This perspective invites expanded elaboration and appropriate application for the benefit of the church today, particularly in its proper understanding of the gracious character of God in the Old Testament.

After providing some select quotes from these early Lutheran fathers, application of their interpretive moves to the text of Jeremiah will be advanced as concrete examples. Lastly, it will be suggested that such a reading provides rich resources for faithful preaching and teaching of the Old Testament today.

Martin Luther (1483–1546)

Martin Luther, in harmony with the church fathers, describes an intimate tie between God's Word (Logos) and God's word (the Scriptures). He writes:

> God has always followed this custom of giving a visible sign, a person, place or spot where He could certainly be found. For if we are not bound and held by a physical external sign, every one of us will seek God wherever he pleases. For this reason the holy prophets wrote much of the Tabernacle, the dwelling place and tent where He willed to be present. Thus God has always done. In like manner He has built us Christians a temple where He would dwell, namely, the spoken Word, Baptism, and the Lord's Supper, which also are perceptible things.[7]

In his *Genesis Commentary*, Luther comments:

> But among this people He reveals Himself; and among this people He wants to be known, praised, and worshipped. He chooses a tabernacle and commands that a temple be built, in order to have a definite dwelling place among the people. To them He reveals Himself through the word, signs, wonders, rites, ceremonies, etc., that they may know that He is present everywhere and may all but feel Him with their hands.[8]

Luther's words are self-evident and profound. The reader immediately notices the striking phrase "may all but feel Him with their hands." Have you ever heard a Lutheran sermon on the tabernacle as God's real and gracious presence for his people? Give that pastor a golden chevron.

---

7. Francis Pieper, *Christian Dogmatics*, vol. 3 (St. Louis, MO: Concordia Publishing House, 1953), 139; cf. WA 3:924.

8. Martin Luther, *Lectures on Genesis 6–14* (1538): vol. 2, p. 225, in *Luther's Works, American Edition*, vols. 1–30, ed. Jaroslav Pelikan (St. Louis, MO: Concordia Publishing House, 1955–76); vols. 31–55, ed. Helmut Lehmann (Philadelphia/Minneapolis: Muhlenberg/Fortress, 1957–86); vols. 56–82, ed. Christopher Boyd Brown and Benjamin T. G. Mayes (St. Louis, MO: Concordia Publishing House, 2009–), hereafter AE.

Ian Hart, an Irish evangelical, has captured Luther's point with great clarity, and so it is worth concluding our consideration of Luther with his words:

> God promised to be as really and intensely present with them in the Tabernacle as he had been at Sinai: just as He had met with them at Sinai through Moses, so now He would meet with them in the Tabernacle through the medium of the priests (29:42f.); and as He had spoken commandments to them on Sinai so now He would speak to them in the commandment from above the mercy-seat (25:22). To confirm this promise that God would stay with them, "the cloud covered the tent of meeting, and the glory of the Lord filled the Tabernacle" (40:34) in the same manner as previously "the cloud covered the mountain" and the "glory of the Lord settled on Mount Sinai" (24:15f.).[9]

MARTIN CHEMNITZ (1522–1586)

We now move from Luther to the second Martin—Martin Chemnitz. In his magisterial *Examination of the Council of Trent*, he provides this inviting comment: "Therefore the institution and use of sacraments did not first begin at the time of the New Testament, but the fathers during the time of the Old Testament, even before the promulgation of the Law, had certain signs or sacraments, instituted by God for this use which were seals of the righteousness of faith."[10]

Another text from the *Examination* makes a similar point: "These things therefore hang together and are clear, . . . that the righteous in the Old Testament no less than we in the New Testament received the benefits of the Gospel which are necessary for salvation not only through the bare promise of grace on account of the coming Messiah, but also through sacraments which had been joined to that promise by divine institution."[11]

It is noteworthy also that Chemnitz views these sacraments as evidence of God's grace over against his Roman Catholic opponents. He writes: "But the papalists are not content with these differences, but simply maintain that God did not offer and convey any grace to the believers

---

9. Ian Hart, "Preaching on the Account of the Tabernacle," *The Evangelical Quarterly*, vol 54, no. 2 (April–June, 1982): 112.

10. Martin Chemnitz, *Examination of the Council of Trent*, 4 vols., trans. Fred Kramer (St. Louis, MO: Concordia Publishing House, 1978), 2:45. "Non igitur Novi Testamenti tempore primum coepit institution et usus sacramentorem: Sed Patres tempore veteris Testamenti imo etiam ante promugationem legis, sua quaedam divinitus in hunc usum instituta habuerunt signa seu sacramenta, quae fuerunt siqulla justitiae fidei." Martinum Chemnicium, *Examen Concilii Tridentini* (Berolini: Sumtibus Gust. Schulauitz, 1861), 236.

11. Chemnitz, *Examination*, 2:52. "Quod scilicet justi in Veteris Testamento, non tantum per nadam promissionem gratiae, propter venturam Messiam: Verum etiam per sacramenta, quae divina institutione promissioni illa annexaerant" (Martinum Chemnicium, 239).

through the sacraments of the Old Testament, even those which have a word of promise attached. This is manifestly wrong."[12]

DAVID CHYTRAEUS (1531–1600)

David Chytraeus, a key person in the framing of the *Formula of Concord* and Professor at the University of Rostock, wrote a commentary on Leviticus, *De Sacrificiis*, in which he comments: "Thus the Levitical sacrifices were also sacraments for the pious." He continues, "They were symbols of the belief in Christ, or signs and testimonies to awaken and encourage faith in God's promised forgiveness of sins, freely given because of Christ's future death on their behalf."[13]

JOHN GERHARD (1582–1637)

John Gerhard's prolific writings provide a wealth of exegetical material. In a very succinct fashion, he writes: "Therefore the sacraments of the Old Testament were also effective means of conferring spiritual blessings on believers."[14]

> In commenting on these Old Testament sacraments, Gerhard specifies some examples: Nevertheless there were more seasonal or temporary sacraments, for instance: passing through the Red Sea, Ex 14:22; staying under the cloud, Ex. 13:22; the eating of the manna, Ex. 16:14 . . . . To this you should also relate that miraculous preservation of the eight souls on the ark at the time of the universal cataclysm, Gen. 7:6, which Peter also compares with baptism as the antitype thereof, 1 Peter 3:21. Relate it also to the dew on the fleece of Gideon, Judges 6, the shadow going backward on the sundial of Ahaz, Is 38, all of which so far fit the sacraments which are salutary means of confirming faith and of sealing the divine promises.[15]

It is interesting that such exegesis ceases in the later Lutheran commentaries. Even the more conservative Lutheran exegetes retreat to the classic messianic texts in their attempt to counter rationalistic expositions. Could they have felt that such exegesis was too difficult to defend? This exegetical trajectory deserves closer examination.

However, for the moment, let us agree with Luther, Chemnitz, Chrytraeus and Gerhard; indeed, it should be noted that these men were by

---

12. Chemnitz, *Examination*, 2:57. "Potiticii vero hisce differentiis non sunt contenti, sed simpliciter volunt, Deum per Veteris Testamenti Sacramenta, etiam quae verbum promissionis annexum haberunt, nullam gratiam exhibuisse et contulisse credentibus, quad maniteste talsum esse . . . ." (Martinum Chemnicium, 241).

13. David Chrytraeus, *On Sacrifice*, trans. John Warwick Montgomery (St. Louis, MO: CPH, 1962), 60.

14. Johann Gerhard, *Loci Theologici*, Tomus Quartus, ed. Eduard Preuss (Berolini: Sumtibus Gust. Schlawitz, 1866), 182.

15. Gerhard, *Loci Theologici*, 182–183.

no means introducing a novel concept by speaking of Old Testament sacramentology. To cite but one source, an Augustinian scholar writes: "Augustine finds numerous sacraments in the Old Testament, most of which come from feasts, historical events, rituals, places and objects and individuals associated with worship."[16]

OLD TESTAMENT SACRAMENTS IN JEREMIAH

The sacramental perspective of early Lutheran theologians recounted above invites consideration of the following question: How would this sacramental perspective on the Old Testament shape its interpretation? Or, put another way, if God's gracious presence is joined to specific aspects of creation such as the tabernacle, how varied and significant might Old Testament sacramentology be? To address this question, Jeremiah provides a good test case.

First, Jeremiah is a Torah-formed prophet. His identity and his mission are given by the God who revealed himself in Moses' Torah. Indeed, Jeremiah with Baruch and a small band are the only ones truly attentive and loyal to the character of God as revealed in the Torah. At the very heart of the Torah, Exodus 25–40, God joins his gracious presence to the tabernacle. The specificity and repeated attention to detail in the manner of its construction, its furniture, and its configuration point to God's intimate involvement in the tabernacle's form and function. The construction reaches its crescendo when the "Glory for the Lord" dwells there rather than in the temples of Egypt or Mesopotamia.

The whole description moves with *sola gratia* action by God. His gracious compassion and love lead him to dwell with his people. For instance, it is written in Exodus 40:34–35, "Then the cloud covered the Tent of Meeting, and the glory of the Lord filled the tabernacle. Moses could not enter the Tent of Meeting because the cloud had settled upon it, and the glory of the Lord filled the Tabernacle."[17] The tabernacle, with its sacrificial system, clearly meets the early Lutheran criteria for an Old Testament sacrament. And, of course, there is solidarity between the tabernacle and the temple as 1 Kings describes: "When all the elders of Israel had arrived, the priests took up the ark, and they brought up the ark of the Lord and the Tent of Meeting and all the sacred furnishings in it" (1 Kings 8:3). And again, "When the priests withdrew from the Holy Place, the cloud filled the temple of the Lord. And the priest could not perform their service because of the cloud for the glory of the Lord filled His temple" (1 Kings 8:10–11). Further, in 1 Kings 9:3, the Lord says to Solomon: "I have heard

---

16. Emmanuel J. Cutrone, "Sacraments," *Augustine through the Ages: An Encyclopedia*, ed. A. D. Fitzgerald (Grand Rapids, MI: Eerdmans, 1999), 742.
17. All translations are my own.

the prayer and plea you have made before me; I have consecrated this temple, which you have built, by putting my Name there forever. My eyes and my heart will always be there." Magnus Ottosson in *The Theological Dictionary of the Old Testament* rightly comments: "A name represents the person who bears it; where God's name is there He Himself is present . . . The presence of Yahweh makes the temple holy."[18]

So, the real and gracious presence of God in tabernacle and temple recommended them as Old Testament sacraments. But, is there even more? The Torah ends with a striking emphasis and invitation: "This day I call heaven and earth as witnesses before you that I have set before you life and death, blessings and curses. Now choose life, so that you and your children may live and that you may love the Lord your God, listen to His voice, and hold fast to Him. For the Lord is your life, and He will give you many years in the land He swore to your fathers, Abraham, Isaac, and Jacob" (Deut 30:19–20). This passage clearly echoes Genesis 1 and 2, emphasizing heaven and earth, life and death, blessings and curse, and the invitation to love the Lord God who is their life! In the context, God promises another Eden where fellowship with him can be lived out, the land he swore to Abraham, to Isaac, and to Jacob.

Could it be that the land itself was to be viewed as a sacrament of God's life and presence for the faithful? The following texts from Jeremiah must be considered. First, in Jeremiah's striking temple sermon, we read this: "The people of Judah have done evil in my eyes, declares the Lord. They have set their detestable idols in the house that bears my name and have *defiled* it" (Jer 7:30). The Hebrew word "אמט" means "to defile, to desecrate." This verb is frequent throughout Leviticus. As Richard E. Averbech notes:

> The impurity of this rebellious nation extended far beyond matters of physical ritual impurity into his religious and moral degradation warned against in Lev. 18–20 . . . . From the start there was an overall concern in Israel that the people pollute the land by murderous bloodshed (Num. 35:33) because to do so would be to 'defile' (pi. Of) the land where I dwell, for I, the Lord, dwell amount the Israelites (Num. 35:34). Thus the concern was not only with the contamination of the tabernacle but also the land as a whole lest even their worship become worthless.[19]

When Jeremiah later describes the messianic epoch of restoration, he states, "there will be heard once more the sounds of joy and gladness, the

---

18. Magnus Ottosson, *Theological Dictionary of the Old Testament*, 16 vols. (Grand Rapids, MI: Eerdmans, 1978), 3:286, s.v. "לְכִיהַ"; hereafter TDOT.

19. Richard E. Averbech, *New International Dictionary of Old Testament Theology and Exegesis*, vol. 2 (Grand Rapids, MI: Zondervan Publishing House, 1997), 372.

voices of bridegroom, and the voices of those who bring thank offerings to the house of the Lord" (Jer 33:10–11). The temple will be restored in the messianic age. Indeed, this note of a restored temple stands in parallel relationship to Jeremiah's description of a restored land:

> Therefore, behold, the days are coming, when people will no longer say, "Therefore, behold, the days are coming, declares the Lord, when they shall no longer say, "As the Lord lives who brought up the people of Israel out of the land of Egypt," but "As the Lord lives who brought up and led the offspring of the house of Israel out of the north country and out of all the countries where he had driven them." Then they shall dwell *in their own land.* (Jer 23:7–8)

Again, the prophet proclaims, "'The days are coming,' declares the Lord, 'when I will bring my people Israel and Judah back from captivity and restore them to *the land* I gave their forefathers to possess,' says the Lord" (Jer 30:3). He writes later, "I will rejoice in doing them good and will assuredly plant them *in this land* with all my heart and soul" (Jer 32:41).

Finally, he writes, "In those days and at that time I will make a righteous Branch, sprout from David's line; he will do what is just and right *in the land*" (Jer 33:15).

As in the case of the temple, the land for Jeremiah has also been defiled: "I brought you into a fertile land to eat its fruit and rich produce; but you came and *defiled* my land and made my inheritance detestable" (Jer 2:7). Again, he writes, "Because Israel's immorality mattered so little, she defiled the land and committed adultery with stone and wood" (Jer 3:9).

Finally, God proclaims by his prophet, "I will repay them double for their wickedness and their sin, because they have *defiled my land* with lifeless forms of their vile images and have filled my inheritance with their detestable idols" (Jer 16:18). A number of scholars have described the dense connection between God and the land: noteworthy are the studies by Walter Brueggemann, W. D. Davies, P. D. Miller, and C. J. H. Wright.

Deuteronomy 6:10–12 is striking: "When the Lord your God brings you into the land he swore to your fathers to Abraham, Isaac and Jacob, to give you—a land with large, flourishing cities you did not build, houses filled with all kinds of good things you did not provide, wells you did not dig, and vineyards and olive groves you did not plant—then you eat and are satisfied, be careful that you do not forget the Lord." Brueggemann comments: "The rhetoric at the boundary is that of pure gift, radical grace. There is no hint of achievement or merit or even planning. It is all given by the Giver of good gifts and the speaker of faithful words."[20]

---

20. Walter Brueggemann, *The Land: Place as Gift, Promise, and Challenge in Biblical Faith*, 2nd ed. (Minneapolis, MN: Fortress Press, 2002), 46.

The intimacy of God's connection to the land is expressed by Magnus Ottosson's summary: "In reality, the land belongs to Yahweh. It is called 'His heritage.' . . . In Leviticus 25:23, this divine claim of possession is emphasized so strongly that the Israelites are regarded as strangers and foreigners: 'The land shall not be sold in perpetuity, for the land is mine; for you are strangers and sojourners with me.'"[21]

Christopher Wright comments on "לחנ", that is, "inheritance": "The term conveyed the special love and care Yahweh had for the land (Ps 68:9–10), and thus the special favor it was for Israel to be given it (Jer 3:19) and the special folly it was for them to mistreat it (Jer 2:7). The precious relationship of the land to Yahweh added poignancy and pain to the destruction of the land the city, and temple."[22] From a slightly different perspective, he maintains: "Given its intimate relationship to both Yahweh and Israel (described, e.g., as the 'inheritance' of both), the land functions as a midterm in the relationship between them. . . . Israel's behavior on the land determines Yahweh's response to Israel in the land, and the land will 'respond' to both."[23]

In a similar way, the temple is expounded in great detail by Manhem Haran in his *Temples and Temple Service in Ancient Israel*. It is a clear set of prohibitions that attend the tabernacle. "A non-priest may not touch any piece of furniture no matter how insignificant in the tabernacle . . . . The non-priest was not even to look at any of the articles of furniture within the tabernacle."[24]

It is worthwhile to recall how this plays out in the narrative of 2 Samuel 6:6–7, "When they came to the threshing floor of Nacon, Uzzah reached out and took hold of the ark of God, because the oxen stumbled. The Lord's anger burned against Uzzah because of his irreverent act; therefore God struck him down and he died there beside the ark of God." The account of Uzzah's death is remarkable for its similarity to St. Paul's admonition concerning the Lord's Supper:

> Therefore, whoever eats the bread or drinks the cup of the Lord in an unworthy manner will be guilty of sinning against the body and blood of the Lord. A man ought to examine himself before he eats of the bread and drinks of the cup. For anyone who eats and drinks without recognizing the body of the Lord eats and drinks judgment on himself. That is why many among you are weak and sick, and a number of you have fallen asleep. (1 Cor 11:27-30)

21. TDOT, 1:401–402, s.v. "אָרֶץ."
22. Christopher Wright, *New International Dictionary of the Old Testament Theology and Exegesis*, 5 vols. (Grand Rapids, MI: Zondervan Publishing House, 1997), 3:79, s.v. "לחנ."
23. Wright, 3:79, s.v. "לחנ."
24. Manhem Haran, *Temples and Temple Service in Ancient Israel* (Winona Lake, IN: Eisenbrauns, 1985), 175, 178.

Jeremiah's view of temple, land, and Zion is congruent with that of his predecessor in the South, namely, Isaiah. Paul Raabe, for example, identifies "Yahweh dwelling in Zion in the temple with the Second person of the Trinity, the pre-incarnate Christ."[25]

Thus, the faithful cannot help but rejoice in God's real presence in temple, Zion, and land! The following psalms give expression to the people's joy:

> Great is the Lord, and most worthy of praise, in the city of our God, his holy mountain. It is beautiful in its loftiness, the joy of the whole earth. Like the utmost heights of Zaphon is Mount Zion, the city of the Great King. God is in her citadels; he has shown himself to be her fortress. Within your temple, O God, we meditate on your unfailing love . . . . Walk about Zion, go around her, count her towers, consider well her ramparts, viewing her citadels that you may tell of them to the next generation. For this God is our God forever and ever; he will be our guide even to the end. (Ps 48:1–3, 12–14)

> In Judah God is known; His name is great in Israel. His tent is in Salem; His dwelling place in Zion. (Ps 76:1–2)

Psalm 126:1–2 displays the deep faith and emotion associated with Zion:

> When the Lord brought back the captives to Zion, we were like men who dreamed.

> Our mouths were filled with laughter, our tongues with songs of joy. Then it was said among the nations, "The Lord has done great things for them."

How do these Old Testaments sacraments—tabernacle, temple, land, and Zion—point to and interpret God's presence in the Messiah? Jesus answers this question in several texts. With respect to the temple, he vividly points to its restoration in him: "I tell you that one greater than the temple is here" (Matt 12:6). Here, Jesus likens the temple to his own bodily presence. This same inherent comparison underlies John 2:18–21:

> Then the Jews demanded of him, "What miraculous sign can you show us to prove your authority to do all this?" Jesus answered them, "Destroy this temple and I will raise it again in three days." The Jews replied, "It has taken forty-six year to build this temple, and you are going to raise it in three days?" but he had spoken of the temple of His body.

---

25. Paul Raabe, "Christ and the Nations—Isaiah's Gentile Oracles," *Concordia Journal* (Winter 2013): 25.

With respect to the land, Jesus provides the "place" where we will be with him in the new heavens and the new earth. In John 14:1–3, Jesus declares "Do not let your hearts be troubled. Trust in God; Trust also in Me. In my Father's house are many rooms; if it were not so, I would have told you. I am going there to prepare a place for you. I will come back and take you to be with me that you also may be where I am." Jesus' reference to a "place" is concrete and tangible, recalling God's meeting with the Old Testament patriarchs. After his vision of the stairway, Jacob acknowledges the sacred character of "the place": "Surely the Lord is in this place, and I did not know it" (Gen 28:16).

CONCLUDING OBSERVATIONS

What theological results come from asserting and recommending this sacramental system as a key part of the Old Testament's witness and structure? I would suggest that several "hermeneutical blessings" flow from the real and gracious presence of God in these Old Testament sacraments: First, the God of the Old Testament is displayed as the God of love, that is, He lavishly bestows his gracious, real presence in concrete components of creation for the saving benefit of his faithful people. Second, the entire structure of Israel's identity is seen as a gift; the tabernacle, temple, theophanies, and the land are all gifts. As Deuteronomy 30:20 so succinctly states: "The Lord is your life." Third, Jeremiah's prophetic challenge and critique assumes the abuse and willful desecration of God's gracious presence in Temple, Zion, Jerusalem, and the land. Fourth, therefore, Jeremiah's portrait of God is not simply that of a sovereign whose abstract laws have been violated; rather, for Jeremiah, God has graciously given Himself for the people, only to have His presence "defiled" by an alien confession, i.e., idolatry and alien behavior that flows from false worship. Finally, the sacramental system of the Old Testament is dense with christological meaning; that is, it is *incarnational* and anticipates the coming of our Lord in the flesh. Horace Hummel made this point with great precision and clarity when he titled his introduction to the Old Testament *The Word Becoming Flesh.*[26] Thus, the incarnation of the Word does not represent something unprecedented or alien to God's character, but is implicit in His relationship to creation from the beginning. The Old Testament sacramental system displays this aspect of God's character with great clarity. ✛

---

26. Horace D. Hummel, *The Word Becoming Flesh: An Introduction to the Origin, Purpose, and Meaning of the Old Testament* (St. Louis, MO: Concordia Publishing House, 1979).

A DEEP SOUNDING OF THE GREEK
OF JOHN'S GOSPEL

CRITICAL FEATURES OF JOHN'S LANGUAGE
IN JOHN 1–6 AND 18–21

✛

It is a pleasure and a privilege to write a contribution to the Festschrift for my good friend and former colleague William C. Weinrich. Bill was my chief interlocutor for interpretive and theological questions during my times on the Concordia Theological Seminary, Fort Wayne, Indiana, faculty (1975–1989), and every discussion with him—often shouting through open doors across a hall dividing our offices—was an enriching experience. This essay, it is hoped, will be of some assistance to him as he continues commentary writing on the Gospel of John.

The motivation for this essay stems from the work underlying my own analysis of the Greek of the Gospel of Mark in the first Mark volume of the Concordia Commentary series, Mark 1:1—8:26.[1] In it I undertook rigorous grammatical analysis of the features of the Greek of the Second Gospel, which I found extremely valuable in many interpretive contexts. It is hoped that what I offer here will provide Bill with similar information to undergird his sure-to-be-extensive exegesis.

PRELIMINARY COMMENTS ON THE GREEK
OF JOHN'S GOSPEL

Many studies of the Greek (= Gk) of the Gospel of John (= GJn) do not analyze its linguistic features in any sort of detail. Most make observations about vocabulary, about synonyms, about the prevalence of parataxis and asyndeton, etc.[2] But John's (= J's) Gk is much more complex than is

---

1. James W. Voelz, *Mark 1:1–8:26* (St. Louis, MO: Concordia Publishing House, 2013), especially 2–24.
2. See, for example, the section entitled "The Language, Text, and Format of the Gospel: Some Considerations of Style," chapter 8, in Raymond E. Brown, *An Introduction to the Gospel of John*, ed. Francis J. Moloney (New York: Doubleday, 2003), in which considerations

generally supposed, and it repays intensive investigation. Here I propose to undertake just that, attempting a thorough analysis of critical features of J's grammar, focusing upon two major sections, chapters 1–6, and chapters 18–21. The former begins the Fourth Gospel and contains many lengthy discourses; the latter concludes it and contains lengthier sections of narrative, especially as that surrounds the capture, death, and resurrection of our Lord. It should be noted that all analysis is done on the basis of the manual investigation of the Gk text of the GJn, as presented in Reuben Swanson's *New Testament Greek Manuscripts: Variant Readings Arranged in Horizontal Lines Against Codex Vaticanus: John*,[3] which means that judgments have been made at numerous points with regard to text critical and interpretive issues.

It is worth observing at the start that, generally, J's Gk evinces many features of more formal Gk (whether that be understood as "Classical" [= C] or "high Koine" [= K][4]) than is usually supposed. Several will be

---

of literary factors occupy almost the entire content of the 28 pages, for example, inclusion, chiasm, ambivalence, irony, explanatory notes, and *relecture/reecriture*. Attention is paid to the phenomenon of two-fold/double meaning. Atypically helpful in this regard is the work of Andreas J. Köstenberger, *A Theology of John's Gospel and Letters: Biblical Theology of the New Testament* (Grand Rapids, MI: Zondervan, 2009), who assembles the work of many authors making comments on John's Greek, especially in section 6, "Johannine Style." Section 6.3 details "Major Johannine Style Characteristics" but includes both grammatical (for example, "Frequent use of the conjunction *hina*" [133], "Frequent use of historical presents" [134]) and literary (for example, "Positive statements followed by converse statements" [133], "Frequent use of double entendre in conjunction with irony and/or misunderstanding" [134]) features. Special mention must be made of the work of E. A. Abbott, particularly his *Johannine Grammar*, first published in London by Black in 1906 and recently reprinted with a new forward and bibliography by K. C. Hanson by Wifp & Stock (Eugene, OR), 2006. This *tour de force* analyzes almost all features of John's Greek, but in a way that is less linguistic than theological (for example, his discussion of the difference between present and aorist subjunctives of the verb πιστεύω proceeds, not to a discussion of verbal aspect, but to one of John's understanding of believing [¶2528], and his comparison of constructions with the infinitive with those of ἵνα proceeds to discuss, not the development of Greek syntax, but the meaning difference sure to exist between the two [¶2495]). Abbott's analyses are extensive but not complete, and they generally do not reflect on patterns of usage throughout the Gospel, (His considerations also extend to John's epistles.) This essay will adopt a more linguistic and literary approach.

3. Reuben Swanson, *New Testament Greek Manuscripts: Variant Readings Arranged in Horizontal Against Codex Vaticanus: John* (Sheffield: Sheffield Academic, 1995). This means that the text adopted by N/A 28 will not necessarily be followed. Swanson gives full details on almost all readings, not simply snippets at the foot of the page in an apparatus.

4. It is probably right to see Hellenistic or K Gk in general as a development of the dialect of ancient Athens; see Antonios N. Jannaris, *An Historical Greek Grammar Chiefly of the Attic Dialect: As Written and Spoken from Classical Antiquity Down to the Present Time* reprint ed. (Hildesheim: Olms, 1968), 6; James W. Voelz, "The Language of the New Testament," *Aufstieg und Niedergang der römischen Welt*, II, Vol. 25/2, 893–977, here 932, moderated by the other dialects, especially Ionic (Voelz, "Language of the NT," 933, including notes), and *written* K Gk as a kind of compromise between "classical" standards and vernacular. In the words of Albert Thumb, *Handbuch des griechischen Dialekte*, 2nd ed. (Heidelberg: Winter, 1932), who himself focused his attention on Modern Gk: "die verschiedenen Formen der hellenistischen Literatursprache . . . sind schliesslich nichts anderes als fortwährende Compromisse zwischen der gesprochenen Sprache und ältere schriftlicher Überlieferung, zwischen Leben und Schule". It is for this reason that the evidence from Aristophanes, whose plays reflect Attic vernacular, becomes important.

considered in depth below, but here we briefly list some of the less notice-able (giving only representative examples):

- Adverbial accusative: 19:39, 21:14
- Accusative of respect: 1:15, 6:71
- ἀκούω + genitive case: 18:37, 19:13
- ἀποκρίνομαι in the aorist middle rather than aorist passive: 5:17, 5:19
- Assimilation of the relative pronoun: 4:14, 21:10
- Crasis to avoid hiatus: 6:15, 6:44
- Neuter plural subjects with singular verbs (regularly): 6:23, 20:30
- Oblique cases expressing time relationships without prepositions (Genitive: 3:2, 18:3; Dative: 6:39, 20:19; Accusative: 2:12)
- Predicate position participles to convey indirect discourse: 19:26, 20:1
- Possessive use of the article: 18:11, 21:17
- Πρός + dative case: 18:16, 20:12

In addition, as in more formal Gk, *variety of usages* appear, as will be seen in detail below. Here we mention as anticipatory examples, the wide use of both Subject-Verb (= S-V) and Verb-Subject (= V-S) word order and wide-ranging uses of tense forms in both indicative and non-indicative moods.

We turn now to the salient specific features of the Gk of the GJn, as exhibited in the 419 verses of chapter 1–6 and 18–21.

SYNTACTIC FEATURES

WORD ORDER: TRANSITIVE VERBS

The general pattern for the placement of an explicit subject (= S) rela-tive to a finite or infinitive transitive verb (= V) form in the GJn is very *flexible*, as it should be in idiomatic Gk writing.[5] See, for example, 19:26–28, in which both S-V and V-S word order occur together:

> Ἰησοῦς οὖν ἰδὼν τὴν μητέρα καὶ τὸν μαθητὴν παρεστῶτα ὃν ἠγάπα, **λέγει** τῇ μητρί· γύναι, ἴδε ὁ υἱός σου. εἶτα λέγει τῷ μαθητῇ· ἴδε ἡ μήτηρ σου. καὶ ἀπ᾽ ἐκείνης τῆς ὥρας **ἔλαβεν ὁ μαθητὴς** αὐτὴν εἰς τὰ ἴδια. Μετὰ τοῦτο εἰδὼς **ὁ Ἰησοῦς** ὅτι ἤδη πάντα τετέλεσται, ἵνα **τελειωθῇ ἡ γραφή, λέγει**· διψῶ.

This is in no way atypical. In fact, in terms of total occurrences in the GJn, there are some 181 instances of S-V word order for transitive verbs

---

5. This is a point made to me repeatedly by Chrys C. Caragounis, native Athenian and retired faculty member of the University of Lund, Sweden. Several of his books on the Greek language are cited below. Note that the present analysis does not include syntax that is "forced" by the basic structure of the Gk language, especially the use of S-V word order after a nominative relative or interrogative pronoun.

in chapters 1–6, and 71 in chapters 18–21, for a total of 252 such instances, while in the first six chapters some 157 instances of V-S word order for such verbs occur, and some 103 in the final four chapters, for a total of 260, or a virtually equal number of occurrences.

There are, however, some distinctive distribution patterns of usage for subjects and transitive verbs in the GJn. The preferred pattern seems to be: *V-S word order in narrative, and S-V word order in discourse.* See, for example,

> 20:19–21: . . . **ἦλθεν ὁ Ἰησοῦς** καὶ ἔστη εἰς τὸ μέσον καὶ λέγει αὐτοῖς· εἰρήνη ὑμῖν. καὶ τοῦτο εἰπὼν ἔδειξεν τὰς χεῖρας καὶ τὴν πλευρὰν αὐτοῖς. **ἐχάρησαν** οὖν **οἱ μαθηταὶ** ἰδόντες τὸν κύριον. **εἶπεν** οὖν αὐτοῖς **ὁ Ἰησοῦς** πάλιν. . .

> 18:20–21: **ἐγὼ** παρρησίᾳ **λελάληκα** τῷ κόσμῳ, **ἐγὼ** πάντοτε **ἐδίδαξα** ἐν συναγωγῇ καὶ ἐν τῷ ἱερῷ, ὅπου **πάντες οἱ Ἰουδαῖοι συνέρχονται**, καὶ ἐν κρυπτῷ ἐλάλησα οὐδέν.

Indeed, of the some 260 V-S occurrences, 204, fully 78%, occur in narrative settings, while of the 252 S-V occurrences, 148 or 59% occur in discourse. The percentage is even higher in sections of the GJn that have a concentration of literary features, for example, in extended conversations between two people. Dialogue sections standardly have some narration and much discourse. When such units are investigated, the pattern V-S for narrative and S-V for discourse is clearly evident. In 4:7–30, the conversation between Jesus and the Samaritan Woman, for example, 19 instances of V-S word order occur, and 14 of S-V.[6] Of the 19 V-S instances, 15 occur in the narrative portions of the pericope, only four in the discourse. Of the 14 S-V instances, two occur in narrative, and twelve in discourse portions. This pattern is even more pronounced for Jesus' interchange with Pilate at his trial, 18:33–38. All of the 18 V-S instances are in the narrative, and all of the seven S-V instances occur in the discourse. See also Jesus and Nicodemus, where five of seven V-S instances are in narrative in 3:1–15, while eight of nine S-V occurrences are in discourse.[7]

There are, however, two major exceptions to what we have described above for transitive verbs. The first concerns the opening of the Gospel. In the magnificent narrative of the first 18 verses (1:1–18) there are *no* uses of explicit V-S word order with such verbs. All explicit expressions of subject

---

6. One might expect more instances of S-V word order, but this investigation requires an *explicit* subject. Often in Greek the subject of verbs is contained in the ending of the verb form itself and is not expressed explicitly. See, for example, the relatively few explicit subjects of transitive verbs in the discourse sections of 4:15–18.

7. It is a question whether Jesus' words stop at verse 15 or continue through verse 21. 7 occurrences of S-V words order suggest extending them, but 6 occurrences of V-S word order argue against it. Is J being coy or ambiguous?

and transitive verbs occur in S-V word order—eleven times—which is not the normal pattern for narrative but, rather, for discourse in the GJn. This is striking, to say the least. Second, in 19:16b—21:25, which describes Jesus bearing his cross, his crucifixion, his burial and his resurrection appearances, and which comprises 82 verses, very little explicit S-V or V-S syntax occurs within its discourses for transitive verbs (only seven altogether). This seems to occasion a shift in V-S usage in this long section, specifically, a shift to somewhat frequent use of S-V word order in *narrative*, and it leads to the observation that S-V word order seems to be used in the narrative portions of the final section of the GJn to highlight the subject of its clause, perhaps by providing contrast. See, for example:

18:28: **αὐτοὶ οὐκ εἰσῆλθον** εἰς τὸ πραιτώριον, ἵνα μὴ μιανθῶσιν ἀλλὰ φάγωσιν τὸ πάσχα.

20:1: Τῇ δὲ μιᾷ τῶν σαββάτων **Μαρία ἡ Μαγδαληνὴ ἔρχεται** πρωῒ σκοτίας ἔτι οὔσης εἰς τὸ μνημεῖον.

See also 19:23, 19:24, 19:26, 19:31, 20:4, 20:15, 20:24, 21:7, 21:8, 21:18, 21:19, 21:23.

Both of the *exceptions* to the normal patterns described in the foregoing paragraph seem to convey *emphasis*, suggesting that these sections are of no small importance to the author, St. John.

WORD ORDER: THE COPULATIVE VERB εἰμί

For the frequent verb εἰμί, the general pattern of placement of explicit subjects relative to the verb form is also *flexible* in the ten chapters of the GJn that we are investigating, as it should be for Gk. Both S-V and V-S word order are in evidence. See, for example,

18:36: **ἡ βασιλεία ἡ ἐμὴ οὐκ ἔστιν** ἐκ τοῦ κόσμου τούτου· εἰ ἐκ τοῦ κόσμου τούτου **ἦν ἡ βασιλεία ἡ ἐμή,** οἱ ὑπηρέται οἱ ἐμοὶ ἠγωνίζοντο ἂν ἵνα μὴ παραδοθῶ τοῖς Ἰουδαίοις· νῦν δὲ **ἡ βασιλεία ἡ ἐμὴ οὐκ ἔστιν** ἐντεῦθεν.

In terms of total occurrences in the GJn, there are some 56 instances of S-V word order in chapters 1–6 and 16 in chapters 18–21, for a total of 72, while in the first six chapters some 38 instances of V-S word order with forms of εἰμί occur, in the final four chapters some 21, for a total of 59, which is a fairly equal number overall, though with a slight preponderance of S-V.

Again, there are distinctive distribution patterns of usage. The preferred pattern is: *V-S word order in narrative, and S-V word order in discourse*, paralleling the pattern detailed above for transitive verb. See, for example, for narrative:

5:1, 2, 5: Μετὰ ταῦτα **ἦν ἑορτὴ** τῶν Ἰουδαίων καὶ ἀνέβη Ἰησοῦς εἰς Ἱεροσόλυμα. **Ἔστιν** δὲ ἐν τοῖς Ἱεροσολύμοις ἐπὶ τῇ προβατικῇ **κολυμβήθρα** ἡ ἐπιλεγομένη Ἑβραϊστὶ Βηθζαθὰ πέντε στοὰς ἔχουσα . . . **ἦν δέ τις ἄνθρωπος** ἐκεῖ τριάκοντα [καὶ] ὀκτὼ ἔτη ἔχων ἐν τῇ ἀσθενείᾳ αὐτοῦ·

And for discourse:

6:41–42: Ἐγόγγυζον οὖν οἱ Ἰουδαῖοι περὶ αὐτοῦ ὅτι εἶπεν· **ἐγώ εἰμι** ὁ ἄρτος ὁ καταβὰς ἐκ τοῦ οὐρανοῦ, καὶ ἔλεγον· οὐχ **οὗτός ἐστιν** Ἰησοῦς ὁ υἱὸς Ἰωσήφ, οὗ ἡμεῖς οἴδαμεν τὸν πατέρα καὶ τὴν μητέρα;

The V-S word order is often seen in narrative with forms of the verb "to be" in first place (or very near first) in its clause, giving a "dummy subject" construction (for example, in English, "There is. . . . There was . . . . There are . . ."). See 5:2 and 5:5, above, as well as, for example, 18:1, 19:14, 21:2. There are, indeed, some twenty instances of forms of εἰμί at or very near the head of the clause, among the 59 total V-S constructions in the GJn.

Of the 72 S-V occurrences, 58 (fully 80%) occur in discourse, while of the 59 V-S occurrences, 41 (almost 70%) occur in narrative. This pattern remains quite constant throughout the Gospel.

When we turn to the placement of a predicate nominative (= Pn), either nouns or adjectives, relative to the verb εἰμί, the pattern is again extremely flexible, that is, either V-Pn or Pn-V word order.[8] See, for example,

21:24: Οὗτός **ἐστιν ὁ μαθητὴς** ὁ μαρτυρῶν περὶ τούτων καὶ ὁ γράψας ταῦτα, καὶ οἴδαμεν ὅτι **ἀληθὴς** αὐτοῦ ἡ μαρτυρία **ἐστίν.**

In fact, in terms of total occurrences, the two patterns are almost identical. The V-Pn order occurs some 56 times in the ten chapters that we are considering, while Pn-V order occurs 55 times. Also, the distribution between discourse and narrative is virtually the same: 42 in discourse and twelve in narrative (of 56) for V-Pn, 39 in discourse and 16 in narrative (of 55) for Pn-V. The only noticeable difference—and this is certainly a matter of interpretive judgment—is that the Pn-V word order in chapters 18–21 seems generally to be *emphatic.* See, for example,

19:35: καὶ ὁ ἑωρακὼς μεμαρτύρηκεν, καὶ **ἀληθινὴ** αὐτοῦ **ἐστιν** ἡ μαρτυρία, καὶ ἐκεῖνος οἶδεν ὅτι ἀληθῆ λέγει. . . .

21:12: λέγει αὐτοῖς ὁ Ἰησοῦς· δεῦτε ἀριστήσατε. οὐδεὶς δὲ ἐτόλμα τῶν μαθητῶν ἐξετάσαι αὐτόν· **σὺ τίς εἶ;** εἰδότες ὅτι **ὁ κύριός ἐστιν.**

8. For the purposes of this analysis, we are not considering periphrastic constructions that employ a form of the verb "to be" + a participle.

See also 18:35, 18:37, 19:21, 21:24, as well as 18:15, 18:17, 18:25, 19:35, 19:42, 20:14, 20:15, 20:31, 21:4, 21:7.

PARATACTIC CONSTRUCTIONS

Parataxis denotes the joining of thoughts, especially clauses, in coordination rather than in subordinated relationships. A coordinating conjunction may appear, or the clauses may relate to one another in asyndeton, that is, without a binding word joining them. It has been observed that J's Gk exhibits parataxis,[9] and this observation is sound. Let us consider the details.

Coordinating Conjunctions: The three chief coordinating conjunctions are καί, δέ, and οὖν, the latter with the meaning "then," which moves a narrative along.[10] Often καί and δέ, the two most well-known such conjunctions, appear in close proximity to one another in J's Gk. See, for example:

2:1: **Καὶ** τῇ ἡμέρᾳ τῇ τρίτῃ γάμος ἐγένετο ἐν Κανὰ τῆς Γαλιλαίας, **καὶ** ἦν ἡ μήτηρ τοῦ Ἰησοῦ ἐκεῖ· 2 ἐκλήθη **δὲ** καὶ ὁ Ἰησοῦς καὶ οἱ μαθηταὶ αὐτοῦ εἰς τὸν γάμον.

οὖν may be added to the mix, with all three appearing together, for example:

19:19–20a: ἔγραψεν **δὲ** καὶ τίτλον ὁ Πιλᾶτος **καὶ** ἔθηκεν ἐπὶ τοῦ σταυροῦ· ἦν **δὲ** γεγραμμένον· Ἰησοῦς ὁ Ναζωραῖος ὁ βασιλεὺς τῶν Ἰουδαίων. τοῦτον **οὖν** τὸν τίτλον πολλοὶ ἀνέγνωσαν τῶν Ἰουδαίων . . . .

The actual details of usage of these three conjunctions are, however, noteworthy.

First, let us consider the meaning of these coordinating conjunctions. The three main coordinating conjunctions καί, δέ, and οὖν are not used interchangeably as far as meaning is concerned. καί normally means "and" and is the most prominent, though at least four examples of the adversative meaning "but" are apparent in the ten chapters under consideration (1:20, 3:32, 4:20, 6:70). δέ may well convey an additional thought and mean simply "and" (for example, 4:6, 5:35, 6:2, 6:12, 6:51, [6:57], 6:71, 19:18, 19:19, 19:23, 19:39, 21:2, 21:8), but usually it denotes a *contrast*, which may be general (for example, 1:12, 2:21, 3:30, 18:23, 18:36, 19:38, 20:17, 21:18 [21:12, 21:23]) but which often involves a switch of subject (for example, 1:38, 2:9, 3:23, 3:36, 4:39, 4:43, 5:11, 5:34, 5:36, 6:10, 18:2, 18:5 *bis*, 18:18 *bis*, 18:22, 19:9, 19:12,

---

9. See Köstenberger, *A Theology*, 131.

10. The use of οὖν to propel narrative is an old usage in Greek, found already in Homer, and apparent in Sophocles and Plato. See LSJM οὖν II, "to continue a narrative," "so, then."

19:19, 19:40, 20:25 [at times preceded by the article alone (for example, ὁ δέ . . . .), for example, 1:38, 2:8, 5:13, 6:20, 18:7, 21:6]), or a switch of scene (for example, 6:3, 6:4, 6:16, 18:5, 18:23, 19:25, 20:1, 20:11, 21:14).[11] οὖν may denote a conclusion = "therefore" (clear examples would be: 3:29, 6:10, 6:13, 18:39, and 21:23, as well as 2:22, 4:48, 4:53, 6:10, 6:13, 18:3, 18:31, 19:1, 19:16, 19:20, 19:38, 21:7, 21:21), but, as noted above, it may well also denote the succeeding action in a sequence = "then, next," for example,

18:17: λέγει **οὖν** τῷ Πέτρῳ ἡ παιδίσκη ἡ θυρωρός . . . .

See also 2:18, 6:11, 18:7, 18:28, 19:23, 20:6, 21:15, as well as 2:20, 3:25, 4:1, 4:5, 4:9, 4:28, 4:40, 6:14, 6:15, 6:19, 18:10, 18:12, 18:27, 18:29, 19:13, 19:16b, 19:26, 19:29, 19:30, 19:31, 19:32, 19:40, 19:42, 20:2, 20:3, 20:21, 21:5, 21:6, 21:7, 21:9, 21:11.[12] (In two cases, οὖν is preceded by μέν in our ten chapters, at 19:24 and 20:30, which seems to convey a sort of grand conclusion to the prior narrative.) Furthermore, to no one's surprise, it is also very often difficult to determine in the GJn the exact meaning of οὖν, which may be used either to continue the narrative or to draw a conclusion; see especially 5:19, 6:21, 6:24, as well as 1:22, 4:6, 4:45, 4:46, 4:52 *bis*, 5:10, 6:28, 6:30, 6:32, 6:34, 6:41, 6:52, 6:60, 6:67, 18:4, 18:11, 18:33, 19:5, 19:6, 19:8, 19:10, 19:15, 19:21, 19:24, 20:8, 20:25.

Second, let us consider the occurrences and distribution of these co-ordinating conjunctions. Surprisingly, καί occurs relatively *seldom* as a conjunction binding clauses (that is, not as a conjunction binding two nouns, pronouns, etc.). Of the 419 verses under investigation in this study, only some 270 instances of καί binding clauses are in evidence, or one every 1.55 verses. As far as distribution is concerned, there are several heavy concentrations of this basic conjunction: eleven occur in 1:1–18, while chapter 20 averages much more than one occurrence per verse, with 41 instances in 31 verses. By contrast, in chapter 6 there are merely 30 instances of καί joining clauses in 71 verses, less than one in every two verses. The statistics reveal that the first six chapters of the GJn show decidedly less frequent usage of καί joining clauses (163 in 281 verses = one every 1.72 verses) than do the final four (107 in 138 verses = one every 1.29 verses), even more so if chapter 1 is excluded from consideration (126 in 281, or one every 1.94 verses).[13]

The more formal conjunction δέ is used only 71 times in the ten chapters of the GJn under consideration (once every 5.9 verses), but rather fre-

---

11. One μέν/δέ occurs, 19:33, as well as one subject switch with ὅς rather than with the simple article, 5:11 (cf. Mark 15:23; cf. Plato *Phaedo* 117B, with καί).

12. οὖν may also occasionally denote the inferential meaning "well, then . . . ." See 1:21, 1:25, 6:62.

13. All occurrences of καί meaning "but" seem to occur in chapter 1–6, however; see statistics above.

quently in the final portion of this Gospel, *viz.*, some 38 times in the 138 verses of chapters 18–21, or once every 3.6 verses. This is about 2.5 times more frequent than its appearance in chapters 1–6, where it appears only 33 times in 281 verses, once every 8.5 verses. Noteworthy is the appearance of δέ only once in 1:1–18 (at 1:12), only four times in the whole of the 31 verses of chapter 20, but 14 times in the 40 verses of chapter 18, and twelve times in the 42 verses of chapter 19. It may be significant that these final chapters are dominated by narrative rather than discourse.

Finally, the conjunction οὖν is more frequent than is δέ in John 1–6 and 18–21 (!), with 91 total occurrences vs. some 71 for δέ, or once every 4.6 verses. οὖν does, however, show a distribution pattern similar to that of δέ: in the first six chapters, which are dominated by discourse, it occurs 39 times in 281 verses (once every 7.2 verses), while in the final four chapters, which are dominated by narrative, it makes 52 appearances in 138 verses, once every 2.7 verses). One may note sections of complete omission: there are no instances in the introduction, 1:1–18, none in the last part of chapter 1 (1:37–51), and none in several important scenes of chapters 20 and 21 (20:11–18 and 21:15–19). One may note that οὖν occurs only five times in the Gospel of Mark and only 32 times in the whole of Luke's Gospel, and that its heavy usage in the GJn is a distinctive trait.

Asyndeton: The lack of a binding word/conjunction may also be said to give rise to parataxis (for example, Julius Caesar's "Veni, Vidi, Vici"). And, indeed, asyndeton is one of the salient traits of the GJn. It occurs no less than 422 times in the chapters under consideration, some 256 times in chapters 1–6 and some 166 times in chapters 18–21, which represents one every 1.1 verses in chapters 1–6 and one every .83 verses in chapters 18–21—overall, a bit more than once every verse (422 in 419 verses)! An astonishing figure, to be sure! See, as typical, the following examples:[14]

> 6:48–50a: **Ἐγώ εἰμι** ὁ ἄρτος τῆς ζωῆς. **οἱ πατέρες** ὑμῶν ἔφαγον ἐν τῇ ἐρήμῳ τὸ μάννα καὶ ἀπέθανον· **οὗτός ἐστιν** ὁ ἄρτος ὁ ἐκ τοῦ οὐρανοῦ καταβαίνων. . . .

> 20:16–17: **λέγει αὐτῇ** Ἰησοῦς· **Μαριάμ. στραφεῖσα ἐκείνη** λέγει αὐτῷ Ἐβραϊστί· **ραββουνι** (ὃ λέγεται διδάσκαλε) . 17 **λέγει αὐτῇ** Ἰησοῦς· **μή μου** ἅπτου. . . .

The distribution of asyndeton is striking and clear. It occurs chiefly in *discourse*, in fact, two-thirds of the time (67.5% [285 of 422]), and that in a way that is constant throughout the Gospel (172 of 256 occurrences [67%] in the first six chapters), 113 of 166 occurrences [68%] in the final four). It

---

14. In the following citation, the first two words of an independent clause are placed in bold print, to indicate that there is no conjunction/binding word either before them or between them.

must be observed, however, that asyndeton is often concentrated in peri-copes in which intense verbal interchange takes place, [15] in which cases it is present both in the discourse and in its accompanying narrative. See especially the citation immediately above from John 20, Jesus and Mary Magdalene, as well as the following: 4:25–26 (Jesus and the Samaritan Woman), 19:15 (Pontius Pilate and the Crowd), 21:16–17 (Jesus and Peter). The inclusion of asyndeton in narrative surrounding verbal interchange is generally *not* consonant with CG usage.[16]

HYPOTACTIC CONSTRUCTIONS

Hypotaxis denotes the subordinating of thoughts to more main thoughts, in contradistinction to parataxis. J's Gk does exhibit hypotaxis, though not, as will be observed, to the degree that other Gospels do. Subordination of thought is achieved by J in several ways.

Predicate Position Participles: A predicate position participle generally functions adverbially, subordinating its thought to that of the main or leading verb of its clause, often conveying a temporal, a causal, or a con-cessive force. This construction is certainly in evidence in the GJn.

Nominative Participle Preceding a Main Verb: The most common predicate position participle construction entails a nominative participle placed pri-or to the main or leading verb. This usually manifests itself rather simply in the chapters of the GJn under discussion, either with no express subject of either verbal form (for example, 19:30: **κλίνας** τὴν κεφαλὴν **παρέδωκεν** τὸ πνεῦμα) or with an express subject of the main verb placed closely be-fore it and after the nominative participle (for example, 18:1: Ταῦτα **εἰπὼν** Ἰησοῦς **ἐξῆλθεν** σὺν τοῖς μαθηταῖς αὐτοῦ). Somewhat frequently, howev-er, J places an express subject, not before the main verb and after the par-ticiple, but *before* both the participle and the main verb (for example, 6:14: **Οἱ** οὖν **ἄνθρωποι ἰδόντες** ὃ ἐποίησεν σημεῖον **ἔλεγον**). Indeed, on two

---

15. Asyndeton characterizes intense interchange in plays of Aristophanes. See, for example, the heated dialogue between the sausage seller (ἀλλαντοπώλης) and Paphlagon in *Knights*, lines 285–88: τριπλάσιον κεκράξομαί σου. Καταβοήσομαι βοῶν σε. Κατακεκράξομαι σε κράζων. διαβαλῶ σ', ἐὰν στρατηγῇς. (I will [have] yell[ed] out three times louder than you! I will shout you down by shouting at you! I will [have] yell[ed] you down by yelling! I will attack your character if you become a general!" (Note that there are no conjunctions and that the future perfect forms imply rapidity and immediate action; see Smyth, *A Greek Grammar for Colleges,* ¶ 1956.) Asyndeton is also present in the Hebrew of the prophets in intense passages. See, for example, Micah 7:9: זַעַף יְהוָה אֶשָּׂא כִּי חָטָאתִי לוֹ עַד אֲשֶׁר יָרִיב רִיבִי וְעָשָׂה מִשְׁפָּטִי יוֹצִיאֵנִי לָאוֹר אֶרְאֶה בְּצִדְקָתוֹ:
"**The wrath** of Yahweh I will bear, because I have sinned against him, until he will plead my case and has accomplished my judgment. **He will make me to go** out to the light. **I will look upon** his righteousness." Words underlined begin a clause directly, without waw or another conjunction.
16. See, for example, Plato *Phaedo* 117 A-E, which consistently begins narrative descriptions between discourse with conjunctions, usually with καί, but also with others.

occasions, he places an express subject *between* two nominative participles that together occur prior to the main verb (for example, 1:38: **στραφεὶς δὲ ὁ Ἰησοῦς** καὶ **θεασάμενος** αὐτοὺς ἀκολουθοῦντας **λέγει** αὐτοῖς; also 5:6). Perhaps surprisingly, *the total number of occurrences of these nominative predicate position participle constructions prior to the main verb is relatively small, only 36 in John 1–6 and 18–21 altogether.* Of these, 15 exhibit the simplest structure of predicate position participle prior to the main verb with no express subject (in addition to 19:30, also 1:36, 2:15, 6:11 6:19, 6:25, 18:38, 19:17, 19:29, 19:33, 20:5, 20:14, 20:20, 20:22, 21:19), five have an express subject (usually closely) prior to the main verb and after the nominative participle (in addition to 18:1, also 1:42, 6:61, 21:20, 21:21), and a surprising 14 display an express subject at the front of the clause, prior to *both* the nominative participle and the main verb (in addition to 6:14, also 4:9, 4:47, 6:15, 6:60, 18:3, 18:4, 18:10 18:22, 19:2, 19:13, 19:26, 19:28, 20:15).

The distribution of these constructions should be noticed. Of the 36 total, only 14 occur in chapters 1–6, and of these, only seven occur before chapter 6. Virtually the same number, 13, occur in merely two chapters containing significant narrative, chapters 18–19.

Nominative Participle Following a Main Verb: This more sophisticated structure, a nominative predicate position participle *following* a main or leading verb, is also present in the GJn. See, for example,

20:20: **ἐχάρησαν** οὖν οἱ μαθηταὶ **ἰδόντες** τὸν κύριον.

Its meaning is often less than clear. At times it may convey *attendant circumstance* with verbs of motion or anti-motion (for example, "remaining, sitting") (for example, 1:31: διὰ τοῦτο **ἦλθον** ἐγὼ ἐν ὕδατι **βαπτίζων**), but usually it either guarantees that the subordinate idea it represents stays subordinate (see 20:20, above) or it conveys a further thought, for example,

5:18: ἀλλὰ καὶ πατέρα ἴδιον **ἔλεγεν** τὸν θεὸν ἴσον ἑαυτὸν **ποιῶν** τῷ θεῷ.

Rarely, as is common in Hellenistic/K Greek, it employs a present (not future) participle to convey purpose, for example,

6:6: τοῦτο δὲ **ἔλεγεν πειράζων** αὐτόν.

This construction occurs less frequently than does a nominative predicate position participle prior to the main verb, *viz.*, 26 times vs. 36,[17] though

---

17. Not included here are the uses of the present participle of λέγω (for example, λέγων/ λέγοντες) before a quotation (8 times) and periphrastic constructions with the verb "to be" followed by a present participle, which gives a continuous force (9 times). Both are evenly distributed.

its distribution is more even within the GJn: 11 in the first six chapters (in addition to 1:31, 5:18 and 6:6, 1:6, 2:23, 3:4, 4:45, 5:44, 6:24, 6:59), and 15 in the final four (in addition to 20:20, 18:18, 18:22, 18:26, 18:32, 19:5, 19:38, 19:39, 20:6, 20:11, 20:18, 21:12, 21:14, 21:29). Of the 26 total occurrences, only three (1:31, 3:4, 5:44) are in discourse.

Genitive/Dative/Accusative Participles: Predicate position participles in the dative and accusative cases are rare in John 1–6 and 18–21, occurring only in 1:48 (ὄντα).[18] The retreat from the use of these oblique cases is not atypical of Hellenistic/K Gk and presages the usage of Modern Gk, which employs an *indeclinable* active present participle form ending in –οντας for all predicate position participial functions.[19] Note that the use of the genitive in 4:39 is also such a rare usage: διὰ τὸν λόγον τῆς γυναικὸς **μαρτυρούσης** ὅτι εἶπέν μοι πάντα ἃ ἐποίησα. It modifies τῆς γυναικός, which itself is genitive because of its modification of τὸν λόγον. (A similar understanding is probable in 4:3).

Unlike 4:39, genitive predicate position participles as part of a *genitive absolute* construction are easily in evidence in John 1–6 and 18–21, and they are used in the CGk way, providing background information. See, for example,

2:3: καὶ **ὑστερήσαντος οἴνου** λέγει ἡ μήτηρ τοῦ Ἰησοῦ πρὸς αὐτόν. . . .

Compared to the number of nominative predicate position participles, the number of such genitive participles in the absolute construction is surprisingly large,[20] *viz.*, twelve (in addition to 2:3, 4:51, 5:13, 6:18, 6:23, 18:22, 20:1, 20:19 *bis*, 20:26, 21:4, 21:11). Indeed, they are used in creative ways, that is, not simply at the beginning of a clause, but often at the end, or even in the middle. See especially:

5:13: ὁ γὰρ Ἰησοῦς ἐξένευσεν **ὄχλου ὄντος ἐν τῷ τόπῳ**. (also 6:23, 20:26)

6:16: ἥ τε θάλασσα **ἀνέμου μεγάλου πνέοντος** διεγείρετο (also 20:1)

Only one does not conform to the strictest standards of being grammatically absolute,[21] *viz.*, 4:51: ἤδη δὲ **αὐτοῦ καταβαίνοντος** οἱ δοῦλοι αὐτοῦ

---

18. This participle could be taken as *supplementary*; see below.

19. Albert Thumb, *Handbook of Modern Greek Vernacular: Grammar, Texts, Glossary*, 2nd ed., trans. S. Angus, (Edinburgh: T&T Clark, 1912), ¶234. That the use of the indeclinable participle form in Modern Gk is not extensive is seen in the fact that Thumb must specifically assert (¶236.1) that such a form need not relate only to the subject of a sentence.

20. Thumb, *Handbook of Modern Greek*, ¶236.2 remarks that Modern Gk rarely uses the indeclinable participle as a "nominative absolute," which would be the equivalent of a genitive absolute in CGk or KGk.

21. See BDF ¶423 and Smyth, *Greek Grammar*, ¶2073.

ὑπήντησαν **αὐτῷ**. . . . In this reticence the GJn does *not* bear similarity to the contemporary papyri.[22]

Two other uses of the participles in oblique cases (usually the accusative) must, finally, be mentioned. First a participle in predicate position that acts as part of the object of the action of the main verb (for example, in English: "I saw him *coming*" [not "while he was coming"]) is a so-called *supplementary participle* and is not, strictly speaking, a hypotactic construction because of its direct connection to the object of the verb (it is not part of a subordinate clause). Nevertheless, it should be observed that J makes use of this construction rather extensively. See, for example,

1:29: Τῇ ἐπαύριον βλέπει **τὸν Ἰησοῦν ἐρχόμενον** πρὸς αὐτὸν . . . .

There are at least 31 instances of supplementary participles in these chapters.[23] Oddly, over one in three (11) occur after chapter 1 after verse 28, while none occurs at all in chapters 3 and 4.

Similar to the supplementary usage is the usage of the participle in predicate position to express indirect discourse (*oratio obliqua*). J seems to evidence such a usage; see especially

19:33: ὡς εἶδον ἤδη **αὐτὸν τεθνηκότα**.

While this might be understood as supplementary (that is, "saw him dead"), it is likely that it conveys the content of what they saw, *viz.*, "saw *that* he was (in a) dead (condition)." See also 20:1.

Attributive Position Participles: J makes regular use of participles in attributive position, whether with the article expressly stated or not. These function normally to convey a subordinate clause that is the equivalent of a *relative clause*, that is, a subordinate clause headed by a relative pronoun. See, for example,

1:29: ἴδε ὁ ἀμνὸς τοῦ θεοῦ **ὁ αἴρων** τὴν ἁμαρτίαν τοῦ κόσμου.

20:8: τότε οὖν εἰσῆλθεν καὶ ὁ ἄλλος μαθητὴς **ὁ ἐλθὼν** πρῶτος εἰς τὸ μνημεῖον . . . .

It is an important question whether this construction is the semantic equivalent of a clause headed by a relative pronoun, to which the answer for J (and for the NT writers generally) is, basically, "No." Generally, the attributive position participle conveys a *restrictive* subordinate clause, that is, one that provides information to narrow possibilities (for example, in 1:29, it is not any lamb that is being referenced but the one specifically

---

22. See Voelz, "Language of the NT," 952, including note 372.

23. In addition to 1:29, 1:32, 133 *bis*, 1:36, 1:37, 1:38, 1:47, 1:51 (3), 2:9, 2:14, 2:9, 5:6, 5:19, 5:38, 6:19 *bis*, 6:62, 18:24, 19:26, 19:33, 20:5, 20:6, 20:7 *bis*, 20:12, 20:14, 21:9, 21:20.

that takes up/away the sin of the world). This is clearly evident in uses that are substantive, that is, without accompanying nouns,[24] for example,

18:21: ἐρώτησον **τοὺς ἀκηκοότας** τί ἐλάλησα αὐτοῖς . . . .

By contrast, a clause headed by a relative pronoun generally conveys a *non*-restrictive meaning, that is, it gives further information about a person, place, or thing—amplifying, but not defining. See, for example,

21:20: ὁ Πέτρος βλέπει **τὸν μαθητὴν** ὃν ἠγάπα ὁ Ἰησοῦς ἀκολουθοῦντα, **ὃς** καὶ ἀνέπεσεν ἐν τῷ δείπνῳ ἐπὶ τὸ στῆθος αὐτοῦ . . . .

J employs some 63 relative pronouns in chapters 1–6 and 22 in chapters 18–21, with virtually all nominatives conveying a non-restrictive force (see further 1:13 and 18:13).[25] Relative pronouns in cases other than the nominative—especially the accusative—may well be non-restrictive, for example,

6:27: ἐργάζεσθε . . . **τὴν βρῶσιν τὴν μένουσαν** εἰς ζωὴν αἰώνιον, **ἣν** ὁ υἱὸς τοῦ ἀνθρώπου ὑμῖν δώσει·

They often, however, convey a restrictive sense, since an attributive position participle can function only as the *subject* of a subordinate thought in Gk (even when it is in the passive voice itself[26]). For a restrictive sense with a relative pronoun, see, again, the passage from 21:20, considered above, this time focusing on the other/first relative pronoun earlier in the verse:[27] ὁ Πέτρος βλέπει **τὸν μαθητὴν ὃν** ἠγάπα ὁ Ἰησοῦς ἀκολουθοῦντα, ὃς καὶ ἀνέπεσεν ἐν τῷ δείπνῳ ἐπὶ τὸ στῆθος αὐτοῦ . . . .

J loves attributive position participles, using them no than 134 times or once every 3.13 verses. The distribution is, however, quite uneven. Of the 134 instances, 112 occur in chapters 1–6 of the GJn (84%), one every 2.5 verses). Furthermore, a large percentage occurs in discourse, especially in these early chapters. Ninety of the 112 or 80% in the first six chapters are found in such a context. By contrast only seven of the 22 in the final four chapters (32%) appear in discourse. It should also be observed that attributive position participles that function as substantives

---

24. Modern Greek employs a participle form ending with -μενος (declinable) to express attributive position participial functions, including that of substantive. See Thumb, *Handbook of Modern Greek*, ¶235.

25. A few exceptions do seem to occur, for example, 4:29: δεῦτε ἴδετε **ἄνθρωπον ὃς** εἰπέν μοι πάντα ὅσα ἐποίησα

26. See, for example, 5:13: ὁ δὲ ἰαθεὶς = "The man *who* had been healed . . . ."

27. A participle cannot be used to express the thought of this clause, if "Jesus" is retained as the grammatical subject of the *active* verbal idea of loving. For a general discussion see the excruciatingly thorough study by Michael Hayes, "An Analysis of the Attributive Participle and the Relative Clause in the Greek New Testament," PhD dissertation, St. Louis, MO: Concordia Seminary, 2014.

are especially frequent in chapters 1–6: 79 of the 112 or 79% can be so classified. By contrast, only eight of 22 in chapters 18–21 are substantives, only 36%.[28] Almost all substantives occur in discourse: Sixty-seven of the 79 in the first six chapters of the GJn, and five of the eight in the final four chapters (62.5%).

Subordinating Conjunctions: J is very comfortable employing subordinating conjunctions in his Gospel, so much so that they seem to compete with participles for the standard means by which to convey adverbial subordinate thoughts. Three are especially frequent.

The use of ὅτε: The most frequent subordinating conjunction, ὅτε, renders the thought "when." J uses it frequently to convey an activity that occurs *prior* to the action of the main verb, the *equivalent of an aorist predicate position participle.* See, for example:

19:8: Ὅτε οὖν ἤκουσεν ὁ Πιλᾶτος τοῦτον τὸν λόγον, μᾶλλον ἐφοβήθη . . . .

This is the equivalent of: ἀκούσας οὖν τοῦτον τὸν λόγον ὁ Πιλᾶτος μᾶλλον ἐφοβήθη. The conjunction ὅτε occurs 15 times in chapters 1–6 and 18–21 of the GJn, with eight in the first six chapters (1:19, 2:22, 4:21, 4:23, 4:25, 4:45, 5:25, 6:24) and 7 in the final four (in addition to 19:8, 19:6, 19:23, 19:30, 20:24, 21:15, 21:18).

The use of ὡς: With the meaning "as" or "when," ὡς could easily be rendered with a present/first principal part participle to convey action at a time congruent with that of the main verb. See, for example,

21:9: ὡς οὖν ἀπέβησαν εἰς τὴν γῆν βλέπουσιν ἀνθρακιὰν . . . .

This is the equivalent of ἀποβαίνοντες οὖν εἰς τὴν γῆν βλέπουσιν ἀνθρακιὰν . . . . ὡς occurs ten times in the ten chapters of the GJn under discussion, six in 1–6 (2:9, 2:23, 4:1, 4:40, 6:12, 6:16), and four in 18–21 (in addition to 21:9, 18:6, 19:33, 20:11).

The use of ὅτι: Used in a causal sense, ὅτι occurs in a number of contexts in which it might seem natural to use a participle, perhaps some seven or eight times in our ten chapters, especially in the first six. Several suggest a normal predicate position participle in the nominative as an alternative, for example,

6:2: ἠκολούθει δὲ αὐτῷ ὄχλος πολύς, ὅτι ἐθεώρουν τὰ σημεῖα ἃ ἐποίει . . . .

---

28. Especially in chapters 1–6, J has noticeable use of one article governing two attributive position participles (1:40, 3:29, 5:24, 5:35, 6:33, 6:40, 6:45, 6:51, 6:54, 6:56), especially in discourse (all but 1:40). Only two occurrences with this structure are evident in chapters 18–21, at 20:29 and 21:24, the first of these in discourse.

This is the equivalent of participial clause with θεωρῶν or θεωροῦντες. See also 3:21, 5:27, 5:39. Several others convey what would be an "absolute" thought, that is, a genitive absolute construction. See, for example,

> 19:42: ἐκεῖ οὖν διὰ τὴν παρασκευὴν τῶν Ἰουδαίων, **ὅτι** ἐγγὺς ἦν τὸ μνημεῖον, ἔθηκαν τὸν Ἰησοῦν.

This is the equivalent of a genitive absolute with ὄντος. See also 3:23, 4:22, and, perhaps, 1:50.

The fairly extensive use of subordinating conjunctions of several types may help to explain the relatively infrequent occurrence of the predicate position participle in the GJn.[29]

ἵνα *and the Infinitive:* J displays a heavy use of ἵνα clauses, and, actually, also of the infinitive. Perhaps surprisingly, his use relative to meaning for both is quite traditional, even "classical." Standardly in the GJn, ἵνα conveys *purpose*, which is the CGk usage.[30] See, for example, 1:7: 7 οὗτος ἦλθεν εἰς μαρτυρίαν ἵνα μαρτυρήσῃ περὶ τοῦ φωτός . . . .

> 20:31: ταῦτα δὲ γέγραπται **ἵνα** πιστεύητε ὅτι Ἰησοῦς ἐστιν ὁ χριστὸς ὁ υἱὸς τοῦ θεοῦ . . . .

As is typical of Hellenistic/K Gk, other usages are also present, including *epexegetical, appositional, object,* and *predicate nominative*. See, for example, in turn:

> 1:27: . . . οὗ οὐκ εἰμὶ [ἐγὼ] **ἄξιος ἵνα** λύσω αὐτοῦ τὸν ἱμάντα τοῦ ὑποδήματος . . . .

> 6:29: **τοῦτό** ἐστιν τὸ ἔργον τοῦ θεοῦ, **ἵνα** πιστεύητε εἰς ὃν ἀπέστειλεν ἐκεῖνος . . . .

> 19:31: . . . **ἠρώτησαν** τὸν Πιλᾶτον **ἵνα** κατεαγῶσιν αὐτῶν τὰ σκέλη καὶ ἀρθῶσιν.

> 4:34: ἐμὸν **βρῶμά** ἐστιν **ἵνα** ποιήσω τὸ θέλημα τοῦ πέμψαντός με . . . .

What is surprising are the numbers and the distribution of ἵνα and its uses. At least 55 instances occur in our ten chapters. *Of these 55, fully 43 convey purpose.* Thus, only twelve evidence the increasingly Hellenistic/K usage, *viz.*, expansion to take over the natural functions of the infinitive. Epexegetical force is seen only in 2:25 and 18:39 (in addition to 1:27, above), appositional only in 6:40 and 18:27 (in addition to 6:29, above), object only in 4:47 *bis* and 19:38 (in addition to 19:31, above), and predicate

---

29. Matthew, for example, has no well attested uses of ὡς in this manner, and Mark only two.

30. Smyth ¶2193 (cf. ¶2209).

nominative only in two instances in 4:34, including the one above. In this the GJn is unlike the Gospel of Mark, which regularly uses ἵνα clauses to express an object relationship between a subordinate idea and the main verb.[31] The uses of ἵνα are evenly distributed throughout the GJn, about once every 9.5 verse, but, oddly, no uses occur in chapter 21, only two in chapter 20 (in the final verse), and just one in chapter 2.

Concomitantly, the infinitive is used in the GJn in very CGk ways, to express both purpose (for example, 1:33) and object (for example, 21:12), as well as subject relationships to impersonal verbs such as δεῖ and ἔξεστιν (for example, 18:31: ἡμῖν οὐκ **ἔξεστιν ἀποκτεῖναι** οὐδένα), and epexegetical relationships to verbs such as δύναμαι (for example, 5:30: Οὐ **δύναμαι** ἐγὼ **ποιεῖν** ἀπ᾽ ἐμαυτοῦ οὐδέν·) and nouns such as ἐξουσία (for example, 19:10: οὐκ οἶδας ὅτι **ἐξουσίαν** ἔχω **ἀπολῦσαί** σε . . . .). The number and the distribution of the infinitive are, again, surprising. Some 60 total occurrences are evident, 45 in chapters 1–6, and 14 in chapters 18–21. Of the 60, 13 are part of object clauses, ten introduce purpose clauses, and the other 37 are central to clauses with various relationships to other verbs and nouns, as detailed above—a frequency demanded by John's hesitancy to employ the ἵνα clause to express these relationships (see the paragraph immediately above). Indeed, the infinitive takes over completely in chapter 21—no example of ἵνα occurs!—to express object (21:12, 21:22, 21:23) and purpose (21:3), and to convey an epexegetical relationship of a clause to a main verb (21:6). *Atypical* of Hellenistic/K and NT and LXX Gk, the articular infinite governed by a preposition is rare in J's usage in these ten chapters, appearing only in 2:24 in the construction διὰ τὸ αὐτὸν γινώσκειν.

PLEONASTIC CONSTRUCTIONS

Several additional syntactical constructions that might be classified as either paratactic or hypotactic (as appropriate) are more helpfully taken together as constructions that include extra words or clauses (hence the term pleonastic).[32]

Appositions: Simplest among these constructions are those that involve the addition of a thought as a piece of further information about a given topic. In such cases, sometimes the material simply amplifies. See, for example the double example in the introduction:

1:14: Καὶ **ὁ λόγος** σὰρξ ἐγένετο καὶ ἐσκήνωσεν ἐν ἡμῖν, καὶ ἐθεασάμεθα τὴν **δόξαν** αὐτοῦ, **δόξαν** ὡς μονογενοῦς παρὰ πατρός, **πλήρης** χάριτος καὶ ἀληθείας.

---

31. See Voelz, *Mark*, 4.
32. Two examples of Semitic pleonastic uses of relative and personal pronouns occur in our chapters, at 1:33 and 5:36, but these do not concern us here.

See also 1:12, 1:18, 1:31 *bis*, 4:45, 5:45, 6:4, 6:8, 6:70, 6:71, 18:15, 21:11. Sometimes it involves presenting a key idea. See, for example,

> 3:13 καὶ οὐδεὶς ἀναβέβηκεν εἰς τὸν οὐρανὸν εἰ μὴ **ὁ ἐκ τοῦ οὐρανοῦ καταβάς, ὁ υἱὸς τοῦ ἀνθρώπου.**

See also 1:45, 4:25, 5:29, 6:27. And several times the construction is quite complex, involving the removal of an element from a subordinate clause and placing it proleptically, that is, before that clause, causing the subordinate clause to give further information regarding the element removed from it. See, for example,

> 4:35: ἐπάρατε τοὺς ὀφθαλμοὺς ὑμῶν καὶ θεάσασθε **τὰς χώρας ὅτι** λευκαί εἰσιν πρὸς θερισμόν.

This might have been worded: . . . καὶ θεάσασθε **ὅτι αἱ χωραὶ** λευκαί εἰσιν πρὸς θερισμόν. See also 5:36 and 5:42.[33]

"Trailer Constructions": Similar to appositions, J often presents additional information almost as an afterthought, or as an aside. See, for example,

> 21:13: ἔρχεται Ἰησοῦς καὶ λαμβάνει τὸν ἄρτον καὶ δίδωσιν αὐτοῖς, **καὶ τὸ ὀψάριον ὁμοίως.**

See also 2:9, 4:2, 4:26, 6:24, 18:16, 19:18, 19:23, 19:24, 20:7, 21:9.

Resumptive Pronouns: J characteristically inserts a demonstrative pronoun into a clause to resume the thought of the express subject. The construction is similar to apposition, but here the pronoun functions as the true subject of the verb—it is not in apposition to what seems to be the "actual" subject that occurs prior—making the prior—"actual"—subject a kind of "nominative absolute." See, for example,

> 1:33: ἀλλ᾽ **ὁ πέμψας** με βαπτίζειν ἐν ὕδατι **ἐκεῖνός** μοι εἶπεν· . . . .

See also 1:12, 1:18, 3:26, 5:11, 5:43, 6:46, 18:12. And 5:35 may also be an example of this construction.

Similar is the placement of a relative pronoun before a demonstrative pronoun, which has the *effect* of making the demonstrative pronoun "resumptive" and the relative pronoun a kind of "accusative absolute." See, for example,

> 5:38: . . . ὅτι **ὃν** ἀπέστειλεν ἐκεῖνος, **τούτῳ** ὑμεῖς οὐ πιστεύετε.

---

33. The GJn has one example of the proleptic placement of a word/phrase before the subordinate clause in a construction similar but not identical to this. See 6:9: ἀλλὰ **ταῦτα** τί ἐστιν εἰς τοσούτους; This represents ἀλλὰ τί ἐστιν **ταῦτα** εἰς τοσούτους; See Acts 19:4 and the placement of the clause εἰς τὸν ἐρχόμενον μετ᾽ αὐτόν *before* the ἵνα clause, though it should go within that clause. Cf. the difficult syntax of Mark 8:24, which probably represents this construction (see Voelz, *Mark*, 517–18).

See also 3:22, 5:19, 18:9 (1:45 may also be analyzed according to this category). This construction mirrors Paul's Gk usage in Romans 7:20: εἰ δὲ ὃ οὐ θέλω **τοῦτο** ποιῶ, οὐκέτι ἐγὼ κατεργάζομαι αὐτὸ . . . . Both of these "resumptive" constructions have a strong rhetorical effect, highlighting the item made "absolute" by the inserted pronoun.

Regarding occurrences, except for apposition, the number is not great for the other constructions, but taken together pleonastic constructions number at least 50. The distribution is, however, of some interest. Twenty-two of 24 appositional examples and 13 of 15 resumptive pronoun constructions occur in the first six chapters of the GJn. None occurs in chapters 19 and 20, and only one is present in chapter 21. The "trailer constructions" are somewhat the opposite. Here, seven of eleven occur in the last four chapters. Furthermore, regarding apposition, all instances involving the presentation of key ideas or the proleptic placement of a noun relative to its subordinate clause occur in discourse. Similar are resumptive pronoun instances, where ten of 15 are in discourse. Again, by contrast, only two of eleven "trailer constructions" are evident in discourse.

HYPERBATON

Hyperbaton, or "split syntax," occurs whenever elements that normally are conjoined (for example, a noun and its modifiers) are separated from one another, "torn apart," as it were. J exhibits this rhetorical feature, usually on a small scale, but sometimes on a larger one, as well. See, for example,

18:38: ἐγὼ **οὐδεμίαν** εὑρίσκω ἐν αὐτῷ **αἰτίαν**.

19:31: **Οἱ** οὖν **Ἰουδαῖοι**, ἐπεὶ παρασκευὴ ἦν, ἵνα μὴ μείνῃ ἐπὶ τοῦ σταυροῦ τὰ σώματα ἐν τῷ σαββάτῳ, ἦν γὰρ μεγάλη ἡ ἡμέρα ἐκείνου τοῦ σαββάτου, **ἠρώτησαν** τὸν Πιλᾶτον ἵνα κατεαγῶσιν αὐτῶν τὰ σκέλη καὶ ἀρθῶσιν.

See also 1:49, 2:15, 4:9, 4:23, 4:36, 4:39, 5:6, 5:20, 6:14, 6:23, 6:30, 6:32, 6:42, 6:55 *bis*, 6:60, 6:63, 18:17, 18:22, 19:11, 19:12, 19:20, 19:35, 19:36 (LXX), 19:42, 21:2, 21:25, and possibly also 19:14. Hyperbaton occurs some 29 times in our chapters, a rather high number for an author not known for writing sophisticated Greek (!). Furthermore, it is present throughout the Gospel, 17 times in chapters 1–6 and twelve in chapters 18–21 (though none occurs in chapter 20). In the first section of chapters, it occurs often in discourse (twelve of 17 instances), while in the second section it occurs chiefly in narrative (eight of twelve). The rhetorical effect of hyperbaton is emphasis, as can well be in in the example from 18:38, above.

MINOR BUT NOTICEABLE FEATURES

Several features of J's syntax are not wide-ranging but are noteworthy. We will examine each very briefly to make their presence known.

Collapsed Relative Clauses: J has a noticeable tendency to collapse the antecedent of a relative pronoun into the relative pronoun itself in the relative clause. See, for example

> 1:26: μέσος ὑμῶν ἕστηκεν **ὃν** ὑμεῖς οὐκ οἴδατε = μέσος ὑμῶν ἕστηκεν **ὁ ἄνθρωπος** ὃν ὑμεῖς οὐκ οἴδατε.

See also 1:15, 1:30, 1:33, 1:45, 3:26, 3:34, 4:18, 5:7, 6:29, 18:26, 19:37 (LXX). In each case the antecedent is quite general, usually "the man" or, in 5:7, "the time." This construction is "classical" and may be labelled "omission of the antecedent."[34] Note also that full construction assumed may well contain the nominative case form that provides the real subject of the main verb (see the example above, as well as 1:33, 3:34, 4:18) or a predicate nominative (1:15, 1:30). The distribution of this construction is of interest. All instances in chapters 1–6 of the GJn are in discourse, while neither of the two in chapters 18 and 19 are.

Placement of Possessive Pronouns: J normally uses "noun/pronoun—possessive" word order, See, for example,

> 20:27: φέρε τὸν δάκτυλόν **σου** ὧδε καὶ ἴδε τὰς χεῖράς **μου** καὶ φέρε τὴν χεῖρά **σου** καὶ βάλε εἰς τὴν πλευράν **μου** . . . .

But it is apparent that on a number of occasions he places the possessive *before* the noun it modifies. See, for example,

> 19:33: οὐ κατέαξαν **αὐτοῦ** τὰ σκέλη.

The reasons for this order seem to be several. The order may be emphatic (see 1:27, 4:16, 4:34, 4:47, 6:53, 19:21, 19:32, 19:33, 19:34, 20:23, 20:25, 21:25), or, it may enable the author to avoid hiatus (!) (in addition to 19:33 above, see 3:19, 3:33, 19:2, 19:29, 19:31, 19:34, 20:25). There are at least 18 instances of this structure in our ten chapters, seven in the first six and eleven in the final four. Among the first seven, all but one are in discourse. Among the final eleven only two are in discourse. The effort to avoid hiatus through this placement of the possessive is especially striking.

SEMANTIC FEATURES

Features of J's Gk that convey non-syntactical meaning are also important and, as we shall see, surprising. They repay close attention and further study.

---

34. See Smyth ¶2509. He understands the antecedent in such constructions to be a demonstrative pronoun, for example, οὗτος.

VERBAL ASPECT

Much ink has spilled over the matter of verb stems and the meanings they convey, within the last twenty-five plus years, with the general consensus that such stems denote—in addition to time in the indicative mood—a perspective on the action. My own understanding is that the aorist stem denotes a *focus upon the act itself* (sometimes as opposed to an alternative act), while the so-called "present" stem, that is, the first principal part stem, conveys a focus upon a *connection* between a doer and the activity.[35] This can be seen in the general difference between the aorist indicative and the imperfect indicative (both past time forms), with the former focusing upon *what* was done, and the latter focusing upon one of several possible "connections" between the doer and the activity in the past, for example, continuously acting, beginning to act, trying to act, habitually acting, etc.[36]

It is striking how wide-ranging is J's use of both first and third/sixth principal part forms aspectually in chapters 1–6 and 18–21 of his Gospel. This is well seen in forms outside the indicative mood, for example, in the infinitive. Indeed, an appropriate contrast is seen between the so-called "present" and the "aorist" stems of the infinitive in 4:7 and 4:15:

4:7: ἔρχεται γυνὴ ἐκ τῆς Σαμαρείας **ἀντλῆσαι** ὕδωρ.

4:15: κύριε, δός μοι τοῦτο τὸ ὕδωρ, ἵνα μὴ διψῶ μηδὲ διέρχωμαι ἐνθάδε **ἀντλεῖν**.

In the first, the focus is on *what* the Samaritan woman came to do (for a similar focus upon act, see 19:11 [ἀπολῦσαι] and 19:12 [σταυρῶσαι]). In the second, the woman focuses on *not wanting to engage herself* in a given activity—and, one could add, *regularly* (for a similar focus upon engaging in an activity, see 21:31 [ἁλιεύειν]; for engaging in an activity, and also regularly, see 4:20, 4:24 [προσκυνεῖν]). Other forces of the "focus on connection" of the 1st principal part infinitive[37] can be seen in the following examples:

6:60: σκληρός ἐστιν ὁ λόγος οὗτος· τίς δύναται αὐτοῦ **ἀκούειν**; = "to keep on hearing" = continuous

3:30: ἐκεῖνον δεῖ **αὐξάνειν**, ἐμὲ δὲ **ἐλαττοῦσθαι**. = "to begin to increase/decrease" = inceptive (see also 18:8)

---

35. See also, Voelz, *Mark*, 280–30, and James W. Voelz, "Present and Aorist Verbal Aspect: A New Proposal," *Neotestamentica* 27 (1993): 153–64.

36. "Connection" between doer and activity is the over-arching category uniting these disparate expressions of focus of the imperfect, in this view. Virtually all interpreters agree on the presence of these disparate expressions or "forces" of the imperfect indicative.

37. Note that these parallel well the various "connections" interpreters regularly see with the imperfect. The imperfect is simply a form of the "focus upon connection" principal placed into past time.

3:2: οὐδεὶς γὰρ δύναται ταῦτα τὰ σημεῖα **ποιεῖν** ἃ σὺ ποιεῖς, ἐὰν μὴ ᾖ ὁ θεὸς μετ' αὐτοῦ. = "actually do" = emphatic (see also 2:24, 3:27)

All instances with μέλλω = "to be about to" employ the "present" in-finitive because a connection is about to be established (see 4:44, 6:6, 6:71, 18:32). It is noteworthy that of the sixty instances of infinitive usage in our ten chapters of the GJn, *the ratio of present/1ˢᵗ principal part stems to aorist/3ʳᵈ+ 6ᵗʰ principal part stems is almost 1:1*: 28–32. This distribution is "classical" and does *not* reflect Hellenistic/K Gk's tendency to prefer the aorist stem.[38]

The use of the subjunctive in ἵνα clauses displays the same verbal as-pect sophistication. For aorists, focusing on *what* the purpose of an activ-ity is, see, for example,

1:8: . . . ἀλλ' ἵνα **μαρτυρήσῃ** περὶ τοῦ φωτός.: describing what the purpose of John's coming was[39]

19:16: Τότε οὖν παρέδωκεν αὐτὸν αὐτοῖς ἵνα **σταυρωθῇ**.: describ-ing for what purpose Pilate handed Jesus over

For the "present" stem, focusing on *connection*, see, for example,

6:28: τί ποιῶμεν ἵνα **ἐργαζώμεθα** τὰ ἔργα τοῦ θεοῦ; = "engage in working"

6:29: τοῦτό ἐστιν τὸ ἔργον τοῦ θεοῦ, ἵνα **πιστεύητε**[40] εἰς ὃν ἀπέστειλεν ἐκεῖνος = "actually believe" or "come to believe"

5:23: ἵνα πάντες **τιμῶσι** τὸν υἱὸν καθὼς τιμῶσι τὸν πατέρα = "begin to honor"

The indicative mood dare not be neglected in this analysis, though, for J uses the imperfect indicative with great precision. See the follow-ing, expressing the several forces of this complex "tense" that focuses on a connection between the doer and an activity in the past:

20:4: **ἔτρεχον** δὲ οἱ δύο ὁμοῦ. = "were running"

6:17: καὶ ἐμβάντες εἰς πλοῖον **ἤρχοντο** πέραν τῆς θαλάσσης εἰς Καφαρναούμ. = began to go"

6:66: Ἐκ τούτου πολλοὶ ἐκ τῶν μαθητῶν αὐτοῦ ἀπῆλθον εἰς τὰ ὀπίσω καὶ οὐκέτι μετ' αὐτοῦ **περιεπάτουν**. = "continued to walk"

---

38. See Jean Humbert, "Verbal Aspect: Has it Evolved from Ancient to Modern Greek?" *The Link* 1 (1938): 21–28, here 22–23.

39. Note in this example that the action of the verb may well have been continuous or regular or repeated, certainly not "one time."

40. A text-critical decision confronts the interpreter here. Reading this stem follows manuscripts. P75, B, L Ψ and others, but many manuscripts read the aorist, πιστεύσητε, which gives a focus on the activity.

21:18: ὅτε ἦς νεώτερος, **ἐζώννυες** σεαυτὸν καὶ **περιεπάτεις** ὅπου **ἤθελες·**= "used to gird"/"used to walk"/"used to wish"

18:18: . . . ὅτι ψῦχος ἦν, καὶ **ἐθερμαίνοντο·**= "tried to warm themselves"

19:3: . . . καὶ **ἐδίδοσαν** αὐτῷ ῥαπίσματα. = "repeatedly gave"

5:18: . . . ὅτι οὐ μόνον **ἔλυεν** τὸ σάββατον, ἀλλὰ καὶ πατέρα ἴδιον **ἔλεγεν** τὸν θεὸν . . . . = "actually broke"/"actually said"

There are no less than 67 instances of the imperfect indicative in chapters 1–6 and 18–21 in the GJn.[41] Of these, only 17 are from verbs of speaking, with 14 from the verb λέγω and three from ἐρωτάω (ἠρώτων). Of the remaining 50 instances, only perhaps 15 convey continuous activity in the past (what most students think is the "basic" meaning of the imperfect). It is noteworthy that only three instances occur in discourse (in Jesus' conversation with Peter in 21:18); all others occur in narrative. Yet the percentage of imperfect indicatives not involving λέγω and ἐρωτάω is identical within the ten chapters we are investigating, approximately one every eight-plus verses, indicating that it is a feature of J's narrative composition.

HISTORICAL PRESENT INDICATIVES

It can easily be observed that the Synoptic Gospel writers employ the so-called "historical present" in their narratives. Mark uses it throughout his Gospel.[42] J is little different. See, for example,

1:29: Τῇ ἐπαύριον **βλέπει** τὸν Ἰησοῦν ἐρχόμενον πρὸς αὐτὸν . . . .

5:14: μετὰ ταῦτα **εὑρίσκει** αὐτὸν ὁ Ἰησοῦς ἐν τῷ ἱερῷ . . . .

21:3: **ἔρχεται** Ἰησοῦς καὶ **λαμβάνει** τὸν ἄρτον καὶ **δίδωσιν** αὐτοῖς . . . .

The effect of this device is to highlight whatever is being described, by foregrounding the activity and making the action vivid to the reader/hearer. This usage is found in CGk.[43]

There are some 109 total historical presents in our set of chapters. The verbs used for these forms are, however, somewhat restricted. Of the 109, fully 84 comprise the verb λέγω, while seven more derive from verbs of seeing (βλέπω four and θεωρέω three), and a further ten from verbs denoting motion (ἔρχομαι nine and τρέχω one). The remaining eight comprise four instances of εὑρίσκω, and one of μαρτυρέω, ἄγω, λαμβάνω,

---

41. In this analysis we omit the imperfects of the verbs ἔχω and εἰμί, since the former employs the forms of the imperfect to express the simple past time meaning "had," that is, "was in possession of" (the aorist has a different denotation), while the latter has no aorist forms.

42. Voelz, *Mark*, 2.

43. Smyth, *Greek Grammar*, ¶1883. Smyth notes that it does not occur in Homer.

and δίδωμι. Regarding distribution, a much greater percentage occurs in chapters 18–21 than in 1–6, 63 to 46. Furthermore, as in the Gospel of Mark, the foregrounding and highlighting of the historical present occur standardly in what appear to be key pericopes.[44] In the GJn, it is those in which Jesus interacts with his close followers. Consider the following distribution against the background of the 109 total occurrences:

21:15–23, Jesus and Peter: 13 historical presents in nine verses

20:1–18, Jesus and Mary Magdalene: 18 historical presents in 18 verses

21:1–14, Jesus and the Eleven at the Sea of Galilee: 11 historical presents in 14 verses

1:37–51, Jesus and Pairs of Disciples Who Follow: twelve historical presents in 15 verses

See also 4:7–30, Jesus and the Samaritan Woman (twelve in 24), and the 2:1–12, Wedding at Cana (six in twelve verses). The first four pericopes represent 54 of the 109 total instances, virtually one-half, and all six 72 of 109, almost three-fourths. It is impossible not to see the occurrences of the historical present and their distribution as highly significant in the GJn.

PERFECT STEMS (PERFECT AND PLUPERFECT FINITE FORMS)

It can easily be observed that J makes liberal use of the perfect stems—the fourth and fifth principal parts—throughout his Gospel. This deserves a much more complete study than can be done here; a thorough investigation is already well under way by Chrys C. Caragounis as part of two monographs.[45] In fact, a full session of the Biblical Greek Language and Linguistics Section at the 2013 Society of Biblical Literature entitled "The Perfect Storm" was devoted to the matter this "tense." Here let us focus simply on *finite* verb forms in the ten chapters of the GJn under consideration.

To this investigator, the semantics of the forms still seem somewhat straightforward: the perfect (indicative) conveys a *present state* or condition that is the *result* of a past action, the pluperfect a *past state* resulting from a prior past action—although it must be recognized that the question of the denotation of the perfect stems is a matter of quite some dispute from several sides.[46] See, for example,

---

44. For Mark, See Voelz, *Mark*, 15–16.

45. *The Development of Greek and the New Testament: Morphology, Syntax, Phonology, and Textual Transmission* (Tübingen, Mohr-Siebeck, 2004), 154–55, and *New Testament Language and Exegesis: A Diachronic Approach* (Tübingen: Mohr-Siebeck, 2014), 135–64.

46. Caragounis, especially, avers (*NT Language*, 135–64) that the perfect has developed toward the aorist in the indicative mood and is beginning to displace it as an expression of the

1:34 κἀγὼ **ἑώρακα** καὶ **μεμαρτύρηκα** ὅτι οὗτός ἐστιν ὁ υἱὸς τοῦ θεοῦ. (= "I have accomplished my task and my job is basically done.")

3:29: αὕτη οὖν ἡ χαρὰ ἡ ἐμὴ **πεπλήρωται**. (= "My joy now stands fully filled.")

6:16: καὶ οὔπω **ἐληλύθει** πρὸς αὐτοὺς ὁ Ἰησοῦς . . . . (= Jesus had not arrived and was not there yet.)

19:19: **ἦν** δὲ **γεγραμμένον·** Ἰησοῦς ὁ Ναζωραῖος ὁ βασιλεὺς τῶν Ἰουδαίων. (= This is what stood in writing: "Jesus the Nazarene, the King of the Jews")

Each example seems to exhibit a traditional understanding of the semantics of perfect and pluperfect forms.

In the GJn finite perfect and pluperfect forms occur some 103 times, about once every four verses. Again, as with the historical present, distribution deserves attention. First, both chapters 1–6 and 18–21 exhibit almost the same percentage of occurrences, 24% and 26% or the verses, respectively. Of the 103 occurrences, fully 71% (74), occur in discourse, with chapters 1–6 exhibiting a significantly larger percentage of its perfect stem forms in discourse (80%) than do chapters 18–21 (55%). Second, it should be noted that 24 of the 103 instances (23%) comprise forms of οἶδα/ ᾔδειν,[47] a verb without a functioning first principal part stem (though only six perfect/pluperfects derive from ἵστημι, whose perfect and pluperfect forms have begun strongly to supplant the present and imperfect middle/ passive forms to convey intransitive present and imperfect meaning, respectively). Third, the remaining 81 forms are distributed rather evenly among a number of other verbs, with *no large-scale pattern of meaning* (for example, verbs conveying motion or perception, perhaps) evident. ὁράω (9), γράφω (8), and ἔρχομαι (7) occur in the perfect/pluperfect in finite forms most frequently, followed by γίνομαι and δίδωμι at six occurrences each, μαρτυρέω with four occurrences, ἀποστέλλω and πιστεύω with 3 occurrences, and finally 19 other verbs occurring only one or two times.[48]

---

simple preterit already in NT times. Constantine Campbell, *Verbal Aspect, the Indicative Mood, and Narrative Soundings in the Greek New Testament* (New York: Lang, 2007), 201, by contrast, understands the perfect to convey an "imperfective aspect" similar to the present stem but with more intensity, with the pluperfect bearing a like relationship to the imperfect (that is, more intensity but more "remoteness"). He argued this also at the SBL session mentioned above. The problem with the Campbell analysis is that the "present" stem is routinely used for intensity. See the discussion of verbal aspect in section 1, two points above. Also, an "historical present" that foregrounds and highlights conveys a certain intensity (see point 2, immediately above).

47. This study did not undertake an investigation of the possible differences between οἶδα and γινώσκω in the GJn in terms of denotation.

48. These are ἀκούω, ἀναβαίνω, γινώσκω, ἐλπίζω, ἐργάζομαι, εὑρίσκω, θεάομαι, καταβαίνω, κοπιάω, κρίνω, κράζω, κρατέω, λαλέω, λέγω, μεταβαίνω, πληρόω, τελέω, τηρέω, τίθημι.

THE CONJUNCTION Γάρ

The simple conjunction γάρ may seem straightforward enough, but J uses it principally in two ways. The first is to express the reason why a statement is made, for example,

4:9: πῶς σὺ Ἰουδαῖος ὢν παρ' ἐμοῦ πεῖν αἰτεῖς γυναικὸς Σαμαρίτιδος οὔσης; οὐ **γὰρ** συγχρῶνται Ἰουδαῖοι Σαμαρίταις.

6:64: ἀλλ' εἰσὶν ἐξ ὑμῶν τινες οἳ οὐ πιστεύουσιν. ᾔδει **γὰρ** ἐξ ἀρχῆς ὁ Ἰησοῦς τίνες εἰσὶν οἱ μὴ πιστεύοντες . . . .

See also especially 6:40 and 19:16.

The second way the conjunction γάρ is used is to express a side comment = "you know."

3:24: οὔπω **γὰρ** ἦν βεβλημένος εἰς τὴν φυλακὴν ὁ Ἰωάννης.

21:8: οἱ δὲ ἄλλοι μαθηταὶ τῷ πλοιαρίῳ ἦλθον, οὐ **γὰρ** ἦσαν μακρὰν ἀπὸ τῆς γῆς . . . .[49]

See also especially 6:27 and 20:9, probably also 4:8, 4:23, 6:6, 6:33, 18:13, 19:31, 19:36. Generally, γάρ is not used to express the direct cause of an activity; that is the realm of ὅτι (see 6:26 and 18:2). Both usages of γάρ detailed above are "classical," including the aside.[50]

The word γάρ occurs 42 times in our chapters, much less frequently than does ὅτι. Of the 35 instances in chapters 1–6, 22 are in discourse, especially discourse by Jesus, while only two of seven in the final four chapters of the GJn are so positioned. Especially in the latter chapters, γάρ clauses provide comments by the "narrator" of the story.

LITERARY FEATURE

One literary feature is well worth noting in the GJn. At important places in the text, statements seem to be made that reveal that the Gospel was intended for *oral presentation*. See especially what seem to be direct indications to an audience in the following:

4:6: ὁ οὖν Ἰησοῦς κεκοπιακὼς ἐκ τῆς ὁδοιπορίας ἐκαθέζετο **οὕτως** ἐπὶ τῇ πηγῇ· (To what does οὕτως point except an action by the presenter?)

19:18: . . . ὅπου αὐτὸν ἐσταύρωσαν, καὶ μετ' αὐτοῦ ἄλλους δύο **ἐντεῦθεν** καὶ **ἐντεῦθεν**, μέσον δὲ τὸν Ἰησοῦν. (ἐντεῦθεν means *there* as a demonstrative adverb [the presenter seems to be gesturing]; it does not mean "on a side" [or, taken together, "one on each side"]).

---

49. Note especially in this example that the γάρ does not express why the statement of its clause is being made or the direct causation of the action described in the prior statement.
50. See Voelz, *Mark*, 5, note 18, and Plato, *Phaedo* 116B.

Concomitant are instances that appear to be "asides" to the hearers/ audience. We have noted the use of γάρ in the section immediately above. See also the "floating ἵνα clause" at 18:32: **ἵνα ὁ λόγος τοῦ Ἰησοῦ πληρωθῇ** ὃν εἶπεν σημαίνων ποίῳ θανάτῳ ἤμελλεν ἀποθνήσκειν. Consider also statements that look like "commentary" for the hearers/audience, because they do not really describe the events of the story.

18:40: μὴ τοῦτον ἀλλὰ τὸν Βαραββᾶν. **ἦν δὲ ὁ Βαραββᾶς λῃστής.**

19:24: **Οἱ μὲν οὖν στρατιῶται ταῦτα ἐποίησαν.**

Both of these are "concluding statements," as it were.

Finally, there are "statements" that describe, not the events of the story, but, rather, the telling of the story by the narrator. See, for example,

19:35: καὶ ὁ ἑωρακὼς μεμαρτύρηκεν, καὶ ἀληθινὴ αὐτοῦ ἐστιν ἡ μαρτυρία, **καὶ ἐκεῖνος οἶδεν ὅτι ἀληθῆ λέγει,** ἵνα καὶ ὑμεῖς πιστεύητε . . . .

21:24: Οὗτός ἐστιν ὁ μαθητὴς ὁ μαρτυρῶν περὶ τούτων καὶ ὁ γράψας ταῦτα, **καὶ οἴδαμεν ὅτι ἀληθὴς αὐτοῦ ἡ μαρτυρία ἐστίν.**

Both of these seem to be commentary by the presenter on the story he is telling, not on the events described by the story themselves.

All of these examples are best understood within a context in which an audience is the direct recipient of an oral presentation of the Gospel of St. John.

CONCLUSION

Let us conclude by drawing comparisons between the features of the Gk of the GJn and the features of the Gk of the Gospel of Mark, which will also allow us to summarize the findings detailed above. It is interesting to compare the two Gospels, because there are clearly relationships between the two, not only in theme, *viz.*, the issue of seeing and believing (cf. Mark 15:32 and John 6:30, 20:25, 20:29), but also in specific content (cf. Mark 14:58 and John 2:19 regarding destroying and rebuilding the temple). The following may be observed—with the proviso that chapters 1–6 and 18–21 of the GJn are being compared with the entirety of the Gospel of Mark.

John is *more "classical"* in his linguistic usage in many respects than is Mark (to the great surprise of this researcher). Chief among his "classical" features are the use of ἵνα clauses (essentially for purpose [Mark's usage is more wide-ranging and Hellenistic/K]), of the infinitive (extensively, especially with object clauses), very strict attention paid to verbal aspect throughout, especially with the infinitives, and very wide-ranging use of the imperfect indicative (Mark evidences verbal aspect concerns principally in the latter chapters of his Gospel), a noticeable use of collapsed relative pronoun clauses (infrequent in Mark), as well as many other small items such as consistent use of singular verbs with neuter plural subjects (Mark is much less strict), the use of the genitive to express the object of the verb ἀκούω (seldom in Mark), consistent use of oblique cases to express time relationships (inconsistent in Mark), accusative of respect (seldom in Mark), and avoidance of hiatus (not as frequent in Mark). J's Gk is *not* more "classical" in the usage of adverbial predicate position participles, which is spare by literary standards and in no way approaches Mark's extensive usage (see, for example, Mark 5:25–27, where seven such participles appear together).

J's Gk is generally more *consistent* in features *throughout the Gospel* than is Mark's. The Gk of Mark changes subtly but markedly as one progresses through his Gospel, so that features of chapters 1–7 are noticeably different than those of chapters 8–16.[51] J does not, for example, change his pattern of usage of S-V and V-S word order, his attention to verbal aspect, or his use of hyperbaton as he moves from the Gospel's beginning to its end (though there is some change in usage of δέ).

It may be noted, however, that J's Gk and Mark's Gk *seem more congruent in the latter chapters* than in the former, in some respects. This may be so for two reasons. First, there is J's *relatively* higher usage of participles in narrative—and there is more narrative in the final four chapters—as well as his noticeable (though still seldom) use of ἵνα to express a direct object relationship between the thought of a main and subordinate clause. Second, in the latter part of his Gospel Mark shows increasing concern with verbal aspect, places nominative predicate position participles *after* the main verb more frequently, and increases his use of hyperbaton. This means that the Gk of each is approaching that of the other, so to speak, when the final days of Jesus are being described. Could usage patterns of both Gospel writers reflect an increasingly settled verbal or even textual tradition of the final days of our Lord?

Concomitantly, J does not with his Gk reflect the social and geographical setting of his scenes, as does Mark.[52] Mark's Gk becomes much more Hellenic and less Semitic as the scenes move from rural Galilee to metropolitan and Hellenistic Jerusalem, a phenomenon not seen in the Fourth Gospel.

In the GJn the Gk of discourse sections is in many respects quite different than that of the surrounding narrative, to a degree much larger than anything seen in the Gospel of Mark—with the exception of asyn-

---

51. Voelz, *Mark*, 11–12, 22–24; James W. Voelz "The Greek of Codex Vaticanus in the Second Gospel and Marcan Greek," *Novum Testamentum* 47 (2005): 209–249, here 246–47.
52. Voelz, *Mark*, 21–22.

deton, which is prominent in both authors in discourse.[53] Indeed, given J's heavier use of the perfect stems and S-V word order in discourse, conversations in the GJn are probably much *less* Semitic than the surrounding narrative, which configuration is not characteristic of Mark's Gospel.

Finally, both Gospels employ the "historical present" in pericopes that appear to be key to their presentations. In the GJn it is 21:15–23, 20:1–18, 21:1–14, 1:37–51 especially, and in the Gospel of Mark it is especially 2:1–12 (Jesus' authority to forgive sins), 4:35–41 (Jesus' authority over nature), 5:22–23, 35–43 (Jesus' authority over death), 14:32–42 (Jesus in the Garden), 15:16–24 (Jesus' passion and crucifixion). It seems that if one follows the present tense indicative forms in narrative, one can follow each writer's focus and points of emphasis.

These, then, are some initial grammatical soundings in the Gospel of St. John, which, I hope, will inspire many others, and which, I trust, Bill, will be helpful to you in your commentary writing. This profound Gospel deserves nothing less than a thorough treatment of its wonderful and much-too-little-respected linguistic usage, a usage that should grab the attention of us all. ✛

---

53. Voelz, *Mark*, 17.

ARTHUR A. JUST JR ✛

JOHN 4 AND THE SAMARITAN
WOMAN AT THE WELL

SCRUTINY AS MISSIOLOGICAL, CATECHETICAL,
LITURGICAL, AND MYSTAGOGICAL

✛

I t was in the fall of 1976 that I first met William C. Weinrich, in the
first year that Concordia Theological Seminary was on the campus
of the Senior College in Fort Wayne, Indiana. I was also taking Greek
at the time—remedial Greek for those who had taken it before. At the
time, the registrar thought I could handle Greek and one other course,
and because I was a history major in college, the course they chose was
Early Church. It was William's second year of teaching, and the powers that be did not know how tough he could be. Greek and Weinrich
turned out to be a lethal combination. Students who have participated
in Christ's suffering by taking Weinrich for Early Church know exactly
what I mean.

As a history and literature major in college, listening to William
sound forth on the early church and all her doctrinal issues was a delight.
A historical geek, I actually enjoyed reading Hans Lietzmann and I remember well taking his second volume with me for Christmas vacation.
I read it in this circular room in the house where my parents lived in
Algorta, Vizcaya, on the northern coast of Spain, as my father was working for General Electric in Bilbao. I enjoyed William so much in Early
Church that I took Medieval Church with him the next quarter. Some
thought I was a glutton for punishment, but I knew from the beginning
that there was something in this man, some wisdom, some hermeneutic
for reading texts that would be the foundation of my theological studies
and my life as a pastor.

This was early in William's teaching career, so he was still developing
his style, but even then, his earthy Oklahoma expressions peppered his
erudite lectures and passionate asides, when he would turn to us and say,
"Gentlemen . . ." There are so many memorable moments with William,

45

but there was one statement of his that I will never forget. Memory is a strange thing, and maybe he never said it quite this way, but this is how I remembered it, and how I have repeated it in almost every class I have taught at the seminary. "Gentlemen," William said, "you can never separate your salvation from the flesh of Jesus Christ." As a first-year seminarian, I knew what those words *said*, but I did not know what those words *meant*, nor that they would become the heart of my teaching. This was William's way of speaking about our Chalcedonian Christology, our sacramentology, our ecclesiology, our eschatology, the key to unlocking the entire Biblical canon.

Festschrifts are about memories, and here are some such memories of William over the past thirty-eight years:

> Joining the faculty in 1984 as he was coming back from sabbatical in Cambridge, Barbara pregnant with John Andrew, while my wife Linda was with Nicholas Paul Arthur.

> Working with C. S. Mann, Winthrop Brainerd, and David Scaer during the dark days of the 1990s on reading the New Testament as an ecclesial, liturgical, catechetical document. The laughter and the level of conversation was unparalleled. Our conversations led to commentaries on Luke, Matthew, and John, setting the stage for the new curriculum at Concordia Theological Seminary.

> Serving alongside him during his brief tenure as acting President, as he and Dean Wenthe began to steady the ship, and his grace as he changed places with Dean, becoming our academic leader for ten years, wrapping the faculty's mind around Farley's *Theologia* and Reinhold Hütter's *Suffering Divine Things,* developing a curriculum centered in the teaching of theology through the pastoral acts, watching him yank us out of an Enlightenment model of teaching theology to one that recognized that we were living in a postmodern world, doing so through the sheer will of his intellect, wisdom, and rhetoric.

> Suffering with him as he faced cancer and triumphed.

> Missing him during his years of "exile" in Latvia, rejoicing when he returned in 2011, team-teaching with him in the *Theologia* courses on Baptism and the Lord's Supper.

I could go on and on, but enough reminiscing.

✠

In the excursus "Baptism as a Central Theme in John's Gospel" in William Weinrich's magisterial commentary, he asserts that ". . . the Gospel narratives are not merely histories *about* Jesus. They are essentially *ecclesial* narratives, precisely because they are narratives concerning Jesus. They are narratives of the life of the church told by way of the life of Jesus. *All Christology is ecclesiology, and all ecclesiology is Christology.*"[1] As narratives of the life of the church, the Gospels were constitutive of the way of catechesis in the early church. The Gospels *catechized* the unbaptized into a life—the life of Christ—by telling them the story of Jesus as *their* story—a story whose *telos* was the font.

This was no easy task, catechumens in the ancient church were coming out of a world that was set against Christ and his church, a world of darkness, a world in the possession of Satan and all his pomp, manifesting itself in what the medieval church would call the seven deadly sins. Consider, for example, the character of the catechumenate in Hippolytus's third century church as they were brought forward to "hear the word," as they were "examined as to the reason why they have come forward to the faith."[2] Catechumens were *scrutinized* by the church from the moment they came as "hearers of the word." Hippolytus gives a litany of the composition of his catechumenate, an inquiry into their "their life and manner of living," that is, whether they are slaves or free, married or unmarried, or if they are possessed with demons, in which case they must be cleansed before they are admitted. What fascinates most readers of Hippolytus is his inquiry into their profession and trades—that some were makers of idols, charioteers, gladiators, pagan priests, soldiers who kill Christians, harlots and licentious men, magicians, enchanters, astrologers, diviners, soothsayers . . . the list goes on and on. All of these must "desist or be rejected," that is "forsake their evil ways and forbidden occupations." There is one exception:

---

1. William C. Weinrich, *John 1:1–7:1*, Concordia Commentary: A Theological Exposition of Sacred Scripture (St. Louis: Concordia Publishing House, 2015), 73. This is the hermeneutic of Weinrich's commentary and CTSFW's interpretation of the Gospels. In the course of reading Weinrich's commentary, I discovered our colleague Peter Scaer's marvelous symposium paper on John 4, Peter Scaer, "Jesus and the Woman at the Well: Where Mission Meets Worship," *Concordia Theological Quarterly* 67, no. 1 (2003): 3–18. In it, he affirms the CTSFW hermeneutic: "The way that one understands the Gospel of John depends, it seems to me, upon the context in which it was written. Is this document written . . . [as] an attempt to demonstrate that the institutions of the church are intimately related to 'what Jesus said and did in his life?' I suggest that the word of John's gospel is not only the foundation of the church, but it was written by a churchman in the context of the church. In a book of the church, we should fully expect to see churchly references to such things as baptism, the Lord's Supper, and the like. Granted, we have entered into a type of hermeneutical circle, but this is the very nature of the New Testament. It is a word of God that comes from Christ's apostles, and thus from the very heart of the church. The word is born of the church, even as it sustains her," 16–17.

2. Cited from E. C. Whitaker, *Documents of the Baptismal Liturgy* (London: SPCK, 1970), 3.

A concubine, who is a slave and has reared her children and has been faithful to her master alone, may become a hearer; but if she has failed in these matters she must be rejected. If a man has a concubine, he must desist and marry legally; if he is unwilling, he must be rejected.[3]

This is not your everyday catechumenate, and the presence of Satan was palpable in the catechumens and in their former lives and occupations. The only way the church knew to deal with such a demonic reality was through catechesis in the Biblical narratives and exorcisms. This engagement with the devil through Scripture and exorcism in early Christian catechesis came to be known as *the scrutinies*. Although the origins of the scrutinies were before Constantine, it was not until later that they became a permanent part of the baptismal rite. Roger Béraudy in his chapter entitled "Scrutinies and Exorcisms" in *Adult Baptism and the Catechumenate* offers this description of this enigmatic part of catechesis:

Scrutiny is the name given to the Lenten Masses during which the exorcisms are administered to those catechumens who are to receive baptism on the following Easter, and who on this account used to form the class of the "chosen." At Rome in the fourth and fifth centuries there were three services of scrutiny, appointed respectively for the third, fourth and fifth Sundays of Lent. The formulas then in use are preserved in the Gelasian sacramentaries.[4]

Edward Yarnold, in his *The Awe-Inspiring Rites of Initiation*, describes the purpose of the scrutinies:

In the early Church . . . it was the community which scrutinized the candidates. Exorcism formed an integral part of the process; in the words of Pope Leo the Great, the elect were "scrutinized by exorcisms." Hippolytus required the bishop himself to perform the last exorcism so that "he may be certain that [the candidate] is purified." St. Augustine, while expecting the elect to scrutinise their own hearts, saw the exorcisms as a means of testing whether they were free from the influence of unclean spirits.[5]

Although often referred to, but rarely described or explained, the scrutinies remain a mystery to most. Perhaps we could dismiss them as part of a bygone era spooked by demons, but they have endured to our

---

3. Cited from Burton S. Easton, *The Apostolic Tradition of Hippolytus* (Cambridge: Cambridge University Press, 1934), 41–43.
4. R. Béraudy, "Scrutinies and Exorcisms," in *Adult Baptism and the Catechumenate,* ed. Johannes Wagner, Concilium Series (New York: Paulist Press, 1967), 57.
5. Edwin Yarnold, *The Awe-Inspiring Rites of Initiation: The Origins of Initiation* (Collegeville, MN: Liturgical Press, 1994), 11.

day, albeit truncated and defanged. The baptismal rites in the *Lutheran Service Book Agenda* preserve Luther's use of exorcisms in baptism that reflect the original scrutinies. Perhaps more universal is the preservation of the Gospel texts associated with the Sundays of scrutiny in the ancient church, namely John 4 and the woman at the well for Lent 3, John 9 and the man born blind for Lent IV, and John 11 and the raising of Lazarus from the dead in Lent V (these Gospels may be found in Series A).

This essay in honor of my dear colleague William Weinrich and his work on John's Gospel in his *Concordia Publishing House* commentary will attempt to ask why these Gospels were associated with the Lenten scrutinies, with special focus on John 4 and the woman at the well.

LUTHER AND THE SCRUTINIES

For modern readers of early catechetical texts, the exorcisms appear almost as exotic and strange as the baptismal rites with their appeal to the senses. Anyone familiar, however, with Luther's baptismal rites knows that he retained two exorcisms in the final baptismal revision of 1526, and in the earlier rite of 1523 he even included exorcisms of the senses—the exsufflation, which was an exorcism of the eyes by breathing under them, and the giving of salt, an exorcism of the mouth. That Luther retained exorcisms in the later rite indicates that exorcisms mattered to him, that in his late medieval world Satan was still as palpable as he was in the early church. For Luther, an engagement with the devil was still a lively pursuit. A certain unease occurs among some Lutherans today with Luther's 1526 rite:

> "Depart thou unclean spirit and make room for the Holy Spirit," and then later, "I adjure you, unclean spirit, by the name of the + Father and of the + Son and of the + Holy Ghost that you come out of and depart from this servant of Jesus Christ . . . Amen!"[6]

I will leave it to others to chronicle how lively this battle with the devil was for Luther, but for many today, such an engagement seems quaint, even superstitious. This modern uneasiness to confess that the unbaptized are still in Satan's grasp is reflected in the sad reality that in the pew edition of *Lutheran Service Book* the exorcisms are missing and may be found only in the Agenda. What remains is the renouncing of the devil and all his works and all his ways as a prelude to the confession of the true faith in the Apostles' Creed. As one who came of age at the height of modernism and rationalism, there remains an unease among my generation about anything supernatural—like a power outside of our

---

6. Ulrich S. Leupold, editor, *Luther Works: Liturgy and Hymns,* Vol. 53 (Philadelphia, PA: Fortress Press, 1965), 107–108.

self like the devil, not to mention God. For postmoderns, however, the devil is real and he is back and there is an apocalyptic war out there in which we are engaged with supra-human powers like sin, death, and the devil, even though some of us may not know it.

AUGUSTINE AND THE SCRUTINIES

The concern for the presence of the devil and the need for exorcisms in the ancient church was reflected in its view of the world. William Harmless, in *Augustine and the Catechumenate*, offers this contextual insight into Augustine's world and that of the early church fathers:

> Both pagans and Christians worked, to some extent, from a common religious topography. As they saw it, the stars and planets moved according to a sublime harmony and order; earth, on the other hand, remained a precarious realm tottering on the edge of chaos. Here below, invisible demonic forces wandered about wreaking havoc. These were responsible, in one way or another, for the vagaries that plagued human well-being: diseases, natural calamities, social ills. Christians tended to interpret these threats as evidence of the power of Satan. His influence seemed everywhere: it masqueraded under the guise of paganism and its accompanying apparatus (idols, sacrifices, amulets, astrology); his pomps were displayed in cultural institutions (the bloody public games, the theaters, the annual festivals); and his dark powers had seeped into every crevice of ordinary social life (whether it be the widespread patterns of usury, drunkenness, or infanticide; whether the land-grabbing habits of the wealthy or the graft of imperial officials).

Harmless continues:

> This world view shaped ancient Christians' vision of conversion. Sometimes, they would speak of *conversio*, of "turning," in terms familiar to us: as a sudden, inner-psychic experience; as a shift in one's institutional affiliation; as an integral process of intellectual, moral, and affective growth. But more often, they envisioned conversion in cosmological terms: it was marked by a metaphysical shift, a transfer of power from the reign of Satan to the reign of God. With this transfer of power came a change of status: the convert ceased to suffer Satan's tyranny and came to enjoy God's magnanimous rule. This awesome transition was necessarily tumultuous. As [Peter] Brown notes [in his biography *Augustine of Hippo*]: "The Christian found himself committed to a wrestling match, an *agon*. This ring was clearly defined: it was the 'world,' the *mundus*. The enemy was specific and external to him, the devil, his angels and their human agents. The 'training' provided by his Church had equipped the Christian for the due reward of vic-

tory in any competition—a 'crown' in the new world. Simple men in the time of Augustine would . . . dream of fighting a wrestling match of horrible violence; they would long to escape from its 'double prison, the flesh and the world.'"[7]

Such a worldview demanded an engagement with the catechumen that was more than noetic. Like the baptismal liturgies of the early fathers, the exorcisms that accompanied the scrutinies engaged the senses. To get the full impact of how serious the early fathers took the devil and how much they engaged body and soul in the catechetical process, we need, again, to hear Harmless, this time in his description of the rite of scrutiny in Augustine and Quodvultdeus:

> The high drama of this turning played out in one of major Lenten rites: the scrutiny (*scrutinium*). In Hippo, this rite took place probably soon after enrollment (or, alternatively, just before the first handing back of the Creed). Augustine alludes to his various elements in *Sermon 216*, delivered to the *competentes* immediately after the rite. However, a clearer picture of it emerges in a series of sermons attributed to Quodvultdeus, a Carthaginian who was a younger contemporary and friend of Augustine. According to Quodvultdeus, the *competentes* would spend the night "not lulled with the delight of sleep nor with minds deceived by dreams . . . but by watching, by praying, by psalm-singing, by brandishing weapons against our adversary, the devil." Then "from hidden places they were brought forward one by one in sight of the whole Church." They would enter with head bowed low and possibly would kneel or prostrate themselves; these gestures symbolized that "pride was destroyed, [and] humility, brought in."

> The *competentes* would strip off their outer cloaks and stand barefoot "upon the stretched-out goatskin." . . . It was a multi-layered symbol. In itself it was a sign of penitence. But the gesture of standing (or perhaps stamping one's foot) upon it was equally important. In this way the *competentes* signaled their renunciation of their sinful inheritance — alluding to the widespread belief that Adam and Eve had worn tunics of goatskin. . . . While standing on the goatskin, the *competentes'* bodies were examined. . . . What this entailed is not clear. Scholars have suggested possible motives for this: to see if they suffered from leprosy or some other contagious disease; to probe for signs of possession inscribed in their flesh; or simply set them free from Satan's physical powers.

---

7. William Harmless, *Augustine and the Catechumenate* (Collegeville, MN: The Liturgical Press, A Pueblo Book, 1995), 260–261, citing Peter Brown, *Augustine of Hippo: A Biography* (Berkeley: University of California Press, 1967), 244.

At some point, an exorcist would come forward, and, according to Augustine, "invoke the name of your redeemer" and "heap well-deserved curses on [the devil]." The invocation included calling down "the lowly, most high Christ" and "the earth-shaking all-powerful Trinity." According to another North African, Optatus of Milevis, the formula of imprecation against Satan was "Cursed one, get out!" Besides these verbal pleas, the exorcist would also breathe upon, or more precisely, "hiss at" the candidate. This gesture, the *exsufflatio,* was a conventional sign of contempt and had become, in Christian circles, a standard exorcistic act. . . . The use of breath was not accidental. For the ancients, one's breath was one's life, one's *spiritus,* the power that animated the flesh. Thus this *exsufflatio* meant spitting out the demonic breath that had invaded the candidates' God-given life-force . . . .

Finally, either at the scrutiny itself or soon after, the *competentes* would give voice to their new-found freedom by formally renouncing Satan.[8]

THE WORLD OF JOHN'S GOSPEL

This worldview of Augustine is a Biblical one. In John's Gospel, it is reflected in the way in which he describes baptism. Although Weinrich points out that "in John . . . there are no exorcisms (in John, the figure of the devil appears only in contexts about Judas and those Jews who reject Jesus),"[9] the "prince of this world" still looms in John's prologue where "the Light continues to shine in the darkness, and the darkness has not been able to put it out" (Jn 1:5).[10] Weinrich notes:

The contrast of between "light" and "darkness" is important in the Gospel of John. "Darkness" characterizes the world estranged from God and opposed to his will and therefore determined by death. As the present passage indicates [Jn 1:5], in the Gospel "darkness" shows itself especially in opposition to Christ and to the life that he offers. Therefore, "darkness" is grounded in unbelief and expressed by the lack of love for the brother (Jn 8:12; 12:35; 1 Jn 2:8–11).[11]

It is the movement from unbelief to faith, founded on the narrative of baptism in John 3, that is at the heart of the catechesis and baptism of adults in the ancient catechumenate. This well-known narrative is filled with the language of conversion described as a transference from the kingdom of darkness into the kingdom of God, through the senses, es-

---

8. Harmless, *Augustine and the Catechumenate,* 261–265.
9. Weinrich, *John 1:1–7:1,* 6.
10. All citations from John are from Weinrich, *John 1:1–7:1.*
11. Weinrich, *John 1:1–7:1,* 145. See also Weinrich's discussion of the "cosmic dualism" of "above-below" in connection to John's use of "flesh," 167.

pecially through the application of water with the Spirit, that moves one across a liminal boundary from one status to another. In his excursus on baptism, Weinrich notes:

> One cannot be a child unless one is begotten. This is the language of new creation through water and the Spirit. . . . The effect of this begetting is that of *"seeing"* or of *"entering into"* the kingdom of God (Jn 3:3, 5). That is *the language of conversion*, what in this Gospel is *a movement from death to life*. . . . The Gospel of John brings together a catena of symbolic opposites: *death and life, darkness and light, blindness and sight*. Finally, we must mention once again *the pervasive appearance and use of water in the Gospel of John*. Water appears in the narrative not only throughout the Gospel but also at every strategic locations in the narrative. It appears at the beginning of the Gospel in John's baptism (Jn 1:26–34), on the occasion of the first sign of Jesus' ministry (Jn 2:1–11), in the first major discourses (Jn 3:5; 4:7–15), in the first scene in the upper room (Jn 13:1–16), and at the climactic moment of Jesus' death (Jn 19:34). This pervasive presence of water in the Johannine account similarly must be accounted for, and a purely symbolic interpretation does not suffice. If we ask in what context these various aspects of John's narrative occur in the literature of the early church frequently and often together, there is but one answer: *in the context of Baptism*.[12]

THE WOMAN AT THE WELL

MISSIOLOGICAL, CATECHETICAL, SACRAMENTAL

In the early church catechumenate, in preparing adults for baptism, the narrative of Jesus with the woman at the well (Jn 4) is the chosen Gospel for the first scrutiny in Lent 3 to which we now turn.[13] Why does the ancient church use the narrative of John 4 to scrutinize the catechumens four weeks before their baptisms at the Paschal Vigil?

To begin, it is important to observe that the rite of scrutiny occurs in the liturgical assembly gathered for worship on Lent 3, so this is not a private matter apart from the community. This is the genius of the ancient catechumenate and today's appropriation of it, namely that catechesis was something the entire community participated in, baptized and unbaptized. Additionally, the act of catechesis was in the Eucharistic liturgy as the baptized were prepared, through the Gospels, to celebrate the paschal

---

12. Weinrich, *John 1:1–7:1*, 72, 74. Emphasis mine.
13. This practice seems to be in place before Constantine, but it is difficult to find a sermon among the church fathers that reflects this reality, although an extended search is necessary to establish this. In the *Ancient Christian Commentary on Scripture IVa: John 1–10*, ed. Joel Elowsky (Downers Grove, IL: InterVarsity Press, 2006), no mention is made of this in the citations by Elowsky.

feast and the unbaptized were in the final preparations of their pre-baptismal, Lenten catechesis before their baptism at the Paschal Vigil.[14]

It cannot be emphasized enough that the Gospel narratives catechized as the final stage of evangelization. What we will now discover about John 4 is that it is *missiological*—Samaritans are called to "come and see" Jesus—it is *catechetical*—Jesus is teaching the Samaritan woman and the Samaritans about his identity as the "I AM," the "Savior of the world"—it is *liturgical*—the Samaritan woman will learn what it means to worship "in Spirit and Truth"—and it is *sacramental*—Jesus is teaching that he is "living water" gushing up to eternal life and that his food is to do the Father's will, namely to offer himself as a sacrifice on the cross. These four themes—mission, catechesis, worship, and sacraments—are inextricably intertwined. They are what the church is all about, what the catechumenate is all about, what John 4 is all about, and how John 4 works as catechesis in the rite of scrutiny.

THE WOMAN AT THE WELL
SCRUTINY AS MISSIOLOGICAL

Catechumens would know that they were at the end of a long process of evangelization as they stood on tunics of goatskin, stamped their feet in renunciation of Satan, and had their bodies examined for evidence of the devil's presence. They had been snatched by the Gospel through the Church out of darkness into light, out of Satan's realm into the kingdom of God. Someone had reached out and evangelized them, calling them to a new life in Christ. They were well aware, therefore, that this first scrutiny signaled that the Paschal Vigil and baptism were near. It would not have been hard for them to see that, as Jesus was reaching out to the Samaritan woman and evangelizing her, so also was he reaching out to them through the catechetical rites of the Church as one of the final acts of evangelization.

As the title of Peter Scaer's *Concordia Theological Quarterly* article indicates, "Jesus and the Woman at the Well: Where Mission Meets Worship," John 4 is about *mission and worship*. Scaer shows how this is "a prime example of evangelism and outreach," and how "missiologists commonly observe that in this story Jesus crosses over a number of cultural bridges: the holy, Jewish man reaches out to a sinful, Samaritan woman. Along the way He breaks down barriers of holiness, ethnicity, gender, and religion."[15]

---

14. Aidan Kavanagh, *The Shape of Baptism: The Rite of Christian Initiation* (New York: Pueblo Publishing Company, 1978), 59, accents this character of the scrutinies: "Nothing less than a formal act of *catechesis* done now no longer apart from the community but with its participation and in its solemn presence."

15. Scaer, "Jesus and the Woman at the Well," 4.

As many have observed, the context of this meeting is most unusual and highly irregular in first-century Jewish culture—a Jew and a Samaritan, a man and a woman, and a well, where men and women court in the ancient world. Here Jesus initiates the mission to Samaria that he will institutionalize before his ascension in Acts 1:8: "But you shall receive power when the Holy Spirit has come upon you; and you shall be my witnesses in Jerusalem and in all Judea and Samaria and to the end of the earth." And Philip makes that mission happen in Acts 8 after the martyrdom of Stephen.

Weinrich notes that Jesus is exhausted by his journey and seeks rest at Jacob's well. This word for exhaustion, κοπιάω, "occurs once more in the Gospel of John, in Jn 4:38 ('to labor, work'), in what is clearly a missiological context." Weinrich also notes that one commentator observed that "it is virtually a technical term in Paul for the missionary labor of himself and others . . . [and thereby] indicate[s] the work of evangelism." Although Weinrich acknowledges that this interpretation is "not impossible," he simply concludes that Jesus' exhaustion is because it is the middle of the day when the heat is most intense, and so this small detail adds "realism" to the narrative.[16]

Fair enough. Jesus, however, is entering mission territory in order to show that he is in fact "the Savior of the nations." As one who works alongside missionaries in Spanish-speaking contexts, I have observed the exhaustion of missionaries after engaging others across cultures, across languages, in a secular, postmodern world. Jesus' exhaustion heightens the missiological context in which he has placed himself at the well of Jacob which, as Weinrich rightly notes, is central to this text.

Both Scaer and Weinrich highlight the marriage imagery in John 4, and that, in Scaer's words, "evangelism is a type of courtship that leads to marriage."[17] Courtship is a perfect image of the catechumenate, of Jesus reaching out/courting the Samaritan woman, a catechumen, and inviting her to the marriage feast of living water and the food that embodies Jesus doing the Father's will of sacrifice. Scaer is particularly expansive on how John 4 is a "Johannine variation on an Old Testament betrothal," "a type of romance," even that this Samaritan woman's many marriages may be "a sly reference to the Samaritan people as whole, who were known for their religious promiscuity," in this case, with other gods, what Josephus named "the gods of five other nations."[18] This fits

---

16. Weinrich, *John 1;1–7:1,* 468 citing T. Okure, *The Johannine Approach to Mission: A Contextual Study of John 4:1–42.* Wissenschaftliche Untersuchungen zum Neuen Testament 2.31 (Tübingen: Mohr, 1988), 86. Weinrich cites Hauck, TDNT 3:829 who claims that κοπιάω is used 19 times for the work of evangelism in Paul's missionary journeys.

17. Scaer, "Jesus and the Woman at the Well," 5.

18. Scaer, "Jesus and the Woman at the Well," 7.

perfectly with the Old and New Testament image of the relationship between Yahweh and Israel, between Jesus and his Church as that of a bridegroom and his bride, as St. Paul so eloquently describes in Ephesians 5. Scaer concludes:

> Five husbands had not brought her any personal satisfaction or ultimate meaning. Earthly water could never satisfy her thirst. False religions could not deliver what she, representative of the Samaritan people, needed. Only Jesus could satisfy her longing. Only Jesus could provide living water. Only Jesus could serve as her true bridegroom.[19]

As in any courtship, a time of scrutiny takes place. Jesus does this with the Samaritan woman at the well as he asks her about her marital life, prompted by his command, "Go, call your husband and come here." (Jn 4:16) She comes clean about her five husbands, and the man she is now living with outside of marriage. Jesus reveals that "the past life of the woman perhaps demonstrated an ethical laxity that bordered on the scandalous."[20] Such scrutiny not only leads to Jesus teaching her the proper way of worship, but sends her out to evangelize others, to "Come! See . . . Could it be possible that this man is the Christ?" (Jn 4:29). She even leaves her water pot behind, for she now has living water.

Her efforts bore fruit: "From that city many of the Samaritans believed [in him] because of the word of the woman as she went about witnessing" (Jn 4:39). But it was Jesus' witness that brought it home for the Samaritans, as he spent two days with them, evangelizing and catechizing (and scrutinizing) them, so that many believed his word and proclaimed: "We believe no longer because of what you said, for we ourselves have heard and we know that this man is in truth the Savior of the world" (Jn 4:42). As Weinrich puts it:

> The mission of the Son is nothing other than the effecting of the Father's will (Jn 4:34). . . . the coming of the Samaritans to Jesus (Jn 4:30, 35) and their eventual confession of him as "the Savior of the world" (Jn 4:42) signal the beginning of that worship in "Spirit and Truth" (Jn 4:23–24) which is itself the acknowledgement of the Father. . . . The acclamation that Jesus is "Savior" is not the acclamation of the Samaritans who go out to meet Jesus (Jn 4:30), but the acclamation of the Samaritans who have come to believe because of the word of Jesus (Jn 4:41–42). Their confession arises from their *hearing* of Jesus and their *knowing* in faith ("we believe," Jn 4:42).[21]

19. Scaer, "Jesus and the Woman at the Well: Where Mission Meets Worship," 8.
20. Weinrich, *John 1;1–7:1*, 489.
21. Weinrich, *John 1;1–7:1*, 505, 527.

THE WOMAN AT THE WELL
SCRUTINY AS CATECHETICAL

Evangelization always leads to catechesis, and the scrutinies at the end of Lent were first and foremost acts of *catechesis*. Aidan Kavanagh puts it well:

> The lenten scrutinies . . . are thus at base major acts of catechesis in which the whole community begins now to take part. . . . The liturgical scrutinies of Lent are therefore both in whole and in each of their parts salient dimensions of the whole catechetical process by which one is formed for full participation in a life of faith."[22]

Weinrich affirms this when he notes that the woman's enthusiastic evangelistic call to her fellow Samaritans to "Come! See!" is in fact a call for them to become catechumens. This echoes Jesus' call to the two of John's disciples to "Come and see" (Jn 1:39) and then Philip's call to Nathanael to "Come and see" (Jn 1:46). Weinrich notes that "such phraseology [to 'Come and see'] was used by rabbis for investigation of *halakah*. It invites to a consideration of the Scriptures."[23]

The woman at the well and her Samaritan kinsmen are catechumens who are being called by Jesus, the rabbi, to consider the Scriptures and prepare them for baptism, which is the entrance into "a new 'way of life,' the *halakah* of the children of God . . . [for] Baptism is the fulfillment of Torah!"[24] This preparation centers on coming to believe in the identity of Jesus as "living water," that is, to identify Jesus as *the* prophet, the one who is worshipped in Spirit and Truth, the Messiah, the Christ, the great I AM, the Savior of the world.

This catechesis is a courtship that begins at the well and then goes out to the city and reaches others. It is dialogical, which continues Jesus' way of teaching that began with his call to Philip and Nathanael in John 1 and his dialogue with Nicodemus in John 3. The dialogue in John 4 begins at the sixth hour, the same hour when darkness covered the earth as Jesus hung from a cross, signaling to us that the goal of the dialogue is cruciform. Jesus enters the darkness of this Samaritan woman to scrutinize her life and then offer to her his life through living water—"a spring of water gushing up to eternal life" (Jn 1:14). But in this living water is also an offer of "my food" that is "[to] do the will of him who sent me and bring his work to completion" (Jn 4:34).

---

22. Kavanagh, *The Shape of Baptism: The Rite of Christian Initiation*, 60.
23. Weinrich, *John 1;1–7:1*, 505.
24. Weinrich, *John 1;1–7:1*, 20.

Jesus begins his catechetical dialogue, and his courtship, with a simple request of the Samaritan woman by Jacob's well: "Give me [water] to drink" (Jn 4:7). She almost seems put out by his forwardness: "How is it that you, who are a Jew, asks from me, who am a Samaritan woman, to drink?" (Jn 4:9). The evangelist needs to explain her response with a parenthetical insertion into the narrative: "(For Jews do not share utensils with Samaritan women" Jn 4:10). Here John acknowledges that Jesus is crossing a cultural boundary that would render him unclean. It is almost as if the Samaritan wants to prevent Jesus from becoming infected with her darkness. But Jesus is not afraid to enter her darkness and scrutinize her: "If you knew the gift of God and who it is who says to you,' Give me a drink,' you rather would have asked him, and he would have given to you living water" (Jn 4:10).

With those simple words—"living water"—Jesus gives her a complete catechesis. Living water is the gift Jesus gives, and "for the rabbis, the gift of God was the Torah," and water "a symbol for the Holy Spirit, for the Torah . . . for revelation and wisdom."[25] Living water as gift, as Torah, as Spirit, as revelation is the perfect image for the final scrutiny of catechumens before baptism, who until their catechesis knew only natural water but will soon, in baptism, "passover" from the devil to Christ by the Spirit. It is as if Jesus, in giving the Samaritan woman "living water" is saying to her: "Depart thou evil spirt and make room for the Holy Spirit." And with this exorcism Jesus makes it possible to participate in his life. Weinrich puts it this way:

> There are two waters, the water from Jacob's well and that water that Jesus will give. The one quenches thirst, but only for a time. The other water is required but once, for through it the Holy Spirit is given, and with the Spirit there is given also the life of the Spirit, which become the inner reality of the child of God (Jn 4:14). Jesus refers to the reception of the Spirit as "drinking" from the living water (Jn 4:14). Such an image is wholly consonant with a baptismal referent. Paul parallels Baptism and being "made to drink of one Spirit" (1 Cor 12:13; cf. 1 For 10:2–4). . . . The life of the Spirit given and received in Baptism is a *life*. As a life it is that which must be lived and necessarily lived in thought, word, and work. The Spirit received in the "living water" is that Spirit which descended upon Jesus and remained on him (Jn 1:32–33). Thus, the gushing water within the baptized is an image of the life of Christ, possessed and lived by those who, animated and guided by the Spirit, are his disciples.[26]

25. Weinrich, *John 1;1–7:1*, 472.
26. Weinrich, *John 1;1–7:1*, 474–475.

The Woman at the Well
Scrutiny as Liturgical

To enter the life of Christ, one has to enter his presence, and in the presence of Christ there are always liturgical rites that mediate that presence. The genius of the early catechumenate and the catechumenate today is that the primary acts of catechesis are in the liturgy. When the scrutinies were first developed, Scripture would be read for as long as an hour and then preached on for another hour. Thus, catechesis took place in the presence of God, in the liturgy of the Word, within the liturgical assembly of the baptized. No wonder it became known as the "Liturgy of the Catechumens." So in the catechumenate, the means of catechesis were the Scriptures heard and interpreted in the liturgy of the church, showing the catechumens the value of liturgical worship.

But many catechumens came from another kind of worship—that of the pagan temple with their idols, their temple meats sacrificed to their false gods, and their temple prostitutes—these were the "sacraments" of pagan worship, that is, the way they communed with their gods. This is why James, the bishop of Jerusalem, insists on the apostolic prescriptions at the Jerusalem council in Acts 15: "that you abstain from what has been sacrificed to idols and from blood and from what is strangled and from unchastity" (Acts 15:29). These were powerful enticements for pagans, and even for Christians after baptism. Although you will not hear sermons today on the urgency of abiding by the apostolic prescriptions of James—as we have no pagan temples with sacrifices to idols and temple prostitutes—such was not the case in early Christianity and you will find many sermons by the early fathers that rail against the pagan temples that are still an attraction to both catechumens and baptized.[27] As Harmless notes, in the time of Augustine, "paganism remained a force to be reckoned with. . . . Maximus, a pagan grammarian from Madaura, could write to Augustine and boast:

> We behold the marketplace of our town occupied by a crowd of beneficent deities; . . . with pious supplications we openly worship our gods, gaining their favor by acceptable sacrifices and taking pains that these things be seen and approved by all.[28]

So a catechumen at the end of Lent is preparing for a radical shift from worshipping false gods to worshipping Jesus, first by being joined to his flesh in holy Baptism, and then by eating and drinking his flesh and blood in the holy Eucharist.

---

27. See Elena Butova, *The Four Prohibitions of Acts 15 and Their Common Background in Genesis 1–3* (Eugene, OR: Wipf and Stock, 2018), 19–39 who provides a survey of the patristic appropriation of these apostolic prohibitions.

28. Harmless, *Augustine and the Catechumenate*, 112.

During the worship wars of the 1980s and 1990s, those of us who were on the front lines of that war needed to learn to address the continuing critique that liturgical worship did not conform with Jesus' command to worship in Spirit and Truth. Liturgical worship was perceived by many to be too formal, preventing "worship of the heart," for that is what Jesus meant when he commanded the Samaritan woman to worship the Father in Spirit and Truth. Scaer sums up their position well: "Worship in Spirit and truth has been accordingly understood as synonymous with a type of heart-felt devotion, in opposition to the ceremonies of Judaism, Catholicism, or, for that matter, liturgical Lutheranism."[29]

Weinrich's exhaustive analysis of the true meaning of worship in Spirit and Truth centers in this reality: that "the confession of Jesus as the Son is the constitutive reality of worship of the Father 'in Spirit and Truth' (Jn 4:23–24),"[30] and that "Jesus is *himself and alone* the one who worships the Father in Spirit and Truth."[31] Weinrich affirms that worship in Spirit and Truth is christological, showing that "heart" worship is not the main point of Jesus' catechesis of the Samaritan woman about true, liturgical worship, but that it points to a shift in the place of worship, from the temple in Jerusalem to the temple of Jesus' body (Jn 2:21), and that to worship the body of Jesus one must be baptized:

> The *place* of the new temple, the new sacrifice, and the manner of the new life is not in the first instance an "interior" reality, but the obedient death of Jesus on the cross. Similarly, therefore, the new worship of the Father by "the true worshipers" is not in the first instance in the interior space of the heart, nor is it in the first instance prayer. Rather, the true worship of the Father is possible only for those who are begotten by water and the Spirit and *so* become children of God, that is, children of the Father (Jn 1:13; 3:3, 5, 7).[32]

For the Samaritan woman to receive this catechesis of Jesus about the worship of Father in Spirit and Truth, she must first be scrutinized by Jesus and begins with his questioning her marital status as "Jesus lays bare the sinful past of the woman."[33] This scrutiny also lays bare for the Samaritan woman that her marital infidelity was echoed in her liturgical infidelity. *She* brings up the question of worship because she sees that Jesus' insight into her past makes him a prophet. *She* wants to know about the true place of worship. This gives Jesus the opening to begin his scrutiny of the Samaritan woman:

29. Scaer, "Jesus and the Woman at the Well," 10.
30. Weinrich, *John 1;1–7:1*, 496.
31. Weinrich, *John 1;1–7:1*, 499. Emphasis Weinrich.
32. Weinrich, *John 1;1–7:1*, 500.
33. Weinrich, *John 1;1–7:1*, 489.

"Believe me, woman," says Jesus, "an hour is coming when neither on this mountain nor in Jerusalem shall you worship the Father. You worship what you do not know. We worship what we know, for salvation is from the Jews. But an hour is coming and is now when the true worshipers will worship the Father in Spirit and Truth." (Jn 4:21–23)

Jesus is scrutinizing the Samaritan woman in his catechesis about true liturgical worship that connects the themes of evangelization, living water, and marital fidelity, a scrutiny that would prepare a catechumen to be baptized and receive the Eucharist—the place where "true worshipers will worship the Father in Spirit and Truth." What the Samaritan woman and all the catechumens who follow her now enter is an eschatological community that is gathered around "the Lamb of who takes away the sin of the world" (Jn 1:29), for that Lamb is the "true locus for worship." Scaer says it best:

Jesus is Jacob's ladder, the true gate to heaven. He is the true temple of God, the place of dwelling. By speaking in this way, Jesus prepared the Samaritan woman for heavenly worship, in which "there is no need of a temple," for the saints stand always in the presence of God and the Lamb.[34]

Weinrich must also have his say as he describes, with the missiological zeal of the prophet Ezekiel, that the Father is seeking others to enter this worship of Spirit and Truth, a community of Jews and Samaritans and Gentiles in one body, the Church:

The theme of living waters flowing from the new temple was an essential element in the prophetic expectation of the ingathering of dispersed Israel and of the nations (Ezek 47:1–2; Zech 14:8). In that day there will be a cleansing from all idolatry and all transgression. God will vindicate his holy name, and redeemed Israel will know that Yahweh is God and will walk in his statutes (Ezek 36:22–36). The restoration of Israel will be, in fact, a new creation, for the land "that was desolate has become like a garden of Eden" (Ezek 36:35; cf. Ezek 36:30; Zech 14:8; Song 4:12–15; Rev 22:1–3). . . . Therefore, Jesus' words that the Father "is seeking" such persons to worship him (Jn 4:23) means nothing other than the Father has sent his Son and has given him over into death so that those who are yet in darkness might in him have light and life (Jn 3:15–17, 21; 6:44; 12:32).[35]

---

34. Scaer, "Jesus and the Woman at the Well," 8–9.
35. Weinrich, *John 1;1–7:1*, 501.

The Samaritan woman was sitting in darkness. Jesus sought her, evangelized her through a catechetical scrutiny, and invited her to become a true worshiper of Father, Son, and Holy Spirit by baptism and faith.

THE WOMAN AT THE WELL

SCRUTINY AS MYSTAGOGICAL

Finally, John 4 as the Gospel narrative for the first scrutiny is *mystagogical*, that is, it explains to the catechumen the meaning of the mystery of Baptism and the Lord's Supper.[36] Jesus at Jacob's well is the mystagogue explaining to the Samaritan woman the theological significance that he is "Living Water," and that she will drink this water once and then live forever. Peter Scaer says as much: "living water serves as catechesis, deepening our understanding of the *sacramental reality* of the church and of worship."[37]

Living water may also be a symbol that unites both baptism and Eucharist. Earlier we noted, with Weinrich, that "Jesus refers to the reception of the Holy Spirit as 'drinking' from the living water," and that he cited Paul's description of Baptism as "being made to drink of one Spirit" (1 Cor 12:13).[38] Our scene of the woman at the well is, after all, about giving Jesus a drink from Jacob's well, and Jesus' countering that he will give her water to drink from which she "will never thirst forever . . . water gushing up to eternal life" (Jn 4:14). Are we to take this literally, that is, in baptism are we made "to drink of one Spirit?"

Perhaps. Hippolytus in his church order *Apostolic Tradition* explains that the newly baptized would receive three cups at their first eucharist:

> The cup of wine mixed with water according to the likeness of the blood, which is shed for all who believe in him. And milk and honey mixed together for the fulfillment of the promise to the fathers, which spoke of a land flowing with milk and honey; namely, Christ's flesh which he gave, by which they who believe are nourished like babes, he making sweet the bitter things of the heart by the gentleness of his word. And the water into an offering in a token of the laver, in order that the inner part of man, which is a living soul, may receive the same as the body.[39]

---

36. This anticipates their fuller catechesis of the sacraments in the post-baptismal, mystagogical catecheses during the eight days of Easter week.

37. Scaer, "Jesus and the Woman at the Well," 14.

38. Weinrich, *John 1;1–7:1*, 474–475.

39. Burton S. Easton, *The Apostolic Tradition of Hippolytus*, 48. See also Everett Ferguson, *Baptism in the Early Church: History, Theology, and Liturgy in the First Five Centuries* (Grand Rapids, MI: Eerdmans, 2009), 333 who explains this custom of three cups in this way: "There was a cup of water (as a sign of washing: 21.29, 33) and a cup of milk and honey (fulfilling the promise of 'the land of milk and honey' and representing nourishment of children: 21.28, 33) in addition to the usual cup of wine (mixed with water) for the blood of Christ (21.27, 33)."

In first Corinthians 10, Paul speaks of baptism in the context of the Exodus and drinking from the supernatural Rock who was Christ. Jean Danielou notes that early fathers understood both "the manna and the water from the rock . . . as figures of the Eucharist." Jean Danielou observes, in *The Bible and the Liturgy*, that Theodore of Mopsuestia and St. John Chrysostom "associated the Rock of Horeb with the manna as a figure of the Eucharist, the manna being a figure of the bread and the water from the rock of the wine."[40] Ambrose, also, in *De Mysteriis* "associates [the Rock of Horeb] with the miracle of the manna to show the superiority of the Christian sacraments:"

> The water flowed from the Rock for the Jews, the Blood of Christ for you; the water slaked their thirst for an hour, the Blood quenches your thirst forever. The Jews drink and thirsted once more; when you have drunk, you need never thirst again. That was a figure, this is the truth. If the figure seems wonderful to you, how much more the reality the figure of which you admire.[41]

But there is more. John records Jesus' disciples encouraging him to eat. And Jesus uses this moment of speaking about eating food, (as he did with the woman at the well about drinking water), to catechize them about how he is "the Bread of Life," anticipating the bread discourse in John 6 where he will say, "Whoever comes to me shall never hunger, and whoever believes in me shall never thirst" (Jn 6:35). Here is what he says in John 4: "I have food to eat that you do not know . . . My food is that I do the will of him who sent me and bring his work to completion" (Jn 4:32, 34).

We began by noting that Weinrich understands that "in this Gospel Christology is also ecclesiology," and we might add missiology, as Weinrich suggests when he says: "*The food which Jesus is to eat has everything to do with the coming of the Samaritans!*"[42] This food is nothing more and nothing less than Jesus fulfilling the Father's will by offering himself up as a sacrifice as the Lamb of God who takes away the sin of the world, a sacrifice we now eat and drink in the holy Eucharist. Weinrich comments on the "intertwining of Christological, sacramental, and ecclesiological ideas in the mention of the 'food' which Jesus was to eat:

> If for Jesus to "eat the food" of the Father's will is for him to reveal himself as the true Lamb of the Passover (Jn 1:29), slaughtered for the life of the world (Jn 3:16–17; 12:47), then it is wholly possible

---

40. Jean Danielou, *The Bible and The Liturgy* (Notre Dame, IN: University of Notre Dame Press, 1956), 150.

41. Jean Danielou, *The Bible and the Liturgy*, 150–151, citing Ambrose *De Mysteriis, 48*).

42. Weinrich, *John 1;1–7:1*, 517. Emphasis Weinrich.

that the image of "food" in John 4 (βρῶσις, Jn 4:32; βρῶμα, Jn 4:34) prepares for the manna discourse of John 6. For there also Jesus speaks of "food" (βρῶσις, Jn 6:27, 55) and of doing the will of him who sent him (Jn 6:38–40). . . . The work of the Father is evidence in the work of the Son . . . The work of the Son entails the life of the church, for as the incarnate Son (Jn 1:14) Jesus is that man who is the perfect expression of the Father's will. Those who come to Jesus and believe in him become one with him in his humanity and *so* become with him the new creation of a new humanity. . . . For Jesus to "eat the food" of the Father's will, that is, for him to die the death for the life of the world, is for him to give himself until faith so that those who believe might eat the "bread" which he is. To think of Christ apart from the salvation he proffers is to think of Christ apart from the mission of his Sonship. In the economy of the incarnation one cannot separate the person of the Savior from those who are saved. Therefore, mention of his food leads Jesus directly to the theme of harvest.[43]

That harvest, of course, is the Samaritan woman and the Samaritans in the village who have been evangelized, scrutinized, and catechized in preparation for baptism and to become true worshipers of the Father in Spirit and Truth in body broken and blood poured out.

What has been done here in John 4 concerning the first scrutiny in Lent 3 could also be done of John 9 in Lent 4 and John 11 in Lent 5, but I will leave that to all the pastors and catechists who might want to follow the ancient church in scrutinizing their catechumens and members for Lents hereafter. ✠

---

43. Weinrich, *John 1;1–7:1,* 519–520. Emphasis Weinrich.

THE CHRONOLOGY OF THE
PASSION IN THE GOSPEL
ACCORDING TO JOHN

✝

Each of the canonical Gospels maintains that Jesus was crucified and died on a Friday.[1] They also all affirm that, two days later, Jesus rose from the dead "on the third day."[2] The Gospels' characteristically inclusive manner of counting the days from Good Friday to Easter Sunday is elsewhere made explicit when Jesus says that he will work "today and tomorrow and on the third day" (Luke 13:32). Likewise, he repeatedly asserts that his resurrection will take place *after* three days."[3] Each of the Synoptic Gospels also maintains that, when Jesus and his disciples gathered on the eve of his crucifixion, they did so to "eat the Passover."[4] The Synoptic descriptions of the Thursday of Holy Week—the meal's preparation, celebration, and aftermath—agree with both canonical and extra-canonical sources regarding the perennial practice of the Jews in observing the highest and greatest of Israel's feasts, "*the* [preeminent] feast of the Jews" (John 6:4): Passover.

In the spring, in what was for the Jews "the first month of the year" (Exod 12:2), the six day observance of the Passover began on the 10th of

---

1. Matt 27:62; 28:1; Mark 15:42; Luke 23:54–56; John 19:31, 42. See further below John 19:14.

2. See τῇ τρίτῃ ἡμέρᾳ in Matt 16:21; 17:23; 20:19; Luke 9:22; 24:7, 46. See also Acts 10:40. See further the equivalent expression τῇ ἡμέρᾳ τῇ τρίτῃ in Luke 18:33. See also 1 Cor 15:4. Contrast "until (ἕως) the third day" in Matt 27:64 and "it is now the third day" in Luke 24:21.

3. See μετὰ τρεῖς ἡμέρας in Matt 27:63; Mark 8:31; 9:31; 10:34. Cf. Luke 2:46; Acts 25:1; 28:17. Therefore, "after three days" means not "three days *later*," but "with the coming of a third day." Similarly, "after [μετά] eight days" in John 20:26 means not "eight days later" (a common mistake), but "a week later" (and so again on the Lord's Day as in Rev 1:10). See D. A. Carson, *The Gospel according to John* (Grand Rapids: Eerdmans, 1991), 657. See further "through (διά) three days" in Matt 26:61; Mark 14:58; and "in (ἐν) three days" in Matt 27:40; Mark 15:29; John 2:19–20. Contrast Jesus' suggestion that "just as Jonah was three days and three nights in the belly of the great fish, so will the Son of Man be three days and three nights in the heart of the earth" (Matt 12:40).

4. Matt 26:17; Mark 14:12, 14; Luke 22:7–8, 11, 15.

Nisan with each Jewish household's selection of a lamb or a goat for the feast (Exod 12:3, 5).[5] The lamb or goat was selected and kept until it was taken to the temple for sacrifice in the afternoon hours of the 14th of Nisan (Exod 12:6).[6] Because the approach of twilight and the setting of the sun marked the end of the day and the beginning of the next day,[7] each household made preparation for a meal that would take place after the setting of the sun in the first hours of the 15th of Nisan (Exod 12:8).[8] If a household happened to be too small for the purchase of a lamb and for its complete consumption (Exod 12:10),[9] then smaller households would join together as one to eat the feast (see Exod 12:4).[10] All leaven was removed from every house in anticipation of the seven-day Feast of Unleavened Bread (Exod 12:15) whose beginning coincided with the day of the *Pascha*, and whose beginning and end were marked with the holding of a sacred assembly

---

5. Cf. in John 11:55 significantly before the 10th of Nisan the many who "went up from the country to Jerusalem before the Passover to purify themselves" in preparation for the sacred six-day-long ritual that would follow.

6. See Exod 12:6, "And you shall keep it until the fourteenth day of this month, when the whole assembly of the congregation of Israel shall kill their lambs toward evening (πρὸς ἑσπέραν)." Cf. Lev 23:5; Num 28:16. According to Philo, *Spec. Laws* 2.145, "After the New Moon comes the fourth feast, [the Passing-Over] [τὰ διαβατήρια], which the Hebrews in their native tongue call 'Pascha.' In this festival many myriads of victims [from mid-day until the evening] (ἀπὸ μεσημβρίας ἄχρι ἑσπέρας) are offered by the whole people, old and young alike, raised for that particular day to the dignity of the priesthood. For at other times the priests according to the ordinance of the law carry out both the public sacrifices and those offered by private individuals. But on this occasion the whole nation performs the sacred rites and acts as priest with pure hands and complete immunity." More specifically, Josephus, *History of the Jewish War* 6.423, observes that normally such sacrifice took place from the ninth to the eleventh hour (that is, from 3:00 PM to 5:00 PM). Alternatively, *m. Pesaḥ* 5.1 mentions the custom of a sacrifice even earlier in the day when the evening of the Passover coincided with the evening of the Sabbath.

7. See "and there was evening (ἑσπέρα) and there was morning (πρωΐ)" identified as a "day" in Gen 1:5, 8, 13, 19, 23, 31. See also "from evening (ἀφ᾽ ἑσπέρας) . . . until evening (ἕως ἑσπέρας)" in Exod 12:18. Thus, the twelve hours of the night followed by the twelve hours of the day (cf. John 11:9) constitute a single day. Hence, John 19:31 suggests the need late in the afternoon Friday to remove the bodies from the crosses before the onset of the Sabbath. Contrast ὀψία, indicating not evening (if we mean by this the first hours of the night), but twilight (meaning the last daylight hour[s] of the day) in John 20:19 (since the verse indicates also that it was still "the first day of the week"; cf. John 20:1). See further Matt 16:2; 27:57; Mark 1:32; 15:42.

8. Raymond Brown, *The Death of the Messiah—from Gethsemane to the Grave: A Commentary on the Passion Narratives in the Four Gospels*, 2 vols., ABRL (New York: Doubleday, 1994), 2:1354, therefore observes that "the slaughtering was at the end of one day (the 14th) and the meal at the beginning of the next (the 15th)." Cf. Jubilees 49:1: "Remember the commandment which the Lord commanded you concerning Passover, that you observe it in its time, on the fourteenth of the first month, so that you might sacrifice it before it becomes evening and so that you might eat it during the night on the evening of the fifteenth from the time of sunset." See also Josephus, *Ant.* 3.248–51, and Exod 12:8, "They shall eat the flesh that night [τῇ νυκτὶ ταύτῃ], roasted on the fire; with unleavened bread and bitter herbs they shall eat it."

9. Exod 12:10, "And you shall let none of it remain until the morning (ἕως πρωΐ); anything that remains until the morning you shall burn" (see also v. 22). Cf. Deut 16:4, 7.

10. Exod 12:4, "And if the household is too small for a lamb, then he and his nearest neighbor shall take according to the number of persons." Josephus, *History of the Jewish Wars* 6.423, observes further that around each sacrifice was a group of not less than ten men, for none were allowed to eat alone, and that many came together in groups of twenty.

(Exod 12:16).[11] Thus, Thursday night's meal and what followed throughout the rest of the evening, morning, and afternoon of the "next day," including the sacred assembly, all took place for the Jews on the same day: the day of the *Pascha* and the first day of the Feast of Unleavened Bread.

Thus, if the passage of a single day is reckoned according to Jewish custom from sundown to sundown, then both the meal eaten Thursday evening and the crucifixion itself are depicted in the Synoptics as having taken place on the day of the Passover: the 15th of Nisan.[12] Jesus' Last Supper with his disciples was a Passover meal. Many, however, have posited that it is precisely here where John and the Synoptics stand in irreconcilable conflict. John, it is argued, offers an alternative chronology of the passion in which Jesus gathers and eats with his disciples not on the day *of* Passover but on the preceding day, in which preparations were then still being made *for* the Passover.[13] Thus, the Passover was eaten not on Thursday evening but on Friday evening. "Attempts to deal with this discrepancy between the Synoptics and John run the gamut from contending that both chronologies are true, through favoring one over the other, to the view that neither is true."[14] This essay will argue that others have been too quick to assert a real discrepancy between the Synoptics and the Gospel of John.

The Gospels were composed for all Christians; therefore, when published, they were quickly distributed as far and wide as the day and circumstances allowed.[15] When distributed, they were immediately studied

---

11. See further Exod 12:18–21. See also Lev 23:5–8; Num 28:16–25; Deut 16:1–8. Thus, Philo, *Spec. Laws* 2.27–28, indicates that the Feast of the Unleavened Bread customarily began on the 15th of Nisan. On the other hand, Brown observes rightly that at times both Josephus and the Gospels will speak differently: "Presumably it is in this imprecise category that Mark 14:12 (copied by Luke 22:7) belongs: 'On the first day of the Unleavened Bread when they sacrificed the paschal lamb,' since technically they sacrificed the lamb on the 14th, and the first day of the Unleavened Bread (when they *ate* the lamb) was the 15th" (*Death of the Messiah*, 2:1355). Apparently, by the first century AD both the day that the leaven would have been removed from each household (the 14th of Nisan) and the first full day of the Feast of Unleavened Bread (the 15th of Nisan) could for evident reasons be called "the first day of Unleavened Bread."

12. Thus, Jesus' resurrection happens during the seven-day-long Feast of Unleavened Bread that began on the 15th of Nisan and ended on the 21st (see Exod 12:18–19). The victorious Jesus emerges from the grave early in the morning and appears to his disciples at the close of Holy Week's 8th day, which was also "the first day of the week" (Matt 28:1; Mark 16:2; Luke 24:1; John 20:1, 19; cf. Acts 20:7; 1 Cor 16:2) and the 17th of Nisan, when all Israel was still in and around Jerusalem for the sake of the feast.

13. See, for example, the translation of John 19:14 in the NAB, NASB, NET, NRSV. John speaks in this way, it is argued, so that the crucifixion of Jesus might happen at the same time that the Passover lambs were being slaughtered in the temple. While it is *grammatically* possible that the statement "it was the day of Preparation *of* the Passover" in John 19:14 means that the morning of Jesus' trial before Pilate was simultaneously a day of preparation *for* the Passover, we shall see that this is hardly the only grammatical possibility and is in all likelihood not the best grammatical possibility.

14. Brown, *Death of the Messiah*, 2:1361.

15. Richard Bauckham, "For Whom Were Gospels Written?" in *The Gospels for All Christians: Rethinking the Gospel Audiences*, ed. Richard Bauckham (Grand Rapids: Eerdmans, 1998), 9–48.

and widely prized as the authoritative testimony of the eyewitnesses of Jesus.[16] By the time the last of the eyewitnesses composed the last of the canonical Gospels,[17] however, the Synoptics had existed for decades.[18] Their content––or, at least the essential content of the initial kerygma of the earliest church as represented in each one of them––had been established tradition for quite some time, and so was reasonably familiar to most, if not all. It is therefore exceedingly implausible that, composing the last of the canonical Gospels in the last years of the first century, the last of the eyewitnesses knowingly contradicted what by then was established and familiar.

This implausibility is especially true when it comes to his testimony concerning the crucial events of the day Jesus suffered and died. The last of the eyewitnesses was himself one of Jesus' first disciples.[19] Charged and sent to proclaim Christ faithfully to the entire world (John 20:21), he first did this in and around Palestine as one of the "pillars" of the earliest church (see Acts 3:1; 4:13; 8:14; Gal 2:9). In the company of other eyewitnesses, when the essential content of the kerygma of the earliest church was a principal concern, he personally contributed to the apostolic kerygma that would later become the narrative tradition of Matthew, Mark, and Luke. In Palestine he lived and served after the death and resurrection of Christ for approximately forty years. Following the destruction of Jerusalem in the year AD 70, he subsequently lived and served in the province of Asia Minor for as many as thirty additional years.

The last of the eyewitnesses was therefore an extraordinary figure. "We need to be interested in his theological thought, which is quite equal to that of Paul," not because it provides "an alleged plurality of apparently contradictory opinions and sketches,"[20] but because he was an exceptional biblical scholar, an impressively discerning and eminently skillful redactor, an exceedingly effective memory artisan, a compellingly persuasive rhetorician,[21] and the last to leave his distinctive imprint on the witness of the New Testament. John was fully conversant with Moses and the prophets (see John 1:49), and the rest of the New

---

16. Richard Bauckham, *Jesus and the Eyewitnesses: The Gospels as Eyewitness Testimony* (Grand Rapids, MI: Eerdmans, 2006).

17. Martin Hengel, *The Johannine Question* (London: SCM, 1990), 30. Hengel posits that John "the elder" (see 2 John 1; 3 John 1) and "beloved disciple" (see John 13:23; 19:26–27; 20:2–9; 21:24) was "a Palestinian Jew who was a contemporary of Jesus" and claimed that he was a physical eyewitness who had "seen with his own eyes and heard with his own ears" (Hengel, *Johannine Question*, 49).

18. Bruce G. Schuchard, *1–3 John*, Concordia Commentary (St. Louis, MO: Concordia Publishing House, 2012), 1–8, 33–58.

19. "The traditional identification of the unnamed disciple [in John 1:35–40] as the Evangelist," observes Carson, *John*, 154, "is plausible enough."

20. Hengel, *Johannine Question*, ix.

21. See most recently Alicia D. Myers and Bruce G. Schuchard, eds., *Abiding Words: The Use of Scripture in the Gospel of John*, RBS 81 (Atlanta, GA: SBL Press, 2015).

Testament Scriptures that by then had stood for decades; he also became the caretaker of the mother of the Lord (see John 19:25–27) and was for some *the* apostle par excellence.[22] Thus, John knew that the last of his works—the Gospel—would be the final eyewitness testimony to be received as Scripture.[23]

Encouraging the faithful so that none would be lost, John was keenly aware that many antichrists and false prophets had gone out into the world and so constantly threatened to deceive. Yet, with the last of his works, John eschewed every novelty and chose instead to focus on the eyewitness testimony that the faithful had heard from the beginning.[24] With the last of his works the last of the eyewitnesses became the last evangelist, so that in his subsequent absence what his children had heard from the beginning might nonetheless endure. The last of the eyewitnesses wrote, then, not to subvert established tradition, but for the purpose of "extending Israel's Scriptures . . . through his authoritative witness to . . . the man Jesus, the Christ, the Son of God."[25] John used elements of standing tradition with a deliberate interest in significantly broadening the church's knowledge of the person and work of Jesus; he proclaimed what it means to belong to Jesus in ways that would be especially meaningful to the faithful, who must soon live in a post-apostolic church looking forward to Christ's return. John, therefore, wrote not to correct or to oppose standing tradition; instead, he wrote to extend and to deepen it.[26] Thus,

---

22. The author, observes Hengel, "was a theological original of fascinating spirituality through and through, an original in the best sense of the word." His works are "an impressive multiform unity derived from 'different christologies.'" He was a "towering creative teacher," the "opposite of a mere tradent" (*Johannine Question*, 104). To Irenaeus, he was the most significant of all of Jesus' disciples (*Johannine Question*, 3).

23. Schuchard, *1–3 John*, 40–43. See further Francis J. Moloney, "The Gospel of John as Scripture," *CBQ* 67 (2005): 454–468.

24. Schuchard, *1–3 John*, 3–4, 55–58.

25. Schuchard, *1–3 John*, 3. "The precise information given by Irenaeus," observes Hengel, "that the Fourth Gospel is also the *last* of the four canonical Gospels, along with the reference to the death of the evangelist in the time of Trajan, and [the Gospel's] last verses, where the end of the beloved disciple is put long after the martyrdom of Peter, should warn us against dating the Gospel too early." Therefore, "we may hardly presuppose a 'final redaction' before 98, that is before Trajan" (*Johannine Question*, 3).

26. Richard Bauckham, "John for Readers of Mark," in *The Gospels for All Christians: Rethinking the Gospel Audiences*, ed. Richard Bauckham (Grand Rapids, MI: Eerdmans, 1998), 147–171. He also observes, "It is a notable, though generally unnoticed, feature of John's narrative sequence that it is both largely compatible with Mark's while also largely avoiding repetition of Mark's narrative. While going its own way, it intersects with and leaves space for Mark's in a way that makes the two Gospel narratives complementary. The nineteenth-century view that John wrote to *supplement* the Synoptics certainly does not do justice to the relationship of John's narrative to Mark's. It is not a mere series of additions to Mark's narrative. It has a narrative integrity of its own. It makes both narrative and theological sense in its own terms, quite independently of Mark. But for readers/hearers of John who also knew Mark, John's narrative can be read as *complementing* Mark's, just as Mark's can be read as complementing John's. The two narratives, each complete in its own terms, intersect with only a minimum of events in common and only a minimum of contradiction in sequence" (170). See also Herman Ridderbos, *The Gospel of John: A Theological Commentary*, trans. John Vriend (Grand Rapids, MI:

John's works "had a profound influence in the mainstream Church of the second century [that] the bulk of modern scholarship has left us entirely unprepared to appreciate."[27] In no way, then, did he intend to correct or contradict the Synoptic chronology of the passion. Jesus and his disciples did indeed eat a Passover meal on Thursday evening in the first hours of the 15th of Nisan. Rightly interpreted, John's Gospel does not speak to the contrary. What follows will examine the texts in John that purportedly speak to the contrary; these texts will be considered in reverse order for reasons that will hopefully become apparent as we proceed, beginning with the suggestion that Pilate ordered the execution of Jesus on "the day of Preparation *of* the Passover" (John 19:14).

THE DAY OF PREPARATION THAT WAS THE PASSOVER (JOHN 19:14)

Many have regularly insisted, often with very little argument, that "the day of Preparation *of* the Passover (παρασκευὴ τοῦ πάσχα)" in John 19:14[28] must refer to a day of Preparation *for* the Passover. Yet, to date, no one has offered evidence of a single instance elsewhere, in which the word παρασκευή refers to a day before the Passover or any other festival day.[29] The proposed sense of John's phrase is nowhere attested.[30] The attempt of some to show that any of the festival days of the Jews had also a παρασκευή "has failed completely."[31] Instead, with every other use of the noun in the New Testament, including its two other uses in John, "the term unambiguously means the day before the Sabbath (Matt 27:62; Mark 15:42; Luke 23:54; John 19:31, 42)."[32] Thus, "day of Preparation" refers to the sixth

---

Eerdmans, 1997), 455, who suggests that John "characteristically omitted what he could assume was generally known among his readers." He adds, "While the fourth evangelist surely meant to lead his readers further and deeper into the significance of Jesus and his story . . . he need not have intended them henceforth to leave [any of the other Gospels] aside and to read only his own Gospel. He did not aim to replace . . . but to write a different kind of Gospel: one which, by selecting far fewer traditions, left space for the reflective interpretation that is the distinctive characteristic of the Fourth Gospel" (169–70).

27. Charles E. Hill, *The Johannine Corpus in the Early Church* (Oxford: Oxford University Press, 2004), 475.

28. Cf. ἡμέρα ἦν παρασκευῆς in Luke 23:54.

29. Carson, *John*, 603–604.

30. "Use of it for the day before the Passover," observes Ridderbos, *John*, 456, "is not known." See Leon Morris, *The Gospel according to John*, NICNT (Grand Rapids, MI: Eerdmans, 1995), 686–687, including n. 104; Craig L. Blomberg, *The Historical Reliability of John's Gospel: Issues and Commentary* (Downers Grove, IL: InterVarsity, 2001), 246–247; and Andreas J. Köstenberger, *John*, Baker Exegetical Commentary on the New Testament (Grand Rapids, MI: Baker Academic, 2004), 537–538.

31. R. C. H. Lenski, *The Interpretation of St. John's Gospel* (Minneapolis, MN: Augsburg, 1943), 1272.

32. Craig L. Blomberg, *Historical Reliability*, 247. Thus, it is "a technical term for the day preceding the *sabbath*," observes Ridderbos, "also called 'the day before the sabbath' [προσάββατον] (Mk. 15:42)" (*John*, 456). Cf. "and the Sabbath was drawing near" in Luke 23:54. Thus, the women mark the place and manner of Jesus' burial, make preparations to complete the work, but first observe the Sabbath before returning to the tomb to do so (Luke 23:55–56).

day of every week that began at sundown Thursday night and ended at sundown Friday night. Every week on this day, the Jews prepared for their observance of the Sabbath, which began at sundown Friday night and ended at sundown Saturday night.[33] There was no day of Preparation for the Passover. There was only the day of Preparation for the Sabbath.

Others have therefore argued that the term "Passover" in John 19:14 refers not to that day's meal, nor to the day itself, but to the seven-day-long Feast of Unleavened Bread that began with the day of Passover and so was regarded by some as "Passover week." Thus, τοῦ πάσχα means "of the Passover feast" or "of Passover week."[34] But how likely is this in the Gospel of John? Nowhere in any of his works does John evince an interest in the days of Unleavened Bread following the Passover. Instead, John consistently exhibits a keen interest in the days leading up to the Passover and to the day of the Passover itself. The proposed solution fails for want of evidence in its support from the Gospel. For John, "Passover" is a day, and a meal, not a week.[35]

Less plausible still are the proposals of those who hold that on Thursday evening Jesus and his disciples celebrated a private, pre-paschal, paschal meal, "in order to anticipate the regular paschal meal to be eaten the next night (which he knew that he could not eat because he would be dead),"[36] or of others who believe that in John Jesus and his disciples follow a calendar different from the Synoptics.[37] That the Synoptics and John describe two Passovers one day apart seems a particularly desperate attempt at a needlessly "unsubstantiated guess"[38] and "pure conjecture."[39] Nowhere do the Gospels suggest that Jesus and his disciples celebrated a private pre-paschal meal. Nor do they offer even the slightest suggestion of a calendrical dispute involving Jesus and his disciples.[40] Rather, the

---

33. BDAG, s.v. παρασκευή, concurs. According to Israelite usage, the day of Preparation "was Friday, on which day everything had to be prepared for the Sabbath, when no work was permitted." For later Christians as well, the term "served to designate the sixth day of the week." It continues to do so in Modern Greek.

34. See the translation of John 19:14 in the NIV. See also Carson, *John*, 603–604; Morris, *John*, 686; Blomberg, *Historical Reliability*, 246–247; and Köstenberger, *John*, 537–538.

35. See especially "six days before the Passover" in John 12:1, "before the feast of the Passover" in John 13:1, "eat the Passover" in John 18:28, and "at the Passover" in John 18:39.

36. Brown, *Death of the Messiah*, 2:1365.

37. See the perspectives of those who have pursued this and other possibilities in Brown, *Death of the Messiah*, 2:1361–1369.

38. Brown, *Death of the Messiah*, 2:1363.

39. Roger T. Beckwith, *Calendar and Chronology, Jewish and Christian: Biblical, Intertestamental, and Patristic Studies* (Leiden, Netherlands: Brill Academic, 2001), 290.

40. Instead, the Gospels uniformly indicate that the Thursday afternoon when Jesus and his disciples prepared for their evening celebration of the Passover was the first day of Unleavened Bread (that is, the 14th of Nisan), when the Passover lambs were all taken to the temple for sacrifice. See "when they sacrificed the Passover lamb" in Mark 14:12; "on which the Passover lamb had to be sacrificed" in Luke 22:7. See also Matt 26:17. With the setting of the sun that night, not some but all ate the Passover.

Gospel descriptions of the constituencies participating in the plot against Jesus consistently presuppose "the same understanding of the feast."[41] The logistical challenges of responding to competing calendars in the same place at the same time when all were together would have been impossible to negotiate.[42] Such differences would have effected, not only each year's observance of the Passover, but also that of every other festival of the Jews, not to mention the weekly observance of the Sabbath. Such a thing may have been possible at Qumran, but not in Jerusalem.[43] The problem with each of these proposed solutions is that there is no evidence to support them: "The solutions have been invented to reconcile [perceived] Gospel discrepancies and cannot call on established Jewish practice for support."[44]

A much simpler and entirely defensible solution is available for explaining John 19:14. The statement, "it was the day of Preparation *of* the Passover," does not mean that the trial before Pilate took place on the day of Preparation *for* the Passover; rather, it means that the trial took place on the day of Preparation (for the Sabbath) *that was* the Passover. The genitive τοῦ πάσχα is another instance of John's fondness for elements in simple apposition[45] and for the genitive of apposition.[46] Therefore, John refers "to the 'preparation' before the Sabbath *at* Passover and not to the day preceding Passover—especially since [John] 19:31 calls the Sabbath following this day of preparation a 'great day,' in accord with the rabbinical custom of calling a Sabbath falling on Nisan 16 'the

---

41. Brown, *Death of the Messiah*, 2:1364.

42. Brown, *Death of the Messiah*, 2:1363. Under what circumstances would authorities in Jerusalem have felt any obligation at all to respond to the external suggestion of an alternate calendar?

43. "What evidence is there," queries Brown, *Death of the Messiah*, 2:1368, "that Jesus at any other time in his life followed anything other than the official calendar? Calendric adherence was a matter of deep religious identity; no accusation against Jesus by his enemies accuses him of Essene sympathies or of calendric irregularities. What would prompt Jesus and his disciples to depart so seriously from the official calendar in this instance? Where did they get the Lamb for Passover?" Thus, "the solution has less plausible basis than most other harmonizations and only creates new difficulties."

44. Brown, *Death of the Messiah*, 2:1364.

45. Daniel B. Wallace, *Greek Grammar beyond the Basics: An Exegetical Syntax of the New Testament* (Grand Rapids, MI: Zondervan, 1996), 48–49, 94, 152–153, 198–199.

46. See Wallace, *Greek Grammar*, 95–100, who labels this usage also the "epexegetical genitive" or the "genitive of definition." The use, observes Wallace, "is fairly common" (95). With it, "the substantive in the genitive case refers to the same thing as the substantive to which it is related. The equation, however, is not exact. The genitive of apposition typically states a specific example that is a part of the larger category named by the head noun" (95). With such a construction, "the head noun: (1) will state a large category, (2) will be ambiguous, or (3) will be metaphorical in its meaning, while the genitive names a concrete or specific example that either falls *within* that category, clarifies its ambiguity, or brings the metaphor down to earth" (95). Examples given are "land of Egypt" (category-example), "the sign of circumcision" (ambiguity clarification), and "the breastplate of righteousness" (metaphor-meaning). Johannine instances of the genitive of apposition include John 2:16 ("house of a marketplace"), 2:21 ("temple of his body"), 11:13 ("rest of sleep"), and 13:1 ("feast of the Passover"). Cf. the genitive in simple apposition in John 7:42 ("Bethlehem, the village").

great Sabbath' since on that day the first fruits were presented"[47] (see Lev 23:11). On the day of "Israel's historical deliverance"[48] (see Exod 12:51), Pilate attempts to release Jesus, something that he customarily did "at the Passover" (John 18:39). While some have argued that the rabbis forbade trials for capital offenses on feast days, or in the course of only a single day, "there is no real evidence that these later Jewish laws were in effect at this time."[49] Jesus was tried, sentenced, and crucified on the day of Preparation for the Sabbath that was simultaneously also the day of the Passover.

Something should finally be said regarding the observation, given also in John 19:14, that when the trial before Pilate came to an end, "it was about the sixth hour" (ὥρα ἦν ὡς ἕκτη). John's comment has for good reason attracted a significant amount of attention. After all, according to Matthew, Mark, and Luke, Jesus was no longer before Pilate at the sixth hour but was instead on the cross. Is the reading "sixth" the unfortunate result of a scribal mistake?[50] Does John offer nothing more than an approximate reference to the time of day?[51] Or must one take John to be right and the Synoptics wrong, the Synoptics right and John to be wrong, or no one evidently right or wrong? None of the previous options provides a satisfactory explanation. Again, John writes not to correct or to otherwise oppose. He writes instead to extend and to deepen.

Jesus is still before Pilate in John 19:14. Pilate has yet to sign Jesus' execution order. Jesus has yet to even begin to make his way to the place of the crucifixion. It will be hours before he is crucified. From Mark it is widely known in the last days of the first century that "it was the third hour (approx. 9:00 AM) when they crucified him" (Mark 15:25). From Matthew, Mark, and Luke, it is widely known that "when the sixth hour (approx. 12:00 noon) had come, there was darkness over the whole land until the ninth hour (approx. 3:00 PM)" (Mark 15:33; see also Matt 27:45;

---

47. Ridderbos, *John*, 456. See also page 606.
48. Rudolph Bultmann, *The Gospel of John: A Commentary*, trans. George R. Beasley-Murray (Philadelphia, PA: Westminster, 1971), 676.
49. Brown, *Death of the Messiah*, 2:1368.
50. See the substitution of "third" for "sixth" in ℵ2 Ds L Δ ψ *l* 844 *pc*. The former, observes Bruce M. Metzger, *Textual Commentary on the Greek New Testament*, 2nd ed. (Stuttgart: Deutsche Bibelgesellschaft, 1994), 216, is "an obvious attempt to harmonize the chronology with that of Mk 15.25 (see the comment there on the converse corruption). Although one may conjecture that the disagreement originally arose (as Ammonius, followed by Eusebius and Jerome, suggested) when copyists confused the Greek numerals . . . the manuscript evidence is overwhelmingly in support of ἕκτη."
51. Carson, *John*, 605, suggests that "more than likely we are in danger of insisting on a degree of precision in both Mark and John which, in the days before watches, could not have been achieved. The reckoning of time for most people, who could not very well carry sundials and astronomical charts, was necessarily approximate. If the sun was moving toward mid-heaven, two different observers might well have glanced up and decided, respectively, that it was 'the third hour,' or 'about the sixth hour.'" In the same vein, see Morris, *John*, 708; Blomberg, *Historical Reliability*, 247; and Köstenberger, *John*, 538.

Luke 23:44), and that "at the ninth hour Jesus cried out with a loud voice" (Mark 15:34; see also Matt 27:46; Luke 23:46) and "breathed his last" (Mark 15:37; see also Matt 27:50; Luke 23:46). Therefore, it makes no sense at all to take John to be referring to a noontime hour.[52] Neither can it be said reasonably that John refers to some rough approximation of a mid-morning time. Instead, "it is possible, indeed likely, in view of the provenance and primary audience of this Gospel that a Roman form of reckoning is being used, in which case the sixth hour is near dawn, at six in the morning."[53] The Romans were known for conducting their legal proceedings in the first hours of the morning. John depicts Pilate as following just such a practice. "This in turn means that Jesus' pretrial hearing and trial before the Sanhedrin likely took place at night and into the early hours of the morning, as the Synoptics suggest."[54]

While it is regularly said that no clear evidence exists for John's use of a Roman scheme (our contemporary scheme) for numbering the hours of the day, there is also no clear evidence that the scheme could not have been used with good effect by John. The scheme existed in the region and was known in John's day.[55] Under what circumstances it was used, and how widely familiar it was, is not entirely known. What may well prove significant in John's case is that the Roman form of time-keeping, which John prefers, was regularly utilized in official proceedings and for legal reasons.[56] John's interest in constructing his Gospel as a story of "Jesus on trial"[57] may well have commended to him the time-keeping scheme that he favors, since just such a scheme was preferred in Roman legal matters. Thus, in John 19:14, John gives the hour of the day that concludes his Gospel's extended and distinguishing narrative of Jesus' trial before Annas (John 18:13–23), before Caiaphas (John 18:24–28), and finally before

---

52. See the translation of John 19:14 in NAB, NET, and NRSV.

53. Ben Witherington, III, *John's Wisdom: A Commentary on the Fourth Gospel* (Louisville, KY: Westminster John Knox, 1995), 294. See also B. F. Westcott, *The Gospel according to St. John: The Authorized Version with Introduction and Notes* (repr., Grand Rapids, MI: Eerdmans, 1981), 282, and the sources that he cites.

54. Witherington, *John's Wisdom*, 294.

55. On the one hand, one must admit, observes Westcott, *John*, 282, "that this mode of reckoning hours was unusual in ancient times. The Romans . . . and Greeks, no less than the Jews, reckoned their *hours* from sunrise. But the Romans reckoned their civil *days* from midnight . . . and not from sunrise, or from sunset (as the Jews)." See Pliny, *Nat.* 5.188, who mentions that the hours of the day were also measured from midnight to midnight by the Egyptians and Hipparchus. "There are also traces of reckoning the hours from midnight in Asia Minor," adds Westcott. "Polycarp is said . . . to have been martyred at Smyrna 'at the eighth hour.' This, from the circumstances, must have been 8 AM Pionius again is said to have been martyred (at Smyrna also) at 'the tenth hour,' which can hardly have been 4 PM, since such exhibitions usually took place before noon. These two passages furnish a sufficient presumption that St. John, in using what is the modern reckoning, followed a practice of the province in which he was living and for which he was writing."

56. See Witherington, *John's Wisdom*, 400–401n39.

57. See Andrew T. Lincoln, *Truth on Trial: The Lawsuit Motif in the Fourth Gospel* (Peabody, MA: Hendrickson, 2000).

Pilate (John 18:28—19:16). When the Roman governor formally orders the execution of Jesus (John 19:13–16),[58] John records the hour in conventionally Roman terms.[59]

The proposed solution is in fact the only one that makes reasonable sense. Jesus is consigned to death and sent out to die with the rising of the sun at six o'clock in the morning. As a new day dawns—the same time that Israel of old, preserved from the threat of death by the blood of the lamb, went out—Jesus, the Lamb of God (see John 1:29, 35–36) and the light of the world (see John 8:12), goes out to be extinguished (see John 9:4)[60] and to make all things new (Rev 21:5); indeed, the dawn that signals his crucifixion points to another dawn when he will manifest himself as the resurrection and the life (see John 11:25).[61] With the "great Sabbath" (John 19:31) that followed his fruitful labor (John 4:34), that is, with his rest (John 19:30; cf. Gen 2:2), comes our rest, the cessation of every labor that burdens a broken people. Together with the day of Preparation for his Sabbath, which was the great and final Passover, comes the great and final restoration of all things and the return of God's rest.[62] How tragic it was on the very day when it came to fruition that those who were "his own" (John 1:11) remained blind to the significance of that day and what it truly meant to "eat the Passover."

SO THEY MIGHT EAT THE PASSOVER (JOHN 18:28)

A second text in John that purportedly pits the Johannine chronology of the passion against the one that we find in the Synoptics is John 18:28.

---

58. "The judge sits on the βῆμα" (see John 19:13), observes Bultmann, *John*, 664n2, "only at the conclusion of the trial."

59. Since the entire Gospel can be reasonably construed as a kind of trial narrative, the case that Westcott, *John*, 282, makes for a Roman understanding of the Gospel's three other earlier references to an hour of the day (see John 1:39; 4:6, 52) should be taken seriously. See also Jack Finegan, *Handbook of Biblical Chronology: Principles of Time Reckoning in the Ancient World and Problems of Chronology in the Bible*, rev. ed. (Peabody, MA: Hendrickson, 1998), 10–11.

60. Bultmann, *John*, 664–665.

61. Note that from the sixth hour at sunset to the sixth hour at sunrise each day what is regularly marked both in John 13–20 and in John 12 (see further below) is the passage of time from the twelve hours of the night to the twelve hours of the day (John 11:9–10). Only with the passing of the night (John 9:4; cf. v. 5) is there the coming of a new day (see John 16:5–6; cf. vv. 16, 20–22). Cf. the description of the first Passover in Exod 12:42 as "a night of watching by the Lord, to bring them out of the land of Egypt."

62. William C. Weinrich, "The Same Yesterday, Today, and Forever: Jesus as Timekeeper," *CTQ* 78 (2014): 3–15. "The true Sabbath rest," observes Weinrich, "foretold in that Sabbath rest of God on the seventh day, is the rest of God whereby he initiates a new day" (4). Weinrich aptly cites Gregory of Nyssa, who writes: "You wonder at the sublime Moses, who by the power of knowledge apprehended the whole of God's creation? See, you have the Sabbath of the first origin of the world being blessed; learn through that Sabbath that this Sabbath is the day of rest which God has blessed above all other days. For on this day the only-begotten God truly rested from all his works, having kept the Sabbath in the flesh through the dispensation befitting death, and returning to what he was by his resurrection he raised again together with himself all that lay prostrate, becoming life and sunrise and dawn and day for those in darkness and death's shadow" (4).

Here, John suggests that when the Jews led Jesus to Pilate in the early morning to be tried by him, they refrained from entering the governor's headquarters, so that (ἵνα) they would not defile themselves and instead might still be able to "eat the Passover" (φάγωσιν τὸ πάσχα). Once again, John's comment suggests to some that the Passover has not yet happened and will not happen until Friday night.[63] To others, "Passover" refers here not to the meal that all would have eaten on the 15th of Nisan, but refers instead to the week-long Feast of Unleavened Bread that began on the 15th and so was regarded by some as "Passover week." "Eat the Passover" refers, then, to what remained of the Feast of Unleavened Bread, which would have continued for another six days.[64] But, again, nowhere does John exhibit an interest in this feast that would have ended on the 21st of Nisan.[65] The problem with the latter possibility "is the fact that there does not appear to be an example of this expression from antiquity that does not mean 'eat the Passover supper.'"[66]

Once more, there is a simpler, defensible solution. While the eating of the Passover customarily began each year with the setting of the sun and with the first hours of the evening of the 15th of Nisan, every Jewish household was also entirely aware that it had until the rising of the sun the next morning for the meal to end.[67] The Jews present for the trial of Jesus by Pilate are depicted by John as having occupied themselves *throughout the night* with the demanding business of Jesus' trial. In their zeal to finally see Jesus' end, in their bid to "feast" first upon him (see John 2:17),[68] they themselves have thus far refrained from eating; standing before Pilate, they still hope to return to their households before the rising of the sun "so they might eat the Passover."[69] If "early morning" refers to a time during the last of the night's four watches (from 3 AM to 6 AM), then they still

---

63. Because a single day's defilement never would have prevented any of the Jews from eating the Passover on Friday night, since the day's defilement would have ended at sundown, it is argued that the defilement was somehow a longer one. We shall see, however, that such distinctions are irrelevant to John's interest.

64. See Carson, *John*, 589–590; Blomberg, *Historical Reliability*, 238–239; and Köstenberger, *John*, 524. "The interpretation here defended," observes Carson, "is not that 'the Passover' refers to the Feast of Unleavened Bread *apart from* Passover [see Morris, *John*, 688–690], but to the *entire Passover festival*. The Jews wanted to continue to participate in the entire feast; they wanted to eat the Passover" (page 590).

65. His focus is instead, we shall see, the six-day-long weeks in Gen 1–2, in John 1–2, and in John 12–19. See further below.

66. Morris, *John*, 688.

67. See Exod 12:10; 34:25; Deut 16:4. See also Exod 23:18; 29:34; Lev 7:15.

68. Steven M. Bryan, "Consumed by Zeal: John's Use of Psalm 69:9 and the Action in the Temple," *BBR* 21 (2011): 479–494, argues rightly that the zeal that consumes Jesus in John 2:17 is the zeal of his enemies. See also Benjamin J. Lappenga, "Whose Zeal Is It Anyway? The Citation of Psalm 69:9 in John 2:17 as a Double Entendre" in *Abiding Words: The Use of Scripture in the Gospel of John*, ed. Alicia D. Myers and Bruce G. Schuchard, RBS 81 (Atlanta, GA: SBL Press, 2015), 141–159; and Bruce G. Schuchard, "Form versus Function: Citation Technique and Authorial Intention in the Gospel of John," in *Abiding Words*, 30n33.

69. Andrew E. Steinmann, *From Abraham to Paul: A Biblical Chronology* (St. Louis, MO: Concordia, 2011), 278–279.

have time.[70] At least they think so. Their first priority, however, will take longer than they are hoping; they will lose the opportunity to eat when Jesus' trial comes to an end at the same time that the night and its meal would have come to an end: at the sixth hour.

The chronology is "extremely tight"[71] *if* one assumes that *both* the Jewish and the Roman legal proceedings happened in the early morning. But if only the Roman legal proceeding took place at this time, then the narrative's timing and the rest of its detail are both eminently sensible and full of suggestion. On the one hand, the sentencing of Jesus comes at a natural time with the end of the night and the rising of the sun. At the same time, the Jews are consistently depicted in potent terms as tragically mistaken at every turn.[72] With the end of the night comes the end of their opportunity, of their need, to eat. One feast is consumed at the expense of the other. Ironically, their misguided zeal to feast first upon Jesus causes them to miss more than the Passover meal. More importantly, they miss the abiding significance of the feast of the Lamb (see John 1:29, 36) that is soon to be given in the daylight hours of the day of Preparation that was the great and final Passover.[73]

---

70. Carson, *John*, 588, notes that the Romans gave to the night's last two watches (from roughly midnight to 3:00 AM and from 3:00 AM to 6:00 AM) the names *alectorophōnia* ("cockcrow") and *prōi* ("early morning"). If πρωΐ is used by John in a technical sense, then Jesus is taken to Pilate sometime before 6:00 AM See further Craig S. Keener, *The Gospel of John*, 2 vols. (Peabody, MA: Hendrickson, 2003), 2:1098–1099. According to Alfred Plummer, *The Gospel according to St. John* (repr., Cambridge: Cambridge University Press, 1906), 328–329, "there is nothing improbable" in Pilate being ready to open his court to the Jews between 4:00 AM and 5:00 AM "In itself," adds Carson, "this is unsurprising: as we have noted many Roman officials began the day very early in the morning and finished their day's labours by 10:00 or 11:00 AM." But then Carson goes on to argue that πρωΐ in John is non-technical in meaning and that the time is later, allowing the Sanhedrin to also meet in the early morning and not at night, which was forbidden, "since Jewish law forbade trying capital cases at night." But this is precisely John's point. The Jews carry out their own interrogation of Jesus under the cloak of darkness throughout the night to avoid the scrutiny of the people. In their zeal to feast upon Jesus, they go against their own cherished traditions to avoid an uprising at the feast (see Mark 14:2; see also Matt 26:1–5; Luke 22:1–2). All Israel is keenly occupied throughout the night with a ritual that keeps their focus on house and home, not on matters happening that night with Jesus. Few are out and about. See "none of you shall go out of the door of his house until the morning" in Exod 12:22. By the time the Jews are up and about the next morning in anticipation of the sacred assembly that would have been next, the dirty deed is already in motion. Jesus has already been tried and convicted and is on his way to the place of the crucifixion.

71. Carson, *John*, 605.

72. "They who had seized the innocent and taken up arms do not enter into the hall of judgment 'lest they should be polluted,'" declares Chrysostom, *Hom. Jo.* 83.3. "Those who paid tithes of mint and anise did not think they were polluted when bent on killing unjustly." "They are about to sacrifice the Passover lamb in accordance with the law, even though the law has no force among them," adds Cyril, *Comm. Jo.* 12 (Maxwell 2:326). "They sentence to death him who knew no sin, bringing down such horrifying ungodliness on their own heads, but they avoid the threshold of the governor's headquarters as though it would cause them to be defiled." Sadly, "they thought that the most shameful of all crimes, unholy murder, harmed them not at all" (327).

73. See especially Jesus' statement "and the bread that I shall give for the life of the world is my flesh" in John 6:51. See further John 6:25–58. Thus, they miss the feast in favor of a feast that becomes a feast of which they know nothing, the feast that knows no end.

BEFORE THE FEAST OF THE PASSOVER (JOHN 13:1)

A third text in John that purportedly pits the Johannine chronology of the passion against the one we find in the Synoptics is John 13:1. For some, the prepositional phrase, "before the feast of the Passover (πρὸ τῆς ἑορτῆς τοῦ πάσχα)," which introduces John 13:1, indicates once more that the meal Jesus and his disciples shared when he washed his disciples' feet (see John 13:2–38) was not a Passover meal. Instead, they contend it occurred the night *before* the Passover.[74] For others, "before the feast of the Passover" simply refers to a time "just before" (that is, moments before) Jesus and his disciples proceeded to eat the Passover.[75] Neither of the two possibilities is satisfactory. First, they fail to adequately explain the use of this prepositional phrase. Second, they do not consider the significance for John of the time when Jesus first "knew that his hour had come to depart this world to the Father" (John 13:1).

Sadly, few interpreters exhibit an awareness of what is grammatically possible. Few ask whether the prepositional phrase, "before the feast of Passover," should be understood to modify the verb of the sentence's main clause (εἰς τέλος ἠγάπησεν αὐτούς) or to modify the Greek participle (εἰδώς) that immediately follows the prepositional phrase. The latter is in fact the more likely possibility;[76] Jesus is first said in John to have known that his hour had come not in John 13, but earlier in John 12 (see Jesus' pronouncement "the hour has come for the Son of Man to be glorified" in John 12:23; see also v. 27).[77] Thus, John 13:1 first recalls that Jesus knew that his hour had come "before the feast of Passover" at the beginning of

---

74. Carson, *John*, 475, notes that many also take Jesus' final word to Judas (see "What you are going to do, do quickly" in John 13:27) and the reaction of Jesus' disciples to it (see "Some thought that, because Judas had the moneybag, Jesus was telling him, 'Buy what we need for the feast,' or that he should give something to the poor" in John 13:28–29) "as evidence that this meal took place twenty-four hours before the Passover." One might, however, rightly wonder, observes Carson, "why Jesus should send Judas out for purchases for a feast still twenty-four hours away. The next day would have left ample time. . . . Moreover, it was customary to give alms to the poor on Passover night, the temple gates being left open from midnight on, allowing beggars to congregate there. . . . On any night other than Passover it is hard to imagine why the disciples might have thought Jesus was sending Judas out *to give something to the poor.*"

75. That John's opening phrase thus places the foot washing "just before" the Passover meal that has yet to begin is suggested by Carson, *John*, 460–461; and Köstenberger, *John*, 401–402.

76. The option is considered by Bultmann, *John*, 463; acknowledged as possible by Morris, *John*, 688; and supported both by Lenski, *John*, 902–903; and by Ridderbos, *John*, 452n3. Cf. Cyril, *Comm. Jo.* 9 (Maxwell 2:117), who appears to break John's single sentence into two sentences: "Before the festival of the Passover, Jesus knew that his hour had come to depart from this world and go the Father. Having loved his own who were in the world, he loved them to the end." Thus, "ἠγάπησεν does not coincide temporally with πρὸ τῆς ἑορτῆς," observes Ridderbos, "but speaks rather of progression in Jesus' display of love, based on the starting point indicated in εἰδώς."

77. See further John 12:31–33, where Jesus declares: "Now is the judgment of this world; now will the ruler of this world be cast out. And I, when I am lifted up from the earth, will draw all people to myself. He said this to show by what kind of death he was going to die." Thus, the hour of Jesus is the appointed time of his suffering and death on the cross. See John 16:32; 17:1.

Holy Week. Then, John transitions to his ultimate interest in the accomplishment of that hour and the completion of its τέλος at the end of the week on the day of Preparation that was the great and final Passover.[78]

I have argued elsewhere that in the second half of the Gospel (John 11–20) John purposefully designs the "Book of Jesus' Hour" so that it

> (1) begins in John 11 and ends in John 20 with a dead man rising and with a troubled Thomas and . . . (2) features in John 12 and in John 13–19 the first and last days of a final six-day-long week of days that begins in John 12 and ends in John 13–19 with an evening meal (see only in 12:2 and 13:2), with foot service (see 12:3 and 13:4–17; cf. 1:27), with an anointing of Jesus for burial (see esp. the framing references to an anointing of Jesus only in 12:3, 7, and 19:38–42), with Judas the betrayer (see 12:4–6 and 13:2, 21–30; 18:1–5), and with the arrival and the consummation of Jesus's "hour" (see 12:23, 27 and 17:1), a week-long "hour," which is the week of the Gospel's third and final Passover.[79]

Therefore, the Gospel's concluding week is not a seven-day week but is instead a six-day week; to this idea, we now turn our attention.

SIX DAYS BEFORE THE PASSOVER (JOHN 12:1)

A final text that supposedly distinguishes the Johannine chronology of Holy Week from the one we find in the Synoptics is John 12:1. Here, John states that "six days before the Passover (πρὸ ἓξ ἡμερῶν τοῦ πάσχα),[80] Jesus came to Bethany, where Lazarus was, whom Jesus had raised from the dead,"[81] and "they made a dinner for him there" (John 12:2; see further verses 2–8). Typically little is made of the time reference in John 12:1.[82]

---

78. "Because he loved his own who were in the world," he therefore loved them like no other to the summing and completing end of the eschatological purposes of the Father in his suffering and death on the cross. That John 13:1 "forms a clear transition to a new section of the Gospel" is affirmed by Ridderbos, *John*, 451. For Ridderbos, "Chs. 11 and 12 increasing[ly] lead into the Passion narrative, especially from 12:23 on." The meal then that begins in John 13:2 "is the opening act of the story of Jesus' death." "A grander opening of the story of Jesus' death," concludes Ridderbos, "is hardly imaginable" (452). See further Chrysostom, *Hom. Jo.* 70.1, who likewise affirms that "to the end" in John 13:1 "means that he left nothing undone that one who greatly loved should do."

79. Schuchard, "Form versus Function," 36–38. See further Schuchard, especially notes 64–66 on pages 37–38 and the illustrations on pages 44–45.

80. While it is grammatically possible for πρὸ ἓξ ἡμερῶν τοῦ πάσχα to be translated "before the six days of the Passover," the more likely meaning of John's slightly "peculiar" and possibly "Hellenistic" expression is attested elsewhere. See BDF § 213.

81. The Gospel's first reference to its third and final Passover appears not in John 12:1, but in John 11:55, where John states: "The Passover of the Jews was near, and many went up to Jerusalem from the country before the Passover in order that they might purify themselves." Their "preparation for the Passover" took place, then, not on the day that was just before the Passover, but in the days that preceded the six-day week of John 12–19.

82. See, however, Köstenberger, *John*, 357, who notes that John's "anointing scene casts a long shadow forward over Jesus' imminent arrest, trial, condemnation, crucifixion, and burial."

If we count the days in an exclusive manner (that is, if Passover is day seven),[83] then six days before the 15th of Nisan would be the 9th of Nisan. If the 15th of Nisan began at sundown Thursday night and ended at sundown Friday night, then six days before the Passover would be the previous week's Sabbath day that began at sundown Friday night and ended at sundown Saturday night.[84] Therefore, sometime during the previous Sabbath day Jesus came to Bethany.[85] Where Jesus was just before he came to Bethany is not specified;[86] nor does John tell us when it was exactly on the 9th of Nisan that Jesus arrived at Bethany.[87]

What seems clear is that the meal they made for him was an evening meal.[88] It happened "on the Saturday evening that preceded Jesus' suffering and death on the cross and followed the Sabbath that would have begun at sundown Friday night and ended at sundown Saturday evening."[89] However, if this is the case, then the dinner happened not on the 9th of Nisan, but on the 10th of Nisan in the first evening hours of the day that began at sundown Saturday night and ended at sundown Sunday. On the 10th of Nisan—the first day of Holy Week,[90] the day that included the events and circumstances of Palm Sunday,[91] the day that began the six day

---

83. Expressing an openness to the possibility that John includes the day of the Passover in the six days and so counts inclusively are Bultmann, *John*, 414n5; Barnabas Lindars, *The Gospel of John*, New Century Bible Commentary (Grand Rapids, MI: Eerdmans, 1972), 415; and Ridderbos, *John*, 412n99. See, however, the seemingly evident exclusive sense of "two years before the earthquake" in Amos 1:1 (LXX).

84. See Carson, *John*, 427; Morris, *John*, 510; and Köstenberger, *John*, 359.

85. The rabbis allowed for modest travel on the Sabbath. Therefore, the Jews accost the man healed by Jesus in John 5 not because he proceeds to depart, but because it is not lawful for him to take with him his bed (see John 5:10). See also the concern of the Jews in John 9:14–16, which has nothing to do with Jesus "passing by" (see John 9:1).

86. See, however, the reference to Ephraim in John 11:54.

87. "He may have arrived just as the Sabbath was beginning, *that is*, on the Friday evening," suggests J. H. Bernard, *A Critical and Exegetical Commentary on the Gospel of John*, 2 vols., International Critical Commentary (Edinburgh: T&T Clark, 1928), 2:415, "or He may have only come from a short distance, and so have refrained from exceeding the limit of a Sabbath day's journey."

88. The term δεῖπνον "can refer to a meal at any time of the day," observes Carson, *John*, 427. In John, however, the referent of its two uses (12:2; 13:2) is consistent and here "is probably connected with the ritual that separated the Sabbath from the rest of the week, including the *Habdalah*, the synagogue service that followed the meal" (see *m. Ber.* 8:5).

89. Schuchard, "Form versus Function," 37n63. See further those cited by Köstenberger, *John*, 360n9.

90. Cf. "the first day of the week" in John 20:1, 19, and "after eight days," meaning "a week later" on another first day of the week, in John 20:26 (see the reading of sys), for a total of three consecutive and concluding first days of the week.

91. "On the next day" (τῇ ἐπαύριον) in John 12:12 refers not to a next calendar day (see 1:29, 35, 43, followed by "on the third day" in 2:1, for a total of six initial days), but to the next morning, as in John 6:22. Therefore, all of John 12 describes the events and circumstances of a single, 24-hour, calendar day, which was the 10th of Nisan and the first of six days, the first day of the week. All of John 13–19 describes the events and circumstances of another single, 24-hour, calendar day, which was the 15th of Nisan and the last of six days, the day of Preparation that was the Passover. Thus, John devotes fully a third of his Gospel's narrative (see John 13–19) to his extended and detailed description of the day of Preparation that was the Passover.

ritual of Passover—they made a meal for him in Bethany.[92] On that day, they set him apart for sacrifice as the great and final Lamb (see John 1:29, 36) of the great and final Passover[93] when they unwittingly anointed him for the day that he was to be buried (see John 12:3, 7 and 20:38–42). Indeed, the day of his burial likewise began with an evening meal (see John 13:2) on the day of Preparation that was the Passover. Thus, the events and circumstances of the beginning of the week on the 10th of Nisan anticipated the week's end on the 15th of Nisan, which was the day of Preparation that was the Passover; the week's end eschatologically completed the paschal foretaste that was the week's anticipatory beginning.[94]

CONCLUDING OBSERVATIONS

The last of the eyewitnesses wrote not to subvert established tradition. Rather, he wrote for the purpose of extending Israel's Scriptures through

---

92. Armand J. Gagne, Jr, "An Examination and Possible Explanation of John's Dating of the Crucifixion," in *The Death of Jesus in the Fourth Gospel*, ed. Gilbert Van Belle, BETL 200 (Leuven, Netherlands: Leuven University Press, 2007), 417.

93. See again the selection of the lamb in Exod 12:3. Thus, Jesus "willed to come five days before the Passover," observes Bede, *Hom.* 2.3 (cf. the reading "five" in 𝔓[66*] so that Jesus' arrival at Bethany and the dinner that they made for him there both happen Saturday night). He did so, "that by this again he might show that he was the stainless lamb who would take away the sins of the world. It was commanded that the paschal lamb, by whose immolation the people of Israel were free from slavery in Egypt, should be selected five days before the Passover, that is, on the tenth day of the month, and immolated on the fourteenth day of the month." See also Cyril, *Comm. Jo.* 7 (Maxwell 2:98), who reads "six" rather than "five," but otherwise finds in John a similar interest: "The Evangelist demonstrates through his narration that Christ does not despise the law. This may be seen in the fact that 'six days before the Passover,' when it was necessary to purchase the lamb and keep it until the fourteenth day, he ate with Lazarus and his friends. Perhaps this was because it was the practice of the Jews, not from the law but from custom, to celebrate a little on the day before [here, meaning the night before and the same calendar day?] the sheep was obtained so that after the sheep was obtained, they might devote themselves to fasting (or at least to limiting their food) and purification until the time of the festival."

94. Nothing is said of the week's intervening days. John's focus is entirely on day one and day six, the beginning and end of the Gospel's concluding and completing week. Cf. the six-day-long week of days with which the Gospel begins in 1:19–2:11 (noted also by Andreas J. Köstenberger, *A Theology of John's Gospel and Letters: The Word, the Christ, the Son of God*, BTNT [Grand Rapids, MI: Zondervan, 2009], 169), which itself ends with the "beginning" (see John 2:11) of Jesus' seven anticipatory signs. See Bruce G. Schuchard, "The Wedding Feast at Cana and the Christological Monomania of St. John," in *All Theology Is Christology: Essays in Honor of David P. Scaer*, ed. Dean O. Wenthe et al., (Fort Wayne, IN: Concordia Theological Seminary Press, 2000), 101–116. See also the sign of Moses in John 3:14. "St. John appears to mark the period as the new *Hexaemeron*," observes Westcott, *John*, 176, "a solemn period of 'six days,' the time of the new Creation. His Gospel begins and closes with a sacred week." See further "the six-day-long first creation whose life-creating labor accomplished by the same creator (1:3) likewise achieved its nuptial telos on day six" in Schuchard, "Form versus Function," 38n67. As with the six days of creation, observes Martin Hengel, "Jesus dies in the evening of the sixth day of the week and thereby finishes God's work (19:30)" (Martin Hengel, "The Old Testament in the Fourth Gospel," in *The Gospels and the Scriptures of Israel*, eds. Craig A. Evans and W. Richard Stegner, JSNTSup 104, SSEJC 3 [Sheffield: Sheffield Academic, 1994], 393). Cf. the sixth hour (19:14) of the sixth day of the week (Friday) of the sixth ritual day of the Gospel's final Passover (the 15th of Nisan), the last of the Gospel's six occasions of a festival of the Jews (see 2:13; 5:1; 6:4; 7:2; 10:22; 11:55).

his own concluding witness to the man Jesus, the Christ, the Son of God. John assumes some elements, retains other elements, and omits still other elements of the standing tradition in order to focus especially on the paschal person and work of Jesus; John wrote not to correct or to otherwise oppose the Synoptic tradition, but to extend and deepen it. He wrote with a pronounced interest in the abiding paschal significance of the final six day week of the Passover that began in customary terms on the 10th of Nisan (day one when Jesus was set apart for the work of the great and final Passover) and ended again in customary terms on the 15th of Nisan (day six when he finished the work of the great and final Passover). This sixth day is followed by the 16th of Nisan (day seven when the Logos of God rested again from all his work that he had done[95]), the 17th of Nisan (day eight when he rose again and reclaimed "the twelve" minus two[96]), and the 24th of Nisan (a week later on another day eight[97] when he finished his work of reclaiming his own,[98] so that his work might now be theirs to do[99]). He wrote with a keen interest in the great and final Lamb of God (see John 1:29, 36) whose concluding and completing work was that of the great and final Passover. ✛

95. See John 1:1–3. Thus, a new beginning, new life and new light, comes through him who was "in the beginning" (John 1:1).

96. See John 6:70–71. See also the proper grammatical antecedent of "them" in John 20:24. See further the names of the seven disciples to whom Jesus comes in John 21:2.

97. See again the Lord's Day in John 20:26.

98. See Thomas in John 20:24–29.

99. See John 13:12–15, 34–35; 15:12–14, 26–27; 17:18, 20; 19:26–27; 20:21–23; 21:1–25.

JESUS, HISTORY, AND THE GOSPEL OF JOHN

✛

For much of the Christian era, there has been a concern and respect for history in the interpretation of the Gospels. All four canonical Gospels were understood to bear witness to people who lived in first-century Galilee and Judea, most notably Jesus of Nazareth. The Gospels were read as testimonies to events that took place in this geographical location and to words that were likely spoken in Aramaic or Greek but written in Greek. With the Enlightenment came the rise of rationalism in biblical interpretation, and with rationalism came radical historical skepticism that culminated in the unhitching of the Jesus of history from the Christ of faith.[1]

Of the four canonical Gospels, it is especially the Gospel of John that has suffered from this historical skepticism in much of New Testament scholarship that came to a climax in the middle of the twentieth century.[2] Among the majority of specialists, Mark is still seen as the earliest Gospel, reflecting some early traditions that are historical.[3] Likewise, because of Matthew and Luke's supposed dependence on Mark as their primarily source, these Gospels are also seen to preserve some historical traditions. The Gospel of John, however, is typically understood to be the least historical of the four Gospels, in part because of its unique content that is often in the form of longer monologues of Jesus' preaching. A. J. B. Higgins offers this succinct yet accurate summary of modern scholarship: "It is still almost axiomatic in some quarters that John's Gospel is so thoroughly in-

---

1. For a brief discussion of this historical process with bibliography, see Charles A. Gieschen, "Confronting Current Christological Controversy," *Concordia Theological Quarterly* 69 (2005): 3–32, esp. 4–7.

2. For a review of the process of "dehistoricizing" the Gospel of John, see Robert Kysar, "The Dehistoricizing of the Gospel of John," in *John, Jesus, and History, Volume 1: Critical Appraisals of Critical Views*, ed. Paul N. Anderson, Felix Just, and Tom Thatcher, Society of Biblical Literature Symposium Series 44 (Atlanta, GA: Society of Biblical Literature, 2007), 75–101.

3. See the history of research on the Synoptic Gospels as summarized in David Laird Dungan, *A History of the Synoptic Problem: The Canon, the Text, the Composition, and the Interpretation of the Gospels* (New York: Doubleday, 1999).

terpretative that it contains little or nothing of genuine historical value."[4] Two other recent scholarly assessments confirm this sad situation. First, Richard Bauckham laments the oft-repeated mantra, "the fourth Gospel is theology, not history."[5] Second, James Dunn offers this conclusion about scholars pursuing any quest of the historical Jesus when he states, "the Fourth Gospel had been effectively knocked out of the quest."[6]

The application of narrative criticism to the Gospel of John, initiated by and exemplified in R. Alan Culpepper's well-known *Anatomy of the Fourth Gospel* in 1983, has been welcomed and embraced by many scholars, including those who characterize themselves as conservative. Narrative criticism focuses on the final form of the text and avoids discussion of historical sources and the historical reliability of the narrated events and words.[7] The focus of narrative-critical approaches is primarily on the author and his literary artistry in developing his characters and events into a plot, not on the characters and events themselves as historical. In retrospect, narrative-critical approaches to John that have come to characterize much of Johannine scholarship for the past three decades have only furthered the characterization of John as a Gospel that presents little history.

Not everyone, however, has dismissed John as an historical source. Even in the midst of the decades when this Gospel was being marginalized due to doubts about its historical value, T. W. Manson gave this hopeful assessment in his contribution to the C. H. Dodd festschrift:

> There is a growing body of evidence that the Fourth Gospel enshrines a tradition of the Ministry which is independent of the Synoptic accounts, bears distinct marks of its Palestinian origin, and is on some points quite possibly superior to the Synoptic record. The question of the historical value of the Fourth Gospel is wide open again.[8]

C. H. Dodd himself stated that previous study on the historical Jesus "proves that a severe concentration on the synoptic record, to the exclusion of the Johannine contribution, leads to an impoverished, one-sided, and finally incredible view of the facts—I mean, of the *facts*, as part of history."[9]

---

4. A. J. B. Higgins, *The Historicity of the Fourth Gospel* (London: Lutterworth Press, 1960), 18.
5. Richard Bauckham, *The Testimony of the Beloved Disciple: Narrative, History, and Theology* (Grand Rapids, MI: Baker, 2007), 93.
6. J. D. G. Dunn, *Jesus Remembered* (Grand Rapids, MI: Wm. B. Eerdmans Publishing Co., 2003), 41.
7. R. Alan Culpepper, *Anatomy of the Fourth Gospel: A Study in Literary Design* (Philadelphia, PA: Fortress, 1983).
8. T. W. Manson, "The Life of Jesus: Some Tendencies in Present-day Research," *The Background of the New Testament and Its Eschatology: Studies in Honour of C. H. Dodd*, ed. W. D. Davies and D. Daube (Cambridge: Cambridge University Press, 1956), 219n2.
9. C. H. Dodd, *Historical Tradition in the Fourth Gospel* (Cambridge: Cambridge University Press, 1965), 446; emphasis original.

Craig Blomberg, in his extensive defense of the reliability of the Gospel of John, states that "one looks long and hard to find careful, convincing documentation of what in many circles has become more a presupposition than the conclusion of a sustained argument. In fact, a surprisingly powerful case for overall historicity and the general trustworthiness of the document can be mounted."[10] Richard Bauckham, in his recent discussion of historiographical characteristics of John, even concludes that "far from appearing the least historical of the four Gospels, to a competent contemporary reader, John's Gospel will have seemed the closest to meeting the exacting demands of ancient historiography."[11] It is noteworthy that the topic of history in the Gospel of John has been the subject of a major section at the annual national meeting of the Society of Biblical Literature in recent years.[12]

This study will follow in the path of those scholars who have recently reasserted the value of the Gospel of John as history. *It will demonstrate that the Gospel of John has an important position alongside the Synoptic Gospels in studying the history of Jesus' life and teaching, and in some cases, even contains what could be considered fuller historical testimony.* It is important to understand that this Gospel's theology is not just in the mind of the author but is also grounded in the history of Jesus' own life and teaching.

EYEWITNESS TESTIMONY

Samuel Byskog has argued that, like ancient historiography, the Gospels were written within the generation of those who experienced the events precisely because the authors wanted to set forth written accounts that could be affirmed by other witnesses who were still living.[13] Reliable historiography was concerned not only with the source of the accounts, but also that it was written within the generation of the events so that other witnesses of the events could substantiate the accounts as reliable. This, for example, is seen in Luke's prologue where he claims to have used material from "the ones who from the beginning were eyewitnesses [οἱ

---

10. Craig L. Blomberg, *The Historical Reliability of John's Gospel: Issues and Commentary* (Downers Grove, IL: InterVarsity Press, 2001), 283.

11. Richard Bauckham, *The Testimony of the Beloved Disciple: Narrative, History, and Theology in the Gospel of John* (Grand Rapids, MI: Baker Academic, 2007), 95.

12. This effort began in November 2002. Some of the essays presented at annual meetings between 2002 and 2004 are presented in Anderson, Just, and Thatcher (eds.), *John, Jesus, and History, Volume 1*. The papers from 2005–2007 have been published in *John, Jesus, and History, Volume 2: Aspects of Historicity in the Fourth Gospel*, ed. Paul N. Anderson, Felix Just, and Tom Thatcher (Atlanta, GA: Society of Biblical Literature, 2009). More recent studies from this section were published in *John, Jesus, and History, Volume 3: Glimpses of Jesus through the Johannine Lens*, ed. Paul N. Anderson, Felix Just, and Tom Thatcher (Atlanta, GA: Society of Biblical Literature, 2016).

13. Samuel Byskog, *Story as History—History as Story: The Gospel Tradition in the Context of Ancient Oral History*, Wissenschaftliche Untersuchungen zum Neuen Testament 123 (Tubingen: Mohr Siebeck, 2000).

ἀπ'ἀρχῆς αὐτόπται]" (Luke 1:2). John's prologue contains no such explicit claim but does imply a similar idea: "The Word became flesh and tabernacled among us, *and we beheld his glory* [καὶ ἐθεασάμεθα τὴν δόξαν αὐτοῦ], glory as of the Only-Begotten from the Father, full of grace and truth" (John 1:14).

In John's Gospel, the important role of eyewitness testimony becomes evident. One reads in John not only of individuals like John the Baptist or the works of the Father bearing witness to Jesus' identity (e.g., John 5:30–36), but also of markers indicating that the author considers himself to be an eyewitness of the person and events that he is narrating in his Gospel.[14] One such marker appears in the epilogue: "This is the disciple *who is bearing witness* [ὁ μαρτυρῶν] to these things, and who has written these things; *and we know that his witness is true* [καὶ οἴδαμεν ὅτι ἀληθής αὐτοῦ ἡ μαρτυρία ἐστίν]" (John 21:24). This claim to be a true witness is preceded by a similar claim a bit earlier in the Gospel at the conclusion of the passion narrative: "But one of the soldiers pierced his side with a spear, and at once there came out blood and water. *The one who has seen it has borne witness—his witness is true, and that one knows what he tells is the truth* [καὶ ὁ ἑωρακὼς μεμαρτύρηκεν, καὶ ἀληθινὴ αὐτοῦ ἐστιν ἡ μαρτυρία, καὶ ἐκεῖνος οἶδεν ὅτι ἀληθῆ λέγει]" (John 19:34–35). Both the statement at the close of the Gospel and this one from the crucial hour of its witness—the death of Jesus—characterize the witness as "true." The assertion that the author was among the eyewitnesses from "the beginning of Jesus' ministry," such as those who served as Luke's sources, seems to be reflected in a statement of Jesus in the Farewell Discourse, where Jesus links the witness of the Spirit with the witness of his apostles: "But when the Paraclete comes, whom I will send to you from the Father, even the Spirit of Truth who proceeds from the Father, he will bear witness to me; *and you also are bearing witness, because you have been with me from the beginning* [καὶ ὑμεῖς δὲ μαρτυρεῖτε, ὅτι ἀπ' ἀρχῆς μετ' ἐμοῦ ἐστε]" (John 15:26–27).

Obviously, the question arises whether the author's understanding of a "true" witness has a direct relationship to what is now regarded as "true" history. A. T. Lincoln, for example, states that a true witness in ancient biography does not mean the same as historical truth in our age.[15] Although that observation is correct, nevertheless these two ideas are not distant or disconnected from each other. As will be demonstrated below, there are many aspects of John's Gospel that support this claim of John

---

14. See the discussion of this theme in Richard Bauckham, *Jesus and the Eyewitnesses: The Gospels as Eyewitness Testimony* (Grand Rapids, MI: Eerdmans, 2006), 384–411. He draws on the work of A. T. Lincoln, *Truth on Trial: The Lawsuit Motif in the Fourth Gospel* (Peabody, MA: Hendrickson, 2000), and "The Beloved Disciples as Eyewitness and the Fourth Gospel as Witness," *Journal for the Study of the New Testament* 85 (2002): 3–26.

15. A. T. Lincoln, "'We know that His Testimony Is True': Johannine Truth Claims and Historicity," in Anderson, Just, and Thatcher (eds.), *John, Jesus, and History, Volume 1*, 186.

being a witness to Jesus' ministry from the beginning. This Gospel gives witness to a fuller chronology for the ministry of Jesus than any of the Synoptic Gospels. This Gospel gives witness to more topographic detail than the others. This Gospel gives more witness about lesser-known apostles like Andrew, Philip, and Thomas. This Gospel gives witness not only to the name of the person whose ear Peter severed at the arrest of Jesus (John 18:10), but it also identifies one of the fireside questioners of Peter as a relative of Malchus (John 18:26). The Synoptic Gospels give witness to Jesus' self-disclosure of his divine identity with two or three uses of ἐγώ εἰμι in the absolute form; John's Gospel, however, testifies to seven of these absolute ἐγώ εἰμι statements, implying there were numerous rather than merely a few occurrences of this formula during Jesus' ministry.[16]

CHRONOLOGY

Most students of the four Gospels are quite familiar with the challenges in trying to lay out a chronology of Jesus' ministry, especially if one attempts to harmonize all the content of the four Gospels into one seamless chronology. The primary challenge has been the lack of time markers in the Synoptic Gospels. The Gospel of John, however, with its mention of Jewish festivals such as Passover, Tabernacles, and Hanukkah, provides a clearer sense of the chronology and length of Jesus' ministry. In the late nineteenth century, the renowned British exegete J. B. Lightfoot stated, "St. John is our authority for chronology of our Lord's ministry. In the Synoptic Gospels it is highly probable that the sequence of events is not strictly chronological, but that in places incidents are grouped according to subject and treatment."[17] To say that the mention of the Jewish festivals in the Gospel of John has a theological function is certainly true, because particular festivals are often the impetus for a discourse by Jesus, such as the Passover being the basis for the Bread of Life discourse (John 6:25–59). This theological function, however, should not override or obscure the function of the references to the feasts as also establishing a historical chronology.

THE MINISTRY OF JESUS MARKED BY THREE PASSOVERS

The Gospel of John has several chronological indicators, the primary being the various Jewish festivals that are mentioned: three Passovers (John 2:13; 6:4; 12:55) with Tabernacles (John 7:2) and Hanukkah (John 10:22) coming between the second and third Passovers. There is one

---

16. These seven occurrences are found in John 4:26; 6:20; 8:24, 28, 58; 13:19; 18:4–8. For this formula as a divine self-disclosure formula, see Charles A. Gieschen, "The Divine Name in Ante-Nicene Christology," *Vigiliae Christianae* 57 (2003): 135–141.

17. J. B. Lightfoot, *Biblical Essays* (Grand Rapids, MI: Baker, 1979 [Reprint of 1893]), 57n2.

unnamed festival (John 5:1), but there is no good reason to claim it is another Passover.[18] The Gospel of John also begins and ends with a week of counted days: the week of manifestation (John 5:19–2:11) and the week of glorification (John 52:1–20:25). There is also a year indicator in the first week: the temple had been under construction 46 years (John 2:20). Although an accurate starting date for Herod's reconstruction of the temple cannot be pinned down, Bauckham draws this conclusion about the significance of this statement for chronology: "The starting date for this calculation may be obscure to us, but it was evidently not to the author. There seems to be no explanation of the precise figure here (forty-six years) other than a claim, at least, to precise chronology."[19] At the conclusion of his study of chronology in the Gospel of John, J. A. T. Robinson suggests the following three-year scheme (next page), with a bit more than two years for Jesus' ministry, depending upon where one places the baptism of Jesus in relationship to Jesus' first Passover visit to Jerusalem.[20]

Jesus' movement back and forth between Galilee and Judea in the Gospel of John is more logical from a historical perspective than the simpler Galilee-to-Judea pattern in the Synoptic Gospels. John's account of Jesus' ministry also explains more fully why Jewish authorities in Jerusalem were familiar with Jesus and were threatened by him long before he enters Jerusalem for his passion. After examining chronological precision in historians like Plutarch and Tacitus, Richard Bauckham offers this conclusion about the Fourth Gospel: "It is surely the case that the prevalence of precise chronology in the Gospel of John would have made it look, to contemporary readers, more like historiography than the Synoptics."[21] It is also noteworthy that this Gospel places these years of chronological history into a broader context. Jesus' narrative has its beginning in creation as mentioned in the prologue (John 1:1–4) and its ending in the *parousia* referenced in the epilogue (John 21:23). This historical frame widens the scope and significance of the history narrated in between.

THE CLEANSING OF THE TEMPLE

Of all the events that pit the chronology of the Synoptic Gospels against John, it is the cleansing of the Jerusalem temple that poses the greatest challenge. All four Gospels testify to this event, but the Synoptic Gospels place it in the last week of Jesus' life after the triumphal entry (Matt 21:12–17, Mark 11:15–19, and Luke 19:45–48), while John has it near

---

18. Bauckham concludes that it is most likely Purim; see *The Testimony of the Beloved Disciple*, 101n29.

19. Bauckham, *The Testimony of the Beloved Disciple*, 100.

20. John A. T. Robinson, *The Priority of John*, ed. J. F. Coakley (London: SCM Press, 1985), 157. There is, obviously, debate about the precise year of Jesus' death that will not be considered here.

21. Bauckham, *The Testimony of the Beloved Disciple*, 101.

AD 27	Autumn (?)	Appearance of John the Baptist
AD 28	March (?)	Baptism of Jesus
	April	In Cana and Capernaum
		In Jerusalem before, and during, *Passover #1* and the Feast of Unleavened Bread (April 28–May 5)
	May	In Judaea baptizing
		Arrest of John the Baptist
		Departure for Galilee
	June–October	In Galilee
	October 23–31	In Jerusalem for Tabernacles
	November–April	In Galilee
AD 29	early (?)	Death of John the Baptist
	April	Desert Feeding, before *Passover #2* (April 18)
	May–September	In Phoenicia, Ituraea and Galilee
	October 15	In Jerusalem for Tabernacles (October 12–19)
	November–December	In Judaea and Peraea
	December 20–27	In Jerusalem for Dedication
	January–February	In Bethany beyond Jordan
AD 30	February (?)	In Bethany in Judea
	March	In Ephraim
	April 2–6	In Bethany and Jerusalem
	April 7	Crucifixion on Day of Preparation for *Passover #3*

the very beginning of Jesus' ministry, during his first Passover pilgrimage to Jerusalem after his baptism (John 2:13–22). Johannine scholars typically state that the Gospel of John rearranges the chronology of the temple cleansing by moving it to the beginning of Jesus' ministry for theological reasons, namely, to establish Jesus as the new temple and sacred place of worship. Others do not struggle with the historical question at all; they conclude that Jesus cleansed the temple at least twice.[22] It is much more likely that all four Gospels are testifying to the same event than to conclude that an event of this magnitude happened twice in in the short span of two years (i.e., the lapse of time between three Passovers).[23]

Certainly, the theological importance of Jesus as the new temple is

---

22. This view was quite widespread in the history of interpretation through 1900; see John F. McHugh, *John 1–4*, ed. Graham Stanton, The International Critical Commentary (London: T&T Clark, 2009), 201n2.

23. James H. Charlesworth considers John's placement of the event more historical than the Synoptic Gospels; see James H. Charlesworth, "The Historical Jesus in the Fourth Gospel: A Paradigm Shift?," *Journal for the Study of the Historical Jesus* 8 (2010): 19.

Certainly, the theological importance of Jesus as the new temple is a significant impetus for the inclusion of the cleansing account in John. However, it is a mistake to dismiss John's chronology of the event for at least three reasons. First, John's emphasis on pilgrimages from Galilee to Jerusalem for major festivals is a logical one for Jesus, since he is defining himself as the fulfillment of Israel's eschatological hopes, not just the hopes of Galilean Jews. The pattern of Jesus as a pious rabbi celebrating major festivals in Jerusalem with his disciples makes good sense, as John 2:13 states forthrightly: "The Passover of the Jews was at hand, and Jesus went up to Jerusalem." Second, the Synoptic Gospels, especially Matthew and Mark, have an extremely compressed portrait of Jesus' movement from a Galilean ministry to Judea. Other than Luke's testimony to Jesus' boyhood travels, the Synoptic Gospels depict one trip to Jerusalem by Jesus. If one is to have a record of Jesus cleansing the temple in the Synoptic Gospels, it must be put at the end of his ministry. Third, although all four Gospels depict a relationship between the cleansing of the temple and the death of Jesus, the Gospel of John presents a more historically convincing reason for the concern of Jewish authorities. Their anxiety over Jesus brews for two years from the cleansing of the temple during the first Passover to the raising of Lazarus near the third Passover. Their concern does not stem merely from his healing and preaching activity in Galilee but especially from his staking claim to the temple early in his ministry as well as healing the lame and blind in the shadow of the temple at Bethzatha and Siloam.

One other observation on the temple should be made. Scholars tend to date the Synoptic Gospels as post-AD 70 writings because they conclude that Jesus' prophecy about the destruction of the temple in Matthew, Mark, and Luke is *vaticinium ex-eventu* ("prophecy from the event"; see for example Matt 24:1–2, Mark 13:1–2, and Luke 21:5–9). But what about John? There is no specific prophecy about the destruction of the temple in John, only the prophetic statement about the destruction of Jesus' body: "Destroy this temple and in three days I will raise it up" (John 2:19).[24] Mark actually substantiates John's testimony when he records a twisted version of Jesus' teaching as presented by *false* witnesses at Jesus' trial: "We heard him say 'I will destroy this temple that is made with hands, and in three days I will build another, not made with hands'" (Mark 14:58). In the

---

24. John A. T. Robinson, *Redating the New Testament* (Philadelphia, PA: Westminster, 1976), 276–278. He gives three pieces of evidence that the temple is still standing when John is written. First, there is no prophecy about the destruction of the temple (cf. John 11:47). Second, John 2:20 mentions that it is in the 46th year of Herod's rebuilding of the temple, but no mention is made of the completion of this project, which took place in AD 63. Third, John 5:2 mentions there is—not "was"—five colonnades of the pool, colonnades that were buried by the Roman destruction of Jerusalem in AD 70 and not rediscovered until recently.

Gospel of John, however, there is much more focus given to temple feasts and worship. Does this focus say something not only about the historical circumstances of Jesus' presence in Jerusalem but also about the historical circumstances of when and where this Gospel was written? Although J. A. T. Robinson's pre-AD 66 date for John has not been widely embraced, his arguments deserve consideration.[25] A setting in Judea before the Jewish revolt when the temple is still standing rather than a late first-century date in Ephesus is certainly possible. This does not mean that the evangelist John did not intend for his Gospel to be read outside of Jerusalem and Judea. His translation of Aramaic terms and explanation of some Jewish customs demonstrate that he wrote for a broad audience.[26]

THE HEALING, FEEDING, AND WALKING ON WATER SIGNS IN JOHN (SIGNS 2–4)

Of the seven signs to which this Gospel gives witness, it is noteworthy that three are accounts of incidents featured prominently in the Synoptic Gospels: healing a young person from the official's household (John 4:46–54), the Feeding of the Five Thousand (John 6:1–15), and Jesus' walking on water (John 6:16–21). It is noteworthy that, although the accounts in John reflect the same incidents recorded in the Synoptic Gospels, there is no firm evidence that the author of John simply adapted these from one or more of the Synoptic Gospels.

In these three miracle accounts, the Gospel of John has some unique details not found in the other accounts.[27] For example, although the healing of the young person from the official's household is found in Matthew and Luke, John refers to the person as an "official" (βασιλικός in John 4:46), not a "centurion" (ἑκατοντάρχου in Matt 8:5 and Luke 7:2), and he calls the young person a "son" (υἱός), not a παῖς (Matt 8:6) or δοῦλος (Luke 7:2). Examples of unique material in John's account of the Feeding of the Five Thousand are that it is not followed by an additional Feeding of the Four Thousand (as in Matt 15:32–39 and Mark 8:1–10) and that it is the only feeding account to mention that the crowd wanted to make Jesus a king by force (John 6:15), a detail that seems to offer a logical consequence that is not mentioned after the other feeding accounts. Finally, it is noteworthy that John's account of Jesus walking on the water is much terser than the accounts in Matthew (14:22–33) and Mark (6:45–52);

---

25. Robinson, *Redating the New Testament*, 254–311. Weinrich proposes this Gospel was written "in Jerusalem during the 40s"; see William C. Weinrich, *John 1:1–7:1*, Concordia Commentary (St. Louis, MO: Concordia Publishing House, 2015), 51.

26. See especially the essays in Richard Bauckham, ed., *The Gospels for All Christians: Rethinking the Gospel Audiences* (Grand Rapids, MI: Eerdmans, 1998).

27. This has been noted by many scholars; for example, see Higgins, *The Historicity of the Fourth Gospel*, 22–39.

if he were drawing on these accounts, one would expect more of their detail in John. In spite of this, John's account includes the unique detail that the disciples had rowed out "twenty-five or thirty stadia" (John 6:19) and ends with an interesting detail not found in Matthew or Mark: "and immediately the boat was at the land to which they were going" (John 6:21). This unique detail may reflect an effort to connect the walking on water with Israel's crossing of the Red Sea, since this detail appears to be echoing Psalm 107:30 (LXX 106:30): "and he brought them to their desired haven."[28] In short, John is clearly familiar with these three events also recorded in other Gospels but does not appear to be drawing on the written accounts of the other evangelists in the recording of these events.

THE PASSION NARRATIVE

There are a few details in the four Gospels that indicate Jesus had been in Jerusalem during his earthly ministry before his passion week. For example, he appears to be well known in Bethany (which is just outside of Jerusalem), he is given a royal welcome into Jerusalem a week before his death, and he knows of a room in Jerusalem where he would eat with his disciples during his Passover pilgrimage. Each of these details makes a few trips to Jerusalem after his baptism and before his death, such as those narrated in the Gospel of John, appear probable.

It is worth observing that John 12:27 gives us a unique interpretation of the Gethsemane passion tradition while still affirming that Jesus is facing none other than drinking the metaphorical cup of God's wrath so vividly discussed by the prophets.[29] As in the Synoptic Gospels, John 12:27 begins with the acknowledgment that Jesus is very troubled by what lies ahead at the cross: "Now is my soul troubled" (cf. Matt 26:38–42; Isa 53:11). Unlike the prayers for removal of the cup found in the Synoptic Gospels (Matt 26:27; Mark 14:36; and Luke 22:42), however, Jesus does not ask to be delivered from this suffering in John's account: "And what shall I say, 'Father, save me from this hour'? But for this purpose I came to this hour" (John 12:27). This same attitude is reflected later in John 18:11 during his arrest in Gethsemane where Jesus says to Peter: "Put your sword back into its sheath. Am I not to drink the cup that the Father has given to me?"

---

28. Given this possible echo of the Ps 107:30 in John 6:21, the wider context of Psalm 107:26–30 is important for the Exodus typology of the entire walking on water account: "They [Israel] mounted up to heaven; they went down to the depths; their courage melted away in their evil plight; they reeled and staggered like drunken men and were at their wits' end. Then they cried to the Lord in their trouble, and he delivered them from their distress. He made the storm be still, and the waves of the sea were hushed. Then they were glad that the waters were quiet, and he brought them to their desired haven."

29. See the discussion in Scot McKnight, *Jesus and His Death: Historiography, the Historical Jesus, and Atonement Theory* (Waco, TX: Baylor University Press, 2005), 368. For a discussion of "the metaphorical cup of God's wrath," see Paul Raabe, *Obadiah*, Anchor Bible Commentary 24D (New York: Doubleday, 1996), 206–254.

Although John presents Jesus as more resolute in facing death than the Synoptic Gospel accounts, John affirms with them the passion tradition that Jesus both struggled with and drank the metaphorical "cup" of divine wrath over sin in his death. This is an interpretation of Jesus' death as atonement of sin that is shared with the Synoptic tradition.[30] Although it is not clear that John is explicitly dependent on parts of one or more of the synoptic passion narratives, it is clear that he was very familiar with the passion narrative tradition found in the Synoptic Gospels.

TOPOGRAPHIC DETAILS

Edgar Goodspeed is a representative example of the many twentieth-century New Testament scholars who dismissed the topographic details found in John's Gospel as a reflection of its ahistorical nature:

> It must be remembered that topography and chronology were among the least of the author's concerns. His head was among the stars. He was seeking to determine the place of Jesus in the spiritual universe and his relations to the eternal realities. These were the matters that interested and absorbed him, not itineraries and time tables, so that practical mundane considerations that might apply to Mark, Matthew, or Luke have little significance for his work.[31]

In contrast, several Johannine scholars have more recently called attention to the accurate nature of John's topographical references.[32] Topographic details in writing history were important, as evidenced by the comments of the ancient historians such as Polybius and Lucian.[33] Lucian states that historians are to report topographic details accurately but not dwell on them.[34] Bauckham notes that John has thirty-one named places, very similar to the total in each of the Synoptic Gospels.[35] Of these thirty-one, however, seventeen are unique to John. Furthermore, Bauckham observes that a greater number of locations are more precise than those found in the Synoptic Gospels. For example, Jesus is not just in Galilee, but at Cana (John 2:1); he is not just in Jerusalem, but at the Pool of Bethzatha (John 5:2). Bauckham also issues this strong challenge

---

30. See Charles A. Gieschen, "The Death of Jesus in the Gospel of John: Atonement for Sin?" *Concordia Theological Quarterly* 72 (2008): 243–261.

31. Edgar J. Goodspeed, *An Introduction to the New Testament* (Chicago: University of Chicago Press, 1937), 310.

32. See especially Bauckham, *The Testimony of the Beloved Disciple*, 93–112; Paul N. Anderson, "Aspects of Historicity in the Gospel of John: Implications for Investigations of Jesus and Archaeology," in *Jesus and Archaeology*, ed. James H. Charlesworth (Grand Rapids, MI: Eerdmans, 2006), 587–618; and Urban C. von Wahlde, "Archaeology and John's Gospel," in *Jesus and Archaeology*, 523–586.

33. Bauckham, *The Testimony of the Beloved Disciple*, 98.

34. For example, see Lucian, *Hist. Conscr.* 24 and 57.

35. Bauckham, *The Testimony of the Beloved Disciple*, 98.

and corrective to the many interpreters who have emphasized a purely symbolic use of topography in John: "As a general feature of the Gospel, its topographical precision is not primarily a matter of symbolism but of realistic historiography."[36] Five examples of topographical detail in John will be briefly reviewed here.

JACOB'S WELL IN SAMARIA (JOHN 4:4–6)

"He had to pass through Samaria. So he came to a city of Samaria, called Sychar, near the field that Jacob gave to his son Joseph. Jacob's well was there." John is the only Gospel that gives any attention to Samaritans as those who were among Jesus' followers.[37] John also shows knowledge of Samaria as an ethnic region, even though it was not a political division established by Rome; Palestine was divided into two regions by Rome (Galilee and Judea), not three. John's reference that the well was near the field that Jacob gave to Joseph is calling on the events narrated in Genesis (33:18–20; 48:22). The name of the town of Shechem near the well probably comes from the tradition that this land was given to Joseph by Jacob as his "portion" (Gen 48:22 MT).[38]

Recent examinations of this site confirm the location of Jacob's well and some of the details noted in John's Gospel. Urban von Wahlde offers these observations concerning the modern-day site:

> There is a well there today, about 250 feet outside the ruins of the town of Shechem. It lies directly on what was the main north-south road in the first century. This made it particularly suitable for travelers. This is, of course, consistent with the fact that Jesus stopped at the well as he was journeying north from Jerusalem to Galilee. In verse 6 of the Johannine text this well is identified as a *pēgē* (a running spring), whereas in verses 11, 12 it is called a *phrear* (a dugout well). The well near Shechem is just such a combination of dugout well and running spring. Thus once again the Johannine text reflects details of the well's location (near Shechem), of the site's history (given to Joseph by Jacob), of its particular makeup (both spring and cistern), as well as of its appropriateness for travelers.[39]

Furthermore, although some have sought to identify John's mention of Sychar as a somewhat strange title for Shechem, it is more probable that

---

36. Bauckham, *The Testimony of the Beloved Disciple*, 100.

37. Luke does record successful outreach to the Samaritans by Philip in the Book of Acts (Acts 8:4–25) but only mentions the rejection of Jesus by the Samaritans during Jesus' earthly ministry (Luke 9:52–56). Luke is the only Gospel writer to record Jesus' parable about "the good Samaritan," but the parable does not indicate any successful mission outreach to the Samaritans during Jesus' ministry (Luke 10:25–37).

38. Joshua 24:32 also notes that Joseph's remains were finally buried there, adding to the significance of this site.

39. Von Wahlde, "Archaeology and John's Gospel," 557.

ancient Sychar was at the site of modern Aschar. There is pre-Christian literary evidence for the town at this location in the mention of the "king of Sakir" in Jubilees 34:1–9.[40]

THE POOL OF BETHZATHA (JOHN 5:2)

"Now there is in Jerusalem by the Sheep Gate a pool, in Hebrew called Bethzatha, which has five porticoes."[41] The vivid description of this pool having five porticoes or colonnades has surprised many interpreters (four porticoes would be more typical for a four-sided pool), yet this description has been substantiated by archaeologists who have uncovered a two-section pool not far from the Sheep Gate with porticoes on each side and one down the middle where the pool was separated into two different sections.[42] Archaeologist Shimon Gibson provides this physical description of the pool:

> There are two large basins: the "northern pool" (53 x 40 meters), which served as a reservoir (the *otsar*) for collected rainwater, and the "southern pool" (47 x 52 meters), which was used as the place for purification (the *miqweh*). The two basins would have been surrounded by porticoes on four sides, with an additional portico extending across the barrier wall separating the two basins. The plastered barrier wall separating the two parts of the pool was partly hewn into the rock and partly built of alternating courses of well-dressed header-and-stretcher ashlars with smothered exteriors, typical of other first-century building ventures in Jerusalem.[43]

The southern pool has steps that would allow a considerable number of people to enter the pool. Water could be let into the southern pool from the northern one via a small opening in the wall that divided the two pools; this may be the source of the stirring of the pool water that is mentioned in the Gospel account (John 5:7). This is another example where the Gospel of John is accurately reporting ancient topological details, even though they may not make sense to the modern interpreter when first read.

THE POOL OF SILOAM (JOHN 9:7)

"'Go, wash in the pool of Siloam' (which means Sent)." This instruction of Jesus given to the blind man who is the focus of John 9 is the only mention of this pool in any of the Gospels. This pool has long been un-

---

40. See von Wahlde, "Archaeology and John's Gospel," 557–558.
41. For a brief discussion of the six variations in spelling the name of this pool, see von Wahlde, "Archaeology and John's Gospel," 560–561.
42. See von Wahlde, "Archaeology and John's Gospel," 560–566.
43. Shimon Gibson, *The Final Days of Jesus: The Archaeological Evidence* (New York: HarperOne, 2009), 75.

derstood to have been at the outlet of Hezekiah's tunnel which was not a ritual washing site. More recently, however, the remains of a pool that was probably used for ritual washings near this site have been uncovered.[44] Von Wahlde offers this intriguing description:

> It was reported in December 2004 that the archaeologists have revealed the full 50-meter length of the pool. The pool is stone lined and has steps leading into it on all sides. On the south side, the retaining wall for the pool was part of the southern wall of the city. On the north side, the steps have been fully revealed and consist of a series of nine steps with every third step being broader than the others and serving as a kind of landing. The archaeologists have also discovered an "elaborately paved assembly area" adjacent to the pool. In addition, a water channel that brought water to the pool from the Gihon Spring has been revealed. Finally, steps leading from the site up the hill toward the Temple have been uncovered.[45]

Von Wahlde goes on to theorize that the relationship between the two pools may be that the pool at the outlet of Hezekiah's tunnel supplied water (*otzer*) to the Pool of Siloam, which was used for ritual washing (*mikveh*).[46]

BETHANY'S LOCATION (JOHN 11:18)

"Bethany was near Jerusalem, about fifteen stadia off." Although Bethany is mentioned in the Synoptic Gospels with the implication that it is near Jerusalem (Matt 21:17; 26:6; Mark 11:1, 11–12; Luke 19:6), only John gives its precise location as being "fifteen stadia" from Jerusalem (about 1.75 miles).[47] This kind of precision is evidence of an eyewitness account. Bethany's close proximity to Jerusalem provides a very logical explanation for the sudden impact of Lazarus' raising on Jerusalem, an impact emphasized in the narrative of John (11:46; 12:10–11, 17–18).

THE PLACE OF THE TRIAL BEFORE PILATE (JOHN 19:13)

"[Pilate] brought Jesus out and sat down on the judgment seat at a place called 'The Pavement,' and in Hebrew Gabbatha." This unique content in the Johannine passion narrative reveals an intimate knowledge of the particular place where Pilate would have rendered judgment (βῆμα means "a step" in the sense of a raised-up place from which judgment was rendered).[48] This place was known as Λιθόσπρωτον ("the stone pave-

44. Gibson, *The Final Days of Jesus*, 63–80. Note also the artist rendering of the Siloam Pool as it may have appeared at the time of Jesus that is found after page 80.
45. Von Wahlde, "Archaeology and John's Gospel," 569.
46. Von Wahlde, "Archaeology and John's Gospel," 570.
47. "A *stadion* is about 218 yards, or one-fifth of a kilometer" (von Wahlde, "Archaeology and John's Gospel," 570).
48. Bauer et al., *A Greek-English Lexicon of the New Testament and Other Early Christian Literature*, 3rd ed. (Chicago: University of Chicago Press, 2000), 175.

ment"), a spot that also had a Hebrew name transliterated into Greek by John as Γαββαθα ("height"). Although there are various opinions on the location of this "judgment seat" where Pilate rendered his verdict upon Jesus, archaeologist Shimon Gibson is convinced that the site is next to a gateway (the Gate of the Essenes) along the wall that was part of the palace complex, which had previously been built by Herod the Great but was later used by Roman officials.[49] The paving stones from this gate area were then robbed in the Byzantine period.[50] The logic of the judgment seat arrangement within this gate area was that such a position would offer the Roman governor significant protection when interfacing with the public on judicial matters. As with other examples discussed above, such knowledge appears to reflect eyewitness testimony by one very familiar with the original historical setting and event.

THE TEACHING OF JESUS

Many scholars have highlighted the significant differences in style and content of Jesus' teaching in the Gospel of John when compared to the Synoptic Gospels. For example, in spite of testimony in the Synoptic Gospels that Jesus used parables in his teaching, no parables are recorded in the Gospel of John. The scholarly tendency, therefore, is to emphasize that the teaching of Jesus in the Synoptic Gospels is more historical while that of the Gospel of John is the creation of the author of John or the so-called "Johannine community."[51] This brief discussion will highlight a few examples of significant common content between the Synoptic Gospels and John that demonstrates historical continuity that is due to its origin in the preaching and teaching ministry of Jesus.

THE KINGDOM OF GOD

A central theme in the teaching of Jesus in the Synoptic Gospels, especially in his parables, is "the kingdom of God" (ἡ βασιλεία τοῦ θεοῦ) or, as in Matthew, "the kingdom of the heavens" (ἡ βασιλεία τῶν οὐρανῶν).[52] For example, each of the Synoptic Gospels summarizes the teaching of Jesus using this terminology (Matt 3:2; Mark 1:15; Luke 4:43). Although the specific mention of the kingdom of God is not prominent in John, neither is it absent. In fact, "the kingdom of God" is a subject featured rather prominently in the Nicodemus dialogue, the first major teaching of Jesus found in John. This dialogue begins by the paral-

---

49. Gibson, *The Final Days of Jesus*, 98–106. Note the reconstruction drawings of this gate area on 102 and 105.

50. Gibson, *The Final Days of Jesus*, 99.

51. For example, see J. Louis Martyn, *History and Theology in the Gospel of John*, Revised and Enlarged (Nashville, TN: Abingdon, 1968).

52. For an excellent analysis of this distinction in Matthew, see Jonathan T. Pennington, *Heaven and Earth in the Gospel of Matthew* (Grand Rapids, MI: Baker, 2009).

lel teaching about "seeing" and "entering" the kingdom of God: "Unless one is begotten from above, one is not able to see the kingdom of God" (John 3:3) and "Unless one is begotten of water and the Spirit, one is not able to enter the kingdom of God" (John 3:5).

Chrys Caragounis has unpacked the common elements in the teaching about the kingdom of God that is found in the Synoptics and John.[53] First, several synoptic texts speak of "entering" the kingdom (Matt 5:20; 7:21; 18:13; Mark 10:23–25) and "seeing" the kingdom (Mark 9:1; 13:28), the verbs used with kingdom language in John 3. Second, John identifies Jesus as "king" with greater frequency (fourteen times) than the Synoptic Gospels (Matthew: eight times; Mark: six times; and Luke: four times). Third, Caragounis also argues that the infrequent synoptic phrase "eternal life" (Matt 19:16, 29; 25:46; Luke 10:25; 18:18, 30) takes on the significance of the language and theology of "kingdom of God" within John's Gospel where it is very frequent ("eternal life" occurs seventeen times; "life" occurs without the adjective "eternal" another nineteen times). Finally, Caragounis notes that the Gospel of John also has a strong future eschatology that is parallel with its realized eschatology; this future eschatology is a strong characteristic of the kingdom of God theology in the Synoptic Gospels. In spite of the brief mention of "kingdom of God" in John, therefore, significant theological connections with the Synoptic kingdom teaching are present.

THE SON OF MAN

One of the clear connections with the historical tradition drawn on by all four Gospels is their preservation of Jesus' use of the title "the Son of Man" (ὁ υἱὸς τοῦ ἀνθρώπου).[54] This title is found primarily on the lips of Jesus—except in John 12:34—and is frequent in all four Gospels.[55] It is clear that "the Son of Man" is not a "confessional title" of the later church, since it is not the content of the major confessions in any of the four Gospels but is Jesus' primary public self-designation used during his earthly ministry.[56] As in the Synoptic Gospels, the frequent use of

53. Chrys C. Caragounis, "The Kingdom of God: Common and Distinct Elements between John and the Synoptics," in *Jesus in Johannine Tradition*, ed. Robert T. Fortna and Tom Thatcher (Louisville, KY: Westminster John Knox Press, 2001), 125–134. The points of contact noted here are drawn from the summary outlined on 125–126.

54. For a good summary of the philological issues, see Joseph A. Fitzmyer, "The New Testament Title 'Son of Man,'" in *A Wandering Aramean: Collected Aramaic Essays*, Society of Biblical Literature Monograph Series 25 (Missoula, MT: Scholars Press, 1979), 143–160. For discussion of the history of scholarship on the subject, see Delbert Burkett, *The Son of Man Debate: A History and Evaluation*, Society of New Testament Studies Monograph Series 107 (Cambridge, UK: Cambridge University Press, 1999).

55. It is found thirty times in Matthew, forty in Mark, twenty-five in Luke, and twelve in John; see Douglas R. A. Hare, *The Son of Man Tradition* (Minneapolis, MN: Fortress, 1990).

56. Jack Dean Kingsbury, *Matthew*, 2nd ed., Proclamation Commentaries (Philadelphia, PA: Fortress Press, 1986), 33–65.

this title in John is grounded in the historical use of it by Jesus himself. Absolutely crucial to understanding the significance of this title in each of the Gospels is seeing the influence of Daniel 7:13 on the later use of this title among first-century (AD) Jews, including Jesus.[57] Daniel 7 was not a marginal text in the canon used by first-century Jews and Christians, as substantiated by Benjamin Reynolds.[58] Both its relationship to the depiction of YHWH as the enthroned likeness of "the man" in Ezekiel 1:26–28 as well as its significant influence upon later apocalyptic texts like *1 Enoch* 37–71, the Book of Revelation (1:13; 14:14), and *4 Ezra* 13 testify to its importance.[59] Many first-century Jews longed for the revelation of the Son of Man.

As in the Synoptic Gospels, the Gospel of John evinces significant interest in the Son of Man; for example, note the comment of Jesus to Nathaniel: "You will see heaven opened, and the angels of God ascending and descending on the Son of Man" (John 1:51). In an obvious allusion to the crucifixion by way of Jacob's comforting vision of God enthroned at the top of a ladder stretching between earth and heaven in Genesis 28, Jesus promises Nathaniel a theophany in which the Son of Man is seen as the ladder stretching between heaven and earth rather than being enthroned at the top of the ladder where one would expect to see him.[60] John also contains a polemic against those who claimed a heavenly ascent to see the Son of Man who is the visible form of God: "No one has ascended into heaven except he who descended from heaven, the Son of Man" (John 3:13).[61] What was puzzling for Jesus' followers was not that he speaks of himself as the Son of Man, but specifically *how* he speaks of himself as the Son of Man. The unique emphasis of the Gospel of John on this subject is that it does not focus on seeing the Son

---

57. Contrary to the assessment of Larry W. Hurtado, *Lord Jesus Christ: Devotion to Jesus in Earliest Christianity* (Grand Rapids, MI: Eerdmans, 2003), 290–306.

58. Benjamin E. Reynolds, *The Apocalyptic Son of Man in the Gospel of John*, Wissenschaftliche Untersuchungen zum Neuen Testament 2:249 (Tübingen: Mohr Siebeck, 2008).

59. *1 Enoch* 37–71 is especially important testimony concerning how the Son of Man of Daniel 7 was being interpreted among first-century Jews as a preexistent person within the mystery of YHWH who would bring deliverance on the last day; see James C. VanderKam, "Righteous One, Messiah, Chosen One, and Son of Man in 1 Enoch 37–71," in *The Messiah: Developments in Early Judaism and Christianity*, ed. James H. Charlesworth (Minneapolis, MN: Fortress, 1992), 169–191. For the identification of the Son of Man closely with the Ancient of Days as the God of Israel in these chapters, see Charles A. Gieschen, "The Name of the Son of Man in *1 Enoch*," in *Enoch and the Messiah Son of Man: Revisiting the Book of Parables*, ed. Gabriele Boccaccini (Grand Rapids, MI: Eerdmans, 2007), 238–249.

60. See Jerome H. Neyrey, "The Jacob Allusions in John 1:51," *Catholic Biblical Quarterly* 44 (1982): 586–605; and Charles A. Gieschen, *Angelomorphic Christology: Antecedents and Early Evidence*, Arbeiten zur Geschichte des antiken Judentums und des Urchristentums 42 (Leiden: Brill, 1998), 280–283.

61. See esp. Charles A. Gieschen, "The Descending Son of Man in the Gospel of John: A Polemic against Mystical Ascent to See God," in *The Open Mind: Essays in Honour of Christopher Rowland*, ed. Jonathan Knight and Kevin Sullivan, Library of New Testament Studies 522 (London: Bloomsbury T&T Clark, 2015), 105–129.

of Man enthroned *in heaven* at the *end* of time but seeing the Son of Man enthroned *on earth* upon the cross *in* time (John 12:23, 32–34).[62]

I AM ABSOLUTE SAYINGS

John's seven "I AM" sayings that use the emphatic personal pronoun formula ἐγώ εἰμι in a predicate nominative construction are well known and widely recognized (e.g., "I AM the Bread of Life").[63] What is not so often recognized are the other seven "I AM" sayings in John where the emphatic personal pronoun formula ἐγώ εἰμι appears in an absolute construction (without any predicate) and is often translated "It is I" or simply "I am." There are also seven occurrences of this form, translated here consistently as "I AM."

1. Jesus said to her [the Samaritan woman], "I Am, the one who is speaking to you" (4:26).
2. But he said to them [the disciples in the boat], "I Am; do not be afraid" (6:20).
3. "You [the Jews] will die in your sins unless you believe that I Am" (8:24).
4. "When you have lifted up the Son of Man, then you will realize that I Am, and that I do nothing on my own, but I speak these things as the Father instructed me" (8:28).
5. "Amen, amen, I tell you, before Abraham was, I Am" (8:58).
6. "I tell you this now [Judas' betrayal], before it occurs, so that when it does occur, you believe that I Am" (13:19).
7. "Whom are you looking for?" They answered, "Jesus of Nazareth." Jesus replied, "I Am." Judas, who betrayed him, was standing with them. When Jesus said to them, "I AM," they stepped back and fell to the ground. Again he asked them, "Whom are you looking for?" And they said, "Jesus of Nazareth." Jesus answered, "I told you that I Am. So if you are looking for me, let these men go" (18:5, 6, 8).

The background for this usage of ἐγώ εἰμι is usually connected to the revelation of the meaning of the Divine Name to Moses in Exodus 3:14 (LXX). Richard Bauckham has argued that a better place to look for the

---

62. See Richard Bauckham, *Jesus and the God of Israel: God Crucified and Other Studies on the New Testament's Christology of Divine Identity* (Grand Rapids, MI: Eerdmans, 2008), 152–181; see also Gieschen, "The Death of Jesus in the Gospel of John," 246-254.

63. The emphatic personal pronoun with the verb is translated "I AM" consistently here because of its relationship to the absolute construction found in John that functions as a divine self-disclosure formula. The predicate nominative constructions are: "I AM the Bread of Life" (6:35, 41, 48); "I AM the Light of the World" (8:12; 9:5); "I AM the Gate" (10:7, 9); "I AM the Good Shepherd" (10:11, 14); "I AM the Resurrection and the Life" (11:25); "I AM the Way, the Truth, and the Life" (14:6); and "I AM the True Vine" (15:1).

antecedent of this usage is in the absolute self-revelation statements at the end of Deuteronomy and the second part of Isaiah (40–66) that are rendered in the LXX as ἐγώ εἰμι or ἐγώ εἰμι ἐγώ εἰμι.[64] Especially noteworthy is the fact that there are nine occurrences in MT and seven in the LXX; John has seven occurrences, but the last one consists of three for a total of nine. The message is clear in John's pattern: Jesus' work (seven signs) is the full revelation of Yhwh's work, his words (seven predicate sayings) are the full revelation of Yhwh''s words of salvation, and his self-declarations (seven absolute sayings) are a complete revelation of himself as the same Yhwh' who made this type of self-declaration in the Old Testament. In summation, his saving works are those of Yhwh', his saving words are those of Yhwh', and his self-declarations are those of Yhwh'. He is, therefore, the visible form of Yhwh' (i.e., the Son) incarnate as the flesh and blood Jesus.

Although not nearly as prominent as in John, the same absolute construction is found in the Synoptic Gospels in the following accounts: the Stilling of the Storm (Matt 14:27; Mark 6:50; but not Luke 8:24); the Eschatological Discourse (Mark 13:6; Luke 21:8; but not Matt 24:23); the Trial before the Council (Mark 14:62; Luke 22:70; but not Matt 26:64); and the Resurrection (Matt 28:20 and Luke 24:39). This evidence indicates that this formula is from the historical proclamation of Jesus rather than an authorial creation in the Gospel of John for purely theological reasons.

THE DIVINE NAME THAT THE SON SHARES WITH THE FATHER

Some scholars have noted that the Gospel of John evinces significant interest in the name that Jesus possesses.[65] It most clearly presents Jesus as the possessor of the divine name in the prayer spoken by Jesus at the close of the farewell discourse in John 17:

> I revealed *your name* to those you gave me from the world. (17:6)

> Holy Father, protect them *in your name* that you have given me, in order that they be one, as we are one. While I was with them, I protected them *in your name* that you have given me. (17:11-12)

> I made *your name* known to them and will continue to make it known. (17:26)

---

64. Bauckham, *The Testimony of the Beloved* Disciple, 239–252; see also Catrin H. Williams, *I Am He: The Interpretation of 'Ani Hû' in Jewish and Early Christian Literature*, Wissenschaftliche Untersuchungen zum Neuen Testament 2:113 (Tübingen: Mohr Siebeck, 2000). The self-disclosure formula in the MT is found in Deut 32:39; Isa 41:4; 43:10, 13, 25; 46:4; 48:12; 51:12; 52:6. This formula in the LXX is found in Deut 32:39; Isa 41:4; 43:10, 25; 45:18; 46:4; 51:12.

65. For further discussion of the divine name in the Christology of John, see John Ashton, *Studying John* (Oxford: Clarendon Press, 1994), 61–79; Gieschen, *Angelomorphic Christology*, 270–293; and Gieschen, "The Divine Name in Ante-Nicene Christology," 135–141.

Several conclusions can be drawn from these petitions. First, the repeated use of the personal pronoun makes it evident that the name discussed here is the divine name of the Father, to whom this prayer is directed.[66] Second, the divine name is twice said to be given to the Son (17:11). Based upon the testimony in this prayer that the Son received the Father's "glory" before the foundation of the world (17:24), the giving of the Father's name is probably also understood to have taken place before creation.[67] Third, Jesus has made the divine name, normally a hidden mystery in this world, known to his disciples.[68] Fourth, the divine name that was revealed to the disciples by Jesus has protecting power (17:11). This power is especially reassuring to the disciples because earlier in the farewell discourse Jesus gives some emphasis to how much they will suffer "on account of my name" (15:21), a theme that is also found in Acts (5:41; 9:16; 15:26; 21:13).

This Gospel unambiguously asserts earlier in its narrative that Jesus shares the name of the Father: "I have come in my Father's name" (John 5:43). This phrase is sometimes interpreted as asserting that Jesus has come by and with the authority of the Father.[69] Although there is certainly a relationship between "name" and "authority," this statement signifies a more intimate and forthright connection: Jesus has come as the one who possesses and shows forth the divine name. This Gospel depicts Jesus demonstrating his true name as the Son by what he says and especially by what does: "The works that I am doing in my Father's name, they bear witness to me" (John 10:25; cf. 14:10–11). This Gospel even depicts Jesus as the embodiment of the divine name of the Father, to the extent that Jesus can pray "Father, glorify *your Name*" (John 12:28). This is not simply a pious prayer that God's name be glorified through Jesus' imminent sacrifice; it is the identification of Jesus as the one who possesses the divine name.

The understanding that this divine name theology has a historical link to Jesus and is not the creation of the author of the Gospel of John

66. Most commentators argue that here "name" denotes the "revealed character and nature of God" rather than the divine name; see Williams, *I Am He*, 280–85. Gilles Quispel argues that these verses refer to the divine name that was hidden but has been revealed by Jesus; see "John and Jewish Christianity," in *John and Qumran*, ed. James H. Charlesworth (London: Chapman, 1972), 148–155.

67. This conclusion is also based upon the identification of the preexistent Word as the divine name in both the prologue and the farewell prayer; see Gieschen, *Angelomorphic Christology*, 271–280. The giving of the divine name in eternity prior to creation may also be the idea behind the Father having "sealed" the Son (John 6:27). For an example of the Son of Man receiving the name of God prior to creation in *1 Enoch* 37–71, see Gieschen, "The Name of the Son of Man in the Parables of Enoch," 238–249.

68. Evidence of the hidden (divine) name of Jesus is also present in Revelation 19:12–13. For this theme in Second Temple Jewish literature and early Christianity, see Gieschen, "The Divine Name in Ante-Nicene Christology," 115–158.

69. For example, Herman N. Ridderbos, *The Gospel of John: A Theological Commentary*, trans. John Vriend (Grand Rapids, MI: Eerdmans, 1997), 205.

is supported by its use in Matthew, especially in the baptismal formula where the same singular divine name is said to be shared by the Father, the Son, and the Holy Spirit (Matt 28:19).[70] Other references in Matthew to the name that Jesus possesses are referring to the divine name, not his personal name "Jesus" (see Matt 10:22; 18:5, 20; and 19:29). The confession of Jesus as κύριος ("Lord") by Jews across the Gospel traditions also supports the historical link between Jesus and the divine name found in John and Matthew, because it is the title κύριος that is consistently used as a substitute for the divine name in the Septuagint.

Finally, how is this evidence of the divine name related to the absolute ἐγώ εἰμι statements discussed earlier? As reverent first-century Jew, Jesus would not have pronounced the divine name, but if he had the self-understanding of possessing the divine name and having a divine identity, he would have expressed this in a reverent manner, such as speaking about his "name" or his "word" or using the divine self-declaration formula.

CONCLUSION

This study began by criticizing both *a historical critical* approach that leads to radical historical skepticism in the study of the Gospels and *a narrative critical* approach that shows little or no interest in the historical light that the Gospels shed on Jesus. Such scholarship is interested in history as evidence for the evangelist's literary and theological artistry as well as the community for which he was writing. J. A. T. Robinson's assessment of the historical skepticism that has characterized the study of the Gospels, especially John during the twentieth century, is incisive: "It is corrosive . . . of our confidence in possessing any firm knowledge about the Jesus of history, who . . . in the twentieth century as in the first, remains an integral part of the Christ of faith."[71] The theology of the Gospels is and remains the theology of the four evangelists, but the works of these evangelists must serve as a historical link to Jesus—to what he actually did and taught—for this theology to be a true witness. The Gospels testify that the Christ of faith is organically grounded in the Jesus of history. It is vital that we use our reason ministerially in rigorous historical research on the Gospels to bear witness faithfully to Jesus Christ as God manifest in human flesh for the salvation of the world. This study has demonstrated that there are solid historical reasons for including the Gospel of John as a historical source for the life and teaching of Jesus, and even for regarding it as eyewitness testimony to Jesus. ✛

---

70. Gieschen, "The Divine Name in Ante-Nicene Christology," 143–146.
71. Robinson, *The Priority of John*, 124.

THE BREAD FROM HEAVEN, THE BREAD OF PRESENCE

REFLECTIONS ON THE INTERPLAY OF FORGIVENESS AND COMMUNION

✛

I will begin with some words of appreciation. William Weinrich holds a very special place for many of us. Reflecting upon my own days at the seminary, I am thankful for studying the Lutheran Confessions and the Reformation. Yet Weinrich took us further back into our church's history and introduced us to fathers such as Irenaeus, Cyprian, Augustine, Athanasius, and Leo the Great. In doing so, he delivered to us the heart of our Nicene faith and brought to our attention matters of the Trinity, the incarnation, and a full and robust sacramental life. Weinrich's teaching is profound, and often, upon leaving his classroom, I would scratch my head and ask, "What did he say?" But even when his teaching was difficult to grasp, I knew he was on to something, and he was always worth hearing again and again. Weinrich especially opened up for us the Gospel of John, helping us to understand more fully what it means that Jesus is the Bread of Life. For Weinrich, Christ can never be reduced to an abstraction or a thought, and the flesh of Christ can never be dematerialized. In eating the bread, we share in things eternal, for his flesh is life-giving. In this essay, I would like to build, in some small way, on Weinrich's case, showing that the eucharistic life is central also to the Synoptic Gospels, which teach that in the Eucharist we feast on Jesus, our Bread from Heaven.

INTRODUCTION

N. T. Wright has (in)famously and repeatedly taken the Western church to task for not incorporating the life of Christ into its theological thinking and ecclesial life. Provocatively, he claims, "I think the Western church has simply not really known what the Gospels were there for."[1] He detects this tendency even in the ancient creedal formulations, writing, "There, the virgin birth is followed directly by Jesus suffering under Pontius Pilate, and Jesus' endless kingdom is placed toward the end of the narrative, appearing to suggest that Jesus will only inaugurate the kingdom at the very end—which contradicts both the Gospels and Paul." Wright holds that the kingdom of God is a present reality. The Gospels are more than background music. Again N. T. Wright observes, "Two or three years ago a book was written which attempted to explain what the Bible says about atonement. It had a lot of Old Testament, and a lot of Paul—but almost nothing about the Gospels. A travesty. The Gospels are not just the back story for Pauline theology."[2]

Wright's observation has been taken up Sarah Hinlicky Wilson, who notes in a recent *Concordia Journal* article that part of Pentecostalism's appeal is that "[i]t emphasizes, first of all, the life and ministry of Jesus that is mysteriously absent from the three great Creeds." Again, Wilson notes that Pentecostalism draws people in by "taking seriously the real presence of the living Christ even today among his people."[3]

We may be tempted to dismiss such critiques. Pentecostalism's miracles too easily become distractions. For good reason, John labeled the miracles as signs pointing to a greater reality. N. T. Wright's complaint might also be ignored, especially as he commonly couples it with a grating critique of the Anselmic atonement and the doctrine of justification by faith. And, as for N. T. Wright's kingdom on earth, it often looks like nothing more than a Christian social program. In typical fashion, Wright summarizes the evangelists as saying, "Jesus is alive again; therefore, new creation has begun; therefore, we have a job to do."[4] (Or as the bumper sticker puts it, "Jesus is coming, look busy.")

But then, Wright and Hinlicky might be onto something. The gospel has to be more than a history lesson. The life of Jesus matters, because it is the flesh-and-blood Jesus who is at the heart of our faith. As C. Kavin Rowe puts it, "The cross is the cross of one who was once a human baby and who went through human life and died as a grown man. The resurrection is the new life that was given to this same human being. Immanuel, God with us, is the one who was killed and raised."[5] God came

---

1. N. T. Wright, "Whence and Whither Historical Jesus Studies in the Life of the Church?," *Jesus, Paul and the People of God* (Downers Grove, IL: IVP Academic, 2011) 133.

2. N. T. Wright, "Whence and Whither Historical Studies in the Life of the Church?," 152.

3. Sarah Hinlicky Wilson, "Six Ways Ecumenical Progress is Possible," *Concordia Journal* 39, no. 4 (2013): 321.

4. N. T. Wright, "Whence and Whither Historical Jesus Studies in the Life of the Church?," 149.

5. C. Kavin Rowe, "Why Easter Needs Christmas," *Faith and Leadership*, March 26, 2013, https://www.faithandleadership.com/c-kavin-rowe-why-easter-needs-christmas.

not only to save us, but to be with us. Without the gospel story, Rowe cautions, "We make Jesus' death and resurrection into mere events that carry with them particular benefits."[6] He continues, "We can never think about the death or resurrection without the human Jesus, without, that is, understanding their significance in the light of God's decision to be with us and for us as a human being."[7] Our very humanity is given meaning by God's Son who becomes one of us.

Happily, Concordia Theological Seminary has addressed the concerns of Wright, Hinlicky, and Rowe. We now put the Gospels front and center in our teaching and curriculum. Instead of requiring one Gospel, we read all four. Still, we might ask, what should we do with the Gospels? With Paul, we "are determined to preach Christ and him crucified" (1 Cor 2:2). And we read the Gospels knowing that "he was handed over for our transgressions and raised our justification" (Rom 4:25). For that reason, I have always been partial to Martin Kähler's oft-quoted observation that the Gospels are passion narratives with long introductions. Then again, when I am reading a book, I often skip the introduction. And so we are back to square one.

Instead of contradicting Wright, we might do well to agree that the Gospels proclaim the kingdom of God as a present reality. To put it another way, what Christ did in the Gospels, he still does. The Book of Acts begins, "In the first book, O Theophilus, I have dealt with all that Jesus began to do and teach" (Acts 1:1). Jesus of Nazareth continues his ministry in an even greater way in the life of the church. "Amen, amen, I say to you, whoever believes in me will do the works that I do; and greater works than these will he do, because I am going to the Father" (John 14:12). Formerly, Jesus cleansed lepers, made the lame walk, opened deaf ears and blind eyes, and even raised the dead. But miracles decrease as Baptism increases. Through Holy Baptism that we are cleansed from our sin (Eph 5:26), we walk in the newness of life (Rom 6:4), ears are opened (Rev 2:17), and the scales fall from our eyes (Acts 9:18). Baptism becomes for us the power of resurrection (Rom 6:1–5).

But is it simply a matter of the church picking up where Jesus left off? How and in what way can we say with the psalmist, "Yea, though I walk through the valley of the shadow of death, I will fear no evil, for thou art with me" (Ps 23:4)? In this study I would like to explore the idea that Christ's presence with his people manifests itself particularly in the bread of the Lord's Supper and at the eucharistic table. And, as a lens through which to see this presence, I would like to consider the Jerusalem temple.

---

6. Rowe, "Why Easter Needs Christmas."
7. Rowe, "Why Easter Needs Christmas."

TEMPLE WORSHIP: A FORGIVEN PEOPLE
IN THE PRESENCE OF GOD

The temple served a twofold purpose. It was at once the place of forgiveness and of presence, of atonement and of dwelling. The temple became the holy mountain of God's dwelling (Ps 48:1–4). Its flora and fauna suggested a new Eden where God once more walked among his people (Gen 3:8). At its heart, the ark of the covenant served as the Lord's dwelling place, and the assurance that the merciful God was on their side (1 Sam 4:3–8).

An elaborate system of sacrifices made possible, as Samuel Balentine puts it, "fellowship with God."[8] Burnt offerings, grain offerings, peace, sin, and guilt offerings were made there. The greatest offering took place on the Day of Atonement when the high priest made his annual appearance in the Holy of Holies. Blood was sprinkled on the mercy seat, and the scapegoat was sent off into the desert. The Lord would not hold the Israelites' sin against them; he would continue to dwell among his people. As John Kleinig puts it, the Day of Atonement made it possible that "sinful Israelites could have safe access to their most holy God."[9]

The temple, however, also had certain limitations. There were plenty of ropes and barriers, curtains, and ushers. Segregation was the order of the day. Regulations were placed upon the unclean, including lepers and menstruants.[10] The temple was divided into zones, as it were, of holiness and presence. Jews could go where Gentiles could not, the priests could go further than the people, and the high priest alone entered the Holy of Holies.[11]

TEMPLE BREAD

Among the strange wonders of the temple is the prominent place of bread. The splattering of blood upon the mercy seat is shocking, yet understandable. Peace comes at a price. But bread, by its nature, is ordinary. At its first biblical mention, bread represents sin's curse, symbolic of toil and mortality in a fallen world: "By the sweat of your face you shall eat bread, until you return to the ground for out of it you were taken; for you are dust, and to dust you shall return" (Gen 3:19). Earthly bread, in contrast to the fruits of Eden, came only through the hard work of planting, harvesting, grinding, milling, and baking. Indeed, bread served as a kind

---

8. Samuel Balentine, *Leviticus: Interpretation: A Bible Commentary for Teaching and Preaching* (Louisville, KY: John Knox Press, 133), 34.

9. John Kleinig, *Leviticus*, Concordia Commentary Series (St. Louis:, MO Concordia Publishing House, 2003), 347.

10. For a helpful mapping of the Temple, see John Elliott, "Temple versus Household in Luke-Acts," in *The Social World of Luke-Acts* (Peabody, MA: Hendrickson, 1991), 213–224.

11. For a helpful description of the temple, see Carol Meyers, "Temple, Jerusalem," in *The Anchor Bible Dictionary,* vol. 6 (New York: Doubleday, 1992), 350–369.

of shorthand for daily sustenance (Prov 6:8), the bare necessity of survival. Bread and water became the diet of prisoners (1 Kings 22:27), and deprivation of bread served as a punishment for the disobedient (Ezek 4:16–17). Yet bread can be found in the temple's two most sacred spaces: the Holy Place and the Holy of Holies (Heb 9:1–5).

MANNA, BREAD FROM HEAVEN

When his wilderness people needed sustenance, the Lord caused manna to rain down from heaven. The people asked, "What is manna?" Moses answered, "It is the bread our Lord has given you to eat" (Exod 16:15). Manna came without sweat or toil. It was bread without price, pure gift (Isa 55:1–2). Manna taught the Israelites to depend on the Lord (Deut 8:3). Even more, manna was heavenly bread: "Yet he commanded the skies above and opened the doors of heaven, and he rained down on them manna to eat, and gave them the grain of heaven. Men ate the bread of angels; he sent them food in abundance" (Ps 78:23–25).

Fittingly, a portion of this bread was to be kept in the Most Holy Place in remembrance of the Exodus deliverance and as a token that heaven and earth were not so far apart. The writer to the Hebrews tells us that it was placed in a golden urn in the very ark of the covenant (Heb 9:4). So Moses instructed,

> This is what the Lord has commanded, "Let an omer of it be kept throughout your generations, so that they may see the bread with which I fed you in the wilderness, when I brought you out of the land of Egypt." And Moses said to Aaron, "Take a jar, and put an omer of manna in it, and place it before the Lord to be kept throughout your generations." (Exod 16:32–33)

Or to paraphrase, "Keep this bread, in remembrance of me."

THE BREAD OF PRESENCE

While manna fell from heaven, the bread of Presence was man-made. It was widely known as the showbread. Even more, it is the "bread of the face," that is, bread set before the face of God.[12] Only a curtain separated the bread of Presence from the Holy of Holies. This bread consisted of twelve loaves which the priests themselves were to bake, using fine flour. The loaves were to be placed upon a table made of acacia wood overlaid with pure gold, and upon the loaves was placed pure frankincense (Lev 24:5–9; Heb 9:2). The use of precious gold signified the utmost holiness of both the bread and the table. Frankincense was offered up as a sacrificial

---

12. The bread of Presence has various names in the Old Testament, including "regular bread," and "rows of bread." See Balentine, *Leviticus*, 187.

aroma, pleasing to the Lord. This bread was offered in recognition of Yahweh's presence within the sanctuary, as if it were the Lord's Supper to eat. This bread of Presence, as Roy Gane has put it, powerfully symbolizes "the Creator in Residence."[13]

While manna remained in the ark of the covenant as a type of relic, the bread of Presence was prepared fresh weekly. The priests dutifully entered the holy place each Sabbath day to offer up new loaves and to eat the bread that had been offered the week before. As Roy Gane writes, "The Sabbath is the common denominator between the 'bread of presence' and creation."[14] Though human hands baked this bread, we are to understand that God as Creator continues to provide for and sustain his creatures (cf. Ps 104:14–15). The bread of Presence consisted of twelve loaves of bread, a number signifying God's covenant with the twelve tribes of Israel (Exod 24:4; Josh 4:1, etc.).[15] The God of creation would care for Israel, even as the people rested.

Gary Andersen has argued that this bread, placed in the presence of God, took within it the very holiness of God.[16] Even the golden table upon which the bread was placed was thought to bear God's presence.[17] Remarkably, as Anderson notes, it became customary for the priests "to bring the table out of the Temple into the courtyard and to display it to the pilgrims."[18] This holy bread was indeed linked to the holiness of the priests, as Leviticus says, "They [the priests] shall be holy to their God and not profane the name of their God. For they offer the Lord's food offerings, the bread of their God; therefore they shall be holy" (Lev 21:6). Strikingly, the bread is made holy by the presence of God, and the bread in turn imparts holiness to the priests.

Bread offerings were common in ancient religion.[19] The Egyptians and Hittites, the Babylonians and Greeks likewise offered up "sacrificial loaves" and libations to the gods.[20] Oppenheim writes, "Food was placed in front of the image, which was apparently assumed to consume it by merely looking at it, and beverages were poured out for the same pur-

---

13. Roy Gane, "'Bread of Presence' and Creator-in-Residence," *Vetus Testamentum* 42, no. 2 (1992): 202.

14. Gane, "Bread of Presence," 202.

15. Additionally, we see the division of the twelve into two groups of six in Deuteronomy 27:11–13, where the Israelites were to divide themselves into two groups of six tribes. Simeon, Levi, Judah, Issachar, Joseph, and Benjamin were to stand on Mount Gerizim to bless the people, while Reuben, Gad, Asher, Zebulun, Dan, and Naphtali were to stand on Mount Ebal for the curse. More specifically, there were twelve loaves, arranged in two groups of six.

16. Gary Andersen, "To See Where God Dwells: The Tabernacle, the Temple, and the Origins of the Christian Mystical Tradition," *Letter and Spirit* 4 (2008): 13–45.

17. This observation is confirmed by Jesus' own word: "For which is greater, the gold or the temple that has made the gold sacred?" (Matthew 23:17).

18. Anderson, "To See Where God Dwells," 25.

19. H. A. Hoffner, *Alimenta Hethaeorum: Food Production in Hittite Asia Minor* (New Haven, CT: American Oriental Society, 1974), 216

20. Jacob Milgrom, *Leviticus 23–27* (New York: Doubleday, 2001), 2092.

pose."[21] The pagan gods were, in a sense, dependent upon this food for their well-being, and the ancients used this food as leverage. Pagan bread offerings implied a kind of *quid pro quo*, with the hope that the well-fed deity would in turn care for the people.[22]

Strikingly, the Israelites offered no libation nor thought of the bread as a divine edible. Indeed, only the frankincense was offered up and, as it were, consumed by God. This practice reflected the biblical tension of God who is both transcendent and immanent; even Solomon asked, "Will God indeed dwell on the earth?" (1 Kgs 8:38). The Lord God of Israel would indeed call the temple home, but he was not like the pagan idols. The Lord scoffs, "Were I hungry, I would not tell you" (Ps 50:12). The priests offered up loaves of bread. And then, remarkably, this bread was given back to the priests as a holy food, which the priests consumed around the table of the Lord: "And it shall be for Aaron and his sons, and they shall eat in a holy place, since is it for him a most holy portion out of the Lord's food offerings, a perpetual due" (Lev 24:9).[23]

In sum, manna came down from heaven and was therefore holy, the food of angels. This bread was inaccessible, separated by the temple curtain. The priests baked the bread of Presence with ordinary ingredients, and yet, by virtue of its proximity to Yahweh, it became a holy and priestly food. Yahweh, who resided on the other side of the curtain, did not participate in the meal offered to him.

THE TEMPLE AND THE NEW TEMPLE IN THE NEW TESTAMENT

Luke painted an idyllic portrait, depicting the temple as the dwelling place of God's people, including righteous and pious figures such as Zechariah, Anna, and Simeon. The boy Jesus appears right at home in his Father's house (Luke 2:46). But during his ministry, Jesus spoke prophetically against temple abuses. Entering the temple, Jesus overturned the tables of the money changers who had turned the house of God into "a house of trade" (John 2:14–17) and "a den of robbers" (Matt 21:13). Jesus prophesied the temple's demise, "Truly, I say to you, there will not be left here one stone upon another that will not be thrown down" (Matt 24:2). He promised to usher in a new era in which worshipers would no longer journey to Jerusalem, for they would "worship the Father in spirit and truth" (John 4:24). Even more, Jesus identified himself as the new temple, the dwelling place of God (Matt 27:40; John 2:20–21).[24]

---

21. A. L. Opppenheim, *Ancient Mesopotamia* (University of Chicago Press, 1964), 191.
22. For further discussion of this idea, see especially Gane, "Bread of Presence," 190–191.
23. Kleinig, *Leviticus*, 517.
24. Commenting on John 2:20–21, Raymond Brown writes, "We are being told that the flesh of Jesus Christ is the localization of God's presence on earth, and that Jesus is the replacement of the ancient Tabernacle." Raymond Brown, *The Gospel According to John 1–12* (New York: Doubleday, 1966), 29.

Given that the Gospels depict Jesus as the new temple, it may be fruitful to consider the role that bread plays in relationship to that temple. In the Gospel of John, Jesus identifies himself as the true manna, the very Bread of Life, who offers his flesh for food (John 6). But today, I would like to consider the Synoptics.

MATTHEW: JESUS OUR IMMANUEL

Matthew served as a kind of catechism for the early church.[25] From the genealogy we learn that Jesus Christ is the Son of David (Matt 1:1). Born into this world, he is given both a name and a title. Matthew writes, "She will bear a son and you shall call his name Jesus, for he will save his people from their sins" (Matt 1:21). Forgiveness and salvation are at the heart of his mission. Even as blood was splattered upon the mercy seat, making atonement for sin, Christ would offer his own "blood of the covenant, which is poured out for many for the forgiveness of sins" (Matt 26:28).[26]

Matthew then adds, "All this took place to fulfill what the Lord had spoken by the prophet: 'Behold, the virgin shall conceive and bear a son, and they shall call his name Immanuel'" (Matt 1:22–23). The name "Immanuel" points to a pervasive theme. In Christ, God came to be with his people. And so the Gospel ends with the promise, "And behold, I am with you always, to the end of the age" (Matt 28:20). Atonement, like a coin, has two sides: Christ became present to make peace with God, and that peace in turn makes possible his continued presence. Or to put it another way, Jesus, like the temple, becomes both the place of atoning sacrifice and of presence, the place of dwelling and of forgiveness, as even his accusers testify by their misunderstanding, "This man said, 'I am able to destroy the temple of God, and to rebuild it in three days'" (Matt 26:61; 27:40).

BREAD IN MATTHEW

Jesus' own teaching on bread is varied. Repeatedly, he downplays the significance of bread. He himself engages in fasting (Matt 4:2). Tempted by the devil, he responds, "Man shall not live by bread alone" (Matt 4:4). In the Sermon on the Mount, Jesus challenged his disciples to set their sight on higher things: "Do not be anxious about what you eat or what you drink, what you will put on. Is not life more than food, and the

---

25. For an assessment of Matthew's reception in the early church, see Edouard Massaux, *The Influence of the Gospel of St. Matthew on Christian Literature before Irenaeus*, ed. Arthur J. Bellinzoni, trans. Norman J. Belval and Suzanne Hecht (Leuven: Peeters, 1990–1993).

26. For a discussion of the Eucharist and atonement in Matthew's gospel, see David P. Scaer, *Discourses in Matthew: Jesus Teaches the Church* (St. Louis, MO: Concordia Publishing House, 2004), 163–164.

body more than clothing?" (Matt 6:25). Instead, he implores, "Seek first the kingdom of God and his righteousness, and all these things will be added to you" (Matt 6:33). Nothing that sustains this body and life can be ultimate. "And do not fear those who kill the body but cannot kill the soul," Jesus says (Matt 10:28). Instead, our Lord urged his disciples to hunger and thirst for righteousness (Matt 5:6). This righteousness is not abstract but is embodied in the one whom Pilate's wife called "that righteous man" (Matt 27:19).[27]

JESUS, THE NEW DAVID, AND THE BREAD OF PRESENCE

But Jesus also speaks of the bread of Presence and in doing so offers a preview of his kingdom. So it happened, when the disciples were hungry, "they began to pluck heads of grain and to eat, but when the Pharisees saw it, they said to him, 'Look, your disciples are doing what it is not lawful to do on the Sabbath'" (Matt 12:2). To answer the charge, Jesus recounted a story of David and the bread of Presence:

> Have you not read what David did when he was hungry, and those who were with him: how he entered into the house of God and ate the bread of Presence, which it was not lawful for him to eat nor for those who were with him, but only for the priests? Or have you not read in the Law how on the Sabbath the priests in the temple profane the Sabbath and are guiltless? I tell you something greater than the temple is here. (Matt 12:3–6)

In one fell swoop, Jesus, the Son of David, revealed himself to be the Lord of the Sabbath, and the new temple.[28] Roy Gane claimed that the bread of Presence was meant to indicate that within the Holy of Holies, the creator himself was in residence. Now, in Christ, the creator is resident in the flesh. Born in Bethlehem, the House of Bread and the city of David, the Son of David ushers in a new kingdom. The first David ate and gave bread to all who were with him (μετ' αὐτοῦ, Matt 12:3). As the narrative unfolds, we will see the new David, our Immanuel, likewise gives bread to all who are "with him."

FEEDING OF THE FIVE THOUSAND: MANNA AND PRESENCE

The Feeding of the Five Thousand directly follows the martyrdom of John the Baptist. King Herod held a feast, and in the reverie he made a foolish promise that resulted in death. The story ends with John's dis-

---

27. Scaer, *Discourses in Matthew*, 179–180.
28. For a nice summary of Jesus, the new David, who is greater than the Sabbath and the temple, see Jeffrey Gibbs, *Matthew 1:1–11:1*, Concordia Commentary Series (St. Louis, MO: Concordia Publishing House, 2006), 53.

ciples taking away his body, foreshadowing the fate of Christ's own body and leading us into the story of a very different king and a very different feast.[29]

And so it happened that when Jesus saw the crowds, he had compassion on them and healed their sick (Matt 14:14).[30] The desert setting hearkened back to Israel's own wandering in the desert.[31] The disciples suggested that the people "go into the villages and buy food for themselves" (Matt 14:15). Yet, as Yahweh fed his sojourning people with heavenly manna, the Lord once more offers bread to his people.[32] Like manna, this bread comes without toil or price (Isa 55:1–2). That night the Lord made the desert holy, as he took bread, blessed it, broke it, and gave it to the people, even as he would on the night when he was betrayed.[33]

This story is about more than food. Desiring to be their Immanuel, Jesus says "They need not go away" (Matt 14:16). Starvation was not the issue; the meal made possible Christ's continued presence with his people. Jesus, the new David, invited the crowds to eat in the presence of one greater than the temple. Even as twelve loaves of bread were placed upon the table of Presence, the disciples return with twelve baskets of bread. The twelve tribes of Israel and the twelve apostles are linked, as Jesus begins to establish his reign over a new Israel. Notably, the bread of Presence was eaten by the priests, but now blessed bread is given to all the children of Israel, including "women and children" (Matt 14:21). Ropes are cut, and barriers fall in anticipation of the curtain that will be torn in two (Matt 27:51). Twelve baskets of leftovers (κλάσματα) invite us to think that still others will be fed with the bread that the Lord has blessed by his word and with his presence.[34]

Yet, his blessed bread did not descend from heaven. Instead, like the bread of Presence, it began with an offering from the disciples, who say, "We have only five loaves here and two fish" (Matt 14:17). As the bread of Presence was brought into the temple having been prepared and baked by

---

29. For a nice discussion of the links between Herod's death and the Feeding of the Five Thousand, see Joel Marcus, *Mark 1–8* (New York: Doubleday, 2000), 403–404.

30. In Matthew, the power of healing is closely related to the power of forgiveness. Jesus is the one who "took our illness and bore our diseases" (Matt 8:17; Isa 53:4). He is the one who raises the paralytic, so that we may know that he "has the authority on earth to forgive sins" (Matt 9:6).

31. As Jeffrey Gibbs puts it, "The Feeding of the five thousand is located along the trajectory from Exodus 16 to the Lord's Supper." Jeffrey Gibbs, *Matthew 11:2–20:34*, Concordia Commentary Series (St. Louis, MO: Concordia Publishing House, 2010), 751.

32. John Koenig writes, "Parallels with Moses and the desert wanderings are surely intentional, especially in Matthew's version of the story." Indeed, Koenig sees this meal as God confirming his ancient covenant with Israel. John Koenig, *The Feast of the World's Redemption* (Harrisburg, PA: Trinity, 2000), 174.

33. For a helpful comparative chart, showing the actions of Jesus in the Feeding Narratives, as well as the accounts of the Lord's Supper, see Marcus, *Mark 1–8*, 410–411.

34. Indeed, κλάσματα becomes the churchly word for the broken pieces of bread offered at the Eucharist. See Didache 9.

the priests, it was returned to them as a gift from God, made holy by its proximity to the Lord and blessed by his word. So, too, here, the disciples offer up bread, and it is given back to them in blessed superabundance. "Blessed are those who hunger and thirst for righteousness, for they shall be satisfied" (Matt 5:6). This supper offered a preview of that ultimate satisfaction: "[T]hey all ate and were satisfied" (Matt 14:20). This was the bread of messianic fulfillment (Ps 132:15; Isa 49:10),[35] a foretaste of the feast to come in Matthew 26, where the New Covenant would be made with the New Israel.

THE COURT OF THE GENTILES: THE BREAD IS SCATTERED

In the Feeding of the Five Thousand, blessed bread was given to the children of Israel. In the story of the Canaanite woman, bread found its way into the court of the Gentiles. It was David who distributed the bread of Presence to those who were with him. Tellingly, a Canaanite woman cried out, "Have mercy on me Lord, Son of David." The new David replied according to the old rules, saying, "It is not right to take the children's bread and throw it to the dogs" (Matt 15:26). In the Lord's Prayer, children call upon their father for bread (Matt 6:11). The son who asks his father for bread, will surely not receive a stone (Matt 7:9). But this Canaanite supplicant pushes at the ropes, saying, "Yes, Lord, yet even the dogs eat the crumbs that fall from their master's table" (Matt 15:27). And indeed, as a father gives good things to the son who asks for bread, so now the new David gives bread to the Canaanite who comes in faith.

The Feeding of the Four Thousand expands the theme of wider distribution. Having offered up crumbs to the Canaanite woman, he continued his healing ministry to a people who are said to have "glorified the God of Israel" (Matt 15:31). Indeed, this new crowd appears to have come from a long distance. Jesus frets that, if sent home, they will faint along the way. Commenting on this, Donald Carson writes, "It is hard to resist the conclusion that in the feeding of the four thousand Jesus is showing that blessing of the Gentiles is beginning to dawn."[36] In the four thousand, we are offered a taste of Christ's promise "that many will come from east and west" and will "recline in the Kingdom of God" (Matt 8:11).

Another detail marks this story as unique. Jesus says, "I am unwilling to send them away hungry, lest they faint on the way" (Matt 15:32). This mention of hunger, absent in the Feeding of the Five Thousand, again recalls the story of King David: "Have you not read what David did when he was hungry and those with him?" (Matt 12:3). Even as David of-

---

35. For a discussion of this bread as "messianic fulfillment," see Jerome Kodell, *The Eucharist in the New Testament* (Collegeville, MN: Michael Glazier, 1988), 97.

36. Donald A. Carson, *Matthew*, Expositor's Bible Commentary (Grand Rapids, MI: Zondervan, 1984), 357.

fered blessed bread to hungry outsiders, so the new David does the same. The story takes yet another twist: in the Feeding of the Four Thousand, there are seven larger baskets left over. Notably, Matthew now uses the term σπύρις for baskets, rather than κόφινος found in the Feeding of the Five Thousand. As Eugene LaVerdiere explains, "Accordingly, the Greek term for baskets, *spurides*, refers to baskets found in Greek or Gentiles settings."[37] Jesus, Lord of the Sabbath and creator of the world, now offers up bread for the world, even as the world was created in seven days, even as the bread of Presence was offered and eaten on the seventh day, as even as now there are seven large basketfuls of κλάσματα (broken pieces) left over (Matt 15:37).[38]

Did the disciples comprehend the implications of the Feedings of the Five Thousand and Four Thousand? As the narrative shows, they did not fully understand much at all. After all the miracles, Peter confessed, "You are the Christ, the Son of the Living God" (Matt 16:16). Yet, he could not comprehend the cross, saying, "Far be it from you, Lord" (Matt 16:22). And if he could not understand the cross, neither was he yet able to understand a meal of body and blood, given in bread and wine.

No, man does not live by bread alone. But the disciples would come to see that Jesus offered up for them a better meal, with a new and blessed bread. This is what precisely Jesus does when, in the Last Supper, Jesus took bread, and after blessing it, broke it, gave it to the disciples, and said, "Take eat, this is my body" (Matt 26:26). Here in this meal, presence and sacrifice are finally brought together in perfection. In the new Holy of Holies, Christ himself offered blood shed for forgiveness, and in the Holy Place, he offers up the bread of his continual presence. He adds, "I tell you I will not drink again of this fruit of the vine until that day when I drink it new with you in my Father's kingdom" (Matt 26:29). So the Gospel ends with a nod to the feast of Christ's present-day presence in his churchly kingdom, "And behold, I am with you always, to the end of the age" (Matt 28:20).

THE GOSPEL OF LUKE: CHRIST'S PRESENCE
IN THE BREAKING OF THE BREAD

In the Great Commission, our Lord promised, "And behold, I am with you always, to the end of the age" (Matt 28:20). Luke's Emmaus story explains how that would be. Jesus came up alongside two of his disciples and asked what they were talking about along the way. The disciples responded, "Concerning Jesus of Nazareth, a man who was a prophet

---

37. Eugene LaVerdiere, *The Eucharist in the New Testament and Early Church* (Collegeville, MN: Liturgical Press, 1996), 57.
38. Joel Marcus sees the number seven as a reference to "eschatological fulfillment." See Marcus, *Mark 1–8*, 514.

mighty in deed and word before God and all people, and how our chief priests and rulers delivered him up to be condemned to death, and crucified him. But we had hoped that he was the one to redeem Israel" (Luke 24:21–24). Jesus opened up the Scriptures and demonstrated that he was in fact the promised redeemer. The disciples pleaded, "'Stay with us, for it is toward evening and the day is now far spent.' So he went in to stay with them" (Luke 24:29). The Lord was "with them," and he would indeed "stay with them." Invited as a guest, he became the host: "When he was at table with them, he took the bread and blessed and broke it and gave it to them. And their eyes were opened, and they recognized him. And he vanished from their sight" (Luke 24:30–31). Even as he vanished, Jesus kept his promise to abide. As the two disciples reported, the Lord was made "known to them in the breaking of the bread" (Luke 24:35).[39] Indeed, Luke 24 is the culmination of Jesus' entire ministry of presence and forgiveness. Jesus is the Lord is one who "visits and redeems his people" (Luke 1:68). He reclines at the table with his redeemed and forgiven friends, and he eats with them.[40]

Luke takes the motif of meal and presence even further than Matthew. Remarkably, as the disciples were talking about the Emmaus experience, Jesus stood "in the midst of them" and asked, "Have you anything to eat?" (Luke 24:41). By the act of eating, the Lord demonstrated that he is not a ghost, an important point for a community gathered around meals of his body and blood. Yet, the fact that he ate "in their presence," tells us more. It fits the pattern of Luke's entire Gospel, in which the Lord desires to eat with his people (Luke 24:43).

CHRIST'S TRUE PASSION

It is often said that the Lukan passion has, in fact, little passion.[41] Jesus faced his death with resolve and equanimity. The loud cry of dereliction is replaced with a prayer of hopeful trust (Matt 27:46; Luke 23:46). But when it comes to the Last Supper, Jesus is hardly the picture of a level-headed stoic. Gathered together with his disciples, Jesus says, "I have earnestly desired to eat this Passover with you before I suffer" (Luke 22:15).

---

39. For a discussion of Luke 24 as the Gospel's culmination, see Arthur A. Just, *The Ongoing Feast: Table Fellowship and Eschatology at Emmaus.*

40. See also Luke 5:29–39; 7:36–50; 9:10–17; 10:38–42; 11:37–54; 14:1–24; 19:1–10; 22:7–38; 24:13–35.

41. In Luke's Mount of Olives scene, Jesus appears to approach his death with a kind of equanimity. Whereas in Matthew, Jesus cries out, "My soul is sorrowful even unto death," and then falls down on the ground to pray three times that the cup of suffering be removed; in Luke, Jesus appears to be in perfect control of himself, showing no signs of anguish, placing his knees on the ground to pray, as if in perfect liturgical posture. And indeed, on the cross, Luke omits Christ's cry of anguish, "My God, My God, why have you forsaken me?" Instead, Jesus dies serenely, offering up a prayer of faith, "Father, into your hands I commit my spirit." For a further discussion of this theme, see Peter Scaer, "The Lukan Passion and the Praiseworthy Death," New Testament Monographs 10 (Sheffield: Sheffield Phoenix Press, 2005), 93–117.

In Greek, the longing is more powerful: "ἐπιθυμίᾳ ἐπεθύμησα," which might be translated, "With passion, I have passionately desired to eat this Passover."

In the Greco-Roman world, the cardinal virtues included prudence, justice, temperance, and fortitude (Plato, *Republic* 427e). Thought to stand in opposition to the virtues were the passions, including distress, fear, delight, and lust (ἐπιθυμίᾳ). The passions were irrational, causing a person to act emotionally rather than reasonably (Luke 15:16).[42] The Septuagint uses the word ἐπιθυμία to translate "covet" in the Ninth and Tenth Commandments. Jesus used this word in the same way when warning against lust (Matt 5:28). Luke himself uses the word to describe overwhelming hunger of the prodigal son who "was longing to be fed with the pods the pigs ate" (Luke 15:16).

So, we see Luke portray Jesus as a man driven by a passion that goes beyond reason. "With great passion have I passionately desired to eat this Passover with you before I suffer. For I tell you I will not eat it until it is fulfilled in the kingdom of God" (Luke 22:15–16). The Lord is the one who fills the hungry with good things (Luke 1:53). But now Jesus himself longs to eat with his people. This is a far cry from the Lord who said, "If I were hungry, I would not tell you" (Ps 50:12). This Lord goes into the desert for forty days, and "he was hungry" (Luke 4:2). This is the Lord pictured in Revelation 3:20: "Behold, I stand at the door and knock. If anyone hears my voice and opens the door, I will come in to him and eat with him and he with me." This is the Lord of Luke 24, who pretends to walk ahead of his Emmaus disciples, as if hoping for an invitation to a supper that he himself will host. This is the Lord who appears again, and asks, "Have you anything to eat?" (Luke 24:42).

LUKE: AT TABLE WITH TAX COLLECTORS AND SINNERS

In the temple's Holy Place, the bread of Presence was placed upon a golden table that was set for YHWH. In the Gospel of Luke, the Lord himself comes to the table and reclines. Luke would have us know that the same Lord who provided bread in the desert also entered into the homes of his people. In this way, Luke's Gospel prepares the reader to understand the ongoing table fellowship of the church.[43]

---

42. Luke is not afraid, however, to depict Jesus as a man driven by an impatient passion. He is like the man who searches out for one lost sheep, and one lost coin, and does not rest until he finds it. He is the one who says, "I came to cast fire on the earth, and would that it were already kindled! I have a baptism to be baptized with, and how great is my distress until it is accomplished!" (Luke 12:49–50). There is desperation, as in the story of the Prodigal Son: "He was longing [ἐπεθύμει] to be fed with the pods that the pigs ate, and no one gave him anything" (Luke 15:16).

43. For a picture of this, see Jerome Neyrey, *The Passion According to Luke* (New York: Paulist Press, 1985), 10.

While Matthew and Mark tell the story of Matthew's call, Luke alone tells us that it led to a "great feast" of tax collectors and sinners. At this, the Pharisees and their scribes grumbled, "Why does he eat with tax collectors and sinners?" (Luke 5:29–30). Jesus responded, saying, "I have not come to call the righteous, but sinners to repentance" (Luke 5:32). And for behavior like this, Jesus was labeled a drunkard and a glutton (Luke 7:34).

For Luke, the table is the place of God's presence, and the banquet of his blessing. While Jesus' wilderness feedings hearkened back to Israel's wandering in the desert, the table scenes pointed forward to a time when the temple would be replaced by house churches, in which Christians would gather together to devote "themselves to the apostles teaching and fellowship, to the breaking of bread and prayers" (Luke 2:42).

At table, Jesus welcomed a sinful woman, who wiped his feet with her hair and received from Jesus absolution (Luke 7:36–50). At table, Jesus dined with Pharisees, teaching them that their understanding of cleanliness was superficial (Luke 11:37–41). At table, he healed a man with dropsy, demonstrating that the Lord of the Sabbath is a Lord of mercy (Luke 14:1–6). Again, at table, Jesus taught about humility, about taking the lowest place (Luke 14:7–11). Indeed, Jesus' teaching about meal etiquette was meant to be applied to the church. As Francis Maloney writes, "This Gospel story also looks to the 'then' of the life of Jesus to question the 'now' of current Christian practice."[44] Jesus says, "Invite the poor, the crippled, the lame, and the blind" (Luke 14:13). This command is meant especially for the church gathered at the Lord's table. If the children of Israel would not come to the table, then the Gentiles would be invited. "Go to the highways and to the hedges and compel people to come in, that my house may be filled. For I tell you, none of these men who were invited shall taste of my banquet" (Luke 14:24).

The kingdom of God becomes a present reality for the church at table. Jesus said, "Blessed are you who are poor for yours is the kingdom of God. Blessed are you who are hungry now, for you will be satisfied" (Luke 6:20–21). In the kingdom of Jesus, the poor and the lame are invited to the feast, with a culminating blessing: "Blessed is everyone who eats bread in the Kingdom of God" (Luke 14:15).

Luke's emphasis on table finds itself in the very institution of the Supper. In fact, of the four institution narratives, only Luke sets the scene by telling us, "And when the hour came, he reclined [at table], and the apostles with him" (Luke 22:14). While all four Gospels record Judas' betrayal, only Luke mentions the table: "But behold, the hand of him who

---

44. Francis Maloney, *A Body Broken for a Broken People* (Peabody, MA: Hendrickson, 1997), 92.

betrays me is with me on the table" (Luke 22:21). As Xavier Léon-Dufour notes, "Luke uses the word 'table' here, instead of 'dish' as in Matthew and Mark, probably in order to emphasize the table fellowship and therefore the terribly contradictory situation of the traitor."[45]

Jesus then proceeded to prepare his disciples for serving at his table, "For who is greater, the one who reclines at table, or the one who serves? Is it not the one who reclines at table? But I am among you as one who serves" (Luke 22:27). This is more than a general exhortation to service, but it becomes a description of the Lord's Supper as the heavenly banquet. Jesus made this point clear, saying, "And I assign to you, as my Father assigned to me, a kingdom, that you may eat at drink at my table in my kingdom" (Luke 22:29–30). This Kingdom is not simply a future hope, but a present reality in the Kingdom ushered in by the new David, soon to be crowned with thorns and crucified under the sign, "Jesus of Nazareth, King of the Jews" (John 19:19).

And so we return again to Jesus' story of David and the bread of Presence. Jesus asks, "Have you not read what David did when he was hungry, he and those who were with him: how he entered the house of God and took and ate the bread of the Presence, which is not lawful for any but the priests to eat, and also gave it to those with him?" (Luke 6:3–4). A few things are striking. First, we see the hunger of David; this ties to the passion of Jesus, who himself hungered to eat with his people. Second, we note the way Luke tied the story more directly to the Lord's Supper. As Arthur Just notes, "Indeed, Luke is the only synoptic to have the *three* words, "taking, he ate, and he gave."[46] Thirdly, we see that Jesus is the new David, and his disciples play the role of those who are "with him." And even more, it is David who expressly "gave it to those with him" (Luke 6:4). Yes, the bread of Presence was a Sabbath day ritual, but a new David had arrived, who himself was the Lord of the Sabbath, and the giver of the bread and a new covenant.

In the temple, the bread of Presence was offered weekly to the Lord, but it was consumed only by the priests. The Lord inhabited the temple, but he was not yet fully with his people. He remained on the other side of the curtain. Only the high priest could enter into his presence, and then only once a year. A weekly meal of bread was offered to him, but he did not partake, for the Lord God of Israel knew no hunger. But now, in the Gospel of Luke, our Lord comes hungering and thirsting, eating and drinking. Luke presents the Lord as one who has a flesh and blood body, who longs to eat with his people. The Lord's death tore open the curtain, and the Lord of Israel, David's greater son, is now able to eat and drink at

---

45. Xavier Léon-Dufour, *Sharing the Eucharistic Bread* (New York: Paulist Press, 1987), 235.
46. Just, *Luke 1:1—9:50*, 257.

table with his forgiven people. And now he eats not only with priests, but with a new and priestly people that includes tax collectors and sinners, the lame and the blind.

MARK: THE BREAD OF PRESENCE, TAKE TWO

In many ways, Mark's teaching about bread mirrors that of Matthew, but he kneads it even further into his narrative. For Mark, "Jesus, the gospel, and the Eucharist were not just a matter of history. In word and symbol, they belonged to the present," writes Eugene LaVerdiere.[47] Again, LaVerdiere notes, "Mark's story of the Eucharist, like other good stories, builds up to a climax, indeed two climaxes, one for each major part of the body."[48] The second climax to which LaVerdiere refers is, as one might expect, the institution of the Lord's Supper. The first climax though, is intriguing. He notes that Mark 6:7—8:21 is often known as the *sectio panis*, or "the bread section," because of its many references to bread. Within this section we hear of our Lord's command to take no bread for the journey (Mark 6:7), the Feeding of the Five Thousand (Mark 6:30–44), the disciples' lack of understanding about the bread, which led to hardened hearts (6:52), Jewish baptismal/cleansing rites and the eating of bread (Mark 7:1–23), the Syrophoenician's desire for bread crumbs (Mark 7:24–30), the Feeding of the Four Thousand (Mark 8:1–9), and finally the story of the disciples who forgot to bring bread upon the boat (Mark 8:14–21).

And so we begin with the boat. While Luke tends to think about the Christian life as a journey, Mark characteristically pictures the church as a boat upon the sea. Jesus first found Peter and Andrew casting their nets, promising to make them "fishers of men" (Mark 1:17). Likewise, he called James and John when they were "in their boat, mending their nets" (Mark 1:19). Jesus looked to the boat as a place of practical safety. Jesus "told his disciples to have a boat ready for him because of the crowd, lest they crush him" (Mark 3:9). The boat also became the seat of teaching: "Again he began to teach beside the sea. And a very large crowd gathered about him, so that he got into a boat and sat in it on the sea, and the whole crowd was beside the sea on the land" (Mark 4:1).[49]

Things, however, get more mysterious in the fourth chapter. Jesus takes the lead, saying, "Let us go across to the other side" (Mark 4:35). The "other side" in this case, is the largely Gentile region of the Decapolis. But then, Jesus becomes, as it were, luggage. Mark writes, "And leaving the

---

47. LaVerdiere, *The Eucharist in the New Testament and the Early Church*, 51.
48. LaVerdiere, *The Eucharist in the New Testament and the Early Church*, 51.
49. Perhaps here, we hear echoes of Psalm 29, where the "voice of the Lord is over the waters" (Ps 29:3) and again, "The Lord sits enthroned over the flood" (Ps 29:10).

crowd, they took him with them in the boat, just as he was" (Mark 4:36). The phrase is enigmatic. James Voelz offers the possibility of translating it, "'as [i.e., in the state that] he was'—perhaps Jesus was exhausted from preaching."[50] The phrase "just as he was" seems to refer to a type or mode of presence. Such a reading would make sense of what follows. The presence of powerful Jesus promised safety for the disciples in a way that is analogous to the Israelites and the ark of the covenant. Yet when a storm rose, and the boat began to take on water, the disciples cried out, "Teacher, do you care that we are perishing?" (Mark 4:38). As both Voelz and Joel Marcus note, the background for this story may be found in the Jonah story, offering a preview of the church as it embarks upon its Gentile mission.[51] Marcus adds that it may reflect "the persecution being experienced by the Markan community."[52] Jesus rose up and rebuked the wind and the wave, demonstrating that he is in fact the Lord of creation, the creator in residence. The disciples need not have feared; Jesus would be their Lord, just as he was, in whatever mode of presence he took.

Shortly after this, we come upon the part of Mark's Gospel that is often referred to as *sectio panis*, the bread section (6:8—8:21).[53] It begins with the command (found only in Mark) that the disciples were not to bring bread along with them on their missionary journey (Mark 6:8). Bread, like clothing, sandals, and other basic necessities, would be provided by their hosts. But, as Joel Marcus notes, "In a deeper sense the disciples will be looked after by God."[54] As Marcus notes, there is significant overlap between the instructions given to the disciples and Deuteronomy 29:5–6: "Your clothes have not worn out on you, and your sandals have not worn off your feet." So Marcus writes, "As the Markan missionaries will not need to bring bread with them, so the Israelites did not take bread, because manna rained down on them from heaven (Exodus 16)."[55] And indeed, as the narrative continues, we see that it is the Lord who would provide.

Mark's Feeding of the Five Thousand runs largely parallel to that of Matthew, but with a few twists. Drawing imagery from Psalm 23, Mark emphasizes Jesus' role as the Davidic shepherd. When Jesus looked upon the crowd, he saw that "they were like sheep without a shepherd" (Mark 6:34). Likewise, Mark adds the detail that Jesus commanded the crowds to recline on "the green grass," recalling Psalm 23, where the Lord as a shepherd "makes me lie down in green pastures" (Ps 23:2). The

---

50. James Voelz, *Mark 1:1–8:26*, Concordia Commentary Series (St. Louis, MO: Concordia Publishing House, 2013), 331.

51. Voelz, *Mark 1:1–8:26*, 338.

52. Marcus, *Mark 1–8*, 339.

53. See LaVerdiere, *The Eucharist in the New Testament and the Early Church,* 51.

54. Marcus, *Mark 1–8*, 389.

55. Marcus, *Mark 1–8*, 389.

theme of superabundance also links the two stories. In Psalm 23, the Lord prepares a table, and the psalmist's cup overflows (Ps 23:5). In the Feeding of the Five Thousand, there is again more than enough.

Indeed, Mark's Feeding of the Five Thousand is not simply bread in the wilderness but is depicted as a messianic banquet. Though the meal is prepared in the desert, we are told that people were divided into plots of hundreds and fifties, πρασιαὶ πρασιαὶ, garden plot by garden plot (Mark 6:40). The garden imagery, like the flora and fauna of the temple, hearkened back to Eden. Though no drink was explicitly offered, the people were told to "recline," as if for a feast. Then the crowds were arranged "συμπόσια συμπόσια." As I have noted elsewhere, a symposium was, in the ancient world, a type of dinner party, a feast in which both wisdom and wine were shared. The word συμπόσια has as its root the sharing of cups. Eugene LaVerdiere notes that Mark's Feeding of the Five Thousand "evokes the banquet setting of a symposium, a formal banquet such as communities held in the home of a member on the first day of the week."[56] The great crowds represent the church universal, and the individual groups, or symposia, represent the eucharistic gatherings found in every congregation. Again, as LaVerdiere puts it, "The scene is that of an assembly of assemblies, a symposium of symposia, for one great eucharistic symposium, as it were, of the universal Church."[57]

This little paradise, however, would be short-lived, and it is followed directly by another boat story, marked by danger, fear, and painful progress. The disciples would have been understandably reluctant to board the boat without the one who could guarantee their safety. Yet mysteriously, "[Jesus] made his disciples get into the boat and go before him to the other side" (Mark 6:45). Jesus then, in a little preview of the Ascension, went up to the mountain to pray. So what we have is a picture, or perhaps some practice for the church, as it lives in a time when the Lord has ascended into heaven, where he continues to pray for his church. As Marcus writes, "The disciples are cut off from Jesus by a great distance; it seems impossible that he should see their distress from miles away in the dark, much less come to their rescue across the roaring sea."[58] Indeed, we are told that once in the boat, "They were making headway painfully, for the wind was against them" (Mark 6:48). Again, Joel Marcus sees this story as a picture of the church persecuted under duress. Indeed, the word Mark uses to describe the painful rowing, βασανίζειν, has a nuance of eschatological tribulation (see also Rev. 9:5; 11:10; 12:2), and it was also used, as Marcus notes, to describe judicial torture, and it is found in

---

56. LaVerdiere, *The Eucharist in the New Testament and the Early Church*, 55.
57. LaVerdiere, *The Eucharist in the New Testament and the Early Church*, 55.
58. Marcus, *Mark 1–8*, 430.

both Jewish and Christian martyrdoms (2 Macc 7:13; 4 Macc 6:6; Polycarp 2:20). But this story of fear turns into one of great hope. Though Jesus appeared to have left his disciples and gone off to a far place, he was in fact a ready and present help in their distress. Revealing himself as Yahweh, "he meant to pass them by" (Mark 6:48). Indeed, this is the same Lord who revealed his glory to Moses by passing by him (Exod 33:17–48). He further revealed his identity, declaring himself to be the great "I AM," saying, "Take heart, I am. Do not be afraid" (Mark 6:50). Why were the disciples afraid? What was the source of their unbelief? Mark writes, "They were utterly astounded, for they did not understand about the loaves/breads" (Mark 6:52).

The boat prepared the disciples for life in the church, and in both stories there is a question as to whether Jesus was truly present for them. How and in what way could the disciples say, "Even though I walk through the valley of the shadow of death, I will fear no evil, for you are with me; your rod and your staff, they comfort me"? They needed to understand the meaning of the loaves.

Mark continues to leave breadcrumbs along the way. In his discourse on true cleanliness, Jesus contrasted his own kingdom with the ways of the Pharisees, who baptize pots and pans and never fail to wash their hands before eating ordinary, earthly bread (Mark 7:1–23). Then, like Matthew, he tells the story of the Syrophoenican woman. He adds the detail that Jesus "went through Sidon to the Sea of Galilee, in the region of the Decapolis" (Mark 7:31), thus underlining the Gentile nature of the Feeding of the Four Thousand.

Mark's bread section then comes to a climax with Jesus in the boat with his disciples (Mark 8:14–21). Mark writes, "Now they had forgotten to bring bread, and they only had one loaf with them in the boat" (Mark 8:14). Clearly, they had not only forgotten the bread, but they had forgotten our Lord's caution against being concerned with earthly bread. Valiantly, Jesus the teacher seeks to elevate the discussion, warning against the leaven of the Pharisees and Sadducees. Paul, ever the precocious student, would later pick up on the theme of leaven as that which disturbs the eucharistic community, urging, "Let us celebrate the festival not with the old leaven, the leaven of malice and evil, but with the unleavened bread of sincerity and truth" (1 Cor 5:8).

The original disciples, having not yet graduated, continue to discuss earthly bread, saying, "We have no bread." Somewhat comically, they begin a discussion as to the fact that they have no bread. Jesus responds in cryptic frustration, "Why are you discussing the fact that you have no bread? Do you not yet perceive or understand? Are your hearts hardened? Having eyes do you not see, and having ears do you not hear? And do you not remember?" (Mark 8:17–18). Then, as a teacher, he sees whether they

THE BREAD FROM HEAVEN, THE BREAD OF PRESENCE ✛

have been taking notes: "'When I broke the five loaves for the five thousand, how many baskets full broken pieces did you take up?' They said to him, 'Twelve.' 'And the seven for the four thousand, how many baskets of broken pieces did you take up?' And they said to him, 'Seven.' And he said to them, 'Do you not yet understand?'" (Mark 8:19–21).

If the disciples had understood about the loaves, they would have understood that Christ was present for them. If they had understood about the loaves, they would have known that Christ only appeared to be sleeping. If they had understood about the loaves, they would have known that Christ, though appearing to be far off, was their ever-present help in time of need. If they had understood about the loaves, they would have known that the one loaf who is Christ is more than enough. If they had understood about the loaves, they would have known that if they had the bread that is Christ, they would have everything they need for life's journey. And so Christ asked his disciples, "Do you not remember?" (Mark 8:18). And he makes his presence known in the sacrament in which says to us, "Do this in remembrance of me." And again, we see that in Jesus is one greater than the temple, and he continues to offer his bread of Presence.

CONCLUSION
A Torn Curtain Leads to Full Communion

The temple was the place of atonement and of presence, but nothing in the original temple was ultimate. The Day of the Atonement came every year, and it had to be repeated to "keep the peace." Communion was granted, but provisionally. Only the high priest could enter into the holy of holies. The manna, the bread from heaven, remained in the holy of holies, but could never be eaten. The bread of Presence was refreshed weekly in the Holy Place, but it could be eaten *only* in the Holy Place, and *only* by the Priests. The Lord himself did not share in this meal. This all comes to an end, or perhaps better, a fulfillment, in Christ who is the new temple. By his atoning death, the temple curtain is ripped open, allowing for full communion with the Creator-in-Residence. Christ now remains for us the Creator-in-Residence, feeding his people with his flesh, the true bread of Presence. As on the road to Emmaus, he longs to be invited to the table, even as he himself invites and becomes our host. He still stands at the door and knocks, so that he may eat with us, and us with him. ✛

NO LONGER ΕΘΝΗ

PAUL'S USE OF THE OLD TESTAMENT
IN 1 CORINTHIANS

✝

The image that I will most remember and appreciate of Dr. William C. Weinrich is the reflection of him standing at the front of one of the classrooms on campus with his beret on the table before him, and an old, tattered *Novum Testamentum* standing alone and open on the podium, with the pages rippled and aged from his constant leafing through the small text.

Of all the things that I appreciate about Dr. Weinrich (and there are many!), his greatest influence on me was his insight into the Scriptures, particularly his Greek acumen. The insight that I gained from him while studying the Greek text is what has driven me as a theologian to spend a lot of time in Greek study. Of all the things I want to be when I grow up, I want to read the Bible like Dr. Weinrich. This essay goes forth in his honor and in the same ambience in which he taught.

INTRODUCTION

My interest in St. Paul's use of the Old Testament increased exponentially in the fall of 2015, when someone dropped off a large statue of Mary in our church's parking lot. To this day, I am not sure if the source of this statue was a zealous Roman Catholic trying to get Lutherans to "see the light" or merely someone who mistook our parish for being Roman Catholic (it has happened before!).

As I studied the figure (it really is a beautiful piece of artwork!), I noticed a serpent wound around Mary's ankles and subtly subjugated under her foot. At first, like any good Lutheran, I was taken aback, because in Genesis 3 the "seed of the woman"—Jesus—crushes the head of the serpent. My first thought was, "Well, there you go! They are always putting Mary in place of Jesus." Then, I remembered Romans 16:20: "The God of peace will soon crush Satan under your feet. The grace of our Lord Jesus Christ be with you." It was at this point that I started to gain a greater appreciation for St. Paul. He was giving commentary on Genesis 3:15 and putting it in the perspective of the church's current situation. St. Paul was teaching the Romans about their lives in the world and their participation in Christ's redemption in Old Testament terms.

Thus, Paul's use of the Old Testament has prompted this study, which considers St. Paul's first letter to the church at Corinth. This essay considers how Paul employs the Old Testament in 1 Corinthians even though he was writing to a non-Jewish audience. In turn, this paper deliberates whether this same approach may be instructive for the church's missionary work in the twenty-first-century Western world.

CORINTH: WERE THEY GNOSTICS
AND DOES IT MATTER?

For a time, a healthy amount of scholarship considered the possibility that the apostle's letter to the Corinthians was intended to combat gnostic thought-forms.[1] Other scholars surmised that Paul was dealing with Stoic, Sophistic, and Epicurean philosophies. What can be demonstrated about Corinth was its diverse culture. Corinth, situated on a narrow isthmus, linked the Greek mainland with the Peloponnese peninsula. The city was known for its wealth; many different cultures passed through this area for trade, commerce, and exploration.

For this reason, Corinth had a very unhealthy reputation. Prostitution was central to the busy port city. It had several temples for goddesses. With so many different cultures and backgrounds in Corinth, religious pluralism was the norm. The people in Corinth were very worldly. Living in Corinth, one did not remain in naïve innocence for long.

First Corinthians is a rich epistle penned in this milieu. The context is central to our consideration because St. Paul addresses issues arising in this unique setting. Our interest is to understand how Paul engages this context as a guide for the church's mission in a similar world today. Twenty-first-century America is not all that different from Corinth in terms of religious and cultural plurality. The task at hand concerns the identity of Paul's particular audience: What were their weaknesses? What were their cultural fixations? And does the apostle's usage of the Old Testament give us insights into how we should go about this today?

Hans Conzelmann elaborates on the Corinthian background. He seems to think that there was an earlier speculative context that preceded Gnosticism. Conzelmann states: "We are merely being superficial if in

---

1. A good article that critiques and summarizes the shift in Corinthian studies from viewing Paul's opponents as gnostic to viewing them as Stoics is Todd E. Klutz, "Re-reading 1 Corinthians after Rethinking 'Gnosticism'," *Journal for the Study of the New Testament* 26.2 (2003): 193–216.

terms of historical causality we trace out external 'influences' of syncretistic, gnostic movements and seek to explain the developments in Corinth thereby."[2] Conzelmann emphasizes a couple key lines of development in 1 Corinthians, "The first and most important factor is the summing up of the 'gospel' in the creed: Christ died and rose again."[3] This summation will lead the student of Paul's letter into a proper understanding of the Old Testament. Conzelmann continues, "Faith then becomes the movement of spiritual ascent along with the Redeemer."[4] Then he speaks of the Spirit and its connection to creedal faith and the gospel. Conzelmann asserts, "The catchwords 'wisdom' and 'freedom,' which Paul had introduced, can also be felt to lead in the same direction."[5] These word choices by the apostle lead the reader into the isagogical issues surrounding the letter.

Other commentators such as Gregory Lockwood take Conzelmann's thoughts further, suggesting that Stoicism and Epicureanism may have been the real combatants. Seeing that Acts 17:18 says that Epicurean and Stoic philosophers spoke with Paul in Athens, it is reasonable to think that these teachings would have been prevalent in Corinth. Lockwood explains: "Epicureanism encouraged the pursuit of pleasure and tranquility, and the avoidance of pain, passions, and superstitious fears, especially the fear of death."[6]

Concerning Stoicism, Lockwood says, "At its worst, it [stoicism] fostered a spiritual pride and (like Epicureanism) a self-centered individualism totally antithetical to the Christian emphasis on the body of Christ, whose members built each other up in love."[7] For the topic at hand, is it possible to connect modern scholarship's premise that Paul is addressing Epicurean, Stoic, and Sophist thought with his use of the Old Testament? Put in missiological terms, the question then becomes: If the apostle is addressing these philosophies by using Old Testament typology, does this give us insight into how we do mission work today? Indeed, the early creedal formulations of the gospel compel the reader to view the Old Testament through the creedal lens. This distinctively Christian hermeneutic is what this essay intends to explore.

PAUL'S USE OF THE OLD TESTAMENT

To the missionary student, Paul may seem perplexing. Often in missionary writings one is told to adjust to the context of the mission field, and to a large extent this is correct. While archaeological findings tell us

2. Hans Conzelmann, _1 Corinthians_ (Philadelphia, PA: Fortress Press, 1978), 15.
3. Conzelmann, _1 Corinthians_, 15.
4. Conzelmann, _1 Corinthians_, 15.
5. Conzelmann, _1 Corinthians_, 16.
6. Gregory Lockwood, _1 Corinthians_ (St. Louis: Concordia Publishing House, 2000), 6.
7. Lockwood, _1 Corinthians_, 7.

that there were Jews in Corinth, nevertheless Corinth was in the midst of the Greek world and dominated by Greek culture. However, in spite of the prevailing Greek culture in Corinth, a careful study of 1 Corinthians proffers evidence of an epistle that brings in many Old Testament thoughts and ideas. The question then arises: Why would Paul use so much Old Testament imagery in a Greek context? If we look at the evidence, perhaps we can begin to piece together the apostle's purpose.

1 CORINTHIANS 1:18—3:23

Paul opens his letter appealing for unity in the church (1:10–17) and then proceeds to speak against factionalism. Richard B. Hays explains: "The first major unit of the letter (1:18—4:21) is directed, as recent studies have convincingly demonstrated, against the Corinthians' infatuation with popular sophistic rhetoric and against their resultant arrogance and competitiveness. The expression σοφία λόγου in 1:17 refers to the eloquent rhetorical presentation of wisdom."[8] Paul responds by proclaiming "the word of the cross," which is the power of God. In verse 19 the apostle expounds the word of the cross with a quote from Isaiah 29:14: "I will destroy the wisdom of the wise, and the discernment of the discerning I will thwart" (1 Cor 1:19).[9] Paul reads the Isaiah passage as a reference to the wisdom of the cross. God's wisdom described in the Old Testament destroys the wisdom of the world's sophists.

The crux of Paul's discussion in this section includes many Old Testament passages. If we look at 1 Corinthians 1:19; 1:31; 2:9; 2:16; 3:19; and 3:20, we observe that these are all passages from the Old Testament that describe God as the One who judges and saves his people.[10] Paul's use of the Old Testament in connection with his explanation of the cross of Jesus Christ makes one wonder what Paul is trying to do. Perhaps the apostle is demonstrating the source of wisdom, that the roots of wisdom do not lie within man himself but within God and are found specifically in the Bible.

Paul is clearly teaching the church in Corinth that the root and source of wisdom come not from philosophers but from God Himself. Hays's remark helps us to see this:

> The threefold reference in 1 Corinthians 1:26 to the Corinthians' lowly status before their calling ("not many were wise [σοφοί] . . . , not many were powerful [δυνατοί], not many were of noble birth [εὐγενεῖς]") mirrors the threefold warning against boasting in Jer.

---

8. Richard B. Hays, "The Conversion of the Imagination: Scripture and Eschatology in 1 Corinthians," *New Testament Studies* 45, no. 3 (1999): 402.

9. See the LXX translation of Isaiah 29:14 and its reference to wisdom, which appears foundational for Paul in 1 Cor 1:19.

10. Hays, "The Conversion of the Imagination," 402–403.

9:22 LXX: "Let the wise man (σοφὸς) not boast in his wisdom, let the strong man (ἰσχυρὸς) not boast in his strength, and let the rich man (πλούσιος) not boast in his riches."[11]

If what Conzelmann, Lockwood, and Hays say is true, namely that Paul is speaking against Stoics, Epicureans, and Sophists, then these verses make sense. Paul is trying to get the Corinthians to forsake wisdom that originates within men and to get them to find wisdom in the Scriptures. This becomes clear in light of Paul's use of Old Testament texts such as Jeremiah 9:22–23.

1 CORINTHIANS 5:1–13

First Corinthians 5 is especially striking in the way Paul appeals to the book of Deuteronomy. St. Paul is specifically engaging immorality in the church. The Greek is particularly helpful for understanding Hays' point; 1 Corinthians 5:1 reads: "Ὅλως ἀκούεται ἐν ὑμῖν πορνεία, καὶ τοιαύτη πορνεία ἥτις οὐδὲ ἐν τοῖς ἔθνεσιν, ὥστε γυναῖκά τινα τοῦ πατρὸς ἔχειν." The apostle speaks of πορνεία which is not even seen among the ἔθνη. This is curious because the Corinthians are Gentiles.

The way Paul proceeds demonstrates how he views the church at Corinth. They are no longer ἔθνη if they are in Christ. So, according to Hays and Guy Prentiss Waters, Paul sees the Christian church at Corinth as Israel.[12] This would explain why Paul quotes Deuteronomy 17:7; 19:19; 22:21, 24; and 24:7. It is striking that Paul's language is nearly identical to the Deuteronomy passages in the Septuagint: ἐξάρατε τὸν πονηρὸν ἐξ ὑμῶν αὐτῶν. Hays's contention follows: "This analysis demonstrates once again that Paul thinks of his Gentile Corinthian readers as having been taken up into Israel in such a way that they now share in Israel's covenant privileges and obligations."[13] Paul instructs them as though they were Jews. They are, after all, the children of Abraham through faith.

1 CORINTHIANS 6:12–20

The apostle continues with concerns over the church's life as he addresses the issues associated with Corinthian confusion within the church. Paul engages the tangible aspects of Christian existence in terms of "glorifying God in one's body." Again, while being Christian, the Corinthians were melding their old ways with their newly found life in the church. Gregory Lockwood notes in his commentary:

---

11. Hays, "The Conversion of the Imagination," 404–405.
12. Guy Prentiss Waters, "Curse Redux? 1 Corinthians 5:13, Deuteronomy, and Identity in Corinth," *Westminster Theological Journal* 77 (2015): 237–250. This article provides a good treatment on this passage that delves further into the issue than Hays does.
13. Hays, "The Conversion of the Imagination," 411.

Another Corinthian slogan that may stem from Stoic or Cynic tendencies is Πάντα μοι ἔξεστιν ("all things are possible for me," 6:12; 10:23). According to the philosophers, the wise (σοφὸς) person enjoys autonomy and may do as he pleases. Hays notes that "in Epictetus there are numerous passages that discuss the freedom of the philosopher, using exactly the same verb [ἔξεστι] that Paul cites here."[14]

It is quite likely, considering the syncretism that was prevalent in Corinth, that the young Christians in Corinth may have tried to merge the freedom of the gospel with a license to do whatever they wanted to do in the name of freedom, merging Epicurean philosophies with Christian teaching. Freedom, according to our beloved apostle, was a reshaped identity; we are set free from the world's bonds and sin's tyranny as we become fastened and connected to the body of Christ and to one another. Concerning sexual relations, St. Paul elucidates on this new union. We are not free in the way the Epicureans thought, but we are set free to serve one another.

In terms of sexual relations, St. Paul quotes Genesis 2:24 in 1 Corinthians 6:16. Again, Paul takes them back to the Torah, and the Greek is similar. As Paul does elsewhere in this epistle, he gives the christological and ecclesiological weight to Genesis 2:24 in verses 15 and 16. He does not merely quote Genesis at length as if the information were unknown to his audience. Rather, Paul instructs the Corinthians concerning what it means to be σάρκα μίαν. Paul's use of Genesis 2:24 in this text is a wonderful example of the apostle's distinctive Christian hermeneutic. Paul writes as though the people have heard this before. They know the account.[15] Thus, Paul reads Genesis 2:24 through the words of Jesus in Matthew 19: "So they are no longer two but one flesh. What therefore God has joined together, let not man separate" (Matt 19:6). Jesus' conclusion, "let not man separate," is the very issue that concerns Paul and underlies his exhortation to the Corinthians forbidding fornication with a prostitute.

1 CORINTHIANS 10:1–33

First Corinthians 10 is also worthy of some attention. The numerous Old Testament references and allusions give one the opportunity to get a sense for how Paul catechized the Christians in Corinth. Lockwood

---

14. Lockwood, *1 Corinthians*, 8.

15. The use of the Greek in 1 Corinthians 6:12–20 is worth highlighting. In terms of the church's life and in consideration of what it means to have the gospel, the careful reader may note that when Paul writes and exhorts the church he does not think of the church as a disembodied reality. In verse 13, for example, Paul speaks of the belly, ἡ κοιλία. The κοιλία is for this world, but the σῶμα is for the Lord, i.e., for the life of holiness here and for the resurrection. Further, when Paul (and Moses) use σάρκα, it is used in a positive sense. Paul is suggesting that σὰρξ is equal to σῶμα in these verses.

considers the opening words of this chapter in this way: "The OT events Paul described in 1 Cor 10:1–5—God's gracious provision for Israel in the wilderness and his judgments on those who rebelled—depict for the Corinthians in a lively way that the God who has called them into communion with his Son (1:9) is the same God."[16] The opening words to the chapter are striking: "I do not want you to be ignorant, brothers, that all *our* fathers were under the cloud and all passed through the sea."[17] Paul recounts the history of Israel in the Torah. Writing to people who are likely of Gentile background, Paul identifies the Corinthian church as children of those fathers who were under the cloud and passed through the sea.

The opening verses remind the reader of several accounts from Moses' writings. Paul demonstrates the centrality of these accounts in verse 6 when he uses the word τύποι, "types." These people are part of God's narrative that teaches about the life of God's people and what happens as a result of sin. By speaking of the fathers of Israel as "types," Paul establishes an intimate familial connection between Israel and the church at Corinth. Consequently, the accounts found in the Torah are immediately applicable to the Corinthian Christians. These chronicles of Israel teach the young church about living the Christian life. What happens when people ignore God's hand, grumble, and fall into sin? One can see what happens in the narrative of the Old Testament, which records God's instruction, admonition, discipline, mercy, and love.

The reader of today, in 1 Corinthians 10:7, is given a clue into Paul's way of bringing the mission of the church to the Corinthian world. It reads: "Do not practice idolatry as some of them did; as it is written: 'The people sat down to eat and drink, and they rose up to have fun.'"[18] Our apostle is thinking of Exodus 32:6, but he does not elaborate, because his readers already know the story. Paul moves onward quickly and reminds them of Numbers 25:1 and 9, as well as Numbers 21:5–6. Paul's exhortation contains one Old Testament account after another, but with a fluidity that demonstrates that the people are accustomed to recounting the narratives. Paul's writing indicates that the Corinthians know these accounts intimately and thoroughly.

Paul continues in verse 10 speaking about "the destroyer." The Greek word, ὀλοθρευτοῦ, is used in the Septuagint in Exodus 12:23 describing the account of the Passover in Egypt and the death of the firstborn. Paul uses this Old Testament reference with theological intent to remind the church that the destroyer continues to work in situations other than with the killing of the firstborn in Egypt.

---

16. Lockwood, *1 Corinthians*, 331.
17. Emphasis and translation mine.
18. Translation mine.

Specifically, in verse 11, Paul says again that these things are "types"; yet, this time he uses a different form of the word, τυπικῶς. Paul focuses on these Old Testament figures by using the word ἐκείνοις, meaning "those," as in "those from antiquity laid out as types for us." Paul speaks of these types as "for our learning," our "admonition." These Old Testament figures and the people of Israel are intended to be objects of instruction (catechesis) for the church.

Paul effortlessly weaves together Old Testament language in order to instruct the church concerning one's proper participation in table fellowship. Hays reminds the reader:

> The Pentateuchal imagery is not confined to vv. 1-13; Paul sustains it through v. 22. The phrase "they sacrificed to demons and not to God" (10:20) is taken directly from the Song of Moses in Deut. 32:17 (and thus it refers, contrary to many English translations, not to 'pagans' but to unfaithful Israel), and Paul's rhetorical question in 10:22 loudly echoes the language of Deut. 32:21: "Or shall we provoke the Lord to jealousy [παραζηλοῦμεν]?"[19]

Paul brings the point back in verse 29 to the Epicurean, Stoic, and Sophistic philosophies that are prevalent among the people. He reminds them of "freedom" and how one's freedom should not destroy the conscience of others. Paul's missionary fervor can be seen in the latter part of this chapter as he shows concern for the conscience of others. How does one live? All should be done "for the glory of God" (1 Cor 10:31). Paul instructs the church through Scripture in order that the church may better understand her life in the world. This leads us to consider the same missionary approach in our contemporary Western culture.

1 CORINTHIANS 14:25

Richard B. Hays emphasizes Paul's view of the church as Israel, especially as it relates to eschatology. Hays comments: "We have become so thoroughly accustomed to thinking of Paul as 'Apostle to the Gentiles' that we may be in danger of overlooking what this self-designation suggests: Paul understood himself as a Jew sent by the God of Israel to the world of Gentile 'outsiders' for the purpose of declaring to them the message of eschatological salvation promised in Israel's scriptures—pre-eminently Isaiah—to the whole world."[20] According to Hays, 1 Corinthians is written to teach the Corinthian church to think eschatologically and to reshape her identity in light of Israel's Scripture.[21]

---

19. Hays, "The Conversion of the Imagination," 400.
20. Hays, "The Conversion of the Imagination," 394.
21. Hays, "The Conversion of the Imagination," 396.

Paul's interest in Isaiah is seen throughout his epistles. Köstenberger offers the remarkable insight that Paul's missionary journeys are not done by randomly picking towns where he wants to vacation. Rather, according to Köstenberger, Paul follows Isaiah 66:18–20.[22] In addition, Paul quotes Isaiah 28:11–12 and Deuteronomy 28:49 in 1 Corinthians 14:21; for Paul, these Old Testament texts prophesy an eschatological reality that is realized in the church's liturgy. Finally, Paul's description of faith and salvation in 1 Corinthians 14:25 is likewise couched in Old Testament references. Conzelmann suggests concerning τὰ κρυπτὰ (the secrets): "Conversion is strictly speaking a work of the Spirit; it becomes manifest in adoration."[23]

Paul's language in 1 Corinthians 14:25 is strikingly reminiscent of 1 Kings 18:39: "And when all the people saw it, they fell on their faces and said, 'The Lord, he is God; the Lord, he is God.'" Perhaps Paul's instruction in verses 20–23 concerning speaking in different tongues and his exhortation to them to be "infants in evil" (1 Cor 14:20) intend to remind them of 1 Kings 18, in which the prophets of Baal are slaughtered and God's people bow down in worship. It is redolent of Elijah's words: "How long will you go limping between two different opinions? If the Lord is God, follow him; but if Baal, then follow him" (1 Kings 18:21). If one pays attention to the tapestry of Old Testament references in Paul's words, a progression reveals itself from prophecy (1 Cor 14:24) to the disclosing of the secrets of hearts (1 Cor 14:25), which in turn leads to worship where one finds that God acts, i.e., that "God is among you" (1 Cor 14:25).

WHAT PAUL'S USE OF THE OLD TESTAMENT MEANS FOR THE MISSIONARY TODAY

A cursory read of Paul's use of the Old Testament may be met with a desultory response. We, after all, are used to the Old Testament. We may not see anything brilliant about its use. A more careful contemplation of Paul's word usage seems to suggest that, though he is writing to a Gentile audience, he sees them as being a part of the true, spiritual Israel. They are the "children of Abraham," and therefore they are not Gentiles. Through faith, they are people of the Scriptures, specifically the Old Testament Scriptures.

Paul's ease in using the Old Testament and the close association of his language with that of the Septuagint indicates that he actively catechized through Old Testament accounts. The church at Corinth knew these ac-

---

22. Andreas J. Köstenberger and Peter T. O'Brien, *Salvation to the Ends of the Earth: A Biblical Theology of Mission* (Downers Grove, IL: Intervarsity Press, 2001), 180.

23. Conzelmann, *1 Corinthians*, 243.

counts, for Paul was reminding the Corinthians of them. This teaches us that Paul and the Christians of Corinth did not regard the Scriptures as dead history. They were alive and offered insight into the church's present life. The Old Testament possesses a didactic quality that leads the church to Jesus Christ.

Since Paul begins the epistle by talking about the "foolishness of the cross," it is only natural to recognize that Paul saw the cross in the Old Testament. Jesus was everywhere in the Old Testament. The church is everywhere in the Old Testament. The instruction contained in the Old Testament speaks to the life of holiness and the threat of judgment today. We are to conclude, then, that the church's life was largely focused on listening to the Scriptures and knowing them.

It would be easy to conclude, like so many do today in mission endeavors, that Paul only needed to fit within the Corinthian context, to let the gospel take shape in that peculiar setting, and to forget the Israel side of the equation. Paul could have easily framed his arguments in language that was different or more relevant to the Greek context. But he chose to teach the Corinthians the Old Testament and to remind them of it. The Old Testament belonged to the church. It is the church's narrative. Truthfully, Paul's perspective is demonstrated in his words, which speak of being "called out of the world," "a new creation," etc. In baptism, the people were stripped of the old world, the old national identity, that they had previously possessed. They now truly belonged to a new homeland; they have left their biological fathers and the world's philosophies in order to be defined by the teachings and life of God's people.

What purpose does Paul's emphasis on the Old Testament mean for missionary activity to the modern and postmodern Western world? Fundamentally, missionaries must teach the church's identity. This is a task that must be treated with great care. Truly, the Western culture today is gravitating towards "tribalism," or "indigenization."[24] This is becoming evident in the secular realm; examples of such indigenization are found in groups such as "Black Lives Matter," "LGBT," and other minority groups coming into America who want to hold onto their culture and resist entering the "great melting pot" of America. Because of modernism's tendency to homogenize everything and everyone, we are seeing a reaction towards this indigenization.[25]

---

24. For a good discussion of indigenization in our Western world, see Carl Raschke, *GloboChrist: The Great Commission Takes a Postmodern Turn* (Grand Rapids, MI: Baker Academic, 2008), 39.

25. The recent decision by Great Britain to leave the European Union, popularly known as Brexit, is yet another Western example of the coming rejection of homogenization. There is a desire to return to one's roots, to recover one's unique identity. While there are many variables for Brexit, the yearning for indigenization should not be ignored.

When the missionary enters the mission field, he must recognize this cultural dynamic of indigenization. Humanity's fallen nature resists being gathered into a body formed in love and mercy. The sinful human condition is inclined toward individualism and fragmentation. This poses a challenge for the missionary; yet there is also great promise if the missionary is able to demonstrate that the church's identity brings its own banner, which Christ holds as he steps out of the tomb of death. The missionary has a great opportunity in the Western world—this ubersecular culture, this overly individualistic culture—to show the love of the Christian family and to demonstrate the church's roots in the Old Testament, finding meaning and centrality in Jesus.

As a culture, we consider ourselves free, autonomous, and in control. In an article by Janice Shaw Crouse, this dynamic is said to be a detriment: "Indeed, a spirit of independence can be a barrier that impedes sharing. Aloofness is the opposite of all of the favorable ingredients necessary for camaraderie. Likewise, pride—the desire to be viewed as a 'winner,' the determination to be 'in control' at all costs—is a quality that isolates us from each other and keeps us from interdependency with our family and friends."[26]

The missionary has ample opportunity to show the heritage of the church, the communal life of the body of Christ, and the identity that is framed in the love and mercy of Jesus. The missionary can and should bring the church's distinct character to those who are looking for identity and still falling short. If anything, this secular emphasis on tribalism provides opportunities. The church's catholicity and creedal life can be demonstrated while exhibiting her unique character in the neighborhood in which she finds her life. The missionary should pay close attention to what St. Paul was doing. He was showing the weaknesses of the Epicurean, Stoic, and Sophistic identities. He was drawing the Corinthians into their newly found identity while pulling them out of their old national background. Paul's emphasis and direction in catechesis—teaching the Old Testament—reminds us of our task today.

CONCLUSION

One of the things that I find remarkable about St. Paul is his depth of wisdom in using the Old Testament. We do not often think about Paul's human considerations towards his own apostolic task. He was a human being like the rest of us, and he had to make decisions and think about how he would address the challenges before him. The challenges that

26. Janice Shaw Crouse, "The Loneliness of American Society," *The American Spectator* (blog), May 18, 2014, http://spectator.org/59230_loneliness-american-society/

the Corinthians brought before him were many! Paul's own meditations on Jesus and his apostolic mission compelled him, a Pharisee who was well-studied under Gamaliel, to think deeply about the Old Testament.

Paul's wisdom and understanding of Jesus and the Old Testament made him a missionary who wisely and with care shepherded the churches he planted. 1 Corinthians is a wonderful piece of Holy Scriptures whereby the Lord used Paul to draw the Christians in Corinth into a new identity grounded in Christ. Receiving this new identity, they could not continue to identify themselves with the world's pedigree. Christ has his own pedigree.

Our task as missionaries is to learn from Paul as we seek to bring the cross of Christ to a culture and a time that seems so alien and unfamiliar. The reality is that the Scriptures have provided us with what we need. If we are willing to be as immersed in the Scriptures as Paul was, then we too will be blessed with the great pearls in the Scriptures that will guide us in our own missionary endeavors to the nations. ✝

PART TWO

THEOLOGIA

OSWALD BAYER AND THE
THEOLOGY OF PROMISES

✦

Theologians advancing Gerhard Forde's Theology of the Cross have found a friend in University of Tübingen emeritus professor and prominent Luther scholar, Oswald Bayer (b. 1939). Bayer's writings are regularly cited by Forde's disciples and often appear along with theirs in the *Lutheran Quarterly* and its monographs.[1] A fundamental influence on Bayer was the British philosopher John L. Austin. Bayer believed that certain aspects in Austin's understanding of language were similar to Luther and could help explain how the Reformer came to his great discovery on justification by faith. Austin's speech act theory divides words into two categories. *Constative* utterances correspond to past events and might be described as informative statements about things that have happened. In contrast, *performative* words bring about or create relations that did not previously exist. This category interests Bayer who says that performative speech "does not refer to a preexisting situation whose existence the sentence merely reveals. Rather, it constitutes and creates a relationship and incorporates features that are both personal and objective."[2] Interpreting early Luther's writings in light of Austin's speech act theory and in connection with the category of performative speech, Bayer hopes to develop a previously unrecognized aspect in the Reformer's theology, namely, that spoken words have a bodily, *leiblich*,[3] aspect and, hence, an objective

1. *Justification Is for Preaching: Essays by Oswald Bayer, Gerhard O. Forde, and Others*, ed. Virgil Thompson (Minneapolis, MN: Lutheran Quarterly Books, 2012). Among the other contributors are Robert Kolb and Steven Paulson. *Living by Faith* is already available, and forthcoming is *Promissio: The Story of the Reformation Turn in Luther's Theology*. Fortress Press provides publishing services for *Lutheran Quarterly*. Articles by Bayer published in *Lutheran Quarterly* include "Justification," *Lutheran Quarterly* 34/3 (Autumn 2010): 337–340; 'God's Hiddenness,' *Lutheran Quarterly* 38/3 (Autumn 2014): 266–279; "Trust," *Lutheran Quarterly* 39/3 (Autumn 2015): 245–261; "The Relationship between Theology and Nature Sciences," *Lutheran Quarterly* 31/2 (Summer 2017): 150–171.

2. Oswald Bayer, *Theology the Lutheran Way*, ed. and trans. Jeffrey G. Silcock (Grand Rapids, MI: Wm. B. Eerdmans, 2007), 126–128.

3. Oswald Bayer, *Living by Faith: Justification and Sanctification*, trans. Geoffrey W. Bromiley (Grand Rapids, MI: Wm. B. Eerdmans, 2003), 47. "From the very beginning human

character.[4] The preached or proclaimed word, particularly in absolution, relieves a believer of having to justify himself, that is, of proving himself to himself, others and God. So, for Bayer, justification has a psychological, liberating affect that in the promises "Christ is present: definite and clear—clearly freeing one and giving one assurance. One cannot remember achieving such freedom and assurance in one's own private, inner monologue."[5] Bayer sees justification not only as one locus in theology but as the overarching one that is applicable even to God and creation.[6]

In a typical dogmatic arrangement, discussion of a system's foundational principle is placed in the prolegomena, i.e., how the theologian comes to know the truth and how the rest of theology flows from this principle.[7] In classical Lutheranism, Scripture is the source of theology, an idea expressed by the Latin *sola scriptura*. Revelation, how God reveals himself, follows the prolegomena in the dogmatic sequence and is often included in it. In classical Lutheran dogmatics, the doctrines of God, creation, and sin are followed by the locus on the person and work of Christ as the God-Man, whose death as an atonement for sin allows God to justify the sinner without offending his moral character. Essential to the classical Lutheran view of the atonement is the incarnation, especially the *genus apotelesmaticum*.[8] "The unified agency of both natures within the unity of Christ's person means that each nature participates in the act of redemption."[9] By the incarnation, Christ's human nature is given

speech is permeated by physicality . . . We are not rational beings first of all; we are primarily speaking beings. Because this is so, we can understand that the deed of God occurs as word and the word as deed. As speaking beings, we can understand the references to God's 'bodily Word,' as in Article V of the Augsburg Confession." Bayer sees AC V, and not AC IV, as determinative for interpreting the confession, as discussed below.

4. Oswald Bayer, *Theology the Lutheran Way*, 125. "In what follows, we will concentrate on this crucial way in which God speaks to us and will consider the unique objectivity of the promise (*promissio*) from the standpoint of hermeneutics and the philosophy of science. Its objectivity of course cannot be understood in a positivistic sense, as if it were a scientific datum open to empirical verification. But, on the other hand, neither can we go to the other extreme in surrendering the objectivity of the promise on the grounds that God and faith are not objective realities that we can grasp but are inaccessible and beyond our reach, as the disciples of Kant maintained, especially in dialectical theology." Compare Steven D. Paulson's *Forward* in Joshua C. Miller, *Hanging by a Promise: The Hidden God in the Theology of Oswald Bayer* (Eugene, OR: Pickwick Publications, 2017), xi. When Bayer speaks of the "incarnate word", he is referring to "the 'external word' of promise," and not the creed's "*incarnatus est de spiritu sancto*" by which the Son of God, the second person of the Trinity, takes up flesh in the Virgin Mary.

5. Oswald Bayer, *Martin Luther's Theology: A Contemporary Interpretation*, trans. Thomas H. Trapp (Grand Rapids, MI: Wm. B. Eerdmans, 2008), 53.

6. Bayer, *Theology the Lutheran Way*, 103–105; Paulson, "Forward," xi. So also, is the observation of Paul Rorem, Forward, Bayer, *Living by Faith*, x and Bayer himself, xiii.

7. Again, Bayer, *Theology the Lutheran Way*, 138. "Our thesis is that the gospel, understood as a particular speech act, is itself the ground of faith. Since the 'essence of Christianity' is a speech act, it must be illuminated, not primarily by an analysis of existence, but by an analysis of language." As discussed below, Bayer makes use of linguistic philosophy of John L. Austin.

8. Jack D. Kilcrease, *The Doctrine of the Atonement: From Luther to Forde* (Eugene, OR: Wipf & Stock, 2017), 47–48, 56–58.

9. Kilcrease, *The Doctrine of the Atonement*, 59–60.

an infinite value so that his death is received by God as a payment or redemption for all sin and all are justified (universal justification). Bayer makes no pretense to follow the classical Lutheran model.

Bayer's foundational principle is justification which, for him, takes place in hearing and accepting God's promises.[10] He does not accept the traditional Lutheran view that the Bible is the formal principle of theology and justification the material principle. Instead, he combines them into one. "In this understanding of the gospel Luther never *formally* answers the question of the authority of the oral, bodily Word in relation to that of the written word of the Bible. Instead, he offers a very *material* answer by pointing out that the preached word that comes to us by the word of mouth is Jesus Christ himself now present with us."[11] One looks in vain for a discussion on the atonement or a citation in the table of contents and indices of his books. He avoids treating the great atonement passages such as Mt 20:28; 26:28; Mk 29:45; Mk 14:24; especially significant is his neglect of Heb 9:12, in which Christ as the great high priest entered the holy of holies with his blood to offer an eternal redemption. This is hardly a slight defect.

Bayer wants to distance himself from the neoorthodox existential understanding of the word of God as advocated by Karl Barth and Rudolph Bultmann.[12] He attempts to distinguish himself from them by offering an objective, substantive, bodily, *leiblich,* understanding of the word of God. Objectivity lies in the word and not outside of it. "Our thesis is that the gospel, understood as a particular speech act, is itself the ground of faith. Since the 'essence of Christianity' is a speech act, it must be illuminated, not primarily by an analysis of existence, but by an analysis of language."[13] Barth proposes that revelation takes place when the believer encounters the preached or proclaimed word of God. This resembles Bayer's view that justification, that is, the believer's awareness that he is justified, takes place in hearing and accepting the promise. Faith becomes the revelatory moment in which the hearer accepts the promise and finds himself at peace with himself, God and all of creation. Until then, the individual is in a state of trying to justify himself.[14] Whether this is really so for everyone is an assumption that never seems to be proven. Personal experience may prove otherwise. Bayer does not identify the Bible with the word of God at least in the sense that the proclaimed word

---

10. For an easy-to-understand description of how Bayer sees the relation between the oral and written word, see his section "Word and Authority of the Bible," in *Living by Faith,* 47–50.

11. Oswald Bayer, *Living by Faith,* 49.

12. Bayer, *Theology the Lutheran Way,* 116, 119. In being bound to the biblical text, Bayer distinguishes himself from Bultmann for whom existence takes precedence over the biblical text.

13. Bayer, *Theology the Lutheran Way,* 138.

14. Bayer, *Justification and Sanctification,* 1–4.

is. This has an uncanny resemblance to Barth that the proclaimed word takes precedence over the Scriptures as the word of God and is the basis of theology.[15] Bayer gives this idea a Lutheran twist:

> Scripture cannot be normative in a formal sense. Rather, *its authority consists in that it works faith*. The Lutheran tradition has articulated this in such a way that its *auctoritas normativa* follows from its *auctoritas causativa*—because of the authority that it has to create faith.[16]

In other words, Scripture's authoritative character is derived from its function in working faith.

Now if what Bayer proposes is so, the word of God could not pronounce any authoritative judgment where it had not effected faith, that is, among those who do not believe. The tail is wagging the dog. Bayer argues from what the word effects to what it is. At a more basic level, this argument is circular where the thing serves as the evidence or the proof of itself. In dogmatic terms, Bayer's perspective is called *fideism*. The Scriptures are self-authenticating, requiring no external proofs, a view not uncommon among the conservatives. For Bayer the bodily word is proof of itself. Like Barth, Bayer does not engage in historical criticism. Like Barth, Bayer's position can be called a 'theology of the word,' because it does not go behind the word to look for external authority. Jesus Christ is the authority in the sense that he is present in the word which is self-contained and not subject to external critique.

Bayer holds up the Old Testament figure of Job, who in the dilemma of his being forsaken sought to justify himself, complaining about how God dealt with him. Similarly, Christ thought that God had dealt with him unfairly, and he struggled against what God was doing to him.[17] Justification is seen as a struggle of the believer with God, just as it was for Christ, over what at the time appeared as untenable circumstances. Bayer has a point; however, he sees these circumstances existentially and fails to recognize that in these struggles, the believer, like Christ, recognizes the hand of God. Thus, he does not take into account that

---

15. Karl Barth, *Christian Dogmatics I: The Doctrine of the Word God Prolegomena to Christian Dogmatics. Part I*, Second Edition, ed. and trans. G. W. Bromiley and ed. T. F. Torrance (Edinburgh: T. & T. Clark, 1975). Barth speaks of three forms of the word of God: preached (88–99), written (99–111), revealed (111–120). "Proclamation must ever and again become proclamation" (88).

16. Bayer, *Martin Luther's Theology*,77.

17. Bayer, *Theology the Lutheran Way*, 207. "Because the church has not understood the importance of complaint, its understanding of the life of Jesus has often suffered from distortion. The passages in the New Testament that are decisive for Christology, the temptation of Jesus, his prayer in Gethsemane as he struggled over the cup of suffering, and his crucifixion, have all been robbed of their emotion and passion under the influence of Stoicism; the same has happened to the miracle stories with their emphasis on Jesus' compassion; see Mark 1:41."

Christ, Job, and the believer rightly expect and receive vindication. The cry of dereliction (Ps 22:1) concludes with the confidence that God comes to the aid of his saints (vv. 24–31). Believers are "looking to Jesus the founder and perfecter of our faith, who for the joy that was set before him endured the cross, despising the shame, and is seated at the right hand of the throne of God" (Heb 12:2).[18] Bayer advances his program, not primarily with biblical arguments, but with Luther's understanding of justification, which was the topic of both his doctoral dissertation and his *Habilitationsschrift*, the more scholarly advanced dissertation. As a Luther scholar, he uses words familiar to Lutherans, such as "promise," "justification," and "word."

Apart from the viability of incorporating Austin's speech-act concept into his theological proposal, Bayer opens himself up to critique with his theory that Luther's great Reformation discovery came as he evaluated Augustine's view of penance. According to Bayer, Luther rejected Augustine's belief that the priest pronounced absolution because he saw that the penitent was already contrite.[19] Absolution did not bring about a change in the one confessing his sins, but only recognized the change that had already taken place. It was, in Austin's terms, *constative* speech, recognizing what was already there. The absolution did not bring about a new relationship or state of affairs between God and the believer. A task for scholars is determining whether Bayer's philosophically informed proposal does justice to Luther.

Bayer's claim that his proposal represents Luther is not unique and does not make it so. Any number of similar theological proposals have been offered beginning with the Enlightenment. Since he acknowledges his use of the speech-act theory as proposed by John L. Austin and Ludwig Wittgenstein, Bayer's readers have to ask whether the speech-act philosophy of language is compatible with confessional Lutheranism. Perhaps even more importantly, readers should ask whether or not it allows for an acceptable method of biblical theology. As it defines itself, speech-act theory does not address past events and so it cannot speak of God's participation in history, for example in the incarnation, miracles, and the resurrection. Speech-act theory does not require the hearer or reader to go behind or beyond the word to a *something* or a *someone* in particular time and place. The spoken word creates the event and is the event itself.

In using philosophy to interpret theology, Bayer is not unique. Yet, the question remains: is speech-act theory compatible with Christianity and Lutheranism in particular? It may not be true, as Paul Tillich

18. Unless indicated otherwise, all quotations from Holy Scripture are from the ESV.
19. Bayer, *Martin Luther's Theology*, 52.

claimed, that theology should be entrusted to answer philosophical questions. Nevertheless, theology must answer those particular philosophical questions that have made their way into the church posing as theological questions, which they are not. It is not saying too much that every doctrinal aberration beginning with Gnosticism and Arianism has a philosophical origin. The Platonic based *finitum non capax infiniti* still prevents Reformed theology from adhering to a robust doctrine of the incarnation and the Lord's Supper. So, in a way, philosophy makes the theological clock tick. Thus, one of the theologian's tasks is to recognize these aberrant philosophical elements. Already during Luther's lifetime, his emphasis on freedom in the gospel was received as a political manifesto and stoked the Anabaptist rebellions. Recruiting Luther in support of new theological insights is what theologians have done since the Reformation and continues in the present. In making use of philosophy, Bayer is hardly unique, and his arguments have to be judged on their own merits.[20]

Choosing justification as a foundational theological principle, as Bayer has done is not without its problems. Bishop Hans Lilje, a former president of the Lutheran World Federation (LWF), noted that Lutherans were unable to come even close to agreement on justification at its 1963 Helsinki convention.[21] It was hoped that the Reformation quincentennial in 2017 would produce clarification of what Luther believed. Instead, Luther studies appear to have gotten worse, going from diversity to downright confusion.[22] Lack of agreement on one or another doctrine would matter little, except that justification, like no other doctrine, defines who Lutherans are and what they believe. In the case of Bayer, it is the foundational doctrine, even for understanding creation.[23] In spite of their disagreements, Lutherans are virtually unanimous in holding up justification as the center of theology and so Bayer's approach has a built-in attraction that we are really dealing with Luther. Scholars are not agreed on whether Luther said that justification is the doctrine by which the church stands or falls or under what circumstances he may have said it. Luther also spoke glowingly of baptism, the Lord's Supper and, perhaps, other doctrines depending on the circumstances.

---

20. Kilcrease shows how this is done by Werner Elert, Gustaf Aulen, Wolfhart Panneberg, Robert Jenson, Eberhard Jungel and Gerhard Forde in his *The Doctrine of Atonement: From Luther to Forde*, 79–165.

21. David P. Scaer, *The Lutheran World Federation Today*, 15.

22. For the frustrating results to the Reformation celebration, see my "Will the Real Martin Luther Stand Up?", 281–297.

23. Bayer, *Living by Faith*, xiii–xiv. "When the article on justification, as suggested in this tractate, is understood in a sense so broad and deep as to encompass even creation and the eschaton, then it does not suffice to speak of this article merely as the *articulus stantis et cadentis ecclesiae*, the article upon which the *church* stands or falls. *Creatio ex nihilo* (creation out of nothing), the basis of the Jewish and Christian doctrine of creation, is to be understood in terms of the theology of justification—and vice versa. God is obliged neither to create and preserve the world nor to forgive sin."

In confronting Bayer's understanding of justification, it is helpful to consider the provincial twentieth century controversy in the LCMS concerning the historical character of the Bible. Both sides in the dispute were agreed that justification, that is, the law and the gospel, was the central Lutheran doctrine without recognizing that they did not agree on its definition. At that time, Rudolph Bultmann was influential with the St. Louis faculty and saw justification as authentic existence. Bayer also has a psychological component in his understanding of justification. He locates objective reality in the promise of justification. Bayer's definition of justification resembles Barth's in avoiding historical criticism of the gospels. From the beginning of his proposal, Bayer raises a red flag when he claims to find parallels in Luther to Wittgenstein's and Austin's theory of language, namely, that the word itself is the event.

Bayer holds that justification provides the certainty of salvation and is the origin and goal of theology. Then he goes one step further and sees self-justification as the overarching reality of all existence. Self-justification determines everyone's personal reality, Christian or not. In all kinds of situations people are justifying themselves.[24] In making this assumption, Bayer has moved the doctrine of justification from its traditional place in Lutheran dogmatics as God's benevolent response to Christ's atoning sacrifice of himself for sin and placed it at the forefront of his program. Each person's desire to be justified replaces the fundamental question of whether God exists and who he is. Justification is not merely one truth into and under which everything else is subsumed.[25] It becomes the standard, by which all other doctrines and practices are normed. Sin is reduced down to the refusal to accept God's word of justification.[26]

In Bayer's proposal, word or promise becomes the basis of the certainty of faith. He presents this proposal within the context of philosophies he finds unacceptable. Bayer recognizes Immanuel Kant's arguments dismantling the certainty of eighteenth century Enlightenment Rationalism that maintained the ability of the mind or the intellect to grasp and to interpret the external, physical world. In place of the discredited external proofs for religion and morality, Kant substituted the moral impera-

---

24. Bayer lays out this program of trust or faith as an overarching reality in "Trust," *Lutheran Quarterly* 29/3 (Autumn 2015) 249–261. For an easy to read overview of how justification determines all of personal reality, see also Bayer, *Living by Faith*, 1–3, e.g., "To be recognized and justified, to cause ourselves to be justified or to justify ourselves in attitude, thought, word, and action; to need to justify our being; or simply to be allowed to exist without needing to justify our being—all this makes for our happiness or unhappiness and is an essential part of our humanity" (p 2).

25. Oswald Bayer, See "Trust," *Lutheran Quarterly* 24/3: 249–261.

26. Bayer, "Trust," 255, "The original temptation, which confronts the human and surges up in him and finds approval, is not to trust God's promise to grant all good and to rescue him in every need, but instead to protect himself radically, to take the root of his existence into his own hands and thereby deny his created and finite nature, and instead to want to be his own creator."

tive that each person had within himself. Friedrich D. E. Schleiermacher built on Kant's subjectivism and proposed consciousness as the source of religious truth and knowledge of God. This philosophical paradigm dominated European Protestant theology until the rise of neorthodoxy led by Karl Barth and Emil Brunner at the end of World War I.

Opposed to Kant's subjectivism on the philosophical spectrum was G. W. F. Hegel who proposed that history was self-revelatory, a philosophical theory fundamental for Karl Marx.[27] In a way this is a return to the old Rationalism that attributed to human reason a confidence in interpreting the world. Bayer wants to steer a middle route between the subjectivity exhibited by Kant and Schleiermacher and an objectivity that can be universally grasped by the mind. For him the word with its promises is the object of faith by which a person is justified. Faith is directed to the word with the promise of God and not to something or someone behind it. The word does not derive its reality from outside of itself. Instead of a *constative* word that informs about something in the past, God's proclamation is a *performative* word doing what it promises.

In *Promissio: Geschichte der refromatischen Wende in Luthers Theologie*, Bayer describes how Luther in 1518 came to this new understanding.[28] Until then, Luther understood justification according to the Augustinian view widely held in medieval Catholicism, namely, that God sees the penitential heart of the believer and finds cause to justify him.[29] In 1518, Luther came to the forensic view of justification that God declares the sinner justified. Bayer argues that the turning point for Luther—what he calls the *die reformatischen Wende in Luthers Theologie*—was his struggle with the medieval Catholic doctrine of penance (*Bussakrament*), which consisted in contrition (sorrow), confession (articulation of sins) and satisfaction (works assigned by the priest).[30] Luther's discovery began when he took issue with the Augustinian view that justification happens within the believer. The promise given in absolution (*promissio absolutionis*) and faith in that promise became foundational for the Reformer's theology.

Before 1518, Luther held to the Augustinian view that the priest in absolving the penitent was merely recognizing that the penitent was al-

27. Kilcrease, *The Doctrine of Atonement: From Luther to Forde*, 87. Robert Jenson adopted certain aspects of Hegel's thought in that "God's activity in history is not really one of pure grace, but actually a means of self-development."

28. Oswald Bayer, *Promissio: Geschichte der reformatischen Wende in Luthers Theologie* (Gottingen: Vandenhoeck & Ruprecht, 1971). Its first part was presented as his doctoral dissertation in 1967 and the second part is his Habilitationsschrift, an advanced dissertation, in 1969 to the University of Bonn.

29. This view was advocated by the Reformation figure Andreas Osiander. It reappeared in America in the nineteenth and twentieth centuries and led to the disruption of the Synodical Conference of the Evangelical Lutheran Church. In the American version, God elects people to salvation *intuitu fidei*, in view of their faith or really because of it.

30. Bayer, *Promissio*, 165.

ready sorry for his sin. Absolution was "a declarative act, or to use Austin's language, a constative speech act, the priest sees the remorse, takes it as a sign of divine justification, the divine absolution that has already occurred in the penitent, without that person knowing it."[31] Until his discovery, absolution for Luther was a constative speech-act, only recognizing what already existed. After his discovery, Luther saw absolution as a performative speech-act bringing about a new state of affairs. It creates a relationship between the one in whose name it is spoken and the one who receives it and believes the promise. Such a speech-act establishes communication, liberates, and gives certainty. Luther calls it *"verbum efficax,"* an active and effective word, "in Austin's terminology, it is a performative speech-act."[32]

Justifying faith arises by trusting in the word as promise.[33] Bayer speaks of the subjective and objective elements of justification, terms familiar to readers of Pieper's *Christian Dogmatics.* However, for Bayer, objectivity rests in the promise, the orally spoken word, what he calls the *mündlichkeitdes Wortes,* and not in anything or anyone beyond or outside of it. Wyller describes Bayer's understanding of faith in this way: *"Glaube ist Vertrauen auf die promissio als Sprachhandlung* (Faith is trust in the promise as a speech act)."[34]

Here is the crucial point. In classical Christian theology, faith is not directed to a self-contained, autonomous word, proclaimed or written, as Bayer proposes. Rather, faith is directed to the thing, person or event, which is reported in the word and from which the saving character of the word is derived. The reported event is made present in the proclaimed or oral word without compromising its character as having happened in history. The apostles proclaimed what they had seen, heard and touched (1 Jn 1:1). Luke claims validity for his gospel from his interaction with those, especially the apostles, who had experienced the things in Jesus's life (Lk 1:1–4; Acts 1:21–23).

Bayer does speak of justification as taking place *extra nos,* but he is not referring to an event taking place in history like the crucifixion or the eternal moment of the atonement, what Lutheran Orthodoxy called objective justification as an inter-trinitarian act. Instead, he is referring to what happens when someone believes the word or promise. This idea is so essential to this theological program that Bayer should speak for himself.

31. Bayer, *Theology the Lutheran Way,* 129.
32. Bayer, *Theology the Lutheran Way,* 130.
33. Wyller, *Glaube und Autonome Welt,* 93. See p 93–101, a section that Wyller entitles "Promissio *Oswald Bayer as Luther-Forscher."* Wyller notes that ". . . Bayers Ausgangspunkt in der Kategorie der promissio [ist] notwendig. Sie ist der Eckstein seines gegenwärtigen systematisch-theologischen Denkens. Bayers Beschäftigung mit der Anredekategorie stammt aus seinen theologiegeschichtlichen Lutherstudien der sechziger Jahre," 93.
34. Wyller, *Glaube und Autonome Welt,* 94.

> In contradistinction to every metaphysical construct of the doctrine of God, God's truth and will therefore are not abstract properties but are a concrete promise, made orally and publicly, to a particular person in a particular situation. "God" is the one whose promise to us in the oral word is such that we can depend on him. God's truth lies in his faithfulness to the word that he speaks.[35]

As a phrase, this can be deceptively attractive to those who are accustomed to hearing preachers summon them to believe the word. However, it must be noted that faith for Bayer is directed not to a *something/someone behind* the word. Faith is not directed toward God's decisive actions in history, like the crucifixion or resurrection, from which the oral word receives its value. Neither does faith find its goal in God or in the person of Jesus of Nazareth, who, while certainly revealing himself through the word, nevertheless has an existence prior to and outside of the word. For Bayer, the theological task does not go behind the text "to a specific concept of human existence," neither does it "cling to the letters in a kind of biblicistic legalism as in theological positivism."[36] In order for Bible passages to be effective, Bayer holds they must be converted into "speech actions"[37] and this can be done by adding the words "for you." For Bayer, formative, constitutive, and declarative acts correspond to Luther's "the blessings of a promise, or faith, and of a gift." Such phrases as *word of absolution, absolve* and *absolving* are for Bayer examples of Austin's speech-acts. By placing the theological weight on the proclaimed word, Bayer has an obvious resemblance to Barth, who held "Finally—and only here do we make the decisive point—the Word of God is the event itself in which proclamation becomes real proclamation."[38]

Bayer holds that the turning point in the Reformation was Luther's redefinition of Augustine's understanding of absolution. However, in addition, Bayer maintains that Luther also questioned Augustine's distinction between the thing signified (called in Latin the *res*) and the sign or signification (called the *signum*). Whether or not Luther made use of it in his theology—and if he did, was this principal characteristic of his entire theology—the distinction between the thing (*res*) and the sign (*signum*)

---

35. Bayer, *Theology the Lutheran Way*, 130–131.
36. Bayer, *Theology the Lutheran Way*, 131. Bayer does not specify who he has in mind, but the last standing group are those who take constative approaches that what the Bible reports really happened, that is confessional Lutherans, Evangelicals and nearly all Catholics and Orthodox.
37. Bayer, *Theology the Lutheran Way*, 131, "In fact, theology is guided only by particular sentences, particular speech acts, none of which, it can be shown, has been chosen arbitrarily and none of which is derived from some principle behind the text. For the Bible itself is full of promises and sentences that can be easily converted into particular kinds of sentences and speech actions without doing violence to the texts."
38. Barth, *Christian Dogmatics I: The Doctrine of the Word God Prolegomens to Christian Dogmatics. Part I*, 93.

is not as easily dismissed as Bayer wants. This grammatical distinction is essential to how life is lived. A person may live on Main Street. However, these words, printed on a street sign or an envelope, are the sign or the *signum* but not the street itself. A particular paved street with houses on both sides is the real thing, the *res*. A newspaper is a collection of signs, *signa*, and the "what" are the things its articles report, the *res*. Written and oral reports, the *signa*, may only partially grasp the things as they are or were in themselves. Indeed, such reports may even distort the reality; but the thing (*res*) has an existence in itself that, contra Kant, can be grasped in some sense. A laboratory experiment would be an example of a *res* and the writing up of the experiment in a report would be the *signum*. As the experiment is repeated, the *signum* may have to be adjusted, but the *signum* and the *res* are not identified with each other. This distinction between the sign (*signum*) and the thing (*res*) is so essential to our social, intellectual, legal and financial lives that without it we could not make sense of them.

Let's assume that Bayer's *signum/res* is philosophically defensible—which it is not—and ask whether it is biblically applicable. As a book or collection of books, the Scriptures qualify as the *signa* and what they report are the *res*. They are not the *res*. Their words remain the *signa* and beckon the hearer to believe in the things (*res*) they report. What is to be believed are things which the words report, something that is made clear in the two endings to John's gospel (Jn 20:30–31; 21:24–25). What is true of the Scriptures is also true of preaching. Hearers trust that what is preached to them corresponds to the things of which the apostles were eyewitnesses (Acts 1:22). The things (*res*) preached give value to the proclamation (*signum*). The gospels, the four accounts of the life, death and resurrection of Jesus Christ, derive their authority from these events (*res*) as they are recorded by the authorized witness of the apostles (Acts 10:41). *Gospel*, as used in Matthew 26:12, Mark 1:1, Romans 15: 9, is more than the proclamation that sins are forgiven, a view essential to Bayer's theology. The gospel, even as the inspired word of God, does not exist as a self-contained autonomous proclamation of justification; rather, it originates in and from those acts in which God was active in Christ.

The distinction between signs (*signa*) and things (*res*) is part of the content and fiber of the Bible, as they are for life in general. One cannot be identified with the other as Bayer claims. The rainbow is the sign that God will not destroy the world by water. The two children promised in Isaiah 7 and 8 are signs pointing to the victory of God's people over their enemies. Swaddling clothes are the sign (*signum*) to the shepherds, identifying the child (*res*) who is Savior of the world. Jonah's release from the fish is a sign of Jesus' resurrection (Mt 12:29–30). The empty tomb is not equivalent to the resurrection but testifies to it. The sign is not the thing itself. Faith involves believing in the sign(s) without first coming face to face with the thing. One first encounters the claims (*signa*) made by and for Jesus of Nazareth and then he may or may not come to faith in him, the thing (*res*) (Jn 20:29).

Bayer claims that the *signum/res* relationship he finds in Luther is the same as what he finds in Ludwig Wittgenstein. "But Luther overcame the distinction [between the *signum* and the *res*] and in doing so shares something in common with the linguistic analysis of the later Wittgenstein."[39] For Luther, according to Bayer, the "thing" and "sign" become one as it was for Wittgenstein. "The speech act with the promise of forgiveness of sins in the name of Jesus is not an 'appearance' but the 'essence' itself."[40] According to him, both Luther and Wittgenstein believed that, "*Essence* is expressed by grammar."[41] Reality now is found in grammar, a discipline that has to do with the structure of language. While Bultmann and others, according to Bayer, "locates the original source of life" in the "pre-linguistic realm", Luther, in Bayer's view, begins "with the external word (*verbum externum*) in the sense of promise, understood as a speech act."[42] So for Bayer, "theology [is done] on the basis of linguistic analysis rather than the analysis of existence," [and so] "we will still preserve what existential interpretation considers important in its privileging of proclamation."[43] So, while Bayer tries to distance himself from Bultmann, he nevertheless agrees with him in understanding faith as an existential event. For Bultmann, faith finds its object within the self as the believer comes to self-awareness. For Bayer, faith finds its object in the bodily word which comes upon the believer from the outside.

Bayer makes a distinction between proclamation, as a performative speech act, and the propositional theology of dogmatics. Performative speech acts, to which the oral word of promises belongs, cannot be judged or evaluated by what they assert but by what they accomplish. They are immune or exempt from historical or philosophical critique. Here Bayer's perspective is similar to Barth's. This point is so fundamental to Bayer's program that the quote below speaks for itself.

> For the sake of clarity, it is necessary in our discussion of this problem to distinguish between two levels or spheres. On the one hand, there is the primary sphere of the performative speech acts, the sphere of the word and faith. On other hand, there is the secondary but related sphere of constative speech acts, the

---

39. Bayer, *Theology the Lutheran Way*, 137.
40. Bayer, *Theology the Lutheran Way*, 137.
41. Bayer, *Theology the Lutheran Way*, 137. Italics original.
42. Bayer, *Theology the Lutheran Way*, 138.
43. Bayer, *Theology the Lutheran Way*, 138.

sphere of theology (in the narrow sense) and its propositions. The statements to which the theological propositions refer, the promises that create faith, are not premises, as we stressed earlier (3). Therefore, they are not propositions that can be checked against what they assert. Rather, their truth and certainty are located in what they are, in what they bring, and in what they constitute. I cannot verify them because they verify me, because they embrace, permeate, and carry my knowledge and actions. I am entirely dependent on them.[44]

With this statement, Bayer has exempted the oral word or the promises from historical or critical examination. The words of promise are true in themselves.

Introducing philosophy, if only as a labyrinth or scaffolding for the biblical substance, comes with its own set of problems. Any dependency on linguistic philosophy poisons the pot from the start. Using Wittgenstein to better understand Luther opens the door to historical agnosticism, since we cannot know with certainty anything from the past. This undermines Christianity, since it has to do with the particular past of God's actions on behalf of Israel and for the salvation of the world through Jesus Christ. Like Austin, Wittgenstein was a linguistic philosopher and held that the essence of life is found in language. Words are without set meanings and one does not have to know what was in the mind of the speaker to derive meaning from what is spoken. Populist philosopher Bryan Magee says,

> [Wittgenstein's method] rejects two traditional theories of meaning. One is that specific words stand for specific things, and have fixed meanings: the true situation is far more protean and fluid than that. The other is that words derived their meanings from the intentions of their users, so that to understand someone you need to know what was in his mind.[45]

Austin saw language as performative in that it does something and does not merely inform about a state of affairs. Proclamation, preaching or word, as Bayer interprets Luther, fits Austin's first category in that the word does something. For Wittgenstein, language is also performative. However, words do not have fixed meanings. Therefore, the hearer may not know and may never know what was in the mind of the speaker when he spoke the word. Essential is what the word does to the hearer and not what the speaker intended. Applied as a theological principle, Wittgen-

44. Bayer, *Theology the Lutheran Way*, 171–172.
45. Bryan Magee, *The Story of Thought* (New York: The Quality Paperback Bookclub, 1998), 205.

stein's method exempts the theologian from asking about the historical origins of the Scriptures and the events and words recorded in them, since ultimately the hearer or the reader determines the meaning. Historical criticism—determining what the writer intended, the circumstances under which he wrote and how the original audience may have understood what he said—is incidental to what the word does now. Theology understood in this way can exist as an abstract system of knowledge and need not depend on anything outside of it. This allows Bayer to hold that the preached word can serve as the word of God in justifying the one who hears it. To repeat, Bayer holds that justification is determinative for all of reality and more specifically the word or the promise is the foundation of all of theology.[46]

Bayer makes use of Luther's metaphor of the death of Christ as "a wondrous exchange or swap of human sin and divine righteousness."[47] At this point, Bayer could present the classical Lutheran doctrine of the atonement—Christ offering himself as a sacrifice to the Father—but he does not.[48] Atonement is not listed in the indices of Bayer's writings as demonstrated in Joshua Miller's assessment of Bayer.[49] Bayer does not locate the redemptive moment in the cross or in the Son offering himself to the Father, but in God's speech act for me in the gospel. By speaking of Christ's death as taking place "for me" or "for you," the salvific moment takes place when the sinner is justified by the word. Atonement for Bayer has an external component; yet this external component is not identified primarily with the historical event of Golgotha or with Christ's eternal sacrifice of himself to the Father, but with the preached word. "This event of Christ's vicarious atoning death and the gift of himself bodily in the sermon, the Lord's Supper and baptism—'for you'—is the criterion of truth for the church."[50] This allows Bayer to hold that "The preaching of the justification of the sinner is the ground and center of the church."[51] At the heart of the human dilemma is self-justification that is resolved by the word of the cross that brings liberation.

---

46. Oswald Bayer, "The Doctrine of Justification and Ontology," *Neue Zeitschrift fur systematische Theologie und Religionsphilosophie* 43:44–53. See also, *Living by Faith,* 9 "The theme of justification is not one special theme, such that there might be other themes alongside it. It embraces the totality. All reality is involved in the justification debate."

47. Bayer, "Justification," in *Lutheran Quarterly* 24/3 (Autumn 2010): 338. This happens in the "event of Christ's atoning death and the gifts of himself bodily in the sermon, the Lord's Supper and baptism 'for you— is the criterion of truth in the church."

48. For an overview of the classical Lutheran doctrine of the atonement, see Kilcrease, *The Doctrine of Atonement*, 51–65.

49. Joshua C. Miller, *Hanging by a Promise*, Forward by Steven D. Paulson (Eugene, OR: Pickwick Publications, 2015), 349. Atonement is listed on page 10 in the index of Oswald Bayer, *Freedom in Response*, trans. Jeffrey F. Cayzer (Oxford and New York: Oxford University Press, 2007), 259, but this page offers nothing on the subject.

50. Bayer, "Justification," 338.

51. Bayer, "Justification," 337.

As I am taken into the wondrous exchange where God takes my place, I am free to look outside myself. I can step out of the context of blame and accusation, leave behind the struggle for mutual recognition and turn to God and the whole creation.[52]

In the same context Bayer says that with a sense of relief "we experience the blessing of a life lived in the splendor of justification."[53] An individual's release from fatal attempts at self-justification is effected "by the word of the cross that brings liberation." Bayer points to Job's unsuccessful attempts to justify himself as an example of self-justification.[54] Justification is an event that takes place when the promise—the word of justification—is heard. This perspective fits the concept that reality is reducible to the word and, therefore, can be defined by linguistic rules. "What God says, God does. The reverse is also true. What God does, God says; his doing is not ambiguous. God's work is God's speech."[55] Reality is reduced to God's verbal promises. This approach is an expression of speech-act theory; things have their existence in their being spoken.[56] Speech-acts for Bayer are not empirically verifiable, a principle resembling Barth's.[57] Bayer acknowledges that he is using the linguistic analysis of Wittgenstein and Austin in order to avoid Rudolph Bultmann's existential interpretation of the Bible, which was taken from Martin Heidegger.[58] Consequently, for Bayer, God's word has an immediate effect of itself and does not redirect the hearer back to the reality upon which it is grounded, "The promise is not only an announcement that will only be fulfilled in the future. It is a valid and powerful promise and pledge that takes immediate and present effect."[59]

In classical Lutheran theology, atonement takes place when the Father offers his Son as a sacrifice and in turn the Son offers himself up as a sacrifice to the Father. It is an eternal inter-trinitarian act historically taking place in one place and time *sub Pontio Pilato*. The Father accepts Christ's death as perfect atonement and, since all men are present in Christ as the new Adam, all are justified. This is called universal justification because *all* are justified. It is also called objective justification, because it is located within God's trinitarian life before and apart from faith. It all happens prior to the hearer coming to faith. Justification realizing itself in faith

52. Bayer, "Justification," 340.
53. Bayer, "Justification," 339.
54. Oswald Bayer, *Living by Faith*, 7–8.
55. Bayer, *Living by Faith*, 43.
56. This approach is attractive to those who find the ultimate reality in the church's worship. See Nicholas Woltersdorff, *The God We Worship: An Exploration of Liturgical Worship* (Grand Rapids, MI: Eerdmans, 2015).
57. Karl Barth, *Church Dogmatics, I, 93*. "Finally—and only here do we make the decisive point—the Word of God is the event itself in which proclamation becomes real proclamation."
58. Bayer, *Theology the Lutheran Way*, 138.
59. Bayer, *Living by Faith*, 51.

is called subjective justification, but faith is not the cause of justification. Without being aware of Bayer's philosophical foundation and scaffolding, his views appear to be consistent with confessional Lutheranism, but they are not.

Bayer's view that justification takes place in accepting God's verdict of justification affects how he views the Augsburg Confession (AC). In an easily undetected move, he identifies the article on the ministry and the sacraments (AC V) rather than the one on justification (AC IV) as its chief article. Favoring one article over the others is not without its drawbacks; but traditionally, the honor has been given to AC IV, that we are justified before God (*coram deo*), not because of our works, but because of Christ. Lack of agreement on justification among Lutherans has not challenged AC IV's position of honor in the doctrinal galaxy.[60] This makes Bayer's claim that, "Article V is the most important article in the Confession," all the more quizzical.[61] AC V is made the hermeneutical key for understanding AC IV. "It [AC V] is the decisive factor for the understanding of justification in Article IV and of good works and the new obedience in Article VI; it tips the balance."[62] This interpretation fits Bayer's contention that justification happens in the proclamation of the promise to the hearer and not in a prior, external event. Apart from what Bayer intends by this maneuver, this shift of emphasis effects how he wants the AC to be understood. Rather, it is to be read in the order it was written and not the other way around. AC III, the article on Christ, and not AC V, determines how justification in AC IV is to be understood.

> There is one Christ, true God and true man, who was born of the Virgin Mary, truly suffered, was crucified, died, and was buried. He did this to reconcile the Father to us and to be the sacrifice, not only for original guilt, but also for all the actual sins of mankind [John 1:29]. (AC III 2–3)[63]

The substance of the article on justification is derived from the prior article on Christology (AC III) and not, as Bayer contends, from AC V, which concerns the means by which justification is made available.

Christ's sacrifice or atonement for sin provides the basis for God's justification of the sinner. So, justification is not a self-contained word spoken by God who in his omnipotence declares the sinner righteous.

---

60. LCMS readers will recall that the St. Louis faculty majority allowed a denial of the historical character of the Bible, especially the gospels, if there was agreement on justification.
61. Bayer, *Living by Faith*, 44.
62. Bayer, *Living by Faith*, 44–45.
63. Paul Timothy McCain, ed., *Concordia: The Lutheran Confessions, A Reader's Edition of the Book of Concord*, 2nd edition (St. Louis:, MO Concordia Publishing House, 2006), 32

If this were the case, he would not be righteous. God's free will and omnipotence are concerned with his interaction with creation, the *opera Trinitatis ad extra*, and not with what God is in himself, the *opera Trinitatis ad intra*. With Bayer's shift from AC IV to AC V as the confession's controlling article, the salvific focus is shifted from Christ's sacrifice for sin (AC III) to the preaching of the word or the promise.

> The most fundamental of all institutions is the "institution" of the Word itself. The world itself depends on it, not just the church, and certainly not just the territorial or local church. It is the institution and the event out of which faith comes, which enables us to see the world as creation—what is possible only through judgment.[64]

Like Calvin and Barth, Bayer reduces each of the means of grace to the common denominator of God's presence in the word.[65]

With justification being made the overriding theological theme, Bayer's proposal has the appearance of an authentic Reformation theology. This appearance must be challenged. From his perspective, justification is understood as an existential moment in which the believer, hearing the word of promise, finds himself free from the need to justify himself in his own eyes or before God. No longer is Christ offering himself at Golgotha as an eternal sacrifice to the Father the defining moment of justification; rather, it is the moment in which one believes the promise. Justification is existentially redefined as one's freedom from the human dilemma. In the new scheme, absolution, not only receives sacramental status, but determines the character of baptism and the Lord's Supper as moments when once again the words are heard: "God forgives you."[66]

Justification (article IV) remains the key to understanding the AC and not the means of grace (article V) as Bayer's claims. Responding to the Judaizers' demand that circumcision was necessary for salvation, Paul saw justification by faith as the chief article. However, in Corinth, the article of Christ's resurrection was more fundamental. "But if there is no resurrection of the dead, then not even Christ has been raised; and if

---

64. Bayer, *Living by Faith*, 45.

65. David P. Scaer, *Baptism*, Confessional Lutheran Dogmatics (St. Louis, MO: Luther Academy, 1999), 175, "Like Calvin, [Barth] saw baptism as he did the Lord's Supper, as a subsidiary form of divine proclamation. This fact should alert Lutherans to the impossibility of exhausting the meaning of Baptism and the Lord's Supper as only subdivisions under the Word, as if one sacrament could be substituted for another or that the content of one is the same as the other. We have been vehement in rejecting such sacramental homogenization that implies one sacrament has the same results as the other."

66. Bayer understands absolution, baptism and the Lord's Supper as the same kind of speech acts as preaching. See "Twenty Questions on the Relevance of Luther for Today," *Lutheran Quarterly* 29/4 (Winter 2015): 441. Barth following Calvin held that the workings and the effects of the word and the sacraments were the same. See David P. Scaer, Baptism, Confessional Lutheran Dogmatics 11, (St. Louis, MO: The Luther Academy, 1999) 175.

Christ has not been raised, then our preaching is in vain and your faith is in vain" (1 Cor 15:13–14). Paul argues that justification by faith comes through preaching the resurrection as a real historical event. Indeed, the historicity of the resurrection is so important that he supplies an impressive list of the witnesses who had seen Jesus risen and alive. Bayer turns this around: "The preaching of the justification of the sinner is the ground and center of the church."[67] This subtle shift places preaching where Christ's resurrection belongs.

Seminary students often find it challenging to read articles and books by theologians, who confer different meanings on words they know from their upbringing in the church, for example, God, Spirit, inspiration, justification, etc. Any word can be given a different or peculiar meaning, of which the reader is unaware.[68] As noted, this property of language is the center piece of Wittgenstein's philosophy. Bayer not only uses words in a different way but also claims he has recovered a previously undeveloped emphasis in Luther's understanding of language. Before the Reformer,

> language [was] a system of signs that point to an object or state of affairs, or that express an emotion. In either case, the sign (*signum*), understood as a statement or expression, is not the reality (*res*) itself. However, Luther's great hermeneutical insight, his Reformation discovery in the strict sense, was that the verbal sign (*signum*) is itself the reality (*res*). This new insight turned the ancient understanding of language on its head.[69]

Luther's great Reformation discovery of justification by faith is now understood to be as much a linguistic discovery as a theological one. In confronting any theological proposal, the uninitiated might ask whether the theologian believes that the events of the creed's second article actually happened: he was conceived by the Holy Spirit, born of the Virgin Mary, crucified under Pontius Pilate, buried, and raised from the dead. Our task is not to question a theologian's faith, including Bayer's, who understands his views as Luther's. Rather, we must address the biblical viability of his theology. Since he says the word or the promise does not depend on external evidences, past or present, he has already eschewed the need to find a foundation in the historical events recorded in the gospels. Like Barth, Bayer addresses neither the historical origin nor character of the gospels nor the events they record. For him, the word of promise is self-contained and virtually autonomous; it is not dependent

---

67. Oswald Bayer, "Justification," *Lutheran Quarterly* 24/3 (Autumn 2010): 337.

68. For an easy-to-read overview of different interpretations, including those offered by Forde, see Kilcrease, *The Doctrine of the Atonement*, 55–165.

69. Bayer, *Theology the Lutheran Way*, 129.

on anything external. Preaching justification is not only the goal of theology but has become its foundation.

In reading Bayer, one is left puzzled whether, or how, the history of Jesus of Nazareth is a determinative factor in his theology. So, we close with this potentially positive but still disappointing section from his essay, "The Word of the Cross."

> Rather, [the narrative of the crucified God] rivets attention to the historical fact of the crucifixion of Jesus of Nazareth in its temporal and spacial determination and does not allow itself to be pried loose from the texts in which it was originally recorded; a "symbolism of the death of Jesus" must keep the texts in mind. The history of the risen crucified remains bindingly written in these texts, having once and for all been done, permits no more further elaboration—without being robbed of its eschatological character.[70]

Does Bayer have it both ways? Jesus lived in a history that is confined to the text but is exempt from critical examination. What we know about Jesus is preserved in the biblical texts; but is it so, as Bayer claims, that, if we examine this history, we rob it of its eschatological character? ✛

---

70. Oswald Bayer, "The Word of the Cross', *Lutheran Quarterly* 9/1 (Spring 1995): 53.

THE EUCHARISTIC MARTYRDOM OF
ST. POLYCARP OF SMYRNA

✛

The final prayer of St. Polycarp of Smyrna, when he is about to be set on fire and burned alive,[1] is comparable to early eucharistic prayers in both its form and content.[2] The eucharistic language and images of the prayer are also reminiscent of the way that St. Ignatius of Antioch described his own anticipated martyrdom several decades earlier.[3] Dr. Weinrich interprets this eucharistic theology of martyrdom in St. Ignatius as a confession of the incarnate Christ, who continues the work of his passion in the Eucharist and in the suffering and death of his saints.[4] In both cases, the crucified and risen Christ is actively present, working in the flesh to reveal the Father, to bestow the Holy Spirit, and to unite the church in his own body unto life everlasting.

Here we explore the ways that Polycarp's martyrdom is presented as a eucharistic sacrifice, offered to the Father in the faith and love of Christ

1. Cf. *Martyrdom of Polycarp* 14.1–3. Unless otherwise indicated, citations herein are from *Polycarp's Epistle to the Philippians and the Martyrdom of Polycarp: Introduction, Text, and Commentary*, edited by Paul Hartog (Oxford: Oxford University Press, 2013); abbreviated *M.Pol.*

2. Polycarp's prayer is "almost certainly based on the eucharistic prayer of the church at Smyrna" (William C. Weinrich, "Death and Martyrdom: An Important Aspect of Early Christian Eschatology," *Concordia Theological Quarterly* 66:4 [October 2002], 336). Cf. David H. Tripp, "The Prayer of St. Polycarp and the Development of Anaphoral Prayer," *Ephemerides Liturgicae* 104 (1990), 97–132; and Maxwell E. Johnson, "Martyrs and the Mass: The Interpolation of the Narrative of Institution into the Anaphora," *Worship* 87:3 (May 2013), 2–22.

3. For example, in his *Epistle to the Romans* (4.1) Ignatius writes, "Let me be food for the wild beasts, through whom I can reach God. I am God's wheat, and I am being ground by the teeth of the wild beasts, that I might prove to be pure bread" (*The Apostolic Fathers: Greek Texts and English Translations of Their Writings*, 2nd ed., tr. J. B. Lightfoot and J. R. Harmer, ed. Michael W. Holmes [Baker Book House, 1992], 171). For a discussion of the point, cf. William C. Weinrich, *Spirit and Martyrdom: A Study of the Work of the Holy Spirit in Contexts of Persecution and Martyrdom in the New Testament and Early Christian Literature* (University Press of America, 1981), 124–127, 137–140.

4. As Dr. Weinrich summarizes, "In the eucharist, the resurrected Christ continues the work of his passion. He continues to act sarkically, for in the eucharist that flesh is given which suffered for our sins and which the Father raised from the dead. In the same way the martyrdom of Ignatius is the activity of the resurrected Christ who works in passion, who works sarkically" (Weinrich, *Spirit and Martyrdom*, 145).

Jesus. The example of his faithful witness unto death is a catechesis and confession of the gospel; it fulfills his pastoral office and, most especially, perfects his celebration of the sacrament of the altar. The ministry and martyrdom of Bishop Polycarp, even to the present day, continues to testify in the record and remembrance of his life and death, glorifying the Lord and strengthening the people of God in the Holy Spirit unto the resurrection of the body and the life everlasting.

ST. POLYCARP OF SMYRNA

Polycarp, the second-century bishop of Smyrna (now Izmir, Turkey), was surely one of the most significant figures of the early church. A "father of the Christians" in his day (*M.Pol.* 12.2), he was remembered and honored for his faithful witness in both life and death (*M.Pol.* 13.2; 19.1; 22.1).

He was an apostolic man, rightly numbered among the "Apostolic Fathers," and provides an important link between the first and second centuries. He was a respected peer and personal confidant of Ignatius of Antioch,[5] and was held in high regard by Irenaeus of Lyons. The latter man recalled from his own childhood that Polycarp had "reported living with John and the rest of the Apostles who had seen the Lord," and that "he remembered their words," so that he was able to proclaim the teaching and the miracles of Christ "in harmony with the Scriptures," as he had learned these things from eyewitnesses of the gospel.[6] It is possible that St. Irenaeus had remembered incorrectly or that he misunderstood the relationship, but there does appear to be some direct or indirect connection between the apostle John and the bishop of the church at Smyrna (Rev 2:8–11). As much or more significant is the way Polycarp's epistle to the Philippians, written in the early second century, draws upon the Epistles of St. John, St. Peter, and St. Paul. The bishop stands on the firm foundation of the apostles.[7]

THE MARTYRDOM OF ST. POLYCARP

As Bishop Polycarp is important in his own right, so is the account of his martyrdom among the most significant documents of the patristic age. Its popularity is not hard to understand; it offers a dramatic narrative, well told, gripping in its details, and full of pathos. The courage of the martyr is undeniable, and the theological interpretation of his death is profound.

---

5. Cf. the epistles of Ignatius to the Smyrnaeans and to Polycarp, and the epistle of Polycarp to the Philippians (*The Apostolic Fathers*, 185–221).

6. Burnett Hillman Streeter, *The Primitive Church* (New York: The MacMillan Company, 1929), 96–97. Cf. Eusebius, *Ecclesiastical History* 4.14; 5.20.

7. Cf. D. Richard Stuckwisch, "St. Polycarp of Smyrna: Johannine or Pauline Figure?" *Concordia Theological Quarterly* 61:1–2 (January–April 1997), 113–125.

The *Martyrdom of St. Polycarp* is typically dated between AD 155 and 170, on the assumption that it was written within a few years of the actual martyrdom (*M.Pol.* 21).[8] It is usually regarded as the earliest of the martyr acts, introducing a new genre and vocabulary of martyrdom.[9] In recent years, Candida Moss has made provocative arguments for reconsidering the dating of the extant document.[10] Yet the witness of the *Martyrdom* remains, whether it was written sooner or later, and here we are concerned with the theology of the text as we have it.[11]

MARTYRDOM ACCORDING TO THE GOSPEL

The key to interpreting the *Martyrdom of St. Polycarp* is discerning what it means to undergo a "martyrdom according to the gospel." The document itself describes what such a death entails (*M.Pol.* 1.1–2; 2.1). It is one that is received and suffered in accord with the word and will of God, as the Lord was crucified and rose again "according to the Scriptures" (1 Cor 15:3–4). As such, it is endured in steadfast faith by the grace of God, and it is borne in conscientious love for others. It is also "an ecclesial event, for through the remembrance of the martyr the Christian community faithfully trains itself for future struggles."[12] A stated purpose of the martyrdom is to commend the example of St. Polycarp, that others should follow in his footsteps "according to the gospel," and thereby imitate Christ Jesus as "partners and fellow disciples" of the faithful martyrs (*M.Pol.* 17.3; 19.1; 22.1).[13]

With a prophetic word from God, the narrative establishes up front that "it is necessary" (δεῖ) for Polycarp to be burned alive (*M.Pol.* 5.2; 12.3). This point is fundamental because evangelical martyrdom is not self-chosen, but the martyr is handed over by God. It is thus with patient acceptance of the will of God that the faithful martyr perseveres with bold courage in the face of death, confident that Christ is present with his word and Holy Spirit (*M.Pol.* 2.2–3; 3.1). Martyrdom "according to the gospel" is offered as a sacrifice of faith to the glory of God, and so also as a service of love in Christ Jesus for the strengthening of the church (*M.Pol.* 1.2).

---

8. Cf. Boudewijn Dehandschutter, "The Martyrium Polycarpi: A Century of Research," and "Research on the Martyrdom of Polycarp: 1990–2005," both in *Polycarpiana: Studies on Martyrdom and Persecution in Early Christianity, Collected Essays*, ed. J. Leemans (Leuven University Press, 2007), 43–92.

9. Cf. Candida R. Moss, "On the Dating of Polycarp: Rethinking the Place of the Martyrdom of Polycarp in the History of Christianity," *Early Christianity* 1 (2010), 539–574.

10. Cf. Candida R. Moss, *Ancient Christian Martyrdom: Diverse Practices, Theologies, and Traditions* (Yale University Press, 2012), 62–72.

11. The text is available in seven Greek manuscripts and in a Latin version (all dating from the tenth to the thirteenth centuries). Significant extracts from the Martyrdom are also preserved by Eusebius in his *Ecclesiastical History* (4.15). Cf. *The Apostolic Fathers*, 222–224.

12. Weinrich, *Spirit and Martyrdom*, 175.

13. Christ has left us an example, that we should follow in his steps (1 Pet 2:21), and St. Paul urges others to imitate him, as he imitates Christ Jesus (1 Cor 11:1; 2 Cor 4:15–16).

The point is made, significantly, by the emphatic contrast between Bishop Polycarp and Quintus the Phrygian who put himself forward and urged others to do likewise. The possible identification of Quintus with an early Montanism has been debated and may be a factor.[14] Such questions aside, it is clear in any case that the voluntary seeking of martyrdom is contrary to the gospel. It is not according to God's will, but is harmful to the neighbor, and is liable to end in apostasy. As Quintus persuades others "to come forward voluntarily," so is he persuaded "to swear and to offer sacrifice" to the idols of Rome (*M.Pol.* 4). It is already a false, self-chosen worship, and therefore idolatry, to hand oneself over to martyrdom. So it is no surprise that in the end Quintus abandons the faith altogether and capitulates entirely.

Whereas Polycarp is contrasted with Quintus, he is positively compared to Christ in a variety of ways. For example, Christ Jesus prays to the Father on the cusp of his passion, "Your will be done"; in the same way, he teaches the church to pray (Matt 6:10; 26:42).[15] So too does Polycarp pray and confess, "The will of God be done," when the police come to arrest him (*M.Pol.* 7.1). Indeed, there are numerous parallels, allusions, overtones, and references to the passion of Christ in the details of Bishop Polycarp's arrest, interrogation, and martyrdom.[16] These narrative echoes, especially in their cumulative literary impact, are indicative of the martyr's faithfulness to his Lord. Nevertheless, these points of similarity do not in themselves constitute a "martyrdom according to the gospel." For the most part, the particular details are circumstantial and coincidental, and therefore not subject to imitation.

Polycarp does what Jesus does, not by mimicry of outward actions or by self-chosen impulses, but as the Lord directs and instructs him. The imitation of his martyrdom should therefore not be understood as the rote repetition of historical events, like some kind of theatrical performance. It is rather a discipleship of following after Christ Jesus within one's own vocation and station in life. Such an imitation is possible for each Christian because Christ has come in the flesh and taken up the cross for his people. The discipleship to which he calls them is a participation in his passion, which takes place by way of his sacraments, and,

---

14. Cf. Gerd Buschmann, *Das Martyrdium des Polykarp* (Göttingen: Vandenhoeck & Ruprecht, 1998), and the book review by William C. Weinrich in *Journal of Early Christian Studies* 8.2 (2000), 300–302; also, Dehandschutter, "The Martyrium Polycarpi: A Century of Research," and "Research on the Martyrdom of Polycarp: 1990–2005."

15. In this way the gospel teaches that we ought to receive all things from the Lord's hand, to go wherever and do whatever he directs (*M.Pol.* 4).

16. Cf. Michael W. Holmes, "The Martyrdom of Polycarp and the New Testament Passion Narratives," in *Trajectories through the New Testament and the Apostolic Fathers*, ed. Andrew Gregory and Christopher Tuckett (Oxford: Oxford University Press, 2005), 407–427; also, Candida R. Moss, *The Other Christs: Imitating Jesus in Ancient Christian Ideologies of Martyrdom* (Oxford: Oxford University Press, 2010), 45–59.

where the Lord so wills, by way of martyrdom according to his gospel. So it is that Polycarp, like Ignatius before him, completes his discipleship through martyrdom (*M.Pol.* 17.1, 3; 16.1–2).

Polycarp lives and dies according to the will and word of God. He is faithful and steadfast in doing so because Christ and his Spirit are with him in life and death. He follows as a disciple in the image and likeness of his Lord because Christ, in the flesh, has given himself to Polycarp in the Eucharist. What is more, as Bishop Polycarp has administered the passion in the remembrance of Jesus, according to the Lord's institution, so does he go to his martyrdom in the same obedience of faith. The Eucharist shapes and defines his pastoral office and ministry as a father and teacher of Christians and as a proponent of the true worship of Christ in opposition to pagan idolatry even unto death (*M.Pol.* 12.2; 16.1).

Martyrdom according to the gospel, therefore, is martyrdom according to the Eucharist. Christ is present with Bishop Polycarp in his martyrdom because the same Lord Jesus Christ is present in and with his church in the Eucharist. The martyr is handed over to his death, as the body and blood of Christ are received and handed over from God in accordance with the word of the Lord (1 Cor 11:23–25). The martyr endures in steadfast faith, just as the passion is efficacious and salutary in its benefits, because Christ the Lord, crucified and risen, is actively present and at work with the fruits of his passion (Matt 26:26–28; Luke 24:30–35). The martyr lives and dies in faith toward God and in love for the neighbor, as the Holy Communion is celebrated with thanksgiving to God and is distributed as divine charity for his church (1 Cor 11:17–34; Acts 2:42–47; 4:32–35). So it is that Polycarp endures unto the end, the Lord is glorified in him, and the church catholic in Smyrna and beyond is strengthened and sustained by his martyrdom (*M.Pol.* 16.2; 19.1–2).

THE EUCHARISTIC SACRIFICE AND SACRAMENT OF CHRIST

The sacrifice of Christ is constitutive and central to the gospel and therefore to the faith and life of the church in communion with God. It is in and with and through the cross and passion of the incarnate Son of God that the Father reveals and gives himself to his people. As the true God is thus made known in the passion of Christ, so is the lordship of Christ established in his passion. The fruits of his passion are brought forth in his resurrection from the dead, and they are presented and distributed to his church in the Eucharist. It is by and with the flesh and blood of the crucified and risen Christ that the Holy Spirit is poured out upon the people of God. He is anointed by the Holy Spirit in his body for the cross and in his resurrection, and the same Spirit remains on him (John 1:32–33; Acts 2:22–33; Rom 8:3–11). He is the great high priest who sacrificed himself once for all and who lives to make intercession for his people before the throne of God (Heb 7:20–28; Rom 8:34). He is the pastor and bishop of his church in all times and places (1 Pet 2:25; Rev 7:17; John 10:11–16; Ezek 34:23).

The sacrament of the altar is the gift and the presence of this great high priest who is himself the sacrifice of propitiation for all sin (Heb 10:5–14; 1 John 2:2; Gal 3:23–25; 2 Cor 5:21), the Christ "who suffered for the salvation of the whole world of the saved, the blameless on behalf of sinners" (*M.Pol.* 17.2). The Eucharist is the giving of his sacrificed body and the pouring out of his sacrificial blood in the life of his church; they are given for Christians to eat and drink as the ongoing feast of his sacrifice in communion with God and man. The supper of Christ is the fulfillment of the Old Testament sacrificial meals—the Passover (Exod 12), the grain offering (Lev 2), and the peace offering (Lev 3). In these sacrificial acts, the meat and grain, offered according to the word of the Lord, were eaten by the people and/or priests in his presence.[17]

The church's celebration of the sacrament is a eucharistic sacrifice, that is, a sacrifice of thanksgiving, which is offered in response to the sacrifice of Christ as the fruits and benefits of his sacrifice are received in the Holy Communion.[18] It does not aim at appeasing an angry God but confesses his salvation and rejoices in his reconciliation. This Eucharist glorifies, honors, praises, and gives thanks to God for his grace and faithfulness in Christ Jesus.

The sacrament of the altar is first of all eucharistic because the Lord Jesus gave thanks in his institution of this sacrament, and his ministers are commanded to do what he has done in their administration of the sacrament in his name (Matt 26:26–28; 1 Cor 11:23–26).[19] The sacrament is further characterized by thanksgiving in view of the good gifts that are given and received. The fruits of the passion of Christ are the sure and certain pledge of the resurrection, the fulfillment of God's good creation, and the first fruits of his new creation in the crucified and risen body of Christ Jesus. Really, the body and blood of Christ are given and received as the fulfillment of all God's promises from the foundation of the world

---

17. Cf. 1 Corinthians 10:16–21; Isaiah 25:6; and Exodus 24:3–9; also, Daniel Brege, *Eating God's Sacrifice: The Lord's Supper Portrayed in Old Testament Sacrifice* (Decatur, IN: published by author, 2009); and John W. Kleinig, *Leviticus* (St. Louis: Concordia Publishing House, 2003).

18. Cf. Ap. XXIV; and Martin Chemnitz, *Examination of the Council of Trent*, vol. 2, tr. Fred Kramer (St. Louis, MO: Concordia Publishing House, 2008).

19. We know the character and content of the Lord's thanksgiving on the night he was betrayed from his "High Priestly Prayer," in which he gives thanks for the name and the glory of God that he received from the Father. He also prays and intercedes for his apostles and his church, in view of the Sacrifice of his cross (John 17). The church likewise gives thanks for the name and the Glory of God, which he causes to dwell in the midst of his people in the body and blood of Christ Jesus, wherein they are united as one body in Christ, in communion with the Father, Son, and Holy Spirit.

to the close of the age, even to life everlasting. And where such gifts are bestowed, there is thanksgiving.

By the same token, genuine thanksgiving at all times and in all places is shaped and defined by the sacrament of the Eucharist. It is offered to God, not from a distance but in his presence, in fellowship with the Holy Trinity, and so also with the household and family of God in a community of mutual charity and love. It is offered to God in love for the neighbor through the sharing of food and drink and in the hospitality of forgiveness given and received.

True thanksgiving is also Christocentric, as surely as the Eucharist is centered in Christ. It echoes and confesses the preaching of Christ Jesus, and it glorifies the Father in the Spirit by the proclamation and remembrance of his cross and passion in particular. It is cruciform in its character and content. In other words, thanksgiving is offered to God in Christ by the self-sacrifice of one's body and life for others. It is a tangible expression of gratitude for the grace of God, which extols the goodness of God's Creation (1 Tim 4:1–5) and embraces the perfection of creation in the incarnation, cross, and resurrection of the Son of God.

There is, therefore, a reciprocal connection between what is received in the sacrament and what is rendered with thanksgiving in a life of faith and love. The Christian who receives the body and blood of Christ becomes, in turn, a living sacrifice offered to God in faith, and a living sacrament offered to the neighbor in love (Rom 12:1; Heb 13:12–16; 1 Pet 2:4–5; Ap. XXIV).

THE EUCHARIST AND MARTYRDOM

The sacrament of the altar is the life-giving fruit of the Sacrifice of Christ. The fruits of the sacrament—the faith and love and thanksgiving of the communicants within their respective vocations and stations in life—belong to the coming of the kingdom of God in Christ Jesus, in, with, and under his cross and passion. Not only the active obedience of good works, but also the patient bearing of the Cross in the confident hope of the resurrection is a testimony to the lordship of Christ. As surely as he is present with the fruits of his sacrifice in the Eucharist, so surely is he present in and with his Christians in their suffering and death for his name's sake.

To drink the cup of Christ is to share in the glory of his cross (Mark 10:35–40), and to partake of the Eucharist is to give thanks and to call upon the name of the Lord in the face of suffering and death for the sake of Christ Jesus. The church is united with Christ in his passion, and she becomes the body of Christ, by the work of the Holy Spirit in Holy Communion, because the sacrament is the self-revelation of God in the flesh and blood of the crucified and risen Christ (1 Cor 10:16–17). So is the same Lord Jesus Christ revealed in the flesh-and-blood martyrdom of his saints (Col 1:24–26; 2 Cor 1:5; 4:7–12; Gal 6:17; 2 Tim 2:11–12).

The testimony of the martyrs to the cross and resurrection is not simply intellectual and verbal, but it is embodied in their life and death as a sacrifice of faith and thanksgiving in Christ Jesus. It is a life-and-death contest of true and false religion, of true and false worship, and of allegiance to the true God versus idolatry (Eph 6:12).[20] Thus, it is a matter of distinguishing the truly pious and faithful from "the atheists" (*M.Pol.* 3.2; 8.2; 9.2; 12.2; 16.1). Repentance is the hinge between true and false worship, but genuine repentance is "to change from harmful things to just things" (*M.Pol.* 11.1). A Christian who has tasted the heavenly gift in the body and blood of Christ (Heb 6:4) fears, loves, and trusts in him above all other gods, and will not forsake his kingdom and his righteousness for the impiety and death of worthless idols.

THE EUCHARISTIC MINISTRY AND MARTYRDOM OF BISHOP POLYCARP

Polycarp is martyred, not only as a Christian disciple, but within his particular vocation and office as the bishop of Smyrna. He has been a father, a teacher, an intercessor, and a celebrant of the church, in the name and stead of Christ (*M.Pol.* 12.2; 16.2). What he was baptized into, and what he received in the Eucharist, he also administered and distributed in his pastoral ministry.

The Eucharist is the heart and center of the pastoral ministry, and of the church's life in Christ. In the sacrament, Christ reveals the Father in himself, bestows the Spirit received from the Father, and unites the church with God in his own crucified and risen body.[21] As Bishop Polycarp has proclaimed the death of Christ in the Eucharist, so now, the passion of Christ is manifested in the eucharistic suffering and death of his servant. The martyrdom of Polycarp is not the termination of his eucharistic ministry, but its culmination and perfection. He thus fulfills "his own lot (*kleron*), becoming a partner (*koinonos*) of Christ" (*M.Pol.* 6.2; 1 Pet 5:1–4).[22]

---

20. "Martyrdom is the refusal to acknowledge false gods by sacrificing to them, and this by way not only of open confession, but by way of one's own death. However, the demand of the earthly authorities that a sacrifice be given is, in fact, paradoxically carried out. The martyr allows the authorities to slay him and so, in that way, to sacrifice him up to the true God. And as a death fully embraced by the faith in the true God, martyrdom is a sacrifice of self fully acceptable to God" (Weinrich, "Death and Martyrdom," 336).

21. Cf. John D. Zizioulas, *Eucharist Bishop Church: The Unity of the Church in the Divine Eucharist and the Bishop During the First Three Centuries*, tr. Elizabeth Theokritoff (Brookline, MA: Holy Cross Orthodox Press, 2001).

22. Cf. Enrico Mazza, *The Celebration of the Eucharist: The Origin of the Rite and the Development of Its Interpretation*, tr. Matthew J. O'Connell (Collegeville, MN: Liturgical Press, 1999), 134–137.

To picture more specifically the continuity between the Eucharist and Polycarp's martyrdom, it is helpful to consider the basic contours and content of the divine liturgy. Justin Martyr, a contemporary of Polycarp in the second century (though in Rome, not Asia Minor), gives a description of the liturgy as he knew it.[23] To summarize, the liturgy comprises (1) The preaching and teaching of the prophetic and apostolic Scriptures by the presiding bishop, who commends to the people "the imitation of these good things," (2) the reception of offerings for almsgiving and for the sacrament, (3) the prayers and intercessions of the church, (4) the consecration of the bread and wine with thanksgiving and the word of Christ, and (5) the distribution of the body and blood of Christ to the communicants (both present and elsewhere).[24] The *Martyrdom of St. Polycarp* significantly follows this eucharistic liturgical pattern.

THE SERVICE OF THE WORD

"The Service of the Word," as we might describe it, does not figure prominently in the events of the *Martyrdom*. However, it is the foundation upon which the whole eucharistic liturgy unfolds in the story of Polycarp's death. His "martyrdom according to the gospel" fulfills the word of God that he receives and speaks according to his pastoral office, just as "every saying that he uttered from his mouth was accomplished and will also be accomplished" (*M.Pol.* 12.3; 16.2).

Bishop Polycarp speaks prophetically because he is "an apostolic and prophetic teacher," a father and teacher of the Christians (*M.Pol.* 12.2; 16.2; 19.1). In keeping with this office and vocation, he even offers to catechize the proconsul in the tenets of Christianity (*M.Pol.* 10.1).

Not only does he teach the word of God, but he also proceeds according to that word, and in doing so he follows the example of Christ Jesus. He does what the Lord Jesus does, just as a presiding bishop administers the sacrament of the altar by obeying the command of Jesus to "Do this" in remembrance of him (1 Cor 11:23–25; Luke 22:19).

As the Words of Institution are the ground and authority on which the church celebrates the Eucharist, so does Polycarp have a revelation from God that establishes his martyrdom. The prophetic word that he speaks, following the vision he receives concerning his death, is the "Institution Narrative" of his eucharistic martyrdom (*M.Pol.* 5.2; 12.3). The voice from heaven that Polycarp receives as he enters the stadium is another word of God that gives him strength and courage to face his death

---

23. There were liturgical differences between Rome and Asia Minor in the second century, of course. Nevertheless, according to St. Irenaeus of Lyons, St. Polycarp visited Rome and was able to celebrate the Eucharist with the church there (cf. Eusebius, *Ecclesiastical History* 5.24). Cf. Mazza, *The Celebration of the Eucharist*, 93–115.

24. Cf. St. Justin Martyr, *First Apology* 65–67.

(*M.Pol.* 9.1). As at the baptism of our Lord (Luke 3:21–22), at his trans-figuration (Luke 9:28–36), and again when "the hour has come for the Son of Man to be glorified," so does the voice from heaven here confirm the will of God for Polycarp (John 12:23–33). It is necessary that he suffer and die as a Christian, which is to say, with bold courage and steadfast faith in the promise of the resurrection.[25]

Polycarp goes to his death in fulfillment of the will of God (*M.Pol.* 2.1; 7.1). That is how and why he is honored and set forth as an example of "martyrdom according to the gospel," with the intention that others imitate his faithfulness and follow in his footsteps (*M.Pol.* 1.1–2; 17.3; 18.3; 19.1; 22.1). His death itself is thus another kind of preaching, a Service of the Word.

THE OFFERTORY RITES

Because he waits upon the Lord and proceeds in faith according to the word of God, Polycarp, steadfast in his faith and confession, endures even unto death. He is strong and courageous in the face of hostility, and free of fear, he gives thanks by word and deed in love for God and man.

Polycarp shows love to others in the way he lives and in the way he approaches his martyrdom (*M.Pol.* 1.2). His own body and life are thus given as alms for his neighbor. What is more, in one brief but poignant example, he demonstrates tangible charity and hospitality to his enemies, although they have come to arrest him and lead him away to the blood-thirsty mobs who are calling for his death (*M.Pol.* 3.2; 6.1; 7.1–2).

Closely connected to his gifts and actions of love, Polycarp also en-gages in notable prayers and intercessions, "as was his habit" (*M.Pol.* 5.1; 7.2–3). This custom of prayer is not simply a matter of personal piety, but it belongs to his pastoral practice, to his office and duty as bishop. It is the prayer of the church. As he had urged the Philippians to pray and intercede for all people (*Pol. Phil.* 12.3), so does he pray and intercede, not for himself, but for the churches throughout the world, and for ev-eryone he ever met, both great and small (*M.Pol.* 8.1). Now his priestly intercessions dovetail with his martyrdom, in which he offers up himself as a prayer of sweet-smelling incense and the evening sacrifice (*M.Pol.* 15.2; Ps 141:2).

It is only after Polycarp has "finished his prayer," that "the hour" comes for "his departure" (*M.Pol.* 8.1). Here is a significant allusion to the "hour of Christ," which marks the hour of his supper and the hour of his cross in the holy Gospels (John 12:23; 13:1). It also indicates that

---

25. Whatever discomfort one may have with the miraculous revelations described in the *Martyrdom* (5.2; 9.1; 12.3; 15.1–2; 16.1), within the context of the story these things distinguish the events as being ordained by God—revealed, directed, and fulfilled by him (*M.Pol.* 14.2)—in contrast to self-chosen paths like that pursued so disastrously by Quintus (*M.Pol.* 4).

the Lord with his liturgist, Polycarp, is the one actually governing these events, not the mounted police who come with weapons to arrest the elderly bishop (*M.Pol.* 7.1–2).

Polycarp's obedience to the will of God (*M.Pol.* 5.2; 7.1) is a confession of divine authority (*M.Pol.* 8.2; 9.3; 17.3; 21).[26] As the narrative states, "it is necessary for us, being very devout, to ascribe to God the authority over all things" (*M.Pol.* 2.1), that is, authority over the Christian, and over all circumstances both good and evil. Even the power of Rome to arrest and execute Christians derives from the true lord and king (*M.Pol.* 10.2), as was also the case with Christ himself before Pontius Pilate (John 19:10–11).

It is not simply submission that Polycarp expresses, but gratitude and allegiance to his faithful king (*M.Pol.* 9.3; 17.3; 21). He pays homage, not to Caesar, but to Christ (*M.Pol.* 8.2). He openly confesses three times that he is a Christian (*M.Pol.* 9.2–3; 10.1; 11.1–2; 12.1). This confession expresses more than his belief and conviction. "A Christian" is who and what he is, his identity and his vocation. He has routinely confessed the Lord Jesus Christ in his preaching, prayer, and praise. Now the witness of his entire life and ministry is sealed by his martyrdom.

As a true and faithful bishop, Polycarp teaches, confesses, and practices the true religion and worship of the true and only God, which sets him in opposition to all false religion and worship (*M.Pol.* 12.2). Consequently, he is confronted with the choice of either offering incense to the emperor or becoming incense to the Lord; either sacrificing to pagan gods or becoming a sacrifice to the one true God (*M.Pol.* 3.2; 8.2; 9.2; 14.2; 15.2; 16.1; 19.2).[27]

He is bound to the wood, not nailed (*M.Pol.* 13.3; 14.1), like Isaac, who was bound to the wood by his father Abraham (Gen 22:9). And the bishop of Smyrna becomes an acceptable whole burnt offering, a choice ram (*M.Pol.* 14.1), and so a "type" of Christ. He acts "like a man" (*M.Pol.* 9.1), or, more to the point, he acts like the true man, Christ Jesus. So do the fire and aroma that attend his death (*M.Pol.* 15.1–2) confirm that his martyrdom is "according to the gospel," offered and received in the image and likeness of Christ. The fire does not destroy the martyr's body, but by the fire of the Holy Spirit his body and his life are transformed into a holy sacrifice (Rom 12:1–2), just as gold and silver are purified by fire (Mal 3:3). So, too, the Christians who witness Polycarp's death

---

26. Consider the bold confession of Shadrach, Meshach and Abednego, who remained faithful to the Lord their God and so refused to obey Nebuchadnezzar or to worship his golden image, even when threatened with the blazing fiery furnace: "Our God whom we serve is able to deliver us from the burning fiery furnace, and he will deliver us out of your hand, O king. But if not, be it known to you, O king, that we will not serve your gods or worship the golden image that you have set up" (Dan 3:17–18).

27. Cf. Weinrich, "Death and Martyrdom," 336.

perceive, not the smell of burning flesh, but "such strong fragrance, like a waft of incense or some other of the precious spices" (*M.Pol.* 15.2; 2 Cor. 2:14–16).

In his death, Polycarp becomes a whole burnt offering (*M.Pol.* 14.1–2; Lev 1). He is also a grain offering (*M.Pol.* 15.2; Lev 2), and a peace offering of thanksgiving (*M.Pol.* 14:2; 17.1–3; 18.2–3; 19.2; Lev 3; 7:11–36). In all three respects, he is offered in continuity with the sacrifice and sacrament of Christ (*M.Pol.* 14.2).[28] The Bishop's body and life are an acceptable and pleasing sacrifice, because he lives and dies in Christ, and Christ abides in him, as the same Lord Jesus Christ is present with the fruits and benefits of his passion in the Eucharist.

THE EUCHARIST

The sacrifice of thanksgiving that Polycarp offers and becomes is not a mute action. It is an embodied and visible word, yes, but one that is accompanied by the voice of faith in the prayer and confession of Polycarp, the fruit of lips that praise his name (Heb 13:15; Rom 10:10).

As previously noted, the prayer of Polycarp on the verge of his martyrdom is clearly analogous to eucharistic prayers of his day; although, in this case, it is the Bishop himself who is consecrated by the word of God and prayer (1 Tim 4:5).[29] Not that he becomes a propitiatory sacrifice for sin, but that he entrusts himself entirely to God, as a sacrifice of thanksgiving, in the confidence and joy of the sacrifice of Christ. His eucharistic prayer and self-sacrifice arise with Christ to the Father in the resurrection and ascension of the incarnate Son of God (Col 3:1–2). With hints of the *Sursum Corda*, he lifts up the eyes of his heart to God in heaven; and, although the Sanctus is not referenced, the fellowship of men and angels in the praise of God is suggested by Polycarp's prayer, as also earlier in the narrative of his martyrdom (*M.Pol.* 2.3; 14.1).

Polycarp addresses and acknowledges "the Lord God Almighty" as the Father of his "beloved and blessed Son Jesus Christ." The Bishop confesses that through this Christ "we have received the knowledge" of the Father, "the God of angels and of powers and of all the creation of the entire race of the righteous." It is through the same Lord Jesus Christ, "the eternal and heavenly High Priest," that Polycarp prays to and praises the Holy Trinity (*M.Pol.* 14.1, 3).

---

28. Daniel Brege has demonstrated the various ways in which the sacrament of the altar is the culmination and fulfillment of all the Old Testament sacrifices. The sacrament is the meal of Christ Jesus, the pre-eminent Sacrifice of God, whose body and blood are given and poured out for his Christians to eat and to drink (Cf. Brege, *Eating God's Sacrifice*; also, Kleinig, *Leviticus*). So, too, that which is fulfilled once for all in Christ Jesus, is also embodied and confessed in the life and ministry, the suffering and death of his servant, Polycarp of Smyrna.

29. Cf. Mazza, *The Celebration of the Eucharist*, 93–115.

Polycarp's eucharistic prayer is thoroughly Christocentric. Not only is Christ the object of the Bishop's praise and thanksgiving, worshiped and glorified together with the Father and the Holy Spirit (*M.Pol.* 14.3; 19.2), but Christ is also the subject of the prayer, the one who prays, because he is the one who reveals the Father to the church (*M.Pol.* 14.1), through whom Polycarp prays to the Father (*M.Pol.* 14.3). It is in the descending of the Son from the Father into the flesh that God is known in the midst of suffering and death, and it is in the ascending of the incarnate Son to the Father that the church's prayer and praise arise like incense before the Holy Trinity (Eph 4:8–10; Rom 10:6–8; John 3:13). It is in the same way that Polycarp himself is also welcomed before God as a rich and acceptable sacrifice (*M.Pol.* 14.2; 15.2; 19.2).

With his confession of Christ Jesus, Polycarp blesses and glorifies the Father, Son, and Holy Spirit, and he gives thanks that he is considered worthy "to receive a portion in the number of the martyrs" (*M.Pol.* 14.2; 19.2). Here Polycarp occupies the place that normally belongs to the bread and wine of the Eucharist. By way of his martyrdom according to the gospel, he enters into the Holy Communion of Christ the crucified, into a participation in the cross and passion of Christ Jesus unto the resurrection of eternal life in both body and soul. With the martyrs who have gone before him, Polycarp's portion is "in the Cup" of Christ (*M.Pol.* 14.2); his body in the fire is like "bread baking" (*M.Pol.* 15.2).

The bishop is poured out like wine into the cup of Christ; he becomes the bread which is the body of Christ. Polycarp is identified with the eucharistic elements because he is conformed to the image of Christ the crucified in his martyrdom, and because the incarnate Christ is present with him in his suffering and death, as surely as he is present with his body and blood in the Eucharist.

Poignantly, not his persecutors but Polycarp is the celebrant of this "Eucharist," since it is only after he "had offered up the 'Amen' and finished his prayer" that "the men attending the pyre lit the fire" (*M.Pol.* 15.1). Recall that the police who came to arrest him earlier in the story did not lead him away until his "hour" had come, when he had finished his extended prayers and intercessions (*M.Pol.* 8.1). It is not that Polycarp is forging his own path or determining the course of events. In his eucharistic prayer, he attributes his martyrdom entirely to the will, revelation, guidance, and accomplishment of God the Father (*M.Pol.* 14.2). But, as a servant of the Lord, "a priest of God Most High" (Gen 14:18), Polycarp is a liturgist in the name and stead of Christ. Therefore, even though he is arrested, tried, and put to death by the enemies of Christ, everything from start to finish actually proceeds according to the word and will of God.

THE DISTRIBUTION OF THE GIFTS

As in the celebration of the sacrament, the bread—in this case, the body of Bishop Polycarp—is first received from the Lord with thanksgiving (1 Tim 4:5) and then handed over in the name of the Lord (1 Cor 11:23), entrusted to God and to his people, to his glory and for their good.

When it became apparent that Polycarp's body "could not be consumed by the fire," he was stabbed with a dagger (as the crucified Lord Jesus was pierced, John 19:31–36), and from his body came both "a dove" and such an "abundance of blood" that it "quenched the fire," causing the crowd to marvel (*M.Pol.*16.1).[30] This description graphically signifies the way that Polycarp "ended the persecution" with his martyrdom (*M.Pol.* 1.1). By his eucharistic death, the bishop of Smyrna has become a sacrament of Christ Jesus, through whom the Holy Spirit is poured out upon the church, bestowing peace such as the world cannot give (John 14:25–28). Perhaps that same point is implied in describing the day as "a great Sabbath" (*M.Pol.* 8.1; 21).

Polycarp enters into the Sabbath rest of Christ by way of his death (*M.Pol.* 17.1; 19.2), and he brings peace and rest to others by his dying. "The elect," who are chosen by God and precious in his sight, although they are despised by the world (1 Pet 2:4–5), are strengthened in faith by the testimony of Polycarp's martyrdom (*M.Pol.* 16.1; 18.3).

"Even before his martyrdom," St. Polycarp was "honored in every respect on account of his good conduct," and the faithful were always eager to assist him in removing his sandals, to see who would "promptly touch his skin" (*M.Pol.* 13.2). Following his death, Polycarp's body is revered all the more, and his bones are gathered to a "fitting" place, to be honored in memory of his death. His remains are more valuable than much gold and many fine jewels, because the body that has suffered and died in the likeness of the Lord Jesus Christ is a more precious and glorious adornment than any kind of earthly wealth (*M.Pol.* 17.1; 18.2–3).

Having participated in the passion of Christ by his martyrdom, Polycarp's body also partakes of the resurrection and glorification of Christ's body (*M.Pol.* 14.2; 19.2; 2 Cor 4:7–12; Rom 6:5–8). For this reason, then, many of the faithful desire to commune (*koinonesai*) with "his holy flesh" (*M.Pol.* 17.1). As the bishop has become a sacrifice of praise and thanksgiving to God in Christ Jesus, so too the remains of his body and the remembrance of his death are the fruits and the "feast" of his sacrifice, now shared with the church for communion with Christ.

---

30. "Now the salvation and the power and the kingdom of our God and the authority of his Christ have come, for the accuser of our brothers has been thrown down, who accuses them day and night before our God. And they have conquered him by the blood of the Lamb and by the word of their testimony, for they loved not their lives even unto death" (Rev 12:10-11).

Just as the church regards the bread and wine consecrated by the word of God and prayer to be the holy body and precious blood of Christ, so do Christians regard the bodies of his holy martyrs, not as they outwardly appear, but according to the promise of his bodily resurrection. The church, therefore, lays them to rest with great care in that same hope and confession.

Polycarp is remembered with thanksgiving by the church, not only in the narrative of his death, but with annual gatherings on "the birthday of his martyrdom" (*M.Pol.* 17.3; 18.3; 21). It is likely that such gatherings were centered in the Eucharist. They commemorate the martyr to the glory of God, and they catechize the Christians by the example of Polycarp, in preparation for a faithful witness unto death. In this way, Polycarp is a link in the chain of discipleship, following the Lord in his passion and providing a pattern for others to emulate in accordance with the gospel and in harmony with the Eucharist (*M.Pol.* 1.1–2; 19.1; 22.1).[31]

With such lofty eucharistic language concerning Polycarp and his martyrdom, and with such explicit comparisons to Christ and his passion, there is the danger and temptation of confusing the martyr with the master. In response to this potential confusion and idolatry, the *Martyrdom* clearly differentiates the worship that belongs solely to Christ, the incarnate Son of God, and the loving honor that is given to the martyrs for his sake (*M.Pol.* 17.2–3). Of course, the clear testimony of Polycarp himself is that Christ alone is Lord and king (*M.Pol.* 9.3).

CONCLUSION: REMEMBERING POLYCARP'S EUCHARISTIC MARTYRDOM

In a day and age when martyrdom is more prominent and visible than ever, the eucharistic life and death of Polycarp of Smyrna remains an instructive example for us. The pattern of his eucharistic ministry as a pastor of the church became the eucharistic pattern of his martyrdom, in which we are also given to see the image and likeness of the cross and passion of Christ Jesus. His martyrdom is a catechesis and confession of the gospel, which still strengthens the faith and life of other Christians all these generations later.

It remains the case that Christian catechesis, flowing to and from the waters of Holy Baptism, is preparation and training for a faithful martyrdom in the confidence of the cross and resurrection of Christ. So, too, the culmination and seal of a eucharistic life are found in such a martyrdom, emulating the sacrifice of our Lord Jesus Christ. As we are baptized into his death, so do we eat and drink the fruits of his passion

---

31. Cf. Robin Darling Young, *In Procession Before the World: Martyrdom as Public Liturgy in Early Christianity* (Marquette, IL: Marquette University Press, 2001), 18–24.

in Holy Communion as the proclamation of his cross in both body and soul. It is not simply that we persevere with patience under persecution, but that, by the bearing of the cross within our own vocations and stations in life, and at the hour of death, we give thanks and praise to God that we are counted worthy to suffer and die in the name and for the sake of Christ Jesus.

All the more so, then, the ministry and life of those who are called to be the pastors and teachers of the church, to be fathers of the faith in Christ Jesus, are eucharistic sacrifices which glorify the God and Father of our Lord Jesus Christ and strengthen his people in the unity and love of the Holy Spirit. Thanks be to God for the gift of his servants, St. Polycarp of Smyrna and Dr. William Weinrich, to the praise and glory of our great high priest, Christ Jesus. ✠

THE SUFFERING OF CHRIST IN THE SERMONS OF LEO THE GREAT

✛

Leo the Great is a figure who looms large in the study of the patris-tics and the history of the church in general.[1] His stewardship of the church in Rome during difficult military and civic times involving the Huns and the Vandals magnified the stature of the bishop in Rome. His energetic defense and advocacy of the primacy of the Petrine office was an important step in the development of the Papacy. His involve-ment in the Nestorian crisis was central to the conflict, and his doctrinal contribution (especially his Tome) is one of the pinnacle achievements of Christology in the Western church. These aspects of Leo's tenure as Pope are well-known and have been investigated by many historians.

What has been less scrutinized until recent decades is his role as a pastor and preacher. While he was a civic leader and an important player on the wider church scene, Leo was primarily the pastor of the church in Rome. In recent scholarship, attention has focused on Leo's role as a pastoral theologian and the effect that his theological vision had on his role as bishop and preacher. Susan Wessel sketches an ambitious portrait of Leo in the context of late antique Rome and sees his pastoral role as central, rather than incidental, to assessing his theological method and significance.[2] Bernard Green focuses on Leo's soteriology and points to Leo's construction of a civic Christianity as the central aim of his career. This building of a Roman vision of Christian community life lived out in the environment of a newly Christian Roman culture is a pastoral task. Green's study is largely based on a close reading of Leo's sermons.[3] Mark Armitage follows a similar course in his study of redemption in Leo. He finds that Leo's two-nature Christology is best understood as a narrative

---

1. The standard biography of Leo in English is still Trevor Jalland, *The Life and Times of St. Leo the Great* (London: Society for Promoting Christian Knowledge, 1941). A more general and more recent biography is Neil Bronwen, *Leo the Great* (London: Routledge, 2009).
2. Susan Wessel, *Leo the Great and the Spiritual Rebuilding of a Universal Rome* (Leiden: Brill, 2008). See especially chapters 3 and 4, 179–250.
3. Bernard Green, *The Soteriology of Leo the Great* (Oxford: Oxford University Press, 2008).

about salvation, "a story about the fulfillment of prophecy and promise" that finds its end in Christ who is one with his Father and one with us.[4]

This emphasis on a more complete picture of Leo as a pastoral theologian naturally spotlights his sermons.[5] Leo's ninety-six published sermons have always been seen as important to his work but were often treated as avenues to understand him as civic leader or in terms of the development of his christological vocabulary. While such enquiries can be valuable, the approach to Leo as pastor and preacher produces a portrayal of Leo as a theologian who was engaged in the work of proclamation to his congregation in Rome. In his sermons Leo treats themes of sacraments and liturgy,[6] sanctification and morality in a congregational setting with Christology at the center of his pastoral theology.

This article seeks to examine one aspect of his preaching, the suffering of Christ, and to locate this theme in the larger pastoral aim of his sermons. Leo's Holy Week sermons on the passion contain the most direct and extensive thoughts of Leo on the suffering of Christ. In these sermons, the importance of the passion of Christ flows out of a focus on the incarnation. But the incarnation and passion point to a third theme intertwined with these: the saving will of the Father and the Son. In his attempts to explicate the paradox of the divine Christ suffering on the cross and to construct a framework for that suffering, Leo consistently returns to a soteriological theme. Christ's suffering is the completion of the divine will to save a lost humanity. This divine will to save is at the center of his attempts to work out the union of the divine and the human in Christ. Further, the suffering of Christ as an expression of God's salvific will is present in the church both as *sacramentum* and *exemplum*— mystery and example. His frequent exhortations to holy living are appropriations of the suffering Christ in the church through preaching, liturgy, church year and sacraments.

THE SUFFERING OF CHRIST AND UNION OF THE NATURES

The union of the divine and human in the one person of the Son is a constant theme in Leo's sermons. His formulas reappear often, and parts

---

4. Mark J. Armitage, *A Twofold Solidarity: Leo the Great's Theology of Redemption*, Early Christian Studies 9 (Strathfield, NSW: St. Pauls Publications, 2005), 20.

5. See also Philip L. Barclift, "Predestination and Divine Foreknowledge in the Sermons of Pope Leo the Great," *Church History* 62 (1993): 5–21. See also Mark J. Armitage, *The Economy of Mercy: The Liturgical Preaching of St. Leo the Great*, PhD dissertation, Durham University, 1997; Bronwen Neil, "Models of Gift Giving in the Preaching of Leo the Great," *Journal of Early Christian Studies* 18 (2010): 225–259; and Francis Murphy, "The sermons of Pope Leo the Great: Content and Style," in *Preaching in the Patristic Age*, ed. David Hunter (New York: Paulist, 1989), 183–197.

6. Tad W. Guzie, "Exegetical and Sacramental Language in the Sermons of St. Leo the Great," *Studia Patristica* 12 (1975): 208–213.

of Leo's sermons are used in his Tome, which insists on the two natures each retaining its own properties in the personal union.[7] However, in the sermons on the Passion, it is apparent that Leo's primary concern is not vocabulary or establishing precise meanings of particular words, but the soteriological aim.[8] The union of the divine and the human in Christ find their ultimate meaning when Christ suffers for the salvation of humanity. Armitage has pointed to the formula of consubstantiality (*consubstantialis patri, consubstantialis matri*) as the most important way Leo accounts for the union. As Armitage notes "What really matters for Leo is not explaining how the Incarnation works but rather if (like Nestorius and Eutyches) we fail to account for Christ's being *consubstantialis patri* and *consubstantialis matri*, we shall be unable to make sense of the narrative which is read to us from the Gospel."[9]

Sermon 65 is a good example of how Leo looks at the union of the natures in light of the suffering Jesus.[10] Leo begins this sermon, preached late in his career on Wednesday of Holy Week in 453 AD, by stating that his aim is to "render service to the Paschal feast" and to combat heresy. He attacks those who deny the reality of Christ's flesh and those who say that such suffering must be an insult to the Godhead. Leo then characteristically asserts the reality and individuality of the two natures while also insisting that all actions belonged to one and the same person. More importantly, Leo goes on to interpret that union of the natures in light of the suffering of Christ. When Christ knocked down the mob sent by the Jewish leaders with a simple word, it was an indication of divine power. Yet the fact that Christ then allowed the soldiers to take him into custody reveals an even greater proof of divinity: the Son of God in human flesh held in check his divine power so that the glory of the passion might be attained. The divine Son of God truly showed himself as Son of God not by flattening the soldiers with power but by surrendering himself to their "wicked hands" so that Christ would suffer. Leo sees this scene as one in

---

7. See Sermons 21.2, 22. 1–2, 23.2, 24.3 and 54.2. See also the analysis of the Tome in Green, *The Soteriology of Leo the Great*, 215–220.

8. Armitage makes the point that Leo displays no great precision in his sermons in using the terms *natura, substantia, forma,* and *status.* They are all interchangeable. His concern is not linguistic precision but doctrinal and ultimately soteriological truth. Armitage, *Twofold Solidarity,* 87–91. However, see Philip Barclift, "The Shifting Tones of Pope Leo the Great's Christological Vocabulary," *Church History* 66 (1997): 221–239.

9. Armitage, *Twofold Solidarity,* 91. See also Basil Studer, "*Consubstantialis Patri, Consubstantialis Matri.* Une antithèse christologique chez Léon le Grand," *Revue des Études Augustiniennes* 18 (1972): 87–115.

10. The Latin text for Leo's sermons is from *Sancti Leonis Magni Romani Pontificis: Tractus Septem et Nonaginta,* ed. A. Chavasse, Corpus Christianorum, Series Latina, vols. 138 and 138A (Turnholti: Brepols, 1973). English translations (unless otherwise noted) are from St. Leo the Great, *Sermons,* trans. Jane Patricia Freeland and Agnes Josephine Conway, Fathers of the Church Series, vol. 93 (Washington DC: Catholic University of America, 1996). Citations are to the tractates and paragraphs in these volumes rather than page numbers.

which Christ "renews our mortal essence through his immortal one" but does so by not asserting his divinity but by suffering in his humanity.[11]

Leo is careful in this sermon[12] (as he is throughout his sermons) to account for both the individuality of the natures and the unity of the person: "What the flesh of the Word suffered was punishment not of the Word but of the flesh. Yet injuries and tortures redounded even onto the one who cannot suffer so that the things which he permitted against his body are appropriately said to have been inflicted on him."[13] After Leo recites the reality of the fleshly post-Easter appearances of Christ to his disciples, he declares why the passion and flesh of Christ are central to his account of the union of natures: "Let us not be torn from our adhesion to the body of Christ. . . . Since the substance of God is incorporeal, how does it dwell in bodily manner in Christ unless the flesh of our race has been made the flesh of the divinity? We filled out in that God [*in illo sumus Deo replete*] in whom we have been crucified, in whom we have been buried, in whom we have even been raised up."[14] The union of the two distinct natures leads to the cross of Christ where that union functions to bring humanity into union with God through the body of Christ. The suffering of Christ is the salvation of Christians, since they are that flesh that died, was buried, and rose. The Christ of the cross shows the Son of God in his strength and in our weakness.[15]

The union of Christ is such that the flesh of human sinners has been made the flesh of the divine and results in a crucifixion and burial and resurrection of Christians. The union of the divine and the human is not a puzzle to be solved for Leo but a mystery that centers on the passion of Christ and that involves the church in salvation. In this passage from Sermon 70, Leo establishes the reality of the natures, their communion in suffering and the ultimate reason for their union in the passion:

> The method of dispensing mercy does not obscure the majesty of the one dispensing it. Through his ineffable power it has come about that while true man is in the inviolable God and true God is in the suffering flesh, glory is conferred upon human beings through shame, incorruption through punishment, life through death.[16]

---

11. *Tr* 65.2.

12. See especially, "No division ever existed between the divine and the human substances. Throughout all the increases of bodily growth, his actions during that whole time belonged to one and the same Person. Yet we do not confuse those things which happened inseparably by mixing them up somehow. Instead, we realize the nature to which any given thing might pertain from its properties. Divine operations do not prejudice human ones, nor do human properties prejudice divine ones. Both join together without the deletion of any proper characteristic of a doubling of the person" (*Tr* 65.1).

13. *Tr* 65.3.

14. *Tr* 65.5.

15. *Tr* 56.2. He also says here, "We worship the Son of God both in his strengths and in our weaknesses."

16. *Tr* 70.3.

It is God who confers glory, but the union of the natures has made it so that this God confers such glory and incorruption through the human things of suffering. The union of the natures is the mechanism by which God chooses to give his glory. It is God himself who is active in the passion and is seen in suffering and weakness. The union of the natures allows the Passion to have its saving force in giving life to human beings.

WHY THE PASSION?

Leo is very interested in proclaiming how the two natures in one person function in the Passion. He wants to answer the question, "Why did Christ have to suffer and why did he have to be both God and man in one person in that suffering?" Leo has two answers to this question.[17] One is that in his incarnation, Christ must be the mediator between God and man. The other is that Christ must be both divine and human in order to overcome the devil.[18] The second of these frameworks for understanding the relationship between the two natures and the suffering of Christ will be treated first.

Leo is fond of the traditional account of the crucifixion that sees the devil overcome by justice and not by power. On account of humanity falling into sin, "the ancient enemy" had justly arrogated for himself "a tyrannical rule over all people. Nor was that dominion unwarranted beneath which he crushed them."[19] The devil, upon seeing Christ, thinks that Christ was a commonplace sinful man. He proceeds to unjustly overwhelm him with sufferings and death, and he thus oversteps his rights and loses his hold on humanity. Here the suffering of Christ functions as part of the divine plan to overcome Satan and free those in his clutches. That plan operated on the level of justice not power, humility not overpowering strength. Leo can sketch the idea as starkly economic: Satan "rages against a nature subject to himself" and takes payment even where no debt is owed, since there is no sin. The cross of Christ then makes void the edict of death that "proclaimed our sale into bondage" and the contractual rights that are now transferred to Christ.[20]

While resting on a theory of rights and what is due to the devil, this overcoming of Satan is for Leo a complete overcoming of Satan's reign. He follows this economic account of the cross with a strong statement of how the nails in Christ's hands and feet have "gouged out everlasting wounds in the devil" and have brought the "killing of hostile powers."[21]

---

17. I am indebted to Bernard Green for this framework. See Green, *The Soteriology of Leo the Great*, 144–158.
18. Leo shares with Augustine the thrust of these accounts of Christ's work. Green, *The Soteriology of Leo the Great*, 150.
19. *Tr* 22.3 (Recension A).
20. *Tr* 61.4.
21. *Tr* 61.4.

The passion is not simply a trick or a commercial transaction but a real crushing of the devil and his reign over humanity. The victory over Satan, however, is achieved in a paradoxical way. Leo presents the account of the devil losing his rights over man[22] in order to emphasize the incarnation and the defeat of Satan's power by the lowliness of Christ, which in an unexpected way displays his divine nature. By "hiding the power of his majesty" Christ displays only the weakness of his assumed human nature. Yet, he does all this "according to the design of His will."[23] In allowing the devil to rage against him, Christ is displaying not weakness, as it appears, but his divine will to save. The Jews and the devil fail to recognize the "mystery of great compassion,"[24] which is being played out on the cross. This awful spectacle is actually the design of God's mercy. By not using his divine strength and glory, Christ triumphs over the devil in a fierce combat whereby the "strength of his humility" wins the victory.[25]

The divine will to save is the center of Leo's conception of Christ's paradoxical victory over the devil when the devil oversteps his rights. It is more than a simple transaction. In Sermon 55, in characteristically terse lines,[26] Leo summarizes the effect of Christ's passion on Satan: "The blood of a spotless Lamb effaced the pact of that ancient transgression. There, the whole perversity of the devil's mastery was abolished, while humility triumphed as conqueror over the vaunting of pride."[27] The two natures here work, as it were, in opposite directions. It is the humble, tormented things of the humanity that gain the victory (they do the work, so to speak), while the divinity does its part in doing nothing, in being hidden and not exercised. This humility of the Godhead is the divine will to save. In hiding and not acting, in allowing the assumed flesh to be punished and killed, God Incarnate abolishes the mastery of Satan and his pride.

The second framework in which Leo sees the suffering of Christ and the union of the natures is Christ as a mediator, uniting the natures in himself. For Leo, the incarnation itself is indicative of this mediatorial role.[28] Yet, when Leo comes to the passion of Christ, the role of mediator is seen through the prism of his suffering. Leo seeks to answer the ques-

22. *Tr* 64.2. He also says here, "While raging against someone he did not hold under the law of sin, the devil lost the right of his wicked rule."
23. *Tr* 62.3.
24. *Tr* 69.4.
25. *Tr* 69.3.
26. For more on Leo's language and style, see W. J. Halliwell, *The Style of Pope Leo the Great* (Washington DC: Catholic University of America Press, 1939).
27. *Tr* 55.3.
28. Leo discusses the incarnation throughout his sermons, but see especially his Christmas sermon (*Tr.* 22) from 441, his Lenten sermon (*Tr.* 54) in 442, his Ascension sermon (*Tr.* 74) from 445, and his Pentecost sermon (*Tr.* 77) for 442.

tion: how can the divine participate in such things as suffering, blood, and death?

In Sermon 54, Leo tackles this question and introduces an image that crystallizes his view: "He had come into this world as the rich and merciful ambassador from heaven."[29] From what precedes and follows this statement, it is evident that Leo sees in the context of the passion this image of the ambassador from heaven as a mediating figure. Leo references 2 Corinthians 5:19 ("God was in Christ reconciling the world to himself") and says that the Creator himself was bearing the humanity that would be restored to the image of its maker. He focuses on the Gethsemane scene (a favorite of Leo's) where Christ is seen as weak and sorrowful and wishes to have the cup pass from him.

Christ's expression of fear and weakness is the context in which Leo develops his image of Christ as an ambassador who is able to give and to bless humanity. The paradox of the divine Son experiencing human weakness forms the way that Leo sees Christ as the strong Redeemer and giver of salvation. Leo maintains that Christ "cured the emotion of our weakness by participating in it and drove away the anxiety in the experience of suffering by undergoing it."[30] By becoming incarnate and allowing himself to know and participate in human suffering, Christ, the divine Son of God, is not weakened or diminished but is in fact expressing his divinity. As Green notes on Leo's soteriology, for Leo "the divine is expressed in the human, humility is not alien to majesty but rather humility is how divine majesty acts in a human life."[31] The strength and the majesty of the divine is expressed in the saving actions of the incarnation and especially the passion. "The Lord trembled with our terror," says Leo, and clothed himself with our weakness but did so in order to wrap us with his strength. The ambassador turns into an image of exchange. For Leo, Christ entered the economy of salvation in order to receive our state and give us his own, to give honors while receiving insults, and to confer "health for pain, life for death."[32]

Leo develops this theme of exchange in Sermons 63 and 64, where he focuses on the experience of the cross. Christ, the sinless one, assumes all our weaknesses that come from sin though without any sinfulness on his own part. He lacks none of the afflictions or hunger or thirst or sadness or tears. Even to the point of death he endured "grievous sorrows."[33] He did all this because no one caught in the snares of death could be freed unless the sinless one allowed himself to be killed.[34] The point of

---

29. *Tr* 54.4.
30. *Tr* 54.4.
31. Green, *The Soteriology of Leo the Great*, 155.
32. *Tr* 54.4.
33. *Tr* 63.4.
34. *Tr* 63.4.

the passion is that by submitting himself to such injuries, Christ brings humanity into participation with the divine nature. Christ's passion, "the shedding of innocent blood for the guilty" establishes freedom and pays the ransom.[35] What follows then is that human beings are attracted to the God who comes in their own flesh and blood and who has opened the way to communion with them. Since he has united himself to human nature, human beings participate in him and in his victory: "He gave his triumph to those in whose body he triumphed."[36] As mediator, Christ's divinity and strength are transferred to his human nature and to those who believe, but this exchange is accomplished through his suffering and by his acceptance of human weakness.

This mediating role means not only that Christ's victory and triumph are given to believers, but also that, as members of his body, they participate in his suffering, death, and resurrection. Christ participates in human suffering not for his own benefit; rather, for Leo, Christ's passion becomes accessible to the church, and the church is joined to that suffering and receives divine gifts. "True worshippers of the Lord's passion" look at Jesus on the cross and see a being of their own flesh.[37] Furthermore, they look at themselves and recognize the divine Son of God who has taken on their flesh. Leo says that as much as we "must not doubt his participation in our nature," neither can we "doubt our participation in his glory."[38] This means that we too are crucified, we too are buried, and we too are raised with him on the third day. As mediator, Christ's incarnation and passion create an exchange whereby Christ, by participating in our sins and weaknesses, gives us his divine glory. This exchange is constitutive of the church's life; as his body, the church participates in his suffering, resurrection, and, finally, ascension into glory.

GETHSEMANE

In Leo's passion sermons, the incarnation is a soteriological matter consisting in the will of God to save humanity. The divine will to save humanity is the will of Christ to suffer and endure the cross, to be the mediator, and to overcome the devil by dying as the Innocent One. The relation between the divine will to save and Christ's will to suffer ultimately consists in the relation between the two natures in Christ. This relationship comes to the forefront when Leo considers the Gethsemane accounts wherein Christ asks his Father to take the cup of suffering from him. Dealing with this scene is an important one for Leo; his exposition

---

35. *Tr* 64.3.
36. *Tr* 64.3.
37. *Tr* 66.3.
38. *Tr* 72.2.

sheds light on his understanding of the divine and human in the passion of Christ and the central role soteriology plays in his thinking.

Leo repeatedly mentions the Gethsemane scene and the problem of the divine and human wills.[39] In Sermon 58, a Palm Sunday sermon, Leo begins by presenting Jesus as a divine figure who, in telling Judas to do quickly what he is doing, was in complete control of the situation. Jesus, who had all power over time, did not delay the coming of the suffering, because he was intent on carrying out his Father's will for saving the world.[40] This sets up Leo's consideration of Jesus' request in the garden to let the cup of suffering pass from him. Leo begins his interpretation of this request by citing John 3:16 and establishing the certainty of the Father's and the Son's will to save: "In saving all by the cross of Christ, the Father and the Son had one will and plan,"[41] and that plan was salvation. Leo puts the will to save at the very center of the divinity. It is the characteristic of divinity to will humanity's salvation.

When Christ asks that the cup pass from him, he is expressing the puzzling truth of the incarnation, namely, that he has taken on human misery, suffering, and weakness. Leo says that Christ has taken on real human lowliness, sadness, and pain in the crucifixion. Christ's prayer expresses the full reality of his assumed human nature. But he is quick to point out why Christ has assumed that nature and weakness: "For this did his mercy undergo the sufferings of our mortality, that he might save it. For this did his strength accept [these sufferings] that he might overcome them."[42] He displays the reality of the nature he has assumed by using "the voice of our nature." Christ then accepts the Passion in saying to the Father, "Thy will be done." Leo can then write this: "This saying of the head is the salvation of the whole body."[43]

What Leo has done is to locate the divinity of Christ in the accepting of suffering. The divinity is not shown in acts of power or might. While Leo is consistently clear in his distinguishing of the natures throughout his sermons, when he comes to the puzzle of the passion, he constructs a picture whereby Christ's divinity is shown in suffering. The important piece of the puzzle is the divine will. For Leo that divine will is John 3:16, the will to save. When Christ asks if the cup be taken away, he speaks with our voice. That human voice is the will to avoid suffering, the voice of fear, and the voice of humanity. When he accepts the cross, that is the divine voice, the divine will. His speaking in that way becomes the salvation of the whole body. The divine nature of Christ is seen in the will to

---

39. See especially Sermons 54, 58, 59, 67 and 68.
40. *Tr* 58.4.
41. *Tr* 58.4.
42. *Tr* 58.4.
43. *Tr* 58.5.

save. That will to save is nothing other than the cross and the acceptance of the cross is both the salvation of the church and the manifestation of the Christ's divinity.

In Sermon 68, Leo presents a similar treatment of Christ's cry of abandonment on the cross. He begins by denying that God could ever abandon him, since such a great union between human and divine exists in Christ. While Leo says that "each substance retained its own proper nature so that the divinity which was in the suffering man was not in the suffering itself."[44] Leo goes on to temper that forceful statement of the division of the natures with an equally forceful statement of the union. He insists that the same one who made all things was taken by the hands of sinful men and pierced by nails and undergoes death.[45] In all this the lowliness and the majesty are seen to be real.

This sets the stage for his consideration of Psalm 22:1 on the lips of Jesus. The reason why Jesus cried out was not that he had been abandoned (which Leo had denied was possible at the beginning of the sermon), but to "make known to all that it was right that he should not be rescued or defended but should be abandoned into the hands of violent men, that is, to become the Savior of the world and redeemer of all people."[46] The cry comes not from "misery," says Leo, but from mercy. It stems from his "decision to die."[47] Leo handles this difficult passage in much the same way he handles the Gethsemane prayer. What might be seen as problematic (how can the divinity be abandoned?) is handled by Leo in terms of God's salvific will. Leo says he cried out on account of his "determination" to die.[48]

Leo thus locates the answer to this perplexing question in the will of God to save: "It was the will of the Father as well as his own will that the Lord should be given over to his passion."[49] The reason that Christ is on the cross is that he, in communion with his Father, has decided to do it. It is the divine will that Christ suffer in order to fulfill the divine plan to "make sinners whole."[50] Paradoxically, the divinity of Christ is manifested precisely in his acceptance of human suffering. Leo locates the revelation of the divinity in God's soteriological decisions. Human reasoning typically locates the divine in the miracles and displays of

---

44. *Tr* 68.1.
45. *Tr* 68.1.
46. *Tr* 68.2.
47. *Tr* 68.2.
48. *Tr* 68.2. In Latin, the passage is "*non per miseriam sed per misericordiam, nec amissione auxilii sed definitione moriendi.*" Freeland and Conway in the Fathers of the Church Series, cited above, translate "*definitione moriendi*" as "decision to die," but it can be rendered more forcefully as "determination."
49. *Tr* 68.2.
50. *Tr* 68.2.

power (and Leo often does as well); yet, when faced with the difficult scenes of Christ's cry of abandonment or his Gethsemane prayer, Leo sees Christ's divinity in and through his humanity in the common will of the Father and the incarnate Son to save. Thus, Leo says in another sermon: "His power and strength have been manifested through the acceptance of weakness."[51]

CHRIST'S SUFFERING PRESENT IN THE CHURCH

Leo's emphases on the divine will to save as well as Christ's suffering become constitutive of his ecclesiology. The saving passion of Christ defines the church's ongoing life. One way he does this is through his use of the related terms *sacramentum* (as well as *remedium*) and *exemplum*. Leo's use of these concepts is a well-known feature of his sermons.[52] The *sacramenta* are the saving actions of his life with the paramount one being his Passion. These *sacramenta* are shared now in the church. They are not merely past events but present realities: "All that the Son of God 'did and taught' for reconciling the world, we have not so much learned from the account of past events as we have felt in the force of present events."[53] Christ, born by the Holy Spirit, fills the church with that same Spirit so that "an innumerable throng of God's children have been born." Through baptism, Leo sees the Christian partaking in the passion of Christ here and now. He sees a "kind of death" and a certain "likeness of resurrection" occurring. Christ is so much present in the church's ministry that after baptism "the bodies of those reborn turn into the flesh of the crucified."[54] This reality is based on the incarnation: "He does not constitute the first fruits of humanity if he does not come from the stock of human nature" but is completed by the passion of Christ in whom Christians are themselves crucified with him.[55] Leo can say that "the flesh of our race has been made the flesh of the divinity."[56] The Lord's Supper is treated in the same way: "The new creature receives food and drink from the Lord himself. This partaking in the body and blood of Christ means nothing else than that we should pass over into what we have taken in."[57] The passion of Christ is present in the church through the saving liturgical acts of the church; the goal of these acts is the transformation of Christians in the suffering Christ himself. Rather than strictly exegetical in

---

51. *Tr* 60.2.
52. See Marie Bernard De Soos, *Le Mystere Liturgique* (Münster, Westfalen: Aschendorff, 1958), 94–98. See also Wessel, *Leo the Great and the Spiritual Rebuilding of a Universal Rome*, 239–242.
53. *Tr* 63.6.
54. *Tr* 63.6.
55. *Tr* 66.4.
56. *Tr* 65.5.
57. *Tr* 63.7.

nature, Leo's preaching is wholly liturgical, presenting the saving events of Christ's life in the church year as a means by which Christ's passion is made present in the church.[58] Through the preaching of the passion, the hearers are joined to that passion. The barrier between past and present is overcome.

Sermon 70 is a striking example of how Leo presents the presence of Christ and his passion in the church. Leo begins by noting the power of preaching to make the Gospel narratives present for the hearers. It is so vivid as to become a "visual aid."[59] For Leo, the evangelical account centers on the fastening of the Son of God, equal to Father, to the cross, condemned and disgraced.[60] This event is presented to believers in the church so that they may strive to be joined to this great mystery.[61] Baptism is the beginning of this union. Thus, Leo introduces a startling image by picturing the waters of baptism flowing out of the empty tomb when the stone has been removed: "When the stone of the sepulcher has been removed, as it were, the water of Baptism brings forth new those souls that the fountain's bosom had received old."[62] This homiletic image captures well Leo's view of the relation of baptism and the church's worship and the cross. They are joined together as source and conduit. What the one provides, the other gives.

The other side of Leo's presentation of the idea of *sacramentum*, the mystery of Christ's passion present in the church's worship, is his use of *exemplum*.[63] Christ and his suffering are not only sacrament but also *exemplum* ("pattern," "model," or "paradigm").[64] The idea of *exemplum*[65] flows directly from the way Leo relates the ancient passion of Christ to the contemporary life of the Christian. For Leo, this relation is firmly fixed in preaching and the sacramental rites of the church. Leo ties together the reality of Christ's passion as both *sacramentum* and *exemplum* this way: "A double remedy has been prepared for us miserable people by the Almighty Physician, one of which is in the mystery (*sacramentum*) the other in his example (*exemplum*). Through the one divine grace is conferred; by virtue

---

58. For Leo's preaching on the liturgical year, see Thomas K. Carroll, "The Genius of the Latin Sermon," *Irish Theological Quarterly* 63 (1998): 349–352.

59. *Tr* 70.1 The Latin says, "*ipsa lectio quaedam facta sit visio*" (literally, "the reading itself has become a kind of vision").

60. *Tr* 70.3.

61. *Tr* 70.4. The Latin says, "*Huic sacramento, dilectissimi, ut inseperabiliter congruamus.*"

62. *Tr* 70.4.

63. For more on Leo's us of *exemplum* (and *sacramentum*) in his scheme of salvation, see Philip Barclift, *Pope Leo's Soteriology: Sacramental Recapitulation*, unpublished dissertation, Marquette University, 1992.

64. Green, *The Soteriology of Leo the Great*, 114.

65. This same dyad of *sacramentum* and *remedium* paired up with *exemplum* (as well *remedium*) is also found in Augustine. See Basil Studer, "'Sacramentum et exemplum' chez saint Augustin," *Recherches Augustiniennes* 10 (1975): 87–141.

of the other human response is required."[66] Christ gives divine grace and then leads his people to be conformed to his example.

This conforming and imitating Christ is for Leo an incarnational and sacramental matter, not one that Christians somehow perform apart from him. The exhortation to follow the example of Christ flows from one's participation in the sacrament of Christ. The Christian's conformity to the pattern of Christ's passion takes place on the basis of Christ's incarnation, his bearing of human suffering, and the presence of that passion in the church's liturgical life. In Sermon 70, Leo, having spoken of Easter and baptism, makes this statement: "What has been celebrated in mystery nonetheless must be carried out in action [*Sed implendum est nihilominus opera quod celebratum est sacramento*], and whatever time remains in the world for children of the Holy Spirit should not be lived without taking up the cross."[67] Here Leo makes several important connections. What has been done in the liturgical worship of the church is lived out in the life of the believer. The new life of the believer—his good works—is precisely the life given at baptism and constituted in the church's worship: "For Leo worship mediates doctrine and praxis."[68] In addition, Leo sees this new life as nothing other than the cross itself being taken up by the believer. So the passion of Christ is the content of baptism causing the rebirth of Christians and the passion of Christ is also the content of the new life that Christians live. The baptized live out the passion in their own lives by taking up the cross. Guzie puts it this way:

> So each time the mystery of the cross is liturgically renewed the worshipper is called to respond by taking his stand on Calvary. In so doing, he is responding at once to the ritual sacrament of Baptism which is part of his personal history and to the word of Scripture which urges him to make his present and future history conform to the total sacramentum which is Christ.[69]

This connection between the new life of the believer and the liturgy that communicates Christ's passion is the context in which Leo exhorts and urges his flock to live the Christian life. His exhortations are often made in an incarnational framework. Leo proclaims, "Be conformed with our Redeemer through his example. He did nothing and suffered nothing that was not for our salvation, in order that the strength that was in the head might also be in the body."[70] Conforming oneself to Christ

---

66. *Tr* 67.5.
67. *Tr* 70.4.
68. David Robinson, "Informed Worship and Empowered Mission: The Integration of Liturgy, Doctrine, and Praxis in Leo the Great's Sermons on Ascension and Pentecost," *Worship* 83 (2009): 540.
69. Guzie, "Exegetical and Sacramental Language in the Sermons of St. Leo the Great," 213.
70. *Tr* 66. 4.

and following his example is an incarnational matter that involves Christ the head imparting his strength to the body. Leo continues in the same section of this sermon, saying that "just as it was our nature (joined into one with the divinity) that the virginity of his Mother brought forth, so it was ours also that the Jewish wickedness crucified. What lay lifeless was ours and what rose on the third day was ours, as well as what ascended above the heights of heaven to the right hand of the Father's majesty."[71] This baptismal union then brings forth the will to "walk in the way of his commandments" and "to confess that which brings our salvation." Exhortation for Leo is Christology and soteriology and sacramental theology. Sermon 53 concludes with a typical exhortation. To seek to live a Christian life is to "embrace the wonderful mystery [*sacramentum*] of the saving Passover."[72] In a string of passive verbs, Leo urges his congregation to be re-formed in the image of the one who became like us in our deformity and be raised to the one who lowered himself on our account. While effort is required of believers (humility, patience, service, and discipline), the underlying reality is that of the incarnation, communicated though the saving acts of the church and experienced in worship. In his sermons, Leo expresses his sincere desire that the reality of the church's worship (which is nothing other than the divine and human in one person, Christ) should be manifested in the lives of those who are members of Christ's body.

CONCLUSION

Leo's treatment of the suffering of Christ in his passion sermons displays his typical focus on the incarnation and the relation of the divine and the human in the one person of Christ. Yet Leo's pastoral interests move him to further situate the divine and the human in the context of soteriology. For Leo, the will of the Father and the Son to save sinful humanity not only forms the foundation for the incarnation and cross but also serves to highlight the relation of the divine nature to human suffering. In the passion sermons, the divinity is paradoxically shown most clearly in the human suffering of Jesus when he accepts his role as crucified Savior and unites the divine and human wills. The suffering of Christ is further presented by Leo as present in the church both as *sacramentum* and *exemplum*, mystery and example. Thus, God's will to save is extended into the life of the church. Finally, Leo's frequent exhortations that his flock lead holy lives are centered in the passion of Christ as his congregation participates in that passion though the church's preaching, liturgy, church year, and sacraments. ✛

71. *Tr* 66.4.
72. *Tr* 53.2.

CRUCIFIED LORD OF GLORY

THEOPASCHITE CHRISTOLOGY
OF THE SCYTHIAN MONKS

✠

O ne contributor to the present festschrift, while teaching at the Seminary in Novosibirsk, remarked, "All I know about Early Church History I've learned from Dr. Weinrich." The author of this article cannot help but concur with this statement. During my time at Concordia Theological Seminary, I made every effort to take all the courses that Dr. Weinrich offered each academic year; and if there was any disappointment, it resulted not from certain sophisticated words and phrases that the lecturer used that made me feel intellectually deficient, but rather from the fact that some courses, while listed in the Academic Catalogue, were not offered at that particular time.

Christ's revelation to Paul in 2 Corinthians 12:9, "My power is made perfect in weakness," comes to mind as a good description for Dr. Weinrich's teaching. Speaking theologically, the event of the cross is where God demonstrates that his greatest power is revealed in the weakness of death. This reality of God dying on the cross for our salvation was summed up in an early Christian aphorism formulated by a remarkable group known in history as the Scythian monks: "One of the Holy Trinity has suffered in the flesh." This orthodox aphorism is the title for this festschrift honoring Dr. Weinrich, because it captures the very heart of his theological perspective.

The Christological thought of the Scythian monks is vital for understanding the theological movements that led to the Fifth Ecumenical Council (AD 553). As it turns out, the Council of Chalcedon (AD 451) was far from being a definitive end to the early Christological controversies that dominated the first five centuries of the church's history. As the sixth century began, the most difficult challenge for the Byzantine church was the rise of Monophysite communities that did not recognize the authority of the Council of Chalcedon.[1] By way of its own state-

---

1. For development of Monophysitism as a separate system and church, see A. I. Brilliantov, "Происхождение монофизитства" [Origin of Monophysitism], in Христианское чтение,

ments, the primary purpose of Chalcedon was to oppose both Nestorianism and Eutychianism. The previous ecumenical council held in Ephesus (AD 431) had been dominated by the influence of Cyril of Alexandria. Under his leadership, Nestorius, the bishop of Constantinople, who was an advocate of the Antiochene theology articulated by Diodore of Tarsus and Theodore of Mopsuestia, had been anathematized. The Christological discourse of Cyril was powerful, but also ambiguous, especially his famous language that there is "one incarnate nature of the Word." Cyril inadvertently borrowed this language from Apollinarius, though he believed the formula to stem from Athanasius. This language was later championed by those loyal to Cyril's Christology, who did not agree with Chalcedon's two-nature formulation.

The Council of Chalcedon (AD 451) was originally called to correct the scandalous "extreme Alexandrian" council of 449 in Ephesus, which was governed by Cyril's successor, Dioscorus. The Roman bishop, Leo I, a strong opponent of Dioscorus and Eutyches, exerted significant influence at Chalcedon. Even though he was not personally present at the council, his legates, assisted by imperial authorities, made sure that Leo's christological emphases would be followed. The Christology of Leo I's famous *Tome* was strictly, forcefully dyophysite, emphasizing two distinct and complete natures in Christ. Therefore, one of the imperatives of the council was to assert a fundamental unity between Cyril and Leo, namely that they taught the same faith. An interesting phenomenon in the conciliar proceedings was that, while the majority of the bishops at the council were Cyrillian in their convictions, they were constrained to use the dyophysite language of Leo to exclude Eutychianism and to please the Imperial authorities.[2]

The Council of Chalcedon in no way satisfied the various churches that were most intimately and passionately involved in the christological struggles of the fifth century. Almost immediately upon the conclusion of Chalcedon, certain bishops and churches in the eastern regions of the empire declared their opposition to the dogmatic formulations of the council. This opposition attacked the dyophysite language inherent in Leo's *Tome* and Chalcedon's *Definition of Faith* and emphasized a natural union of divinity and humanity in Christ. Therefore, this opposition, asserting the "one nature" of Christ, has become known by the name of Monophysitism.

1905, 793–822; W. A. Wigram, *The Separation of the Monophysites* (London: The Faith Press, 1923); W. H. C. Frend, *The Rise of the Monophysite Movement* (Cambridge: James Clarke & Co., 1972). Not all scholars are satisfied with this terminology, e.g., Patrick T. R. Gray, *The Defense of Chalcedon in the East (451–533)*, Studies in the History of Christian Thought 20 (Leiden, Brill: 1979). Gray prefers to use the language of Chalcedonians and non–Chalcedonians throughout his work.

2. Gray, *The Defense of Chalcedon in the East*, 13–16.

The Scythian monks, led by the Archimandrite John Maxentius, accepted all of Chalcedon, including its controversial "in two natures" formula expressed in the *Definition of Faith*. However, being loyal to Cyril of Alexandria, the Scythian monks sought to interpret the Chalcedonian definition in light of the unitive Christology, for which the bishop of Alexandria was famous. In contrast, most Western interpretations of the council were strictly guided by the two-nature emphasis of Leo as expressed in his *Tome*, which was directed against Eutyches and accepted by the bishops gathered at Chalcedon.[3] The Scythian monks wanted the "reconciling of Leo and Cyril,"[4] which was the original posture of the conciliar gathering at Chalcedon. Their famous "Theopaschite" formula, "One of the Holy Trinity has suffered," and its accompanying Christology, were intended to refute certain Nestorianizing tendencies in their homeland, as is evident in their dispute with Paternus, the Bishop of Tomi. In addition to refuting Nestorianism, the Theopaschite formula also encouraged a theological and political reconciliation with some Monophysite communities.

PRESENTATION OF THEOPASCHITE CONFESSION

Scythian monks figured prominently in the events of AD 519–520, after which they disappear from the scene as an organized group, though their literary activity continued beyond that time. Like a meteor crossing the night sky, the activity surrounding the Scythian monks spans from Constantinople to Rome and from the mouth of the Danube River to Roman North Africa. Among the participants involved in the short history of the Scythian monks were the following: the Roman Bishop Hormisdas, the Emperor Justin I, his nephew, the future Justinian I, Count Vitalian ("*master militium*"), the Roman deacon Dioscorus, and the Roman legates who were present in Constantinople at the time.

The Scythian monks came from the region of the Black Sea that is south of the mouth of the Danube River, which was then a Roman Latinized province of Scythia and is a territory of modern Romania.[5] They are sometimes also referred to as the Gothic monks, because a mixed

---

3. E.g., John A. McGuckin, "The Theopaschite Confession," *Journal of Ecclesiastical History* 35 (April 1984): 240. Cf. John A McGuckin, *St. Cyril of Alexandria: The Christological Controversy: Its History, Theology, and Texts*, Supplements to Vigilae Christianae 23 (Leiden, Brill: 1994), 240–241.

4. Richard Price and Michael Gaddis, trans., *The Acts of the Council of Chalcedon: Volume 2* (Liverpool: Liverpool University Press, 2007), 24–25. As witnessed in the acclamations at Chalcedon, e.g. in Session 2, 23: "Leo taught piously and truly. Cyril taught accordingly. Eternal is the memory of Cyril. Leo and Cyril taught the same. Leo and Cyril taught accordingly." The purpose of the Scythian monks was to restore "Cyril" in the proper part of the equation.

5. Cf. R. V. Sellers, *Council of Chalcedon* (London: S.P.C.K., 1953), 305. Sellers mistakenly considers Scythopolis in Galilee as their home.

culture resulted in that land due to the penetration of Goths into territory traditionally occupied by the Scyths.[6] Their leader, Archimandrite John Maxentius, was from the city of Tomi, which was the center of that region. They spoke and wrote in Latin, although at least some of them have known Greek as well,[7] and they were thoroughly Cyrillian in their theology.

They make their first public appearance in Constantinople at the end of 518 or the beginning of 519, which coincided with the end of the thirty-seven-year Acacian Schism that had disrupted church fellowship between Constantinople and Rome. While Scythia maintained formal relations with the Roman church, the Imperial See of Constantinople had greatly increased in importance after the decisions of the Councils of Constantinople in 381 and Chalcedon of 451.[8] To complicate matters, the church in Scythia remained in communion with Rome during the Acacian schism, resulting in an estrangement from Constantinople and other Eastern churches.[9] Thus, it could be that the Scythian monks appeared in Constantinople because they hoped to find a positive reception and imperial support for their opposition to their own bishops.[10] Thus, the Scythian monks first presented their *Confession* in Constantinople.[11] The principal and most controversial line of their confession was "One of the Trinity has suffered in the flesh."[12] The immediate context for this confession was the Scythian monks' disagreement with their bishop, Paternus, as well as with some other bishops in their area who may have been sympathetic to Nestorianism. Thus, the Scythian formula seems intended to be a test for measuring orthodox Christology within a Nestorian context. The Scythian monks apparently believed that their formula would serve as a helpful, perhaps even essential, addition to the Chalcedonian *Definition of Faith*. Rather than replacing the Christological definition of Chalcedon, the

---

6. Aloys Grillmeier, *Christ in Christian Tradition. Vol. 2, From the Council of Chalcedon (451) to Gregory the Great (590–604). Part Two: The Church of Constantinople in the Sixth Century* (Atlanta, GA: John Knox Press, 1996), 320.

7. E.g., Scythian Monks, *Disputatio XII capitulorum Cyrilli Alexandrini et sic dictorum Nestorii anti anathematismorum*, Corpus Christianorum Series Latina 85A (Turnholt: Brepols, 1978), 199. The author of the treatise seems to be able to knowledgeably discuss the nuances of the meanings of Greek words.

8. Norman P. Tanner, ed., *Decrees of the Ecumenical Councils*, 2 vols. (Washington DC: Georgetown University Press, 1990). See Canon 3 of Constantinople (Tanner, *Decrees of the Ecumenical Councils*, 32) and Canon 28 of Chalcedon (Tanner, *Decrees of the Ecumenical Councils*, 99–100).

9. John Maxentius, *Responsio adversus epistulam quam ad Possessorem a Romano episcopo dicunt haeretici destinatam*, CCL85A, 137.

10. David Russel Maxwell, *Christology and Grace in the Sixth-Century Latin West*, (PhD diss., Universoty of Notre Dame, 2003), 78. Maxwell holds that they wanted to appeal to the emperor not to the Bishop of Constantinople.

11. Most likely the *Libellus fidei*, the earliest remaining document of the controversy. CCL85A, 5–25.

12. *Libellus fidei* XI (20), CCL85A, 17.

Scythian aphorism sought to ensure the true meaning of the Fourth Ecumenical Council. Specifically, it promoted Cyril's christological vision as articulated in his writings, especially the *Twelve Chapters*, as the standard for an orthodox confession of Christ.[13] While Cyril was recognized in the East, his standing was less significant among Western bishops, who were loyal to Leo's Christology as expressed in the *Tome*. However, if the promotion of Cyril's christological vision was their intent, it was by no means universally appreciated. Almost immediately, the Scythian monks incurred powerful opposition. This opposition attacked the Scythian monks at their most vulnerable point—the implication that an addition to the *Definition* was necessary. For their opponents, the Scythian monks were in effect making the claim that Chalcedon was not sufficient to stave off the contamination of the Nestorian heresy. Given the sensitivities of the time, the Scythian formula was seen as an implicit attack on Leo's *Tome*. This characterization of the Theopaschite formula ensured the immediate opposition of the Roman deacon, Dioscorus, who would become the archenemy of the Scythian monks.[14] Dioscorus clearly understood that the Scythians were introducing a different *way* to interpret Chalcedon, namely through the lens of Cyril.[15]

Opinions in Constantinople were divided. Among the opponents of the Scythians were the deacon, Victor, and initially Justinian, the young nephew of the emperor, Justin I. In support of the Scythian monks there was Count Vitalian, the military general, who was strong enough to resist Anastasius and was likely of Scythian lineage himself.[16] Vitalian was presented as a relative of Leontius, which probably refers to Leontius of Jerusalem. Vitalian wholeheartedly supported the monks' initiative, and his military power made him a formidable figure.

After the Roman legates sent by the pope Hormisdas (two bishops, a presbyter and two deacons) appeared in Constantinople,[17] the Scythian monks addressed them as well as Bishop John of Constantinople with formal complaints against the Scythian bishops and the deacon, Victor,

---

13. Cf. Asterios Gerostergios, *Justinian the Great: The Emperor and saint* (Belmont, MA: Institute for Byzantine and Modern Greek Studies, 1982): 99. The "mia physis" formula of Cyril, with which Gerostergios seeks to establish connection, was not as central to their argument as the Twelve Anathemas, especially the last of them.

14. He even believed them to be under direct influence of the devil. Dioscorus, *Suggestio ad Horm.*, quoted in Fr. Glorie, *Prolegomena to Maxentii altorumque Scytharum Monachorum necnon Ioannis Tomitanae urbis episcopi*, CCL 85A, XXVI.

15. Dioscorus, *Suggestion to Pope Hormisdas* of 15 October 519, in CA, ep. 224, no. 7: CSEL 35, 686, quoted in Grillmeyer, 2.2., 321. As a Roman, Dioscorus saw in Chalcedon Leo and Leo alone. The Scythian monks saw in Chalcedon primarily Cyril and his Christology, which does not mean that they ignored Leo and thought of him as heretical.

16. PL 63, col. 472AB, quoted in M. Oksiuk, *Theopaskhitskie spory*, in Trudy Kievskoi Dukhovnoi Akademii, 1 (1913), 534.

17. John Maxentius, *Libellus fidei*, CCL 85A, 5. Their names are given in the very beginning of *Libellus*.

whom they publicly accused of heresy.[18] At a formal session organized through the influence of Count Vitalian and Justin I, the monks' argument failed to persuade, and their formula was not accepted as a necessary criterion of orthodoxy. Vitalian himself prevailed upon the Roman legates to refrain from entering the dispute, which aided the Scythian monks' cause. However, Dioscorus' reaction showed that he was bound to tradition and that he interpreted the christological decisions of the ecumenical councils only through the lens of Leo's theology. Cyril received no recognition in his pronouncement. He writes, "The Scythians then began to speak against him: 'Let the phrase "One of the Trinity" also be added.' But we spoke against this saying: 'We can neither say nor add that, which was not defined in the four councils or in the letter of the blessed Pope Leo.'"[19] Thus, the Scythian monks did not gain the favor of the Roman legates. Nonetheless, their leader, John Maxentius, presented them with two of his writings in the attempt to convince them of their allegiance to Chalcedon and orthodoxy in general.[20] However, his writings could effect no change in the Roman representatives. It was obvious to the Scythian monks that the Roman legates were hostile to their intentions and would give a negative estimate of their theological formula to Pope Hormisdas.[21]

Meanwhile, through the involvement of the Emperor Justin, Count Vitalian reconciled with Paternus, the Scythian bishop with whom the monks were in dispute. Reconciliation between the Scythian monks and their bishop was, however, to prove a more complex matter. The Scythian monks were not prepared to surrender their confession. In the words of the Roman legates: "These monks, however, fallen by means of their flight, preferred to depart from the city rather than reach the peace."[22] Again revealing his support, Count Vitalian was instrumental in organizing the escape of the Scythian monks from Constantinople.[23] However, the reputation of the Scythian monks was further harmed before they arrive in Rome. Hormisdas received negative reports about their mission, not only from his own legates, but also from Justinian, who blamed them as trouble-makers interested in disrupting the peace of the church.[24] Hormisdas does not appear to have been a profound theological thinker. Like

18. Grillmeier, *The Church of Constantinople in the Sixth Century*, 321. Also see Glorie, *Prolegomena*, XXIV.

19. Dioscorus, *Suggestio ad Horm.*, quoted in Glorie, *Prolegomena*, 25. Other examples of the same attitude abound, e.g. Glorie, *Prolegomena*, 26, 28.

20. John Maxentius, *Epistula Scytharum Monachorum ad Episcopos*, CCL 85A, 157–172; John Maxentius, *Professio Brevissima Fidei*, CCL 85A, 33–36.

21. Glorie, *Prolegomena*, 27. The legates accused the monks of being stubborn and that by their action they supported the cause of the Monophysites in Antioch.

22. Legati apost. sedis, *Epist. ad Horm.* die 29.vi.519, quoted in Glorie, *Prolegomena*, 27–28.

23. Glorie, *Prolegomena*, 28.

24. Justinian, *Ep. ad Horm.* die 29.6.519, quoted in Grillmeier, *The Church of Constantinople in the Sixth Century*, 322.

some of his predecessors, he was a pragmatic church leader, bound to tradition above all costs and preoccupied with political power struggles. His initial response to the Scythian monks, which had been positive,[25] gave way over time to a growing frustration. He hesitated to render a verdict in the case. Without an able advisor at his disposal, Hormisdas noted in a letter to both deacon Dioscorus and Justinian that he would have preferred to send the case back to Constantinople.[26]

However, an interesting change occurred in the mind of Justinian. While Pope Hormisdas was becoming more critical of the Scythian monks, Justinian was becoming more supportive. In his initial letter to Hormisdas, which he wrote after the departure of the monks from Constantinople, Justinian complained that they were "monks in name only" and that because of their partisan spirit, "discord to them is greater than love and peace of God."[27] In this initial letter, Justinian seemed to be in full accord with Dioscorus and perhaps under his influence. Speaking in a manner similar to the Romans, Justinian accused the monks of wishing to introduce into the church "novelties" that are not found in the four ecumenical councils or in the letter of Leo. However, following this initial letter, Justinian seems to have completely changed his opinion concerning the Scythian monks. Whether or not this change of mind happened due to the influence of Count Vitalian, who in preceding years organized nothing less than a major scale revolt, we cannot be sure. In any case, the change in Justinian's theological assessment must have been profound and cannot be attributed merely to political reasons, as demonstrated by his continuing support of the monks in future years. Justinian quickly penned a new letter, which he hoped would save the Scythian monks from harsh treatment due to his first letter. In this letter, Justinian repeatedly referred to the monks as "religious" and asked Hormisdas to send the monks back to Constantinople.[28] It may be that this change in Justinian's attitude was to some extent encouraged by the positive opinion of the monks in Constantinople, which left the Roman legates increasingly isolated.

In Rome, on the other hand, the attitude toward the Scythian monks was quite different. The initial approval of the monks now gave way to different tactics, perhaps due to the influence of Dioscorus.[29] In his correspondence with Pope Hormisdas, Dioscorus made unwarranted and hostile accusations and misrepresentations, and this greatly increased

25. John Maxentius, *Libellus fidei*, CCL85A, 5. It is indicated by the superscription under the title of *Libellus fidei*.
26. Glorie, *Prolegomena*, 31.
27. Justinian, *Epist. Ad Horm.* die 29.6.519, quoted in Glorie, *Prolegomena*, 28–29.
28. Justinian, *Epist. ad Horm.* in 7.519, quoted in Glorie, *Prolegomena*, 29.
29. John Maxentius, *Resp. Adv. Epist. Horm.*, 6, CCL85A, 132. Also see Glorie, *Prolegomena*, 30.

the confusion over the actual position of the Scythian monks. Dioscorus writes, "Yet those Scythians declare that 'all accepting the Council of Chalcedon are Nestorians,' saying that 'the Council is not sufficient against Nestorius' and thus 'the Council should be received in the way that they themselves explain it.'"[30]

For his part, Hormisdas would not allow the case concerning the Scythian monks be tried again in Constantinople. As a result, Hormisdas suggested that Dioscorus and other dissenting parties should come to Rome so that the case could be heard in the presence of the contending sides.[31] The indecisiveness of Hormisdas may reflect the inconsistent behavior of Justinian. Justinian was now asking Hormisdas to render his dogmatic verdict *ex cathedra* on whether the Scythian formula had to be preached from the pulpits and whether it was necessary to uphold it.[32] Hormisdas seemed reluctant to react theologically. In any case, he decided to delay any decision until his Roman legates returned and rendered their own assessment of the monks' theological posture.

However, as these events unfolded, other events happened that undermined the balance of power and put the Scythian monks into jeopardy. Count Vitalian, the monks' most powerful and consistent supporter, was assassinated in Constantinople; in addition, Vitalian's assassination was accompanied by the death of John, the bishop of Constantinople. In view of these events, Rome became the sole judge of the matter. Since Rome was not positive toward them, the Scythian monks sought support elsewhere in the West and sent their confession formulations to the bishops of North Africa.[33] The most prominent theologian among them was Fulgentius of Ruspe, who finally endorsed their confession. Then, in the middle of AD 520, the monks decided to leave Rome, since their enemy Dioscorus was about to assume the position of judge in their case. Prior to their departure, however, they published their *Chapters against Nestorius* as a witness to the people of Rome concerning their orthodoxy.[34]

Pope Hormisdas became understandably furious after their departure. He wrote an angry letter to the African bishop, Possessor, who lived in Constantinople at the time. In this letter, he called the monks disobedient, disruptive, and disrespectful of church authorities.[35] In some manner John Maxentius was able to learn of the contents of this letter and wrote a witty response, pretending not to recognize the Pope as the author of the letter and claiming that it was penned by some

---

30. Dioscorus, *Suggestio ad Horm.* die 15.10.519, quoted in Glorie, *Prolegomena*, 31.
31. Hormisdas, *Epist. ad Justinian*, PL 63, col. 478A, quoted in Oksiuk, 551.
32. Justinian, *Epist. ad Horm.* die 15.10.519, quoted in Glorie, *Prolegomena*, 32.
33. John Maxentius, *Epistula scytharum monachorum ad episcopos*, CCL 85A, 157–172.
34. John Maxentius, *Capitula contra Nestorianos et Pelagianos as satisfactionem fratrem*, CCL 85A 29–30. Opinion that the chapters were published in Rome belongs to Oksiuk, 554.
35. Hormisdas, *Epistula ad Possessorem episcopum Africae*, CCL 85A, 116–117.

anonymous heretic.[36] Through this subterfuge, John Maxentius was able to reply to the Roman bishop[37] in sharp tones while at the same time preserving himself from the charge that he was knowingly disrespectful toward the Pope. As it happened, Maxentius' response to Hormisdas brings this chain of events to an end. Following this response, the Scythian monks as a group fade from view and receive scant attention in our historical sources.[38]

CHRISTOLOGICAL EMPHASES OF THE SCYTHIAN MONKS

In the previous section of this essay, the historical events and theological conflict that formed the immediate context for the Scythian Theopaschite formula were considered. In this section, a thematic survey of Archimandrite John Maxentius and the Christology of the Scythian monks is examined. This survey is by no means complete; nevertheless, it provides a general picture of Scythian Christological emphases evident in their writings.

UNITY OF CHRIST

The unity of Christ's person was of greatest importance for the Scythian monks, just as it was for Cyril of Alexandria. This unity appeared to them compromised by the assertions of Nestorianizing theologians, who understood it only in the "social" sense,[39] that is, as a union based primarily on moral grounds that presupposed the existence of a separate and quasi-independent human subject in Christ united to the Second Person of the Trinity through the benevolence of the latter. This perspective resonates with the Antiochene tradition epitomized by Theodore of Mopsuestia that viewed the union in Christ as occurring κατ' εὐδοκίαν, that is, as a union by grace. According to the Scythians, Nestorians claimed that Mary gave birth to the flesh only, that is, to a pious man in whom God dwelled.[40]

The main concern of the Scythian monks was to defend the teaching of Cyril concerning the unity of the person of Christ, and this concern confronts the reader of their works at every turn. Echoing Cyril, the Scythian monks repeatedly claim that the Nestorian interpretation in-

---

36. John Maxentius, *Resp. ad Ep. Horm* 6, CCL 85A, 132.

37. Cf. Tixeront, J. *History of Dogmas. Volume III. The End of the Patristic Age (430–800),* 2nd ed. (St. Louis and London: B. Herder Book Co., 1926), 126. Tixeront characterizes response of Maxentius to Hormisdas as "violent" and "unjust," which seems to be an exaggeration.

38. A. A. Vasiliev, *Justin the First: An Introduction to the Epoch of Justinian the Great.* Dumbarton Oaks Studies 1 (Cambridge, MA: Harvard University Press, 1950), 196.

39. Cf. John Maxentius, *Brevissima adunationis ratio verbi Dei ad propriam carnem,* CCL 85A, 40. Maxentius also speaks of the "natural union of the Word" as opposed to the "social" union of Nestorians.

40. Scythian monks, *Disputatio XII capitulorum Cyrilli Alexandrini et sic dictorum Nestorii anti anathematismorum,* CCL 85A, 207.

evitably divides Christ into two and results in two subjects in Christ.[41] Likewise they charge that the Nestorian interpretation results in two sons, one by nature and another by grace.[42] Nestorius and his followers are also blamed for introducing yet a third element into Christ, a nature peculiar to him alone.[43] Nestorianizing theologians tended to divide Christ into several elements or aspects; whether there are three of them as in the case of Arius and Apollinarius (soul, body, God) or four (soul, body, mind, God) does not change their fundamental incapacity to view Christ as one.[44] They rightly inquire how Nestorians can even proclaim Christ to be Lord if he is not also God the Word.[45] In all of these elaborations a thorough-going concern for the unity of Christ's person is self-evident.

PROPER UNDERSTANDING OF THEOTOKOS

The Scythian monks charged Nestonianizing theologians with hypocrisy concerning their use of *theotokos* ("Mother of God") as a title for Mary. For instance, the monks criticize the Acoimetae monks of Constantinople for claiming to recognize the *theotokos*, but in reality, only paying lip service to the concept. In his *Dialogue against the Nestorians*, John Maxentius claimed that, while such persons do not explicitly reject the *theotokos*, they do not explain it to mean that Mary gave birth to God according to the flesh, but merely that she gave birth to a man who was united with God.[46] In the *Libellus fidei*, Maxentius thoroughly rejects the Nestorian notion, which goes back to Theodore of Mopsuestia, that the Trinity "dwelt in Christ"; for, if this were the case, then Christ would have existed outside the Trinity.[47]

In their theological writings, the Scythian monks also ridicule the Nestorian understanding of the title, Immanuel. In their discussion, they are clearly guided by Cyril's insight concerning the eucharistic implications of the incarnation, an understanding foreign to the Nestorian perspective.[48] Accordingly, the monks distinguish sharply between the way God is "with us" ordinarily, "whenever we invoke" his name, and

---

41. Scythian monks, *Disputatio XII*, CCL 85A, 197.

42. Scythian monks, *Disputatio XII*, CCL 85A, 200.

43. Scythian monks, *Refutatio quorundam Nestorii dictorum*, CCL 85A, 214. Cf. Nestorius who thought he found an ideal diplomatic solution in the language of "Christotokos" avoiding what he thought were the undesirable extremes of "theotokos" and "anthropotokos."

44. Scythian monks, *Refutatio quorundam Nestorii dictorum*, CCL 85A, 214.

45. Scythian monks, *Refutatio quorundam Nestorii dictorum*, CCL 85A, 216.

46. John Maxentius, *Dialogus Contra Nestorianos*, CCL 85A, 53.

47. John Maxentius, *Libellus fidei* IX (14), CCL 85A, 14.

48. An interesting picture emerges in comparing interpretations of Cyril of Alexandria and Theodore of Mopsuestia of John 6: their attention to the Eucharistic implications in the text is markedly different.

the concrete presence of God in the incarnation.[49] In their argument the Scythians make use of their opponents' admission that, finally, Nestorius himself confessed the *theotokos*.[50] However, the question remains, who is the "God" to whom Mary gave birth? Their answer is clear: not a different God, not a "recent or strange God" but rather God the Word.[51]

The Scythian monks claimed that Nestorian theology is in effect a reappearance of the theology of third century Adoptionist Paul of Samosata who described Christ as a man elevated to divine status through the election and benevolence of God.[52] For Nestorians, Immanuel is God, not by nature but merely by grace. For the Scythian monks, Nestorian Christology implies that the unity of the humanity and divinity in Christ is similar to the communion of any human being with God.[53] The Scythian monks, of course, do not dispute the term Immanuel as such, but rather the meaning attributed to it by their opponents. For Nestorians, Immanuel does not refer to God's true presence with us in the flesh but becomes merely an empty title given to the man Jesus.[54] Therefore, they accuse the Nestorians of declaring that Christ displayed divine glory merely as a pretense, not as a true reality.[55]

"ONE INCARNATE NATURE" VS. DYOPHYSITE CHRISTOLOGY

The support of the Scythian monks for Cyril's Christology and even his language, "one incarnate nature of God the Word," reveals more than any other their approach to the council of Chalcedon. They were faithful proponents of the Chalcedonian definition: "We truly confess one substance[56] or person in two natures of God the Word who became incarnate and was made man, which the venerable council of Chalcedon handed down to us."[57] While insisting on the fullness of Incarnation, the Scythian monks are careful to maintain the completeness of the humanity in Christ.[58] Nevertheless, they allow for the term "one incarnate nature of God the Word," since it means nothing other than "one subsistence or person in two natures."[59] Thus, the Scythian monks present

---

49. Scythian Monks, *Disputatio XII capitulorum Cyrilli Alexandrini et sic dictorum Nestorii anti anathematismorum*, CCL 85A, 196.
50. Scythian Monks, *Disputatio XII*, CCL 85A, 196.
51. Scythian Monks, *Disputatio XII*, CCL 85A, 196.
52. It was typical in Christological polemics to trace all heresies and deviations to a common root or origin by comparing them to each other; whether the views of Paul of Samosata resembled those of later extreme Antiochene theologians is outside of scope of this paper.
53. Scythian Monks, *Disputatio XII*, CCL 85A, 198.
54. Scythian Monks, *Disputatio XII*, CCL 85A, 205. This is an explanation of Anathema 7.
55. Scythian Monks, *Disputatio XII*, CCL 85A, 199.
56. Subsistentia stands for Greek ὑπόστασις.
57. John Maxentius, *Libellus fidei*, CCL 85A, 13.
58. Scythian monks, *Refutatio*, CCL 85A, 222.
59. Scythian monks, *Refutatio*, CCL 85A, 222.

an interpretation of this controversial Cyrillian phrase solely within the framework of the two-nature Christology formulated at Chalcedon.

Thus, the Scythian monks demonstrate a desire to reconcile the Chalcedonian definition with Cyril's christological vision. In the letter of the Scythian monks to Fulgentius and other bishops of Africa, they once again claim that both "one nature" and "two natures" terminology is acceptable with a certain caveat. Some dyophysites "cunningly" admit only the "two nature" terminology revealing their Nestorian sympathies.[60] At the same time, while addressing monophysites the Scythian monks speak from a different perspective, they demand acceptance to the two natures and firmly claim that "there are without any doubt two natures in Christ after uniting."[61]

This terminological flexibility should not be viewed as a sign of inconsistency, but rather as a conscientious attempt to reconcile tensions that transpired at the Council of Chalcedon and subsequently resulted in the alienation of the Monophysites. Reinterpretation of Chalcedon within a Cyrillian framework is perhaps most clearly seen in the Scythian declaration of Christ as "God and Son of God, from and in two natures united without confusion."[62] At the Council of Chalcedon a majority of the bishops loyal to Cyril attempted to express Cyrillian Christology using language compatible with the dyophysite emphasis of Leo's *Tome*. The confession of Christ as ἐκ ("from") two natures and ἐν ("in") two natures were both under consideration at Chalcedon. The undesirable association of ἐκ with the contemporary heresy of Eutychius, as well as pressure coming from both imperial representatives and Roman legates, led to the adoption of the "in two natures" formula, causing tremendous unrest in a great part of the Christian East.[63] To further complicate the problem, the western reading of the Chalcedonian definition through the lens of the Leo's Tome has become the normative interpretation of many subsequent Chalcedonians; this narrow interpretation only confirmed the prejudices and suspicions of non-Chalcedonians that the council of Chalcedon was a departure from Cyril's Christology. Thus, the language of the Scythian monks seeks to amend this unfortunate situation and restore the proper balance. The confession of Christ as both "out of" and "in" two natures peacefully coexist here; each of them interprets and reinforces the other, while not allowing for any polarization.

---

60. John Maxentius, *Epistula scytharum monachorum ad episcopos*, CCL 85A, 159.
61. John Maxentius, *Responsio contra acephelos*, CCL 85A, 44.
62. John Maxentius, *Dialogus contra Nestorianos (libri II)*, CCL 85A, 63.
63. Account of the Cyrillian character of the council can be found, e.g., in Gray, *Defence of Chalcedon*, 7–16. Cf. J. N. D. Kelly, *Early Christian Doctrines* (San Fransisco: HaprerCollins, 1978), 340–341.

CHRIST AS COMPOSITUS

The Scythian description of Christ as composite served the purpose of promoting a unitive Christology. Yet, it also provided a healthy alternative to the Monophysite Christology, which emphasized one "theanthropic" nature. Describing Christ as composite is intended to retain a certain dyophysitism, but to focus on Christ as a single being.[64]

In the *Dialogue,* the Scythian monk (self-designated as Catholicus) claims the following: "Indeed I confess God and man, Son of God, but I quickly run away from those who do not confess one and the same Christ the Son of God who is both incomposite before the Incarnation and composite after the Incarnation."[65] His opponent Nestorianus counters with the statement that, in this scheme, Christ seems "imperfect" because composite implies parts and suggests that God the Word is just a part of Christ. This idea of parts is absolutely alien to the unitive Christology of the Catholicus, who writes, "God the Word is nothing less than Christ, because He himself is Christ."[66] To be passible, that is, capable of suffering, Christ must be composite; a simple and incomposite nature is not passible. Thus, for Catholicus, one has to insist on Christ as composite in order to safeguard the reality of the cross and his impassible suffering.

GOD BECAME CHRIST; CHRIST DID NOT BECOME GOD

Another point of confession for John Maxentius and the Scythian monks against the "followers of Theodore of Mopsuestia" is that "God has become Christ, not that Christ has become God."[67] This maxim is intended to safeguard the unity of Christ, in whom there are not two separate beings. The one anointed was truly God: "God indeed is anointed, because he himself is the one made man, not another God, another man, but the same God, the same man."[68]

For Nestorians, the thought that God could be anointed was utterly ridiculous; surely it was the "boy" who was born of the Virgin Mary that was anointed. Yet for the Scythian monks, God truly was anointed, even though it sounds strange to human reason, because the "boy Jesus" was none other than God.[69] There is one Christ, not two. No concessions are given to Nestorians in this area. Thus, when Nestorianus interprets

---

64. John Maxentius, *Epistula ad episcopos* 6, CCL 85A, 160; *Capitula* 9, CCL 85A, 30; *Responsio contra acephalos* 3, CCL85A, 44.

65. John Maxentius, *Dialogus* 2.2, CCL 85A, 78.

66. John Maxentius, *Dialogus* 2.2, CCL 85A, 81.

67. John Maxentius, *Capitula* 7, CCL 85A, 30; *Libellus* 25, CCL 85A, 20; *Epistula ad episcopos* 11, CCL 85A,163.

68. John Maxentius, *Epistula ad episcopos* 11, CCL85A, 163–164. Cf. Chapter 7, 30.

69. John Maxentius, *Dialogus* 1.8, CCL 85A, 63.

Acts 2:36 to mean that Jesus (as one separate from God) was made Lord and Christ,[70] Catholicus understands it in connection with Philippians 2:6–7. He demonstrates that the one who was Lord in eternity took upon himself the "form of slave" and was crucified.[71]

THEOPASCHITE CHRISTOLOGY OF IMPASSIBLE SUFFERING

The paradox of impassible suffering lies at the heart of the Scythian monks' christological vision. This paradoxical language flows directly from their insistence on the unity of God the Word incarnate. It is God who suffered for us on the cross.[72] To be sure, this suffering is understood in the sense that God the Word suffered in his flesh, while his divine nature remained impassible. To explain the paradox, the Scythian monks employ an analogy that stemmed from Cyril of Alexandria: when a human person suffers, the soul itself may suffer no pain according to its own nature, yet we say that the whole person has suffered.[73] Like Cyril before them, the monks cite the Nicene Creed as support for their conviction that the one subject of all that Christ experienced is true God from true God. In this way, Scythian Christology simply reiterates the logic that was foundational for Cyril's theology in his dispute with Nestorius: "Thus we say that he also suffered and rose again, not that the Word of God suffered in his own nature . . . . But since his own body, which has been born, suffered these things, he himself is said to have suffered them for our sake. For, he was the one, incapable of suffering, in the body which suffered."[74]

Likewise, the Scythian monks, while commenting on the final chapter of Cyril's *Twelve Chapters,* once again assert that the suffering of Christ is not to be attributed to the divine nature in itself.[75] The impassible suffering of the divine Word forms the very center of the Scythian monks' Christology and expresses yet another implication of the *theotokos* language: the One who was born of the Virgin Mary is the same One who suffered for us on the cross.

Another reiteration of Cyril's twelfth chapter and the paradox of impassible suffering appears in the *Epilogue.* The chief concern of the Scythian monks is to promote the cross of Christ as the concrete place where the mind of God is revealed; only in the cross does man come to

---

70. John Maxentius, *Dialogus* 2.9, CCL 85A, 86.

71. John Maxentius, *Dialogus* 2.9, CCL 85A, 88.

72. Scythian monks, *Disputatio,* 202.

73. Scythian monks, *Disputatio,* 202. Cf. Cyril of Alexandria, *Letter to Clerics at Constantinople* (Letter 10), Fathers of the Church 56, 56.

74. Cyril of Alexandria, *Second Letter to Nestorius* (Letter 6), FC 76, 40.

75. Disputatio, 213. 12th anathema of Cyril is also used by the Scythian monks in support of their Theopaschite formula in Epist., 162.

know God's mind, heart, and essential character. If one refuses to con-fess the true suffering of God the Word, as is the case with Nestorians, then he shows himself to be ashamed of the cross.[76]

There are several ways Nestorian theologians attempted to remove suffering from God. They insisted that God could not have in any way suffered in the flesh, "because this is nowhere said in the Scriptures, but rather Christ suffered in the flesh."[77] In turn, the Scythian monks are eager to confess both realities: that Christ has suffered in the flesh means nothing other than the suffering of God himself in the flesh.[78] To reject the suffering of God is to deny that Christ is God.[79]

Another argument used to protect God from human suffering was to limit the suffering to the flesh; it was not God that suffered, but only the flesh of Christ.[80] Again, the unitive Christology of the Scythian monks drives them to the obvious conclusion: if the flesh of Christ has suf-fered, then God has suffered in the flesh. When describing the cross, the Scythian monks seem compelled to employ paradoxical language: "He who is eternal life, wisdom and power of the Father . . . suffered, was crucified, and died according to the flesh."[81] In the *Dialogue against Nestorians* Scythian monks further elaborate on how "the one who is life was crucified and died."[82] The dialogue continues with this exchange:

"Nestorianus: And how is life itself able to hang on the cross?

Catholicus: By the way of belief that God, who is true life, has become man."[83]

God has been crucified precisely because he is God made man; one and the same is true life and made man. Life and death are incompatible, but in Jesus' flesh Life himself submits to suffering and interacts directly with death.

THEOPASCHITE FORMULA:
"ONE OF THE HOLY TRINITY HAS SUFFERED IN THE FLESH"

The most famous aphorism of the Scythian monks, the Theopaschite formula, is also highly paradoxical; it must be understood as an organic expression of their unitive Christology. It was meant to be a christologi-cal litmus test, uncovering crypto-Nestorians from among formal pro-ponents of Chalcedonian Christology. Theologians sympathetic to the

76. Scythian Monks, *Epilogus*, CCL85A, 232.
77. John Maxentius, *Dialogus* 2.9, CCL 85A, 88.
78. John Maxentius, *Capitula* 6, CCL 85A, 30.
79. John Maxentius, *Dialogus* 2.9, CCL 85A, 89.
80. John Maxentius, *Dialogus* 2.12, CCL 85A, 92.
81. John Maxentius, *Professio brevissima catholicae fidei* 5, CCL 85A, 35.
82. John Maxentius, *Dialogus* 2.6 VI, 84.
83. John Maxentius, *Dialogus* 2.6 VI, 85.

Nestorian perspective would find it very difficult to accept this formula in good conscience. These theologians claimed that the phrase "one of the Trinity has suffered for us in the flesh" divided the Trinity.[84] To this the monks aptly retorted that "one of the Trinity" does not divide Trinity any more than the Nicene phrase "God from God."[85] Likewise, Mary did not give birth to the Trinity but to God who is "one of the Trinity."[86] After all, "Catholics know no other God apart from the Trinity."[87]

According to John Maxentius, the heretics asserted that Christ is "one person of the Trinity," but they refused to admit that he is "one of the Trinity."[88] In response, the Scythians felt compelled to anathematize the Nestorian formula.[89] The Nestorian preference for the phrase "one Person Christ of the Trinity" was based on a general observation that "three persons are the Trinity."[90] While the difference between the Nestorian and Scythian phrases seems trivial, much was at stake here. For Nestorians, the language of the Scythians, which made an exact identification between Christ and "one of the Trinity," failed to protect the whole Trinity (and God in general) from suffering. For Scythian theologians, on the contrary, the Nestorian phrase "one Person of the Trinity," while by no means heretical by itself, was open to Nestorian interpretation. Christ's association with the Trinity is left ambiguous and could mean that God the Word simply abides in the person of Christ. This interpretation failed to assert an exact identification of God the Word with the person of Jesus.[91] According to John Maxentius, "if God the Word is Christ, and Christ God the Word, just as the Catholic faith teaches, how then is Christ not one of the Trinity, but rather God the Word just one person of the Trinity?"[92]

The Scythian christological formula seeks to expound the confession that is already fully present in the Nicene Creed, namely that the one who is "true God from true God" suffered by us and for our salvation. God the Word is not from the substance of the Trinity according to the flesh.[93] He received his flesh in time from the Virgin Mary, the *Theotokos*. However, it is "God the Word, our Lord Jesus Christ, with his own flesh" that one must confess as one of the Trinity.[94] And it is this divine person

---

84. John Maxentius, *Libellus* 20, CCL 85A, 17.
85. John Maxentius, *Libellus* 20, CCL 85A, 17.
86. John Maxentius, *Libellus* 21, CCL 85A, 18.
87. John Maxentius, *Libellus* 21, CCL 85A, 18.
88. John Maxentius, *Responsio adversus epistulam quam ad Possessorem a Romano episcopo dicunt haeretici destinatam* 1.8, CCL 85A, 135.
89. John Maxentius, *Capitula* 4, CCL85A, 29.
90. John Maxentius, *Dialogus* 2.21, CCL 85A, 105.
91. John Maxentius, *Responsio* 1.8, 135.
92. John Maxentius, *Responsio* 1.8, 135.
93. John Maxentius, *Dialogus* 2.22, CCL 85A, 106.
94. John Maxentius, *Dialogus* 2.22, CCL 85A, 105.

who has suffered for us in the flesh. Every attempt to separate God from suffering and the cross is thwarted; for the Scythian monks, God's ultimate revelation takes place precisely where He wills to be found—at the cross, in the suffering that he assumed for us and for our salvation.

CHRIST AND THE HOLY SPIRIT

Fully grasping the unity of Christ and the incarnation of God the Word are essential also for confessing the proper relationship between Christ and the Spirit. Is Christ the bearer of the Spirit essentially from eternity or does he depend on a later descent of the Spirit to perform his works and miracles? The Christology of the Scythian monks leaves no room for any adoptionist christological schemes.

Nestorianizing opponents of the Scythian monks refused to admit that Christ could have performed signs and wonders from himself without the mediation of the Holy Spirit; for the Scythian monks, Christ bears the Spirit in himself. His possession of the Spirit was not the result of a mere filling, a temporary inspiration, or a gracious empowerment, giving Christ the ability to perform wonders only through the Spirit's external mediation.[95] Indeed, turning Christ into an external agent dependent on the power of the Spirit introduces the separation of Christ from the Spirit. According to the Cyrillian Christology of the Scythian monks, Christ is one of the Holy Trinity who is inseparably united to the Spirit as well as to the Father, and so his activity by the Spirit comes from himself and not from an external source of grace.

EUCHARISTIC IMPLICATIONS: FLESH OF CHRIST AS LIFE-GIVING

It is very important for the Scythian monks to demonstrate that the flesh of Christ is not feeble. Like Zwingli centuries later, Nestorians stumble on the words from John 6:63 that "the flesh profits nothing." A eucharistic reading of John 6 enables Scythian monks to show that Nestorians have interpreted the phrase out of context when they refer it to the flesh of Jesus.[96]

In the *Dialogue*, Catholicus and Nestorianus argue concerning the way God inhabits the temple of Christ's body.[97] The question is whether it is man or God to whom the body belongs. Did God assumed the body that belongs to Mary's son or did God assume his own body directly from Mary in accordance with the Christology of Cyril? Catholicus thus claims: "I proclaim not God in a man, but God in a body."[98]

---

95. Scythian monks, *Disputatio*, CCL 85A, 207.
96. Scythian monks, *Disputatio*, CCL 85A, 210–211.
97. John Maxentius, *Dialogus contra nestorianos* 2.4, CCL 85A, 83–84.
98. John Maxentius, *Dialogus contra nestorianos* 2.4, CCL 85A, 84.

At this point, Nestorianus asserts that John 6 speaks about "the flesh of the Son of Man" rather than "the flesh of God." Catholicus's response leaves no room for doubt: "This flesh is truly the flesh of God; otherwise, how could it give life?"[99] This assertion is once again driven by the Scythian monks' fervent concern for the unity of Christ. In no way can the flesh of Jesus be detached from God the Word incarnate; the flesh of Jesus, present on the church's eucharistic altar, is truly life-giving because it is truly the flesh of God.

CHRISTOLOGICAL LEGACY OF THE SCYTHIAN MONKS

During the Theopaschite controversy, in which the Scythian monks were central participants, both negative and positive reactions to their Christological proposal abounded. In the West, the disapproval of the papal legate, Dioscorus, and of Pope Hormisdas was balanced by the positive reception of their Christology by Fulgentius of Ruspe and the North African bishops. In the East, as already noted, Justinian changed his attitude from an initially critical posture to a positive and supportive one. Justinian later fully embraced the Christology of the Scythian monks, which was nothing other than the Christology of Cyril expressed within the framework of the Council of Chalcedon.[100] In AD 533 Justinian issued two decrees that were directly related to points the Scythian monks desperately tried to promote some fourteen years earlier. These decrees stated that the faith of Chalcedon must include the confession of the Scythian formula "one of the Trinity suffered" as well as the concept of the "union according to hypostasis" (ἕνωσις καθ' ὑπόστασιν).[101] When the Acoimetae monks opposed these decrees, as was expected, Justinian did not hesitate to use the authority of the Roman bishop at the time, Pope John II. As described by Justinian in his inquiry to the pope, the matters of dispute in which the Acoimetae monks were involved closely resembled the concerns expressed earlier by the Scythian monks.[102] Pope John II proved quite different from his predecessor Hormisdas. He did not hesitate to approve the decrees of Justinian and consequently the formula of the Scythian monks. Thus, he promoted the formula's recognition in the Roman West. The Acoimetae monks were anathematized for their Nestorian inclinations.[103]

---

99. John Maxentius, *Dialogus contra nestorianos* 2.4, CCL 85A, 84.

100. Cf. Kenneth Warren Wesche, *The Defense of Chalcedon in the Sixth Century: The Doctrine of "Hypostasis" and Deification in the Christology of Leontius of Jerusalem* (PhD, Fordham University, 1986), 27–28. Wesche admits that Justinian was not original in his thought while noting that he recognized implications of the theopaschite formula.

101. Codex Justinianus I, 1, 6 (7–8) and I, 1, 7 (8–10), in Gray, 57.

102. Denzinger, *Enchiridion symbolorum, definitionem at declarationem de rebus fidei et morum* (Rome, 1967), 138–139, quoted in Glorie, 38. The three matters of dispute included 1) "one of the Trinity" formula, 2) impassible suffering, and 3) confession of true *theotokos*.

103. "Aquimatos vero, qui se monachos dicunt, qui Nestoriani evidenter apparuerunt, Romana etiam damnat ecclesia." ACO IV, 2, 210, quoted in Gray, 57.

Thus, in the end the Acoimetae monks lost their theological struggle with the Scythian monks. The famous "Three Chapters controversy" of the sixth century had a very close relationship to the concerns of the Scythian monks. Thus, the fifth Ecumenical Council of Constantinople (AD 553) provided the ultimate vindication of the Scythian monks' christological vision. It is especially evident from Anathema 10 of the Council, which directly quotes the formula of the Scythian monks:

> If anyone does not confess his belief that our Lord Jesus Christ, who was crucified in his human flesh, is truly God and the Lord of glory and one of the members of the Holy Trinity: let him be anathema.[104]

Since Justinian and the fifth ecumenical council, the Christology expressed in the Scythian formula has been universally recognized as orthodox. As already pointed out, the Scythian monks were not original thinkers; they were but loyal followers of Cyril of Alexandria, whose Christology they faithfully confessed in the context of the early sixth century. Therefore, it is not always possible to describe their direct influence on later developments and dogmatic formulations. While recognizing this caveat, we cannot help but notice the profound impact of this Christology on the Lutheran Reformation a thousand years later. The Christology of Martin Luther bears a striking similarity to the convictions of the Scythian monks. Moreover, these christological expressions are not uncommon in Lutheran hymnody today:

> The Virgin Mary's lullaby calms the infant Lord Most High; Upon her lap content is He, Who keeps the earth and sky and sea.[105]

These lines are a poetic summary of the christological doctrine expressed by John Maxentius:

> It ought to be confessed that God was born from a woman, not according to the divinity, but according to the humanity; that God was laid in a cradle and wrapped in sordid clothes and the He grew and progressed in age and wisdom, according to the humanity, not according to the divinity; that God hungered and thirsted and became tired from a journey and rested, not according to the divinity

---

104. Tanner, *Decrees of the Ecumenical Councils*, 118.

105. *Lutheran Service Book* (St. Louis, MO: Concordia Publishing House, 2006), 382. A number of other similar expressions may be deduced from Luther's writings, e.g: "The Infant lying in the lap of His mother created heaven and earth and is the Lord of the angels. I am indeed speaking about a man here. But 'man' in this proposition is obviously a new word and, as the sophists themselves say, stands for the divinity; that is, this God who became man created all things" (Luther, *Lectures on Galations* 1535, *LW* 26:265).

but according to the humanity; that God was seized by impious hands, judged, condemned, crucified and that his side was pierced with the sword, not according to the divinity but according to the humanity; that God, with his own flesh, ascended into heaven and sits at the right hand of the Father and, with the flesh, from there will come again in glory to judge the living and the dead.[106]

Martin Chemnitz was consciously aware of this Christology; he refers not only to Cyril[107] and the decisions of the ecumenical councils, but even quotes John Maxentius on two occasions in his *De Duabus Naturis in Christo*. The first quote, which is found in the chapter entitled "Concerning the divine nature in Christ incarnate," emphasizes part of the Scythian christological confession ("one of the Trinity"). This Scythian formula is presented by Chemnitz as a quote from Proclus: "Mary gave birth not to the Trinity, but to one of the Trinity."[108] The second time Chemnitz quotes Maxentius is in the chapter entitled, "The ancients spoke that the Logos with his own flesh is the second Person of the Trinity": "If anyone is not willing to confess that Christ is one of the Trinity together with his own flesh, let him be anathema."[109]

This last quotation is taken from the fourth anathema of the *Twelve Chapters of John Maxentius against the Nestorians and Pelagians*.[110] Both times J. A. O. Preus translates it into English as "one person of the Trinity,"[111] yet it is more correct to render it in accordance with the Scythian formula, "one of the Trinity," in order to preserve its full Theopaschite power. Finally, it is remarkable that in the very beginning of the *Catalogue of Testimonies there are listed four of Cyril's anathemas including the twelfth anathema, so central to the Scythian monks' Theopaschite convictions*.[112] By listing Cyril's anathemas, which were so foundational for the Christology of the Scythian monks, as canons of the Third Ecumenical

---

106. John Maxentius, *Professio brevissima catholicae fidei*, CCL 85A, 34.

107. Martin Chemnitz, Loci Theologici, tr. J. A. O. Preus, Vol. I (St. Louis, MO: Concordia Publishing House, 1989), 117–126. It is remarkable that Chemnitz quotes one by one the anathemas of Cyril, anathemas of Nestorius, refutations of Theoritus, and replies of Cyril, following it with both letters of Cyril to Successus. In this we can see Chemnitz standing in line of tradition exemplified by the output of the Scythian monks.

108. "Non Trinitatem, sed unum ex Trinitate genuit Maria." Martin Chemnitz, *De Duabus Naturis in Christo*, 6 (reprint of the Latin original by the Lutheran Heritage Foundation, 2000). J. A. O. Preus has translated "unum ex Trinitate" of John Maxentius as "one person of the Trinity."

109. "Si quis non asquiescit confiteri Christum unum de Trinitate cum carne propria, anathema sit." Chemnitz, *De Duabus Naturis in Christo*, 165.

110. Attribution is not given in J. A. O. Preus's translation of Chemnitz. Martin Chemnitz, *The Two Natures in Christ*, tr. J. A. O. Preus (St. Louis, MO: Concordia Publishing House, 1971).

111. Martin Chemnitz, *The Two Natures in Christ*, tr. J. A. O. Preus (St. Louis:, MO Concordia, 1989), 40, 405.

112. *BSLK*, 1104.

Council, our Lutheran fathers inadvertently fulfilled the aspirations of those Eastern theologians in the fifth and sixth centuries, who interpreted the canonical decisions of the Council of Chalcedon through the lens of Cyril's unitive Christology.

Even though the Scythian monks were unable to effect political and theological unity among the adherents and opponents of Chalcedon, their christological legacy is still alive. The church opted to preserve their documents for a reason, and so we may be grateful to God for our ancestors in the faith, with whom we commune in the liturgy as we gather "with angels and archangels and the whole company of heaven." ✛

BEGOTTEN, NOT MADE

SCRIPTURE AS BAPTISMAL NARRATIVE
IN ATHANASIUS'S DEFENSE OF NICAEA

✝

M y first encounter with William C. Weinrich was in his "Early Church History" class, required of every first-year seminary student. This class was much more than a typical history course and much more than merely an intellectual exploration into the artifacts of ancient cultures, past traditions, and dead theologians. Rather, his course was an initiation, even a rite of passage, into the living theological conversation of the one, holy, catholic, and apostolic church. Yet for Weinrich, this theological conversation is not like a free-floating ship moving on the surface, bobbing with the waves, and drifting according to the direction of prevailing winds; rather, the church is meant to be an ark that has come to rest on a firm rock or has been rendered stable by a long and weighty anchor. For Weinrich, the church's theological anchor penetrates beyond post-Reformation dogmaticians, beyond the Lutheran Confessions, and even beyond the ecumenical councils and creeds of early Christian fathers; this anchor extends through the Scriptures themselves into the very flesh of Jesus, the Son of God, who draws his own eternal being from the Father. As the study of John's Gospel emphasized for Weinrich, the *arche* or source of the church's theological reflection is not grounded merely in the created realm, but in the *Logos* himself, who "became flesh and dwelt among us" (John 1:14).

Thus, if the Lutheran church is to recognize her true identity in and with the one, holy, catholic, and apostolic church confessed in the creeds, then she must first recognize the true source of her being and life. For Weinrich, it was especially significant that the Lutheran Confessions themselves begin with that which precedes Reformation history. The ecumenical creeds are the first confessions in the Book of Concord and, therefore, are given theological priority in relation to every subsequent confession. In addition, the Augsburg Confession counts it of first importance to confess the Triune God in full accord with "the decree of the

Council of Nicaea" (AC I, 1). Thus, in this essay, I am pleased to explore, in honor of Weinrich, the theological conversation represented in the creed that is given birth at Nicaea (AD 325), finished at Constantinople (AD 381), and finally recognized as the symbol of orthodox Christianity at Chalcedon (AD 451). As its history demonstrates, the Nicene Creed is the only confession that is truly ecumenical and can lay legitimate claim to full catholicity. In this essay, Athanasius' theological exposition of Proverbs 8 will be considered in order to show that the Nicene Creed was not merely an imperial law forced upon the church for political reasons, but an authentic expression of the church's baptismal identity.

ARIUS: READING SCRIPTURE AGAINST THE SABELLIANS

As Khaled Anatolios points out, Arius did not represent a foreign invasion into fourth-century Christianity. Anatolios refers to the theological culture of the ancient church as "the flow of Christian experience,"[1] and Arius, as a well-respected presbyter in Egypt, must be interpreted as one moving within the momentum of the Christian stream. By all accounts, Arius's perspective sought to be rooted in the reading of Scripture. Arius was not, first of all, a philosopher trying to corrupt Christian doctrine with pagan philosophical ideas. He was a preacher and teacher, who shepherded a flock and sought to root Christian identity in the Scriptures. It is perhaps in this scriptural context that Arius's theological vision should be interpreted. In a letter representative of his early conflict with Alexander, bishop of Alexandria, Arius makes the intriguing assertion that "there are three *hypostases*."[2] Concerning this assertion, Anatolios entertains an interesting question: where, precisely, do the three persons subsist for the presbyter of Egypt? Clearly, for Arius, it is not in God that they subsist, since Arius's God is an absolute monad; nor is it merely in general reality, since, as noted by Anatolios, there are many more than three persons or *hypostases* in general reality.[3] Anatolios suggests that Arius is referring to the Christian confession, in which the three persons are the objects of Christian faith. While Anatolios is undoubtedly correct, it may be worthwhile to push this a little farther. The three persons confessed in the church's creed are the three names listed in the liturgy of Baptism and the three main actors in the salvific narrative of Holy Scripture.

---

1. Khaled Anatolios, *Retrieving Nicaea: The Development and Meaning of Trinitarian Doctrine* (Grand Rapids, MI: Baker Academic, 2011), 42–43.

2. Arius, *Letter to Alexander*, in Athanasius, *De Synodis* 16. Cf. Philip Schaff, ed., *Nicene and Post-Nicene Fathers*, 14 vols., *Second Series* (Peabody, MA: Hendrickson, 1994), 4:458; hereafter *NPNF2*. Cf. Rowan Williams, *Arius: Heresy and Tradition* (Cambridge: Wm. B. Eerdmans Publishing Co., 2001), 48–61. Williams places this creedal letter at the very beginning of the controversy.

3. Anatolios, *Retrieving Nicaea*, 44.

Thus, Arius's assertion that "there are three *hypostases*" arises from his administration of Baptism and his preaching of the Scriptures. If this perspective is correct, then it may be supposed that Arius's theological vision is not the product of a philosophical conviction but rooted in his pastoral interest to combat the dangers of heresy. Indeed, the first picture of Arius given by Socrates, the church historian, portrays a presbyter zealous to combat the heresy of Sabellius.[4] Modalistic Monarchianism was a persistent heresy that many early Christian theologians found seductive throughout the third century. Most fundamentally, modalism was a theological hermeneutic that offered a way to relate the unity of divine revelation to the changing narrative of Scripture; it provided a reading of sacred texts that reconciled the diversity of divine actors with the Christian confession of one God. Early in the second century, Marcion attempted to give the distinction between the two covenants its full force. For the Christian covenant to be truly and authentically new, its newness must be rooted in its divine author. For Marcion, the Scriptures must be read as direct revelations of God's own being; diversity in the scriptural narrative demands a diversity of divine beings.

Horrified at Marcion's teaching, most Christian preachers and teachers repudiated his conviction that a schism originating in the divine realm underlies the diversity inherent in the scriptural narrative. However, the strength of Marcion's perspective was the seriousness with which he read Scripture; he gave the diversity of the scriptural narrative a fullness of meaning that preached with radical implications. Thus, Christian theologians, in order to combat Marcion, needed to meet his perspective on the battleground of the scriptural narrative. The hermeneutic of theological schism had to be challenged by a hermeneutic of theological unity. A modalistic hermeneutic seemed to offer a solution and, therefore, became a natural tendency for many Christian preachers. Modalism made a distinction between God's internal being and his external revelation to creation. This distinction allowed Christians to confess the absolute oneness of God's being in spite of the changeable character of Scripture. The diversity of covenants and variety of concrete actors in the biblical narrative are merely external manifestations of one and the same God.

However, in the course of this argument, the modalist hermeneutic presented a scriptural narrative that was fundamentally different from that of Marcion. For Marcion, the Scriptures were a direct and authentic revelation of God's own being. The way God is presented in the Scriptures is precisely the way he is at the depth of his nature. Thus, Marcion read Scripture with a literal or substantive emphasis that compelled him to root diverse texts and distinct covenants in the very being of their

---

4. Socrates, *Ecclesiastical History* 5. Cf. *NPNF2* 2:3.

divine authors. To reject the distinction between the just god of the old covenant and the loving, gracious god of the new is quite simply a failure to take the letter of the Scriptures seriously. Modalism, on the other hand, offered a scriptural narrative that was rhetorically nuanced and metaphorical. In an effort to communicate with his creation, the transcendent God revealed himself in and through types and images that fit humanity's limited state. In the same way that a single, eternal archetype can make an endless number of impressions in malleable tissue, so the one God uses a variety of earthly metaphors and bodily images to manifest himself to those incapable of comprehending him truly.

However, for many theologians and, no doubt, Arius as well, the Sabellian reading of Scripture possessed serious deficiencies. While modalism promoted a theological unity against Marcion, it left the church with a scriptural narrative that was ambiguous, unstable, and unreliable. Indeed, Tertullian, at the beginning of the third century, follows Praxeas's modalistic perspective to the absurd conclusion of patropassianism. The suffering of the Son either reaches the one God himself, bringing the charge of patropassianism, or it is merely a temporary mode of God's self-manifestation. Both paths lead to unsatisfactory ends. The diversity inherent in the Scriptures offers only external, momentary revelations of what God is like. Modalism could not offer an authentic and eternal knowledge of God as he truly is; indeed, the God who manifested himself rhetorically under various images could easily manifest himself under a new metaphor or through a different actor in the future. Modalism endorsed a biblical narrative that was external to God's being and, therefore, was an ever-changing text subject to the forces of corruption.

There is simply not enough primary source material to detail the Arian perspective in relation to the Marcionite and Sabellian readings of Scripture. However, it is quite evident as the conflict unfolds that Arius, along with others who share his theological vision, was deeply concerned with the Scriptures and the Christian knowledge of God. Thus, it seems at least probable that the diverse readings of Scripture promoted by Marcion and Sabellius affected Arius's own exegesis. Indeed, the conjecture of this present study is that Arius's emphasis on the Son's ontological subordination to the Father is not, first of all, a foreign philosophical conviction that he imposed upon the Scriptures; rather, it is an organic consequence of his anti-Sabellian understanding of the biblical narrative.

According to Rowan Williams's reconstruction of Arius's *Thalia*, the Alexandrian presbyter begins with the fundamental principle that "God himself is inexpressible to all beings."[5] This principle may agree with neo-Platonism and the momentum of the philosophical perspectives pre-

---

5. Williams, *Arius*, 101.

vailing among Arius's contemporaries. However, it may also offer a clue to the way Arius understood the diverse readings of Scripture prevalent in his time. Both the Marcionite and Sabellian perspectives assume that God seeks to reveal his own being in and through the biblical narrative. For those favoring the Marcionite perspective, the two covenants represent true and authentic revelations that must be read as direct, literal testimonies to their divine authors. Two covenants proceed from two divine principles. In Arius's day, Manichees and other "Gnostic" groups certainly shared this hermeneutic of theological diversity. On the other hand, those favoring the Sabellian perspective gave more attention to the limitations of the human reader. Modalist readers shared the assumption of Marcion that God sought to reveal his own being in and through the Scriptures. However, for the Sabellians, the limited character of creation acted as a barrier that prevented the direct, literal revelation promoted by Marcion. The best that God could do is to offer glimpses of his nature in and through different images and metaphors, with which humanity could relate.

For Arius, both perspectives lead astray because they share the assumption that the Scriptures are revelations of God's inward being. It is this assumption that Arius rejects at the beginning of his *Thalia*. God's essence is "inexpressible to all beings." This "inexpressible" character is a theological absolute for the Alexandrian presbyter. God's essence is incommunicable, not only to humanity, but also to the Son. "To put it briefly," Arius goes on to explain, "God is inexpressible to the Son, for he is what he is in himself, and that is unutterable, so that the Son does not have the understanding that would enable him to give voice to any words expressing comprehension."[6] This passage is remarkable for its emphasis on the inability of the Son to give an authentic revelation of God as he is in himself. In his *Thalia*, Arius comes across as a true mystic. The divine essence is inaccessible, not due to the blindness of sin or the natural limitations of humanity, but because God is an absolute monad for whom "inexpressibility" is an essential attribute. This perspective undermines both Marcionite and Sabellian interpretations of Scripture. For Arius, Scripture is not given by God as a revelation of his inward being; it is a revelation of his external will as it moves toward creation and gives life to all things.

If the above conjecture has some merit, then it seems that Arius has turned the Sabellian distinction between God's inward being and his external revelation to creation into a radical schism. Sabellian readings of Scripture introduced the distinction based on the limitations of the flesh; God desires to reveal his being and life to his people, yet the weak-

6. Williams, *Arius*, 103.

ness of humanity simply would not allow a direct and naked revelation to take place. Thus, God resorted to fleshly, visible images in order to offer concrete representations of his divine character that fit the needs of his creatures. However, for Arius, the distinction between God's essence and the economy of his revelation was not due simply to creaturely limitation, but to divine necessity. God's essence, by definition, is inexpressible and incommunicable. This fundamental conviction meant that the Scriptures have nothing to do with the revelation of God as he is in himself. Holy Scripture consists simply in the revelation of God's creative will. The Scriptures are not direct revelations of the divine being as Marcion claimed, nor are they even rhetorical images or metaphors of the divine essence as Sabellians thought. Rather, the Scriptures are the proclamation of the divine will as revealed in the external activities by which God creates, catechizes, and redeems the world.

Thus, for Arius, the Christian knowledge of God reduces down to creation. God is creator and can never be known in any other way than as the one who made heaven and earth. All theology must take place within the economy of God's creating energy. Thus, even the Son's very ontology must subsist within the economy of God's creative work. Here again, Arius's emphasis on creation offers a stark contrast with Marcionite and Sabellian readings of Scripture. For Marcion, creation and the old covenant belong to a different god than the new covenant and the Christian gospel. In a similar way, the Sabellians, while maintaining the old covenant, are tempted toward supersessionism; new modes of divine revelation represent a progress that moved humanity beyond old dispensations. For Marcion and Sabellius, creation is merely the beginning of an ancient narrative; for Arius, creation is the very setting that undergirds the whole biblical narrative and, therefore, controls God's relation to humanity from beginning to end.

ATHANASIUS: THE SCRIPTURES AS BAPTISMAL NARRATIVE

The heart of Athanasius's response to the Arian perspective is found in his most profound theological work, *Discourses against the Arians*. After recognizing that Athanasius's *Discourses* have been "relatively neglected," Anatolios maintains that these orations represent "a wide-ranging trinitarian hermeneutics that certainly includes soteriological concerns but advances further into a broad reading of Scripture."[7] It is the hermeneutical character of Athanasius's Trinitarian theology that will be considered here, especially as it relates to his reading of Proverbs 8:22–31. In the first two *Discourses*, Athanasius is clearly interested in refuting his opponents'

---

7. Anatolios, *Retrieving Nicaea*, 108.

proof texts. However, for Athanasius, the problem with the Arian reading of Scripture is not lexical, grammatical, or textual; the problem is not historical—a failure to recognize the original context of the author; nor is the problem methodological—a failure to follow proper rules of interpretation. Rather, for Athanasius, his Arian opponents fail to recognize the theological "sense" that underlies the entire biblical narrative and the spiritual "scope" toward which the narrative moves. Thus, Frances Young in her insightful analysis of patristic exegesis concludes that the key to Athanasius's reading is the "canon of truth." "But fundamentally it is his sense of the overarching plot," Young writes, "a sense inherited from the past and ingrained in the tradition of the Church, which allows him to be innovative in exegetical detail and confident of providing the correct and 'pious' reading."[8]

In this quote, Young references language used by Athanasius, who prefers to describe the Arian reading of Scripture as "impious (ἀσεβὴς)." This language is ecclesial and spiritual in character and, therefore, suggests an implicit connection between the reading of Scripture and the liturgical life of the church. For the bishop of Alexandria, the Arian reading is "impious," not because it fails to meet proper scientific standards of exegesis, but rather because it undermines the church's sacramental life, her victory over evil, and the formation of virtuous piety in her children. For Athanasius, the gathering of the baptized around the flesh of Christ is the proper setting for the reading of Scripture. In this context, the "canon of truth" referenced by Young is not merely a set of intellectual doctrines, but the true presence and effective operation of the Father, Son, and Holy Spirit.[9] The flesh of Christ is the ground of humanity's relationship to the Holy Trinity and the foundation of the church's divine knowledge. Thus, the body of Jesus is the geographical landscape within which the church hears the Scripture and the site in which the plot of salvation unfolds. Since this plot reaches resolution in the crucified, risen, and ascended body of Jesus, it establishes the "scope" toward which the biblical narrative moves. This eschatological scope that unites the Scriptures into a single narrative is ecclesial and consists in the generation of the baptized as sons of God and their eschatological perfection in communion with the Father through the Son in the Spirit.

---

8. Frances Young, *Biblical Exegesis and the Formation of Christian Culture* (Peabody, MA: Hendrickson, 2002, reprint), 43.

9. Concerning the criterion for Athanasius's reading of Scripture, cf. Peter J. Leithart, *Athanasius* (Grand Rapids, MI: Baker Academic, 2011), 39–40. Leithart suggests that "Christ himself—understood in the Athanasian sense of the Word made flesh—is the criterion of appropriate reading" (40). Leithart maintains that this leads to circular reasoning; however, this is only true if the Word made flesh has no subsistence distinct from the scriptural text. I am arguing that for Athanasius the Word made flesh is most properly identified with the church's Eucharist. While the Eucharist is not independent of Scripture, it does signify an ontological subsistence of Christ's body that fixes scriptural texts.

CALLING GOD "FATHER":
BAPTISM AS THE SETTING FOR PROVERBS 8

The assembly of the baptized around the flesh of Jesus is the setting for the dramatic plot of God's relationship to humanity. This ecclesial setting is introduced in Athanasius's first *Discourse*. From the beginning of this discourse, Athanasius argues that the Son's essential connection to the Father is absolutely necessary to maintain the Son's character as true "image" of the Father.[10] In *Discourse* I.20, Athanasius even makes the interesting claim that the Son is not only the image through which humanity sees the Father, but the image by which the Father knows himself.[11] He says, "For God's image is not delineated from without (οὐ ἔξωθέν γραφομένη), but God Himself hath begotten it (αὐτὸς ὁ Θεὸς γεννητής); in which seeing Himself (ἐν ᾗ ἑαυτὸν ὁρῶν), He has delight, as the Son Himself says, 'I was his delight.' When then did the Father not see Himself in His own image? . . . and how should the Maker and Creator see Himself in a created and originated essence? for such as is the Father, such must be the Image."[12] For Arians, on the other hand, the Son can only be an arbitrary image that subsists within the Father's external, creative will: "If the Son be not all this, but, as the Arians consider, originate (γενητός), and not eternal, this is not a true Image (οὐκ ἔστιν ἀληθὴς εἰκὼν) of the Father, unless indeed they give up shame, and go on to say, that the title of Image, given to the Son, is not a token of a similar essence (οὐχ ὁμοίας οὐσίας), but His name only."[13] For Athanasius, the Arian schism between the essence of God (what he is in himself) and

---

10. Concerning the Son's role as image, cf. Christopher Beeley, *The Unity of Christ: Continuity and Conflict in Patristic Tradition* (New Haven, CT: Yale University Press, 2012), 146–147. Beeley interprets Athanasius's image theology in contrast to Origen, thus his presentation portrays Athanasius as one controlled by philosophical considerations. It seems more likely, however, that Athanasius's "image theology" connects in a fundamental way with the church's baptismal and eucharistic life. In Baptism, the church reads Scripture from within the intimate exchange between the Father and the Son. It is precisely the intimacy of this theological setting that the Arian vision undermines.

11. The idea of the Son as the image by which the Father knows himself returns to prominence at the end of the second discourse (*Discourse* II.82). He writes, "And in whom does the Father rejoice, except as seeing Himself in His own Image, which is His Word? . . . And how too has the Son delight, except as seeing Himself in the Father?" (*NPNF2* 4:393). Concerning Athanasius's unique reading of Proverbs 8:30, cf. Peter Widdicombe, *The Fatherhood of God from Origen to Athanasius* (Oxford: Clarendon Press, 1994), 206–207. Widdicombe maintains that Athanasius develops the Father's "delight" in the Son beyond his Alexandrian predecessors. According to Widdicombe, Athanasius "takes Proverbs 8:30 to signify that the delight that the Father has in the Son is the same joy as that with which the Son rejoices in the Father. Their delight in each other is fully reciprocal and complete. . . . Their mutual delight is grounded in, and an expression of, the communion of nature that exists between them" (Widdicombe, *The Fatherhood of God*, 207).

12. Athanasius, *Discourses* I.20. Translation of Athanasius's *Discourses* comes from Schaff, *NPNF2*, cited above. The original Greek can be found in J. P. Migne, ed., *Patrologia Graeca*, 162 vols. (Paris, 1857–1886). Hereafter cited in the following way: *Discourse* I.20 (*NPNF2* 4:318; PG 26:53).

13. *Discourse* I.21 (*NPNF2* 4:318; PG 26:55).

the economy of his external will (how he relates to creation) undermines the Christian claim to a more intimate and truthful knowledge of God. The knowledge that comes from the Son cannot be qualitatively different from the revelation that has its origin in any other part of creation.

From this perspective, Athanasius's complaint concerning the Arian use of "unoriginate" as a title for God becomes more understandable, for it expresses a certain impious agnosticism concerning God that reduces Christian theological knowledge to the level of pagan Greeks. "If they had any concern at all for reverent speaking," Athanasius says, the Arian would call God "Father" rather than "unoriginate":

> For, in calling God unoriginated (ἀγένητον), they are, as I said before, calling Him from His works (ἐκ τῶν γενομένων ἔργων αὐτὸν), and as Maker only and Framer (ποιητὴν μόνον καὶ δημιουργὸν), supposing that hence they may signify that the Word is a work (ποίημα) after their own pleasure. But that he who calls God Father, signifies Him from the Son (ἐκ τοῦ Υἱοῦ σημαίνει) being well aware that if there be a Son, of necessity through that Son, all things originate (τὰ γενητὰ) were created. And they, when they call Him Unoriginated (ἀγένητον), name Him only from His works, and know not the Son any more than the Greeks; but he who calls God Father, names Him from the Word (ἐκ τοῦ Λόγου σημαίνει).[14]

In this passage, Athanasius argues that the Arians have changed the proper setting in which the church reads Scripture and communes with God. The Arians ground the church's relationship with God in his external creative will; the Arian church speaks to God merely as creatures calling upon their Creator. Yet, for Athanasius such worship is no better than any other creature's attempt to know its Maker from an external position. The Arian perspective implies that the church's knowledge of God sprouts from the same soil as pagan idolatry. In contrast, Athanasius argues that the Son is not merely the content of the church's divine knowledge, but the proper setting within which she hears, speaks, and lives.

Thus, Athanasius's reasoning leads him to the very ground of his argument, the sacramental life of the church:

> "Unoriginated (ἀγένητον)" is a word of the Greeks, who know not the Son; but "Father" has been acknowledged and vouchsafed by our Lord (παρὰ τοῦ Κυρίου ἡμῶν). For He, knowing Himself whose Son He was, said, "I am in the Father, and the Father is in Me;" and, "He that has seen Me, has seen the Father," and, "I and the Father are One;" but nowhere is He found to call the

Father unoriginated (ἀγένητον). Moreover, when He teaches us to pray, He says not, "When ye pray, say, O God Unoriginate (Θεὲ ἀγένητε)," but rather, "When ye pray, say, Our Father, which art in heaven." And it was His will that the Summary of our faith (τὸ κεφάλαιον τῆς πίστεως) should have the same bearing, in bidding us be baptized, not into the name of Unoriginate and originate, nor into the name of Creator and creature, but into the Name of the Father, Son, and Holy Ghost. For with such an initiation (τελειούμενοι) we too, being numbered among works, are made sons (υἱοποιούμεθα), and using the name of the Father, acknowledge from that name the Word also in the Father Himself.[15]

Athanasius's appeal to the Lord's Prayer, the Creed, and Baptism is not simply for the sake of illustration, as if the church's sacramental practice were extraneous to the substance of his argument. Rather, for Athanasius, whose very episcopal identity is rooted in the performance of these ecclesial rites, such an appeal represents the essential foundation of his conviction. The baptismal liturgy establishes the setting for the church's theological confession precisely because it makes visible and real the theological scope that gives purpose to the entire biblical narrative. Only the baptized call God "Father," because only they subsist within the Son. As the baptized, the church is given a place within the intimate dialogue that moves eternally between the Father and the Son. Thus, when they call God "Father," the baptized do not speak metaphorically or figuratively of their Creator; rather, they speak truly, confessing the Father as he is known by the Son and naming God as he truly is at the depth of his being.

Athanasius's critique of his Arian opponents begins, not with the scriptural text itself, but with the setting in which they hear and interpret. For Athanasius, Arians have failed to recognize the distinction between creation and Baptism. While his Arian opponents hear the words of Scripture as creatures relating to their Creator, Athanasius hears the same texts as a son relating to his father. This distinction is fundamental to Athanasius's argument in the second discourse. In his second discourse, Athanasius seeks to engage the most effective proof texts used by his opponents. It is clear that Proverbs 8:22–31 is perceived by the Alexandrian bishop as the central pillar on which the Arian doctrine rests. Indeed, Athanasius's refutation of the Arian reading of Proverbs 8 occupies almost the whole of the second discourse. However, before he engages in a detailed reading of the text itself, he spends several sections introducing the text and his exegesis. In this introduction, Athanasius seeks to establish the proper setting in which this text is to be heard and interpreted. "Let us proceed afresh," Athanasius says, "to take up the

---

15. *Discourse* I.34 (*NPNF2* 4:326; PG 26:81–84).

question of the sense (τὸν νοῦν) of these [passages], to remind the faith-ful (πιστοὺς ὑπομνήσωμεν), and to shew from each of these passages that they [the Arians] have no knowledge at all of Christianity."¹⁶

Athanasius begins by grouping Proverbs 8 with Hebrews 3:2, Acts 2:36, and John 1:14, all of which employ the language of "created," "made," or "became" in reference to Christ. Athanasius is convinced that his Arian opponents read these verbs as ontological absolutes. These verbs do not merely represent a certain sequence of events through which the Son passes; rather, these verbs testify to an ontological setting, the boundaries of which cannot be transgressed. The Son's very essence subsists within God's creating and making. For Athanasius, the absolute character of the Arian view of creation leads to an absurd dualism between God's essence and his external will. According to the Arian position, the will of God is generative, but his essence by definition is without generative character. In this way, the will of God becomes an arbitrary and capricious choos-ing that remains external to God's inward being and does not reveal God as he truly is in himself. Athanasius seeks to expose and challenge this dualism from the very beginning of his second discourse:

> For if the Divine Essence be not fruitful itself (μὴ καρπογόνος ἐστὶν αὐτὴ ἡ θεία οὐσία), but barren (ἔρημος), as they hold, as a light that lightens not, and a dry fountain (πηγὴ ξηρὰ), are they not ashamed to speak of His possessing framing energy (δημιουργικὴν ἐνέργειαν)? . . . For if they attribute to God the willing about things which are not (τὸ βούλεσθαι περὶ τῶν μὴ ὄντων), why recognise they not that in God which lies above the will (ὑπερκείμενον τῆς βουλήσεως)? now it is something that sur-passes will (ὑπεραναβέβηκε τῆς βουλήσεως), that He should be by nature (πεφυκέναι), and should be Father of His proper Word (πατέρα τοῦ ἰδίου Λόγου).¹⁷

For Athanasius, God's power to generate life cannot be limited to his creative work but must have its root in God's essence. The Word by which God creates "must surely be the living Will of the Father, and an essential energy (ἐνούσιος ἐνέργεια), and a real Word (Λόγος ἀληθινὸς), in whom all things both consist (συνέστηκε) and are excellently gov-erned."¹⁸ Athanasius then concludes his thought:

> No one can even doubt, that He who disposes (ὁ ἁρμίζων) is prior to the disposition (τῆς ἁρμονίας) and the things disposed (τῶν ἁρμοζομένων). And thus, as I said, God's creating (τὸ δημιουργεῖν) is second to His begetting (τοῦ γεννᾶν); for Son implies something

16. *Discourse* II.1 (*NPNF2* 4:348; PG 26:148).
17. *Discourse* II.2 (*NPNF2* 4:349; PG 26:149).
18. *Discourse* II.2 (*NPNF2* 4:349; PG 26:149).

proper to Him and truly from that blessed and everlasting Essence (ἐκ οὐσίας); but what is from His will (ἐκ βουλήσεως), comes into consistence from without (ἔξωθεν), and is framed through His proper Offspring which is from It.[19]

For Athanasius, his Arian opponents have made creation an end in itself; the external work of creating becomes a closed setting that severely limits the range of divine revelation in the Scriptures and the theological knowledge that can be derived from them. Humanity can only know God from his external works and, therefore, can at best know him as Creator. God's fatherhood and sonship can only be interpreted by Arians as metaphors or images of God's creative will. In response, Athanasius seeks to establish a different setting for the biblical narrative. Rather than interpreting divine fatherhood and sonship within the setting of God's creation, Athanasius interprets God's creative work within the setting of his generative essence.[20]

By limiting the generation of life to God's creative will, the Arians allow no distinction between "begetting" and "creating," understanding them to be synonymous. Thus, Athanasius's task is to support the distinction between "begetting" and "making" that lies at the heart of the Nicene Creed, which confesses the Son as "begotten, not made." However, of equal importance to Athanasius in this discourse is the intimate connection between these verbs. At the depth of his being, God is Father who subsists in the eternal begetting of the Son. Yet, God's fatherhood is not confined within the limits of the divine essence, but begins to reveal itself in the economy of his relation to creation:

> If then that which comes first (πρότερον), which is according to nature (κατὰ φύσιν), did not exist, as they would have it in their folly, how could that which is second come to be, which is according to will (κατὰ βούλησιν)? for the Word is first and, then the creation. . . . For through Him did creation come to be, and God, as being Maker, plainly has also His framing Word, not external (οὐκ ἔξωθεν), but proper to Him (ἴδιον ἑαυτοῦ); for this must be repeated. If He has the power of will (τὸ βούλεσθαι), and His will is effective (ποιητικόν ἐστι), and suffices for the consistence (πρὸς

---

19. *Discourse* II.2 (*NPNF2* 4:349; PG 26:152).
20. Peter Widdicombe concludes that "Athanasius went beyond Origen in making fatherhood the subject of systematic analysis" (Widdicombe, *The Fatherhood of God*, 255). He continues: "Taking his starting-point from the belief that descriptions of the Son as Son and of the Father as Father were essential to an adequate understanding of the Christian experience of salvation, Athanasius argued that the priority of the description of God as Father made sense both of the idea of God as the unoriginated first principle, an idea to which the Alexandrian tradition was deeply committed, and of the idea of God as directly involved in the process of salvation. God's nature as God, his perfection as God, the source and goal of all existence, turned for Athanasius on the conception of God as inherently generative."

σύστασιν) of the things that come to be, and His Word is effective, and a Framer, that Word must surely be the living Will of the Father (ἡ τοῦ Πατρὸς ζῶσα βουλή), and an essential energy.[21]

Implicit in this passage is Athanasius's assumption that God created all things *ex nihilo*. God's creative work does not consist in the synthesis of external materials; rather, by his will alone, God calls forth the very substance of created things. For the will of God to manifest such power, its effective energy must originate in God's inward being. For Athanasius, the Arian schism between God's will and his essence not only destroys God's fatherhood, but also undermines God's creative work. For Arians, creation becomes a purely external operation, which, as Athanasius charges, turns God into "an artificer, not a Maker (τεχνίτης, οὐ ποιητής)."[22] "For how, if, as you hold, He [the Word] is come of nothing," Athanasius asks, "is He able to frame things that are nothing into being?"[23] For Athanasius, the confession of God as Father does not replace the confession of God as Creator. Rather, God's fatherhood ensures and protects God's creative work by rooting the divine will that creates all things *ex nihilo* within God's generative essence.[24] The generation of creation does not originate arbitrarily in God's external choice but is an expression of his true being as Father.

In this way, Athanasius intends to establish the Father's begetting of the Son as the theological setting in which the economy of his creative work is interpreted. However, God's true identity as Father, whose being subsists in the eternal begetting of the Son, is by no means a philosophical notion or speculative presupposition for the bishop of Alexandria. Rather, God's fatherhood, as the interpretive setting in which the church hears the Scriptures and understands the economy of his relation to creation, is constituted for the church in the act of Baptism. It is for this reason that Athanasius ends his introduction to Proverbs 8 with reference to the church's baptismal liturgy.

In *Discourse* II.18–30, Athanasius introduces his reading of Proverbs 8 with an emphasis on the intimate relation between the Word's creation of all things and his eternal sonship as one begotten of the Father and proper to his essence. The Son was not brought forth "for us," as an instrument serving the end of creation. Rather, humanity was created by the Son and, therefore, is intended to subsist within his sonship.

---

21. *Discourse* II.2 (*NPNF2* 4:349; PG 26:152).
22. *Discourse* II.22 (*NPNF2* 4:359; PG 26:192).
23. *Discourse* II.21 (*NPNF2* 4:359; PG 26:189–192).
24. Cf. Anatolios, *Retrieving Nicaea*, 114. Anatolios writes that "Athanasius comes to the startling conclusion that to deny the Son a place within the divine essence is effectively to deny that God is Creator."

But the sentiment of Truth (τό τῆς ἀληθείας φρόνημα) in this matter must not be hidden, but must have high utterance. For the Word of God was not made for us, but rather we for Him, and "in Him all things were created." Nor for that we were weak, was He strong and made by the Father alone, that He might frame us by means of Him as an instrument (δι' ὀργάνου); perish the thought! it is not so. For though it had seemed good to God not to make things originate, still had the Word been no less with God, and the Father in Him.[25]

For Athanasius, the Word's sonship is an end in itself; he is not begotten by the Father for the purpose of creation or for any other end beyond himself. Thus, his sonship not only precedes the creation of all things, but it is the eternal setting within which his creation of all things *ex nihilo* takes place.

For Athanasius, the Son's eternal and essential relationship to the Father is the "sentiment of truth" that underlies the whole of Scripture. In *Discourse* II.32, Athanasius begins to demonstrate that the intimate relationship between the Father and the Son is the theological context for the church's reading of Scripture. While Arians read the Scriptures as words of the Creator spoken to his creatures, Athanasius reads them as originating within the intimate correspondence between the Father and the Son. The Arian reading of Scripture is not merely a dispute with Athanasius, but with God himself. "For if the voice were ours which says, 'This is My Son,'" notes the Alexandrian bishop with thick sarcasm, "small were our complaint of them; but if it is the Father's voice (τοῦ Πατρός ἡ φωνὴ), and the disciples heard it, and the Son too says of Himself, 'Before all the mountains he begat me,' are they not fighting against God (θεομαχοῦσι) . . . ? For they neither feared the voice of the Father, nor reverenced the Saviour's words, nor trusted the Saints."[26] In this text, Athanasius connects Wisdom's words in Proverbs 8 with the Father's words at Jesus' baptism in order to present them together as a reciprocal testimony within the Godhead. At his baptism, the Father testifies to his Son, and in Proverbs 8 the Son testifies to his Father. This reciprocal correspondence, manifested in Jesus' baptism, becomes the very root from which the prophetic and apostolic Scriptures grow.

The Scriptures, therefore, do not contain external or arbitrary images and names for God, but images rooted in the eternal and essential correspondence that binds together the Father and Son. Indeed, for Athanasius, the trustworthy character of Scripture as the foundation of the church's knowledge of God is compromised by his Arian opponents. If

---

25. *Discourse* II.31 (*NPNF2* 4:364; PG 26:212).
26. *Discourse* II.32 (*NPNF2* 4:365; PG 26:213–216).

the words of Scripture are to be trusted, they must subsist within that Word, who himself subsists eternally and essentially within the Father:

> We understand in like manner that the Son is begotten (γεννώμενον) not from without (οὐκ ἔξωθεν) but from the Father (ἐκ τοῦ Πατρὸς), and while the Father remains whole (ὁλόκληρον μένοντα), the Expression of His subsistence is ever (χαρακτήρατ ῆς ὑποστάσεως) and preserves the Father's likeness and unvarying Image (εἰκόνα ἀπαράλλακτον), so that he who sees Him, sees in Him the Subsistence too (ὑπόστασιν), of which He is the Expression. And from the operation (ἐκ τῆς ἐνεργείας) of the Expression we understand the true Godhead of the Subsistence (τὴν τῆς ὑποστάσεως ἀληθῶς θεότητα), as the Saviour Himself teaches when He says, "The Father who dwelleth in Me, He doeth the works" which I do.[27]

While the Arians set the Scriptures in the external correspondence between the Creator and his creatures, Athanasius sets them within the Son as the eternal image begotten from the Father's own being.

For Athanasius, to read the Scriptures from within the reciprocal dialogue of the Father and the Son is simply to read the Scriptures as the baptized. The Arian reading of Scripture undermines the church's baptismal identity. Since Baptism takes place in the Trinitarian name, Athanasius believes that Baptism gives creatures, which are external to God, a place of sonship within the divine fellowship of the Holy Trinity. However, by emptying the names of the Father and the Son of their true meaning, the Arians destroy the reality of Baptism.

> And these [Arians] too hazard the fulness of the mystery, I mean Baptism; for if the consecration (τελείωσις) is given to us into the Name of the Father and Son, and they do not confess a true Father (Πατέρα ἀληθινὸν), because they deny what is from Him and like His Essence (ὅμοιον τῆς οὐσίας), and deny also the true Son (τὸν ἀληθινὸν Υἱὸν), and name another of their own framing as created out of nothing, is not the rite administered by them altogether empty (κενὸν) and unprofitable, making a show, but in reality being no help towards religion (εὐσέβειαν)? For the Arians do not baptize into Father and Son, but into Creator and creature, and into Maker and work. And as a creature is other than the Son, so the Baptism, which is supposed to be given by them, is other than the truth, though they pretend to name the Name of the Father and the Son, because of the words of Scripture, for not he who simply says, "O Lord," gives Baptism; but he who with the Name has also the right faith (τὴν πίστιν ὀρθήν).[28]

27. *Discourse* II.33 (*NPNF2* 4:366; PG 26:217).
28. *Discourse* II.42 (*NPNF2* 4:371; PG 26:236–237).

Yet, for Athanasius, the Arian doctrine not only undermines the origin of Baptism in the Father's begetting of his Son, but it also destroys the eschatological purpose of Baptism—the incorporation of humanity into the fellowship of the Holy Trinity:

> In thinking to be baptized into the name of one who exists not, they will receive nothing; and ranking themselves with a creature (κτίσματί συντασσόμενοι), from the creation they will have no help, and believing in one unlike (ἀνόμοιον) and foreign to the Father in essence, to the Father they will not be joined (οὐν συναφθήσονται), not having His own Son by nature, who is from Him, who is in the Father, and in whom the Father is, as He Himself has said; but being led astray by them, the wretched men henceforth remain destitute (ἔρημοι) and stripped (γυμνοί) of the Godhead.[29]

In these texts, the intimate connection between the Scriptures and Baptism is unveiled. As the setting in which the biblical narrative is to be read and the economy of God's relationship to his creatures is to be understood, Baptism is much more than merely a passive assumption that colors the church's reading of texts. Rather, Baptism supplies the plot that Athanasius sees moving at the depth of the Scriptures, uniting them into the single drama of salvation. Baptism also governs the eschatological scope or resolution, toward which Athanasius believes the sacred narrative to be driven by the energetic force of the Spirit.

"CREATED" AND "BEGOTTEN": BAPTISM AND THE PLOT OF PROVERBS 8

In *Discourse* II.18–43, Athanasius introduces his reading of Proverbs 8:22–31. For the Alexandrian bishop, Proverbs 8 is the central passage or proof text around which the argument of his opponents revolves. Thus, an orthodox reading of this text is crucial for thwarting the Arian cause. Yet, this text is especially difficult for Athanasius, because the LXX uses the verb "created" alongside the verb "begotten" in reference to God's Wisdom, a divine figure all parties identified with Christ. The use of these two verbs in close proximity to one another compels Athanasius to answer certain fundamental questions. How are these verbs to be interpreted? What is the relationship between them? At first appearance, the verbs seem synonymous, an understanding promoted by Arians. Thus, Athanasius's task is, not merely to refute the Arian reading, but primarily to offer an interpretation that harmonizes with Nicene orthodoxy. John O'Keefe and R. R. Reno argue that "Athanasius does not so much

---

29. *Discourse* II.43 (*NPNF2* 4:371–372; PG 26:240).

'prove' the Nicene doctrine as demonstrate its exegetical effectiveness."[30] In the Nicene Creed, the Son is confessed as "begotten, not made." This distinction meets its most profound challenge from the Arian reading of Proverbs 8 and their insistence that "creating" and "begetting" share a common meaning. Thus, Athanasius must supply a reading of Proverbs 8 that preserves the fundamental distinction articulated at Nicaea, yet also adequately defines the intimate relationship between God's creating and begetting implicit in Proverbs 8.

For Athanasius, a reading that agrees with Nicaea is quite simply a reading that conforms to the church's liturgy and practice of Baptism. Therefore, Athanasius ends his introductory comments with an emphasis on the baptismal liturgy. Athanasius acknowledges that "the course of the discussion has led us also to mention holy Baptism."[31] Within this context, Athanasius wants to begin his exposition of Proverbs 8 with this fundamental question in mind: "Why too in the baptismal consecration (τῇ τελειώσει) is the Son named together (συγκατονομάζεται) with the Father?"[32] After establishing Baptism as the foundation for his reading of Proverbs 8, Athanasius begins his exposition of the text in *Discourse* II.44. His exegesis does not begin with the text, the grammar, or lexical considerations; rather, he begins with the genre of *Proverbs* in order to emphasize that the true meaning of such proverbial statements is not always as it first appears: "Since, however, these are proverbs (παροιμίαι), and it is expressed in the way of proverbs, we must not expound them nakedly in their first sense, but we must inquire into the person (τὸ πρόσωπον), and thus religiously put the sense on it [or: with piety fit the sense to him] (μετ᾽ εὐσεβείας τὸν νοῦν ἐφαρμόζειν αὐτῷ)."[33] For Athanasius, since the person precedes the words he speaks, one cannot interpret the words without first recognizing who it is that speaks them. However, for the bishop of Alexandria, it is not a mere angel that speaks the words of Proverbs 8:22, but the Wisdom of God himself.

By establishing Wisdom as the subject of the text, Athanasius is able to interpret Proverbs 8:22 in connection with 9:1, which refers to Wisdom building a house. Since it is clearly "our body" that is the house Wisdom builds for himself, Athanasius maintains that Proverbs 8:22 can be interpreted in the same fashion. Like the verb "build," so also the verb "created" can be understood to refer, not to "the Essence of His Godhead," but to "His manhood and His economy (οἰκονομίαν) toward us."[34]

30. John O'Keefe and R. R. Reno, *Sanctified Vision: An Introduction to Early Christian Interpretation of the Bible* (Baltimore, MD: John Hopkins University Press, 2005), 61.
31. *Discourse* II.41 (*NPNF2* 4:370; PG 26:233).
32. *Discourse* II.41 (*NPNF2* 4:370; PG 26:233).
33. *Discourse* II.44 (*NPNF2* 4:372; PG 26:240).
34. *Discourse* II.45 (*NPNF2* 4:372; PG 26:241).

Athanasius's main purpose is to provide an alternative way to understand the verb "created." While Arians understand the verb "created" as a description of Wisdom's ontological origin, Athanasius maintains that the verb can possess an alternative meaning when used of one who pre-exists. He refers to Psalm 102:18, Psalm 51:12, Ephesians 2:15, and Ephesians 4:22 as examples of scriptural passages where "created" is used of pre-existing things. In such circumstances, the verb "create" does not necessarily refer to "the essence and mode of generation (τὴν οὐσιαν καὶ τὴν γένεσιν)."[35] In Psalm 51, David does not pray for the construction of a heart different in essence from the one he already possesses. Rather, in such a passage, the verb "create" means "renovation according to God and renewal (τὴν κατὰ Θεὸν ἀνανέωσιν καὶ ἀνακαίνισιν)."[36] In this way, Athanasius undermines the Arian insistence that the verb "create" can only have a single meaning. His purpose is to broaden the range of meaning attached to the verb "create" so that his own reading can at least be entertained. The purpose of his long introduction to Proverbs 8, which emphasized the pre-existence of the Father's essential begetting of the Son in relation to his creative work, then becomes clear. The verb "create" must not be seen as an absolute expression that becomes a controlling hermeneutic for all other descriptions of the Son. Rather, the meaning of the verb must be adapted to the person, who is being described.[37]

Having broadened the possible meanings for the verb "create," Athanasius is ready to offer his reading of Proverb 8. While the verbs "created" and "begotten" appear in close proximity in the text, Athanasius intends to argue for a fundamental distinction between them. Athanasius understands the Arian reading of Proverbs 8:22–31 to give the verb "created" a dominant role. While the Arians assert the synonymous character of both verbs, it is the verb "create" that expresses most literally and fundamentally Wisdom's relation to God. The "begetting" of Wisdom mentioned in Proverbs 8:25 becomes merely a metaphor for his origin as the beginning of God's creative work. The verb "create" controls the meaning of the verb "begets." Athanasius challenges this Arian hermeneutic by demonstrating that the verb, "create," is not so narrowly defined as his opponents claim. Secondly, the bishop of Alexandria argues that the verbs, while both referring to Wisdom, are employed with a grammatical

---

35. *Discourse* II.46 (*NPNF2* 4:373; PG 26:244).
36. *Discourse* II.46 (*NPNF2* 4:373; PG 26:245).
37. Cf. *Discourse* II.3, where Athanasius makes this hermeneutical point. He writes, "For while it is confessed what His nature is, what word is used in such instances need raise no question. For terms do not disparage His Nature; rather that Nature draws to Itself (εἰς ἑαυτήν ἕλκουσα) those terms and changes them (μεταβάλλει). For terms (λέξεις) are not prior to essences (τῶν οὐσιῶν), but essences are first and terms second" (*NPNF2* 4:349; PG 26:152). In such a text, Athanasius seems to understand the Arians as holding to a kind of biblicism that makes a single word or statement from Scripture a controlling hermeneutic for the whole of Scripture and for the mystery of the Son's relation to the Father.

difference. To the verb "created" a qualifying purpose is added, while no such qualification is attached to the verb "begets":

> On this account then the reason (ἡ αἰτία) of "He created" is added, namely, the need of the works (τῶν ἔργων ἡ χρεία); and where the reason is added, surely the reason rightly explains the lection [i.e., term]. Thus here, when He says "He created," He sets down the cause, "the works;" on the other hand, when He signifies absolutely (ἀπολελυμένως σημαίνων) the generation from the Father (ἐκ τοῦ Πατρὸς γέννησιν), straightway He adds, "Before all the hills He begets me;" but He does not add the "wherefore (οὐ διὰ τί)," as in the case of "He created," saying, "for the works," but absolutely (ἀπολελυμένως), "He begets me," as in the text, "In the beginning was the Word."[38]

For Athanasius, this grammatical difference between the verbs is a clue signifying the distinctiveness of each verb and their relationship to one another. Proverbs 8:22 qualifies the verb "created" with the phrase "for the sake of his works (εἰς ἔργα αὐτοῦ)." This grammatical structure signifies, according to Athanasius, that "the works" must pre-exist Wisdom's creation. Thus, if the Arian reading is correct and "created" signifies the origin of Wisdom's being, then Proverbs 8:22 teaches an absurdity. The Arian reading suggests that Wisdom's very existence depends upon humanity and the works of creation.[39] This teaching has already been the subject of Athanasius's critique in *Discourse* II.29–30. "First, the Son appears rather to have been for us brought to be," Athanasius writes, "than we for Him . . . . And we were brought into being that we might be, but God's Word was made, as you must hold, not that He might be, but as an instrument for our need; so that not we from Him, but He is constituted from our need."[40]

However, challenging and criticizing his opponents' interpretation is not Athanasius's main goal; rather this critique simply lays the groundwork for his own positive reading of Proverbs 8:22–25. The fact that "created" is qualified by the phrase "for the sake of his works" and that the verb "begets" is without qualification signifies their distinctiveness and their relationship within the narrative of salvation. Athanasius's interpretation focuses on the three verbs used in Proverbs 8:22–25: "the Lord created me (ἔκτισέ)," "he founded me (ἐθεμελίωσε)," and "he begets me (γεννᾷ)." For Athanasius, these three verbs trace the narrative of Wisdom's relationship

---

38. *Discourse* II.56 (*NPNF2* 4:379; PG 26:265–268).

39. Cf. Anatolios, *Retrieving Nicaea*, 47. Anatolios argues that, for Athanasius, Arius pushed his soteriological emphasis to an extreme. Indeed, the Word's very essence is defined as being "for us." Thus, Anatolios finds it "ironic indeed that Athanasius should complain that Arius's theology is too soteriological."

40. *Discourse* II.30 (*NPNF2* 4:364; PG 26:210).

to the Father. The Arian reading, because it makes the verbs "founded" and "begets" synonymous with "created," lacks movement or any dynamic character; Proverbs 8:22–25 becomes a static text, in which the three verbs are merely three ways of saying the same thing. However, for Athanasius, the three verbs move backwards from his incarnation, in which he undergoes creation for the sake of humanity, to his founding, in which he is made the foundation for humanity's creation in the image of God, to his begetting, in which he has his eternal origin in the Father.

By emphasizing the movement of the narrative,[41] Athanasius is able to establish the present tense verb, "begets (γεννᾷ)," as the fundamental setting in which the aorist verbs, "created (ἔκτισέ)" and "founded (ἐθεμελίωσε)" take place. Athanasius exploits the temporal difference between "created" and "begets" to emphasize the Nicene distinction between creatures and sons. "And there is this difference, that the creatures are made upon the beginning (ὑπὸ τὴν ἀρχὴν) and have a beginning of existence connected with an interval . . . . But the Word of God, not having beginning of being (ἀρχὴν τοῦ εἶναι), certainly did not begin to be (ἤρξατο τοῦ εἶναι), nor begin to come to be (ἤρξατο γίνεσθαι) but was ever (ἦν ἀεί)."[42] Athanasius continues,

> The being of things originate (τῶν γενητῶν) is measured by their becoming (ἐν τῷ γίνεσθαι μετρεῖται), and from some beginning (ἀπό τινος ἀρχῆς) does God begin to make them through the Word, that it may be known that they were not before their origination; but the Word has His beginning, in no other beginning than the Father (ἐν τῷ Πατρὶ), whom they allow to be without beginning (τῷ ἀνάρχῳ), so that He too exists without beginning in the Father (ἀνάρχως ὑπάρχῳ ἐν τῷ Πατρὶ), being His Offspring, not His creature.[43]

Athanasius's narrative reading is clever and innovative, allowing the bishop of Alexandria to maintain a fundamental distinction between the verbs "created" and "begets," but also to establish an intimate relation between them.[44] Yet, as ingenious as his reading is to this point (*Discourse*

---

41. Cf. James D. Ernest, "Athanasius of Alexandria: The Scope of Scripture in Polemical and Pastoral Context," *Vigiliae Christianae* 47 (1993): 341–362. Ernest maintains that "the history of the incarnation of the Word of God for the sake of human salvation . . . is Athanasius's only real exegetical principle and his only hermeneutical rule."

42. *Discourse* II.57 (*NPNF2* 4:379; PG 26:268–269).

43. *Discourse* II.57 (*NPNF2* 4:379; PG 26:269).

44. The narrative framework that gives continuity to his interpretation of Proverbs 8 is missed by some scholars. Cf. Christopher Beeley, *The Unity of Christ* (New Haven, CT: Yale University Press, 2012), 155. Beeley asserts that Athanasius has a "dualist Christology," and that he imposes a "binary metaphysical scheme" upon the Scriptures. Beeley focuses on the ontological distinction between Creator and creature and fails to recognize the narrative continuity in which the Word becomes fully human in order to bring humanity into his own divine sonship. Thus, in Athanasius there is a unity of subject in that one and the same Son of God is eternally begotten of the Father and, for the redemption of man, undergoes a creation that identifies him fully with humanity.

II.57), it appears to be rather arbitrary—a capricious bending of the text to win an argument. However, in the following sections, the root and breadth of his narrative reading unfolds. In *Discourse* II.58, Athanasius introduces Moses' song as recorded in Deuteronomy 32:6 where the verbs "create" and "beget" are again placed in close proximity to one another. However, in Deuteronomy the two verbs do not refer to the Word or Wisdom, but to the people of God. For Athanasius, since the verbs "create" and "beget" are used with reference to both divine Wisdom and the people of God, their meaning must be located in the dynamic narrative of salvation in which the divine Word enters into reciprocal communion with humanity.

In his reading of Deuteronomy 32:6, Athanasius emphasizes the order of the verbs in Moses' song. First, the text speaks of humanity as "created" and "made," then, lastly, it employs the language of "begets." For the bishop of Alexandria, the verbs in Deuteronomy 32 (as in Proverbs 8) relate dynamically in the narrative of salvation:

> For God not only created (οὐ μόνον ἔκτισεν) them to be men, but called (ἐκάλεκεν) them to be sons, as having begotten (γεννήσας) them. For the term "begat" is here as elsewhere expressive of a Son, as He says by the Prophet, "I begat sons and exalted them;" and generally, when Scripture wishes to signify a son, it does so, not by the term "created," but undoubtedly by that of "begat." And this John seems to say, "He gave to them power to become children of God, even to them that believe on His Name; which were begotten not of blood, nor of the will of the flesh, nor of the will of man, but of God (ἐκ Θεοῦ ἐγεννήθησαν)." And here too the cautious distinction is well kept up, for first he says "become," because they are not called sons by nature (διὰ τὸ μὴ φύσει) but by adoption; then he says, "were begotten," because they too had received at any rate the name of son. . . . But this is God's kindness to man (φιλανθρωπία), that of whom He is Maker (ποιητὴς), of them according to grace He afterwards becomes Father also; becomes, that is, when men, His creatures, receive into their hearts, as the Apostle says, "the Spirit of His Son, crying, Abba, Father."[45]

For Athanasius, the whole of Scripture is united around a single salvific plot, which is fundamentally baptismal in character. Within this narrative, the verbs "create" and "beget" are distinct, yet intimately related. The narrative of God's relation to humanity begins with his creation of them in his own image and likeness; yet this narrative opens up to the mystery of sonship accomplished through the Word's incarnation and the gift of the Spirit, in whom the baptized call God "Father."

---

45. *Discourse* II.59 (*NPNF2* 4:380; PG 26:272–273).

In this way, Athanasius refuses to read Proverbs 8 as a single, isolated passage; rather, he connects it to the soteriological plot that, according to the bishop of Alexandria, underlies the whole of the Bible. By connecting Proverbs 8 to other passages where the verbs "create" and "beget" are placed in close proximity with one another, Athanasius is able to root his reading in a much broader and more catholic context. The reader simply will not understand Proverbs 8 if he does not engage the whole of Scripture and the Christological plot that lies in, with, and under every text. For Athanasius, this soteriological plot consists in a reciprocal communion between the *Logos* and his creation. In Deuteronomy 32 and John 1:12–13, God's relation to humanity is emphasized; these texts move from God's creation of humanity to his begetting of them in the waters of Baptism through the gift of the Spirit. However, in Proverbs 8, the other side of this plot is in view as it uses the verbs "create" and "beget" with reference to divine Wisdom. For the Son of God, "begetting" precedes his submission to the act of creation for the sake of humanity.[46]

> God, being first Creator, next, as has been said, becomes Father of men, because of His Word dwelling in them. But in the case of the Word the reverse; for God, being His Father by nature (φύσει), becomes afterwards both His Creator and Maker, when the Word puts on that flesh which was created and made, and becomes man. For, as men, receiving the Spirit of the Son, become children through Him (γίνονται τέκνα δι' αὐτοῦ), so the Word of God, when He Himself puts on the flesh of man, then is said both to be created and to have been made (κτίζεσθαι καὶ πεποιῆσθαι).[47]

Athanasius's narrative reading of Proverbs 8 is not merely an innovative tactic designed to win the argument. Rather, in *Discourse* II.58 it is clear that Athanasius's reading sprouts from his practice and confession of Baptism. Baptism is not only the setting in which he reads Proverbs 8, but also the fundamental plot that allows Athanasius to read the Scriptures as a single, unified narrative.

---

46. Cf. also *Discourse* III.33 where this reciprocal relation between begetting and creating is considered in connection with the Virgin birth and Baptism. Athanasius writes, "Whence also, whereas the flesh is born of Mary Bearer of God (γεννωμένης τῆς σαρκὸς ἐκ τῆς Θεοτόκου Μαρίας), he himself is said to have been born (γεγεννῆσθαι), who furnishes to others an origin of being (γένεσιν εἰς τὸ εἶναι); in order that he may transfer our origin into himself (τὴν ἡμῶν εἰς ἑαυτὸν μεταθῇ γένεσιν), and we may no longer, as mere earth, return to earth, but as being knit (συναφθέντες) into the Word from heaven, may be carried to heaven by him. . . . For no longer according to our former origin in Adam do we die; but henceforth our origin and all infirmity of flesh being transferred (μετατεθέντων) to the Word, we rise from the earth, the curse of sin being removed, and of him who is in us, and who has become a curse for us. And with reason; for as we are all from earth and die in Adam, so being regenerated (ἀναγεννηθέντες) from above of water and Spirit, in the Christ we are all quickened (ζωοποιούμεθα); the flesh being no longer earthly, but being henceforth made Word (λογωθείσης), by reason of God's Word who for our sake 'became flesh'" (*NPNF2* 4:412; PG 26:293–296).

47. *Discourse* II.61 (*NPNF2* 4:381; PG 26:276–277).

"THE BEGINNING OF WAYS":
BAPTISM AND THE SCOPE OF PROVERBS 8

To this point in his *Discourses*, it is evident that Athanasius's reading of Proverbs 8 does not consist in a grammatical or methodological argument. Indeed, for both Athanasius and his Arian opponents, the grammatical text functions within a larger narrative of God's relation to humankind. As a biblical text, Proverbs 8 must fit properly, even aesthetically, into the narrative's setting and plot. For Arians, the setting is identified with creation; the transcendent and almighty God, by means of his external will, creates all things. This setting is absolute and acts as a fundamental boundary that can never be transgressed. God is Creator, and therefore his relation to humanity will always be defined in terms of his creative, electing, and moral will. In this way, the setting determines the plot that underlies the Scriptures. As Creator, God manifests his perfect will through the obedient submission of Jesus Christ. This emphasis on Jesus' obedience is demonstrated in the Arian reading of Philippians 2:9–10. In *Discourse* I.37, the Arians maintain that Jesus is "exalted" and receives the title of Lord as a "reward" for the fulfillment of his work. Thus, for Arians, Jesus is called God and Lord, not on the basis of his nature or essence, but because of his perfect obedience.

For Athanasius, the proper setting for the Scriptures is not simply God's creative work, but his eternal generation of the Son. It is precisely in this regard that the Christian reading of Scripture is distinctive. Indeed, Athanasius claims that the Arian confession of God as "unoriginate" is no better than the devotion of pagan Greeks. In addition, in refuting the Arian reading of Philippians 2, the bishop of Alexandria maintains that the opinion of his opponents is "a device of our present Judaizers."[48] Like the Jewish reading of Scripture, Arians make creation the setting for the biblical narrative, and the fulfillment of his external, legal will becomes the underlying plot in which every text functions. For Athanasius, Christians read Scripture as the baptized. Baptism reveals the true theological setting that precedes God's creative work, namely, the eternal begetting of the Son. God is Father even before he is Creator; indeed, creation itself cannot be properly understood unless it is seen as the expression of God's generative essence. The baptismal confession of God as "Father," establishes not only a new setting for the church's reading of Scripture, but also a fundamentally different plot that underlies biblical texts and unites them into a single narrative. For Athanasius, Jesus is not merely the embodiment of God's creative and moral will, but the only begotten Son who ontologically assumes humanity into his own eternal sonship. Born of woman, humankind begins life as a creature, but, baptized in the Spir-

---

48. *Discourse* I.39 (*NPNF2* 4:329; PG 26:92).

it, Christians are joined to the body of Jesus and subsist within his eternal sonship calling God "Father." In this way, Baptism calls the church to read Scripture from within a new setting and according to a new plot.

However, Baptism not only supplies a new setting and plot, but it also establishes a new "scope" toward which the biblical narrative moves.[49] In their interpretation of Philippians 2:8–11, the Arians refer the exaltation of Christ to the Word's very essence. In Athanasius's opinion, the Arian reading is problematic for two reasons. First, as expected, Athanasius finds it revolting that his opponents so easily ignore Jesus' statements concerning his own changeless and eternal nature. If the Word changes, then his revelation of God is unstable and untrustworthy. Yet, it is not only the Word's relation to the Father that is compromised by the Arian perspective. Indeed, for Athanasius, even more problematic is how the Arian reading of Scripture destroys the Son's relationship to the humanity. By ascribing the exaltation to the Word's nature, the Arian reading of Scripture fails to understand the soteriological character of the Word's incarnation, death, and resurrection. Athanasius recognizes that in the Arian reading the Son "seems Himself not to have promoted the flesh at all, but rather to have been Himself promoted through it (αὐτὸς δι' αὐτῆς βελτιωθεὶς)."[50] For Athanasius, the narrative of Scripture is here turned upside down. Instead of the Son emptying himself for the sake of humanity in order to exalt it into communion with the Father, the needy Son descends in order to promote himself through his association with the body.[51] Thus, the Arian reading alters the plot that underlies the Scriptures and supplies a radically different scope to govern the momentum of the biblical narrative.

Athanasius returns to this emphasis on the scope of Scripture in his reading of Proverbs 8. In *Discourse* II.59, Athanasius relates the verbs "created" and "begets" to one another within the larger framework of the baptismal plot that underlies the Scriptures. Created humanity and the eternally begotten Son relate in a dynamic, reciprocal narrative. "For as men, receiving the Spirit of the Son, become children through Him, so the Word of God, when He Himself puts on the flesh of man, then is

---

49. In his helpful article on Athanasius' references to the "scope" of Scripture, James Ernest rejects the vague translation of "scope" as "general drift" (Ernest, p 344). Instead, Ernest maintains that "scope" connects to Athanasius understanding of the salvific narrative consisting in the Word's incarnation for the sake of humanity.

50. *Discourse* I.38 (*NPNF2* 4:328; PG 26:89).

51. Concerning the theological contours of the reciprocity between the Son's condescension and humanity's ascension, cf. Khaled Anatolios, *Athanasius* (London: Routledge, 2004), 43–56. Anatolios characterizes the alternative readings of Scripture presented by Athanasius and Arius in this way: "Either the Son is by nature true God who humbled himself in order to bring about our exaltation, so that his salvific work is the result of the abasement that he undertakes for our benefit; or he was himself "promoted" to divinity as a reward for his work in the flesh. The choice then is between the God of loving condescension and the self-promoting, upwardly mobile God!" (Anatolios, *Athanasius*, 53–54).

said both to be created and to have been made."[52] This reciprocal relationship between the begotten Son and created humanity establishes the scope toward which the Scriptures move. It is this eschatological scope that occupies Athanasius's attention in *Discourse* II.65.

Having established the narrative relation between the verbs "created" and "begets," Athanasius moves to consider the qualifying expression that Wisdom was created as the "beginning of ways."[53] Athanasius begins his exposition of this phrase with an emphasis on the newness of the way that begins in Christ.

> For when the first way (ἡ πρώτη ἡ . . . ὁδός), which was through Adam, was lost (ἀπώλετο), and in place of paradise we deviated unto death (ἐξεκλίναμεν εἰς τὸν θάνατον), and heard the words, "Dust thou art, and unto dust shalt thou return," therefore the Word of God, who loves man (ὁ φιλάνθρωπος), puts on Him created flesh (τὴν κτισθεῖσαν σάρκα) at the Father's will, that whereas the first man had made it dead (ἐνέκρωσεν) through the transgression, He Himself might quicken it in the blood of His own body (ἐν τῷ αἵματι του ἰδίου σώματος ζωοποιήσῃ), and might open "for us a way new and living (πρόσφατον καὶ ζῶσαν)," as the Apostle says, "through the veil, that is to say, His flesh."[54]

In this section, Athanasius identifies the "beginning (ἀρχή)" and the "way (ὁδός)" with the flesh of Christ. Through sin, Adam "inclined (ἐξεκλίναμεν)" or moved his body toward death and corruption. Thus, his flesh became a descending way, a vain and circular path by which those who are from the dust return to the dust. Yet, in Jesus' flesh a new way is established. Athanasius interprets Proverbs 8, where Wisdom is created as the "beginning of ways," in connection with John 14 and Colossians 1. In these texts, "way" and "beginning" are used as titles for the incarnate Christ as he relates to the church. Jesus' body is the "beginning (ἀρχή)," not as the temporal, historical start to a new path, but as the ontological source from which it proceeds.

By identifying the "beginning" of the new way with the flesh of Jesus, Athanasius is able to establish the resurrection as the foundation for his reading of Proverbs 8: "For if, as has been said, because of the resurrection from the dead He is called a beginning (ἀρχή), and then a resurrection took place when He, bearing (φερῶν) our flesh, had given Himself to death for us (δέδωκεν ἑαυτὸν ὑπερ ἡμῶν τῷ θανάτῳ), it is evident that His words, 'He created me a beginning of ways,' is indicative not of His essence (οὐσίας), but of His bodily presence (τῆς ἐνσωμάτου

---

52. *Discourse* II.61 (*NPNF2* 4:381; PG 26:277).
53. *Discourse* II. 65 (*NPNF2* 4:383–384; PG 26:285)
54. *Discourse* II.65 (*NPNF2* 4:384; PG 26:285).

παρουσίας)."[55] With this emphasis on the concrete flesh of Jesus, Athanasius is not merely referring to the historical narrative of salvation—a narrative that lies in the past. Rather, he is highlighting the ongoing presence of Jesus' flesh in the church as the foundation of her life and the source of her identity as the people of God. "For since the Savior was thus created according to the flesh . . . and had our first fruits (τὴν ἀπαρχὴν), viz. that human flesh which He took to Himself, therefore after Him, as is fit, is created also the people to come."[56] This ecclesial emphasis fits Athanasius's eucharistic vision of the church. The flesh of Jesus is not only the historical cause of salvation, but also the place or location in which salvation eternally subsists. Athanasius's argument moves from the baptismal setting and plot of the Scriptures to the goal of the baptismal liturgy—the joining of the baptized to the eucharistic flesh of Jesus.[57]

However, for Athanasius the body of Jesus is not a static presence, but a dynamic path that moves from a beginning toward an eschatological fulfillment. In *Discourse* II.65, Athanasius emphasized that the way of Christ is a "new" way, yet in the next section (*Discourse* II.66) the language of "newness" gives way to the language of "perfection." The movement of the incarnation does not end with the virgin birth and the Word's bodily presence among men; rather, it moves from his generation in the womb of Mary toward the eschatological perfecting of humanity through the sacrifice of his own flesh to the Father. "The perfect Word of God (ὁ τέλειος τοῦ Θεοῦ Λόγος)," writes Athanasius, "puts around Him an imperfect body (τὸ ἀτελὲς σῶμα), and is said to be created 'for the works;' that, paying the debt in our stead, He might, by Himself (δι' ἑαυτοῦ), perfect what was wanting to man (τὰ λείποντα τῷ ἀνθρώπῳ τελειώσῃ)."[58] Athanasius refers to John 17:4 and 5:36, both of which employ the language of "perfection (τελειώσας)." Through his passion, Jesus does not merely restore humanity to its original condition; he "perfects" it according to the eschatological fulfillment of his Father. From the beginning, the Word created humanity in order to bring it into his own filial

---

55. *Discourse* II.66 (*NPNF2* 4:384; PG 26:285).
56. *Discourse* II.66 (*NPNF2* 4:384; PG 26:288).
57. Cf. Anatolios, *Athanasius*, 56–61. In his insightful study, Anatolios demonstrates that Athanasius' emphasis on "offering" and "sacrifice" takes place with what he calls an "implicitly Eucharistic framework" (59). Antolius, then, concludes, "Moreover, once again we cannot ignore the implicit Eucharistic overtones of his assertion that Christ's offering of his own body as a sacrifice applies to us through our 'kinship' (*Or. Ar.* 1:43) with his body and our being 'co-bodied' (*sussōmoi*) with him (*Or. Ar.* 2:74)" (61). It is my point in this section that, for Athanasius, the Eucharist is the very goal or scope, toward which the baptismal liturgy moves. In the same way that the scope of the virgin birth and incarnation of the Word is his sacrifice on the cross and his ascension to the Father's right hand, so the scope of Baptism is the offering of the baptized in communion with Christ to the Father.
58. *Discourse* II.66 (*NPNF2* 4:384; PG 26:288).

relation to the Father; it is precisely this fulfillment that is constituted in the crucified and risen flesh of Jesus.

In the following section (*Discourse* II.67), Athanasius begins to define more concretely what he means by the Word's perfection of humanity. The Alexandrian bishop knows that his reading shifts Proverbs 8 from a description of God's creative work to his soteriological purpose in and through the incarnation. "Therefore it remains for us to say that when He has become man, then He took the works (ἔλαβε τὰ ἔργα). For then He perfected them (ἐτελείωσεν), by healing our wounds (ἰασάμενος) and vouchsafing to us the resurrection from the dead (χαρισάμενος ἡμῖν τὴν ἐκ νεκρῶν ἀναστασιν)."[59] Here Athanasius describes the Word's "perfection" of humanity in terms of two specific aspects. First, the Word "heals," which signifies the Word's restoration of humanity to a condition pure of sin's traumatic wounds. Yet, secondly, the Word "bestows" the resurrection from the dead, which signifies the fulfillment of humanity in an exalted condition that rises above its original formation. Athanasius continues,

> Because the works were become imperfect (ἀτελῆ) and mutilated (χωλὰ) from the transgression, He is said in respect to the body to be created; that by perfecting them and making them whole (τελειώσας καὶ ὁλόκληρα ποιήσας), He might present the Church unto the Father (παραστήσῃ τῷ Πατρὶ τὴν ἐκκλησίαν), as the Apostle says, "not having spot or wrinkle or any such thing, but holy and without blemish." Mankind then is perfected in Him and restored (τετελείωται καὶ ἀποκατεστάθη), as it was made at the beginning (κατὰ τὴν ἀρχὴν), nay, with greater grace (μείζονι μᾶλλον χάριτι). For, on rising from the dead, we shall no longer fear death (οὐκέτι φοβούμεθα θάνατον), but shall ever reign (βασιλεύσομεν ἀεὶ) in Christ in the heavens. And this has been done, since the own Word of God Himself, who is from the Father, has put on the flesh, and become man. For if, being a creature, He had become man, man had remained (ἔμενεν) just what he was, not joined to God (οὐ συναφθεὶς τῷ Θεῷ).[60]

In this passage, Athanasius defines perfection in terms of the scope of Jesus' incarnate narrative. Jesus defines the path of sonship, which reaches its goal in being "offered to the Father" and "joined to God." Within the death, resurrection and exaltation of Jesus' flesh, the church lives and moves and has her being. In the fellowship of his body, the church is being "offered to the Father," delivered from "the fear of death," and finally "joined to God."

---

59. *Discourse* II.67 (*NPNF2* 4:385; PG 26:289).
60. *Discourse* II.67 (*NPNF2* 4:385; PG 26:289).

Athanasius recognizes that, for his Arian opponents, the biblical narrative can only end where it first began. Creation controls the movement and purpose of Scripture so that the eschatological horizon for humanity remains closed and limited. Humankind ever remains a creature, whose relationship to the Creator can always be reduced to God's external will. Thus, Athanasius begins *Discourse* II.68 referring to an apparent objection of his Arian opponents: "'Yet,' they say, 'though the Savior were a creature, God was able to speak the word only and undo the curse (μόνον εἰπεῖν ὁ Θεὸς καὶ λῦσαι τὴν κατάραν).'"[61] This Arian aphorism identifies salvation with a transcendent act of power. The plot of salvation becomes nothing more than the Creator reasserting his supremacy over a rebellious creation. Yet, while Arians speak of what God is "able" to do, Athanasius points to the scope of God's purpose for humanity. The Arian reading focuses on the almighty power of the Creator's will, but it leaves humanity bound to the weakness of its original ontology. In the Arian perspective, humanity can do nothing better than offer a slavish submission to its omnipotent Maker.

However, for Athanasius, the "scope" of the scriptural narrative is not determined by what God has the power to accomplish, but by what God in his supreme love accomplishes for the benefit of humanity: "We must consider [that it is necessary to observe the scope of] (σκοπεῖν δεῖ) what was expedient for mankind (τὸ τοῖς ἀνθρώποις λυσιτελοῦν)."[62] For Athanasius, Scripture is not a narrative about the almighty will of God asserting its dominance; rather, it reveals a Father who condescends in love to form humanity for communion with his Son. The Alexandrian bishop refers to Noah, Moses, and the ancient Judges to demonstrate God's intent to work in and through humanity. Even the ancient law was not declared from the transcendent heavens, but from Sinai. God condescended to the mountain so that Moses might "ascend (ἀναβῆναι)" the mountain and that Israel might be formed in "hearing the word [that was] near them."[63] For Athanasius, the biblical narrative is not oriented toward the recovery of a lost past, but toward a future eschaton, already begun in the exalted flesh of Jesus, that will surpass all human imagination.

Thus, for Athanasius, the salvation of humanity demands more than the speaking of an external, creative word that returns all things to their pristine origin; rather, salvation demands the incarnation of God's own Word:

> If God had but spoken, because it was in his power, and so the curse had been undone, the power of the one giving the command would

---

61. *Discourse* II.68 (*NPNF2* 4:385; PG 26:292).
62. *Discourse* II.68 (*NPNF2* 4:385; PG 26:292).
63. *Discourse* II.68 (*NPNF2* 4:385; PG 26:292).

be demonstrated (τοῦ μὲν κελεύσαντος ἡ δύναμις ἐπεδείκνυτο), but man would remain what Adam was before the transgression, receiving an external grace (ἔξωθεν λαβὼν τὴν χάριν), and not having it fit together with the body (μὴ συνερμοσμένην ἔχων αὐτὴν τῷ σώματι). For such was his condition when he was placed in Paradise.[64]

In this intriguing text, Athanasius maintains that even before sin Adam's relationship to God was defined by his creation. Humanity possessed a creaturely existence rooted in the will of the Creator. Athanasius describes this creaturely relation in spatial terms; his relationship was one of "external grace."[65] Yet, through the incarnation, death, and resurrection of Christ, humanity is internalized by the eternal Word who is proper to the Father's essence. In Christ, humanity possesses a relation to God that is new, unprecedented, and perfect.

The contrast between Athanasius and his opponents regarding the scope of the biblical narrative could not be greater or more profound. The Arians present a salvation narrative that moves in a circular pattern, a mere restoration of the beginning. Athanasius points out the obvious weakness, namely, that this perspective implies an "interminable (ἄπειρον)" repetition of events, in which man is ever being seduced by the serpent, ever enslaved to sin, and ever in need of forgiveness. However, for Athanasius, the scope of Scripture moves from a beginning in God's creative work toward an eschatological perfection that has its "source (ἀρχὴ)" in the resurrected flesh of Jesus. In Christ, human flesh along with its passionate movements is given a permanent and eternal dwelling within God's consubstantial Son. Through his crucified and risen humanity, all who are one body with him are truly "free from sin and from the curse which came upon it, and might truly abide forever (διαμείνωσιν εἰσαεὶ), risen from the dead and clothed in immortality and incorruption."[66]

Above all else, for Athanasius, the internalizing of humanity along with its passionate movements renders salvation firm and eternal. The

---

64. *Discourse* II.68 (*NPNF2* 4:385; PG 26:292).

65. Concerning this emphasis on the inadequacy of an "external grace," cf. *Discourse* III.31–32. In this passage, Athanasius emphasizes the importance of the verb "carried" or "bore" in Isaiah 53. He writes, "And the Word bore (ἐβάσταζεν) the infirmities of the flesh, as His own, for His was the flesh (αὐτοῦ ἦν ἡ σάρξ); and the flesh ministered (ὑπούργει) to the works of the Godhead, because the Godhead was in it, for the body was God's. And well has the prophet said "carried (ἐβάσταξε);" and has not said, "He remedied our infirmities (ἐθεράπευσεν)," lest, as being external (ἐκτὸς) to the body, and only healing (ἰασάμενος) it, as He has always done, He should leave men subject still to death; but he carries our infirmities, and He Himself bears our sins, that it might be shewn that He has become man for us, and that the body which in Him bore them, was His own body; and, while He received no hurt Himself by "bearing our sins in his body on the tree," as Peter speaks, we men were redeemed from our own affections (τῶν ἰδίων παθῶν ἐλυτρούμεθα), and were filled with the righteousness of the Word (τοῦ Λόγου δικαιοσύνης ἐπληρούμεθα)" (*NPNF2* 4:410–411; PG 26:389).

66. *Discourse* II.69 (*NPNF2* 4:386; PG 26:293).

salvation narrative presented by the Arians lacks stability, because humanity remains infirm and is dominated by the erratic motions of fear. "Had the Word been a creature (κτίσμα)," writes Athanasius, "the devil, himself a creature (κτίσμα), would ever continue the battle (ἀεὶ τὴν μάχην) and man, being between the two (μέσος), had been ever in peril of death (ὕποπτος ἀεὶ τῷ θανάτῳ), having none in whom and through whom he might be joined to God (συναφθεὶς τῷ Θεῷ) and delivered from all fear (ἐλεύθερος παντὸς φόβου)."[67] In Christ, humanity moves toward a new eschatological goal.[68] Through the sin of Adam, humanity becomes enslaved to a passionate movement away from God, which ends in the dust of corruption. However, through the incarnation of the Word, corruptible humanity is given a place within the only begotten Son, and through his passionate self-abasement, humanity is moved toward God being offered to the Father and found acceptable in his sight.

> For therefore the union (συναφὴ) was of this kind, that He might unite what is man by nature to Him who is in the nature of the Godhead (τῷ κατὰ φύσιν τῆς θεότητος), and his salvation and deification (ἡ σωτηρία καὶ ἡ θεοποίησις) might be sure (βεβαία). Therefore let those who deny that the Son is from the Father by nature and proper to His Essence (ἴδιον αὐτοῦ τῆς οὐσίας), deny also that He took true human flesh of Mary, Ever-Virgin; for in neither case had it been of profit to us men, whether the Word were not true and naturally Son of God, or the flesh not true which He assumed. But surely He took true flesh, though Valentinus rave; yea the Word was by nature Very God, though Ariomaniacs rave; and in that flesh has come to pass the beginning of our new creation (ἡ ἀρχὴ τῆς καινῆς κτίσεως), He being created man for our sake, and having made for us that new way (τὴν ὁδὸν ἡμῖν ἐκείνην ἐγκαινίσας).[69]

For Athanasius, the essential relationship between the Father and the Son makes salvation firm and permanent precisely because the flesh, which is naturally unstable and subject to the motions of fear, has been brought into the eternal fellowship of the Father and the Son. The Father's eternal generation of the Son establishes both the proper setting, from which the biblical narrative proceeds, and the scope, in which it comes to fulfillment. Baptism is more than merely a beginning or initiation; it proclaims the mystery of the eschatological fulfillment that awaits the church, namely, to be knit into the fellowship of the Holy Trinity through communion with the flesh of Jesus.

---

67. *Discourse* II.70 (*NPNF2* 4:386; PG 26:296).

68. Concerning the passionate movement of humanity in Athanasius thought, cf. M. C. Steenberg, *Of God and Man: Theology as Anthropology from Irenaeus to Athanasius* (London: T&T Clark, 2009), 158–159.

69. *Discourse* II.70 (*NPNF2* 4:386; PG 26:296).

CONCLUSION

After examining Athanasius's reading of Proverbs 8, scholars often conclude with some appreciation for his creative, even innovative, interpretation; however, these academic evaluations usually contain the judgment that his exegesis is forced and highly manipulative. This accusation reveals more about the academy than about Athanasius himself, for it judges Athanasius according to those characteristics the academy finds especially valuable—the use of unbiased, scientific methods that produce moderate and balanced results. Missed in this evaluation is the character of Athanasius himself.[70] The bishop of Alexandria does not have the luxury of moderation; he cannot listen to his Arian opponents from a transcendent perch nor judge their interpretation of Scripture with intellectual detachment. Athanasius is a passionate warrior, immersed in a very public battle with paganism and Arianism for control of the culture. This conflict is more than an intellectual squabble among the Christian elite; rather, it is a fierce battle involving emperors, politicians, philosophers, theologians, and every member of the church. This conflict, therefore, is a cultural battle that involves cities, institutions, and every aspect of public life.

Thus, Athanasius's exegesis is not a benign intellectual exploration into the historical meaning of an archeological artifact; it is, rather, a tool or weapon to be wielded in a much larger battle. For the bishop of Alexandria, orthodox Christians, loyal to the Trinitarian confession of Nicaea, are under attack from two fronts. First, since the Edict of Milan, the Christian church has been ushered into a public, institutional, and political battle for the culture of the Roman Empire. Before Constantine's rise to power, Christians could withdraw from public life and enjoy the benefits of relative obscurity. However, Christianity's new place in the world required them to engage with the advocates of traditional civic religious practices and assume some responsibility for the character of public culture. Receiving power in the world demands the moral exercise of that power for the good of humanity. Second, the church not only faced paganism's attack from without, but also Arianism's attack from within her own borders. Yet, this battle with Arianism was no less public, political, and profound than Christianity's struggle with paganism. Indeed, from Athanasius's perspective, Arianism has enjoyed the political support and coercive power of the imperial court. Athanasius knows that his interpretation of Scripture will not merely be heard by intellectuals, but by politicians, civic magistrates, common laity, and perhaps even the emperor himself.

---

70. Concerning judgments of Athanasius's character, cf. Anatolios, *Athanasius*, 33–34.

Therefore, at the heart of Athanasius's reading of Scripture is not a method of interpretation, an intellectual formulation or an abstract hermeneutic. Rather, most prominent is Athanasius's passionate loyalty to Christ, his pastoral heart for the church, and his sense of episcopal duty to publicly confess the truth and refute heresy. For the bishop of Alexandria, the orthodox faith is not merely an abstract idea; it has a concrete geography, a geography being threatened with invasion from the external forces of paganism and usurpation from the internal forces of heresy. Thus, Athanasius defines himself geographically as one who has been called to govern the church by standing at a baptismal font, presiding at an altar, and filling a pulpit. To occupy this place in the church is to be rooted in the theological soil of Jesus' body. It is precisely the theological significance of Jesus' body that Athanasius seeks to defend with his exegesis and with the whole of his argument. Thus, the intimate connection between the Scriptures and the church's sacramental life is not a hermeneutical choice for the bishop of Alexandria; it is the most fundamental of theological assumptions that conditions his reading of Scripture.

In this essay, Athanasius's reading of Proverbs 8 was considered as it unfolds in his second discourse against his Arian opponents. In the course of this examination, it was argued that the bishop of Alexandria saw his conflict with the Arians as a battle for the reality of Baptism. Athanasius does not refer to Baptism as an arbitrary rhetorical device designed to manipulate his hearers. Rather, Baptism is naturally assumed by the bishop of Alexandria to be the proper setting for the whole biblical narrative. Even before he acts to create the world, God is Father who subsists within his eternal generation of the Son. Thus, in the Creed, God is confessed as "Father," even before he is confessed as "Creator of heaven and earth." When the baptized call God "Father," as they do in the Creed and the Lord's Prayer, it is no mere empty metaphor that proceeds from their mouths; rather, they speak truly, for they speak from within the very body that the only-begotten Son has made his own from the Virgin Mary. The reality of Baptism, for Athanasius, does not proceed from the Creator's will as an arbitrary legal command. The *arche* or ontological source of the church's Baptism is nothing other than the Father's eternal generation of the Son. This essential relation, through which the Father and Son dwell in and with each other, is not simply a philosophical idea developed by Athanasius to combat his rivals. It is the eternal foundation, upon which the church's baptismal identity depends and the fundamental setting for her reading of the Scriptures.

The Father's begetting of the Son, as the baptismal setting for the Scriptures, manifests itself in two ways. First, the eternal generation of the Son establishes the salvific plot that undergirds the biblical narrative uniting the various actors, scenes, and texts into a single drama. Second, it also provides the eschatological scope, toward which the biblical narrative moves and in which the salvific plot is perfected. Since the Arians do not accept the Son's essential divinity, their understanding of the plot does not begin with the *kenosis* or self-emptying of the Son for the sake of his creation. The Arian plot consists in the restoration of the Creator's lordship through the power of his almighty will perfectly embodied in the obedient submission of Jesus. For Athanasius, the incarnation, suffering, and death of Jesus are not signs of his ontological subordination to his Creator, but manifestations of his love for humankind (*philanthropia*), by which he sets aside his glory and abases himself in order to unite with his fallen formation. This loving condescension leads to the glorious exaltation of humanity into the mystery of divine sonship. In this way, Baptism establishes a dynamic, reciprocal exchange, in which the eternally begotten Son undergoes a creation in the flesh so that those created in the flesh might become sons through the gift of his Spirit. Thus, the confession that the Son is "begotten, not made" is not merely a technical distinction used in philosophical speculations about Jesus. Rather, for Athanasius, it defines the very reality of Baptism, by which the church receives "the power to become children of God, generated not from blood, nor from the desires of the flesh, nor from the desires of man, but from God" (John 1:12–13). ✛

PART THREE

ECCLESIA

LUTHER'S TWO KINGDOMS
IN THE HOUSE POSTILS

✠

One of the most impressive elements in William Weinrich's career is that he combined theological scholarship and teaching at the highest level with ongoing service to church and state as a chaplain in the Air Force Reserves and Indiana Air National Guard for over thirty years. Given the significance of the military chaplaincy for his ministry, I am offering the following in his honor—an essay that treats Luther's theology of the two kingdoms.

Not surprisingly, much has been written about the two kingdoms since it is a theme that recurs frequently in the Reformer's writings. Many scholars have used the terminology to refer primarily to Luther's ideas regarding spiritual and temporal authority (including, but not exclusively, political authority).[1] In both realms, God is in charge but exercises his authority in very different ways. In addition to this distinction, however, Luther also used the language of two kingdoms to describe an even more fundamental distinction in his theology, the kingdom of Christ and that of the devil, the world.[2] Whereas the first distinction designates two different but complementary modes of divine power, the second emphasizes the radical hostility of the forces of evil directed against Christ, the means of grace, and his people, the church. The second duality as well as

---

1. See, for example, Quentin Skinner, *The Foundations of Modern Political Thought*, 2 vols. (Cambridge: Cambridge University Press, 1978), 2:14; J. M. Porter, "Introduction; The Political Thought of Martin Luther," in J. M. Porter, ed., *Luther: Selected Political Writings* (Philadelphia, PA: Fortress Press, 1974), 1–21; and Mark E. Sell, "Appendix: Two-Kingdom Theology, Civil Righteousness, and Civil Religion," in *The Anonymous God: The Church Confronts Civil Religion and American Society*, David L. Adams and Ken Schurb, eds. (St. Louis, MO: Concordia Publishing House, 2004), 265–287.

2. Robert Kolb, "Luther's Hermeneutics of Distinctions," in Robert Kolb, Irene Dingel, and L'ubomír Batka, eds., *The Oxford Handbook of Luther's Theology* (Oxford: Oxford University Press, 2014), 178. Kolb distinguishes *three* uses of the "two kingdoms" language in Luther: (1) "rarely" for institutions of church and secular government; (2) God's rule vs. Satan's; and (3) two spheres (vertical and horizontal) of human life, in both of which God rules and Satan works to corrupt. Since the first is a particular instance of the third, I am treating them together under one heading, the distinction between temporal and spiritual authority.

the first appeared early in Luther's work,[3] and both made their way into the Lutheran Confessions.[4] One can also find them both in Luther's later works.[5] But in this essay, I am proposing to trace this double duality of the kingdoms in Luther's *House Postils.*[6]

The *House Postils* are a collection of sermons on the traditional Gospel lessons of the church year and represent an effort by one of Luther's earliest disciples to make the Reformer's preaching available to ordinary people. The development of Luther's theology into that of the Lutheran Church is a complicated story that includes many disparate elements besides Luther himself—among them Veit Dietrich, the editor of the first version of the *House Postils.* For many years, Dietrich was close to Luther and assisted him in many ways. He spent several years in Wittenberg (1522–1535) and actually lived with the Reformer at the Black Cloister. When Luther debated the Zurich reformer, Huldrych Zwingli, at Marburg in October 1529, Dietrich was there. And the next year, when Melanchthon went off with the princes of Saxony to the Diet of Augsburg, Dietrich remained with Luther at Coburg Castle (April to October, 1530). Among the tasks that Dietrich undertook for Luther and his cause were organizing Luther's correspondence, taking dictation for future publications, transcribing the "table talks," and recording Luther's sermons and lectures. Not surprisingly, one of the editors of the Weimar edition of Luther's works, Albrecht Freitag, has identified Veit Dietrich—along with Georg Rörer—as the "most significant" of those who constructed the "Luther tradition."[7]

---

3. Both are present, for example, in *Temporal Authority: To What Extent It Should Be Obeyed* (1523) in *LW* 45:75–129 (WA 11:314–36). See also Luther's sermons on the same subject from the fall of 1522 in WA 10III:371–385.

4. For the antagonism between God and the devil, see Ap VII & VIII, 16–19; LC IV, 25; FC SD X, 20; Ap XII, 55; and SC III, 3. For the distinction between temporal and spiritual authority, see AC XXVIII, 4; Ap XVI, 1–3, 6–8; and LC I, 164. See Paul Timothy McCain, ed., *Concordia: The Lutheran Confessions,* 2nd ed. (St. Louis, MO: CPH, 2005, 2006). Unless otherwise noted, all English translation for the Lutheran Confessions will be from this version. For the original languages, see *BSLK.*

5. For the distinction between temporal and spiritual, see "Against the Roman Papacy: An Institution of the Devil, 1545," *LW* 41:298, 301; and "Against Hanswurst, 1541," *LW* 41:225, 226. For the kingdom of the devil at enmity with God, see "Against the Roman Papacy, 1541" *LW* 41:335, 338, 365; "On the Councils and the Church, 1539" *LW* 41:10, 164, 168–169; and "Against Hanswurst," *LW* 41:193, 218, 247.

6. Volume 52 of Weimar edition consists entirely of the first edition of Luther's *House Postils* from 1544. That is the edition I have used for this paper. There is a 19th century English translation, Martin Luther, *Sermons on the Gospels for the Sundays and Principal Festivals of the Church,* ed. M. Loy, 2 vols. (Rock Island, IL: Augustana Book Concern, 1871). This has been helpful but the translation in the text is my own.

7. Albert Freitag, "Veit Dietrichs Anteil an der Lutherüberlieferung" in Karl Drescher, ed., *Lutherstudien zur 4. Jahrhundertfeier der Reformation veröffentlicht von den Mitarbeitern der Weimarer Lutherausgabe* (Weimar: Hermann Böhlaus Nachfolger, 1917), 171. For Dietrich's biography, see Bernhard Klaus, *Veit Dietrich: Leben und Werk* (Nürnberg: Verein für bayerische Kirchengeschichte, 1958); and Hans J. Hillerbrand, ed., *The Oxford Encyclopedia of the Reformation,* 4 vols. (New York: Oxford University Press, 1996), s.v. "Dietrich, Veit."

One element in that "tradition" has been Luther's house postils that Dietrich first published in 1544, just a few years before Luther's death. These postils are sermons on the traditional Gospel lessons for festivals and Sunday services.[8] For reasons of health, Luther limited his public preaching from 1531 to 1535, but he continued to preach to the members of his own household—relatives, friends, boarders, and servants, as well as his wife and children.[9] By doing this, Luther felt that he was carrying out his duties as a "house father" by instructing his servants (*gesinde*) in how to be Christians.[10] But once he had delivered these sermons, Luther forgot all about them. Veit Dietrich, however, thought they were worth remembering, so he took notes on them, and some years later decided to publish them. Luther agreed to supply an introduction.

After their initial appearance in 1544, the *House Postils* were frequently reprinted. There were eleven editions just in 1544 and 1545, including two editions in low German and one in Latin. John Frymire has compiled a chronological listing of ninety-four printings of the *House Postils* from 1544 to 1609.[11] In 1559, Andreas Poach published another version of the *House Postils*, based on Georg Rörer's notes, not Dietrich's.[12] Poach was highly critical of Dietrich's work, but by 1559 Dietrich's edition had already been printed thirty-five times, not including the eight low German and four Latin versions that were based on it. The Rörer/Poach version appears only seven more times in Frymire's list.[13] In the formative years of Lutheranism, therefore, the house postils, especially Dietrich's version, were available as models for Lutheran preaching and teaching. Emil Hirsch has described them as the postils from which entire generations of Lutheran clergy learned about Luther's doctrine and preaching.[14]

---

8. They are not all "Gospel" lessons. The list of 94 texts for the church year, compiled by the editors of the Weimar edition, includes these exceptions: Gal 4:4–7 for New Year's Day; 1 Cor 11:23–26 and 27–34 for two sermons on the sacrament during Holy Week; Rom 5:8–11 on the suffering of Christ also during Holy Week; Isa 9:2–7 for Christmas; and three texts from Acts: 2:1–4 for Pentecost; 6:1–15; 7:1–2, 44–59 for the Martyrdom of St. Stephen; and 9:1–25 for the Conversion of St. Paul. Dietrich also included 8 postils on the Passion of Our Lord, each with a text from Matthew. See WA 52:XII–XXVI.
9. Martin Brecht, *Martin Luther*, 3 vols. (Philadelphia and Minneapolis, MN: Fortress Press, 1985–1993), 2:204.
10. WA 52:1.4–6.
11. John M. Frymire, *The Primacy of the Postils: Catholics, Protestants, and the Dissemination of Ideas in Early Modern Germany* (Leiden: Brill, 2010), 546–548.
12. Poach's version appeared several years after Luther died and demonstrates the enmity that set in during the decades after Luther's death among those who claimed to be his theological heirs, for Poach charged Dietrich with numerous inaccuracies. Modern editors have agreed that Dietrich did not publish an exact copy of Luther's original preaching (which was hardly possible) but incorporated non-Luther elements into the *House Postils*, including some of his own material. For background to both versions, see the introduction by Georg Buchwald in WA 52:VII–XII. The Weimar edition also provides data on the relationship between Dietrich's edition and Rörer's still extant manuscript notes. See also, Emanuel Hirsch's introductory comments to each version in *Luthers Werke in Auswahl*, vol. 7: *Predigten* (Berlin: Walter de Gruyter, 1962), 69, 84.
13. Frymire, 546–548.
14. Hirsch, 69.

Luther himself acknowledged them as authentic in the introduction he prepared for the first edition, "I have preached these sermons from time to time in my house for my household" after the example of the patriarchs and according to the command of Christ to the apostles that they preach first of all in houses, to which, Luther suggested, neighbors might also come.[15] In Luther's case, these particular house sermons derived from a time in the early 1530s when he did not feel up to preaching in the city church on account of ill health but nonetheless felt responsible for leading his servants and children through the Gospel readings appointed for each Sunday and festival of the church year.[16]

Also, according to Luther's introduction, he did not originally intend their publication. In fact, he did not realize that they were being taken down when he preached them. Once delivered, he thought, they were "completely forgotten."[17] But not so; Veit Dietrich was recording Luther's sermons at home as he preached them. At least that is Dietrich's claim in the dedication to the city fathers of Nuremberg that accompanied his publication of the *House Postils* in 1544, "I alone recorded them . . . and have kept them until the present." Luther called them "crumbs" and "fragments," but Dietrich saw them as a "treasure," especially on account of their simplicity and brevity—perfect, he thought, for ordinary folk:

> These sermons were presented in a fine, short, and simple fashion and are especially serviceable for young, simple folk. For with such people, one must not employ great artistry but should present the teaching briefly and simply and with words so impress them that they can grasp and mark something of the teaching.[18]

So Dietrich intended them for "unlearned" clergy who often pastored poor peasant parishes. If their pastors were not capable of preaching, such churches should be content if they would just read materials like the *House Postils* that presented pure doctrine in an orderly, simple, and understandable way.[19] He was also concerned that heads of households who could not get to church on a Sunday would have appropriate materials to hear or read at home for the hallowing of the Sabbath with God's word.[20] Finally, Dietrich offered the postils to those who still lived under bishops and other unreformed clergy and so had no expecta-

---

15. WA 52:1.3–29.

16. Although right from the beginning these sermons were called "*Haus*postil," Luther apparently felt up to preaching at times in the city church during these years. According to the editors of the Weimar edition, 25 of the 94 postils were preached "publice." See WA 52:XII–XXVI.

17. WA 52:2.4.

18. WA 52:2.5; 5.40–6.4.

19. WA 52:6.5–7, 17–19.

20. WA 52:6.20–26.

tion of hearing true doctrine in their churches that they might at least read it at home.[21]

A main objective of Dietrich was "pure doctrine."[22] These sermons provided just that and, of course, had the advantage of coming from Luther himself, whom Dietrich praised as the one through whom "God has brought the Scriptures and knowledge of God to light, has abolished the terrible abuses that the papacy introduced into the Church, and has established both pure doctrine and right worship in the Church."[23] Dietrich was convinced that exposure to these sermons would produce much "fruit," viz., strengthen faith, improve lives, and so offer praise and thanks to God.[24]

As a summary of what pure doctrine entails, Dietrich singled out Luther's doctrine regarding baptism, the sacrament of the altar, and the true knowledge of Christ and of God as well as other articles. For, as he insisted, "where this teaching is, there will be the forgiveness of sins and the privileges of the Church, no matter how weak it may otherwise be."[25]

But what about the two kingdoms doctrine, the subject of this essay? Although Dietrich himself did not specify it in his introduction, he nonetheless made use of it by distinguishing two spheres of God's activity: temporal and spiritual. Thus, when praising a good ruler as one who looks out for his own people more than for himself, Dietrich wrote that this is a "glorious and excellent gift of God" that brings down God's blessings upon the land, whereas a selfish ruler who neglects his office merits God's displeasure. However, this gift—like all those intended for temporal existence—cannot be compared to the interpretation of Scripture (and the office of the ministry) that brings the Holy Spirit who changes our hearts, cleanses us through the forgiveness of sins, establishes us in true obedience, and saves us forever.[26] So there are definitely two distinct realms in which God operates and accomplishes different purposes in each.

Interestingly, however, Dietrich concluded his introduction, i.e., his dedication to the governing officials of Nuremberg, with a prayer that God would move them not only to value his word but also to protect his church in order that God's name would be hallowed, his kingdom come, and his will be done, so that God might also provide good fortune and well-being to the state. For Dietrich, the two realms might be distinct, but they were hardly separate.[27]

---

21. WA 52:7.35–8.13.
22. WA 52:6.31–38.
23. WA 52:5.21–25
24. WA 52:6.17–19; 8.22–24.
25. WA 52:6.33–38.
26. WA 52:4.14–22, 28–36.
27. WA 52:9.5–11.

But this is Veit Dietrich, so what about Luther—or Dietrich's version of Luther in the *House Postils?* Not surprisingly, Luther's sermons reflect the same point of view. But how accurately did Dietrich present Luther's preaching in this work? In one sense, the question does not matter, because the Luther of publications like these was the Luther to whom people had access. From another perspective, however, the question is most important: Was the Luther whom his students presented to the public an authentic representation of the real Luther? In other words, did "Lutheran" theology as it developed after Luther reflect the actual views of the historical Luther as he himself presented them in his own publications, or did it somehow go in different or even contrary directions? Many have addressed this question through the years,[28] and this essay hardly proposes a comprehensive answer. However, we *can* provide still another piece of the puzzle by comparing Luther's treatment of the two kingdoms to Veit Dietrich's presentation of this theme in Luther's *House Postils.*

Even that, however, is still too much, since Luther used the distinction throughout his lengthy career. So instead of trying to do all of Luther, I propose restricting our attention to just two documents, Luther's *Temporal Authority: To What Extent It should be Obeyed* (1523)[29] and his *Commentary on Psalm 82* (1530)[30]—the first because it is an early, clear, and thorough treatment of the topic, and the second because it demonstrates a major shift in Luther's thinking about the proper role of the government in "spiritual matters."[31] Since the *House Postils* come even later in Luther's career, we might expect them to reflect the second document rather than the first—and they do.

As is generally true of Luther's works, his 1523 treatise reflects the particular context of its composition. In this case, that means a growing divide among the ruling elite of the Holy Roman Empire of the German Nation between those who supported Luther and those who did not. Although

---

28. Arguments over Luther's legacy began shortly after his death. See Irene Dingel, "Luther's Authority in the Late Reformation and Protestant Orthodoxy," in Robert Kolb, Irene Dingel, and Ľubomír Batka, eds. *Oxford Handbook of Martin Luther's Theology* (Oxford: University Press, 2014), 525–539. Philip Melanchthon often gets the "blame" for corrupting Luther's original insights. See Ken Schurb, "Twentieth Century Melanchthon Scholarship: With Particular Reference to 'The Melanchthonian Blight,'" *Concordia Theological Quarterly* 62 (1998): 287–307. A good example of the debate over the authentic Luther recently has involved the doctrine of justification no less, especially with the emergence of the so-called Finnish school that emphasizes the motif of "union with Christ" in Luther over against the "imputation" language of Melanchthon and others. See Aaron O'Kelley, "Luther and Melanchthon on Justification: Continuity or Discontinuity?" in Michael Parsons, ed., *Since We Are Justified by Faith: Justification in the Theologies of the Protestant Reformations* (Milton Keynes, Bucks, UK: Paternoster, 2012), 30–43.
29. *LW* 45:75–129 (WA 11:314–36).
30. *LW* 13:39–27 (WA 31I:189–218).
31. For an excellent description of how Luther's views regard church and state shifted over the years, see James M. Estes, *Peace, Order and the Glory of God: Secular Authority and the Church in the Thought of Luther and Melanchthon, 1518–1559* (Leiden: Brill, 2005).

Frederick the Wise continued to provide him with protection in electoral Saxony, Emperor Charles V had already condemned Luther in the Edict of Worms (May 1521), and other temporal rulers were taking steps against him and his writings. In particular, Frederick's cousin and the ruler of ducal Saxony, George the Bearded, had condemned Luther's translation of the New Testament and prohibited its sale in his realm just weeks after its publication.[32] Other rulers were still on the fence. So, in view of what princes were considering or actually doing about Reformation issues in their territories, Luther penned a treatise to instruct a Christian ruler in both his obligations and his limits in the exercise of his authority.[33]

For our purposes, it is important to note that *Temporal Authority* differentiates very carefully between *both* versions of the two kingdoms and employs a distinctive terminology to distinguish them. Luther describes the duality of good versus evil as two "kingdoms [*Reiche*]" and defines them this way:

> We must divide the children of Adam and all mankind into two classes, the first belonging to the kingdom of God, the second to the kingdom of the world. Those who belong to the kingdom of God are all the true believers who are in Christ and under Christ, for Christ is King and Lord in the kingdom of God.

A few paragraphs later, Luther adds, "All who are not Christians belong to the kingdom of the world."[34]

This stark dichotomy between Christians and non-Christians has a long history in theology. Augustine, of course, made it a theme in his *City of God*,[35] but it goes back to the Bible itself, e.g., John 15:19 ("If you were of the world, the world would love you as its own; but because you are not of the world, but I chose you out of the world, therefore the world hates you.") and John 18:36–37, Jesus' answer to Pilate's question about his kingship, "My kingdom is not of this world. . . . You say that I am a king. For this purpose I was born and for this purpose I have come into the world." So Luther's use of the first dichotomy in this treatise does not represent anything novel, except perhaps his implication that the hierar-

---

32. According to Brecht 2:108, those of George's subjects who had purchased a testament were supposed to turn it in to the government and get a refund. The Bible came out around the middle of September; George's prohibition began 7 November 1522.

33. For background to *Temporal Authority*, see Estes, 30–41.

34. *LW* 45:88, 90 (WA 11:249.24–27, 251.1–2).

35. "This [human] race we have distributed into two parts, the one consisting of those who live according to man, the other those who live according to God. And these we also mystically call the two cities, or the two communities of men, of which the one is predestined to reign eternally with God, and the other to suffer eternal punishment with the devil." Philip Schaff, ed., *A Select Library of the Nicene and Post-Nicene Fathers of the Christian Church*, 1st ser., vol. 2: *St. Augustin's City of God and Christian Doctrine*, reprint ed. (Grand Rapids, MI: Wm. B. Eerdmans Publishing Co., 1956), 284.

chical church[36] of his day (bishops, pope, etc.) belongs to the kingdom of the world rather than that of God, "It is not the church but the devil's apostles who command such things, for the church commands nothing unless it knows for certain that it is God's word."[37]

Similarly, the second dichotomy—temporal and spiritual authorities—has a long history prior to Martin Luther. Luther calls them the two "governments [*Regimente*]" in *Temporal Authority*, but the distinction itself went back at least to Gelasius I (pope, 492–496), who articulated the so-called "two swords" theory:

> [Christ] has made a distinction between two roles, assigning each its sphere of operation and its due respect. . . . Christian emperors were to depend on priests for their eternal life, priests were to profit from imperial government for their historical existence. . . . God's soldier does not involve himself in secular affairs . . . , while those involved in secular affairs are seen to have no charge of divine affairs.[38]

This distinction too has biblical foundations. Perhaps not Luke 22:38 ("And they said, 'Look, Lord, here are two swords.' And he said to them, 'It is enough.'"),[39] but certainly Matthew 22:21 ("Render to Caesar the things that are Caesar's, and to God the things that are God's."). Well before Luther, therefore, the question was not whether there were two God-given authorities but what was the relationship between the two?[40]

Luther's contribution to the discussion of two kingdoms and two governments in his *Temporal Authority* is itself twofold. First of all, he develops the first dichotomy, church and world (believers and unbelievers), into a rationale for the second dichotomy, spiritual and temporal authority. God established the two *governments* on account of the two *kingdoms*.

---

36. Luther was not the first to condemn the hierarchy and name the pope "antichrist." In the 14th century, for example, Spiritual Franciscans identified John XXII as the Antichrist. See Malcolm Lambert, *Medieval Heresy: Popular Movements from the Gregorian Reform to the Reformation*, 2nd ed. (Oxford: Blackwell, 1992), 210–211.

37. *LW* 45:106 (WA 11:262.33–34). See also *LW* 45:109 (WA 11:265.20–22), "They [temporal authorities] blithely heap alien sins upon themselves and incur the hatred of God and man, until they come to ruin together with bishops, popes, and monks, one scoundrel with the other." Here again, there was medieval precedent. According to Lambert, 280–281, Lollards in England in the 14th century identified the visible, hierarchical church that persecuted them as the Church of Antichrist.

38. Gelasius I, "The Bond of Anathema," in Oliver O'Donovan and Joan Lockwood O'Donovan, eds., *From Irenaeus to Grotius: A Sourcebook in Christian Political Thought, 100–1625* (Grand Rapids, MI: Eerdmans, 1999), 178–179.

39. According to Patrick Healy, *The Chronicle of Hugh of Flavigny: Reform and the Investiture Contest in the Late Eleventh Century* (Burlington, VT: Ashgate Publishing Co., 1988), 150–151, it was Peter Damian in the 1060s who "first imbued the 'two swords' in Luke with a political significance."

40. For an excellent introduction to this oft-treated topic, see John Kilcullen, "Medieval Political Theory," accessed on August 13, 2018, https://www.mq.edu.au/about_us/faculties_and_departments/faculty_of_arts/mhpir/staff/staff-politics_and_international_relations/john_kilcullen/medieval_political_theory/. See also Gerald F. Gaus and Chandran Kukathas, eds., *Handbook of Political Theory* (London: SAGE Publications, 2004), 338–354.

Secondly, he very carefully defines the nature of each government so as to limit each to its own sphere. Temporal authority, especially, has responsibility for what goes on here on earth. Therefore, it should not interfere with the authority that is concerned with a right relationship with God that lasts for eternity. This sounds like separation of church and state, but it turns out that in Luther's thinking, this is not the case.

As far as the first point is concerned, connecting the first dichotomy to the second, Luther's argument is straightforward. Those who belong to the kingdom of the world require the restraints of the law. That is the essential function of temporal authority. Luther writes, "It is certain and clear enough that it is God's will that the temporal sword and law be used for the punishment of the wicked and the protection of the upright." Luther compares non-Christians to "savage wild beasts [*den wilden bösen thieren*]." Without civil government, "they would devour one another, seeing that the whole world is evil. . . . No one could support wife and child, feed himself, and serve God. The world would be reduced to chaos."[41] In order to restrain them, God has established temporal authority.

At this point in his thinking, Luther is remarkably optimistic about believers: "If all the world were composed of real Christians, that is, true believers, there would be no need for or benefits from prince, king, lord, sword, or law."[42] Empowered by the Holy Spirit, their conformity to the will of God is automatic. They need no law, so their submission to civil authorities is voluntary and for the sake of their neighbors:

A true Christian lives and labors on earth not for himself alone but for his neighbor. . . . Because the sword is most beneficial and necessary for the whole world in order to preserve peace, punish sins, and restrain the wicked, the Christian submits most willingly to the rule of the sword, pays his taxes, honors those in authority, serves, helps, and does all he can to assist the governing authority.[43]

Luther later changed his mind about the relationship of the Christian to civil government. Submission was not, after all, voluntary but mandatory insofar as a Christian lived in time as well as for eternity and therefore had temporal responsibilities, in respect to which he was under government.[44] Nonetheless, Luther's main point about the nature of temporal au-

---

41. *LW* 45:87, 91 (WA 11:248.29–31; 251.12–15, 26). Luther's description reminds one of Thomas Hobbes's well-known description of mankind without civil government, "The life of man [is] solitary, poor, nasty, brutish, and short." See Thomas Hobbes, *Leviathan or the Matter, Forme and Power of a Commonwealth Ecclesiastical and Civil* (New York: Collier Books, 1962), 100.
42. *LW* 45:89 (WA 11:249.37–250.1).
43. *LW* 45:94 (253.23–29).
44. For example, "[Christians'] government is a spiritual government, and . . . they are subjects of no one but Christ. Nevertheless, *as far as body and property are concerned*, they are subject to worldly rulers and owe them obedience" (emphasis mine). "Whether Soldiers, Too, Can be Saved," *LW* 46:99.

thority remained constant. God had established it for temporal purposes. Therefore, it was good, and Christians could participate in it as rulers, soldiers, hangmen, or whatever else was needed—all with a good conscience.

But what were the limits to temporal authority? That too was a question of importance in 1523, and Luther supplies an answer in *Temporal Authority:* "The temporal government has laws which extend no further than to life and property and external affairs on earth, for God cannot and will not permit anyone but himself to rule over the soul." For the Reformer, "ruling over the soul" means principally prescriptions for the faith,

> When a man-made law is imposed upon the soul *to make it believe this or that* as its human author may prescribe, there is certainly no word of God for it . . . with such a wicked command the temporal power is driving souls to eternal death.[45]

What to believe is solely a matter for God's word. This is the authority of the spiritual government, not the temporal, and therefore those who administer spiritual authority, "priests and bishops," do not use law or the sword, "Their ruling is rather nothing more than the inculcating of God's Word. . . . Christians can be ruled by nothing except God's Word, for Christians must be ruled in faith, not with outward works."[46]

When temporal authority exceeds its limits by trying "to coerce the people with laws and commandments into believing this or that," it is behaving most wickedly, for "whoever believes something to be right which is wrong or uncertain is denying the truth, which is God himself. He is believing in lies and errors, and counting as right that which is wrong."[47] To explain what he means by forcing false faith, Luther specifies a command "to side with the pope . . . or to get rid of certain books" and then mentions specifically what was going on in some of the German territories, viz., "the tyrants have issued an order that all copies of the New Testament are everywhere to be turned in to the officials."[48] Authorizing or prohibiting books sounds like a temporal matter, but when the book promoted (or was) the word of God, it was no longer temporal but spiritual and so beyond the legitimate control of the government.

But what about the opposite situation? Does Luther think that a temporal authority should protect his people from false doctrine and heretics? True to his premise that temporal authority should *not* concern itself with spiritual matters, Luther's position—in 1523—is that government should stay out of the heresy-hunting business: "Heresy can never be restrained by force. . . . Heresy is a spiritual matter which you cannot hack to pieces

45. *LW* 45:105 (WA 11:262.7–10, 16–18, 24–25; emphasis mine.
46. *LW* 45:117 (WA 11:271.15–18).
47. *LW* 45:105 (WA 11:262.14–15, 28–30).
48. *LW* 45:111, 112 (WA 11:267.1–3, 15–16).

with iron, consume with fire, or drown in water." There is only one remedy for false doctrine, and it is in the provenance of the clergy, viz., the word of God. "God's Word must do the fighting," Luther contends and then goes on to explain, "If you wish to drive out heresy, you must find some way to tear it first of all from the heart and completely turn men's wills away from it. With force you will not stop it, but only strengthen it. . . . God's word . . . enlightens the heart, and so all heresies and errors vanish from the heart of their own accord."[49]

Such optimism about the power of the word apart from the power of the state successfully to suppress heresy did not last long. The Peasants' War especially was a major turning point. However, Luther continued to maintain the "two governments" (or "kingdoms") framework for discussing the extent and nature of political authority in regard to the Church. He did not, however, maintain the same limitations on that authority as he had presented them in *Temporal Authority*. Instead, he maintained that temporal rulers who were Christians should use their God-given authority to advance the interests of the church. Their job was not to preach but to create and maintain the earthly conditions for the proper proclamation of God's word.

This was a position that Luther advocated already in 1520 in his *Address to the Christian Nobility of the German Nation*, and one to which he returned in his preface to the *Visitation Articles* of 1528. By 1530, Luther was becoming quite comfortable with the development of a state church when he helped to prepare and encourage the princes for their presentation of the Augsburg Confession. This is also evident in his *Commentary on Psalm 82*, first published in the spring of 1530, which Luther used to present his current thinking regarding temporal and spiritual authorities. Although he continued to distinguish them, Luther did not separate them. In fact, he presented each of them as working in the interests of the other.[50]

Most of the commentary is about temporal rulers, but Luther also addresses spiritual authorities, the clergy: "[God] has appointed priests and preachers, to whom He has committed the duty of teaching, exhorting, rebuking, comforting, in a word, of preaching the Word of God."[51] Luther argues that faithful preachers should aim that word publicly right at government officials as well as the people to admonish and correct their faults, "The first verse [of the psalm] teaches that to rebuke rulers is not seditious, provided it is done . . . by the office to which God has committed that duty, and through God's Word, spoken publicly, boldly, and honestly." Luther explains that this is a matter of importance for the entire community as an inoculation against rebellion, "It would be

---

49. *LW* 45:114, 115 (WA 11:268.22–23, 24–25, 27–28; 269.9–12, 14–15).
50. For background, see Estes, 180–188.
51. *LW* 13:49 (WA 31I:196.7–8).

far more seditious if a preacher did not rebuke the sins of the rulers; for then he makes people angry and sullen, strengthens the wickedness of tyrants. . . . God might be angered and might allow a rebellion." Much better therefore when the preacher goes after "the lords . . . as well as the people, and the people as well as the lords," for "a preacher is neither a courtier nor a hired hand. He is God's servant and slave, and his commission is over lords and slaves."[52] God's word applies to all, and the clergy are supposed to make that application by their preaching.

And that is exactly what Luther does in his commentary—apply God's Word, Psalm 82, to the temporal rulers of his day, both because he has the office of preaching and because secular government is God's institution. By 1530, Luther was very much concerned with "unauthorized" preaching. In fact, he blamed the Peasants' War on those who—without call or command—would "sneak and creep" into other men's houses and parishes to spread their poison.[53] At the same time, however, he was also sensitive to the charge that he was going way beyond his own call as a preacher in Wittenberg by giving instructions to the entire world. To this he responded by pointing to his call—from pope and emperor, no less—as a "Doctor of Holy Scripture" at the university, which, he contended, authorized him to expound the Scriptures "for all the world" and to teach everyone. Even as a preacher in Wittenberg, he added somewhat disingenuously, he had the right to teach his people through publications. If others outside of Wittenberg wanted to read them, who was he to deny them? He certainly did not insist that anyone should read his writings.[54]

As far as government was concerned, Luther taught, as before, that God had established it in order to maintain temporal peace among men, for "where there is no peace, no one can keep his life or anything else, in the face of another's outrage, thievery, robbery, violence and wickedness."[55] Because God desired to preserve what he has already made— creatures, works, and ordinances—now threatened by human wickedness, he also instituted and still preserves earthly government and has committed to it "the sword and the laws." The divine origin of temporal authority means, first of all, that men must obey it,[56] and secondly, that rulers are responsible to God for the exercise of their office.[57] It also means that they should carry it out under God's word, "It is [God's] will that they be subject to His Word and either listen to it or suffer

---

52. *LW* 13:50–51 (WA 31I:197.29–32, 33–198.3–4, 12–15).
53. *LW* 13:64 (WA 31I:210.36).
54. *LW* 13:66 (WA 31I:212.9, 12–13).
55. *LW* 13:45 (WA 31I:192.22–23).
56. *LW* 13:44 (WA 31I:192.9–12), "Men ought to obey [rulers] as His officers and be subject to them with all fear and reverence, as to God Himself."
57. *LW* 13:45 (WA 31I:193.3–4), "God Himself will punish wicked rulers and impose statutes and laws upon them. He will be Judge and Master over them."

all misfortune. . . . For God's Word appoints them, makes them gods, and subjects everything to them. Therefore . . . they are to be subject to it and allow themselves to be judged, rebuked, made, and corrected by it."[58] Thus, when preachers instruct rulers in God's word, the latter are supposed to obey it.

Besides connecting the two governments by means of the word that the one preaches and the other obeys, Luther also uses Psalm 82 to show that the relationship works the other way too. When the temporal authorities carry out their God-given responsibilities, the church also benefits. For one thing, amidst the evils that characterize a world without government, Luther includes the following, "Much less will there be room to teach God's Word and to rear children in the fear of God and His discipline."[59] Temporal peace makes it possible for the clergy as well as parents to carry out their responsibilities.

But there is more—much more. For Luther brings the two governments closer together in this commentary than he did in *Temporal Authority* by arguing that the word of God supplies temporal blessings as well as eternal. That makes promotion of the word an essential element in the exercise of temporal authority by a Christian ruler. Luther writes:

[One true, pious, God-fearing pastor or preacher] can help many thousands of souls, both in eternal life *and in this life*. For by his word he can bring them to God and make of them able and apt people, serving and honoring God *and wholesome and profitable for the world*.

Given such positive consequences for this life and world, Luther contends that promoting and protecting God's word follows automatically from a ruler's God-given responsibility to provide justice for the godly and to repress the ungodly: "If God's Word is protected and supported so that it can be freely taught and learned, and if the sects and false teachers are given no opportunity and are not defended against the teachers who fear God, what great treasure can there be in the land?"[60]

The prince does not do the preaching, but he makes it possible for a pastor to do so. By such preaching, the latter not only "fills heaven with saints," but also "preserves peace and unity, raises fine young folks, and plants all kinds of virtue in the people. . . . A pious prince or lord who supports or protects such a pastor can have a part in all this." "Indeed," Luther continues, "this whole work and all the fruits of it are his, as though he had done it all himself, because without his protection and

58. *LW* 13:48 (WA 31I:195.33–196.3).
59. *LW* 13:45 (WA 31I:192.24–25).
60. *LW* 13:52 (WA 31I:199.7–11); emphasis mine.

support the pastor could not abide." Thus, the right use of temporal power enables good preaching, and good preaching brings temporal as well as spiritual blessings. Prince and preacher have different roles, but they share a common goal, viz., to advance the complete well-being of the people.[61]

Later in this commentary, Luther reveals just how far he has departed from his position of 1523 by addressing the question of whether rulers may also "put down opposing doctrines or heresies" when they undertake "to advance God's Word and its preachers." After all it is one thing to make sure that an orthodox preacher has a living and quite another to silence his heretical opponent. In *Temporal Authority*, Luther was quite clear that the clergy should combat false doctrine by the word and that secular authorities should stay out of it since, after all, physical measures cannot force the faith on anyone.[62] Luther's answer in 1530 is quite different. Although still acknowledging that "no one can be forced to believe," he offers four scenarios in which a ruler may properly use temporal authority against false teachers: (1) heretics who are openly seditious and reject temporal authorities and arrangements, for example, private property and marriage; (2) those who commit blasphemy by publicly rejecting the doctrines held by all Christendom, such as the resurrection of Christ; (3) when two preachers establish rival pulpits and so disturb the public peace by arguing over doctrine; and (4) when two opposing parties argue about ceremonies and man-made laws, and one of them binds consciences regarding matters that are left free in Scripture.[63]

From a modern perspective, freedom of speech would trump Luther's concerns in all four categories, even the first. But from his own perspective, what justifies Luther in appealing to government are the *social* consequences in each of the situations he describes, even in the second case of public blasphemy. This is a speech-crime that Luther groups with cursing, swearing, reviling, abusing, defaming, and slandering. Blasphemy is a crime against one's neighbor, for the perpetrator takes "from God and the Christians their doctrine and word, and he would do them this injury under their own protection and by means of the things all have in common. . . . He who makes a living from the citizens ought to keep the law of the city, and not defame and revile it."[64] Openly denying the doctrine that is held by a Christian community is an insult and offense to the community, an abuse of the privileges that one enjoys when living in such a place. Therefore rulers should not tolerate it.

Luther's description of these four situations shows that he has embraced the widely held opinion of the early modern period that a com-

---

61. *LW* 13:52–53 (WA 31I:199.28–29, 31–32, 34–200.1).
62. *LW* 45:114, 115 (WA 11:268.22–23, 24–25, 27–28; 269.9–12, 14–15).
63. *LW* 13:61–64 (WA 31I:208.1–210.8).
64. *LW* 13:62 (WA 31I:208.32–34, 35–36).

mon religion constitutes a kind of social glue for a community, large or small. Of course, Luther sees this as a characteristic of *orthodox* religion only, but the point remains. A well-ordered state requires a public faith, and the temporal authorities should maintain it. So while Luther's dichotomy of temporal and spiritual authorities survived in his mature theology, as Luther now formulated it, there was no longer even a hint of our contemporary separation of church and state, but rather their closest support and cooperation.

But what about Luther's other version of the two kingdoms, the kingdom of Christ versus the kingdom of this world and of the devil? That dichotomy also remains firmly in place. Although not especially prominent in Luther's *Commentary on Psalm 82*, it surfaces right at the conclusion. Referring to the last verse of the psalm—an appeal to God to come and judge the earth—Luther comments that "worldly government will make no progress. The people are too wicked and the lords dishonor God's name and Word continually." Therefore, there is need for a better "government and kingdom," and that is the kingdom of Christ. Almost his last words, Luther writes, "Over and above the righteousness, wisdom, and power of this world, there is need for another kingdom, in which there is another righteousness, wisdom, and power. For the righteousness of this world has an end, but the righteousness of Christ and of those who are in His kingdom abides forever."[65]

While Luther's understanding of the hostility between Christ and Satan remained constant, his *Commentary on Psalm 82* showed that by 1530, his other two kingdoms theology had developed substantially from what it was in *Temporal Authority*. Things had changed in the Reformer's thinking about church and state. This was certainly evident in what we may call his public theology, i.e., in works that he published in order to advance the cause of Reformation in Saxony and beyond, such as this commentary. Nor was this work unique. From this point forward at least, one may safely conclude that Luther accepted the commonly held notion that the *ius reformandi* belonged to the civil authorities.[66]

But what about the theology that Luther preached? Did the two kingdoms make it into sermons and if so, how? At last, we come to the *House Postils* in order to answer these questions. And what we find is that the "two kingdoms"—both kinds—are clearly evident in the sermons that Veit Dietrich published on the basis of sermons that Luther preached.

---

65. *LW* 13:72 (WA 31I:218.31–35).

66. Implicit already in the Augsburg Confession, Melanchthon states it explicitly in the Apology (Ap XXI, 44) and cites Psalm 82 in order to justify it, "It is your [the Emperor's] special responsibility before God to maintain and to propagate sound doctrine and to defend those who teach it. God demands this when he honors kings with his own name and calls them gods (Ps 82:6), 'I say, You are gods.'" See Estes, 189–212.

Consider the most fundamental of Luther's dichotomies—the kingdom of Christ and the kingdom of this world (ruled by Satan). Everywhere in the *House Postils*, Luther depicts the human experience as a battle between God and the devil, the church and the world. True enough, he does not always use *kingdom* (*Reich*) terminology to express this reality but often he does, especially if there is something in the text itself that leads to it. "Kingdom" terminology is prominent in the gospels,[67] so it occurs naturally in many homilies derived from texts that include it. For example, in the very first sermon of the collection, the text for the first Sunday in Advent (Matt 21:1–9)[68] includes a quotation of Zechariah 9:9, "Behold, your king is coming to you." Not surprisingly, therefore, Luther's postil discusses in detail the nature of Christ's kingship and kingdom. Texts like these almost require the preacher to explain what Jesus meant by the "kingdom," but not necessarily "two" kingdoms. So in this homily, Luther emphasizes the contrast between Christ the king and worldly kings, not the devil as "ruler" of this world. Even so, however, Luther points to the devil as the enemy of Jesus and his kingdom, "For the devil and his servants will leave no stone unturned in order to oppose this kingdom and either to destroy or to falsify the Word."[69]

Parables are a special instance of "kingdom" texts, since Jesus announced to his disciples that the purpose of his parables was to reveal to them "the secrets of the kingdom of heaven" (Matt 13:10–11). By my count,[70] the Gospel lessons for the Sundays of the church year in the *House Postils* include thirteen parables, and five of them explicitly identify "the kingdom of heaven [or God]" as their subject. Luther's sermon for the twentieth Sunday after Trinity on Matthew 22:1–13 is an excellent example of how two kingdoms terminology could lend itself to the explication of a "kingdom" parable, in this case, the parable of the marriage of the king's son. Right at the outset, Luther equates the "kingdom of heaven" with the "kingdom of our Lord Christ where the Word of God and faith are." Those who belong to this kingdom have the forgiveness of sins and deliverance from death and hell. Elsewhere, Luther replaces

---

67. The term "Kingdom of God" occurs 4 times in Matthew, fourteen times in Mark, thirty-two times in Luke, and twice in the Gospel of John. In addition, Matthew employs "kingdom of heaven" thirty-four times. In addition, Jesus is called "king" thirty-four times in all four. See W. F. Moulton and A. S. Geden, *A Concordance to the Greek Testament* (Edinburgh: T & T Clark, 1978), s.v. "βασιλεία" and "βασιλεύς."

68. In the Weimar edition, while the designation for each postil includes the biblical book and chapter, the editors have added the verse numbers in brackets.

69. WA 52:15.16–18. See also in the same sermon, WA 52:12.4–8, and 12.27–29 include references to the devil as an enemy from which Christ delivers us.

70. It is debatable what one should actually consider a parable. Martin Scharlemann, *Proclaiming the Parables* (St. Louis, MO: CPH, 1963), 18–19, records scholarly enumerations that range from thirty to seventy-nine. Here I am using the term for the illustrative narratives that characterized Jesus' preaching. So, for example, I have included Luke 16:19–31 (the rich man and Lazarus) even though Jesus did not explicitly call it a "parable."

"hell" by "devil" in describing the work of Christ to "free us from sin, death, and devil, and give us eternal life."[71]

As one might expect with a text that offers excuses for turning down the king's invitation, Luther uses it to discuss the many ways that people reject God's word. This word is important because it delivers the blessings of the kingdom, including protection from Satan. Luther writes, "God promises and speaks to you: 'If you hear and mark my Word diligently, you will be a master of the devil. He will have to flee from you and will not be able to come near you at all. For wherever my Word is, there am I also. But where I am, the devil cannot be found but will have to go away.'"[72] Luther, however, also includes a warning in this sermon, "Through His promise and great grace God attracts us and through great punishment He terrifies us. If these two means will not accomplish it, then the abominable devil will help and will also do it." Obviously, the only alternative to Christ and his kingdom is the power of Satan.[73]

In addition to biblical texts that themselves use kingdom terminology, Luther also uses it to explicate texts that do not employ it. For example, in the third sermon of the collection, the text is Matthew 11:2–10, which treats John the Baptist's sending disciples to Jesus with the question, "Are you the One who is to come?" Luther uses the text to explain extensively what kind of a king Jesus is and what kind of kingdom he has.[74] Although Luther presents our Lord as a king "who wants to help poor, miserable people, suffering in body and soul," his emphasis is on spiritual blessings, for "Christ is such a king who wants to help the dead, sinners and those imprisoned under the Law, to eternal life and righteousness." Luther describes preaching the gospel to sinners as the "greatest miracle." The law cannot save from sin; but Jesus can, for God commissioned him to be the king of sinners and preach the gospel to the "poor," i.e., those who despair of finding help in themselves or anywhere else.[75]

Here as elsewhere the opposition to Jesus is "the whole world [Welt]," which "is offended at this King and wishes that the devil would just take away this heretic." Luther equates their offense at Jesus with a rejection of the gospel. For what bothers the world so much is that Christ "turns everything upside down. . . . He wants to shove the pious and righteous into hell and not permit them into his kingdom. However, he wants to raise sinners into heaven." For Luther, then, the world hates the message

---

71. WA 52:505.28–30 and WA 52:511.4–5.

72. WA 52:509.24–28. Luther adds that one may employ the Ten Commandments and the Lord's Prayer to drive Satan away and keep him from harming a person (WA 52:509.34–39).

73. WA 52:514.7–10. Among the alternatives to Christianity, Luther cites Islam ("the devil's *Dreck*," WA 52:509.4–5) and Enthusiasts and Anabaptists whose sacraments the devil introduced (WA 52:509.10–12).

74. WA 52:24.24–26, 29–30.

75. WA 52:24.29–30; 26.4–6; 26.13, 14–16; 26.37–39.

of God's free grace to sinners and prefers its own works-righteousness. This leads it to lie about Christ and his followers as if they were against good works. Not so. "For if you would listen to our dear Lord Christ correctly and want to enter His kingdom, you would learn that they do not forbid good works. . . . One should do them and busy himself with them seriously so that one does not violate God's Word or his conscience." The problem is not with the doing but rather with relying on them when we die and enter eternity. For that, we must "look to our Lord Christ and firmly rely upon His work and merit so that through Him we may find grace and eternal salvation in that life."[76]

Luther continues to identify "the world" as Christ's opposition in this sermon;[77] and refers to "the kingdom of the devil" just once when he describes the Law as saying, "Whoever is a sinner belongs to *the kingdom of the devil* and of death [emphasis mine]."[78] In other sermons, however, the devil figures much more prominently as the principal opponent of Jesus. Luther's second sermon for Christmas is an excellent example of this, for the Reformer explains the angel's message to the shepherds, "For unto you is born this day a Savior," as a proclamation of rescue from the devil's control. In one place, Luther describes this control as "a horrible devil's kingdom [*Reich*]" and in another, he characterizes the work of the Savior as "powerfully attacking the government [*Regiment*] of the devil and taking His own to Himself."[79] Elsewhere, he refers to people as the "devil's prisoners" who lie under his "tyranny"[80] and maintains that everyone must confess that "the devil has violated and throttled me and all men, thrown me under God's wrath and into eternal judgment."[81]

Of course, sin is the most obvious manifestation of the devil's power over mankind.[82] But Luther is clear that his control includes all the consequences of sin as well—temporal and eternal:

> You have been up to now prisoners of the devil who has plagued you with water, fire, and pestilence. Indeed, who can recount all the misfortunes? Here all you poor people lie under his tyranny. He misleads the soul with lies that are infinitely more harmful to the soul than any pestilence can ever be to the body. Although

---

76. WA 52:27.17–20; 27.26–30, 37–40.

77. WA 52:28.31; 28.40; 29.8–9; 29.22–23; and 29.31.

78. WA 52:26.17–18. In Luther's thinking, the two are always related, for example, "That is the kingdom of the world that the devil impels and rules" (WA 52:56.3–4). See also WA 52:292.14–15 and 296.10–12.

79. WA 52:42.20–21; WA 52:47.32–33. See also WA 52:44.4–5 ("in the kingdom of the devil and under the power of death"); 52:44.16–17 ("possessed by the devil").

80. WA 52:45.37–39. See also WA 52:48.4 ("the devil's servants").

81. WA 52:42.36–37.

82. "The devil has through sin thrown us men down very low and produced extraordinary misery." WA 52:42.10–11.

now he is thus tormenting soul and body, nevertheless eternal death still lies hidden behind.[83]

Here, once again, as in the case of a hostile "world," Luther maintains that the only answer to the devil's power is the Lord Christ.[84]

Christ versus the devil, Christ's kingdom against his, remains prominent in the *House Postils*,[85] but what about the other two kingdoms motif—temporal power and spiritual? This too occurs regularly in these sermons both in texts that suggest the distinction and those that do not. As examples of the former, we can cite Matthew 22:15–22 ("Render unto Caesar.")[86] or Luke 16:36–42 ("Judge not and you will not be judged.").[87] But Luther also discusses this distinction in connection with texts that do not immediately lend themselves to it, such as Luke 2:21 (the circumcision of Jesus)[88] or Luke 2:41–52 (the boy Jesus in the temple).[89] It also occurs incidentally as an example or application throughout these sermons.[90]

Furthermore, the doctrine that Luther preached in the *House Postils* about the distinction between the temporal and spiritual authorities is the same as he was teaching in publications like *Temporal Authority* and the *Commentary on Psalm 82*. Of course, as we noted above, in the latter, Luther was allowing for a much greater role in the affairs of the church by civil government than he did in the former. So in the *House Postils*, sometimes he sounds like the early Luther and sometimes the late. But since these are homilies—not doctrinal essays—one can understand that there were times when he wanted to emphasize some themes in his teaching and not others. For example, in the last few pages of his sermon on Matthew 22:15–22, Luther sets out to describe the "difference" between "the kingdom of the world" and "the kingdom of our Lord Christ" and concludes that "these two kingdoms should remain distinct and not be mixed up together."[91] This sounds like the early Luther. The two king-

---

83. WA 52:45.37–46.2.

84. Luther also contends that what the devil does, he does under the authority of God who uses him, for example, to punish sinners. See WA 52:388.22–26; 439.3–4; and 498.5–6.

85. Here are just a few examples: WA 52:19.26–29; 20.35–36; 57.1–6, 11–15; 147.19–20; 183.5–12; 190.28–37; 230.31–34; 238.4–10; 289.16–17; 292.24–27; 329.21–25; 394.22–25; and 477.10–16.

86. WA 52:529.9–533.24.

87. WA 52:383.24–394.16.

88. WA 52:82.30–86.16.

89. WA 52:104.10–110.18.

90. For example, WA 52:26.6–16; 66.38–67.5; 84.31–38; 107.1–9; 133.37–134.2; 158.10–21; 189.18–25; 268.1–12; 278.38–279.2; 358.28–34; 396.22–26; 411.14–21; 454.1–9; 471.2–6; 492.9–17; and 521.32–522.11.

91. In these two passages, WA 52:533.1–2 and 536.25–26, Luther uses *"Reich"* for both entities. But in these postils, Luther does not observe the same care for terminology as he did in *Temporal Authority*. Thus, in the same postil under discussion here, Luther employs both *"Regiment"* and especially *"Oberkeit [Obrigkeit]"* for temporal authority. In a single paragraph explaining how it is that the "two kingdoms" are to remain distinct, he uses *"Regiment"* twice (WA 52:536.30, 36) and *"Oberkeit"* seven times (WA 52:536.29, 31, 33, 35, 37; 537.2, 3).

doms are essentially different, and he is not interested—at this point—in discussing how temporal rulers can assist the church. No. They are fundamentally distinct in their purposes—one is concerned with earthly matters and the other with a person's relationship to God:

> Give to God also what is God's, that is, believe in Jesus Christ, listen to the holy Gospel and accept it. Continue to fear God and to obey His commandments. Be merciful, friendly, and patient. Let this be your sacrifice to God, and He will be satisfied. But so far as the body is concerned—your property, class, and calling—there let Caesar participate. In this way, God and Caesar can remain in harmony with one another.[92]

Civil government is a part of God's arrangement for this life, and Luther lists it along with other God-given institutions: "Our Lord God does not condemn the worldly kingdom but confirms it along with house, estate, food, the married estate and all estates that Caesar must have." He then names various callings—some civil (citizen, nobleman, prince), others economic (farmer, servant, maid), and still others family (wife and husband) before enjoining all to stay in their class and not rob Caesar of his kingdom.[93]

What is implicit in this sermon, Luther states explicitly elsewhere: *God* has established all such arrangements, including government. In contrast to the Savior from sin, who came only after centuries of prophecy and waiting, "God had already established saviors in temporal matters, such as worldly authority in civil government, father and mother in the home, physicians for times of sickness, and jurists to handle legal matters." But these are a different kind of savior than the child Jesus. Rulers, parents, and all the rest "are themselves sinners and cannot protect even themselves from death." Jesus is the only kind of Savior who can do that.[94]

Because God has established temporal authorities of every sort, Christians can exercise vocations like parent, government official,[95] or employer and know that it pleases God. Luther makes this point over against Anabaptists who rejected Christian participation in such insti-

---

92. WA 52:533.17–22. This distinction also leads to radically different modes of behavior. In the kingdom of Christ, "there should be no anger but pure friendliness and love"; but in temporal and domestic administration, there "hand and mouth according to one's status and office should inflict injury and harm on those who misbehave and do not do what they are told" (WA 52:412.3–7).

93. WA 52:533.2–4.

94. WA 52:158.9–17. For other passages in which Luther attributes temporal authorities to God's ordinance, see WA 52:26.21–22; 54.8–10; 66.39–67.2; 83.11–18; 137.7–10; 358.28–32; 396.22–26; and 471.2–4.

95. Even the public executioner; see WA 52:407.1–4; 411.25–29; and 483.22–32.

tutions, "They despise worldly government as an unchristian estate."[96] In this same passage, Luther compares Anabaptists to monks who also invented their own works of righteousness and disdained participation in the temporal arrangements that God had established. Such criticism of monasticism comes up in other places as well.[97] On at least one occasion, Luther also says that Christians can use the justice system, "It is good if someone can maintain his legal rights and life in an orderly and moderate way," but he does so in a context of rebuking the faithful for refusing to suffer injustice at the hands of others when they have deserved much worse at the hands of God who forgives them. As God has forgiven them, they also should forgive others.[98]

When Luther discusses the two kingdoms in his postil on Matthew 22, after distinguishing the state from the church, his main purpose is to insist that each kingdom should keep to its own sphere—temporal and spiritual, respectively. Luther's understanding of "temporal" is comprehensive. It includes "life and property, . . . body and property, house and estate." To take care of such things, God has established a variety of offices—"king and emperor to protect their subjects against their enemies; father and mother to support and educate their children, . . . physicians to advise us and assist us in our bodily sicknesses, etc."[99] Though he warns against rulers devolving into tyrants in this sermon,[100] his main concern is when civil authorities (ironically, even bishops[101]) intrude on spiritual matters:

> It is a serious, great sin when the temporal authority insists on such obedience from its subjects that they cannot offer to God the obedience that belongs to Him. For example, when they forbid true doctrine or punish their subjects for receiving the Sacrament as Christ has established it or force the people to participate in idolatrous practices like masses for the dead and indulgences.[102]

Luther explains that God demands first and foremost from his people that they remain faithful to his word.[103] Although Luther is emphatic

96. WA 52:424.39.
97. WA 52:424.34. See also WA 52:115.4–13; 172.2–11; and 533.11–15.
98. WA 52:531.25–532.3.
99. WA 52:83.13–16.
100. "Also in temporal matters, so long as it concerns money and property, a limit must be maintained, for there must remain a difference between temporal authority and a tyrannical regime . . . for the government was not established to make men beggars" (WA 52:536.27–37).
101. "The bishops . . . are nothing more than temporal princes" (WA 52:535.14–15).
102. WA 52:534.36–41. In another passage, WA 52:535.21–33, Luther adds to his indictment the appointment of false preachers, forbidding the reading of good books, the invocation of saints, pilgrimages, the sacrifice of the mass, and various other works to obtain forgiveness of sins.
103. WA 52:533.31–33; 534.2–3. Faithfulness to God's word arises frequently in the *House Postils*. See, for example, WA 52:171.25–34 and 192.24–26.

about the obligation of subjects to obey their government,[104] that obedience must stop when the state oversteps it bounds: "If temporal authority should oppose its subjects' following God's Word, the subjects should not obey but rather suffer on this account whatever they can suffer." So Christians do not take up arms but endure even to the point of losing their freedom—or their lives.[105] If there is a conflict between obedience to God and to the state, Christians should also remember that God can punish with "hell fire and eternal death." Much better—"a thousand times" better—therefore, to anger the emperor who can subject his people to temporal punishment only.[106] Moreover, Luther threatens the rulers themselves who go beyond the temporal to interfere with God's kingdom that he can and will punish in this world as well as the next:

> God wants His kingdom undisturbed and His service unhindered. But whoever dares otherwise will run forward with his head and bring all to destruction, as one can see has always happened everywhere with even the greatest emperors, kings, and lords. As soon as they wanted to have everything and leave to God nothing, God has maintained his own and they, tyrants, have lost all and perished.[107]

If one reads Luther's postil on Matthew 22 casually, it may sound as if the Reformer is advocating separation of church and state, "For these two kingdoms must remain distinct and not be mixed up together so that to God should remain what is God's and to Caesar what is Caesar's."[108] He also explains that "God wants to make body and property, house and estate subject to Caesar, but that the heart should remain only for Him, and that He should rule in the heart through His Word and Spirit."[109] Significantly, however, Luther's examples of the temporal authorities' interfering in the spiritual kingdom *all* have to do with the imposition of false doctrine and practices. So for example, if government authorities forbid true doctrine, punish the people for insisting on receiving the sacrament as Christ instituted it, or pressure them into participating in masses for the dead or in indulgences, "In these and other things, they go beyond their office and want to prevent the obedience that is owed to God."[110] Likewise, if a ruler, not content with having power over body

---

104. WA 52:533.11–12; 535.39–536.4. Luther specifies taxes and rent as normal parts of obedience and, where necessary to maintain public peace, adds body and property (536.37–537.3).
105. WA 52:533.35–36; 534.8–9.
106. WA 52:533.36–41; 534.1–4, 15–21.
107. WA 52:536.11–16. Luther later adds (537.5–7) that God punishes tyrants "through rebellion, through foreign enemies, and in other ways."
108. WA 52:536.25–27.
109. WA 52:536.4–7.
110. WA 52:533.39–534.2.

and property, wants to have authority "over the heart" as well and insists that "people should believe and do in divine things what he wants and not what God has taught and commanded in His word," evil consequences must follow.[111] So rulers violate the two kingdoms principle when they demand a false faith and piety from their people.

But what if they promote true doctrine and practice—that which is in accord with God's word? Luther does *not* understand that situation as a breach of the two kingdoms doctrine. Quite the contrary. This is exactly what Christian temporal authorities are supposed to do. In a sermon for Maundy Thursday, Luther applies the virtue of "washing feet" to rulers in their service to the people for whom they are responsible:

> If kings and princes want to be Christians, they must wash the feet of their subjects. . . . First of all, they should supply their subjects with faithful Church servants and should see to it that the Word of God is presented truly and faithfully to them, that they are defended from idolatry, and that the true worship of God is established.

This is not an option for temporal authorities, "They are responsible to God for these things."[112]

It is important to remember also that the power of the state is the power of the sword, so elsewhere, Luther points out that temporal authorities may use force in carrying out such duties. There are two kinds of mercy, Luther contends, responding to two kinds of need, "spiritual and bodily [*geistlich und leiblich*]." Spiritual need occurs when the soul is suffering as, for example, "a young man who is growing up and cares not at all for preaching, is unable to pray, behaves indecently, and is full of vice." Such a person needs correction "with words, blows, and rods." That, Luther contends, is a spiritual mercy that rescues someone from "the devil and his kingdom." It concerns "eternal life." It is a matter not of the body but of the soul. And it belongs principally to parents in the home and to "government with their subjects."[113]

Luther extends the concern of the state to heresy and heretics. As in his *Commentary on Psalm 82*, here in the *House Postils*, Luther understands heresy as leading to temporal calamities. He calls "false doctrine and wrong worship of God" the "most dangerous and most horrible offense." A Christian government must deal with it since it brings all kinds of misfortune and "ruin to the state." Nor can rulers be indifferent to errors that dishonor Christ or hinder the salvation of souls, "for the sake of their office, nothing is more fitting than that temporal authority use the

---

111. WA 52:536.7–11.
112. WA 52:222.27–34.
113. WA 52:482.15–16, 19–21, 24–25, 29–30, 34–35; 483.2–4.

sword and all its power to maintain pure doctrine and true and unfalsified worship of God."[114]

Luther also believes that God will punish temporal powers for any failure to maintain true religion, "For how could God give good fortune and well-being to those who do not care about His Word but impose public idolatry and false worship upon their subjects?"[115]

In another place, Luther singles out especially the training of children in the word of God. This is a responsibility that belongs both to parents and to government, "It is not enough that father and mother, princes and lords, only maintain the peace for their children and subjects and fill their bellies. They should also nourish their souls and lead their children and households to the truth and knowledge of God's Word in order that they become God-fearing, pious, and saved." Luther explains that "the highest and best work and the foremost worship that we can do on earth is to bring other people—especially those entrusted to us—to the knowledge of God and to the holy Gospel."[116] But this is not just a job for the church and her clergy. Temporal authorities, including the state, are involved as well.

Therefore, distinguishing the two kingdoms means anything but separating them—far from it. In Luther's theology, church and state are supposed to work together in the cause of true doctrine and right worship, the first by right use of the word, the second by law and force. In a passage that concludes Luther's homily on the Parable of the Wheat and the Tares (Matt 13:24–30), the Reformer maintains:

> Each [of the two kingdoms] should give a hand to the other. The spiritual government with the Word and excommunication, but the temporal government with the sword and power should each help the people to be pious and protected from every offense. If it goes this way, it will be fine and God will give success to both governments. But whatever wicked fellows still survive, who care nothing for the Word and remain unpunished by temporal authority, they shall receive their judgment on the last day.[117]

Luther clearly keeps the two kingdoms distinct even though they have a basic goal in common—to get people into heaven. The spiritual kingdom uses spiritual means (the word), but the temporal kingdom uses physical means (pain and punishment). Cooperation, not competition, is Luther's ideal situation.

---

114. WA 52:135.2–5, 21–26. See also WA 52:57.16–20 for Luther's joining the sects to social disruptions.

115. WA 52:222.35–37.

116. WA 52:415.13–17, 18–20.

117. WA 52:135.26–32.

The *House Postils* provide a wealth of material for analyzing Luther's theology,[118] preached in the 1530s and shaped for publication by his erstwhile student, Veit Dietrich, about a decade later. The two kingdoms are a motif throughout this collection of sermons. When Luther preaches about the two kingdoms in terms of the combat between God and the devil, he is presenting a fundamental element in his worldview, something that enables him to make sense of reality as he experienced it (why it was so bad) and as he read about it in the Scriptures (why Christians could still have hope in Jesus Christ). When he uses that same terminology of two kingdoms to distinguish between temporal authority and spiritual, he is presenting another key point in his thinking, this time showing how God rules the world through men (and so too frequently corrupted by sin) and on behalf of men (and so mediating God's blessings both for this life and for the next).

Luther's two kingdoms terminology includes a wide range of topics in his thinking, some that challenge our own materialistic presuppositions regarding the universe and others that test our commitments to separating church and state. For Lutherans today, that is probably more than enough. ✛

---

118. See, for example, my essays, "Martin Luther Preaches Salvation to His Friends: Justification by Faith in the Mature Reformer," in Michael Parsons, ed., *Since We Are Justified by Faith: Justification in the Theologies of the Reformation* (Milton Keynes, Bucks, UK: Paternoster Press, 2012), 16–29; and "No Alternatives to Jesus: Luther's Understanding of Idolatry as Evident in His *House Postils*" in Michael Parsons, ed., *Aspects of Reforming: Theology and Practice in Sixteenth Century Europe* (Milton Keynes, Bucks, UK: Paternoster Press, 2013), 16–32.

PULPIT GREETING AND BLESSING

✛

And he rolled up the scroll and gave it back to the attendant and sat down. And the eyes of all in the synagogue were fixed on him. And he began to say to them, "Today, this Scripture has been fulfilled in your hearing." (Luke 4:20–21)

Wat is the proper way to begin and end a sermon? One can observe a variety of appropriate ways in which pastors introduce and conclude their sermons. Some practices reflect the theological nature and purpose of the preaching task and office (*Predigtamt*, AC V). Politicians, talk show hosts, comedians, academicians, and other public speakers understand the importance of following the correct protocol. Similarly, Lutheran pastors should understand the liturgical context in which they are speaking and how it shapes the preaching task.

Some preachers simply rise from their seat, go directly to the pulpit and start talking—Luke 4:20–21 in reverse. Others take a moment to bow toward the altar or kneel for silent prayer. Some re-read a key portion of the sermon text or the text in its entirety. Some begin with an apostolic greeting such as Ephesians 1:2 and end with the Votum from Philippians 4:7. Some add an extemporaneous pulpit prayer or a brief commentary on the nature of the Bible as God's inspired Word. Some follow the practice which they learned at their home congregations. Others point to what they were taught in homiletics class or observed in the seminary chapel or on vicarage. Some begin with a cheerful "good morning," or humorous attempts to warm up and connect with the congregation. Finally there are those who enter the Holy Ministry and their first pulpit having given the matter little or no thought.

We have all seen pastors who lead the liturgy as if they are doing little more than reading words printed in liturgical books. It is precisely because words are the most important element of the rite that pastors must distinguish how they are being used in each part of the liturgy. The liturgy is a heavenly conversation with God and his holy ones. In the liturgy, words are proclaimed (holy absolution, Scripture readings, and sermon); they are prayed and chanted (petition, praise, and thanksgiving); they are spoken or sung in succinct expressions of acclamation (Alleluia, Thanks be to God) and assent (Amen); they are announced in Trinitarian Invocation and exchanged with others in reconciliation (Peace be with you). Words are also used to give greetings (The Lord be with you; Grace to you and peace from God our Father . . .) and blessings (Post-Sermon Votum, Pax Domini, Communion Dismissal, Apostolic and Aaronic Benedictions).

The Liturgy is not a concatenation of randomly selected liturgical elements that may be shuffled about like a deck of cards. This is obvious when considering the major parts of the liturgy. One would not move the Old Testament Reading after the Holy Gospel,[1] the Sanctus forward into the Service of the Word,[2] or permit the Agnus Dei to hop about the liturgy like a little lost lamb who can be found anywhere except at home after the consecration.[3] However, while these major liturgical acts have a stable consistency, the Liturgy also contains various movable elements that by nature are able to fit the theological and ritual flow at numerous points. This is particularly true of short acclamations and responses such as "alleluia," "amen," "Thanks be to God," and "Lord have mercy."

Another element found at various locations throughout the Divine Service and Daily Office is the ancient Salutation and Response in which the pastor greets the congregation, "The Lord be with you," and the people reply, "And with your spirit." On the positive side, such traditional liturgical responses unite the congregation in her corporate worship with others—past, present, and future. They also carry biblical and theological freight which is consistent with Christian worship. On

---

1. Naturally, this can occur where it is the custom to read the entire sermon text from the pulpit and the pastor is preaching on the assigned Old Testament Reading.

2. In addition to the unionistic distribution formula (nehmet hin und essen, *spricht* unser Herr und Heiland Jesus Christus, das ist Mein Lieb . . .), criticism of the liturgical revisions in the Berlin Agendas of 1822 and 1829 (Kirchen-Agendas of the infamous Prussian Union) included "especially the insertion of the Preface also in the divine service without communion (*inbesondere die Einflügung der Präfation auch in einen Gottesdienst ohne Abendmahl).* Alfred Niebergall, "Agenda," in *Theologische Realenzyklopädie*, Vol. 2, ed. Gerhard Krause and Gerhard Müller (Berlin: Waalter de Gruyter, 1978), 57. The Preface included the Sanctus and was found as an option in the 1822, 1829 and 1895 Prussian Agendas. See *Kirchen-Agenda für die Hof- und Domkirche in Berlin* (1822) and *Agenda für die Evangelische Landeskirche* (1895) in Herbst, Wolfgang, ed. *Evangelischer Gottesdienst: Quellen zu seiner Geschichte* (Göttingen: Vandenhoeck & Ruprecht, 1992), 172–192.

3. The Agnus Dei is seldom found in Reformed Communion services. Its historic position following the consecration encourages its use as a hymn of adoration to the body and blood of Jesus, the Lamb of God, who now comes to us in the bread and wine and is present on the altar. Lithuanian Lutheran scholar Darius Petkunas has documented that the Agnus Dei was found in the Polish Reformed communion liturgies; however, its position in the liturgy was constantly changing. For example, the 1637 Agenda placed the hymn earlier in the service after the Confession of Sins. See Darius Petkunas, *Holy Communion Rites in the Polish and Lithuanian Reformed Agendas of the 16th and Early 17th Centuries* (University of Helsinki, 2004 and Klaipėdos Universtetas, 2007), 338–341.

the negative side, they can become hollow recitation if the pastor and people are not taught the meaning behind the words and actions. Sadly, it is often the clergy who foster dead ritualism because they are unaware of the liturgy's rich theological history and meaning or simply disinterested in liturgical matters.

What does it say when a pastor keeps his head down and eyes in the hymnbook while greeting his people, "The Lord be with you," and then turns to the altar with his back to the people while they are responding, "and also with you." At its worst, it is insulting. At its best, it displays ritual cluelessness. For nearly 2000 years pastors have exchanged this greeting with the faithful. The greeting expresses the understanding that the risen Lord Jesus is truly present in the Divine Service. He is giving out his gifts through the Word and Sacrament. The people respond, "and with your spirit" which expresses the understanding that worship is the gift of the Holy Spirit; indeed, the Holy Spirit is with the spirit of their pastors as they impart the gifts of God "in words not taught by human wisdom but taught by the Spirit, interpreting spiritual truths to those who possess the Spirit" (1 Cor. 2:13). Without the Holy Spirit, neither pastor nor people are able to pray. "Likewise the Spirit helps us in our weakness; for we do not know how to pray as we ought, but the spirit himself intercedes for us with sighs too deep for words" (Rom. 8:26).

At the beginning of the Service of the Word, the congregation prayerfully responds to the pastor's greeting with the words "And with your spirit." With this response the people acknowledge the necessity of the Spirit who promises to work through Word and Sacrament. The pastor must have the Spirit (with his spirit) because he is distributing the gifts of the Spirit in Word and the Sacrament. This is acknowledged in the Rite of Ordination which includes the account of our Lord's establishment of the holy ministry under the title, "The Institution of the Office of the Holy Ministry," "And with that he breathed on them and said, 'Receive the Holy Spirit'" (John 20:22).[4] The Service of Holy Communion also begins with the same Greeting and Response which again confesses the true presence of the body and blood of our Lord given out for the forgiveness of sins, life and eternal salvation. In *The Lutheran Hymnal*, the Greeting and Response was exchanged yet a third time to introduce the conclusion of the liturgy. The conclusion was short, consisting of merely the Salutation, Benedicamus and Aaronic Benediction. The concluding benediction with the thrice repetition of the Holy Name is a blessing bestowed by the LORD himself yet again as the people take leave into the week and to their vocations.

---

4. *Lutheran Service Book Agenda*, The Commission on Worship of the Lutheran Church—Missouri Synod, (St. Louis, MO: Concordia Publishing House, 2006), 162.

The historic Salutation ("The Lord be with you") and pulpit Greeting (Ephesians 1:2) are both greetings and blessings. The repeated historic dominical salutation, post sermon votum, concluding Aaronic and apostolic blessings shape the entire service with the biblical understanding that when blessings are spoken, they actually do something, that is, the words bestow what they say, blessings actually bless. The insertion of "may" into the texts (*May* the peace of God which passes all understanding, keep . . .) introduces a wishful intention which diminishes the clear and comforting distribution of the peace. The repeated use of blessings permeates the entire liturgy and influence the way the texts are linguistically phrased. Liturgy and sermon texts are more than mere historical reports and abstract theological allocution. They make present and distribute the Blessed Trinity and his saving gifts. God is not a "theory of everything." He is a person—that is to say, three persons yet one God. The repeated use of blessings that bless also shapes the way the pastor speaks when giving pastoral care throughout the week.

In the early church the ancient salutation and response was thick with incarnational and sacramental freight and was used repeatedly throughout the Divine Liturgy, including prior to the sermon. St. John Chrysostom (349–407), patriarch, renowned preacher and contributor to the development and beautification of the Divine Liturgy used at the Hagia Sophia in Constantinople, expounded the meaning of the response, "and with your *spirit*", in a sermon he preached in the presence of Bishop Flavian of Antioch. He explained "that if there were no Holy Spirit there would be no pastors or teachers, who became so only though the Spirit," He then explained the importance of the preacher giving the peace before entering the pulpit.[5]

> If the Holy Spirit were not in this common father or teacher [Bishop Flavian] when he *gave the peace* to all shortly before ascending to his holy sanctuary, you would not have replied to him all together, *"And to your spirit."* This is why you reply with this expression not only when he ascends to the sanctuary, nor *when he preaches to you*, nor when he prays for you, but when he stands at his holy altar . . . "[6]

The Lutheran Church retained the ancient greeting and response in the Divine Service, Matins and Vespers; however, it was translated into the vernacular so the people could exchange the greeting with understand-

---

5. The Eastern liturgies normally used the greeting, "Peace be with you," and response "And with your spirit." The west used both "Peace be with you," and "The Lord be with you." Both "Peace" and "Lord" refer to the same risen Lord Jesus who is with the apostles, that is, with his church on Easter evening giving them his Peace. The response in both the East and West is consistently, "And with your spirit."

6. Geoffrey J. Cuming, Hippolytus: A Text for Students with Introductions, Translations, Commentary and Notes (Bramcote Notts, England: Grove Books, 1976).

ing. Thus Wilhelm Loehe could say, "Every time [the greeting and response is exchanged] the knot of love and unity between pastor and congregation is tied anew."[7]

PULPIT GREETING AND BLESSING

In addition to beginning the Service of the Word with the ancient Christological Salutation, many Lutheran pastors greet the congregation a second time with an apostolic salutation from Ephesians 1:2 when they enter the pulpit to preach the Word. Similarly, in addition to the final Benediction at the close of the service, many pastors also bless the people from the pulpit after the sermon with a Pauline blessing from Philippians 4:7. Like the ancient Salutation and Response, the pulpit salutation and blessing can also become perfunctory and mindless ritual. If this is true for the pastor it will likely be true for the congregation.

The pew edition of the *Lutheran Service Book (LSB)* contains no rubrics concerning a pre-sermon greeting or post-sermon blessing in Divine Services 1, 2, 4, and 5. Divine Service 3, which is an updated revision of the Service of Holy Communion in *The Lutheran Hymnal,* contains no pre-sermon Apostolic Greeting, but does include the *TLH* rubric, *"After the Sermon, the pastor may say:* The peace of God, which passes all understanding, keep your hearts and minds in Christ Jesus. *Philippians 4:7"*[8] No rubrics are given in the *LSB* Daily Offices, the Service of Prayer and Preaching or Occasional Services. However, the *LSB Altar Book* includes the following rubrics in all five Divine Services.

Before the Sermon, the pastor may say:

P Grace to you and peace from God our Father and the Lord Jesus Christ. Ephesians 1:2

C Amen

After the Sermon, the pastor may say:

P The peace of God, which passes all understanding, keep your hearts and minds in Christ Jesus. Philippians 4:7

C Amen

The above greeting and blessing are remnants of a Pulpit Office, that is, a "pulpit service within a service" found in many Lutheran Agendas whose shape goes back to the office of Prone in the Middle Ages.

---

7. "Sich jedesmal der Knoten der Liebe und Eintracht zwischen Pfarrer und Gemeinde aufs Neue schurzt." W. C. van Unnik, "Dominus Vobiscum: The Background of a Liturgical Formula," *Sparsa Collecta. The Collected Essays of W. C. van Unnik,* part 3, Supplements to *Novum Testamentum* 31 (Leiden: E. J. Brill, 1983), 362.

8. *Lutheran Service Book,* The Commission on Worship of the Lutheran Church—Missouri Synod (St. Louis, MO: Concordia Publishing House, 2006), 192.

The Prone was a vernacular medieval preaching service inserted into the Latin Mass consisting of the Gospel, announcements, homily, bidding prayers and *other devotions.*[9] In the *Formula Missae* (1523), Martin Luther shows that he is still living with Prone when he writes, "Likewise, we do not think that it matters whether the sermon in the vernacular comes after the Gospel or before the Introit of the Mass . . . ."[10] Here Luther was simply reflecting current church practice. However, three years later in the *Deutsche Messe* (1526), Luther eliminated the pre-service location as an option: "After the Gospel the whole congregation sings the Creed in German: 'In One True God We All believe.' Then follows the sermon on the Gospel for the Sunday or festival day."[11] The *Deutsche Messe* still retained the Medieval "mini-pulpit service." Following the sermon, and still from the pulpit, Luther added a public paraphrase of the Lord's Prayer and admonition on the sacrament (*"other devotions"*), general prayers and Lord's Prayer.

> After the sermon shall follow a public paraphrase of the Lord's Prayer and admonition for those who want to partake of the sacrament . . . Whether such paraphrase and admonition should be read in the pulpit immediately after the sermon or at the altar, I would leave to everyone's judgment. It seems that the ancients did so in the pulpit, so that it is still the custom to read general prayers or to repeat the Lord's Prayer in the pulpit.[12]

The "mini-pulpit service" within a Divine Service survived in many Lutheran agendas. It included the sermon, announcements, Prayer of the Church, and a blessing (*Votum*) after which a hymn or hymn verse was sung while the pastor went to the altar to prepare the altar and begin the Service of Holy Communion with the traditional Preface.

In the nineteenth century, a Confessional Movement arose in European Lutheranism which sought to address the disintegration of Lutheran liturgical worship which occurred in the seventeenth and eighteenth centuries under the influences of rationalism and pietism. The task included the restoration of the Prayer of the Church. Both the location

---

9. "History of Preaching," in *Concise Encyclopedia of Preaching,* ed. William H. Willimon & Richard Lischer (Louisville, KY: Westminster John Knox Press, 1995) 196.

10. Martin Luther, *An Order of Mass and Communion for the Church in Wittenberg* (1523): vol. 53, pp. 25, in *Luther's Works, American Edition,* vols. 1–30, ed. Jaroslav Pelikan (St. Louis, MO: Concordia Publishing House, 1955–76); vols. 31–55, ed. Helmut Lehmann (Philadelphia/Minneapolis: Muhlenberg/Fortress, 1957–86); vols. 56–82, ed. Christopher Boyd Brown and Benjamin T. G. Mayes (St. Louis, MO: Concordia Publishing House, 2009–), hereafter AE.

11. Luther, AE 53:78. See also, Luther, AE 53:68, in Wittenberg, the sermon was preached on the Epistle at Sunday morning Matins (5:00 AM) "chiefly for the sake of the servants . . . since they cannot be present at other sermons." The Gospel reading was preached at the 8:00 or 9:00 AM Mass and the Old Testament (chapter by chapter) on Sunday afternoon Vespers.

12. Luther, AE 53:78, 80.

from the pulpit and the manner in which it was prayed fostered confusion about the nature of the liturgical act, contributed to inferior forms, and ultimately led to the loss of meaningful participation by the congregation. Theodosius Harnack, one of the leading liturgical scholars of the nneteenth century, addressed the issue in volume one of his influential *Praktische Theologie* where he refers to the Prayer of the Church (*Kirchengebet*) as the "true congregational act of prayer (*der eigentliche Gemeindegebtact*)," in which the effects of the Word are manifest. The prayer follows the sermon and is a sacrificial response to the sacramental gift given in the Word. In view of the flow of the liturgy, Harnack describes how the Prayer of the Church looks both backward and forward.

> On the basis of the newly experienced and acquired grace, the congregation now has the power and authority and desire to pour out her heart before God, and to offer him her spiritual sacrifice of praise and thanks, of requests and supplications for herself and her members, as well as for all of Christendom and all mankind. At the same time, such a priestly sacrifice of worship (*Opferdienst*) is the proper preparation for the reception of the following Sacrament, the proper evangelical Offertorium.[13]

Unfortunately, as Harnack points out, the old Lutheran praxis of using the Litany at the altar had deteriorated in present practice to where the prayer is nothing more than an act of the preacher who reads it out loud from the pulpit. Harnack argues for the restoration of congregational prayer on the basis of church history. He explains, "The ancient Church distinguished, as we know, between *Epiklese* and *Prosphnese*, and so also did the old Protestant praxis distinguish between collects and admonitions to prayer.[14] Harnack further clarifies that *Epiklese* and Collects are direct prayers addressed to God, and ought to be prayed from the altar, while *Prosphonese* and Admonitions to Prayer are addressed to the congregation, that, with or without corresponding prayers, become pronouncements for prayer. The current "inappropriate and inadmissible position" (*unpassende und unstatthafte Stellung*) of praying the general prayer in the pulpit evolved from the practice of offering the admonition for prayers, which are not directed to God, from the pulpit. Harnack is adamant:

13. Theodosius Harnack, *Praktische Theologie I* (Erlangen: Verlag Von Andreas Deichefrt, 1978), 625. "Auf Gruind der neu erfahrenen und angeeigneten Gnade hat nun die Gemeinde Machte und Recht und lust, ihr Herz vor Gott auszuschütten, und ihm ihre geistlichen Opfer des Lobes und Dankes, der Bitte und Fürbitte wie für Glieder, so für die ganze Christenheit und alle Menschen, darzubringen. Zugleich ist solch priesterlicher Opferdienst die rechte Vorbereitung zum Empfang des darauf folgenden Sacraments, das rechte evangelische Offertorium."

14. Harnack, *Praktische Theologie I*, 626. "Die alte Kirche unterschied, wie wir wissen zwischen Epiklese und Prosphonese, und so unterscheidet auch die alt-protestantische Praxis zwischen Collecten und Vermahnungen zum Gebet."

If one wants to allow the customary bad habit to continue, then no other choice remains for us, than either to change the prayer again into an admonition to prayer and relinquish it then to the pulpit, or, what is more advisable, to retain the form of direct prayer which is then moved to the altar. So, as it now abides, it can and may not remain.[15]

Under the leadership of Harnack, the liturgical commission was successful in moving the Prayer of the Church from the pulpit to the altar as an independent congregational activity. The rubrics, however, did allow for the pastor to pray the prayers from the pulpit "Where the acoustic in the Church are inadequate, or other existing local conditions demand it on convincing grounds . . ." The 1883 Livonian Agenda served as the basis for the 1897 Imperial Agenda which was the first common agenda uniting the Lutheran Churches in the Russian Empire.[16] As was the case among the Lutheran churches in Europe, so also the Lutheran Church in the Russian Empire entered the nineteenth century in liturgical chaos,

"without a single church order, a single liturgy, and without a single religious and theological viewpoint or confession . . . . On paper the Lutheran Church was the Church of the Augsburg Confession and the Church of Luther's Small Catechism, but in fact little attention was given to either. Each territorial church had its own liturgy and in each church the prescribed liturgy (in whatever languages it appeared) was altered and adapted according to the whims of pastors and patrons. Not only did the liturgy differ from one consistorial district to another, but from parish to parish as well."[17]

Church agendas in the nineteenth century often included lengthy, detailed rubrics. The 1883 Livonian Agenda is a typical example and reflects the changes taking place in the liturgy during the confessional revival. It also paints a picture of what worship looked like, particularly what was going on in the pulpit during the "Pulpit Office."

---

15. Harnack, *Praktische Theologie I*, 626. "Will man nun nicht die hergebrachte Unsitte fortbestehen lassen, so bleibt uns keine andere Wahl, als entweder das Gebet wieder in eine Vermahnung zum Gebet zu verwandeln und es dann der kanzel zu lassen, oder, was sich mehr empfiehlt, die Form eines directen Gebets beizubehalten, aber dasselbe dann auch an den Altar zue verlegfen. So wie es jetzt gewöhnlich ist, kann und darf es jedenfalls nicht bleiben."
16. The full title of the Livonian Agenda is *Agenda für die evangelisch-lutherischen Gemeinden im russischen Reich: Revidirt im Auftrage der livländischen Provincial-Synode des Jahres 1883* (Dorpat: H Laakmann's Buch- und Steindrucherei, 1885). Hereafter referenced as follows: *Livonian Agenda*. The Imperial Agenda is *Agenda für die evangelisch-lutherischen Gemeinden im russischen Reich. I Theil,* (St. Petersburg: R. Golicke, Spasskaya Str. № 17, 1897).
17. Darius Petkūnas, *Russian and Baltic Lutheran Liturgy in the Nineteenth and Twentieth Centuries* (Klaipėda, Lithuania: Klaipėdos Universteto Leidykla, 2013), 648.

1883 LIVONIAN AGENDA

The congregation sings the Chief Hymn (*Hauptlied*).

During [the hymn] the pastor goes to the pulpit and after an **Apostolic Greeting** and **Reading the Text**, the **Sermon**.

Note: The **homiletical Prayer** (*homiletische Gebet*) ends in the words: Sanctify us in your truth, your Word is truth.

The congregation sings the so-called **Pulpit Verse** (*sog. Kanselvers.*) after the sermon.

After this follows, where it is the custom of the congregation, the citation by name, not merely the proclamation of the newly married couples, but also the births, baptisms, pregnant women (*sechswöcherinnen*, women expecting a child within six weeks), the sick, the deceased and also the communicants and bereaved of the deceased, who are commended to the congregation for intercession or a prayer of thanksgiving respectively, after which then either a short **Votum** is said (ct. page 99) and the petition that is included in the Prayer of the Church itself, or also immediately at the pulpit a **Free Prayer** (*freies Gebet*) can be added.

Where the acoustics in the church are inadequate, or other existing local conditions demand it on convincing grounds, the general Prayer of the Church can also be [held] from the pulpit at this point in the Divine Service, and then also freely as needed. (*Wo mangelhafte Akustik der Kirche oder andere, in den locale Verhältnissen liegende, triftige Gründe es verlangen, kann das allgemeine Kirchengebet auch auf der Kanzel an dieser Stelle des Gottesdienstes, und dann nach Bedürfniß auch frei gehalten warden*).

The **Concluding Votum** now follows, and after a silent prayer, the pastor leaves the pulpit.

The congregation sings a short hymn (*kurzes Lied*)

The liturgist goes to the altar during this [hymn] and prays (turned toward the altar) the **Prayer of the Church** (*Kirchengebet*) (see page 111), in which the participation of the congregation through singing the responses indicated [on page 111] is desirable. On the days which bear the character of repentance and mourning, as the Day of Repentance, Good Friday etc. and in times of particular trial, the liturgist prays the Litany (see page 105)—he speaking (or singing) the congregation always singing.[18]

In *Praktische Theologie I* (1877), Harnack argued for moving the Prayer of the Church from the pulpit to the altar. As precedent he pointed out

---

18. *Livonian Agenda*, 16–17. Bold and italicized words are as they appear in original Agenda.

that it was restored to its ancient, natural and independent place after the sermon at the altar in the Prussian Liturgy (1822) as well as by Bunsen, Höfling, and Löhe (1844).

1822 PRUSSIAN AGENDA

The 1822 Prussian (Berlin) Agenda[19] moved the Prayer of the Church to the altar but located it before the sermon. The order is as follows: Gospel, Creed, Preface, Sanctus (by choir), Prayer of the Church, Lord's Prayer, and Congregational Hymn during which the minister enters the pulpit.[20] "After a brief entrance prayer the sermon text follows immediately for both of which the congregation stands to hear as well as standing to receive the spoken blessing at the close of the sermon."[21] Following the sermon the minister (*Geistliche*) speaks the Aaronic Benediction and the choir responds by singing the triple amen. A congregational hymn follows with the rubric "When no communion takes place after the divine service, it ends here." The Berlin Agenda was revised in 1829 and again in 1895. In 1895 the Prayer of the Church was moved after the sermon and to the altar. The order now being Gospel, Creed, Sermon Hymn (*Predigtlied*), Pulpit Greeting (*Kanzelgruß*), Sermon, Hymn Verses (*Liedervers.*), Intercessions and Announcements (*Fürbitten und Abkündigungen*), and Pulpit Blessing (*Kanzelsegen*). The congregation then sings a stanza of a hymn during which the minister goes to the altar. When there is no communion the service concludes with the Dialog and Preface, Sanctus, Prayer of the Church and Benediction. Where communion is celebrated the Dialog, Preface and Sanctus are moved to the Service of Holy Communion following the Lord's Supper hymn and Admonition.[22]

LOEHE'S 1844 AGENDA

Johannes Konrad Wilhelm Loehe (1808–1872) was a leader of the confessional movement in southern Germany where he served as pastor in Neuendettelsau, Bavaria from 1837 until his death in 1872. Shortly after arriving in Neuendettelsau, Loehe began an extensive study of historic

---

19. The Agenda was commonly referred to as either the Berlin or Prussian Agenda and went through three editions or revisions in 1822, 1829 and 1895. The exact title was *Church Agenda for the Court and Cathedral Church in Berlin*.

20. *Kirchen-Agenda für die Hof- und Domkirche in Berlin* (1822), in Herbst, Wolfgang, ed. *Evangelischer Gottesdienst: Quellen zu seiner Geschichte*, (Göttingen: Vandenhoeck & Ruprecht, 1992),176–178. Hereafter referenced as follows: *Evangelischer Gottesdienst, 176–178*.

21. *Evangelischer Gottesdienst,* 178. "Nach einem kurzen eingangsgebet folgt sogleich der Text zur Predigt, welches beides die Gemeine stehend anhort, so wie stehend empfangen wird, der am Schluss der Predigt gesprochene Segen [Aaronic Benediction]."

22. *Evangelischer Gottesdienst,* 178. "Gemeinde: Liedervers, während dessen der Geistliche an den Altar tritt. Dass große Dankgebet mit den Wechselsprüchen am Eingang und dem schließenden Heilig der Gemeinde kann an dieser Stelle eintreten, wenn es nicht in der Kommunionfeirer seinen Platz findet."

liturgies, examining over two hundred old agendas in order to find the best *Hauptgottsdienst* for use by the Lutheran church living in an age of Rationalism and spiritual apathy. His goal was to produce an order of service that was faithful to the old Lutheran agendas. His work was influential in both Germany and among the Lutheran churches to the east in the Baltic countries and Russian Empire. He was further inspired to complete the task when he received a request from Pastor F. C. D. Wyneken for a liturgy to be used by the Lutheran missionary pastors in North America. In 1844 Loehe completed his *Agenda für christliche Gemeinden des lutherischen Bekenntnisses.*[23] The Ancient Salutation (The Lord be with you) and Response is exchanged four times in the service: (1) Before the Collect of the Day; (2) Before the Holy Gospel, (3) In the Preface, and (4) Before the closing Aaronic Benediction. Once in the pulpit the minister begins his sermon with the Apostolic Greeting and concludes it with the Gloria Patri. The full Pulpit Office then follows concluding with the Votum.

> While the Creed is being sung or said the minister ascends the pulpit. At the end of the Creed he greets the congregation with the Apostolic Salutation, and preaches the Sermon. If he concludes the Sermon with the Gloria Patri, the congregation shall say: Amen.
>
> After the Sermon the minister admonishes the congregation to prayer, and gives notice of special requests for intercessions, e.g. For the sick, dying, tempted, bridal couples, etc. Especially is it the duty of the minister to admonish to thanksgiving, when a believer has peacefully departed in Christ; and also, where it is custom, for the birth of a child. A few of the prayers, used on the above occasions are here given. [Loehe includes the full text of three prayers]
>
> Other announcements of spiritual nature may also be made at this time e.g., festivals, days of prayer, Christian meetings, excommunications or restorations. At the conclusion of the announcements the minister admonishes to benevolence and almsgiving, according to 1 Cor. 16; 2 Cor. 8:9; Gal. 6. He then pronounces the VOTUM, to which the congregation responds with an Amen, after which he leaves the pulpit.
>
> While descending from the pulpit the congregation begins to sing the Offertory.[24]

During the Offertory, the offerings are gathered and also, "the minister places the bread and wine upon the altar; or, if these have been there

---

23. The third edition of Loehe's Agenda was translated into English in 1902. J. K. Wilhelm Loehe, *Liturgy for Christian Congregations of the Lutheran Faith*, trans. F. C. Longaker, (Decatur, IL: Repristination Press, 1997).

24. Loehe, *Liturgy*, 20–21.

from the beginning of the service, he now reverently uncovers them, and prepares himself through prayer and meditation for the administration of the Sacrament."

LITURGICAL MANUALS AND THE CONDUCT OF THE LITURGY IN TWENTIETH-CENTURY NORTH AMERICA

The restoration of the liturgy in the language of the people in the sixteenth century eliminated the need for a vernacular Prone amid the Latin mass. Over time, the sermon was integrated into its natural place as part of the Service of the Word rather than in a semi-independent pulpit service. The Prayer of the Church was moved to its proper place at the altar, the Hymn of the Day preceded the sermon, and announcements were moved to the end of the service or printed in a bulletin. By the twentieth century, the following elements remained: prayer, pre-sermon greeting/blessing/invocation, reading of the text or a portion of the text, sermon, concluding blessing/Votum. Pastors in America now consulted English liturgical manuals and textbooks for instruction on the conduct and nature of the sermon. Paul Zeller Strodoch's *A Manual on Worship: Venite Adoremus* (1946) makes no mention of the Apostolic Greeting at the beginning of the sermon.[25] He does, however, strongly recommend that during the singing of "*the* Hymn of the Service" before the sermon, rather than a silent prayer at the altar, "the minister may enter the sacristy for devotions preparatory to the Sermon, or he may occupy the stall nearest the pulpit."[26] Strodoch judges prayers by the minister in the chancel as "pious gestures" which are too often "ostentatious" and "rushed." On the other hand it can be argued that disappearing into the sacristy will strike some as odd. An exception might be where the church architecture requires the preacher to pass through the sacristy on his way into the pulpit.

Luther Reed disagrees with Strodach. In *The Lutheran Liturgy* (1947) he writes: "The minister should be seated in the chancel during the singing of the hymn and join in the singing, or at least follow the text. Retire-

---

25. Paul Zeller Strodach, *A Manual on Worship: Venite Adoremus* (Philadelphia: Muhlenberg Press, 1946 rev. ed.) (NB, the first edition was published in 1930) Strodach does instruct the preacher to conclude the sermon with the Apostolic Blessing (Votum) from Philippians 4:7 and states: "It is proper to raise the right hand in gesture of blessing as it is pronounced. Immediately after it has been said, the minister should leave the pulpit and go to and face the altar during the singing of the Offertory Sentences." Strodach, *Manual on Worship*, 225.

26. Strodach, *Manual on Worship*, 223–24, continues: "The quiet of the sacristy is the place for a moment's devotion before entering the pulpit. In this seclusion one can reach for that grace which is so much needed . . . Here too, is the *best* place for devotions and not on the altar steps or bowed over the pulpit desk. These latter places mean ostentation and hurry in devotions, and too often look like mere pious gestures, and can hardly be classed as good example. Quiet and alone-ness are what are needed, and the entire period of the singing of the Hymn offers a far richer opportunity for the seeker. Leave the sacristy during the last stanza of the Hymn and enter the pulpit immediately."

ment to the sacristy breaks the unity of the Service and the continuity of leadership."[27] Luther Reed recommends,

> Before entering the pulpit the minister may offer silent prayer at the altar while the congregation concludes the hymn.
>
> While the liturgy does not prescribe it, the minister, after entering the pulpit and before beginning the Sermon, may conform to the *general custom in Lutheran churches abroad,* (emphasis added) and give the apostolic greeting: "Grace be unto you, and peace from God our Father and from our Lord Jesus Christ" (Eph. 1:2). Or, in place of this he may say; "In the Name of the Father, and of the Son, and of the Holy Ghost, Amen."
>
> The Sermon ended, the minister pronounces the Votum—"The Peace of God," etc., —with uplifted hands. Anciently it was customary to end the homily with an ascription of praise. The Votum as we use it today is a benediction (Phil. 4:7), invoking the promised blessing of peace upon all who stand fast in the Lord and worship him. It fittingly concluded the second part of the Office of the Word and leads into the Offertory.[28]

Reed goes on to explain that the Service of the Word ends with the Votum after the sermon and that the Offertory is not a conclusion to the sermon but the beginning of a new part of the liturgy.[29]

The year 1965 saw the publication of two influential books by Arthur Carl Piepkorn and Paul H. D. Lang. In *The Conduct of the Service,* Piepkorn opines: "The preacher need not enter the pulpit until the end of the hymn," and adds, "The traditional text for the sermon at the Service is the Gospel for the Day."[30] He then explains:

> It is an ancient custom in the church to begin the sermon with the words; "In the Name of the Father and of the Son and of the Holy Ghost. Amen." While saying these words, the preacher should make the sign of the Holy Cross upon himself. If he has used this invocation, he ought not to follow it with another after reading his text, such as "In the Name of Jesus."
>
> The sermon ended, the congregation shall rise, and the Minister shall say; "The peace of God, which passes all understanding, keep your hearts and minds through Christ Jesus." There is no authority given to vary this formulation. Although the General Rubrics of *The Lutheran Liturgy* (p. 421) authorizes the preacher to raise his

27. Luther D. Reed, *The Lutheran Liturgy: A Study of the Common Liturgy of the Lutheran Church in America,* (Philadelphia, PA: Fortress Press,1947), 305.

28. Reed, *Lutheran Liturgy,* 307.

29. Reed, *Lutheran Liturgy,* 308, 309.

30. Arthur Carl Piepkorn, *The Conduct of the Service,* (Fort Wayne, IN: Redeemer Press, 2006). (Original printing 1965, Concordia Seminary Print Shop, St. Louis), 19.

hand in blessing and make the sign of the Holy Cross when saying the Votum at the close of the Sermon, it is better not to avail
oneself to this privilege. The preacher may end his sermon with
the Trinitarian Invocation, or he may close his sermon with an
ascription of praise to the Holy Trinity.[31]

Concluding the sermon with an ascription of praise to the Holy Trinity was very common among the early church fathers. There are a few
examples that demonstrate this practice. Cyril of Jerusalem concluded
a Mystagogical Catechesis on the Rites before Baptism: "Now to God
the Father, with the Son and the Holy Ghost, be glory, and power, and
majesty, for ever and ever. Amen."[32] Augustine ended a sermon on the
Trinity in the Baptism of Christ with a blessing and doxology:

> May then the power of His mercy strengthen our heart in His
> truth. May it confirm and calm our souls. May His grace abound
> in us, may He have pity on us, and remove obstacles from before
> us, and from before the Church, and from before all those who are
> dear to us, and may He by His power, and in the abundance of His
> mercy, enable us to please Him forever, through Jesus Christ His
> Son our Lord, Who with Him and with the Holy Ghost lives and
> reigns world without end. Amen.[33]

In a sermon on the Holy Spirit, Basil the Great concludes with a prayer,
exhortation, and doxology:

> For myself, I pray that I may depart to the Lord holding fast to
> this profession; and I exhort them also, to preserve the faith in-
> violate till the Day of Christ, to maintain the Spirit undivided
> from the Father, and from the Son, and observe the faith of their
> baptism, both in their profession of faith, and in giving praise to
> God, Father, Son and Holy Ghost, to Whom be praise and glory,
> world without end. Amen.[34]

John Chrysostom:

> Thus shall we overcome all dangers and come to our imperishable
> crown, to which may we all alike attain, by the grace and mercy of
> Our Lord Jesus Christ, to Whom be glory and empire and honour,
> now and forever and ever. Amen.[35]

---

31. Piepkorn, *Conduct*, 20.
32. St. Cyril of Jerusalem, *Lectures on the Christian Sacraments: The Procatechesis and the Five Mystagogical Catecheses,* ed. F. L. Cross (Crestwood, New York: St. Vladimir's Seminary Press, 1977), 58.
33. Augustine's sermon is found in the following collection: *The Sunday Sermons of the Great Fathers*, vol. 3, trans. and ed. M. F. Toal (Swedesboro, NJ: Preservation Press, 1996), 81.
34. Augustine, *Great Fathers*, 10.
35. Augustine, *Great Fathers*, 88.

In *Ceremony and Celebration*, Paul H. D. Lang also instructs the preacher to go to the pulpit at the close of the hymn, bowing at the center of the altar if he crosses in front of it on his way to the pulpit. His pulpit rubrics agree with Piepkorn: "[He] begins the sermon with 'The grace of our Lord Jesus Christ, etc.' or the Trinitarian Invocation. At the end of the sermon he says, 'The peace of God, etc.' and while saying it, he may raise his hand in blessing and make the sign of the cross, although it is better not to do this." While the congregation sings the Offertory chant the minister goes to the altar to distribute the offering plates and prepare the elements for the Blessed Sacrament.[36]

EPHESIANS 1:2 AND PHILIPPIANS 4:7

What is the proper way to begin and end a sermon? To understand this question as a quest for a singular, correct practice may reveal a proclivity toward narrow rubricism and repristination. It is more helpful to phrase the question, why it is that usage of the Apostolic Greeting from Ephesians 1:2 and Blessing from Philippians 4:7 are so widespread? What is the theological and liturgical significance and benefit of using these texts? What are the other options and what do they communicate?[37]

The *Lutheran Service Book Altar Book* includes the following rubric in all five settings of the Divine Service: "*Before the Sermon, the pastor may say:* Grace to you and peace from God our Father and the Lord Jesus Christ." The congregation responds Amen." The full salutation in Ephesians 1:1–2 reads:

Paul, an apostle of Christ Jesus by the will of God,
To the saints who are in Ephesus, and are faithful in Christ Jesus:
Grace to you and peace from God our Father and the Lord Jesus Christ.

The Epistle to the Ephesians follows standard epistolary form, yet as with all the Pauline epistles, it is unlike any other letters written in the first century. Paul is not an official messenger (*schluchim*) of his teacher Gamaliel (Acts 22:3) or another prominent religious leader. He is not an

---

36. Paul H. D. Lang, *Ceremony and Celebration* (St. Louis, MO: Concordia Publishing House, 1965; Reproduced by Redeemer Lutheran Church, Fort Wayne, Indiana and Emmanuel Lutheran Church, Adell, Wisconsin, 2004), 100.

37. For example, Reed, *Lutheran Liturgy*, 308, states without references or comment: "It is an ancient custom in the church to begin the sermon with the words: 'In the Name of the Father and of the Son and of the Holy Ghost. Amen.'" It is understandable that this usage connects the sermon with the creedal confession and makes it clear to all that the preacher rejects the Christological heresies threatening the ancient churches. Concluding with an ascription of praise to the Holy Trinity is also an appropriate response. A clear Trinitarian greeting is equally beneficial in the 21st century as the Church continues to face a plethora of Christological and anti-Trinitarian heresies. Another option practiced in many churches is the addition of Easter Greeting and Response, "Christ is risen; He is risen indeed," during the Easter season.

ambassador for the emperor or another political authority. He is an apostle of Christ Jesus, the Messiah who fulfilled everything written in the Law of Moses and the Prophets and the Psalms (Luke 24:44).

Paul, formerly Saul, never dreamed he would be an apostle of Jesus of Nazareth to the Gentiles. Saul had no desire or intention to follow Jesus. He was committed to destroying the Church. He was not with the apostles on the evening of the day of our Lord's resurrection when the risen Lord appeared to them and said, "Peace be with you. As the Father has sent me, (ἀπέσταλκέν) even so I am sending you (πέμπω)." (John 20:21) Paul's desire was to persecute the church, but he became an Apostle (a sent one) "by the will of God," when the Lord Jesus appeared to him on the road to Damascus. His call as an Apostle was an immediate call from the risen Lord Jesus. He refers to himself as "one untimely born," that is, a "spiritual miscarriage" (ἐκτρώματι), nevertheless, he was an Apostle—by grace. Paul described himself as the "least of the apostles, unworthy to be called an apostle" because he persecuted the church of God. "But by the grace of God I am what I am, and his great grace toward me was not in vain. On the contrary, I worked harder than any of them, though it was not I, but the grace of God that is with me." (1 Cor. 15:10) The primary form of his hard work was preaching—preaching the gospel; delivering of first importance that Christ died for our sins in accordance with the Scriptures and was raised on the third day in accordance with the Scriptures. Even Paul, who was a witness to the risen Lord Jesus, preached the Word "according to the Scriptures" (1 Cor. 15:1–11). When pastors are called and ordained into the Holy Ministry through the Lord's Church, they are called to preach the Word of Christ. They are also authorized and sent by Jesus to deliver his "peace," to forgive sins in his stead, to baptize and to administer his risen, life giving body and blood in the Blessed Sacrament.

It is one thing to read Paul's Epistle to the Ephesians, but what does it mean when a pastor greets the congregation from the pulpit with the Apostolic Greeting written by Paul to be heard by members in the congregations in Ephesus when they gathered for the Divine Service? It is presumptuous for a pastor to take it upon himself to speak as an apostle. On the other hand, if he has been placed into the office of the apostolic ministry by the Lord, it is both humbling and a great honor to speak the apostolic greeting.[38] Apostles do not make themselves apostles. They do not call and send themselves any more than one can take it upon himself

---

38. Given its Apostolic nature, the use of the Ephesians 2:2 Salutation by non-ordained preachers (seminary fieldworkers and vicars) is best avoided in favor of the Trinitarian invocation or simply, "In the Name of Jesus." It is also consistent with the LSB *Altar Book* which assigns the Apostolic Greeting and Votum to the Presiding Minister (P) and not an Assisting Minister (A) or Leader (L).

to travel to a distant country and introduce himself as a self-appointed ambassador of the President of the United States. At ordination, a man is called and placed into the holy ministry not because of his own will or desire, but "by the will of God." The epistolary salutation identifies from whom the words are coming and by what authority they are being spoken. A letter from Caesar carries a lot of authority. One disregards what the emperor says at one's peril. A letter from God our Father and the Lord Jesus Christ is from the highest authority above which there is no higher authority. It is by this authority that a pastor preaches, administers the sacraments, forgives and retains sins. When the preacher begins his sermon with the Apostolic Salutation, he is putting all on notice that he is not speaking on his own authority. Thus Luther is bold to write, ". . . the office of preaching the Gospel is the greatest of all and certainly is apostolic."[39] Furthermore, the apostolic preacher does not speak his own words and opinions, but the pure and efficacious Word of God, that is, the Word of the Father's only begotten Son Jesus Christ. "It is one of the more dramatic assertions of Luther that the Word of God spoken among us is performative, that is, it actually does what it declares. 'His Word bestows what it says. In short, *the Word announces and then actually bestows the gift of God's grace.'*"[40]

When the preacher faithfully proclaims the biblical Word, it is indeed the *viva vox Dei*, the *viva vox Christi*. It has been said that the Word of God becomes the voice of God in the sermon. In "Luther on Preaching the Word of God," Ronald Feuerhahn describes the Lutheran understanding of preaching as the Word of God, as God's voice. "The ministry [office] is Christ's continued activity on earth. In the pulpit he speaks through the mouth of the preacher, at the font he himself is the Baptist, at the altar he imparts the remission of sins through the hands of the minister."[41] Feuerhahn articulates the Lutheran understanding of preaching and the Word of God with nine quotes from the Apology of the Augsburg Confession, Martin Luther and Martin Chemnitz. For example, from Luther, ". . . let us not despise the services of the men whom *God uses as intermediaries . . . pastors* have been appointed in the church. *When you hear them, you hear God . . .*"[42] From the Apology,

> [Pastors] do not represent their own persons but the person of Christ, because of the church's call, as Christ testifies (Luke 10:16),

39. Luther, *Brief Instruction on What to Look for and Expect in the Gospels* (1521), AE 35:122.

40. Ronald R. Feuerhahn, "Luther on Preaching the Word of God," in *You, My People, Shall Be Holy: A Festschrift in Honour of John W. Kleinig*, ed. John R. Stephenson & Thomas M. Winger (St. Catharines, Canada: Concordia Lutheran Theological Seminary, 2013), 40.

41. Feuerhahn, "Luther on Preaching," 42. Feuerhahn is quoting Vilmos Vajta, *Luther on Worship: An Interpretation* (Philadelphia: Muhlenberg, 1958) 112.

42. Feuerhahn, "Luther on Preaching," 43. The quote comes from Luther, AE 4:72 (Luther on Genesis 21:22); emphasis added by Feuerhahn.

"He who hears you, hears me." When they offer the Word of Christ or the sacraments, they do so in Christ's place and stead. Christ's statement teaches us this in order that we may not be offended by the unworthiness of ministers.[43]

For Lutherans, the Word of God is living, the *viva vox*. Where the Word is, there is the Spirit. ". . . there is no real separation between Christ and the Holy Spirit, between the Christological and the Pneumatological. For the Spirit of God is always serving us with the Father and the Son."[44] In contrast for the Reformed, especially those of Calvinist background, the Word is static. Feuerhahn illustrates the difference with a quote from the great Princeton theologian, Charles Hodge dating from the end of the nineteenth century: ". . . the power of the Word of God is 'not due to any inherent, permanent power, according to [as it is in] the Lutheran doctrine.'"[45] Feuerhahn continues,

> For the Reformed there is that Docetic problem about God being wrapped in humanity, even in human words. The Spirit has to be added; He cannot be part of the Word as He is for Luther. For the Reformed the Spirit is attending the Word, not in it. He is, in the words of Hodge, "accessary" to the Word. The Reformed tradition therefore prescribed that the sermon be introduced with a prayer calling upon the presence of the Holy Spirit. The Lutheran preacher was confident that the word he spoke was God's Word and would be accompanied by the Spirit of God.[46]

Similarly, the Wesleyan/Methodist perfectionism tradition has had a great influence on American Christianity, including American Lutheranism. John Wesley wrote:

> Whosoever . . . imagines there is any intrinsic power in any means whatsoever, does greatly err, not knowing the Scriptures, neither the power of God. We know that there is no inherent power in the . . . letter of Scriptures read, the sound thereof heard or the bread and wine received in the Lord's Supper; but that it is God alone who is the Giver of every good gift, the Author of grace; that the whole power is of Him whereby, through any of these, there is any blessing conveyed to our souls.
>
> We know likewise, that God is able to give the same grace though there were no means on the face of the earth. In this sense we affirm that with regard to God there is no such thing as means;

---

43. Ap. VII/VIII, 28–9, Tapert 173.28; KW 178.28).
44. Feuerhahn, "Luther on Preaching," 48.
45. Feuerhahn, "Luther on Preaching," 40.
46. Feuerhahn, "Luther on Preaching," 41.

seeing he is equally able to work whatsoever pleaseth him, by any, or by none at all.[47]

The opening Salutation in the Epistle of Ephesians also identifies the recipients of Paul's apostolic message: "To the saints who are in Ephesus, and are faithful in Christ Jesus." Today the city may be different, but the recipients are the same; members of the *Una Sancta*, the one holy catholic church, "the saints who are . . . faithful in Christ Jesus." The people, for whom preachers compose their sermons today, and at whom they look while speaking from the pulpit, share the same relationship with him as the faithful Ephesians shared with St. Paul. Both congregations are made up of people who have been called out of sin and darkness and made holy through their baptism into Christ Jesus. Both are "faithful in" Christ Jesus, "believe in," and "trust in" Christ Jesus— πιστοῖς ἐν Χριστῷ Ἰησοῦ can be translated either way. Immediately following the Salutation Paul goes on to give thanks to God the Father for every spiritual blessing bestowed upon the Ephesians. He includes the comforting doctrine of predestination of grace which is founded upon the "riches of his grace which he lavished upon us." (1:7–8) Paul is then highly complementary of the faith of the Ephesians: "For this reason, because I have heard of your faith in the Lord Jesus and your love toward all the saints, I do not cease to give thanks for you, remembering you in my prayers." (1:15–16) Pastors who love their people do well to imitate Paul. They will not be afraid to give thanks to God for the fruits he has worked in them. Pastors will not hesitate to compliment their people as good fathers do their children and pray continuously for them.

With this in mind, the pastor greets his congregation with a beautiful Apostolic Salutation which is more than merely a greeting. It is a greeting and a blessing all wrapped into one. And it is more than just a repetition of historical words written two thousand years ago by a man named Paul. The pastor is not merely reading a script as if he is performing on stage. The grace and peace do not come from Paul. They do not come from the preacher. They come ἀπὸ θεοῦ. They come "from God our Father and the Lord Jesus Christ."[48] This is what pastors as "servants of the Word" and "servants of Christ" are given to do. Like the Apostle Paul, pastors are unworthy to hold such an office, yet like Paul, by grace they have been authorized to distribute God's blessings through his Word. It is not about cleaver rhetoric and powerful speech. The Greeting shapes the sermon as well as the expectations of the hearers and gives confidence to the pastor.

---

47. John Wesley and John Emory, Bp., *The Works of the Rev. John Wesley*, vol. 5, 3rd American Complete and Standard Ed. (Cincinnati, OH: Canston and Curts, 1825), 187–188.

48. The Apostolic Greeting also sends a remarkable message to visitors who may have never heard anyone speak like this before.

"Grace" is the first word out of the preacher's mouth—then comes ὑμῖν, the plural dative "to you." With this he delivers the divine gift. Then comes "and peace" as the pastor delivers the same gifts given from the mouth, side, and hands of the risen Jesus to his disciples in the locked room on the first Easter eve. This grace and peace are not from the pastor. He has been sent merely to speak on behalf of Jesus Christ who was sent by the Father. Grace and peace come from Jesus. Next comes the preaching of repentance and the forgiveness of sins. By using the Apostolic Greeting, the pastor will have at least delivered the gifts in his opening sentence if, heaven forgive, the sermon takes a complete nosedive thereafter. On a good day, the pastor will continue to shape his sentences in a manner which lets Jesus speak. That is why it is the tradition to preach on the Gospel at the Divine Service every Sunday. The red letters are found in the Gospels. Before we partake of our Lord's body and blood, we should hear what he has to say to us today. This does not mean that pastors only preach about grace and peace, namely, the Gospel. Sermons must include both law and Gospel if they are to faithfully proclaim all of our Lord's words and saving works. The Epistle to the Ephesians, as do all the epistles, includes considerable law. For example, chapters four and five are filled with warnings about avoiding sin and immorality.

Jann Fullenweider has crafted a vivid description of the need for preaching the law in today's culture where people demand a diet of "meet my needs" cotton candy Gospel.

> We preach to call people to the Trinitarian bath to be initiated into the countercultural body of Christ and daily to live deeply into the meaning of the identity they have received in the bath. Such preaching means preaching people upside down, shaken up, inside out of their current lives, and rehearsing the peace of God now present in a world that knows no peace. There is nothing entertaining, pleasant, dispassionate, spectatorial, or democratic about this kind of confrontation, any more than there is about discovering you are the center of the action in a shock-trauma unit.

> Perhaps it is time for North America assemblies to admit to ourselves that preaching is more like awakening in a shock-trauma unit than it is like being lulled in a swinging cradle. We make our familiar contented proposals about God and fail to hear the voice that rebuked Peter in love so long ago, "Get behind me, Satan" (Matt 16:23).[49]

---

49. Jann Fullenweider, "Proclamation: Mercy for the World," in *Inside Out: Worship in an Age of Mission*, ed. Thomas Schalttauer (Minneapolis, MN: Fortress Press, 1999) 33–35.

STANDING FOR THE GREETING AND VOTUM

Should the congregation stand when the pastor enters the pulpit? Some German agendas in Europe (for example, Berlin Agenda) instructed the people to stand for the reading of the text, the Apostolic Greeting and the concluding Votum. In the *Lutheran Service Book,* Settings 1, 2, 3 and 4, the sermon follows the Hymn of the Day. Unless the final stanza is a Trinitarian doxology, the congregation will be seated when the pastor enters the pulpit. In Setting 5 the sermon follows the Creed after which the *LSB* has inserted the rubric *"Sit"* between the Creed and Sermon. Therefore, the congregation will most likely be in the process of sitting down as the pastor enters the pulpit. Thus in all five settings, the congregation will be seated unless it has become a local tradition to stand, or the people are invited by the pastor to stand. Some congregations continue this practice of standing simply because it is a long practiced custom. Few, including the pastor can explain from whence the practice arose. Some pastors appear uncomfortable, even a bit confused, as to what they should be doing at this point. In some churches, the congregation stands for all the Scripture readings, not only for the Holy Gospel. This practice has been introduced in some Lutheran Churches in Africa. In some churches the entire text of the pericope is read from the pulpit if it is serving as the sermon text, regardless of whether it is the Holy Gospel, Old Testament, Epistle, or another text. When asked why they stand, both people and pastor respond that it is out of respect for the reading of Holy Scripture, that is, God's Word.

The practice in some Lutheran Churches, going back to its European roots is for the people to stand when the pastor enters the chancel at the beginning of the service. This is a simple act of respect for the man who will begin the liturgy with the Triune Invocation or salutation. If the pastor begins the sermon with the Invocation or with the Greeting, it is fitting for the congregation to respectfully stand as it receives the Divine Name or the Apostolic and Christological Greeting/Blessing. If such respect is shown to earthly leaders and magistrates when they enter the room, how much more is it due one who has been placed into the office to proclaim Christ's words of eternal life.

THE APOSTOLIC GREETING AND VOTUM MAKE
CHRIST AND HIS GIFTS CONTEMPORARY

The Apostolic Greeting and Votum act as book ends, keeping the body of the sermon from falling apart into disorder and confusion. First, the opening greeting shapes the introduction to the sermon.

> The often-repeated rules for the introduction of a sermon are two: it should win attention; it should gain interest. The verbs are *to attend* and *to interest.* Both are transitive verbs. People do not simply

attend; they attend to something or somebody. We do not simply interest people; we interest them in something or in someone, ourselves or somebody else.[50]

The Apostolic Greeting points the attention and interest to the grace and peace which come from the Father and Jesus Christ. It takes the attention off of the hearers and the pastor and puts it onto Jesus Christ and what he is saying and doing to us today. It makes Christ and the giving out of his gifts to us contemporary. Thus the first words spoken by the pastor following the Salutation when preaching on John 20:19–31 (Easter 2) continue in the present tense. For example, the pastor might begin, "*Today* Jesus is among us and greets us as he did the Apostles on the evening in the upper room. Jesus says to us, "Peace be with you." He shows us his hands and side from which blood was shed to atone for our sins and make peace between us and God. When you hide behind the walls and locked doors of sins, guilt, shame, denial, and excuses; as spiritual claustrophobia closes in around you, Jesus says to you, "Peace . . . Peace be with you." Following an exposition of the text in the body of the sermon, the preacher points the hearers to Jesus' greatest beatitude by saying, "Today Jesus says to you, 'Blessed are those who have not seen and yet believed.'" The pastor then blesses the people with the Votum, "The peace of God, which passes all understanding, keep your hearts and minds in Christ Jesus." The people acknowledge and receive the peace by saying "Amen." The "Amen" is said by the congregation, not by the pastor.

The sermon for Easter 2 on John 20 which describes the risen Lord Jesus speaking peace to his disciples thus begins with the pastor, in the stead of Christ distributing peace, speaking peace into the ears and hearts and souls of the congregation. It ends with the pastor once more speaking the living words of Christ and his peace to the people with the Votum. There are many appropriate ways in which to begin and end the sermon. However subtle, the Apostolic Greeting from Ephesians 1 and Votum from Philippians 4 foster "real presence" preaching in which the risen Lord is present with his Words, body and blood, or as Luther puts it, preaching in which Christ is brought to us and we to him.

> When you open the book containing the gospels and read or hear how Christ comes here or there, or how someone is brought to him, you should therein perceive the sermon or the gospel through which he is coming to you, or you are being brought to him. For the preaching of the gospel is nothing else than Christ coming to us, or we being brought to him.[51]

---

50. Henry Grady Davis, *Design for Preaching* (Philadelphia, PA: Fortress Press, 1958), 186–87.
51. Luther, AE 35:121.

CONCLUSION

Prone and the subsequent Pulpit Office no longer exist. With the possible exception of (1) re-reading a pertinent verse or verses from the sermon text, (2) an introductory greeting or invocation and, (3) a concluding Votum or doxology, there is no need to include the many elements found in the medieval vernacular Prone or later Lutheran Pulpit Office such as a pulpit prayer, Lord's Prayer, General Prayer, reading of the entire text, hymn stanza, announcements etc. Instead of being encased in a separate Pulpit Office, the sermon is now an integral part of the Service of the Word and located amid the liturgical flow of Readings, Creed, Hymn of the Day, and Sermon. It could be argued a pulpit greeting and blessing are redundant in view of the fact that the Divine Service already begins with the traditional greeting, "The Lord be with you" and concludes with the Aaronic Blessing. On the other hand, a case can be made to include additional greetings appropriate to the sacramental acts.

Sermons preached in the Divine Service are liturgical sermons and are developed from and shaped by the liturgy on many levels. The individual personality of the pastor is expressed more in the sermon than any other place in the liturgy. Here the pastor writes a new text or composition for each service—both content and delivery are involved. In order to prepare his sermon, he must engage and understand the biblical text using a hermeneutic that is theologically sound and Lutheran, that is, Christological, sacramental, and eschatological. He must understand the text within the liturgical context, which includes the structure and theology of the liturgy, the church year and lectionary. When composing his sermon, he must choose his words in view of the congregation. The relationship of the sermon to the liturgy has been addressed numerous times. The very titles of two influential works summarize this understanding of the homiletical task. In 1844, Theodosius Harnack titled his Magisterschrift "The Idea of the Sermon Developed from the Nature of the Protestant Cultus" (*Die Idee der Predigt, entwickelt aus dem Wesen des protestantischen Cultus*). In 1957 Bishop Bo Giertz wrote an excellent paper titled, "The Meaning and Task of the Sermon in the Framework of the Liturgy." Both works articulate how the sermon is shaped by the liturgy.

Sermon preparation begins with the preacher squarely focused on the text. The text consists of words lying silently on the pages of a book. The process begins as a mental, academic activity involving the careful reading of the text, translation from the original, examination of isagogical matters, word studies, grammar, syntax, parallel passages etc. The task then moves on to consultation with dogmatic and confessional works and commentary from early church, medieval, reformation and contemporary exegetes and preachers. Some pastors preach with a manuscript in which each word has been carefully crafted and written down on paper. Others preach without a manuscript. Whether one uses a manuscript or not, the end result is the same—a spoken, oral proclamation from the mouth of the preacher to the ears of the gathered people. Over the past few decades, studies in the area of orality and performance criticism in the early Church help us to appreciate the distinction and interplay between the written text and oral proclamation. That said, caution is in order against pushing things to extremes.[52] In short, one must avoid pitting the written word against oral word. Both are the Word of God. Both have their place. Both are gifts from the Word made flesh to his Church. Both are present in the historic liturgy.

The Apostolic Greeting serves as a *transition from* the written text (which was silently contemplated by the pastor in his study during the week) and the Readings (spoken out loud from the lectern) *to* the proclamation of the words he speaks from the pulpit. The preached Word of God then enters the ears of the people. The Apostolic Greeting from Ephesians One sees to it that the first word from the preacher's mouth is grace. He does not simply utter theological concepts. He gives God's grace and peace to those who have ears to hear. It is made clear from the start that this is no ordinary grace and peace but comes from God the Father and the Lord Jesus Christ. The sermon then explains and extols this grace and peace in concrete, real life, down to earth textual proclamation. Preaching unfolds the text and makes Jesus Christ and his gifts of grace and peace present in the liturgy and in the lives of his people. ✝

---

52. Larry Hurtado counters performance critics who assert that texts were "performed" not read in the early church. "Advocates of 'performance criticism' are right to pose questions about how texts functioned in earliest Christianity, and to emphases the place of the spoken word in the Roman era. But it is important to avoid oversimplifications and ensure that we develop an accurate picture of matters. There is no basis for claiming that texts played a minor role in the Roman era, serving as mere adjuncts to 'orality,' or that in early Christian circles texts were typically delivered from memory and not read out, or that they were composed in performance. Texts of all kinds, including particularly literary texts, were central in practically all areas of Roman life, and nowhere more so than in the circles that comprised earliest Christianity." Larry Hurtado, "Oral Fixation and New Testament Studies? 'Orality', 'Performance' and Reading Texts in Early Christianity," *New Testament Studies,* vol. 60, (Cambridge University Press, 2014), 339. See also Thomas M. Winger, "The Spoken Word: What's Up with Orality?" *Concordia Journal,* vol. 29:2 (April 2003), 133–151. Winger concludes: "I would not want to propose that the oral proclamation of Scripture is 'better' than modern silent study, but neither would I accept the reverse. One must take care not to suggest in a quasi-Barthian manner that the written Scriptures only become God's Word when they are spoken aloud . . . ." Winger, "Spoken Word," 151.

IN HIS IMAGE

THOUGHTS ON THE
WORTHINESS OF MAN

✤

From a Christian perspective any discussion on "who man is" will only achieve its purpose if it moves forward from creation to soteriology. Within the framework of protology and eschatology is man placed into a relationship with God (*coram Deo*) through the word that justifies. That event alone offers the proper talk of man, and without it any philosophical descriptions of the purpose and destiny of humans remain incomplete. This is Martin Luther's point, which he voiced in particular in his "*Disputation concerning Man*." Arguing against philosophical and medieval-scholastic depictions, Luther individualizes anthropology, which receives its true identity from nothing and no one else but through God, in view of the encounter of Jesus Christ through the word. Luther's focus on salvation according to its historical and eschatological dimensions is often diminished by theological attempts that still seek to define "who man is" retrospectively from a disposition that man has received as an endowment from the past event of creation and continues to possess after the fall. Instead, Luther looks strictly forward where man's true being is received extrinsically as a gift from God. Philosophy and other human sciences must step aside for that theological narrative and let it take central stage.[1] In what is to follow we shall shed light on that narrative and reflect on a human structure that can best be accommodated in it, especially in light of the image of God debate.

---

1. In recent years theological anthropology has been driven by ethics, which makes the theological direction more attuned to current ethical issues concerning the devaluing life and the integration of technology. This may explain why Werner Elert placed his theological anthropology in *The Christian Ethos* and not in his dogmatics, *Der christliche Glaube*. Werner Elert, *The Christian Ethos*, trans. Carl J. Schindler (Philadelphia:, PA Fortress Press, 1957), 23–48; Werner Elert, *Der christliche Glaube*, 6th ed. (Erlangen: Martin-Luther-Verlag, 1988). For explicit ethical concerns over technology, see Noreen Herzfeld, *In Our Image: Artificial Intelligence and the Human Spirit* (Minneapolis, MN: Fortress Press, 2002).

HUMAN IMAGE UNDERSTOOD AS SUBSTANTIVE
ONTOLOGY AND DEFINED FROM CREATION

Still all these implementations of art, brain, senses, and hands, would have remained ineffective, even in the upright form, if the creator had not given us a spring to set them all in motion, the *divine gift of speech*.[2]

This divine gift of speech is essentially what Johann Gottfried Herder, in his *Outlines of a Philosophy of the Theory of Man*, came to conclude as the distinguishing mark of man from other "beasts," as he called them. However, he placed humans on a forward path guided by an image of God that God has impressed on the human mind and that leads humans on their path forward in history towards self-improvement and fulfillment: "We are not yet men, but are daily *becoming* so."[3] In this teleological orientation man's image is developing and never coming to full blossom, so that fulfillment is found in the end with God, the creator.[4] Wolfhart Pannenberg identifies Herder as the watershed figure in philosophical anthropology for taking this eschatological perspective that places man's destiny (German: *Bestimmung*) in his excentric anticipation to interact with events in history.[5] The thought of an evolving image of God in the course of history seems plausible insofar as we humans, traveling through time diachronically, must interact with circumstances that lead us to a better self-understanding.[6] However, the question for Pannenberg is whether humans are not fully endowed at a certain point in time synchronically with an image of God in Christ that restores an active relationship with God.[7]

Even among those anthropologists for whom human life has evolved from matter, the search continues for individual qualities that distinguish

---

2. Johann Gottfried Herder, *Outlines of a Philosophy of the Theory of Man*, vol. 1, bk. 3, trans. T. Churchhill (London: Luke Hanfard, 1803; New York, 1966), 154; emphasis added.

3. Herder, *Outlines of a Philosophy of the Theory of Man*, 229.

4. Herder, *Outlines of a Philosophy of the Theory of Man*, 123.

5. Wolfhart Pannenberg, *Anthropology in Theological Perspective*, trans. Matthew J. O'Connell (Philadelphia, PA: The Westminster John Knox Press, 1985), 45.

6. "Self-understanding does not come with the contemplative act of immersion in the self but only with an outward movement, with action in the world and the encounter with history." Helmut Thielicke, *Being Human . . . Becoming Human*, trans. Geoffrey W. Bromiley (New York: Doubleday, 1984), 18.

7. Pannenberg's denial of the radical impact of the fall as a loss of the image allows man to continue with the possession of the image that in history—and not salvation history—is always "becoming." The image is on its path of a destiny with God and thus always in the "subjunctive." Not only Herder but also Pannenberg understand the image purely diachronically and eschatologically, not synchronically, one restored in Christ and practiced in a relationship. Wolfhart Pannenberg, *Systematic Theology*, 2 vols., trans. Geoffrey W. Bromiley (Grand Rapids, MI: William B. Eerdmans, 1994), 2:202. See Thorsten Wapp, *Gottebenbildlichkeit und Identität: Zum Verhältnis von theologischer Anthropologie und Humanwissenschaft bei Karl Barth und Wolfhart Pannenberg* (Göttingen: Vandenhoek & Ruprecht, 2008), 46, 380–388.

man from the rest of creation and that exist apart from God.[8] Theological attempts are also offered to make humans other than beasts. Because of their distinct dualistic structure of body and soul, flesh and spirit, it has been argued that humans, unlike animals, possess a degree of God-consciousness. Augustine helps us here: Man finds himself in an "in-between status" as an integrated whole of mind, soul, and body who is above the beasts but "a little lower" than the angels and endowed with a mind or *animus* which is also capable of contemplation.[9] This thought of man's capacity towards self-transcendence is invoked by Reinhold Niebuhr,[10] and Gilbert Meilaender in his book *Neither Beast nor God: The Dignity of the Human*[11] draws from that tradition as well. However, for Martin Luther the dualism of body and soul, spirit and flesh did not become distinguishing marks for humans over against the rest of creation, but rather realities of spiritual warfare borrowed from the apostle Paul and from self-experience.[12] And in view of that warfare and the loss of what originally had been set perfectly in place between Adam and his creator, humans are in fact rebellious, wild, and ferocious beasts, only to be restored in Christ (FC SD II, 17–19, 24, 59). Here the image of God (*imago Dei*) receives focal attention, which, having taken its seat not in the body but the soul, is no longer in possession of the true knowledge of God and the original righteousness, and thus it switches to the image of Satan, *imago diaboli* or *satanae*.[13]

---

8. Next to language, other abilities are listed: 1. Self-consciousness, especially the ability to look very far ahead into the future; 2. A moral being that has the ethical intuitions of right and wrong and assume responsibilities that follow from these insights; 3. The use of conceptual tool of language; 4. Exercise of rational skills, especially the scientific and mathematical abilities. See John Polkinghorne, "Anthropology in an Evolutionary Context," in *God and Human Dignity*, ed. R. Kendall and Linda Woodhead (Grand Rapids, MI: Eerdmans, 2006), 96–98. For additional and similar qualities, see Joel B. Green, *Body, Soul, and Human Life* (Grand Rapids, MI: Baker, 2008), 42.

9. Augustine, *On the Trinity* 15.1.8. St. Augustine, *The Trinity*, trans. Stephen McKenna, The Fathers of the Church, vol. 45 (Washington, DC: The Catholic University of America Press, 1963), 451, 470. Augustine, an individual substantive supporter of the image, writes: "Then no one can doubt that man has been made to the image of Him who created him, not according to our body, not according to any part of the mind, but according to the rational mind where the knowledge of God can reside" (Augustine, *On the Trinity* 12.7.12; McKenna, 354). See Herzfeld, *In our Image*, 16, 101.

10. Reinhold Niebuhr, *The Nature and Destiny of Man*, vol. 1 (Louisville, KY: Westminster John Knox Press, 1996), 161–162. One should note that Augustine thinks of rationality not only being an act performed, but as a neo-Platonist he also includes contemplation. However, he presupposes faith as the "intellectual cognition (or contemplation) of eternal things" as superior to "the rational cognition of temporal things" in that act of contemplation (Augustine, *On the Trinity* 12.15.25; McKenna, 368; see also Niebuhr, *The Nature and Destiny of Man*, 157).

11. Meilaender, *Neither Beast nor God: The Dignity of the Human Person* (New York: Encounter Books, 2009), 4, 38–42.

12. Luther addressed the issue of *spirit-caro-totus homo* with Romans 7:14–20, realizing that where *spirit* and *caro* are set up as opposites, each applies to the entire person and his life. Thus, original sin "is a total lack of uprightness and of the power of all the faculties both of body and soul and of the whole inner and outer man" (*LW* 25:299).

13. In his *Lectures on Genesis*: "These and similar evils are the image of the devil who stamped them on us" (*LW* 1:63). Also in an undated sermon, Luther writes, "Aber das selbe bilde [Gottes] ist nu untergangen und verderbet und an des stat des Teuffels bilde auffgericht, aber durch

Thus, any talk spent on the image of God for post-Fall humans apart from the restoration and relationship in Christ would not be a part of Luther's anthropology. He might be open to entertain the idea of some value of humans in relation to the "things below," in which humans through the use of reason make valuable contributions. And yet, in relation to God there is this nothingness.[14] To some, that may seem an unfair devaluing of post-Fall human life, making them out to be in fact nothing else but mere animals. What softens the blow, is that the soul, albeit corrupted and enslaved to sin, conveys the idea that man is still *anthropos* (Rom 5:12). Even after the fall, man possesses a "formal-structural responsibility," which indicates that fallen man, while he lives in rebellion against God, cannot be equated with animals. This is the argument that many theologians—and it is the majority of them—who follow Luther's teleological orientation still wish to make.[15] The Lutheran Confessions point out that man remains an object of God's love and a being in whom God unlocks something in order to engage a *modus operandi* for conversion and redemption in Christ.[16] Even as sinner man still remains human. Thus, the argument of original sin as an *accidental* and not *substantive* reality helps to underscore that very point, for otherwise God would have to shun the entire sinner (FC SD I, 45).

To preserve this sense of uniqueness for humans, some Lutherans have posited an image in the broad or wider sense "according to which man, in distinction from the animals, is still a rational being even after the fall."[17] This would mean that the natural image of God has remained

Christum ist es widder bracht und verneuet, durch wilchs blut wir errettet sind von sund, tod und Teufel und durch den heiligen geist, durch ihn erworben, gerecht, wahrhafftig, grundgut im hertzen und inns ewige leben gesetzt werden," in Martin Luther, *Luthers Werke: Kritische Gesamtausgabe [Schriften]*, 65 vols. (Weimar: H. Böhlau, 1883–1993), 24:153; hereafter WA. See also Albrecht Peters, *Der Mensch* (Gütersloh: Gütersloher Verlagshaus Mohn, 1979), 45, 194.

14. Luther, as does Pieper, takes *şelem* and *dĕmût* as synonyms for image. Thus, the loss of state of integrity implies the total removal of the image of God not only of the *dĕmût* (LXX: *homoiosis*, Vulg.: *similitudo*) but also the image itself, *şelem* (LXX: *eikon*, Vulg.: *imago*). *LW* I, 337–338. Pieper, *Christian Dogmatics*, 3 vols. (St. Louis, MO: Concordia Publishing Company, 1950–1953), 1:515.

15. Emil Brunner presses this point: "Likewise this distinction between a formal-structural responsibility which *cannot be lost*, and the responsibility which finds its fulfilment—materially—in existence in love, is such that it can only be derived from the false decision, from sin." Emil Brunner, *Dogmatics, Volume II: The Christian Doctrine of Creation and Redemption*, trans. Olive Wyon (Philadelphia, PA: The Westminster Press, 1952), 73; emphasis added.

16. "That does not mean that the human being after the fall is no longer a rational creature, or that human beings can be converted to God without hearing and thinking about the divine Word, or that they cannot understand or freely do or refrain from doing what is good and evil in external, temporal matters" (FC SD II, 19). Moreover, in distinction to other animals, the human has a capacity on which God works albeit a passive capacity (FC SD II, 23), and God does not coerce to conversion (FC SD II, 60), as if man were a robot or stone, and yet it remains all God's doing through the Holy Spirit and the word (FC SD II, 71).

17. It is unfair to criticize the Lutheran Orthodox theologians who do so, such as Baier or Quenstedt, of not fully teaching total corruption; FC SD II, 59. Pieper, *Christian Dogmatics*, 1:519.

with man in spite of the fall, which Scriptures seem to indicate (Gen 5:3; Gen 9:6; James 3:9; 1 Cor 11:7; Acts 17:28).[18] But the thought of an *imago* remnant intensifies the tension between the christocentric and pneumatological orientation and the philosophical approach that pleads for rational powers. Yet, the philosophical perspective plays into the hands of those who wish to preserve the Humanist tradition of a positive estimate of natural man like Philip Melanchthon and John Calvin.[19] Since the extant image (*imago Dei late dicta*) is understood as the use of rational powers or freedom of the will, the conclusion is drawn that its loss comes only through insanity.[20]

However, as we will determine later, associating rational thought and an intellect of man as such in a static-substantive sense ignores the relationship with God: "The image of God in man consisted in much more than in his possession of intellect and will, in his knowledge of God and the will to do only God's will."[21] While the Reformers do not go so far, slumbering in their idea of a remnant image is an emancipatory power of reason ready to be taken to a new level. That indeed has happened with philosophy, particularly with Immanuel Kant, who has man rise to independence by calling him to emerge from his self-imposed tutelage or self-incurred immaturity and to declare himself supreme, independent with rights and powers and accountable only to himself.[22] Theologically speaking, however, that route is erroneous: "When we say that being human is something we *have*—we 'own' it—then we are saying that we are human *apart from God*."[23] Instead, theologians have clung to a both/and

---

18. This is Pannenberg's point on which he builds his entire scheme. Pannenberg, *Systematic Theology*, 2:214.

19. See here Albrecht Peters, *Der Mensch*, 66, 83.

20. "Das Ebenbild Gottes im weiteren Sinne (*imago Dei late dicta*), das natürliche Ebenbild, besteht in vernünftigen Denken und in der Freiheit des Willens. Dasselbe ist unverlierbar und gehört zur Substanz des Menschen; denn wenn das Vermögen zu denken und zu wollen fehlte, würde der Mensch aufhören ein vernünftiges Wesen zu sein. Dies natürliche Ebenbild ist trotz des Sündenfalles geblieben und kann nur vom Wahnsinn verdüstert werden." Wilhelm Rohnert, *Die Dogmatik der evangelisch-lutherischen Kirche* (Braunschweig und Leipzig: Verlag von Hellmuth Wollermann, 1902), 197.

21. Pieper, *Christian Dogmatics*, 1:517.

22. "Enlightenment is man's emergence from his self-incurred immaturity. Immaturity is the inability to use one's own understanding without the guidance of another. This immaturity is self-incurred if its cause is not lack of understanding, but lack of resolution and courage to use it without the guidance of another. The motto of enlightenment is therefore: *Sapere aude!* Have courage to use your own understanding!" Immanuel Kant, *An Answer to the Question: "What is Enlightenment?"* Konigsberg, Prussia, 30 September 1784; Immanuel Kant, *Kant: Political Writings*, ed. H. S. Reiss, trans. H. B. Nisbet, 2nd ed. (Cambridge: Cambridge University Press, 1991), 54. For an examination of the consequences, see R. Kendall Soulen and Linda Woodhead, eds., "Contextualizing Human Dignity," in *God and Human Dignity* (Grand Rapids, MI: Eerdmans, 2006), 1–24. Already sixty years before Kant, Blaise Pascal (1623–1662) affirmed the capacity for rational agency in humans though not yet liberating man entirely from God.

23. Michelle J. Bartel, *What It Means to Be Human* (Louisville, KY: Geneva Press, 2001), 36.

structure for humans that reflects the tradition since Irenaeus[24] of arguing for an extant formal *imago* and a loss of the material principle that *similitudo*, which is the upright relationship (*rectitudo*) with God through the Fall. But what could this formal *imago* be understood as? Martin Kähler refers to the image of God as a "disposition . . . that includes the task of realizing it," implying that man as a personality has the ability (*Fähigkeit*) to step in a relationship with God.[25] Paul Althaus is less explicit on possession but rather conveys the idea of an endowment or constitution in man "in which man is destined for fellowship with God."[26] Oswald Bayer argues similarly: "Accordingly being in the image of God is not completely lost but it is radically corrupt. It behaves like a radio receiver which still functions but picks up the wrong station: the community of communication is disrupted; the human can no longer hear or know God even if it wants to. It only picks up static."[27]

Perhaps all these attempts to define an extant image would come close to what Luther calls the "*capacitas passiva*" (passive capacity), or what the Formula holds as a human's substance that is distinct from that corrupting disease, original sin. However, Luther does not intend to convey the thought of neutrality or only a half-spiritually-dead person, and he does not identify that passive capacity as the image of God (FC SD II, 23, 89). Instead, Luther speaks of a total loss both of the formal *imago* and the content *similitudo*.[28] It seems that attempts among theologians to hold fast to a both/and structure inevitably invite a discussion similar to that which was led between Emil Brunner and Karl Barth, where the former strongly emphasized the restoration of a relationship with God in Christ but that this restoration connects (*Anknüpfungspunkt*) to something latent in man. Brunner affirmed both a formal concept of the image and a

---

24. Those that distinguish between a formal remnant and material loss would be in the tradition of Irenaeus, (*Adversus Haereses* IV, 38, 12; V, 6, 1), in that the Platonic distinctions apply. The *eikon* is the image or copy, and the *homoiosis* the actual communion with God, and the gift of grace that the first humans received and was lost through sin and restored in Christ. Medieval Latin Scholasticism is known for maintaining this distinction. See Pannenberg, *Anthropology in Theological Perspective*, 48.

25. An "Anlage . . . , welche eine zu erfüllende Aufgabe in sich schließt." Martin Kähler, *Die Wissenschaft der christlichen Lehre von dem evangelischen Grundartikel aus im Abrisse dargestellt*, 2nd ed. (Leipzig: A. Deichert'sche Verlagsbuchhandlung, 1893), 262, 300; cited in Pannenberg, *Systematic Theology*, 2:228.

26. "Verfassung des Menschen . . . in die er bestimmt ist zur Gemeinschaft mit Gott . . . im zweiten, christologischen Sinne bezeichnet es die erfüllte Bestimmung." Paul Althaus, *Die christliche Wahrheit: Lehrbuch der Dogmatik*, 2 vols., 2nd ed. (Gütersloh: Bertelsmann, 1949), 2:93; Pannenberg, *Systematic Theology*, 2:227.

27. Oswald Bayer, "Being in the Image of God," *Lutheran Quarterly* 27, no. 1 (Spring 2013): 86.

28. In his *Genesis Lectures*, Luther took ṣelem and dĕmûth as synonyms based on the fact that Scripture in Gen 1:26 switches to use only one word for image (*LW* 1:337–338). This placed Luther in the predicament of interpreting texts such as Gen 5:1–3 and 9:6, which spoke of an extant image against the doctrine of the loss of the image. Still he remains consistent in that he interprets them as images to be renewed in word and Spirit. Peters, *Der Mensch*, 45n45.

Christologically defined material one.[29] Barth dismisses this ontological idea of a formal remnant, claiming that Brunner cannot have it both ways. For Barth, such a connection would not be possible. First, it detracts from the deeply entrenched hostility of man, and second, it limits God's sovereignty, since he would become dependent on something outside of himself.[30] Barth writes, "For the man who is with Jesus—and this is man's ontological determination—is with God," and man outside of God exists as a mere shadow of himself.[31]

Defining the ontology of man apart from God's restoration in Christ, be it the capacity towards self-transcendence, reason, will or responsibility, all in some ways tie into the classical Aristotelian definition of man as *"animal rationale"* (ζῷον λογον ἔχον) who is in possession of the life-giving the "soul" (*anima vegetativa*).[32] And that ontology also looks back retrospectively to the biblical creation narrative in attempt to salvage some "leftovers" for man that have not been entirely lost through the Fall. From a scriptural point of view, that attempt is not without warrant. After all, texts such as Genesis 5:3; 9:6; 1 Corinthians 11:7; James 3:9; and to a degree also Acts 17:28 all seem to affirm an extant image for humans. This perspective, which we may call the protological-Adamitic orientation, is accompanied by the Christological-eschatological orientation where texts such as 2 Corinthians 4:4; Colossians 1:15; and Hebrews 1:3[33] affirm Christ as the image (εἰκών), through whom all believers are

29. Emil Brunner references the formal concept of the image to 1 Cor 11:7 and James 3:9, and Acts 17:28: "Something is meant which distinguishes man, always and forever, which is not affected by the contrast between sin and faith," but then that formal concept of being responsible must be complemented by the material concept in the New Testament "something which sinful man, by the very fact that he is a sinner, no longer possesses; which, however, is given back to him in the new life he receives from Jesus Christ . . . the actual (material) fulfillment of responsibility." Emil Brunner, *The Christian Doctrine of Creation and Redemption, Dogmatics*, vol. 2, trans. Olive Wyon (Philadelphia, PA: The Westminster Press, 1952), 76.

30. See here Karl Barth, *Church Dogmatics*, 4 vols. (Edinburgh: T&T Clark, 1956-1975), III/2, 128. The debate would also include his famous response "Nein!" to Brunner in 1934. Emil Brunner, *Man in Revolt*, trans. Olive Wyon (New York, 1939), 172.; See Peters, *Der Mensch*, 121.

31. Barth understands man being in God as the only true ontological reality which sin cannot destroy: "Godlessness is not, therefore, a possibility, but an ontological impossibility. Man is not without God but with God. This is not to say, of course, that godless men do not exist. Sin is undoubtedly committed and exists. Yet sin itself is not a possibility but an ontological impossibility in man." Barth, *Church Dogmatics*, III/2, 136. Restoration and relationship with God occurs through God's election of Christ and man into Christ to which man is summoned though the word. In contrast to Luther, Barth does not maintain the same intense focus on the cross and justification. Barth places the second Adam before the first and so the actual event of cross and justification lose their significance and seem to come as an afterthought. Barth, *Church Dogmatics*, III/2, 142-150; Peters, *Der Mensch*, 135.

32. Aristotle also ascribed to a generic understanding of the soul, and not so much a mark of individual personality, in that souls are also in plant life and animals. Aristotle, *On the Soul*, trans. W. S. Hett, Loeb Classical Library 307 (Cambridge, MA: Harvard University Press, 1935), 87. See also Norman Melchert, *The Great Conversation*, 4th ed. (Boston, MA: McGraw Hill, 2002), 331.

33. Image and glory seem to complement one another. The Hebrews text speaks to Christ as the radiance of God's glory (Hebrews 9-10). Conversely, according to Paul in Romans 3:23,

restored (Rom 8:29; 1 Cor 15:49; 2 Cor 3:18) and endowed with knowledge, righteousness, and holiness (Col 3:10; Eph 4:24). This leads us to
conclude that the loss of image of God must be understood as precisely
the lack of the knowledge of God and of the original righteousness and
holiness. It is a spiritual loss that had formerly been located in the soul.[34]
As such it would then be wrong to posit the image as a physical or bodily
entity that distinguishes man from woman or husband from wife along
the lines of gender and sex.[35]

What the scriptural evidence points out is that for a human to attain
salvation and restoration into Christ's image, it becomes not a matter of
looking back at creation trying to salvage as best as possible something in
the form of possession, but rather forwards towards the goal, that is, the
renewed relationship with God in Christ from which flow capacities such
as knowledge, love, and the exercise of righteous living in God's sight.[36]
Thus, the individual-ontological concept, also called the substantive or
structural understanding of the image of God, which goes back to Aristotle and is associated with rational powers or similar capacities that man has
in his possession, cannot satisfy scripturally or theologically. For Luther,
too, "the image of God refers to a total orientation of the human toward
God, a total relationship. As such it cannot be divided or parceled out."[37]

A number of reasons may speak in support of this. First, if we were to
parcel out the image, giving parts of it to man and some to Christ, then
the devil himself would represent the truest image of God, having been
very rational and endowed with a great intellect as he demonstrated in
the temptation narrative (Luke 4). Second, and this seems to be of recent
provenance, there is the cultural and ethical issue increasingly raised by
concerned Christian ethicists. For if the image were to be understood
as an ontological, rational capacity, it leads humans, as history sadly has
shown, to draw comparisons with one another and then to elevate some
over others. Outstanding thinkers or artists who exhibit greater capacities and powers are thus thought to be more human than those who
do not possess the same abilities, such as the unborn and incapacitated
(sometimes called vegetables). The ethical debate has brought into the
image of God debate the question of the value of life and has sensitized
theologians to reassess their descriptions of the image in view of human

---

all humans have lost that glory as a result of sin and then are restored back through Christ into
that glory and holiness.

34. See here Ap II, 18–22; FC SD I, 10.

35. Pieper, *Christian Dogmatics*, 1:524.

36. Pieper writes, "To call man the image of God because he possesses reason and will
and leave out of consideration what he is to become in Christ is to stretch a point." Pieper,
Christian Dogmatics, 1:520.

37. Carl E. Braaten and Robert Jenson, eds., *Christian Dogmatics*, 2 vols. (Philadelphia,
PA: Fortress Press, 1984), 1:332–333.

value or dignity.[38] Third, should a human's extant image be defined as a rational and intellectual power, then that understanding could easily influence soteriology and offer a synergistic concept of spiritual renewal. Indeed, this has always been a decidedly Lutheran concern and, as the history of theology shows, a legitimate one. Forms of Pelagianism have plagued the church for as long as it has existed, and that danger persists in projects that demythologize the biblical account of Creation and Fall, and thereby diminish the full impact of the Fall and original sin.[39]

This latter concern is brought out in a study some decades ago by Wilfried Joest "*Ontologie der Person bei Martin Luther,*"[40] who has demonstrated that the pre-Reformation, medieval-scholastic theology operated in general with an individual-substantive concept by determining such to exist in post-Fall man via the analogy of being (*analogia entis*). By comparing man to God, the human being is said to be in possession of a static immutable element that he may call his, either his intellect and reason (*via antiqua*) or his will (*via moderna*).[41] Thus, this substantive or ontological approach finds something within the individual human, irrespective of his actions or surroundings: "Substantive interpretations tend to approach the question of what is the image of God in human beings from the bottom up, beginning with an examination of the human person and looking from there for what represents the highest and best in our innate nature, and what separates us from the rest of creation."[42]

Against this philosophical-theological attempt, which he addresses in his "*Disputation concerning Man,*" Luther puts forth a narrative that declines a static-substantive fixation of the image from the past and instead re-orientates it christocentrically and eschatologically grounding it in such texts as 1 Corinthians 15:44–49.[43] Luther invites the necessity of an encounter with the Word and Holy Spirit only after which man is raised out of his spiritual rebellion to God and clothed with the only true

38. Such concerns are voiced clearly by Noreen Herzfeld, *In Our Image*, 10–32.

39. Paul Tillich's existential interpretation denies the historicity of the actual fall. As a result it would be unclear what may have caused what he calls "the total estrangement from God." It just seems to be there as part of every human. Paul Tillich, *Systematic Theology*, vol. 2 (Chicago: The University of Chicago Press, 1957), 44–59; see especially 29, 57. The same applies to Pannenberg for whom the fall is a myth, and so his understanding of sin is far cry from that radical destructive reality as Luther understood it. Pannenberg, *Systematic Theology*, 2:212; Wapp, *Gottebenbildlichkeit und Identität*, 397.

40. Wilfried Joest, *Ontologie der Person bei Luther* (Göttingen: Vandenhoek & Ruprecht, 1967), 237.

41. The emphasis on reason reflects the *via antiqua* tradition associated with the medieval scholastic theologian Thomas Aquinas, whereas the association with the will goes back to the *via moderna* tradition with William of Occam. The latter tradition was skeptical of the Aquinas scheme of establishing analogy between man and God, but for Luther it found its demise by falling on the human will in soteriology.

42. Herzfeld, *In Our Image*, 19.

43. See *LW* 1:65 and a sermon on 1 Cor 15:44–49, delivered in February 1533 (WA 36,663–669); Peters, *Der Mensch*, 47.

substantive image, Jesus Christ (Col 3:10; Eph 4:24; Rom 8:29). It is from Christ that knowledge, fear, and trust of God (the First Commandment) as well as the proper ethical functions of becoming "a Christ" for the neighbor are born.[44] Any analogy of being is intercepted and modified by the cross itself and faith in Christ; it now becomes an *analogia fidei* and *relationis.*[45] Human existence is defined futuristically as that "material of God for the form of his future life" and that which is materially grounded in the person of Jesus Christ through faith.[46] In search for that essence of humanity we would find it embedded in the history of salvation, in particular in the event of justification:

> The decisive insight in this anthropology lies in its defining the realm of the "spirit" or the "heart" or "conscience" as initially not an anthropologically given which then secondarily relates to God by means of faith. Rather, there is only one way in which human beings exist, by being in relationship with another person than the self, by means of "relying" (*sich verlassen*).[47]

In the end, the descriptions of how that restoration into the image occurs would not only belong to soteriology but to missions as well. The former would inform the latter on what it is and what it should do.[48]

The point here is that this extrinsic dependency to Christ continues throughout a believer's life. The posture of passivity and receptivity remains. This extrinsic relation with Christ as *telos* is one the believer can never turn his back on or define as his possession apart from faith. Faith remains one of appropriation (*fides apprehensiva*), grounded in the person of Christ. Any alternative anthropological model that would want to see an "*unio cum Christo*" with the soul in a "real-ontological" manner would abandon the one described above, where the correct posture is "*extra se*" and a faith that "*ponit nos extra nos*" (places us outside of ourselves).[49] Thus

---

44. Luther, *The Disputation concerning Man* (1536), Theses 21–23, 32, 38 (*LW* 34:139–141).

45. Karl Barth, *Church Dogmatics*, III/2, 221, 323. In the first article sense, that relationship becomes one of thanksgiving. This is where Karl Barth follows Luther (*Church Dogmatics*, III/2, 172). In contrast to Barth, however, the analogy of being cannot be dismissed. In fact, as Brunner rightly points out, too a degree, the analogy of faith is preceded by the analogy of being illustrated with the example of speaking: "When we say that we can only speak of God aright because God has spoken to us in His revelation, we have already made the tacit admission that there is a fundamental analogy between what 'speaking' means in the divine and in the human sense." Emil Brunner, *Christian Doctrine*, 2:24. Peters, *Der Mensch*, 123–124.

46. Theses 35–38 (*LW* 34:139–140).

47. Notger Slenczka, "Luther's Anthropology," in *The Oxford Dictionary of Martin Luther's Theology*, ed. Robert Kolb, Irene Dingel, and L'ubomir Batka (Oxford: University Press, 2010), 216.

48. Klaus Detlev Schulz, *Mission from the Cross* (St. Louis, MO: Concordia, 2009), 100–101.

49. One can safely say that the majority of Luther scholars have rejected the transformative and ontological attempts of the Mannermaa school by revisiting the texts in Luther that purportedly speak of such. See, for example, Martin Luther's 1535 *Lectures on Galatians* (*LW* 26:166) and Slenczka, "Luther's Anthropology," 220.

the Lutheran tradition has dismissed the substantive understanding of the image in favor of an understanding that defines it as "accidental" perfection restored to the soul through the relationship with Christ, the substantive image. If understood any other way, the image could, for example, be transmitted through birth from one being to the next. It seems here that the dichotomy of soul and body is still an important one to operate with even in view of theologians criticizing it for being a "disembodied version of the image," which Genesis 1:26–28 does not seem to indicate.[50] However, that does not mean that the relationship between soul and body is impermeable as if the body remains unaffected by sin and a neutral entity all along. The plea to think of humans more holistically in terms of well-being is also bought to theology from the medical field.

THE FUNCTIONAL UNDERSTANDING OF THE IMAGE EXPRESSED THROUGH REGENCY

When it comes to the subject of theological anthropology and the image of God, some exegetical treatments have shifted gears from an individual-substantive (structural or ontological) concept to a functional one that posits the image as a capability to rule over other life forms, animate and inanimate. Now, it is no longer what we have *within* us, but rather what we are to *do*. That connection is established with the *dominium terrae* mandate, in which man's uniqueness and superiority is underscored in terms of function and abilities to rule. Here scholars argue that the so-called priestly writer (P), to whom they attribute Genesis, is informed by his immediate surrounding world like Egypt and Mesopotamia where king and royalty generally represent their god.[51] With some grammatical finesse applied to Genesis 1:26, Gerhard von Rad and others argue that man is invested with God's power to function as his representative.[52] This functional regency of exerting one's dominion allows humans not only to follow what God has obliged humans to do but also to use the earth as the means to ensure their survival. Indeed, this understanding does bear a strong Lutheran component that calls for all humans to become God's agents, as masks or channels of God, who in their vocation, whether they do so knowingly or not, bestow God's blessings to others (LC I, 26). For exegetes such as Gerhard von Rad and Hans Walter Wolff, that function-

50. Marc Cortez, *Theological Anthropology* (New York: T&T Clark International, 2010), 21.

51. The Priestly (P) writer's connection to his surrounding world is one of conjecture and doubtful according Westermann, who follows more a relational concept. Claus Westermann, *Genesis 1–11: A Commentary*, trans. John Scullion (Minneapolis, MN: Augsburg, 1984), 153.

52. Gerhard von Rad prefers the translation of the "beth" in Gen 1:26 to read "as the image of God", rather than "in the image of God" which conveys the idea that the whole person and not just something in him serves as God's image. Gerhard von Rad, *Genesis: A Commentary*, trans. John H. Marks (Philadelphia, PA: Westminster, 1961), 56. Herzfeld, *In Our Image*, 23.

ality explains the image of God.[53] Von Rad writes, "The divine likeness is not to be found either in the personality of man, in his free Ego, in his dignity or in his free use of moral capacity, etc."[54] Humans rule the world, and they are allowed to live from the life around them by taking from it.

The downside of this anthropocentric, even anthropomonistic, depiction of regency over creation has as its by-product the exploitation of the earth's resources, or what some call ecological imperialism.[55] Consequently, environmental concerns have made theologians and denominations more wary of human exploitation of the earth and assert a more conscious sense for environmentalism.[56] In some cases these concerns go to the extreme—whether motivated for religious, philosophical, or ecological reasons—of collapsing man's superiority over the rest of creation and summoning everyone to show a greater reverence for all of creation. Often that path has led to an ecological monism, which has removed God and declared man to consist of matter only. This ecological materialism is also called naturalism or physicalism. Holistic traditions such as New Age reflect a pantheistic monism having been inspired from Eastern religions such as Buddhism and ancient Gnosticism.[57] However, where the superiority of humans is collapsed into a more inclusive approach, a series of problems arise. Not only is man thereby denied his special status and honor, but this reverence for all that lives on earth has difficulties justifying of any life form, even the pathogenic or disease-causing agents. While one of the side effects of anthropocentrism can become a self-centered manipulation of creation and its resources, the other side, which bestows sanctity and honor to all of life, cannot argue convincingly why human life still receives preferential option over the rest of creation. Theological anthropology seems to be juxtaposed between these two extremes, and it must argue clearly that it is not because of the biblical worldview of creation that humans exploit creation but rather because of their habitual sinfulness.[58]

53. "Nicht in selbstherrlicher Willkür, sondern als verantwortlicher Geschäftsträger nimmt er die Aufgabe wahr. Sein Herrschaftsrecht und seine Herrschaftspflicht sind nicht autonom, sondern abbildhaft." Hans Walter Wolff, *Anthropology of the Old Testament*, trans. Margaret Kohl (Philadelphia, PA: Fortress Press, 1974), 160. See also Douglas John Hall, *Imaging God: Dominion as Stewardship* (Grand Rapids, MI: Eerdmans, 1986).
54. Gerhard von Rad, "The Divine Likeness in the Old Testament," in *Theological Dictionary of the New Testament*, ed. Gerhard Kittel, trans. Geoffrey W. Bromiley (Grand Rapids, MI: Eerdmans, 1964), 391. See also Herzfeld, *In Our Image*, 20–25.
55. See, for example, Lynn White, "The Historical Roots of our Ecological Crisis," *Science* 155 (March 10, 1967): 1203–1207.
56. *Together with All Creatures: Caring for God's Living Earth*, A Report of the Commission on Theology and Church Relations of the Lutheran Church—Missouri Synod (2010).
57. Sire's description of naturalism holds true: "Space and time (all we know of reality) come into being together. Moreover, nothing spiritual or transcendent emerged from this cosmic event. It makes no sense to say there was a *before* the singularity. In short, matter (or matter/energy in a complex interchange) is all there is. Ours is a *natural* cosmos." J. W. Sire, *The Universe Next Door*, 5th ed. (Downer's Grove, IL: InterVarsity Press, 2009), 69.
58. Wilfried Härle, *Dogmatik,* 2nd ed. (New York: Walter de Gryter, 2000), 427.

Unlike the individual-substantive view that seems to be static and highlights the image within humans as intellectual abilities over those of the body, the functional image of regency allows man to see himself as God's sovereign representative in a holistic fashion, including his upright posture: "It is the whole person, both physical and intellectual, that exerts dominion over the earth."[59] The concerns with this functional understanding are similar to the previous, ontological one, and in addition to those concerns, the Lutheran retort would be that the understanding of the image of God as exercising dominion is not part of but an immediate consequence of possessing the divine image. The close juxtaposition of "in our image" and "let them rule" in Genesis 1:26 does not imply that the latter defines the former and places a functional identity on the first humans. Luther himself in his radical sense concluded that human sovereignty after the Fall is only a caricature of what it once was; it is nothing but a "mock sovereignty."[60] Instead, the attainment of true functionality in exerting one's dominion could be perceived teleologically as a goal (*Bestimmung*) or final cause,[61] and as a consequence of the restored image.[62]

LUTHER'S DISPUTATION CONCERNING MAN: SALVATION HISTORICAL AND ESCHATOLOGICAL RESTORATION

In his 1536 *Disputation concerning Man* (*Disputatio de homine*), Luther does not seem to contest the classical and traditional insight that "philosophy or human wisdom defines man as an animal having reason, sensation, and body" (Thesis 1).[63] Indeed, reason "is the most important and the highest in rank among all things and, in comparison with other things of this life, the best and something divine" (Thesis 4). Thus, in Luther's anthropology, reason does have an important place in understanding who man is. Not only does it belong to man; it has also been put to good use: "It is the inventor and mentor of all the arts, medicines, laws, and of whatever wisdom, power, virtue, and glory men possess in this life" (Thesis 5). Reason belongs to man and, because of it, man "is distinguished

---

59. Herzfeld, *In Our Image*, 24; Von Rad writes, "One will do well to split the physical from the spiritual as little as possible: the whole man is created in God's image." Von Rad, *Genesis*, 56.

60. Pieper, *Christian Dogmatics*, 1:522.

61. Westermann supports the approach of Peters, *Der Mensch*, 200. Westermann, *Genesis 1–11*, 158.

62. "It is a creation that longs for its complete renewal when we, God's children, are revealed in glory. In the meantime the Gospel has set us free to embrace our human creatureliness, and with it, our care for all of our fellow creatures, both human and nonhuman. Our faith should be at home with this earth, which after all is the realm of the new creation through Christ's work of redemption." *Together with All Creatures*, 23.

63. For this and following citations, see *LW* 34:137. Other places worth noting are Luther's explanation of Paul's explicit references to the topic in the letter to the Romans and Galatians, as well as the resurrection chapter in 1 Corinthians 15. Then there is also Luther's interpretation of Genesis as well as his first Article of the Creed; see Peters, *Der Mensch*, 27.

from the animals and other things" (Thesis 6). In addition, man is given the "*dominium terrae*" (Thesis 7), and so reason is used positively as "a kind of god appointed to administer these things in this life" (Thesis 8). Also, man did not lose reason after the Fall; "after the fall of Adam," God did not "take away this majesty of reason, but rather confirmed it" (Thesis 9).

What is important for our exercise is that Luther embraces the definition of man both as a rational being as well as in the task of exercising dominion over creation; and yet, Luther disassociates himself from making these ontological and functional definitions part of the image. Defining man in terms of possessing reason or using function is not unique to theology. Human philosophy, and we could add all human sciences, concludes who man is from mere empirical observations, which Luther calls facts that are gathered *a posteriori*.[64] Theology by contrast operates with a far broader and deeper picture of who man is by drawing from outside evidence *a priori*: "Therefore, if philosophy or reason itself is compared with theology, it will appear that we know almost nothing about man."[65] To demonstrate that distinction, Luther is willing to take the approach of integrating philosophy's jargon on the subject, even when he says on one occasion that it should, because of its limited scope, be given a "bath" and "baptism."[66] To make his point, Luther goes to battle with philosophy as it has come to him through the traditional Aristotelian and medieval-scholastic interpretations of the four causes.[67]

---

64. Theses 3 and 10 (*LW* 34:137). For Luther, philosophy is knowledge of the world attained through a rational exercise that humans do by and for themselves (German: *rational autogenes Weltwissen*). It is a knowledge gained through observation of inner-worldly phenomena through one's senses and reason. The *sensus* and *ratio* are the two parts that make up philosophy or any human endeavor. Luther calls the effort of reason *intellecta*, but he would also know of an *intellecta fidei* that is totally different to that of reason. The *intellecta fidei* is an understanding attained only through the Holy Spirit and faith, and thus comes in no way natural to man. Joest, *Ontologie der Person bei Luther*, 104–107.

65. Thesis 11 (*LW* 34:137). By looking at a number of places in Luther's writings that span his entire life, Luther's stance towards philosophy is fairly consistent on this point; Joest lists these places as following: First lectures on Psalms (1513–1515); Lecture on Romans (1515–1516); Operations in Psalms (1519–1521); The Magnificat (1521); De servo arbitrio (1525); Lectures on Galatians (1531); Lectures on Genesis (1535); Theses on the Disputation concerning Man (1536). Joest, *Ontologie der Person bei Luther*, 89–93.

66. In "Promotionsdisputation von Palladius und Tilemann (1537)," WA 391:229, 23; Peters, *Der Mensch*, 31.

67. In his *Physics* II.3 and *Metaphysics* V.2, Aristotle offers his general account of the four causes. This account applies to everything that requires an explanation, including artistic production and human action. Here Aristotle recognizes four types of things that can be given as an answer to a why-question: The material cause: "that out of which", e.g., the bronze of a statue. The formal cause: "the form," "the account of what-it-is-to-be," e.g., the shape of a statue. The efficient cause: "the primary source of the change or rest," e.g., the artisan, the art of bronze-casting the statue, the man who gives advice, and the father of the child. The final cause: "the end, that for the sake of which a thing is done," e.g., health is the end of walking, losing weight, purging, drugs, and surgical tools. See here Aristotle, *Phys.* II.3, 195a6–8; II.3, 195b21–25, trans. Ogle. Cf. *Met.* V.2, 1013b6–9, as quoted in Melchert, *The Great Conversation*, 170–172.

Based on inner-worldly observation, philosophy relates both final and efficient causes inadequately to the "peace of this life" (final cause) and not God himself (efficient cause).[68] At best, it can make out the other two causes, the material and formal causes. When it comes to the information *a priori*, which speaks of the pre-Fall condition of man, Luther posits it as perfect,[69] but in the situation after the Fall he lists as negative.[70] And as much as one would want to think of creation after the Fall in positive terms, the fact stands: "That the whole man and every man, whether he be king, lord, servant, wise, just, and richly endowed with good things of this life, nevertheless is and remains guilty of sin and death, under the power of Satan" (Thesis 25). This recognition of creation as being tainted after the Fall escapes philosophy's insights.[71] The solution that theology proposes for man is that "he can be freed and given eternal life only through the Son of God, Jesus Christ (if he believes in him)" (Thesis 23). In contrast, philosophy not only denies the reality of the Fall (Thesis 26), and even if it admits that fact, it nonetheless offers a false solution, namely that man does what is in him in order "to merit the grace of God and life" (Thesis 27).[72] Instead, Luther's emphasis concerning salvation is on the act of justification by grace through faith alone (Thesis 32–33). Thus, it is clear that a return to the original state as it once was is possible only in Christ: "He can be freed and given eternal life only through the Son of God, Jesus Christ (if he believes in him)" (Thesis 23).

Luther looks at anthropology teleologically in keeping an eschatological perspective on man's ultimate destiny, that is, he describes the final cause in Theses 37–38: "And as earth and heaven were in the beginning for the form completed after six days, that is, its material, so man is in this life for his future form, when the *image of God has been remolded and perfected*." Here Luther has taken into account the loss of the εἰκόν,

---

68. "For philosophy does not know the efficient cause for certain, nor likewise the final cause" (Thesis 13; *LW* 34:138). Luther reflects at length on Aristotle and the causes in his *Lectures on Genesis* by taking him to task for not knowing the final and efficient cause: "Aristotle declares: 'Man and the sun bring mankind into existence.' Well said. But follow this wisdom, and you. But what sort of wisdom and knowledge is it that knows nothing about the final cause and the efficient cause? . . . Therefore let us learn that true wisdom is in Holy Scripture and in the Word of God. . . . Without the knowledge of these two causes our wisdom does not differ much from that of the beasts, which also make use of their eyes and ears but are utterly without knowledge about their beginning and their end." *LW* 1:124–125, 127; Joest, *Ontologie der Person bei Luther*, 97.

69. "Theology to be sure from the fullness of its wisdom defines man as whole and perfect: namely, that man is a creature of God consisting of body and a living soul, made in the beginning after the image of God, without sin, so that he should procreate and rule over created things, and never die." (Theses 20–21; *LW* 34:138).

70. "But after the fall of Adam, certainly, he was subject to the power of the devil, sin and death, a twofold evil for his powers, unconquerable and eternal" (Thesis 22; *LW* 34:138).

71. "Therefore those who say that natural things have remained untainted after the fall philosophize impiously in opposition to theology." (Thesis 26; *LW* 34:139)

72. See also Theses 29–30; *LW* 34:139.

of the spiritual and physical integrity and perfection that man once had and posits a restoration of it in the future time, received through faith in Christ and then fully restored at the time of our resurrection. Though Luther has emphasized eschatological finality as strong as no other theologian before him, man progresses towards his final goal as sinner and saint constantly renewed through a life already realized through faith in Christ.[73]

Luther presents us with a narrative anthropology, a narrative that draws in the following stations that have creedal overtones: man created in the image of God, estranged from God, called to restoration in Jesus Christ, and through justification and sanctification brought back on the path towards the final goal; which, in short, is summarized with the doctrine of justification and restoration of righteousness in Christ through faith.[74] While we have no *carte blanche* indictment against theologians who wish to secure a formal remnant, Luther would caution them against such an attempt, especially where it associates itself with a quality that can be found *internally* and integrally to man and that he can exercise freely.[75] The christological *telos* and the image of God's restoration in God himself through justification pull us away from such reasoning. In order to be a true human, such reality comes about *externally* with God who creates and redeems humanity, and that image is preserved and honored only while in the relationship with God.[76]

The idea of the image of God as one to be received in the future and understood in the context of a relationship with God established through Christ and faith in him makes the value of life for all humans lie in their destiny (*Bestimmung*) and purpose. Helmut Thielicke follows Luther's depiction of the future in Theses 35–38 by beginning the theme of humanity and finitude with the "Whither first" and only then the "Whence"[77] and radically adds to that an important ethical concern:

> The certainty of the divine likeness is thus grounded in our final relationship, in what we call our alien dignity. If we base our dignity on our biological origin, we are simply made into more highly organized animals. If we base it on our immanent value, on our functional abilities, we are sacrificed to animality. For when we

---

73. Joest, *Ontologie der Person bei Luther*, 323, 352–253.

74. Peters, *Der Mensch*, 31, 56. The dividing line between theology and philosophy is the cross. One may see his *Heidelberg Disputation*, where Luther draws out this split that exists between a philosopher's and a theologian's approach to the cross (Theses 19–23; *LW* 31:40).

75. Joest, *Ontologie der Person bei Luther*, 126.

76. For Augustine humankind is made after the image of God with respect to the rational or intellectual soul. However, that image is preserved only in relation to God and only in that relationship to be considered honorable (Augustine, *On the Trinity* 12.11; McKenna, 358). Origen, too, would agree (Soulen and Woodhead, "Contextualizing Human Dignity," 10).

77. Thielicke, *Being Human . . . Becoming Human*, 374.

lose our usefulness, we lose our right to life. Only that relation establishes the inviolability of our humanity—only the fact that we
are the children of God, the apple of his eye, bought with a price.[78]

The emphasis here is on the restoration of the vertical relationship between God and humans from which the horizontal relationship between
humans also follows. One can invoke a relational concept of the *imago
Dei* in Luther's sense only on the basis of the vertical restoration through
the word as a necessary prerequisite. Man is turned against God, and so
he is, with his conscience and heart, called out (*rapi*) through the word
from his inwardly focused state. The entire life of a Christian remains
in that receptive mode of listening (*auditus fidei*).[79] Those who attempt
to one-sidedly promote a relational concept of the image from creation
or solely transfer it into eschatology as always-in-the-becoming, yet outstanding, forget that Luther already makes it a present reality enacted
through the Christ-bearing word and faith.[80]

In terms of what the image actually is, we would have to posit that
image as a moral restoration of a certain, true knowledge of God (*noti-
tiam Dei certiorem*), fear of God (*timorem Dei*), trust (*fiduciam Dei*), and
a rectitude and ability "to grasp God and reflect God" (*aut certe rectitu-
dinem et vim ista efficiendi*) or as being "created in truth, holiness, and
righteousness" (Ap II, 18–22; FC SD I, 10). In it man becomes true man,
and it finds its reflection in works of responsibility and love towards the
other, male and female included.[81] From that restored relationship with
God flow acts of response so that "we are in duty bound to love, praise,
and thank him without ceasing, and in short devote all these things to
his service, as he has required and enjoined in the Ten Commandments"
(LC II, 19). Being restored once again into the image of God, man enters a communicative and ethical relationship with God and his fellow
neighbor and in so doing becomes a "Christ" for all people.[82] Negatively
speaking, the loss of the image in man had caused a break-down in
precisely three areas of human relations: humans towards God (Gen

---

78. Thielicke, *Being Human . . . Becoming Human*, 407.

79. Joest, *Ontologie der Person bei Luther*, 222–224.

80. Again we mention this as a concern over a radical eschatology such as that of
Pannenberg, who forgets the restored reality in Christ.

81. The argument that by the creation of male and female God underscored the image to
be relational would, however, not mean the differences between sexes is part of the image as
Barth claims, or that the woman holds the image only derivatively. Barth, *Church Dogmatics*,
III/1, 195–196; Pieper, *Christian Dogmatics*, I:523. See here Augustine: "For he [author of
Genesis] says that human nature itself, which is complete in both sexes, has been made to the
image of God, and he does not exclude the woman from being understood as the image of
God" (*On the Trinity* 12.7.10; McKenna, 352).

82. It has been common to talk of an "I" and "Thou" relationship which since Martin
Buber has been invoked by a series of theologians such as Bonhoeffer. See Herzfeld, *In Our
Image*, 105n84.

3:8), towards one another (Gen 3:7, 12, 16), and towards creation (Gen 3:18–19). The restoration of a relationship that was severed through the fall brings to the attention that Christ serves as the nexus and endows man with the image as a gift. What was once lost can become a reality again.[83] And as argued earlier, it remains a relationship of dependency on Christ, and the mode of receptivity exists throughout the believer's life. Thus, for Luther it cannot be divided or parceled out. Indeed, the idea that man is to love, fear, and trust God but has also lost those abilities does—unlike Arminian and Pelagian approaches—point to the need for a restored relationship into the image of God, which again returns those abilities back to man.[84] As Oswald Bayer puts it:

> Relational anthropology informed by the biblical-reformational tradition balks at any self-contained rationalistic, monistic, or individualistic definition of the human. Instead, the human is to be seen fundamentally as an essence called into communication with its creator. There is an ontological breadth to being justified by faith: to live an undeserved, completely beholden existence. . . . The being of the human is its elementary dependence on God's activity, in that life and what is necessary for life "against all danger" is provided to it anew every second—it can have no continued existence in and of itself at any moment.[85]

CONCLUSION

Is there not an understanding of a remnant of the image that is needed for us to express the value or dignity of man, for those in particular who find themselves outside the relationship with God in Christ? The concept of teleology that operates with the fall and restoration in Christ could be criticized for devaluing human life as such. Not necessarily so we must counter. First, in a context where the value of human life was placed on utility, Bonhoeffer simply argued that the fact that bodily life is born from another human already warrants its protection and value.[86] Second, the focus on teleology and the salvation-historical interpretation of the image is precisely making all humans the object of divine love *here and now*, as we saw in the statement from Thielicke, where providential

---

83. Pannenberg is radical in teleology, separating himself completely from those who wish to stick to the image as an endowment from creation. But it seems that Pannenberg places the restoration more in history than in salvation history, so that it takes an evolutionary and processional note—never found as a goal. That would go against the image of being in fact an endowment from God in Christ, even if eschatology reminds us of something yet to come. See Thorsten Wapp, *Gottebenbildlichkeit und Identität*, 456.

84. Stanley J. Grenz, *The Social God and the Relational Self: A Trinitarian Theology of the Imago Dei* (Louisville, KY: Westminster John Knox, 2001).

85. Bayer, "Being in the Image of God," 77.

86. Bonhoeffer, *Ethics* (New York: Simon & Schuster, 1995), 162.

care and the cross become divine expressions of love towards all humans, albeit in view of their restoration. We saw that the salvation historical concept of the image restoring a relationship with God is also in the forefront with Althaus, Kähler, Bayer, and Brunner; it still affirms a remnant of the image in humans that, though corrupted, still exists. To some degree, such an attempt seems to corroborate with Luther's concept of a *capacitas passiva,* which points out that God chooses to work on humans and not on other life. Humans are not robots nor are they coerced in their conversion (FC II, 60, 64). This leads us to consider humans as valuable precisely because there is something that they have in their possession. Just as a potter who holds his shattered clay pot in his hands lovingly with the intention of bringing it back to its original shape, so too humans are objects of God's love whom he desires to bring out of their broken existence. However, Luther does not identify that *capacitas passiva* as the image of God, even if it does provide the notion of something special with regards to humans in contrast to other forms of life.[87] He held steadfast and radically to a synthetic and monergistic understanding of a concept of the image that sees it only put in place in the restored relationship with God through Christ. To ask questions on who man is outside of that context would extend his scope, and he was in principle dismissive of any responsory capacity associated with an extant image because of the convoluted system brought to him via the philosophical and theological tradition, and thus Luther chose to put it to rest once and for all.[88] ✝

87. "Wir sehen ihn dann, wenn wir verstehen, daß das Wort, das der Antwort ruft, für Luther nicht der Appell an eine eigenständige geistige Reaktion des Menschen ist, sondern der Zuspruch des schlechthin tragenden Mit-seins Gottes, der den Menschen gerade aus seiner Seinsisoliering befreit, in der er meint, Gott gegenüber ein Zentrum eigenständiger Reaktion sein zu sollen" (Joest, *Ontologie der Person bei Luther,* 304).

88. Of course speaking this way also has contemporary value: "This is good news, for it means that what matters most in our humanity is not our intelligence, which is, after all, given to us in different measures and too soon taken away by illness or death. Rather, the image of God is found whenever two or three meet in authentic relationship. Computers cannot replace us, for each of us, as a participant in these relationships, is irreplaceable. In each moment when we follow Jesus' call to love God or to love one another, we imagine the Triune God in a unique way," (Herzfeld, *In Our Image,* 94).

LET US MAKE MAN

A CRITIQUE OF TRANSHUMANISM

✦

Universal Studios released a film version in 1931 of Mary Shelley's classic novel, *Frankenstein*. Before the opening credits, one of the characters comes on screen and makes this prefatory statement: "We are about to unfold the story of Frankenstein, a man of science who sought to create a man after his own image without reckoning upon God. It is one of the strangest tales ever told. It deals with the two great mysteries of creation—life and death. I think it will thrill you. It may shock you. It might even—horrify you."[1]

The story of Frankenstein's monster is embedded in our culture. There have been at least four hundred movies based on Shelley's novel, the first being a production of The Edison Company in 1910.[2] The most enduring version is still the 1931 Universal classic directed by Frank Whale and starring Boris Karloff. Jon Turney says that Shelley's story about finding the secret to life became one of the most important myths of modernity and the governing myth of modern biology.[3] The novel effectively warns of the dangers of careless scientific overreach. What the novel fails to do is answer its own dominant unspoken question, what is a human being?

Transhumanist philosophers and scientists at the beginning of the twenty-first century, like Victor Frankenstein, are on the quest for the secret of life, but it is a dangerous path. They believe they can redefine what it means to be a human being. Dr. Gregory Stock delivered a TED Talk in February 2003 in which he stated, "Using technology upon ourselves is going to completely revolutionize medicine and healthcare; that's obvious. It's going to change the way we have children. It's going to change the way we manage and alter our emotions. It's going to probably change

---

1. *Frankenstein: The Man Who Made a Monster*, directed by James Whale (Universal City, CA: Universal Pictures, 1931), film.

2. Jon Turney, *Frankenstein's Footsteps: Science, Genetics and Popular Culture* (New Haven and London: Yale University Press, 1998), 28.

3. Turney, 3.

the human lifespan. It is really going to make us question what it is to be a human being."[4] The problem is not that Transhumanists or Victor Frankenstein are "playing God." All physicians, as healers, are masks of God at work in the world. The problem is that a number of their solutions are based upon a flawed understanding of the nature of human beings. We cannot know *how* to treat a thing unless we know *what* it is.

We live in a time of astounding technological accomplishment and promise. From charting the human genome to nanotechnology, scientific discovery is making it possible for us to heal and prevent illness at a cellular and sub-cellular level. Beyond healing, however, human enhancement is sought.

Transhumanism is the philosophical basis for those well-funded researchers at world-class institutions who are attempting to merge technology with the human body to give it new capabilities. For example, Raymond Kurzweil, author of *The Singularity Is Near: When Humans Transcend Biology*, promises that we will be able to fill our bloodstream with nano-machines that will carry oxygen to our cells with greater efficiency than our red blood cells, making it possible to run a mile while hardly taking a breath. He says that we will be able to hold our breath underwater for hours.[5] Cambridge researcher, Aubrey de Grey claims that we will arrest the aging process so that human life may be extended by decades or even centuries.[6] We will, they promise, become a race of immortal supermen.

Aristotle said in his *Poetics* that every *ethos* implies a *mythos*. Our way of life and our assumptions, behaviors, and hopes are reflected and also shaped by the stories we tell ourselves. Imaginative narratives often cast light on issues in ways that non-fiction prose cannot. Allen Verhey explains that "Myths help us to map our world and our place in it. They serve to orient us, to locate us; they enable us to interpret and to see the significance of the things and events around us."[7] Cultural expressions like folklore, song, and art help to assign meaning to birth, life, family, and death.

Theologian Elaine L. Graham, in her book, *Representations of the Post/ Human*, examines the significance of stories "for furnishing Western culture with influential—perhaps definitive—narratives of what it means to be human."[8] She argues that science fiction and horror books and films,

---

4. Gregory Stock, "To upgrade is human," TED Talk, February 2003, last accessed December 3, 2018, https://www.ted.com/talks/gregory_stock_to_upgrade_is_human?language=en.

5. *Plug & Pray*, dir. Jens Schanze, perf. Joseph Weizenbaum, Raymond Kurzweil, Hiroshi Ishiguro (Germany: United Docs, 2010), DVD.

6. Aubrey de Grey, "A roadmap to end aging," TED Talk, July 2005, last accessed December 3, 2018, https://www.ted.com/talks/aubrey_de_grey_says_we_can_avoid_aging.

7. Allen Verhey, *Nature and Altering It* (Grand Rapids, MI: Wm. B. Eerdmans Publishing Co., 2010), 14.

8. Elaine L. Graham, *Representations of the Post/Human: Monsters, Aliens, and Others in Popular Culture* (New Brunswick, NJ: Rutgers University Press, 2002), 19.

in particular, are socially beneficial because they serve to soften our prejudices toward marginal beings.[9] Stories that feature sympathetic aliens, androids, and monsters help us to empathize with the other.[10]

Is a foundational definition of humanity possible? Pope John Paul II taught that the human body is revelatory of God. He was speaking primarily of sexuality, that our bodies are designed to be given to a complementary partner in love and that this one-flesh union, and the life that proceeds from it, echoes the type of fellowship that exists between the members of the Holy Trinity. As beneficial as this understanding of sexuality and marriage is, the church must attend to a multifaceted theological anthropology. It must articulate a more expansive theology of the body, a *somatology*, in order to respond to some of the soteriological and eschatological promises of transhumanist philosophy.

Mary Timothy Prokes writes that a theology of the body that can answer contemporary challenges will consider these, and other, questions:

- How should the lived body be described?
- What is the meaning of human embodiment?
- What is the relationship of the human body to the rest of the material universe?
- What does bodilyness contribute to an understanding of being made in the "image and likeness of God?"
- Why do Christians affirm that the ultimate divine revelation has been given in and through the Incarnate Christ?
- What is the meaning of suffering, illness, aging and dying?
- What is the destiny of the body-person after death?[11]

An additional question is whether there is such a thing as a fixed human essence that deserves respect and what it means for our treatment of the body. No single essay can tackle all of these topics. Our goal is to address theological somatology using Mary Shelley's novel, *Frankenstein*, as a basis for our analysis.

In his book, *Nature and Altering It*, Allen Verhey identifies sixteen definitions of the word "nature." The question of nature is important in speculative fiction because it determines who qualifies for inclusion in the human community. The first meaning comes from the ancient Greeks, who used the term (φύσις) to mean "the kind of thing a thing

---

9. She explains, "literature about monsters, as well as genres such as the fantastic, the Gothic, or utopian and speculative fiction, may serve to dislocate the reader from an over familiarity with the present" (Graham, 59).

10. Graham's book includes chapters on *Star Trek*, the film *Gattaca*, and the Jewish legend of the Golem among other topics, but a sizeable portion of the book deals with Mary Shelley's *Frankenstein*.

11. Mary Timothy Prokes, *Toward a Theology of the Body* (Grand Rapids:, MI Eerdmans, 1996), 26.

is."[12] Elaine Graham points out that for many, "'Nature' comes to mean the essential, basic constitution of the world, embodying fundamental and immutable physical (and moral) qualities."[13] When we examine Dr. Frankenstein's creation, the nature or essence of his creature is called into question. The novel is preoccupied with this question.

Is there, in reality, a fixed nature for a thing, or are our classifications just imposed and perpetuated by cultures? Elaine Graham follows French philosopher Michel Foucault's view that nature is not ontological, but rather a social construction. Thus human nature is not so much about *what* you are as it is about *how* you are understood and described by yourself and others.

BOUNDARIES BETWEEN CATEGORIES

Graham utilizes the phrase "ontological hygiene." It refers to a protective attitude people have toward their presumptive categorizations of the world. When their ontologies are threatened, they feel discomfort. We do not trust marginal or liminal beings. "The erosion of clear boundaries between humans and non-humans can either be interpreted as a threat to the 'ontological hygiene' of humanity or a rendering transparent of the very constructed character of the parameters of human nature," she says.[14] Monster stories cast doubt on our ontological certainties. They expose the fragility of the very "taken-for-grantedness" of such categories as male or female, human or animal, human or machine, and living or dead. They require us to rethink our belief that the categories we use to understand the world are true and static.[15]

Traditional interpreters of the Genesis creation account find clearly defined taxonomies in chapters one and two. "So God created mankind in his own image, in the image of God he created them; male and female he created them" (Gen 1:27). Not only are the boundaries between male and female distinct in Genesis, so are the boundaries between human and animal,[16] animate and inanimate, and Creator and creation. The categories are sharp and inviolable.

---

12. Verhey, 2.
13. Graham, 31.
14. Graham, 20.
15. "The human imagination, by giving birth to fantastic, monstrous and alien figures, has in fact always eschewed the fiction of fixed species. Hybrids and monsters are the vehicles through which it is possible to understand the fabricated character of all things, by virtue of the boundaries they cross and the limits they unsettle." Graham, 37.
16. Cf. H. G. Wells, *The Island of Dr. Moreau* (London: Heinemann, Stone & Kimball, 1896). Wells's novel a late Victorian example of a science fiction narrative blurring the boundaries between human beings and the animal kingdom. In the story, Moreau asserts that he has devoted his life to "the study of the plasticity of living forms." Unlike, Victor Frankenstein, Moreau possesses none of the humanitarian motives Victor Frankenstein began with. The "plasticity of living forms" is precisely the basis for Gregory Stock's and Raymond Kurzweil's Transhumanist agenda. Turney, 57.

Beings whose bodies have not fit neatly into presumed categories have, at times, been labeled monsters. Though he is called "creature," "wretch," "fiend," "daemon," and "devil," "monster" is Dr. Frankenstein's favorite epithet for his creation. The word derives from the Latin *monstrum*, which itself derives from the root *monere*, "to warn." The idea originally referred to strange births, where mothers gave birth to offspring that appeared inhuman or less than fully human. In antiquity, such "monstrous" births were considered warnings from the gods.[17] By the late Middle Ages, however, the view had changed. Such births went from being warnings of coming misfortune to being instances of God's wrath.[18]

Later, naturalistic explanations were sought. It was thought that malformations were caused by something that occurred externally to the mother during pregnancy. This belief was still prevalent in nineteenth-century England when the grotesque features of the so-called Elephant Man, Joseph Merrick, were attributed by some to the belief that his mother had been startled by a circus elephant while he was *in utero*.

Such "monsters" are liminal beings. This terminology derives from the Latin word *limen*, which means threshold. If you stand on the threshold, you are neither inside nor outside the room. You are in between. Liminal beings are those that stand between categories. They are taxonomically imprecise. This is why they make us uncomfortable.

THE GOLEM

Tales of man-made life forms, including animated men of metal or stone, date from ancient times and come from Greece, Rome, India, and China. The question has been often considered whether a living being could be built the same way that one might build a house. Two significant representations of the fabricated humanoid in Western culture are the Jewish folkloric figure of the Golem and the creature in Mary Shelley's *Frankenstein*.[19]

In Genesis 2:7–8, God forms the first man from the soil. The Hebrew word for God's action is רַצָּי (*yatsar*), the same word used of a potter fashioning formless clay into a cup. This is distinguished from אָרְבַ (*bara'*), God's creative act of making something new. In Hebrew usage, only God can *bara*, but both God and man can *yatsar*.

Medieval Jewish mystics speculated that certain righteous men might be able to discover and duplicate God's technique for fashioning (*yatsar*) living beings from pre-existing lifeless matter.[20] It is believed that God

---

17. Graham, 47.
18. Graham, 48.
19. Graham, 61.
20. Bob Curran, *Man-Made Monsters: A Field Guide to Golems, Patchwork Soldiers, Homunculi, and Other Created Creatures* (Pompton Plains, NJ: New Page Books, 2011), 51.

revealed this knowledge to Abraham and the other patriarchs. Some believed a word of power could be utilized to instill life into inanimate material, corresponding to God breathing life into Adam's clay.

Of course, any such contrivance of man, even were it to succeed in simulating human life, would still be far from the perfect creative work of God. This anthropomorphic clay creature was called a Golem (סלוג) in Jewish folklore. In every part of the tradition, the Golem is humanlike but always less than human. It has no spirit. Only God himself could bestow that. A Golem cannot, therefore, make moral judgments and so could be instructed to harm or even kill. In some stories, it is used for manual labor like a robot or Haitian zombie. In others, it becomes a protector of the Jews. The threat that it could turn on its maker is always present.[21]

The most famous story of the Golem is the sixteenth century Golem of Prague fabricated by Rabbi Judah Loew ben Bezalel, the chief rabbi of the city, who made the creature to defend the Jewish community during a period of persecution. Initially intended to protect the Jewish people, it became increasingly violent, and some versions of the story have it turning on the Jews themselves.

The Golem remains a popular cultural image in the Czech Republic and has throughout the years continued to make periodic appearances in both literature and film.[22] The Golem stories betray a kind of dualism, in which the man of clay can live and function without a spirit. In Christian theology, a human body without a spirit is, by definition, a corpse. There is no biological life for a man apart from his spirit.

Dualism has a long pedigree in Western civilization. Plato (428–348 BC) taught a bifurcated view of reality, the material world versus the world of ideas. Whenever there is a sharp division between matter and spirit, the tendency is to denigrate one and exalt the other. In Platonism, material reality, including the body, is considered inferior to immaterial reality. The immaterial realm of ideas and spirit is considered good and changeless. The material realm is considered illusory and subject to change. Certain extreme dualistic interpretations of Platonism can undermine the Christian understanding of God as the Creator of both the material and immaterial worlds. As we say in the Creed, he is the maker of all things, "visible and invisible."

The philosopher, René Descartes (1596–1650), considered the body a mere machine. In his *Treatise of Man*, he declared that the difference be-

---

21. Curran, 54.
22. Cf. Gustav Meyrink, *Der Golem*, (Leipzig, Germany: Kurt Wolff, 1914). Director Paul Wegener made a silent horror film entitled *Der Golem* in 1915. In it, as in Meyrink's novel and as in the case of the legend of the Golem of Prague, a holy and learned rabbi constructs a clay figure that he brings to life with the intent of protecting his persecuted congregation but with tragic result.

tween a living body and a dead body is analogous to a watch being wound or unwound.[23] He wrote: "I assume their body is to be but a statue, an earthen machine. . . . We see clocks, artificial fountains, mills and similar machines which, though made entirely by man, lack not the power to move, of themselves, in various ways."[24] For Descartes, the rational soul governs the body like an engineer might regulate the actions of a mill; the body is a vehicle for the mind.[25] One type of dualism makes the body and mind utterly separate. The preferable Christian model could be called a wholistic dualism that understands a perichoresis between body and soul. The emphasis here is on the body and soul together.

The Jewish mystics who speculated about building a living humanoid believed they could learn to wind the Cartesian watch, so to speak, but they were clear about their limitations. For them, no amount of human creativity could instill a soul into clay. The Golem was a purely mechanical type of lifeform.

FRANKENSTEIN AND ITS IMPLICATIONS

The second great man-making myth is Frankenstein. The question of the creature's soul is never answered in the story. No mere automaton, however, the monster has reason, feelings, and desire. Shelley's book is a preeminent myth for modernity precisely because Victor achieves his goals from the perspective of scientific materialism, entirely apart from anything supernatural. Early in the book, Victor flirts with mysticism but he rejects it as unscientific nonsense. He is initially enamored with alchemy but eventually puts all that aside. The secret of life in Frankenstein is not so mysterious that it cannot be discovered and manipulated.

Mary Shelley was born Mary Godwin in 1797, the daughter of two celebrated intellectuals of the day, William Godwin and Mary Wollstonecraft. She grew up in an unconventional household with poets and thinkers coming and going. Her most famous novel's genesis came about in 1816 when she and her soon-to-be husband, Percy Shelley, were visiting their friend, Lord Byron, and his other guests at a house on Lake Geneva, Switzerland. Over three rainy days in June, Byron challenged his guests to each write a fantastic tale for their mutual entertainment.[26]

---

23. Turney, 15.

24. Descartes, *Treatise of Man*, trans. Thomas Steele Hall (New York: Prometheus Books, 2003), 2–4. In a similar way, Descartes writes, "Moreover, breathing and other such actions which are ordinary and natural to it, and which depend on the flow of the spirits, are like the movements of a clock or mill which the ordinary flow of water can render continuous" (*Treatise*, 22).

25. Descartes writes, "And finally when there shall be a rational soul in this machine, it will have its chief seat in the brain and will there reside like a turncock who must be in the main to which all the tubes of these machines repair when he wishes to excite, prevent, or in some manner alter their movements" (*Treatise*, 22).

26. Incidentally, Byron's personal physician, John Polidori, wrote a story called "The

Mary's contribution was the story that was developed into the novel *Frankenstein, or The Modern Prometheus*, published in England in 1818.

The novel's secondary title, *The Modern Prometheus*, is revealing. In Greek mythology, Prometheus is the Titan who formed man from clay and gave him his upright stature like that of the gods. Prometheus later stole fire from the gods and gave it to mankind. Fire represents that which divides civilized man from brute beast. It represents the light of hearth and science. Enraged by this transgression, Zeus sentenced Prometheus to be shackled with an eagle eating out his liver for eternity. Prometheus is both the heroic creator and the eternally tormented transgressor and is a popular figure amongst the Romantic poets. Frankenstein is the man of science who defies the gods and creates life. And for his trouble, he loses everything he loves.

As is often noted, the chief title *Frankenstein* refers to the mad scientist figure, Victor Frankenstein—not to the creature he produced. The creature, in fact, remains nameless throughout the novel. With no name, it is robbed of any semblance of family, heritage, clan, tribe, or nation. With no name, he stands outside the family of man. At times, the novel refers to him as a creature, which is quite telling. A creature implies a creator. Victor is the anti-God, the father who rejects his progeny, the creator that abandons the work of his hands. The creature's outrage at being so unjustly forlorn is the motivation of his many subsequent offenses. The creature is a type of Adam, a new man, whose fall is precipitated by the godlike figure who does not love his creation.[27] In one reading of the novel, Victor is the true monstrous being.

There is no reason to assume the novel was merely the product of a vivid teenage imagination. The text of the novel itself provides evidence that Mary Shelley was "extremely well acquainted with the science of her time."[28] There are several historical figures who may have provided inspiration for Shelly's story, including Johann Konrad Dippel and Giovanni Aldini.

In the seventeenth century, Johann Konrad Dippel was born in Castle Frankenstein in Darmstadt and occasionally went by the name Frankenstein. His dates are August 10, 1673 to April 25, 1734. Dippel was the

Vampyre," inspired by fragments of a story by Byron himself. "The Vampyre" was later published as a novella in 1819, seventy-eight years before Irishman Abraham Stoker unveiled his gothic masterpiece. It is one of the earliest examples of the Romantic vampire figure. In one rainy holiday, the two greatest gothic monsters of English literature were born.

27. "Remember that I am thy creature; I ought to be thy Adam, but I am rather the fallen angel, whom thou drivest from joy for no misdeed. Everywhere I see bliss, from which I alone am irrevocably excluded. I was benevolent and good; misery made me a fiend. Make me happy, and I shall again be virtuous." Mary Wollstonecraft Shelley, *The Annotated Frankenstein*, annotated ed., ed. Susan J. Wolfson and Ronald L. Levao (Cambridge, MA: Belknap Press, 2012), 171.

28. Turney, 22.

son of a Lutheran pastor but became highly critical of the church and traditional dogma. A dabbler in alchemy, he even developed a reputation for black magic and necromancy.[29] Hair-raising rumors about Dipple abounded, including that he had a secret laboratory at Castle Frankenstein where he performed experiments on human corpses. Though she never mentions the castle or the story of Konrad Dippel in her journals, it is known that Mary Shelley travelled through this area of Germany in 1814. Many sources theorize that she may have heard the stories of his experiments and was inspired by them. Her version of Frankenstein, however, employed no black magic. He was a true rationalist.

Another likely influence on the Frankenstein story is Giovanni Aldini, who was born into a wealthy and noble family in Bologna, Italy, in 1762. He was the nephew and collaborator of the scientist Luigi Galvini. Together they experimented with the effects of electrical currents on the nerves and muscles of dead animals. They established the theory known as "galvanic electricity," which postulated that the muscles and limbs of animals are animated by a type of electricity circulating in their bodies.

Aldini was a showman as well as a scientist and raised money for his research by holding public spectacles using electricity to cause dead animals' body parts to twitch on stage. According to Curran, Aldini's central theory was that galvanic electricity might be used to bring people back from the dead.[30] On January 17, 1803, Aldini attempted to reanimate the corpse of executed criminal George Foster in London. Though the experiment was unsuccessful, it was widely publicized and discussed in London. Aldini published a book about it that was circulated in London in 1804 and 1805.

Mary Shelley would unquestionably have been aware of this and other experiments using galvanic electricity. Dr. Henry Cline, the Godwin family physician, was celebrated for his own success in reviving a coma patient using electrical current. We know from Mary's diaries that Percy Shelley and Byron had discussed galvanic experiments during their time on Lake Geneva.

While it does occur on a rainy night, the animation scene in the novel is a good deal less dramatic than the 1931 James Whale adaptation with its thunder and lightning. Shelley writes simply: "I collected the instruments of life around me, that I might infuse a spark of being into the lifeless thing that lay at my feet."[31] Earlier in the novel, in chapter two, a young Victor witnessed the destructive power of lightning, and a visiting scholar explained to him the properties of electricity and the theories of

---

29. Curran, 44.
30. Curran, 28.
31. Shelley, *The Annotated Frankenstein*, 114.

Galvini. Most contemporary readers would have connected the dots and known that he used electricity to awaken his profane experiment.

There are many themes at work in *Frankenstein*. The first is the now well-worn motif of the mad scientist. The corruptive power of knowledge occurs in world mythologies and religions from Prometheus to Adam and Eve. Mary Shelley broke new literary soil,[32] but over the next hundred years other important novels appeared that examined the potential dark side of medical science, notably *The Strange Case of Dr. Jekyll and Mr. Hyde* by Robert Louis Stevenson in 1886 and *The Island of Dr. Moreau* by H. G. Wells in 1896. One popular novelist in the late twentieth century who focused often on the perils of unfettered biological experimentation was Michael Crichton, a medical doctor himself. His biomedical thrillers include *The Andromeda Strain*, *Jurassic Park*, *Lost World*, *Congo*, *Prey*, and *Next*.

Like a lot of science fiction, Frankenstein is cautionary. "Learn from me," Victor Frankenstein intones, "if not by my precepts, at least by my example, how dangerous is the acquirement of knowledge and how much happier that man is who believes his native town to be the world, than he who aspires to become greater than his nature will allow."[33] Turney observes that myths that relate to the acquisition of knowledge almost always end badly. When the knowledge in question has to do with the creation of life, the stakes are particularly high.[34]

As in a Greek tragedy, Victor Frankenstein exhibits hubris toward heaven. In one place he exclaims: "It was the secrets of heaven and earth that I desired to learn."[35] His confidence in his scientific prowess was boundless: "my imagination was too much exalted by my first success to permit me to doubt of my ability to give life to an animal as complex and wonderful as man."[36] Interestingly, the creature exhibits the same hubris toward his creator as Victor shows to God. In their encounter where the monster demands that Victor fabricate a mate for him, he says, "You are my creator, but I am your master; obey!"[37] The lesson of the Greek tragedies is that such arrogance always results in the protagonist's undoing. Film critic E. Michael Jones states: "All monster stories, beginning with Frankenstein, the first of the genre, are in effect protests against the Enlightenment's desacralization of man."[38] Shelley warns

---

32. "Mary Shelley's Frankenstein is often identified as the first modern work of science fiction—the 'first great myth of the industrial age' . . . —thus spawning an entire genre in which the literary imagination sought inspiration from science and technology. . . . More fruitfully, it offers reflections on the fundamentals of human identity." Graham, 14.

33. Shelley, *The Annotated Frankenstein*, 109.

34. Turney, 14.

35. Shelley, *The Annotated Frankenstein*, 347.

36. Shelley, *The Annotated Frankenstein*, 110.

37. Shelley, *The Annotated Frankenstein*, 257.

38. Stephen T. Asma, *On Monsters: An Unnatural History of Our Worst Fears* (Oxford: Oxford University Press, 2009), 196.

of the perils of scientific overreach and the potentially dehumanizing effects of technology.

One of the things that makes Mary Shelley's novel unique, especially for its time, is that it examines the idea of creating artificial life without the aid of any deity or supernatural agency.[39] It is surprising that though he regrets his actions, Victor never has a point of awakening where he humbles himself before the Almighty. The functional atheism of Victor goes hand in glove with his unfettered scientific exploration. Unlike Goethe's Faust, who knowingly makes a deal with the devil to acquire forbidden wisdom and later experiences divine intervention, the materialist Victor Frankenstein dies for his sins in unbelief.

The novel's creature is presumably "born" a tabula rasa. His murderous behavior is not the result of an inherent quality but the result of his experiences—nurture, not nature. He is one of Rousseau's noble savages corrupted by heartless modernity. In this view, society's ills are not endemic to human nature, but merely a result of unjust systems of power that oppress those who did not have the good fortune to be high-born. Graham and others speculate that Shelley's original motivation for writing was to express sympathy for the socially and politically oppressed. In later editions of the novel, however, her introduction places the emphasis not upon social equity but upon the hazards of renegade science.[40]

The creature in *Frankenstein* is a misunderstood outcast who represents every marginalized outsider. Our sympathies are torn between Victor and his monster. It is hard not to sympathize with the scientist early on. Deeply affected by the early death of his mother,[41] he dreamed of overcoming sickness, aging, and even death itself. Vainglory, it seems, was as much a motivation as altruism. He says, "what glory would attend the discovery if I could banish disease from the human frame and render man invulnerable to any but a violent death!"[42] And later, "I thought that if I could bestow animation upon lifeless matter, I might in process of time (although I now found it impossible) renew life where death had apparently devoted the body to corruption."[43]

What made Victor's creature monstrous? Was it his strange origin? Was it his physical appearance? Shelley described the creature as being

---

39. Asma, 14.

40. Turney supports the consideration that Shelley's concerns might have been more socio-political than scientific. He says the novel's shape "is marked, equally clearly, by the turbulence of the era. Mary grew up at a time when it seemed that the French Revolution might be followed by the overturning of the established order in Britain" (Turney, 19).

41. Cf. *Transcendent Man*, dir. Barry Ptolemy, perf. Ray Kurzweil (Sherman Oaks, CA: Docurama, 2009), DVD. In this documentary film, the death of his father is portrayed as influential in Raymond Kurzweil's Transhumanism, the belief that human beings can overcome their mortality by means of biotechnology.

42. Shelley, *The Annotated Frankenstein*, 93.

43. Shelley, *The Annotated Frankenstein*, 110.

eight feet tall, with translucent yellowish skin pulled so taut over the body that it "barely disguised the workings of the vessels and muscles underneath"; and with watery, glowing eyes, flowing black hair, black lips, and prominent white teeth. The creature considers whether his appearance and his otherness are linked: "My person was hideous and my stature gigantic. What did this mean? Who was I? What was I? Whence did I come? What was my destination? These questions continually recurred, but I was unable to solve them."[44] In *Frankenstein*, physical beauty and moral goodness are linked. Stephen Asma points out that there is something deep within us that both attracts and repulses us about extraordinary bodies.[45] The anthropologist Mary Douglas demonstrates in her book *Purity and Danger* that human beings universally organize their world. Boundaries are safe. Ambiguous things are threatening. The monster's physical repulsiveness is central to understanding people's reactions to him and how his inner moral character is shaped by this experience.

Frankenstein's creature is not human in the conventional sense. But it is difficult to say that it is completely inhuman. It is truly a liminal being. It has the form of a man. Materially, it is indistinguishable from human beings, a patchwork of corpses robbed from graves and morgues. It has the faculties of reason, speech, a sense of self, and a sense of right and wrong. But it has no mother or father. Frankenstein is referred to as the creature's father but he did not beget it. He fashioned it in a laboratory. He constructed it. It is an assemblage of parts, the fruits of man's artifice instead of the fruit of any man's loins—made, not begotten. In these ways, he is not unlike our primeval progenitor.

Our monster found a copy of *Paradise Lost* and found himself in its pages. Like Adam, the creature was never in a womb, was not born, and did not have a childhood.[46] Frankenstein's creature is a new Adam, but a desecrated version. He himself speculates whether he bears greater resemblance to the first constructed man or perhaps to the fallen angel.[47] Yet even Satan is not so wretched, he postulates, as he.[48]

---

44. Shelley, *The Annotated Frankenstein*, 208.

45. Asma, 5.

46. Yet Adam did have parentage. In the Gospel of Luke, Adam is called the son of God (Luke 3:38).

47. Cf. Shelley, *The Annotated Frankenstein*, 209. "Like Adam, I was apparently united by no link to any other being in existence; but his state was far different from mine in every other respect. He had come forth from the hands of God a perfect creature, happy and prosperous, guarded by the especial care of his Creator; he was allowed to converse with and acquire knowledge from beings of a superior nature, but I was wretched, helpless, and alone. Many times I considered Satan as the fitter emblem of my condition, for often, like him, when I viewed the bliss of my protectors, the bitter gall of envy rose within me."

48. Cf. Shelley, *The Annotated Frankenstein*, 210. "'Hateful day when I received life!' I exclaimed in agony. 'Accursed creator! Why did you form a monster so hideous that even *you* turned from me in disgust? God, in pity, made man beautiful and alluring, after his own image; but my form is a filthy type of yours, more horrid even from the very resemblance. Satan had his companions, fellow devils, to admire and encourage him, but I am solitary and abhorred.'"

ENTER TRANSHUMANISM

Compare the words of Shelley's book to those statements from modern scientist and inventor, Ray Kurzweil: "In my view, it's only technology that has the scale to address the pressing problems we have today. . . . Whereas biology is very intricate and very clever, it's also very sub-optimal compared to what we ultimately will be able to design with nano-technology."[49] Kurzweil, like Frankenstein, believes that science and technology are changing many of the assumptions that we have about human life, including the assumption that, before the *parousia*, we have to die.[50]

In the documentary, *Transcendent Man*, one of Kurzweil's former college friends is quoted saying that Kurzweil's goal was always to invent things so the blind could see, the deaf could hear, and the lame could walk.[51] Indeed many marvelous medical developments have improved the lives of sick and handicapped people. Kurzweil himself has had a hand in some of them. The messianic quality of modern medicine is inescapable. Raymond Kurzweil, Gregory Stock, and others claim that humankind will attain a type of immortality by means of technical advances. These and other Transhumanists readily acknowledge that their goals overlap with the objectives of religion. For them, science replaces all need for religion.

In the past, people speculated that a living replica of man could be generated by mystical practices, e.g., the Golem. Today people profess that with science, all things are possible. But are they beneficial? As artificial intelligence and robotics technologies develop, fundamental questions about human nature, identity, consciousness, and personhood are raised. Alan Turing's test of machine intelligence says a computer is "thinking" if extended discourse with it proves indistinguishable from discourse with a living person. In the German documentary *Plug & Pray*, Joseph Weizenbaum, Professor Emeritus of Computer Science from MIT and Stanford, argues against the endeavor of creating a human-like robot. When chided on a panel for being a little bit negative toward Artificial Intelligence, Weizenbaum said:

> I'm not a little negative. I'm very negative. I've spent half my life teaching at what might be the world's most advanced university (MIT). . . . There and at Stanford and Carnegie Mellon University and many others . . . they work hard and spend lots of money, much of it coming from the military, to build robots, that is, human-like robots. I recall a famous scholar saying, "In 50 years, we

49. *Plug & Pray*, DVD.
50. *Plug & Pray*, DVD.
51. *Transcendent Man*, DVD.

will have human-like robots. . . . And people will marry these human robots. But when I meet such a beautiful woman, she doesn't have . . . she may have a nice body and whatnot, yet she was never a child. Thus she doesn't have a history, that makes up a person, whatever the material is. Which brings up the question: do we need all that?"[52]

Weizenbaum notes that what is most remarkable is not the assertion that such technology may one day exist but the belief that we understand human beings well enough to make one.

Frankenstein's monster learns the story of Adam and Eve where the Lord states that it is not good for man to be alone, so God made the woman for him. This plants the idea that his creator is obligated to make a female companion for him. His objective is to experience social community. He wants relationship. He wants a family, and there is nothing remotely monstrous about that: indeed it is a very human impulse. His anger at being rejected by his creator is what leads him to commit atrocities in an attempt to hurt the scientist. When he demands that Victor give him a mate, the scientist at first agrees but then refuses for fear that they would reproduce and begin a parallel race that could spell the destruction of humanity. Denied a mate by his creator, he murders Frankenstein's wife on their wedding night.

The creature's appearance is so repellant that he cannot connect with any human being. Graham posits, "the bodily imperfection of Victor's creature serves as a clue to his ontological status. His hideous being, with its physical oddities, places him beyond the pale of human culture."[53] The only human being with whom he is able to establish a friendship is the blind man in the cottage, a relationship that comes to a violent end when the man's family returns.

The monster of the novel, unlike that of most film presentations, is not an inarticulate imbecile. He is sensitive. He is intelligent. He craves to have community. He begs his creator to give him a companion, a woman, one like himself, who will not be repulsed by him. Film representations of the monster sometimes go beyond the novel by denying it rationality and speech, two key indicators of humanity.

Shelley's novel portrays Victor Frankenstein, on the other hand, "as an arrogant, egocentric individual with a prodigious intellect who is obsessed with his own brilliance, imagining himself to have almost God-like abilities who becomes terrified at the success of his experimentation."[54] Victor is obsessively preoccupied with cheating death. Graham

---

52. *Plug & Pray*, DVD.
53. Graham, 64.
54. Curran, 21.

asks, as noted earlier, whether he might not be, "in his narcissistic obsession with controlling nature, the true monster of the tale?"[55]

THE HUMAN BODY AS MEANS OF REDEMPTION

In the 1935 film, *The Bride of Frankenstein*, one character toasts the dawning age of scientific marvels saying, "To a new world of gods and monsters." Are we the gods or the monsters? When human beings grasp god-like status, the outcomes are always monstrous.

Biophysicist Dr. Gregory Stock, author of *Redesigning Humans: Choosing Our Genes, Changing Our Future*, had this to say in a TED Talk from February 2003:

> What we do with our biology is going to shape our future, and that of our children and that of their children. Whether we gain control of aging; whether we learn to protect ourselves from Alzheimer's and heart disease and cancer. . . . What we're doing is seizing control of our evolutionary future. We are essentially using technology to just jam evolution into fast-forward. *And it's not at all clear where it's going to take us.*[56]

The hubris only gives way to a sort of chilling fatalism: "It's obvious to everyone that if we can do this, we absolutely will do this, whatever the consequences are." Stock's faith in science is blind and he is asking us to take the Kierkegaardian leap with him. *Frankenstein*, and stories like it, shape our moral understanding of what is good about science and what is dangerous.

Transhumanists like Stock think of the body as raw material, not as the locus of God's action. If your automobile or personal computer wears out, you replace the worn parts. You upgrade the software to get more life out of it. And if you plan well and expense is no object, there is no reason your device or appliance could not last almost indefinitely.

Of course, this raises questions of continuity. If you continually replace parts, a time will come when none of the original remains and it is fair to ask whether it is still the same object. If Pete Townsend retires, is it still *The Who*? It depends on what you identify as the essence of the band. Is it necessary for all of the same players to be present? Is not the essence of *The Who* the music? Maybe. Or maybe it is the music played and sung by these particular players. In Transhumanism, the real self is not identified with the body but with the mind. Not the players, but the music.

A dualist may identify the spirit or soul as the true self, and the body as merely an instrument that is occasionally in need of an upgrade. As

55. Graham, 14.
56. Stock, "To upgrade is human," emphasis added.

materialists, Transhumanists struggle to identify the essence of a person. A materialist believes that the body is all there is, and yet they disdain our present bodies. They also believe that there can be continuity of the true self even if every molecule of the body is replaced with something artificial. For them, the mind or the consciousness emerges from the highly complex system of the brain. All that you are, your dreams, your memories, and your desires, boil down to etheric information, the organic equivalent of ones and zeros. Information can exist continually even if the substrate changes. You may possess ten different computers, each more sophisticated than the last one, but your data files remain essentially the same. They just keep getting transferred from one machine to the next. Transhumanists see no reason that something similar could not be done with human minds.

If the nature of a man is nothing more than material, then there must be a materialistic explanation for human consciousness. Your memories and personality are nothing more than codes imprinted in your neurons. With time, we should be able to read and store that code in man-made devices. Indeed, we should be able to write new code for artificial memories, desires, and personalities, to alter ourselves or construct synthetic humans with minds that are indistinguishable or superior to our own.

Our definition of nature is the thing that a thing is. If the nature of man is spiritual as well as material, then even if we could exactly duplicate the structures and functions of the brain, as we can do for simpler organs, it would still not be a human being.

Transhumanist philosophy is a brand of neo-Gnosticism. Whereas ancient Gnosticism challenged the goodness of the body, the Transhumanists disavow the goodness of these particular bodies. They do not deny the reality of physical existence, but they do harbor disdain for the body as we know it.

The church must occupy itself with the questions posed by Prokes such as, "What is the meaning of human embodiment?" and further ask, "What is the meaning of these particular bodies of which we consist?" Many Westerners are functional dualists. We see the human body as little more than an elaborate vehicle for the real self. Experience shows that whenever body or spirit is exalted, the other is degraded. We betray a mechanistic view of humanity when we think we can master life and death by means of *techne*. Human dignity is diminished when we shift the body from being subject to being object.

If John Paul II is right, the "givenness" of one's particular body has theological significance. Genesis 1 and 2 require a great deal more theological reflection than as reaction to Charles Darwin. These are not simply verses that record events of the primordial past. They identify that

God is the Creator. As Martin Luther explains in the First Article of the Apostles' Creed in his Small Catechism: "I believe that God has made me and all creatures; that He has given me my body and soul, eyes, ears, and all my members, my reason, and all my senses, and still preserves them." The reason I do not want to "transcend biology" is because my biology is who I am. Our biological nature is a gift from God. God inhabits our biology, "The body is for the Lord and the Lord is for the body" (1 Cor 6:13). It is as an embodied person that I will be glorified.

So what is a human? A mere assemblage of parts? An elaborate machine? A container for the soul? Or something much richer and deeper? The body is not an obstacle course for the mind. It is the divinely intended enabling condition of human life. Indeed, in Genesis, man is described as the image of God. Most often, in the Old Testament, "image" refers to statues, idols, three-dimensional replicas. Human beings are the three-dimensional representation of God in the world. We are physical beings who stand in the physical world as God's own. Jesus is the paradigm for our humanity, our anthropology. Transhumanism fails because it leaves Christology behind.

The Incarnation of the Divine Logos tells us that the material of our lived existence is important. We must ask how the Word-made-flesh might influence our attitudes toward biomedical technologies that attempt to fundamentally redefine human life without overreacting against ethically permissible medical interventions. Christ is true man and his embodied life, death, and resurrection have organic importance to those incorporated into his body by means of his body. In an age of editing genetic codes, three-parent IVF embryos, and Transhumanist fantasies about overcoming death with nanobots in our bloodstream, the message of Christianity proclaims that the body is not merely a suboptimal product of mindless forces, but rather the means of God's saving work. ✛

THE "WILLIAM WEINRICH" PRINCIPLE

✛

Dr. William Weinrich and I served together as LCMS vice-presidents. During his term as President, Rev. Al Barry assigned Dr. Weinrich to attend and represent him and the Synod at an inter-denominational dialogue.

At the next meeting of LCMS vice-presidents, LCMS President Barry asked Dr. Weinrich to give his report. In his opening remarks, Dr Weinrich emphasized the following point: When you are in discussion or dialogue with other people—especially those coming from a different theological perspective—always do this first: Try to understand *why* people say what they do; or *why* they confess and practice what they do.

Dr. Weinrich was making this point: In Biblical and theological discussions, don't be "trigger-happy." Instead, it's better to go at it a little more slowly. Be a little more patient and sympathetic in your discussions. Try to understand what makes others in a dialogue express their faith—and practice their faith— in the manner that they do. Then, as Dr. Weinrich emphasizes, a meaningful and even fruitful dialogue becomes possible, even though you do not fully agree with them; such sympathetic dialogue enables you to become more aware of the underlying principles of another's belief, his way of thinking, and his confession.

THE "WEINRICH PRINCIPLE"—POPE BENEDICT

Here is an example of the "William Weinrich Principle." Some years ago my family and I were traveling south of Chicago towards St. Louis. At one point, we listened to a religious radio program. A Roman Catholic priest was explaining his work in his parish. He told about three young Catholic ladies, his parishioners, who went off to the university. At the university, these young ladies attended an interdenominational Bible study. Upon their return to their parish, these troubled young ladies asked their priest this question: "Father, people at these Bible studies ask us 'Why do you as Catholics pray to Mary and to saints?" Then they added: "This is not found in the Bible."

To his radio listeners in central Illinois, this Catholic priest then simply and warmly stated: I simply explained to these young ladies: "Not everything is in the Bible!" In other words, to the surprise of even many Catholics today, the official teaching of the Roman Catholic Church is this: The highest authority in spiritual matters is not Scripture alone. Rather, the teachings and pronouncements of the Roman Catholic Church *share the authority, and are equal to*, the Scriptures. "The Church . . . does not derive her certainty about all revealed truths from the holy Scriptures alone. Both Scripture and Tradition must be accepted and honored with equal sentiments of devotion and reverence."[1]

Maintaining consistency regarding the question of exactly who/what has authority in the church is not always easy. The highest authority is not always as immovable as sometimes thought. On 2 May 2005, *US News & World Report* opened a few eyes concerning how "authority" vacillates in the Catholic Church. According to this magazine article, it works sort of like a card game: It all depends on who has the highest bid, and therefore the "trump card!" In an article on Joseph Ratzinger who later became Pope Benedict XVI, *US News & World Report* references John Allen, Ratzinger's biographer, who notes the change in Ratzinger's position. According to Allen, "In 1966, Ratzinger wanted to recover the role of Scripture as a tool for assessing church teaching and practice." By 1997, however, as he edged closer to the title of Pope Benedict XVI, Ratzinger warned that the use of Scripture to evaluate church teaching "was one of the most dangerous currents to flow out of Vatican II."[2]

Sound familiar in the LCMS? LCMS pastors loudly champion "Scripture alone!" However, upon being elected District President (Bishop), or LCMS President (Archbishop), the tare seeds of human imagination (Matt 13:25) can sometimes begin to take root in the heart and mind. LCMS Resolutions and the pronouncement of the *LCMS Handbook* can take on a Pope Benedict glow, becoming a higher authority than Scripture!

These are rather simple examples. Yet, in each case, they explain the value of the "Weinrich Principle." In dialogue with Roman Catholics, Protestants, or even other LCMS Lutherans, use the Weinrich Principle. Drill down and listen carefully. What are they claiming as their highest authority? Roman Catholics are part of a church body that bases its the-

---

1. *Catechism of the Catholic Church*, (Liguori, MO: Liguori Publications, 1994), 26.
2. Jay Tolson, "Defender of the Faith," *U.S. News & World Report Magazine* 138, no. 16 (May 2, 2005), 38.

ology and confession, not on Scripture alone, but on the Bible *and* church tradition. Satan tempts Lutherans to hedge on God's Word no less than he does Catholics.

THE "WEINRICH PRINCIPLE"—JOHN STOTT

Here is a second example reflecting the need for the "Weinrich Principle." For 25 years, Rev. Dr. John Stott was the rector of All Souls Church in London. For a quarter century Stott was also the chaplain to the queen of England. He had great influence in England; however, arguably, Stott had even greater worldwide influence. For years, Stott was the most widely-read writer for InterVarsity. His first best seller came off the press in 1958, titled: *Basic Christianity.* This small format paperback has been reprinted endless times and translated into 63 languages, and climbing. Other Stott books followed with similar success.

NYT columnist and PBS TV news commentator David Brooks, a self-proclaimed Jew, wrote that Stott is the "Pope of the Evangelicals." Consequently, Brooks noted: Whatever Stott wrote, or said, was totally believed by evangelicals, *without question*!

Stott was also often the main speaker at the annual worldwide Intervarsity Christmas conferences. These meetings, taking place during Christmas vacation at Champaign-Urbana, drew 20–25 thousand university students. When Stott spoke to the 25,000 students at the Urbana, Illinois meetings, you could hear a pin drop. Rapt attention. No one spoke. Like the arrival of Santa Claus, "Not a creature stirred, not even a mouse!" Thirty years ago, then already ordained, I attended these conferences. I was impressed. "When I was a child, I used to speak as a child, think as a child, reason as a child; when I became a man, I did away with childish things" (1 Cor 13:11)—including the writing and thinking of John Stott.

I used the Weinrich Principle: Drill, baby, drill! Patiently and courteously drill down and try to understand *why* Stott said what he did? Why Stott taught and wrote *what* he did? Using the "Weinrich Principle," it becomes clear that Stott denies the miraculous power of God's Word. In what way? In his many writings, Stott marginalizes, undermines, or outright denies God's miracles in His Sacraments. When you deny the power of the Sacraments, you deny God's living Word— the heart, engine, and Seed of the Sacraments. When you separate Christ from His living Word (John 6:63) you then have a "divided" Christ (1 Corinthians 1:13). Regarding Stott and other so-called Bible teachers: "You will know them by their fruits" (Matt 7:16).

DRILL BABY DRILL!

So, today, when you get into discussions about religion with both your non-Lutheran, and also your Lutheran friends, first, be charitable. Secondly, as you prepare for these discussions—or even in the midst of the discussion—never misrepresent anyone. Drill down, keep gently probing. As you do your probing, use the *William Weinrich Principle*: Always try to figure out *why* people are saying what they say regarding their religious convictions. Your discussions will be less confrontational and more richly blessed by the Spirit. "Whoever is wise, let him understand these things; Whoever is discerning, let him know them. For the ways of the LORD are right . . . ." (Hosea 14:9). ✝

A HYMN

IN HONOR OF

WILLIAM C. WEINRICH, DOCTOR JOANNIS

✛

I am deeply indebted to Dr. Weinrich in more ways than I can express here. He, like every good teacher, is interested not in his own praise and glory but with the inculcation of truth in his students. Most of all, like every good churchman, he is interested in the proclamation of Truth, namely, our Lord Jesus Christ, for the sake of the Church. Because of his dedication to his office as professor and out of deep personal gratitude for what he has taught me personally about St. John's Gospel, the Blessed Trinity, and the sacramental life of the Church, I am pleased to present this hymn in his honor. May God be glorified for many more years to come by the work Dr. Weinrich has done and continues to do.

THE LADDER WHICH GOD'S ISRAEL SAW

1. The ladder which God's Israel saw
Saves mankind from death's hellish maw.
It is the staircase angels tread,
Upon which hung the Church's Head.

2. Isaiah in the temple cried,
"God's glory I have truly spied."
What saw this Prophet of the Lord,
If not the throne of Christ the Word?

3. Did Pilate know he'd raised up high
The throne of God into the sky?
Over Christ's head, these words were seen,
"King of the Jews, the Nazarene."

4. And from the Temple's riven side
Poured forth our life which hid inside.
The water and the blood which flowed,
The Church's life to her bestowed.

5. O Christ, you are our glorious Light,
    Who from the cross is shining bright.
    We praise you, Father, for your Gift.
    Your name, O Spirit, high we lift.

Text: Gino R. Marchetti II
Tune Name: Wo Gott Zum Haus (Public Domain)
Tune Source: Geistliche Lieder auffs new gebessert, Wittenberg, 1535, ed. Joseph Klug
Setting: The Lutheran Hymnal, 1941; Lutheran Service Book, 2006
Meter: LM
Date: + The Eve of the Feast of the Reformation, 2019 AD +

✝